Programming in Modula-3

Springer
Berlin
Heidelberg
New York
Barcelona
Budapest
Hong Kong
London
Milan
Paris
Santa Clara
Singapore
Tokyo

László Böszörményi
Carsten Weich

Programming in Modula-3

An Introduction in Programming with Style

Foreword by Joseph Weizenbaum

 Springer

László Böszörményi
Carsten Weich

Universität Klagenfurt
Institut für Informatik
Universitätsstraße 65-67
A-9022 Klagenfurt

With 61 figures

The software environment was created with the kind support of Springer-Verlag, Digital Equipment Corporation, and Raiffeisenverband Kärnten

Translated from the German edition *Programmieren mit Modula-3* by Robert Bach, Traunkirchen, Austria

ISBN-13: 978-3-642-64614-0   e-ISBN-13: 978-3-642-60940-4
DOI: 10.1007/978-3-642-60940-4

CIP-data applied for
Die Deutsche Bibliothek CIP-Einheitsaufnahme
programming in Modula-3: an introduction in programming with style /
László Böszörményi; Carsten Weich. Foreword by Joseph Weizenbaum [Transl. from
the German ed. by Robert Bach]. - Berlin; Heidelberg; New York; Barcelona; Budapest;
Hong Kong; London; Milan; Paris; Santa Clara; Signapore; Tokyo: Springer; 1996
  Dt. Ausg. u.d.T.: Böszörményi, László: Programmieren mit Modula-3
  ISBN-13: 978-3-642-64614-0
NE: Weich, Carsten:

© Springer-Verlag Berlin Heidelberg 1996
Softcover reprint of the hardcover 1st edition 1996

Typesetting: Camera-ready by authors; Cover illustration: Hegedus Miklos
Cover design: Künkel + Lopka Werbeagentur, Ilvesheim
SPIN:10426494   33/3020-5 4 3 2 1 0 - Printed on acid-free paper

To Joseph Weizenbaum

Foreword
by Joseph Weizenbaum

Since the dawn of the age of computers, people have cursed the difficulty of programming. Over and over again we encounter the suggestion that we should be able to communicate to a computer in natural language what we want it to do. Unfortunately, such advice rests upon a misconception of both the computer and its task. The computer might not be stupid, but it is stubborn. That is, the computer does what all the details of its program command it to do, i.e., what the programmer "tells" it to do. And this can be quite different from what the programmer intended. The misunderstanding with respect to tasks posed to the computer arises from the failure to recognize that such tasks can scarcely be expressed in natural language, if indeed at all. For example, can we practice music, chemistry or mathematics without their respective special symbolic languages?

Yet books about computers and programming languages can be written more or less reasonably, even if they are not quite poetic or lyrical. This book can serve as an example of this art and as a model for anyone attempting to teach inherently difficult subject matters to others.

Klagenfurt, April 1995

Preface

Striving to make learning to program easier, this book addresses primarily students beginning a computer science major. For our program examples, we employ a new, elegant programming language, Modula-3. However, most of the concepts that we introduce apply and are relevant independently of the specific programming language.

This book can either accompany an introductory lecture on programming or serve self-study purposes. Both cases absolutely demand hands-on programming practice in addition to reading the book. Perusing a book on programming in dry dock without ever navigating the challenging waters of programming would be like reading about how to play a violin without ever touching the instrument. Learning to program means mastering both theory and practice, preferably simultaneously.

Newcomers to a computer science major bring with them a broad range of different backgrounds. Some have no computer literacy, while others can handle certain application programs such as word processors or spreadsheets. Still others have programming experience, although the breadth and depth of their skills varies greatly. This book assumes no particular prerequisites. A reader armed with normal high school mathematics and rudimentary computer literacy should be able to understand this book. We begin with fundamental concepts and only stepwise introduce the more difficult, higher-level concepts that build on them. To avoid the risk of boredom, students with a higher level of programming experience should feel free to skim over exhaustive explanations that are already clear to them.

Organization of the Book

The book consists of five parts:

1. *Introduction*
   In the first chapter we cast light on the term programming from various perspectives and show their relative importance in the field of computer science. The second chapter introduces a formal notation for the precise specification of the syntax of programming languages.

2. *Introduction to Programming*

Chapters 3 to 10 introduce the classical programming concepts. Beginning with a sequence of statements and many simple and user-defined static types, these chapters move on to arm the reader with procedures, functions and modules to be able to correctly structure even complex problems. On completion of Chapter 10, the reader should be able to write many challenging programs.

3. *Advanced Programming*

Here we introduce a number of concepts that particularly support the development of program systems that need to react to ever changing sets of data. We present dynamic data structures as well as recursion at the algorithmic and data-structure level. The reader also becomes familiar with persistent data and exception handling. Chapter 13 treats object-oriented programming, which has conquered an ever growing share of the field of software system development. Another steadily rising field, parallel programming, highlights Chapter 16.

4. *Appendices*

Through the appendices we have striven to ease the task of Modula-3 programming. Appendix A describes a complete non-trivial program to manage music CD's. Appendix B, intended as a reference for the pros, offers a complete but very compact description of the semantics of Modula-3. It is a reprint of the original Modula-3 language definition [CDG+89]. Further appendices describe the most important interfaces to the Modula-3 development environment and provide concise descriptions of various such environments. The appendices also include detailed instructions on installing and configuring a Modula-3 development environment and the software included with this book.

5. *Included Software*

All examples in the book have been tested. They are either executable themselves or parts of executable programs. We provide these to the reader at no charge. All Modula-3 programs (including the Modula-3 compiler) can be started from an integrated, interactive, user-friendly environment.

Acknowledgments

Our foremost gratitude goes to Roland Mittermeir, who profoundly contributed to the production of this book. Significant texts and examples in Chapters 10 to 12 come from him. He is actually a co-author of this book.

We also owe special thanks to Hans-Peter Mössenböck, Peter Rechenberg, Johann Eder and Karl-Heinz Eder; they assumed the enormously work-intensive and thankless task of thoroughly proofreading the original German manuscript. We likewise wish to express our gratitude to Michael Dobrovnik for his comments on our example program in the appendix. Their criticisms and comments taught us a great deal, and without their contributions it would have been impossible to complete this book. Naturally the authors retain full and sole accountability for any errors.

Our gratitude also goes to the researchers at Digital Systems Research Center, Palo Alto, who developed Modula-3 and made it available. We especially thank Marc Najork, for his support. We are also grateful to Greg Nelson and Bill Kalsow.

We also extend our appreciation to Springer-Verlag, Digital Equipment Corporation, the University of Klagenfurt and the Raiffeisen Bank of Carinthia for their generous support of the development of our user-friendly Modula-3 environment and to Miklós Szabó for his development work.

We also offer our sincere thanks to Silvia Nedizavec for her meticulous preparation of the figures in this book and to Michael Vrbicky for his help in formatting the English edition.

Last but not least, we thank our patient families, who spent many evenings and weekends without us during the two years in which we wrote this book.

We offer the reader this book as the fruits of our labors in the hope that it proves to be a useful learning instrument and that it provides some fun and pleasure along the way.

Contents

1 What is programming?   **1**
- 1.1 An informal introduction 1
  - 1.1.1 Algorithms 2
  - 1.1.2 Switches and symbols 4
  - 1.1.3 Turing machine 6
  - 1.1.4 Computability 7
- 1.2 The von Neumann computer 9
- 1.3 Rigid thought structures 11
- 1.4 Programming in the small 14
  - 1.4.1 Software production methods 14
  - 1.4.2 Writing simple programs 17
- 1.5 Levels of programming 18
  - 1.5.1 Formal and human languages 18
  - 1.5.2 Assembler 20
  - 1.5.3 High-level programming languages 21
- 1.6 Programming and computer science 24
  - 1.6.1 The responsibility of computer scientists 25

2 Metalanguages   **27**
- 2.1 Definition of formal languages 27
- 2.2 Digits and numbers 29
- 2.3 Names 30
- 2.4 Arithmetic expressions 31
- 2.5 Extension for Modula-3 syntax 33

3 The structure of programs   **35**
- 3.1 Structuring 35
- 3.2 Language environment 36
- 3.3 The statics and dynamics of a program 38
  - 3.3.1 Data and data types 39
  - 3.3.2 Algorithms and procedures 41
- 3.4 Structure of Modula-3 programs 42
  - 3.4.1 The module 42

3.4.2   Hello, world   44
3.4.3   Source code   46
3.4.4   Computing the arithmetic mean   47
3.4.5   SIO interface   50

4   Predefined data types   **53**
4.1   Integers   53
4.1.1   Range   53
4.1.2   Operations   54
4.2   Logical type   60
4.2.1   Range   60
4.2.2   Operations   60
4.3   Characters   63
4.3.1   Range   63
4.3.2   Operations   65
4.4   Texts   67
4.4.1   Range   67
4.4.2   Operations   68
4.5   Floating-point numbers   72
4.5.1   Range   73
4.5.2   Floating-point literals   74
4.5.3   Operations   75
4.5.4   Input and output of floating-point numbers   78

5   Statements   **83**
5.1   The assignment   83
5.2   Structured statements   84
5.3   Sequence   87
5.4   Branches   87
5.4.1   If statement   87
5.4.2   Case statement   92
5.4.3   Equivalence of If and Case   96
5.5   Loops   97
5.5.1   While loop   97
5.5.2   Loop invariants 102
5.5.3   Repeat loop 105
5.5.4   For loop 108
5.5.5   Loop statement 110
5.5.6   Equivalence of the repetition statements 112

6   User-defined simple types   **115**
6.1   Enumeration 115
6.1.1   Predefined enumerations 117

	6.1.2	Range	117
	6.1.3	Operations	118
6.2	Subranges		120
	6.2.1	Operations	122
	6.2.2	Predefined subranges	122

7 Expressions and declarations 125

7.1	Expressions		125
	7.1.1	Syntax of expressions	125
	7.1.2	Evaluation of expressions	127
	7.1.3	Evaluation of logical expressions	128
7.2	Declarations		129
	7.2.1	Constant declarations	129
	7.2.2	Type declarations	131
	7.2.3	Variable declarations	132
7.3	Equivalence of types		133
7.4	Subtypes		134
7.5	Assignment compatibility		135
7.6	Expression compatibility		136

8 Composite static types 139

8.1	Arrays		140
	8.1.1	Unidimensional arrays	141
	8.1.2	Multidimensional arrays	142
	8.1.3	Array constructors	144
	8.1.4	Operations on arrays	145
	8.1.5	Example: Schedule	148
	8.1.6	Linear search in an array	150
	8.1.7	Sorting an array	152
8.2	Records		154
	8.2.1	Record selectors	156
	8.2.2	Record constructors	157
	8.2.3	Operations with records	160
	8.2.4	With statement	160
	8.2.5	Example: Student data management	162
8.3	Sets		163
	8.3.1	Range	164
	8.3.2	Set constructors	165
	8.3.3	Operations on sets	165
	8.3.4	Example: Input of numbers	168
8.4	Comparison of arrays, records and sets		170
8.5	Packed data types		170

9   Structuring algorithms   **173**
  9.1 Block structure   173
  9.2 Procedures and functions   177
       9.2.1 Procedure declaration   179
       9.2.2 Procedure invocation   181
  9.3 Modes of parameter passing   183
       9.3.1 Value parameter   185
       9.3.2 Variable parameters   185
       9.3.3 Read-only parameters   186
       9.3.4 Information transfer via global variables   187
       9.3.5 Comparing the kinds of parameters   188
  9.4 Identifying the procedures   192
  9.5 Name, type and default value of
       a parameter   193
  9.6 Eval statement   194
  9.7 Procedure types   195
       9.7.1 Operations with procedures   195

10 Modules   **201**
  10.1 Structure   206
       10.1.1 Interface   207
       10.1.2 Implementation   208
       10.1.3 Compilation units   210
  10.2 Using modules   210
       10.2.1 Structuring the data space   212
       10.2.2 Type creation   215
       10.2.3 Creating toolboxes   219
  10.3 An example with graphic elements   219
  10.4 Modularization   223

11 Dynamic data structures   **227**
  11.1 Dynamism in static data structures   228
       11.1.1 Implementation of stacks as arrays   228
       11.1.2 FIFO queues in arrays   231
       11.1.3 Example: Rotating shifts   234
       11.1.4 Explicit address management with pointers   235
       11.1.5 Address management by the system   238
  11.2 Dynamic data in Modula-3   241
       11.2.1 Allocation and deallocation   241
       11.2.2 Operations with references   245
       11.2.3 Open (dynamic) arrays   246
       11.2.4 Arrays of references   247
  11.3 Subtypes   248

11.3.1 Subtype rule for references 249
11.3.2 Subtype rule for arrays 250
11.4 Abstract and encapsulated data types 251
11.4.1 Opaque data types 252
11.4.2 Revelation 254
11.4.3 An abstract and a generic stack 257
11.4.4 Rules for the design of encapsulated data types . . . 260
11.5 Dynamic structures 261
11.5.1 Lists 262
11.5.2 Kinds of lists 263
11.5.3 Singly linked, sorted linear list 264

12 Recursion **271**
12.1 Recursive algorithms 273
12.1.1 Fundamentals of recursive programming 273
12.1.2 Using recursion 278
12.1.3 Quicksort 281
12.1.4 The Towers of Hanoi 282
12.1.5 Recursive list management 285
12.2 Recursive data structures 287
12.2.1 Trees 287
12.2.2 Binary trees and search trees 290
12.2.3 Binary search trees 292
12.2.4 Traversing a tree 294
12.2.5 Implementation of the binary search tree 296

13 Objects **305**
13.1 Object-oriented modeling 305
13.2 Object-oriented programming 308
13.2.1 Encapsulation 308
13.2.2 Inheritance 309
13.2.3 Polymorphism 310
13.2.4 Dynamic binding 310
13.2.5 Object-oriented applications 311
13.3 Object types in Modula-3 312
13.3.1 Declaration of object types 313
13.3.2 Implementation of objects 314
13.3.3 Implementation of methods 315
13.3.4 Accessing object components 317
13.3.5 Creating objects 317
13.3.6 Subtyping rules for objects 318
13.4 Encapsulation of object types 319
13.4.1 Inheritance 323

13.4.2 Polymorphism and dynamic binding 325
13.4.3 Generalization 328
13.4.4 The tree class hierarchy 339
13.4.5 Subclasses of binary trees 344

14 Persistent data structures   349
14.1 Files 350
    14.1.1 Accessing files 350
    14.1.2 Access functions 351
    14.1.3 Files and main memory 352
    14.1.4 File types 352
14.2 Files in Modula-3 353
    14.2.1 Input and output streams 353
    14.2.2 Fmt and Scan 357
    14.2.3 Simple-IO 360
14.3 Persistent variables 362
    14.3.1 Implementation 364

15 Exception handling   371
15.1 Exceptions in a program 371
15.2 Exception handling in Modula-3 375
    15.2.1 Exceptions, run-time errors,
            programming errors 375
    15.2.2 Declaration of exceptions 376
    15.2.3 Generation of exceptions 376
    15.2.4 Exception handling 376
    15.2.5 Delegating exceptions 377
15.3 Delaying exception handling 379
15.4 Strategies for exception handling 382

16 Parallel programming   385
16.1 Motivation for parallelism 385
16.2 Parallel programs 388
16.3 Threads in Modula-3 390
    16.3.1 Schedulers of Modula-3 environments 390
    16.3.2 Creating threads 391
16.4 Shared variables 397
    16.4.1 Data-parallel algorithms 397
    16.4.2 Critical regions and mutual exclusion 400
    16.4.3 Type Mutex and the Lock statement 402
    16.4.4 Monitor 405
    16.4.5 Semaphores 413
16.5 Message passing 418

      16.5.1 Client/server model 418

      16.5.2 Synchronous message communication 419

      16.5.3 Asynchronous message communication 419

      16.5.4 Channels 420

A A small database   **427**

  A.1 The task 427

  A.2 The object model 428

  A.3 Interfaces of the object model 431

      A.3.1 Interface of the base object 431

      A.3.2 The specific interfaces 432

  A.4 User interface 433

      A.4.1 Input strategy 433

      A.4.2 Output 435

  A.5 Implementation 436

      A.5.1 Persistent sets 437

      A.5.2 Sets 438

      A.5.3 Object lists 439

      A.5.4 Auxiliary modules 439

      A.5.5 Selections 439

      A.5.6 Implementation modules of the object model 440

      A.5.7 Input 441

      A.5.8 Queries 442

  A.6 Interfaces 443

  A.7 Implementation modules 447

B Language Definition   **469**

  B.1 Definitions 469

  B.2 Types 470

      B.2.1 Ordinal types 470

      B.2.2 Floating-point types 471

      B.2.3 Arrays 472

      B.2.4 Records 473

      B.2.5 Packed types 474

      B.2.6 Sets 474

      B.2.7 References 474

      B.2.8 Procedures 475

      B.2.9 Objects 477

      B.2.10 Subtyping rules 480

      B.2.11 Predeclared opaque types 482

  B.3 Statements 482

      B.3.1 Assignment 483

      B.3.2 Procedure call 484

B.3.3   Eval   485
B.3.4   Block statement   486
B.3.5   Sequential composition   486
B.3.6   Raise   486
B.3.7   Try Except   487
B.3.8   Try Finally   488
B.3.9   Loop   488
B.3.10 Exit   488
B.3.11 Return   489
B.3.12 If   489
B.3.13 While   490
B.3.14 Repeat   490
B.3.15 With   490
B.3.16 For   491
B.3.17 Case   492
B.3.18 Typecase   492
B.3.19 Lock   493
B.3.20 Inc and Dec   493
B.4 Declarations   494
B.4.1   Types   494
B.4.2   Constants   494
B.4.3   Variables   495
B.4.4   Procedures   495
B.4.5   Exceptions   496
B.4.6   Opaque types   496
B.4.7   Revelations   496
B.4.8   Recursive declarations   497
B.5 Modules and interfaces   498
B.5.1   Import statements   499
B.5.2   Interfaces   500
B.5.3   Modules   500
B.5.4   Generics   501
B.5.5   Initialization   503
B.5.6   Safety   503
B.6 Expressions   504
B.6.1   Conventions for describing operations   504
B.6.2   Operation syntax   505
B.6.3   Designators   506
B.6.4   Numeric literals   507
B.6.5   Text and character literals   508
B.6.6   Nil   508
B.6.7   Function application   508
B.6.8   Set, array, and record constructors   508

B.6.9   New 509
B.6.10 Arithmetic operations 510
B.6.11 Relations 513
B.6.12 Boolean operations 514
B.6.13 Type operations 514
B.6.14 Text operations 516
B.6.15 Constant Expressions 516
B.7 Unsafe operations 516
B.8 Syntax 518
B.8.1   Keywords 518
B.8.2   Reserved identifiers 518
B.8.3   Operators 518
B.8.4   Comments 518
B.8.5   Pragmas 518
B.8.6   Conventions for syntax 519
B.8.7   Compilation unit productions 519
B.8.8   Statement productions 520
B.8.9   Type productions 521
B.8.10 Expression productions 521
B.8.11 Miscellaneous productions 522
B.8.12 Token productions 522

C Library interfaces   **525**
C.1 Standard interfaces 525
C.1.1   Text 525
C.1.2   Thread 527
C.1.3   Word 528
C.1.4   Real 530
C.1.5   Float 530
C.1.6   FloatMode 533
C.2 Formatting 534
C.2.1   Fmt 534
C.2.2   Scan 538
C.3 Input and output streams 538
C.3.1   Rd 538
C.3.2   Wr 540
C.3.3   Simple input/output (SIO) 542
C.3.4   Simple Files (SF) 545

D Modula-3 language environments   **547**
D.1 The DEC/SRC language environment 547
D.2 A language environment for PCs 548
D.2.1   Installation 548

D.2.2 The programming editor 549
D.2.3 The browser 550
D.2.4 A graphical user interface 550
D.2.5 Restrictions 551

Bibliography   **553**

Index   **557**

Chapter 1

What is programming?

1.1 An informal introduction

The question seems superfluous: Programming means writing programs, right? But what are *programs*? In essence, programs contain a sequence of instructions that produce desired behavior on a computer. This still sounds simple. Does this mean that programming is also simple? Unfortunately, we cannot answer this question in the affirmative just like that.

Just what is the difficulty in programming? We can most readily formulate it as follows: Programming is difficult because humans are so intelligent and computers so unintelligent. As a result, there seems to be a general difficulty in issuing instructions: If we try to issue instructions to an intelligent being, we encounter the problem that the affected being might not agree with our intentions – precisely because the being is intelligent. If we issue instructions to an unintelligent being (such as a computer), then we must assume that it does not even understand our instructions. If we want to assure that our instructions are actually and impeccably executed, then we must descend to the level of the unintelligent being. In other words, we must provide very precise *specifications* of our wishes, down to the last detail. And here we encounter the difficulty of programming: Humans must communicate their wishes with unaccustomed precision, which more or less contradicts the very nature of most people.

Does this make programming hopelessly formidable? This is not the case. As we shall see, people can learn to structure programs so systematically that even a very complex set of instructions can be reduced to a comprehensible structure. Thus we can decompose our programs into correspondingly small and comprehensible units, allowing us always to concentrate on the essential.

Here the notation that we use is particularly important. We know that the ancient Greeks did not posses our modern mathematical notation [Col69]. Although they practiced mathematics on a very high level, their computational skills were by no means as efficient as what we have today. (Perhaps efficiency was not even their goal, but that is another story.) For lack of adequate notation, they calculated in a way akin to when we do computations in our head today. The semiautomatic (and hence only semiconscious) calculations that we carry out with pencil and paper, e.g., when we multiply two larger numbers, was made possible only through the introduction of modern notation.

1.1.1 Algorithms

How we apply a set of exact rules, e.g., to multiply larger numbers, can also be termed *algorithmic computation*.

> An algorithm is a precise, unambiguous specification of a finite, effective procedure.

But what does this statement mean? Let us first clarify some of the terms.

- The essence of a *procedure* is that it can be *executed* stepwise – by a human or even a machine.

- *Finite* has dual meaning: First, the *description* of an algorithm must be finite. Second, its execution must be finite; i.e., it must *terminate* at some time.

  You might wonder why it is necessary to require that a description must be finite. You might assert that an endless description cannot be produced anyway; that would require endlessly long paper! This is not the case. A description might contain a loop, e.g., from which there is no exit.

  A student once behaved very conspicuously during a written examination until the examiner finally approached him and found a suspicious paper on his desk. The following words were written on the paper: "Perpetuum mobile – description on the reverse side". The examiner turned the paper over to find the words: "Perpetuum mobile – description on the reverse side". This is not an algorithm (unfortunately, or we would have implemented the perpetuum mobile). Neither the description nor the procedure terminates.

  In the following example the description terminates, but the procedure does not always terminate. We give someone instructions on how to find the way out of a systematically structured labyrinth:

  > "Go to the first possible branch. If it goes left, follow it. Otherwise continue straight. Keep going straight until you reach a T-junction and then take a right turn there.

> Repeat the whole procedure until you see the light. If you
> reach a dead end, then turn around and continue as though
> the interruption had not occurred."

Whether this procedure terminates depends on the labyrinth. If it
has no exit, the procedure does not terminate. Hence this is no algorithm. Since in computer science inexhaustibly looping procedures
are often very important, they are sometimes called *nonterminating
algorithms*.

- *Effective* means that the algorithm actually has an effect, returns a
  result. Some twenty years ago, when computer time was very expensive, a good friend of one of the authors wrote an excellent program that carried out important computations with utmost precision.
  The program ran a whole weekend around the clock. However, the
  programmer forgot to write the output instructions that would have
  printed the results. This was not exactly effective, and his boss was
  not at all pleased.

  Effectiveness is closely related to finiteness: An endless function certainly does not return a result. However, it can have an effect, a *side
  effect*. If the author of the above program had forgotten the instructions that terminate the program instead of the output instructions,
  then the program would have been very effective, exhausting all the
  paper in the printer, yet without a result. His boss would have been
  no more pleased in this case.

- *Unambiguous* means that with every step the executing agent knows
  exactly what is to be done and always has exactly one next step. When
  the Oracle of Delphi tells me, "Know thyself", then this is certainly
  great wisdom, but not unambiguous and hence no algorithm. There
  is no unambiguous procedure for this purpose. Probably there can
  be no such procedure, for while I try to know myself, I change as a
  consequence of the search. Perhaps this is exactly the purpose of the
  instruction.

- The meaning of *precise* naturally depends on the receiver of our instructions. For example, we might request of a high school graduate,
  "Please tell us how many months you have lived." Although we have
  formulated the task with sufficient precision, we have said nothing
  about the procedure. In such a case we have formulated only the
  function, but not the algorithm. By contrast, we could say, "Multiply
  your age in years by the number of months in a year and add to that
  the number of months that have elapsed since your last birthday."

Here the procedure (the algorithm) for how to proceed is also formulated precisely. Yet if we confront a computer, such a formulation in everyday language would lack sufficient precision.

There have been efforts in the realm of *artificial intelligence* to make computers "intelligent" enough to execute such instructions formulated in human language. We do not treat this research here.

This brings us to the point where we inevitably need to turn to the subject of computers. Above we defamed computers as unintelligent beings. Why? Computers are praised as the most intelligent of machines! Computers actually do enjoy a unique position among machines because they possess amazing flexibility. Consider one of the most wonderful machines, the clock. The clock has a well defined function for which it can be used. It can tell us what time it is, but nothing more. Somewhat more flexible devices do exist. A table, e.g., permits us to store a variety of things on it (although not everything). Despite the endless variety of applications for tables, their function remains clearly defined and restricted.

1.1.2   Switches and symbols

Let us illustrate the flexibility of the computer with the following comparison. Take a simple light switch; its function is very much restricted in that it turns a light on or off. Now imagine a light switch that is not connected to a light. If we assign some arbitrary meaning to the *up* and *down* positions (*states*), then we can employ it for various functions. For example, we could make an agreement with our children: "If the switch is *up*, then please do not disturb me. If it is *down*, we can go out and play." We could invent any number of such interpretations. And if a single switch does not suffice, we can simply use more.

We thus achieve enormous flexibility by liberating the switching function to allow any assigned interpretation. For a wired light switch, its *interpretation* is inherent: *up* means a lighted room and *down* means dark (or vice versa). But severed from their usual function, these two states can mean anything.

Actually a computer consists of nothing more than a vast number of (very fast, minute) switching elements. Part of these switches constitute the *central processing unit* (CPU, which consists of the *arithmetic/logic unit* (ALU) and the control unit) and the rest form the *memory*.

The switching elements of the processing unit have predefined functions: The CPU can execute a set of predefined primitive instructions (including, e.g., addition of two numbers according to a specified algorithm). The CPU is the active element, or the engine of a computer.

The switching elements of the memory unit can again be classified into two parts: the *program region* and the *data region*.

Programs employ the instructions of the CPU to describe certain behavior. If we liken the CPU to the engine of an automobile, then the program is the map that guides us to various destinations. The *execution* of a program corresponds to a specific excursion. To carry out a given trip, the driver must *interpret* this map. Similarly, the CPU interprets the instructions of a program. (Here we neglect the fact that humans generally interpret more intelligently than computers: A quick glimpse at the map might suffice for a human, while the CPU must process the instructions step by step.)

The engine (CPU) for a certain automobile (computer) remains the same. However, the map (program) can change any number of times as new maps become necessary for new destinations. Also, a specific route (program execution) can be repeated any number of times.

The instructions of a program relate to data in the *same* memory unit (called working storage or main memory). This means that every execution of a program with different data can produce somewhat different results. For example, if we write a program to determine the arithmetic mean of two numbers, then the program should return 3 for 2 and 4, and for 10 and 20 the result would be 15. Or, to continue the auto simile, we could consider the state of traffic lights, other automobiles, and the streets to be traveled as our data. The traffic situation changes with each trip.

Our data comprise a set of possible states, the *state space*. We usually perceive this state space as consisting of smaller state units – *state variables*. Each such unit represents one dimension in this hypothetical space. Each traffic light, for example, has its possible states (red, amber and green), and ten traffic lights form a ten-dimensional state space.

At any given time, the state space has a certain configuration (the current state of the lights) which represents the *current state*. For example, if our data region consists of two switches, then the total state space contains four possible configurations: both up, both down, the first down and the second up, and the first up and the second down.

> The alert reader might ask what the current state is if we are just in the process of toggling a switch. Obviously we need to introduce infinitely many intermediate states in order to be able to do justice to the process of switching itself. To avoid this, we prefer to refine our statement that the state space has a certain configuration at any given time. *At any moment* only means at any moment when the switching elements have fixed their states. In the interim periods, when the state space is in the process of changing from one state to the other, we will simply look the other way.

We identify state variables by *name* or by *address*. We call the contents of a state variable (a concrete configuration of a smaller state unit) its *value*.

☐ Read/ write head

Figure 1.1: *Turing machine*

As indicated, these values can represent, or *symbolize*, anything. Therefore computers are often called *symbol-manipulating machines*.

If we view all of memory as one unit, then we can say that during the execution of a program computers can change their own state space *automatically* – either in an endless loop or until some point is reached that is regarded as *end state* or *termination state*. Hence computers are often called *automata*. The name automobile reflects the fact that the vehicle propels itself as a horseless carriage. Because the computer controls itself, a computer resembles an automobile that reads maps itself, selects and drives the route independently, and eventually even controls the traffic lights as well. (Perhaps the future will offer such automobiles.)

Before examining the architecture of modern computers in more detail, we should ask what all a computer can compute.

1.1.3   Turing machine

In his famous paper [Tur36] Alan Turing developed a *hypothetical* computer that could do the following (Figure 1.1):

- Read symbols from a tape of infinite length where at least two different symbol values must be possible, e.g., 0 and 1.

- Replace an existing value with a new one.

- Move the tape left or right.

- Make a transition to a new state based on the existing state and the value that was read.

The machine begins at a certain position on a tape that contains the input. The machine's respective action depends on the input symbol at this location and on the current state of the machine itself. The machine has only a fixed number of states between which it can change back and forth (depending on the contents of the tape). With every state transition, it writes a new symbol onto the tape (i.e., at every processing step), and the tape is moved on. The action might also be to stop the tape and thus the machine; the tape content at this time represents the result.

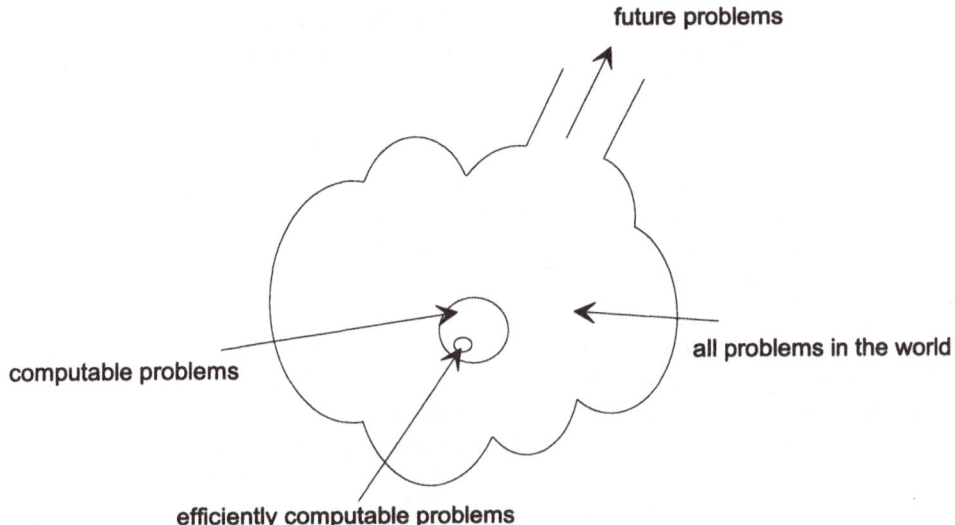

Figure 1.2: *Computability*

The *interpretation*, i.e., the specification of which symbol triggers the writing of which new symbol and which movement, is stored on the same tape (expressed with similar symbols), e.g., by storing state numbers. Thus one tape (we could call it a program) can turn the machine into an adding machine, while another tape makes the same machine a prime number generator, and so on.

Naturally the Turing machine is no real computer; it is a mathematical abstraction that requires in-depth study to understand it in full [Tur36, Hop79]. It represents the first successful attempt to formalize the term *computability*.

1.1.4 Computability

As unlikely as it might seem, this apparently simple machine can, in all probability, compute everything that is computable. We add the constraint "in all probability" because this hypothesis, made by Alonso Church, has yet to be proven or refuted. The constraint "that is computable" indicates that by no means everything is computable. This even applies in mathematics, where we might expect otherwise. Many scientists, beginning with Kurt Gödel, have proven this. We can even say that more things are uncomputable than are computable.

Even such a "simple" function as one that can decide whether *arbitrary* functions *always* terminate cannot be computed. For if we had such a function f_1, then we could define another function f_2 that terminates precisely and exclusively at that point when f_1 claims that f_2 does not terminate. Now if we ask f_1 whether f_2 terminates, then either f_1 responds in the affirmative – in which case f_2 does not terminate – or vice versa. This is quite amazing, isn't it?

The number of uncomputable functions is non-enumerably infinite, while the number of computable functions is "only" enumerably infinite [Hop79]. And this does not encompass what is uncomputable outside of mathematics.

Furthermore, many computable functions can only be computed very inefficiently. The time required to compute many functions rises exponentially (e.g., by a power of two) with the size of the problem. Assuming that a function requires 4 time units for 2 data values, then 3 data values would escalate the time to 8, and 4 values would demand 16. For 10 data values the function exceeds 1000 time units. Although such functions might be theoretically computable, in practical terms they prove impossible to process for larger problems. Problems that we handle as programmers must be not only *finite* but also *efficiently computable* (Figure 1.2).

This indicates that the domain of programming is definitely restricted. This needs to be stated at the beginning of an introductory textbook to programming. Still, we hope that this realization will not deflate anyone's motivation to learn programming. The use of computers makes it possible to produce many things to make one's own life and others' lives easier. However, when the computer is applied to domains that are principally uncomputable, this application becomes senseless and even damaging. Most domains of human life are uncomputable – and they should not be made computable by force. Nothing is more boring than a conversation in which we always know what the partner will say next. On the other hand, nothing can be finer than a conversation in which the participants grace each other with new, unexpected ideas. The experience is intensified if we ourselves give birth to new ideas. The value of human life is its very uncomputability (whereby we do not mean hysteria).

The difference between medication and poison often depends on the dose. The same applies to the application of computers. People who study computer science should be aware of this fact in order to be able to promote the reasonable use of computers and to prevent their senseless application.

"A machine only becomes useful when it has grown independent of the knowledge that led to its discovery," Dürrenmatt stated ironically in his drama *The Physicists*. And he draws the consequences: "Hence today any fool can make a light bulb glow – or an atomic bomb explode." We hope that our book will help to foster the reader's capability to understand both the power and the limits of programming.

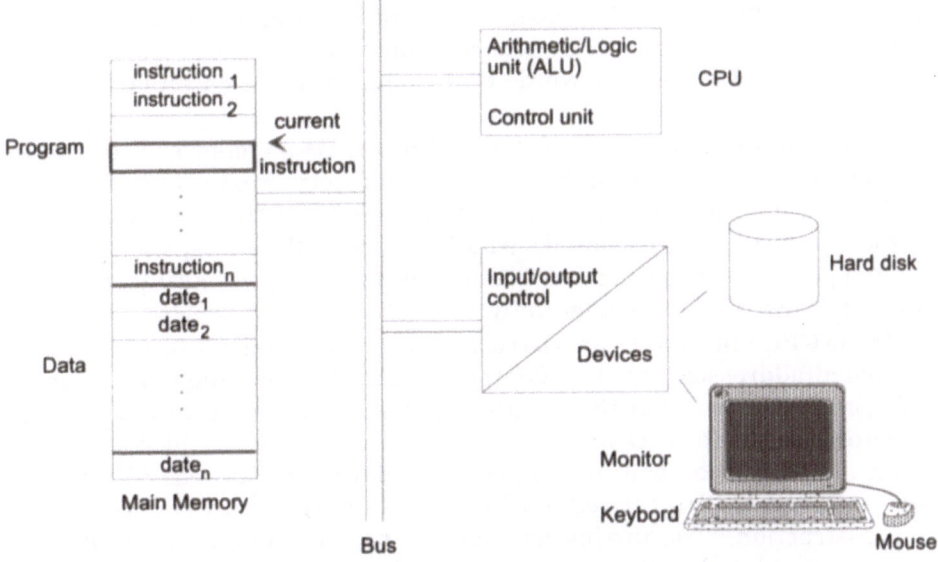

Figure 1.3: *Structure of a computer*

1.2 The von Neumann computer

Alan Turing's computer was never built in the form described above (page
6) (for one reason because a tape of infinite length proves rather difficult
to realize). The first modern computers that appeared in the late 1940s
had a somewhat different architecture. The classical *von Neumann* computer (see Figure 1.3[1]), named after the Hungarian-American mathematician John von Neumann consisted of:

- Memory

- Central processing unit or CPU (= arithmetic/logical unit (ALU) +
  control unit)

- Input and output units (I/O)

The memory can represent any state space, and it can be modified arbitrarily. This memory is divided into *memory cells* (also called *words*), which can
be *addressed* individually.

The memory cells consist of smaller atomic units called *bits*. A bit corresponds to a single switch and can have two states, which are represented

---

[1]The original von Neumann architecture had no bus, but all modern computers do have
a bus system.

as 0 and 1. The bit is the smallest unit of representation in the *binary number system* [AU92]. Eight bits combine to form a *byte*. Most modern computers employ memory words that consist of 32 or 64 bits (i.e., 4 or 8 bytes).

The computer depicted in Figure 1.3 functions as follows: From an input unit we load an initializing state into memory. Part of this state (the *program*) remains unchanged in storage as long as the instructions that it specifies are being executed. Another part of the state, the *data*, can be changed. The execution is governed by the CPU, which interprets the program's instructions sequentially.

If the CPU encounters an instruction, e.g., which tells it to add the data located at addresses 100 and 200, then it loads the operands into its internal *registers*, carries out the addition, and stores the result in an internal register. Then the CPU processes the next instruction, which might tell it, e.g., to write the result of the previous addition to address 300 of memory. Instructions are carried out in this way until the CPU encounters a halt instruction. The intriguing aspect is that the program and its data are accommodated in the same memory. Hence we can imagine programs that process other programs (or even themselves) as data. Here we begin to perceive an exciting flexibility.

"This idea often scared me in the beginning," stated Konrad Zuse [Zus92], the designer of one of the first – if not the very first – modern computers. "Because until then with the computers Z1-Z4 one could understand what was going on. You could even follow the calculations. In the moment that I allowed the computed data to influence the program – for that only a small wire connection the arithmetic unit and the stored program is required – I could no longer monitor the calculations. I had a lot of respect for that little wire, because I felt as soon as this wire is there, Mephisto stands behind me. ... With it a programmer can do the most amazing things."

> Note here that in this context Zuse did not mean exactly the same thing with *"stored program"* as we understand today. He meant in particular the ability to recompute the *addresses* (or *indices*) of the data, which he considered to be a program modification.

The programs of a von Neumann computer consist of the basic instructions of the computing machine. The most important of such instructions are:

- Simple arithmetic operations (such as addition and multiplication)

- Logical operations (such as comparison)

- Assignments (where one storage cell accepts the state value of another)

- Conditional and unconditional branches (the condition usually being the result of the preceding operation)

The architecture of the von Neumann computer is very powerful, almost as powerful as the Turing machine. However, there are important differences:

- Storage is finite for the von Neumann computer.

- The von Neumann computer has a general concept of input/output, which enables *communication* with the user.

- Von Neumann computers are relatively easy and efficient to implement.

- More important (at least from the viewpoint of programmers) is that the von Neumann is relatively easy to program – even though programming in the early years of the computer (the 1950s) in retrospect seems unbelievably difficult, inefficient and especially error-prone.

If we try to employ a Turing machine to program even simple mathematical functions (i.e., to translate them into the basic instructions of the Turing machine), we find that this soon becomes quite cumbersome and clumsy.

1.3 Rigid thought structures

The instructions of a von Neumann machine more closely resemble human thinking. This is no wonder, as they were derived from thought structures. We can program a von Neumann computer with such instructions as:

Instruction i1:
  Take a symbol x and compare it with a symbol y.
  If they are equal, jump to instruction i2; else jump to instruction i3
  ⋮
Instruction i2:
  ⋮
Instruction i3:
  ⋮

The actual notation that must be used is not as relaxed as in our example. We show the actual appearance of such a program later.

The basic arithmetic operations (addition, multiplication) and predicate logic (negation, conjunction, disjunction) are fundamental elements of the instruction set. The basic structure of programs is essentially based on such constructs as: "if ... then ..." and "repeat ... until ...". These constructs reflect certain thought patterns.

It is noteworthy that these rigid thought structures are stored in the computer independently of the respective content. We must emphasize that it is by no means as self-evident as it might seem to be able to store thought structures. This requires that humans formulate these structures abstractly and independently of the content. This in turn requires the capacity of humans to observe their own thinking process, yet this contains a fundamental contradiction [Küh84, Küh90]. We can observe our thinking only with our thinking itself – no other tool is available. How can thinking observe itself? When we attempt such observation, then we note that the observing thinking always comes too late – thoughts are already present. Thinking cannot grasp the *process* of thinking. However, it can apparently observe its own *past*. Once the thought is there, we can observe it in terms of both content and structure. Hence thinking seems to be occurring in at least two dimensions: in the present, where it is currently active, and in the past, where what has been thought becomes conscious and observable from the perspective of the present.

This leaves the question of why the present dimension escapes observation. It would be a contradiction to say that such observation is principally impossible. First, we cannot doubt the existence of the present because the past could not exist without a corresponding, preceding present. Second, we cannot principally preclude the possibility of observing something that surely exists – to make a certain statement in that direction would require already having observed it. Hence we are confronted with a *practical* impediment: Our attention does not suffice to consciously grasp the presence of thinking – actually our own present. Our attention remains dark at first, and the light of consciousness always comes too late and shines on the already frozen dimension of the past. Therefore many thinkers doubt the existence of this present and try to derive the origin of thinking from something beyond thinking, such as from philosophical *matter* or the *collective unconscious*.

Consider, however, that the process-oriented, present form of thinking cannot be darker than the light of consciousness – indeed, it could be that this light is so bright that it blinds us at first. The results of thinking – our own thoughts – are clear to us, which is the only thing that is really clear to us. Thus the origin, the source of thinking cannot be *principally* unclear, unapproachable, incomprehensible. We cannot trace thinking to something that is principally incomprehensible. The "darkness" of philosophical matter or of the collective unconscious is principal in nature (so defined), while the darkness of present thinking is only practical. People cannot think something that they do not understand themselves. (They can say things that they do not understand, but that is another matter.) In order to cast our own light on the moment of origin of understanding, we would have to remove practical impediments.

These practical impediments consist of the weakness of our attentiveness. This is reflected in the fact that our attentiveness is too weak, too scattered to stick to a specific subject for an arbitrarily long time. Normally even a short time proves impossible; our attention is quickly diverted. In order to bear its own presence in its *living*, process-oriented character, our attentiveness would have to be much stronger. Enhancing our attentiveness and thus leading it to its own present dimension – to *our own* present dimension – could be achieved nowadays by any halfway healthy person by *practice*. Whether we do this is a matter of free choice. In *A Guide for the Perplexed* [Sch78] E. F. Schumacher writes that today's humanity and today's science have lost their vertical component. Finding it again is within the realm of free choice.

The usual form of thinking known today is thus perhaps not its final form – and probably not the first. Small children apparently have a consciousness different from that of adults. Likewise earlier humankind also seems to have had a different, more "archaic" consciousness that encompassed different abilities, different *qualities* [Küh84, Küh90]. The ancient Greeks were excellent mathematicians, but they did not invent the computer. They also did not compute as efficiently as we do. Instead, they experienced the qualities of numbers; e.g., for Pythagoras mathematics had the character of a cult or religion. The history of mathematics bears witness to an ever increasing ability to abstract [Col69], always associated with the loss of certain other qualities. The computer appears at a certain phase of our development in which the ability to abstract has reached its highest level and is also generally accessible.

Computers can store rigid thought structures and thus simulate intelligent behavior. They can effectively emulate the past dimension of intelligence, which is the mechanics that have loosed themselves from the process. However, this is not intelligence, for computers lack at least two fundamental features of intelligence:

1. The ability to produce new ideas

2. The capacity to make free decisions

The "intelligence" of a computer always derives from human intelligence and cannot regenerate itself [Bös89]. In response to the frequent question of whether a computer can emulate human behavior such as human thinking, we can respond: In its highest forms, as when we discover something new, certainly not. However, we humans can become so mechanical and schematic in our thinking and behavior that little difference remains

between us and a computer. Yet even at our worst we have the potential
to free ourselves from such automation and to direct our intellect in completely new directions.

1.4   Programming in the small

For the programmer the most important consequence of the above considerations is that programming, viewed very generally, is nothing more than
the translation of ideas into an unusually precise form. The programmer
must cast human concepts into the mold prescribed by the structure of the
computer.

This general definition of programming takes on a broad variety of concrete forms. In computer science much effort was expended to make this
translation easier through the development of both *methods*, and *programming languages*.

1.4.1   Software production methods

Let us first define the scope of the term *programming* as we employ it in
this book. We shall outline the phases in the development of an idea to a
complete program, indeed to a *program system*, or *software* system.

Conception of an idea

First an idea emerges on the part of us or our client. We first need to
examine whether this problem lends itself to solution by computer. If the
problem is principally uncomputable, then we must forsake our search for
a computer solution. Of course, this basic uncomputability might only arise
later. We might also find that the problem could be solved by computer, but
we decide that we prefer not to solve it, e.g., because the solution would
cause harm to persons. In this case we should also abandon our search for
a solution.

This aspect was addressed as follows by J. Weizenbaum in a lecture
in Budapest. If you go to a doctor and ask to have a finger removed, the
doctor would certainly ask why. If you respond that your head hurts, then
the doctor will surely want to examine you for the cause of your headache.
By contrast, if a client approaches a software developer with the request
to produce software to compute the ballistic trajectory of objects with high
precision, then the software developer normally only asks when the client
needs it and how much the client is willing to pay. It would be better if the
software developer would also first ask why. If the client expresses a desire
to improve a weapons system to finally obliterate a neighboring country

from the face of the earth, then the technical problem becomes a complex social and moral problem that cannot be solved at a technical level.

In the absence of such impediments, we can advance to the next phase.

Analysis

The fundamental question is: What are the actual requirements? Frequently a client can only formulate wishes very vaguely, such as an improvement in bookkeeping or increased productivity in the company's manufacturing. These are admirable wishes, but they do not suffice to derive a program. We need to study the complete production process and formulate the rough requirement in the form of a number of smaller constituent requirements. We need to localize bottlenecks where we can employ automatic controls to achieve improvements. However, we must note that a local optimization can have unexpected negative side effects on the overall system: For example, the bottleneck might move from the improved production station to its successor, which might be overwhelmed by the improvement.

A client might also approach a software developer with a very specific wish: Produce software that does this and that. In such a case the developer should also ask why. One of the authors of this book was once contracted to produce software to implement a certain communication protocol. The work would have easily taken a year. But the author first determined the actual requirement behind the wish. The result was that the client did not need the new software at all, and the requirements could be met by slight adaptation of existing software within two days.

In summary, in this phase we analyze the problem to be solved, at first completely independently of the details of the final the solution.

Specification

Once we have understood the problem in detail, we derive a number of specific requirements. Now we are able to say exactly *what* we want to achieve. We formulate our problem solution as a (possibly very large) set of subfunctions. We normally describe such a subfunction by specifying possible input data (*parameters*) of a function and stating which results (*output*) the function should produce. Furthermore, we specify the conditions that the inputs and outputs must fulfill. Outputs of subfunctions serve as inputs for other functions. Since it is difficult to assure that the set of outputs of one function are compatible with the set of inputs of the next, we can employ computer-aided tools and dedicated *specification languages*[PST91].

This phase usually overlaps chronologically with the preceding phase. The result is a document that should contain all components to be realized.

Design

This phase produces a detailed plan for the *solution* of the of the specified problem. Here is where we begin to consider *how* to solve the problem. This plan should remain as independent as possible of concrete implementation details, but we do need to consider the requirements on the computer system. From the data set, the functions, and the nature of utilization (e.g., around the clock, once daily, once annually; by a certain client, by many clients, etc.) we can determine the necessary capacity, performance and security of the computer system. Which specific type of computer affords these features should not affect the design in this phase. The costs of the solution must be compatible with the client's budget.

Implementation

Now the design is translated into a form that the computer can process. Here we might first check which software components are already available (either from the client or from third-party vendors); these can be reused, perhaps in modified form. *Reuse* is possible already during specification or design; reuse is still practiced seldom, yet increasingly.

The missing components must be programmed. The actual programming occurs rather late in the *software life cycle*[Som92], and it is frequently a smaller part of the time investment. This is a general rule which – like all rules – does not always apply. The individual components must be *validated*: We must be convinced of their correctness. This can occur via formal methods (the proof of a software component similar to a mathematical theorem), or by thorough testing (to determine how the software reacts to certain typical and atypical inputs). We are best advised to use a reasonable combination of both approaches.

Integration and testing

The individual components must be synthesized and the overall system must be tested. An important quality attribute of the design, as well as of the software tools employed, is whether this step is easy or – as so often happens – it becomes hopelessly complex. In the latter case we would need to begin a redesign – or we put poor software on the market, which certainly has been known to happen.

Installation and maintenance

Last but not least, the software is installed for use. It begins a second life: Software must often be *maintained* over years or decades. For poorly planned projects, the errors begin to emerge here. Either some detail fails to work that was not detected during implementation, or something has been omitted. Now the nature of the errors determines the consequences: If the analysis was sloppy, this might now necessitate rethinking and re-designing large parts of the software system. The farther back in the development process that an error occurred, the more difficult and expensive is the remedy.

Detected errors and new wishes need to be handled continuously. Almost never are programs written once and then put into service without modification. Particularly the design of the system must thus pay attention to *modifiability*. Typical modifications include extensions and adaptations to newly purchased hardware.

Top-down and bottom-up

The distinction between the development phases is not always clear, and we sometimes need to repeat certain phases. The method outlined here is only one of many possibilities for carrying out a software project. It basically represents a *top-down* approach: First we view the whole, decompose and refine it, and then sequentially solve the subproblems. The opposite direction, a *bottom-up* approach, means obtaining or constructing functional components that can hopefully combine to a useful whole. For certain problems this proves quite practical: If we have a store of pre-fabricated parts, we can sometimes simply assemble them. This requires that we can slightly modify the problem to be solved so that it matches our available parts. (For more about the software development process, see [Som92]).

> We could say that the *top-down* method puts analysts and designers in a "divine" position: They attempt to create a world from above. The opposite approach (*bottom-up*) in its extreme form regards the world from an ant's perspective, seeing only the details and hoping that they fit together to a whole. As in the Indian saying where different people are confronted with different parts of an elephant's body — one holding the tail, another the trunk, the third a leg — each individual is convinced that elephants look like what they are perceiving.

1.4.2 Writing simple programs

This book concentrates primarily on the production of relatively simple programs where at least the specifications are already available. Design and validation will usually be quite simple. Hence this book is restricted to *programming in the small*. Our primary concern will be devising algorithms and corresponding data structures for given problems. Thereby we further restrict the yet too general definition of programming. We define *programs* according to Niklaus Wirth as follows:

| Programs consist of data structures and the algorithms that operate on them.

The restriction to programming in the small does not mean that we want to develop our programs ad hoc. Quite the contrary:

| We shall practice in the small how to design programs systematically and with good style.

Good style in this context has less to do with aesthetics, but is a *quality attribute* that is most difficult to define. A program reflects good style if it is structured comprehensibly and economically. In the words of E.F. Schumacher, "Small is beautiful" [Sch89]. This applies even if the scope of the problem is quite large: We must particularly assure that large problems are decomposed into multiple smaller ones and that the overall structure of the solution as a whole remains comprehensible. We adapt Schumacher's quotation for the purposes of this book: "Clear is beautiful." This principle will pay off in the development of large software systems!

1.5 Levels of programming

1.5.1 Formal and human languages

Programming today differs radically from that of the early days of the computer in the 1950s due to the introduction of various *formal languages*. Formal languages used for programming are called *programming languages*. Their purpose is to make programming easier, more efficient and especially more secure (less error-prone).

Note that the expression *formal language* (and the derived expression *programming language*) can be confusing because it gives the impression of affinity to human languages. In part they were actually derived from the observation of human languages by researchers such as N. Chomsky. Formal languages also have an *alphabet* (the set of characters that may appear), a *syntax* (a set of rules that govern correct sentence formation) and *semantics* (rules that attempt to distinguish meaningful from meaningless sentences). However, there are fundamental differences.

The rules of formal languages – similar to those of a game – are determined *in advance*. *Before* playing chess, we must study the rules. In the immensely more complex "game of language", as Ludwig Wittgenstein calls it, we participate before we learn any rules. The rules of human languages are determined *along the way*. Not a single human language possesses a complete grammar, and the usage of human grammars is unconscious (or what terms *superconscious* [Küh90]). A small child of five or so can usually speak its native language(s) perfectly (is *competent*, in Chomsky's terms). But the child has no idea of grammar and is not even aware of its existence. With *formal languages* the opposite is true. Here the alphabet, syntax and semantics, all rules, are determined in advance. Using a formal language requires (especially at first, similar to learning a foreign language) that these rules be applied very *consciously*.

Furthermore, human languages are inherently *ambiguous* – otherwise there would be no poetry, no puns or other humor. The purpose of formal languages, and so of programming languages, is that their grammar is specified *unambiguously*. Although some formal languages fail to fulfill this requirement, we consider this their shortcoming rather than some enrichment. The requirement of freedom from ambiguity again shows the fundamental difficulty of programming: In human communication, ambiguity can often be the most important component (imagine the intolerable poverty of life without poetry and humor). Yet communication with the computer demands unambiguity. Although unambiguity is often required in human spheres as well, it is never completely achieved there, not even in the military.

However, there are significant commonalities between good programming languages and human languages. A true wonder of linguistics is that children learn their native language from surprisingly little data. A great deal can be guessed – even if some errors occur in the process. This is possible because human languages, despite all exceptions, are as consistent as from a casting. Good programming languages are also consistent in this sense – seeing a given property, we can, with a certain level of experience, infer another. Still, we discourage this approach to learning a programming language and suggest instead a systematic method, whereby theoretical considerations should always precede trial and error! With chess it is also better to learn the rules first, then perhaps some methods of the grand masters; only later can one develop into a real chess player. Simply trying aimlessly quickly exhausts a partner's patience. The computer is more patient in this sense, but observe that we also write our programs for people, usually other people.

For human languages we have deliberately avoided the widespread expression *natural language*. We consider human languages far from natural. This is reflected in the fact that they are not inherited. A baby can learn any language as its native language. If a child grows up without a human environment, it does not learn to speak – it does not even walk upright [Küh90]. While a deaf dog barks exactly like other dogs, a deaf child does not automatically learn a language. This leads us to ask: If human languages are neither artificial (like formal languages) nor natural (like dog barking), where do they come from? We leave this question open as a stimulus.

1.5.2 Assembler

Above we mentioned the programming style of the pioneering period of computing. Today we call this style *low-level programming*, or programming close to machine level. At the lowest level of programming the basic instructions of the computer and the addresses of the data are mapped, or *coded*, directly onto the internal switching elements of the computer. Such programs are only sequences of numbers or *codes*. This is the level of machine language or *machine code*.

The next step is known as *assembly language*, or *assembler*, where the basic instructions can be specified in the form of short, easy-to-remember names. Also, the data addresses need not be written directly; instead, the programmer uses short, symbolic names (as is the practice in mathematics), which are automatically mapped onto concrete addresses by the *program translator* (the *assembler*). This programming style dominated programming for decades. Although its importance has declined over time, it will likely remain necessary for certain purposes.

The following is the short program segment that was loosely formulated on page 11, here in a typical assembler notation:

```
i1:  LOAD x
     CMP y
     BEQ i2
     BRA i3
i2:
     ⋮
i3:
     ⋮
```

The first instruction loads the storage cell at address x into the central processor, into the *accumulator register* of the arithmetic/logic unit. The second instruction (where CMP means *compare*) compares the contents of the storage cell at address y with the value in the register. If the comparison indicates equality, control jumps to i2 (BEQ means *branch on equal*). Otherwise program flow continues at i3 (BRA stands for *branch*). Machine code would look even worse, consisting of nothing but a sequence of numbers (binary numbers coded in octal or hexadecimal form – quite inhuman).

1.5.3 High-level programming languages

Programming languages on a higher level of abstraction (*high-level* programming languages) afford more complex commands and data structures.

> Various taxonomies can be applied to high-level programming languages. Some authors distinguish generations of languages. However, we do not discuss this further here.

This book explains programming with the help of a new, modern programming language, the high-level programming language *Modula-3* [Nel91, Har92]. It was developed at the Systems Research Center (SRC) of Digital Equipment Corporation (DEC) in Palo Alto, California. The most important attributes of Modula-3 are:

- It is an *imperative* programming language.

- It has a secure *type system*.

- It is a *structured* programming language.

- It is *object-oriented*.

Imperative programming languages

Imperative programming languages focus on the algorithm. The programmer must specify the algorithm precisely (as in the example on page 3, where we specified the method for computing age in months: "Multiply your age in years by the number of months in a year ..."). The programming language offers many aids for expressing an algorithm, but the programmer bears sole responsibility for the correctness of the algorithm itself.

> A more than two decade old story tells of a fledgling computer user who complained indignantly to the system programming group of his computing center: The computer failed to give an error message when he erroneously entered the sine function in a formula instead of the cosine! Even today such errors are seldom detected automatically. The computer can check whether sine is written correctly and whether the parameter values are in a permissible range, but not whether the programmer meant to write sine.

A fundamentally different approach (or *paradigm*) employs only *functions*. Here the user does not want to deal with memory and commands at either a low or high level, but simply enters mathematical functions in the usual form. With an adequately powerful function concept built particularly on *recursion* (see Chapter 2), this approach can actually be implemented. This paradigm is employed in *functional programming languages*.

The *logical programming languages* represent a different paradigm. Here the programmer must specify initial statements and derivation rules so that the computer can automatically derive the correct consequences.

We do not discuss the *functional* and *logical* paradigms further in this book. We refer interested readers to the literature (e.g., [WH83, CM81]).

Imperative programming languages (often called *procedural*) are the oldest form and are particularly useful for an introduction because they require the programmer to express the algorithms explicitly. Functional and logical programming languages partially hide the inner behavior of the computer. Although this might often be useful, for a novice it is particularly important to become familiar with the details.

The imperative programming languages have seen a very interesting development. The first such programming language, *Fortran*, (from *For*mula *trans*lator) made an important breakthrough at the end of the 1950s. Fortran represented the first successful attempt at translating a formal notation that very much resembled the accustomed mathematical formulas, automatically and efficiently into machine language. This began a new dimension for programming because for the first time the programmer was freed from many details of machine language and could better concentrate on the content of the algorithm.

The programming language *Cobol* brought another development by enabling easier expression of commercial applications rather than mathematical formulas. Cobol emphasized such aspects as easy generation of formatted tables.

After the initial euphoria, difficulties soon emerged with the new languages. They were not defined precisely enough. Furthermore, they contain a number of features that encourage certain programming errors and make them hard to detect. An attempt to build larger software systems with these languages soon reveals their drawbacks.

> This makes it all the more surprising that Fortran and Cobol are still so widespread today. These programming languages do not even represent the technology of yesterday, but reach back even farther. The improvements made in these languages over the years have been cosmetic in nature and tend more to disguise the errors than to remedy them. Without a doubt, the most important reason for the longevity of these dinosaurs is the large installed base (estimated as hundreds of thousands of programs consisting of billions of lines of code). At any rate, universities have been responsible for assuring that development continues and that new and improved programming languages continue to gain acceptance.

Formally defined languages

Such experience caused researchers to think about the precise specification of programming languages. This led to the *Backus-Naur* notation (presented in Chapter 2), which is a *metalanguage* (itself a formal language) that helps to specify further formal languages. Naturally this only makes sense if the metalanguage is significantly simpler than the formal languages being described. Although Backus-Naur notation can describe (without extreme complexity) only the *syntax* of a programming language, it still brought important quality improvements in programming languages.

The language *Algol-60* was the first programming language with a formally specified syntax, making its definition concise and unambiguous. Even today Algol-60 remains exemplary in many ways. For a long time Algol served as the publication language for precisely specifying algorithms in scientific literature. Many other languages borrow from Algol-60 (the *Algol family*), e.g., Algol-68 and especially Pascal.

> The significant difference between Pascal and Algol-68 is not so much Pascal's introduction of new concepts, but rather its restraint in the use of new concepts, which enabled the realization of compilers for Pascal programs with comparably little effort. What is more important, this made it easier for a programmer to learn such a language and to completely master it.

A strict type system: the Pascal family

Pascal [Wir71] has itself become the progenitor of a series of languages (the *Pascal family*), such as *Modula-2* [Wir82], *Oberon* [WG92, RW92], *Oberon-2* [Mös93] and the language used in this book, *Modula-3* [Nel91, Har92]. Pascal's most significant innovation over Algol-60 was that Pascal vested great importance not only in control structures but also in the design of data structures.

Pascal was the first widespread language with a strict type system. On the one hand, this means (in simplified form) that for all data the programmer must *declare* in advance the type – the permissible value range and the allowed operations. This enables the compiler to check the correct use of the data. It is no longer possible to add apples and oranges, as with earlier programming languages. This is an important example of how restriction can achieve increased security. On the other hand, Pascal compensates for this strictness by providing flexibility in the *definition* of new data types. In Pascal the programmer can define custom types beyond the *predefined* types built into the language.

Structured programming

Modula-3 is a *structured* programming language.

The theory of structured programming builds on the works of E.W. Dijkstra and O. Dahl [Dij68a, DDH72]. We do not explain structured programming here, but do note that all languages of the Pascal family incorporate this theory. We can summarize the essence of the theory by saying that it restricts programming to constructs that form closed and well understood units. The advantage of this approach is that we can check the correctness of smaller components individually and then construct a larger system from such checked components. This requires rules of composition that assure that we do not destroy the already tested components during the synthesis.

Structured programming languages provide special constructs, *structures*, for structured programming. In Modula-3 the classical concepts of structured programming have attained a very high degree of maturity.

Object orientation

The newest members of the Pascal family – including Modula-3 – are *object-oriented*. Pascal recognized the importance of data structures and elevated the design of data structures to equal importance with control structures. Object-oriented programming languages go farther: They combine associated data structures and operations into a syntactic and semantic unit. Details of object-oriented programming are covered in Chapter 13.

Note that in object-oriented programming languages a very important aspect of programming comes to light: modeling. Computers, as the name indicates, were originally conceived as computing machines. (To be more specific, during World War II the goal was to decode encrypted enemy messages.) Due to their flexibility, computers are capable of representing abstract *models* of very different systems. Both the structure and the behavior of systems can be modeled on computers. Naturally the model must be conceived by humans, but just as models can be built from wood or plaster, they can be constructed as software. Object-oriented programming languages provide especially expressive concepts for modeling the structure and behavior of systems.

1.6   Programming and computer science

Programming (in the restricted sense above) is only a modest aspect of computer science. Some use the term *informatics* nowadays instead of computer science to emphasize that this is a science with a spectrum that extends beyond the computer itself. While on the one hand increasingly many people spend an increasing amount of time on a computer, the activity of many computer scientists is shifting to tasks (e.g., analysis, specification, etc.) that only indirectly involve a computer. You can study many aspects of computer science without ever having seen a computer.

1.6.1 The responsibility of computer scientists

Even programming does not necessarily require a computer. One of the most important computer scientists, Edsger W. Dijkstra, proposes a method [DFS88] by which programming should be learned as a purely mathematical discipline, initially only with the help of pencil and paper (and thinking, of course). The correctness of programs is not tested on a computer but verified by means of mathematical proof. The underlying idea is that the programmer should learn to accept complete responsibility for the correctness of a program. The availability of (ever faster) computers creates an immense temptation to immediately test programs on the machine instead of thinking them through to the last detail. However, we can never exhaustively test a complex program. Testing helps us to detect a certain number of errors. Still, we can never preclude additional errors that were not detected during testing. Only careful thinking can give us greater certainty. Thinking is also error prone, for to err is human. Still, if we ourselves as authors of a programs cannot comprehend it, then how can we expect it to function properly as if by magic?

Such a position would also be morally dubious. In a lecture in Zurich Edsger W. Dijkstra said: "An adult with a healthy hand is responsible for his own handwriting." Likewise, authors are responsible for their own programs and should not attempt to shift this responsibility to the computer.

In this book we do not assume the computerless approach of Dijkstra. However, we do assume his position of moral responsibility.

Chapter 2

Metalanguages

As stated in the introduction, the syntax of a formal language should be
defined with the help of a simple *metalanguage*. The syntax specifies the
rules for correct sentence construction. Human communication allows a
great deal of liberty, but communication with a computer demands following strict rules. Yet if the rules themselves are defined imprecisely, this
makes following them almost impossible.

> The lack of a formal definition of Fortran syntax actually created a
> great many difficulties in the construction of the first Fortran compiler.

2.1 Definition of formal languages

To start with an example, let us take a formal language, a notation familiar
to everyone: the notation of arithmetic. We all know that arithmetic allows
us to use numbers and symbols that stand for numbers. In addition, we
can form arithmetic expressions with the help of operators. We know that
a + b or (a + b) * (c - 2) are legal expressions[1]. Expressions like a + b * c
and a * b / c are also legal, although it is not necessarily clear

- Whether a + b * c should be interpreted as $(a + b)c$ or as $a + (bc)$ —
  that is, whether multiplication has higher *precedence* than addition,
  or vice versa, or whether they have equal precedence.

- Whether a * b / c should be interpreted as $\frac{ab}{c}$ or as $a\frac{b}{c}$; that is, assuming that multiplication and division have equal precedence, as usual,
  whether evaluation is to proceed from left to right (*left-associatively*)
  or from right to left (*right-associatively*). If b is not divisible by c without a remainder, this makes a significant difference!

---

[1]The * character is used in computer science for multiplication.

We also understand that expressions such as a + * + b) and a + $% are incorrect. The assimilated rules that we apply in the evaluation of the correctness of such expressions are usually quite unconscious and incompletely formulated. Can we formulate these rules explicitly, concisely and unambiguously? For this purpose we introduce another *formal language* – a *metalanguage* – that serves to define other formal languages. Naturally it must be simpler (significantly simpler, if possible) than the formal languages that it is to define; otherwise we lose more than we gain.

The first such formalism employed to define programming languages (for Algol-60 in 1960) was the *Backus-Naur form* (BNF). Later it experienced many extensions (*extended Backus-Naur form* EBNF). We first introduce the language scope of the original BNF; however, we use the notation of the newer and more widespread EBNF. We base our introduction to BNF on *Methodology of Programming* by Edsger W. Dijkstra and W. H. J. Feijen [DFS88].

The following symbols can occur in a BNF definition:

- Symbols of the BNF itself, called *metasymbols*.

- Symbols belonging to the language being defined. These are written in quotation marks ("). They stand for themselves alone; that is, they are utilized in the same form as they appear in the definition.

- Names of syntactical units that are then themselves described with BNF rules.

A BNF definition resembles a mathematical equation. To the left of the equal sign (=) we have the name of the syntactical unit to be defined (original BNF employed the symbol ::= to underscore the difference from the usual equal sign). At the right we have the symbols that define the syntactical units at the left. These can be any BNF symbols. The following rules apply:

1. Two or more consecutive symbols (e.g., x y z) form a *sequence* that must appear in exactly the same order on application of the definition (x before y before z without omission).

2. Two symbols separated by the metasymbol | designate alternatives from which to choose in applying the definition. Sequence binds stronger than the alternative; thus x y | z means that either xy or z is possible, but not xyz or xz.

3. Definitions terminate with a period.

This suffices for now in order to precisely define the syntax of quite complex formal languages.

2.2 Digits and numbers

Our first example is the definition of digits:

Digit = "0" | "1" | "2" | "3" | "4" | "5" | "6" | "7" | "8" | "9" .

This definition states that a digit consists of either a 0 or a 1 or a 2, etc.

This was simple so far. Now let us define the syntax of a natural (non-negative) number. A number consists of any number of digits. Can we express this in BNF? We write as follows:

NaturalNumber = Digit | Digit Digit | Digit Digit Digit.

This allows precise definition of numbers under 1000. But how do we continue? Since we could have infinitely long numbers, we would need to write the definition on endlessly long paper. Instead, we introduce new symbols, the curly braces { and }, as repetition symbols. Everything within { and } can be repeated any number of times (including zero). Now we can write:

NaturalNumber = Digit {Digit} .

This definition states that a number consists of at least one digit, followed by any number of additional digits. Note that the following definition would be incorrect because a number cannot consist of no digit at all:

NaturalNumber = {Digit} .

Introducing the braces is practical, but not absolutely necessary, to master the problem of infinite repetition. The following definition would also suffice:

NaturalNumber = Digit | Digit NaturalNumber.

Perhaps this looks curious. The same syntactical unit (NaturalNumber) appears on both sides of the definition. Such definition, where one element is defined in part by itself, is called *recursive*. Can something be defined by itself? Certainly this *alone* does not suffice! Such a definition as the following is senseless:

NaturalNumber = NaturalNumber.

However, the unit to be defined can be included in its own definition. This allows us to express infinite definitions in finite (and usually very short) form. The above recursive definition states that a natural number consists of either a single digit or a digit followed by a natural number. This constituent natural number again consists of either a single digit or a digit followed by a natural number, and so on any number of times. At some point, however, the first alternative (NaturalNumber = Digit) must apply so that the digit generation terminates.

Any digit from 0 to 9 thus is a natural number itself (e.g., 2 is a natural number). If we write a digit in front of it, we still have a natural number (e.g., 62 is another natural number). If we place another digit in front of this, we still have a natural number (e.g., 862), and so on.

It should be clear that it does not matter whether we generate numbers by adding digits to the front or the back. Thus the following definition proves just as adequate:

NaturalNumber = Digit | NaturalNumber Digit.

2.3   Names

Now let us approach the task of precisely defining the syntax of arithmetic expressions. In order to be able to use symbolic names (for variables) in addition to numbers, we need to define letters and names.

Letter = "a" | "b" | $\cdots$ | "z" | "A"| "B" | $\cdots$ | "Z".

The ellipsis ("$\cdots$") serves as an abbreviation for an obvious case. To be absolutely precise, we would have to list all letters (which is no problem since their number is finite). The ellipsis spares us a bit of writing; it belongs neither to BNF nor to the notation we are defining.

Our definition states that a letter can be any lower-case or upper-case character in the alphabet. We can further define a name (or identifier) following the pattern of the numbers. Let us begin as follows:

Name = Digit | Name Digit | Letter | Name Letter .

This definition states that a name consists of any sequence of letters and digits. This means that a1, 1a, x, and xyz as well as 1 and 625 are all valid names. However, this is inconvenient because we cannot distinguish numbers from names.

> Exact definition alone does not protect us from errors: Our definition provides a precise syntax, but falters semantically. It is not even in- herently incorrect, but only clashes with our definition of numbers.

To solve this problem, most such grammars require that names begin with a letter, which can then be followed by digits and/or letters. Thus a1 would be valid, but not 1a.

Hence we must amend our definition slightly:

Name = Letter | Name Letter | Name Digit .

This definition states that a name consists either of a single letter or a sequence of letters and/or digits beginning with a letter. A name must always begin with a letter.

We could also express the definition of names without recursion with the help of braces:

Name = Letter {Letter | Digit }.

2.4 Arithmetic expressions

Now we can define the syntax of arithmetic expressions. Arithmetic expressions consist of terms connected by additive operators. The terms contain factors bound by multiplicative operators. A factor can be a number, an identifier or an expression in parentheses. Our definition in BNF takes the following form:

```
1 addop      = "+" | "−" .
2 mulop      = "*" | "/" .
3 Expression = Term | Expression addop Term .
4 Term       = Factor | Term mulop factor .
5 Factor     = NaturalNumber | Name | "(" Expression ")".
```

Now let us examine the examples of incorrect expressions given on page 28: The expression a + * + b) is invalid because a term cannot begin with *. A + (an addop) must always be followed by a term (see rule 3). The expression a + $% is even easier to reject because the characters $ and % are not valid.

What about the interpretation of a + b * c? Can our syntax answer this question? Does it express the precedence of operators? Which is the correct interpretation, $(a + b)c$ or $a + (bc)$? Let us test this by deriving the expression from the rules according to both interpretations. For our derivation we assume that we have a valid expression and then attempt to replace the names of the syntactic units with the help of the rules until we reach the character string that we want to interpret, or until we fail. If we need to replace multiple names, we will always take the one at the extreme left.

In the first case $((a + b)c)$ we could derive our expression from the definition as follows:

Expression → *Term* → *Term mulop Factor* → ?

First we apply the first alternative of rule 3 (since we are striving for the interpretation $(a + b)c$, the second alternative does not apply). Then we choose the second alternative of rule 4 to represent our expression as a product. Here we reach a dead end because a + b is not a valid term.

Now let us try our derivation with the interpretation $a + (bc)$:

> *Expression* → *Expression addop Term* → *Term addop Term* →
> *Factor addop Term* → *Name addop Term* → a *addop Term* → a
> + *Term* → a + *Term mulop Factor* → a + *Factor mulop Factor* →
> a + *Name mulop Factor* → a + b *mulop Factor* → a + b * *Factor*
> → a + b * *Name* → a + b * c.

With the second interpretation we have succeeded in finding a corresponding alternative of the definition to derive the expression a + b * c from the definition. On the basis of this example it seems that our formal definition also expresses the precedence of operators: The precedence of multiplicative operators is higher than that of additive operators.

If we examine the *expression* syntax more closely, it becomes clear why this is so: In the second alternative of rule 3 we see that the additive operators can connect only whole expressions and terms. The multiplicative operations must already be combined as a term.

Now let us consider the expression a * b / c. Do we interpret it as $a\frac{b}{c}$ or as $\frac{ab}{c}$? The second alternative of rule 4 states that a term is always to the left and a factor to the right of a multiplicative operator. Likewise the second alternative of rule 3 states that in additive operators the expression is to the left and the term to the right. Given equal precedence, operators are left-associative (they combine from left to right to become operands). In our example the first case would be right-associative; hence the second case conforms to the definition. We can derive the expression as follows:

> *Expression* → *Term* → *Term mulop Factor* → *Term mulop Factor mulop Factor* → *Factor mulop Factor mulop Factor* → *Name mulop Factor mulop Factor* → a *mulop Factor mulop Factor* → a * *Factor mulop Factor* → a * *Name mulop Factor* → a * b *mulop Factor* → a * b / *Factor* → a * b / *Name* → a * b / c.

Our syntax definition thus also expresses the rule of left-associativity for operators with equal precedence.

Note that in this case the recursive definition cannot be replaced by the use of repetition symbols. The case where any number of parentheses can appear before or after a symbol – e.g., (X))) – is easy to describe. However, if the parentheses are to appear only pairwise as in mathematical expressions – e.g., (((a + b) * c) + 1) – then we cannot express this with repetition symbols alone.

Notation	Meaning
x y	*Sequence* (y follows x)
x | y	*Alternatives* (either x or y)
[x]	*Option* (x not at all or once)
{x}	*Repetition* (x not at all or any number of times)
(x)	*Group* (combines a set of symbols)
"abc"	*Terminal* (abc is a symbol of the grammar to be defined)

Table 2.1: EBNF *definition*

2.5 Extension for Modula-3 syntax

Here we add a BNF extension that we will later use in the introduction of Modula-3. We base Table 2.1 on [Har92, Nel91] to show its definition, whereby x and y are intended to represent an arbitrary syntactic unit. This definition contains some redundancy. The advantage of this extended definition (as will later become obvious) is that the syntax to be defined (here Modula-3) becomes more concise and readable.

Chapter 3

The structure of programs

The intention of this chapter is to provide an overview of program components that will be explained in detail in later chapters. We introduce the structure of computer programs and the most important structuring concepts in general and for Modula-3 in particular. In the last part of the chapter we develop our first Modula-3-programs. This chapter addresses almost everything, but finishes explaining almost nothing. The readers should retain questions for the next chapters, and on completion of the book should be able to answer them.

3.1 Structuring

The programs of the 1950s were monolithic chunks of code, all one piece. As long as a program consists of not more than 100 lines and executes a single (albeit complex) computation, this approach can work well. However, once the programs grow larger, they must be structured. Today's software systems consist of tens of thousands, even hundreds of thousands or millions of lines of code. Under such circumstances, structuring the programs becomes a necessity that is decisive for the quality of nontrivial software. Novices frequently fail to understand when a program is rejected in an exercise or an examination even though it "works" – it was just somewhat "dirty". Dirty, i.e., poorly structured, programs create chaos and cause immense damage as soon as they have to work together with other parts of a larger system. Since the end of the 1960s, this awareness has increasingly found its way into the consciousness of computer scientists and has formed a foundation of university education in programming.

> The basic idea of structured programming is to construct programs from components whose correctness can be checked independently of other components. A correctly functioning component must not sabotage others, i.e., must not affect their correctness.

Smaller and larger components must all comply with this principle. Thereby we achieve a division of labor and can decompose a complex problem into smaller ones that are easier to solve. The smallest components of problem solutions are variables, simple types and individual instructions; larger components include procedures, objects and modules. Some of these are introduced in this chapter, and the remainder of the book handles them in detail. But first let us examine the path a program takes from its development to its execution on a computer.

3.2   Language environment

Programming languages are *formal languages* that permit us to precisely express problem solutions. Programming languages have another important characteristic: Source code in a programming language can automatically and efficiently be brought into a form that a digital computer can execute. Such source code is translatable and executable.

This is a fundamental property of programming languages. Formal languages that lack this characteristic are not real programming languages. When we speak of programming languages, we mean automatically and efficiently translatable formal languages. For historical reasons, the automatic translation of programs is called *compilation* and the translator is called a *compiler*. Compilation means the assembly of various components. The expression stems from times when programs were not translated, but only certain subfunctions were automatically incorporated. Compiler technology has experienced immense evolution over the last three decades and now is one of the theoretically best founded areas of computer science. Here we only discuss some elementary points. The interested reader should refer to the literature [ASU85].

> The purpose of translating a formal language is not always the generation of an executable computer program. Formal languages are also used to precisely specify problems and, as explained in Chapter 2, to represent other formal languages. The purpose of automatic translation in this context (if it is done at all) is to check the completeness and consistency of the specification.

A system that transforms program code written in a certain programming language into executable programs is called a *language environment*. The purpose of a language environment is to transform programs from the form in which they were written (a form adapted to human needs) into a form that a computer can process. Thus programs have various phases of transformation (see Figure 3.1).

Figure 3.1: *Phases of program translation*

1. *The program text or source code*
   The text written in a programming language such as Modula-3 is called program text or source code. The source code is normally written by a programmer.

   > There are systems that can automatically generate source code of a high-level programming language from a formal specification language that is on a higher abstraction level than the programming languages we present here. We do not discuss such systems here. Furthermore, there are even systems (compiler-compilers) that can generate the source code for compilers for other programming languages [ASU85].

   Large programs are normally not compiled as one unit, but in smaller *compilation units*. The particular decomposition depends on the programming language.

2. *The compiled program*
   The compiler translates the source code into a form that comes close to the machine language and proves nearly unreadable for humans (aside from determined hackers and compiler developers). The compiled code (or object code) is enriched with additional control information that is necessary, e.g., to link programs components that were compiled separately, to a single program. Additional control information assists the program loader.

3. *The loadable program*
   The *linker* generates the loadable program. The main function of the linker is to link the separately compiled program components. In the loadable program, the (separately compiled) compilation units are already linked.

4. *The executable program*
   The executable form of a program generally ensues only upon *loading* into main memory. The program must be started from the language environment. During execution an executable program receives *run-time support* from this environment.

Corresponding to these forms, the conversion of source code to an executable program usually encompasses four main steps:

1. *Compilation*

2. *Linking*

3. *Loading*

4. *Execution*

In various language environments these functions can be implemented in different ways. Often individual functions are merged. Some systems embed linking in the loader, i.e., link at load time. This saves the explicit link step and adds flexibility. Some very new systems even incorporate part of the translation in the linker/loader [Fra94], adding even more flexibility.

Most systems distinguish these four steps internally, but the user receives interactive help to combine several steps into a sequence. Compiling and linking, as well as loading and execution, are each controlled with a single command[1].

3.3   The statics and dynamics of a program

The previous section showed on the one hand that a program is textual source code and on the other hand that it can be executed by a computer after appropriate translation. The structuring of a program thus has two aspects: static and dynamic. The static aspect regards the structuring of the source code, while the dynamic aspect affects program execution.

We illuminate these aspects with the following example: A company has a static structure that determines its management hierarchy, departments, groups, etc. This structure changes relatively seldom; it is tuned to the company's underlying global goals. However, the various units must cooperate with one another, and how this cooperation takes place is by no means determined by the static structure. Instead, it depends on the respective tasks, which departments interact with which, who provides and consumes services, how information and materials flow between organizational units, etc. The static structures (at least for healthy companies) tend to be much simpler than the dynamic rules, which adapt to changing demands.

Accordingly, programs also have a static structure that reflects the underlying goals and that only seldom change for a correctly designed program. The dynamics of a program, resulting from the respective input data that reflect demands, builds on the static structure.

---

[1]Our language environment, e.g., provides commands for automating the compilation of multiple components and their linking; see Appendix D.

3.3.1 Data and data types

As Chapter 1.1 showed, programs contain instructions that manipulate data. We also saw that a computer can store the data in the form of a state space, with freedom in the interpretation of the individual states. This flexibility proves to be too great to allow us to reasonably handle it. We want to restrict the possible interpretations. We categorize the data and define *data types*. Some programming languages are quite relaxed in this sense. They provide more flexibility at the expense of security. We prefer strict languages like Modula-3 that permit only typed data. Every programming language has some predefined (built-in) types, and most permit the programmer to use *type constructors* to create additional types.

Data types

- A data type defines a *set of permissible values*.

- It specifies the *set of operations* on these values.

One data type, e.g., that occurs in practically every programming language defines the set of whole numbers. This type is usually called INTEGER and is usually predefined. The numbers 0, 1, 625 and -2300 are all of this type, but real numbers such as 2.5 are not. The set of integers is always finite (in contrast to the set of whole numbers in mathematics) because a computer can only store finite sizes. Most programming languages specify a general integer type and leave it to the respective language environment to set the limits of this set. This approach can create difficulties if different environments offer a programming language with different value ranges. This can mean that a number might be legal in one environment, but create a range overflow in another. In order to create software that can be *ported* to any other environment (with the same programming language), we need to pay particular attention to this aspect.

In addition to integers, most programming languages provide other built-in types, such as:

- real numbers

- readable text

- characters

- logical values

In addition to the set of permissible values, data types also define the *operations* allowed on the data of a given data type. Even if we know that integers are whole numbers within a certain range, this does not unambiguously restrict which operations are permissible. We consider it self-evident

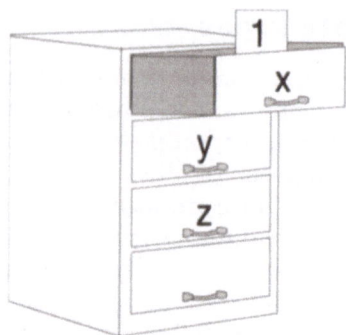

Figure 3.2: *Variables in computer science*

that addition and subtraction are permitted on whole numbers. However, we need to clarify what happens when we add two numbers whose sum leads to an overflow of the integer range (because it cannot be *represented*). Another question is whether multiplication for two integers is defined in advance, or whether it needs to be realized by repeated addition. Division presents a more complicated problem. How do we divide numbers that are not divisible without a remainder? How do we obtain the remainder? What is the remainder when we divide a positive number by a negative number?

Another example is the logical type, usually called *Boolean* after the English mathematician George Boole. Here the complete range consists of two values: *true* and *false*. We will see how useful this type is after we specify the operations (such as logical ∧ and ∨ relations).

Hence we conclude the following: A type is really defined only when we specify the set and semantics of the allowable operations in addition to the permissible range. The definitions of such types are often called *abstract data types* (see Section 11.4).

Data types serve to categorize data. They define a general *pattern*, or scheme, the type. We still need to *create* (or *instantiate*) the concrete data itself, i.e., the *examples* or *instantiations* belonging to a type.

Variables

The concept of *variables* in programming is quite different from that in mathematics. In mathematics a variable x stands for a *value*. If we say about a right triangle that $a^2 + b^2 = c^2$, we mean that if a, b and c assume the values of the length of sides and the hypotenuse of a right triangle, then the above equation applies. An equation such as $x = x + 1$ does not apply for any real value.

In computer science variables are *containers* for values [AU92]. They have a name, a type and a stored value (see Figure 3.2). The name x represents a container *and* a value. The semantics of a programming language always clearly define what is meant in each case.

All programming languages contain an *assignment operation* that resembles an equation, but means that the *value* of the right side is assigned to the variable designated in the left side. An assignment such as x = 1 means that the *container* x is to store the *value* 1. The assignment x = x + 1 indicates that 1 is added to the *value* of x and the result is stored in *container* x. Thus the purpose is to increment the value stored in x by 1. This has nothing to do with the mathematical interpretation. To underscore the difference between these interpretations, many programming languages, including Modula-3, replace the equal sign with a special assignment operator (:=) (see Section 3.4.4).

All variables together constitute the *state space* of a program. The variable containers can be created as fixed or be generated at run time. (The scope of the state space can change dynamically; see Chapter 11.)

Constants

Constants are values that are set on creation of a program and do not change during program execution. All values written directly into the source code (such as numbers and texts) are constants. We call such constants *literals*. However, we can also assign names to constants and access their values via their names; such constants are often called *symbolic constants*. Like variables, constants have a type.

3.3.2 Algorithms and procedures

In the introduction we discussed the algorithm, which precisely and unambiguously expresses a finite, effective procedure. Programming languages provide constructs to express algorithms. Whether such algorithms are really finite, effective, unambiguous, etc. rests in the hands of the programmer.

In most programming languages the essential building block for formulating algorithms is the *procedure* or the *function*. With the help of their own data and statements, procedures define an algorithm (or subalgorithm). We can assign names to procedures and functions and *parametrize* them to make the algorithms reusable. On each execution of the procedure, we can substitute new parameter values to allow application of the algorithm to different data of the same type. The mathematical formula $y = f(x)$ expresses that for various x values f defines corresponding y values. $f(a)$ represents $f(x)$ for a certain a. In an imperative programming language f(a) means that at the position where f(a) occurs in a program, the function f starts with the current value of a, executes, and returns the result.

Consider the example of the arithmetic mean of two numbers. The algorithm is very simple: Add the two numbers and divide the sum by two. The function construct permits us to assign this algorithm a name such as Mean. The function requires passing two parameters for the two numbers to be averaged, and it returns the mean. The statement

```
z := Mean(x, y)
```

starts the computation and, after execution of the function, assigns the result to the variable z.

Procedures have many more applications than for computations in the form we showed here. Also, they do not necessarily return a value. A *function* or *function procedure* is a special procedure that returns a value – it stands for a value. Procedures that do not return a value (sometimes called *pure procedures*) form a statement. Chapter 9 handles both variants in detail.

3.4   Structure of Modula-3 programs

To make these considerations more concrete, we need an overview of the most important structuring elements in Modula-3. In the process, we will develop our first Modula-3 programs. These programs will not do much of practical use, but that is not our goal initially. We begin by equipping ourselves for our later launch to distant planets.

By way of preview, we list the most important structuring elements:

- *Module:* A program consists of modules.

- *Block:* A module contains blocks.

- *Declaration:* A block contains declarations (definitions) ...

- *Statement:* ... and statements (instructions to the computer).

3.4.1   The module

A Modula-3-program consists of a number of modules. The module is the smallest *compilation unit* in Modula-3.

> Many programming languages support the module concept, e.g., Modula-2, Oberon-2 and Ada. In Ada they are called *packages*. The name of the programming language Modula is an abbreviation of *Modular Language*.

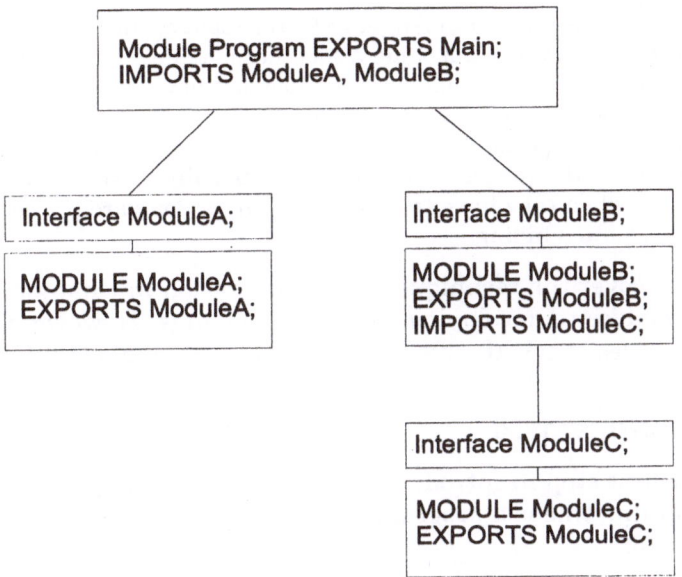

Figure 3.3: *A module hierarchy*

A program is a *main module* that relies on the services of other modules. These service modules in turn can employ the services of additional modules, etc. This creates a module hierarchy. The root of this hierarchy is always the main module. In principle, modules could exchange services bidirectionally (e.g., module A employs the services of module B and B those of A); however, in a good design, this is very rare.

Theoretically a Modula-3 program could consist of a single module (the main module). As we soon will see, even the smallest practical programs already consist of two modules. The number of modules rises rapidly with the complexity of the tasks that a program must fulfill.

A module normally has two parts, an *interface* and an *implementation*. These are stored in separate files. The interface specifies the elements that it provides (*exports*) to other modules, i.e., the services that a module offers. Other modules can *import* and employ these services. The implementation contains the realization of the exported elements. The internal details of the implementation are hidden from the environment (*information hiding*). Other modules can only access the interface of a module, but not its implementation. This corresponds to the basic requirement of structured programming: It must not be possible to sabotage a functioning module from outside it.

> By sabotage we mean introducing programming errors, not malevo-
> lent sabotage. Likewise information hiding does not imply classified

government secrets, but a language feature that *syntactically* protects the internal details of a module from other modules. Information hiding is practical even if one programmer develops all modules alone. Here this programmer knows all the details of the implementations, yet applying information hiding can significantly reduce the error-proneness of the program. Programmers usually learn to appreciate this only when they have to carry out a larger software project without information hiding.

Until we cover the technique of modularization in Chapter 10, we will restrict ourselves to developing only main modules. However, we will employ the services of certain available modules (e.g., module SIO).

3.4.2   Hello, world

A frequent first step in introducing a programming language is the *Hello World* program. This is a program that outputs a greeting ("Hello, world!") on the monitor:

Example 3.4: *Hello World program*

```
MODULE Hello EXPORTS Main;
  IMPORT SIO;
BEGIN
  SIO.PutText("Hello, world!\n")
END Hello.
```

In the simplest manner, this program demonstrates the use of module building blocks. We developed a module named Hello. It exports the predefined, empty interface Main; this labels it as a main module. The IMPORT statement indicates that we intend to employ the services of the module SIO, which means "simple input/output". The module provides services to the input/output of data, including the procedure PutText for output of text. The text is the parameter of the procedure and is specified here as a constant. Character strings enclosed in quotation marks are text constants. The character string "\n" has a special meaning: It moves the *cursor* to the start of the next line (a carriage return with line feed). We can compile, link, load and execute the module Hello. (SIO need not be compiled; it is part of the language environment and ready for use). We receive the following output on the monitor:

```
Hello, world!
```

It is probably quite easy to understand how the Hello module works. But how do we know that we have to write "IMPORT SIO" to import SIO?

"Use module SIO" would say the same thing. This is a matter of syntax, i.e., the rules for how to write Modula-3 source code. To define the syntax, we use EBNF, as described in Chapter 2:

Simplified syntax of modules[2]

$$Module_3 = \text{"MODULE" Ident}_{89} \, [\, \text{"EXPORTS" IDList}_{87} \,] \, \text{";"}$$
$$\{ \, Import_{10} \, \} \, Block_{12} \, Ident_{89} \, \text{".".}$$

The identifiers MODULE and EXPORTS are symbols of the programming language itself; i.e., they are used in Modula-3 source code exactly as they occur within the quotation marks in the syntax. The character strings MODULE and EXPORTS constitute *keywords*; these strings are reserved and may only be used for their intended purpose (e.g., MODULE to introduce a module definition). Most programming languages have such keywords, which are usually rather few in number. With a little programming experience they tend to be learned automatically. In Modula-3 all keywords are written in all capital letters (hence "Module" is *not* a keyword because Modula-3 is case-sensitive).

The syntactic unit $Ident_{89}$ stands for any name specified by the programmer (compare Section 2.3), whereby keywords are precluded. It indicates the name of the module. The same name must be repeated at the end of the module. The requirement that the name be the same at the beginning and end of the module is *not* evident from the syntax (because $Ident_{89}$ in the syntax stands for any name). Therefore we have to describe this requirement verbally.

Names chosen by the programmer can be in any mix of upper-case and lower-case characters. However, we should avoid names consisting of only capital letters in order to keep keywords optically distinguishable.[3] In this book module names always begin with a capital letter.

Such rules constitute important *conventions* that make source code more readable. The compiler processes all names in the same way. Another aid promoting readability is textual indentation of the source code after BEGIN and the undenting after END in a block. This makes the block optically distinguishable (for human readers) and easier to understand.

A module consists of its name followed by an optional list of exported interfaces, then a number of optional imports and finally a block. We have

---

[2]The syntactic constructs are provided with indices to simplify orientation in the complete syntax description of the language (see Appendix B.8.)

[3]The first module that we encountered, SIO, is the first exception to the rule. We use the module as though it were part of the system and thus use the capital letters in the name.

already mentioned that a module must have (i.e., export) at least one interface. If a module does not specify its list of exported interfaces, then it is assumed that it exports an interface equivalent to the name of the module.

The syntax of a block is very simple:

Syntax of a block

Block$_{12}$ = { Declaration$_{13}$ }"BEGIN" Stmts$_{23}$ "END".
Stmts$_{23}$ = [Stmt$_{24}$ { ";" Stmt$_{24}$ } [";"]].

Stmt$_{24}$ stands for a statement (see page 49), Stmts$_{23}$ for a sequence of statements. Our statement in the Hello World program is the invocation of the procedure PutText from module SIO. We do not discuss the syntax of the import list or the procedure invocation here. It suffices to say that the keyword IMPORT can be followed by a list of module names (separated by commas) and a semicolon. Since our first example imports not an individual procedure but the whole interface of SIO, when we use the procedure PutText in the body of the procedure, we must precede its name with the name of its module. We call this *qualifying* the name of the procedure with the name of the module. We write the parameter of the procedure (the greeting text) between parentheses after the procedure name.

> Interested readers can check the syntax definition in Appendix B.8 to determine whether the IMPORT statement and the procedure invocation in the example abide by the syntax.

3.4.3 Source code

The source code (the text) of a program must serve human needs and the machine (more precisely, the translation program) equally well. This whole book deals with how to formulate programs properly so that we obtain the desired results after compilation. To make the source code comprehensible for human readers, we use blanks, blank lines and tabulators (collectively called *white space*). We indent certain parts and group elements of the source code that belong together (see Example 3.5). We can insert any amount of white space *between* syntactic units.

We can also insert explanatory comments directly in the source code. The symbol pair (* and *) serves as special bracketing for enclosing a *comment*. Comments can be placed wherever white space is allowed. Comments serve to inform the human reader of source code. They are not strictly part of the program (the compiler simply skips everything between commentary brackets). Commentary can significantly increase the readability of a program. In the next example we use comments to explain the purpose of each line of the program.

```
MODULE Mean EXPORTS Main;                    (*Author: LB, October 15, 1994 *)
(*The program computes the arithmetic mean of three numbers. *)

  IMPORT SIO;                                (*We import the services of Simple I/O *)

  VAR
    x, y, z: INTEGER;      (*x,y and z contain the values whose mean we will compute*)
    mean: INTEGER;                   (*We store the result in the variable mean *)

BEGIN                                        (*This begins the statement part*)
  SIO.PutText("Arithmetic mean of three numbers\n");    (*Greeting text on the monitor*)
  SIO.PutText("Please enter three numbers: ");          (*Prompts the user for inputs*)

  x:= SIO.GetInt();                                      (*Reads a value into x*)
  y:= SIO.GetInt();                                      (*Reads a value into y*)
  z:= SIO.GetInt();                                      (*Reads a value into z*)

  mean:= (x + y + z) DIV 3;      (*Computes the mean and stores it in the variable mean*)

  SIO.PutText("Arithmetic mean = ");
  SIO.PutInt(mean);                                      (*Outputs the arithmetic mean*)
  SIO.PutText("\n");                  (*Moves to the start of the next line on the screen*)
END Mean.
```

Example 3.5: *Arithmetic mean of three numbers*

Comments can be used in many ways. If multiple programmers are working on a project, comments prove to be one of the most important aids for reading source code written by someone else. All source code should bear a header with the name of its author and the date of completion as well as a brief description of its purpose. Project team members decide what else is to be commented, or commentary policy is dictated by company regulations. Usual objects of commentary include the purposes of variables and procedures as well as the logic of difficult algorithms.

Commenting can be exaggerated. Comments also inflate the source code and can, if they reiterate the obvious, devalue the readability of source code.

In this book comments serve to support explanations in the text. Comments such as "This begins the statement part" are certainly out of place in real programs!

3.4.4   Computing the arithmetic mean

Next we examine how variables and assignments are used in Modula-3. We will write a program to compute the arithmetic mean of three numbers. Again we provide the solution (Example 3.5), which we discuss in this section.

Declarations

Example 3.5 demonstrates the use of variables in Modula-3. As we showed above (page 46), a module contains a *block* which consists of *declarations* and *statements*. The idea of a declaration is to define names (*identifiers*) for later use. The following lines declare the names x, y and z as variables of type INTEGER.

```
VAR
  x, y, z: INTEGER;
```

This declaration also creates containers for the declared names, whose values are initially *undefined*.

The programmer must *initialize* each variable, i.e., provide it with a start value.

In our example initialization takes place by reading the values via SIO.GetInt().

Simplified syntax of variable declarations

$$\text{Declaration}_{13} \quad = \cdots \mid \text{"VAR" VariableDecl}_{17} \text{ ";" } \mid \cdots$$
$$\text{VariableDecl}_{17} = \text{IDList}_{87} \text{ (":" Type}_{48} \mid \cdots \text{) .}$$
$$\text{IDList}_{87} \qquad = \text{Ident}_{89} \text{ \{ "," Ident}_{89} \text{ \}.}$$

This excerpt from the syntax of declarations shows that the declaration of variables follows the keyword VAR. This declaration takes the (simplified) form of a list of (variable) names, a colon and a type. (We do not discuss the syntax of types here. In our example the name of the type is the predefined type INTEGER.)

In Modula-3 all variables that are used in the statement part of a block must be declared. This is not the case in every programming language (e.g., Fortran and PL/1). However, the requirement to declare all variables has important advantages:

1. The Compiler can test whether we use only variables that we intend to use (rather than artifacts ensuing from spelling errors).

   It is a well known story that a Venus rocket was lost in space because a Fortran program with a guidance function contained a spelling error that created a phantom variable that stole the value of the intended variable. Such an error is impossible in languages like Modula-3, which require explicit declaration.

2. The compiler can test whether a variable is used only according to its type. (By contrast, some programming languages allow the "addition" of a text with a number. The result is naturally nonsense.)

3. The compiler knows how to reserve storage for the variables.

Not only all variables but also all types and procedures must be declared. Generally speaking, declarations associate a name (which is visible only within the block in which it is declared) and a definition.

Statements

With statements we have collected the most important components of Modula-3 programs: We have a module that contains a block. The block consists of declarations and a statements sequence (see page 46).

Simplified syntax of statements

$$\text{Stmt}_{24} \quad = \text{AssignStmt}_{25} \mid \text{CallStmt}_{26} \mid \cdots$$
$$\text{AssignStmt}_{25} = \text{Expr}_{66} \text{ ":=" } \text{Expr}_{66}.$$

A statement (Stmt_{24}) can be an assignment (AssignStmt_{25}), a procedure call (CallStmt_{26}), or another kind of statement not listed above. We have already seen that the statement part can contain a sequence of statements separated by ";". The statements of a statement sequence are executed sequentially. The output of the two texts with which Example 3.5 begins is such a statement sequence consisting of two procedure calls (SIO.PutText):

```
SIO.PutText("Arithmetic mean of three numbers\n");
SIO.PutText("Please enter three numbers: ");
```

The following statement is an assignment (AssignStmt_{25}):

```
x:= SIO.GetInt();
```

The expression (Expr_{66}) to the left of the assignment operator (:=) must specify a variable container to which the expression on the right side can be assigned. For now let us assume that the expression is simply the name of a variable. The right side is an expression that determines the value. In this case we have a *function call*. SIO.GetInt() reads a number from the keyboard and returns the value. The effect of the statement is that the number that the user enters is assigned to the variable x.

The following statement is also an assignment:

```
mean := (x+y+z) DIV 3
```

```
INTERFACE SIO;                              (*Simple Input/Output 13.04.94. LB*)
  ⋮
PROCEDURE GetText(): TEXT;
(*Reads a sequence of nonblank characters and returns them. *)

PROCEDURE PutText(t: TEXT);
(*Writes the characters from t to the output stream. *)

PROCEDURE GetInt(): INTEGER;
(*Reads all adjacent digits from the input stream and returns the result
  as an INTEGER. *)

PROCEDURE PutInt(i: INTEGER; length := 3);
(*Outputs i as a sequence of digits to the output stream.
  If the number of digits in i is less than length, then blanks are added at the beginning
  to bring the total output characters to length. *)

PROCEDURE Nl();
(*Outputs a line feed.*)
  ⋮
END SIO.
```

Example 3.6: *Simplified excerpt from the SIO interface*

Here the expression on the right is an arithmetic expression (compare Section 2.4) quite similar to the familiar ones from mathematics. The only unusual element is the keyword DIV, which represents integer division. DIV divides the first operand $(x + y + z)$ by the second (3). The result is stored in the variable mean.

The program ends by outputting the result. SIO.PutInt outputs an integer. One possible execution of this program is the following[4]:

```
Arithmetic mean of three numbers
Please enter three numbers:  -4 9 28
Arithmetic mean = 11
```

3.4.5   SIO interface

How can we use the name SIO.PutText and others in Example 3.5 without declaring them? Obviously, specifying the import list serves this function:

IMPORT SIO

Thereby we import a number of declarations into our module, i.e., make them visible in the module. These declarations define the services of the

---

[4]User input is in italics.

module, in our case, input/output procedures. The part of the module SIO that is public (i.e., visible for other modules) – its interface – is stored in a separate source code file. Figure 3.6 shows a (simplified) excerpt from the SIO interface.

Commentary is absolutely essential in interfaces in order to explain the provided services to users of the module. The interface exports the listed procedures. The Get procedures read from the keyboard and return a corresponding function value. The Put procedures output the value of their parameters on the monitor. (Section 14.2.3 shows how the same procedures can also read from and write to *files*.) The complete interface is printed in Appendix C.3.3.

Chapter 4

Predefined data types

Section 3.3.1 introduced some predefined data types. Now we handle all predefined data types in Modula-3 individually.

4.1 Integers

Without a doubt the most basic and most frequently used data type is that of the *whole numbers*. The type for whole numbers in Modula-3, as in most programming languages, is called INTEGER. Modula-3 defines a separate type for non-negative whole numbers, CARDINAL. INTEGER numbers can assume any whole-number value within the range (upper and lower limits) imposed by the language environment. CARDINAL numbers can assume any whole-number value between 0 and the upper limit imposed by the language environment.

Ordinal types

These whole number types are *ordinal types*, which means that they are ordered: Every whole number, excepting the limit values, has exactly one predecessor and one successor (smaller or larger by one, respectively). We will encounter a number of other ordinal types. However, there are data types that do not reflect this property (e.g., character strings and floating-point numbers, presented in this chapter).

4.1.1 Range

We specify the range of whole-number types in square brackets: [lower limit .. upper limit], whereby the two limit values are inclusive.

> In the PC environment for Modula-3, the range of INTEGER numbers is [-2147483648..2147483647] and for CARDINAL numbers [0..2147483647].

The values of these remarkably large numbers might seem completely arbitrary. However, some insight into the fine points of binary representation [AU92] quickly shows that these values expressed as powers of two seem much rounder: $[-2^{31} .. 2^{31} - 1]$ and $[0 .. 2^{31} - 1]$. The range for type INTEGER reflects that 1 bit of a storage word is used for the sign, the rest for the numeric value. 64-bit computers provide a range of $[-2^{63} .. 2^{63} - 1]$.

A Modula-3 programmer need not know anything about the details of the internal representation (although this knowledge certainly does no harm). The programmer only needs to know that INTEGER numbers are whole numbers in the specified range. If a particular computation might exceed the range of type INTEGER, the limits can be checked in the program with predefined (built-in) functions.

4.1.2   Operations

As mentioned, in addition to its range each predefined data type has a set of operations permissible on it. For whole numbers Modula-3 offers a group of arithmetic and a group of relational operations. In addition, there are a number of predefined functions for whole numbers.

Most of these operations (such as addition, testing for equality, etc.) are also defined for other data types (such as floating-point numbers), but with different semantics.

Predefined functions

The predefined function FIRST returns the lowest value of an ordinal type; the function LAST returns the highest. We can query these values as normal INTEGER values in our computations and assure that their range is not exceeded. The function LAST also lets us define the type CARDINAL more precisely: Its range is [0 .. LAST(INTEGER)].

Since whole number types are ordinal, it makes sense to be able to simply specify the *next* or the *previous* number for a given x. This can be done with the predefined procedures INC and DEC.

        INC(x)   is equivalent to x:= x + 1.
        DEC(x)   is equivalent to x:= x − 1.
        INC(x, y) is equivalent to x:= x + y.
        DEC(x, y) is equivalent to x:= x − y.

This might seem extraneous: Why do we need a predefined procedure for operations that can so readily be derived from existing operations? The

```
MODULE MinMax EXPORTS Main;                    (*Ranges. October 20, 1994. LB*)

  IMPORT SIO;

  CONST MaxPlaces = 11;                        (*Maximum number of decimal places*)
BEGIN
  SIO.PutText("MinInteger = ");
  SIO.PutInt(FIRST(INTEGER), MaxPlaces); SIO.Nl();

  SIO.PutText("MaxInteger = ");
  SIO.PutInt(LAST(INTEGER), MaxPlaces); SIO.Nl();
END MinMax.
```

Example 4.1: *Outputting the range limits of type INTEGER*

importance of INC and DEC is that they apply to all ordinal types (see also
Sections 6.1 and 6.2).

> Furthermore, these built-in procedures are usually more efficient than
> arithmetic expressions because the variable only needs to be accessed
> once. In the expression x:= x+1 the variable is accessed twice: to read
> its value and to write the new value.

The predefined function ABS provides the absolute value of an INTEGER
number.

> Note that ABS(FIRST(INTEGER)) cannot be represented because of the
> asymmetry of the upper and lower bounds of INTEGER numbers. The
> explanation points to the coding of INTEGER numbers as twos comple-
> ments [AU92].

Example 4.1 outputs the range limits of type INTEGER on the monitor.
Output is right-justified because the second parameter of PutInt has been
set accordingly.

The example also shows the advantages of using symbolic constants.
The value of MaxPlaces is the maximum number of decimal places plus one
place for the possible sign. This value depends on the respective language
environment and finally on the underlying computer. On a 32-bit computer
the maximum number of places is 10, while a 64-bit computer allows 19.
To port the program to a computer with a different number of maximum
places, it suffices to adapt the value of this constant (e.g., MaxPlaces = 20
for a 64-bit computer) and recompile the module. Nothing else changes.

The monitor output on a 32-bit computer is:

```
MinInteger =  -2147483648
MaxInteger =   2147483647
```

Arithmetic operations

Modula-3 predefines the following arithmetic operations (in parentheses we provide the notation used in the language):

- addition (+)

- subtraction (–)

- multiplication (*)

- integer division (DIV)

- remainder after integer division (MOD)

The result of an integer expression is always an integer. The + and – signs can also be used as unary operators (signs). We can omit the unary + sign (+x equals x).

Rules of precedence (compare Sections 2.4 and 7.1) are defined as usual: Addition and subtraction have the least, *, DIV and MOD medium, and the unary sign has the greatest connective strength.

If x is divisible by y without a remainder, then x DIV y yields exactly the quotient; otherwise x DIV y returns the nearest whole number that is less than the quotient.

MOD computes the remainder for integer division. The semantics of MOD are defined so that the following equation always applies:

$$x \text{ MOD } y = x - y * (x \text{ DIV } y)$$

If $y > 0$, then x MOD y returns a result in the range [0 .. y – 1]; for $y < 0$ the result is in the range [y + 1 .. 0].

> MOD is often used to determine whether a number is even or odd. x MOD 2 always yields 0 for even and 1 for odd x, even if x is negative.

The following table provides an overview of the behavior of DIV and MOD for positive and negative operands:

x	y	x DIV y	x MOD y
9	4	2	1
–9	–4	2	–1
9	–4	–3	–3
–9	4	–3	3

It is important to note that the semantics of arithmetic operations often deviate from the meaning familiar from mathematics. The reason is the fact that a computer can store only finitely large numbers.

Hence, e.g., the associative law of addition does not always apply:

$$(x + y) + z = x + (y + z)$$

Consider the following statement sequence:

```
VAR
    x, y, z, w: INTEGER;

    x:= LAST(INTEGER);
    y:= 1;
    z:= -2;
```

a) w:= x + (y + z);   *b)* w:= (x + y) + z;

In case a) y + z is computed first (yielding −1), which can easily be added to the maximum INTEGER value (yielding LAST(INTEGER) − 1). In case b) x + y is computed first, attempting to add one to the maximum INTEGER value. Thus the interim result cannot be represented in the system. What happens? The language definition of Modula-3 (and most programming languages) leaves this question open, and the decision is left to the language environment. Either program execution can be terminated with an *overflow*, or computation continues. For efficiency reasons, language environments usually choose the second variant.

By the way, in the above example the second variant works with no problem; w has the same value in both cases. The reason is two's complement representation [AU92]. The essence of this representation is that the number line joins at the two ends, actually forming a circle. This means:

```
LAST(INTEGER) + 1  = FIRST(INTEGER)
FIRST(INTEGER) − 1 = LAST(INTEGER)
```

Thus case b) yields:

(x + y) + z = FIRST(INTEGER) − 2 = LAST(INTEGER) − 1

This attractive property only affects additive operations. (x + y) * z with the original values, e.g., would lead to a nonsensical result (0). In this case terminating the program due to overflow would be more adequate than continuing computation.

Another example shows that we must proceed with caution with integer division as well.

(x * y) DIV y = (x DIV y) * y = x

```
MODULE Integers EXPORTS Main;              (*Integer operations, Sept. 12, 1993. LB*)

  IMPORT SIO;

  VAR
    i, j: INTEGER;

BEGIN                                                   (*Statement part*)
  SIO.PutText("Basic arithmetic functions\n");
  SIO.PutText("Please enter two numbers: ");

  i:= SIO.GetInt();                        (*Assigns the entered number to i *)
  j:= SIO.GetInt();                        (*Assigns the entered number to j *)

  SIO.PutInt(i); SIO.PutText(" + "); SIO.PutInt(j); SIO.PutText(" = ");
  SIO.PutInt(i + j); SIO.NI();

  SIO.PutInt(i); SIO.PutText(" – "); SIO.PutInt(j); SIO.PutText(" = ");
  SIO.PutInt(i – j); SIO.NI();

  SIO.PutInt(i); SIO.PutText(" * "); SIO.PutInt(j); SIO.PutText(" = ");
  SIO.PutInt(i * j); SIO.NI();

  SIO.PutInt(i); SIO.PutText(" DIV "); SIO.PutInt(j); SIO.PutText(" = ");
  SIO.PutInt(i DIV j); SIO.NI();

  SIO.PutInt(i); SIO.PutText(" MOD "); SIO.PutInt(j); SIO.PutText(" = ");
  SIO.PutInt(i MOD j); SIO.NI();
END Integers.
```

Example 4.2: *Integer operations*

only applies if x is divisible by y without a remainder. Let us examine what happens with the following values:

x:= 11; y:= 4;
a) z:= (x * y) DIV y;   b) z:= (x DIV y) * y;

In case a) the result is z = 11 (or z = x), but in case b) z = 8. If we begin with x = 8, the result is the same in both cases (z = 8). If x starts with the value LAST(INTEGER), then case a) would produce an error because x*y obviously cannot be represented. (Here again an overflow error would be preferable over an erroneous result.) Example 4.2 permits the user to play with the basic operations. Here is a possible sequence:

```
Basic arithmetic operations
Please enter two numbers:  12 -5
  12    +    -5  =      7
  12    -    -5  =     17
  12    *    -5  =    -60
  12  DIV    -5  =     -3
  12  MOD    -5  =     -3
```

x = y	is *true* if x and y have the same value, otherwise *false*.
x # y	is *true* if x and y do not have the same value, otherwise *false*.
x < y	is *true* if the value of x is less than that of y, otherwise *false*.
x > y	is *true* if the value of x is greater than that of y, otherwise *false*.
x >= y	is *true* if x = y or x > y, otherwise *false*.
x <= y	is *true* if x = y or x < y, otherwise *false*.

Table 4.3: *Relational operations*

Relational operations

Modula-3 also specifies a group of relational operations for integers.

- equal (=)

- unequal (#)

- greater than (>)

- less than (<)

- greater than or equal (>=)

- less than or equal (<=)

Many of these operators are defined for multiple types. The operators = and # apply to all types. The semantics of the operations depend on the type, so we explain them separately in each context. The result of a relational operation is always either *true* or *false* with no other possibility. Thus the logical data type BOOLEAN (see Section 4.2) serves as the result type for relational operations.

Relational operations are defined for INTEGER values in the accustomed way (see Table 4.3). x <= y is equivalent to y >= x. If both x < y and x > y prove *false* then x = y is *true*. Hence if x = y is *true*, then x # y must be *false* and vice versa. Since whole numbers represent an ordinal type, all relational operations are unambiguous.

> For floating-point numbers, as we will see in Section 4.5, this is not always so simple.

We will consider examples of relational operations later, in the next subsection along with the logical data type, and particularly with statements that contain a condition.

4.2   Logical type

4.2.1   Range

The type name for logical values in Modula-3 is BOOLEAN. Logical data
can assume only one of two predefined values *true* and *false*. For logical
values Modula-3 predefines the constant values TRUE and FALSE.

> Many programming languages (such as Fortran, Algol-60 and C) lack
> the logical data type. The range is so minute that many believe that
> logical values can be simulated easily with integers. We could inter-
> pret the value 0 as *false* and the value 1 as *true*, and this would take
> care of the logical data type. However, the logical data type incorpo-
> rates much more semantics.

The presence of an explicit logical type has the following advantages:

1. Logical values can be explicitly distinguished from arithmetic values.
   This makes programs more readable and less error-prone. This also
   precludes happening to interpret the same variable once as a logical
   value and another time as a number.

2. The operations of Boolean algebra can be defined for logical data.

4.2.2   Operations

The following logical operations are defined (with Modula-3-notation in
parentheses):

- Negation (NOT)

- Or (OR)

- And (AND)

The meaning of these operations can most readily be depicted in a *truth
table* (where p and q are of type BOOLEAN):

p	q	NOT q	p OR q	p AND q
true	*true*	*false*	*true*	*true*
true	*false*	*true*	*true*	*false*
false	*true*	*false*	*true*	*false*
false	*false*	*true*	*false*	*false*

```
MODULE Booleans EXPORTS Main;          (*Boolean operations, Sept. 14, 1993. LB*)

  IMPORT SIO;

  VAR
    p, q: BOOLEAN;

BEGIN                                                        (*Statement part*)
  SIO.PutText("Basic Boolean functions\n");
  SIO.PutText("Please enter two Boolean values: ");

  p:= SIO.GetBool();
  q:= SIO.GetBool();

  SIO.PutBool(p); SIO.PutText(" OR "); SIO.PutBool(q); SIO.PutText(" = ");
  SIO.PutBool(p OR q); SIO.Nl();

  SIO.PutBool(p); SIO.PutText(" AND "); SIO.PutBool(q); SIO.PutText(" = ");
  SIO.PutBool(p AND q); SIO.Nl();

  SIO.PutText("NOT "); SIO.PutBool(p); SIO.PutText(" = ");
  SIO.PutBool(NOT p); SIO.Nl();
END Booleans.
```

Example 4.4: *Boolean operations*

In words (where $x \Leftrightarrow$ *condition* is an abbreviation for: "x is *true* if and only if *condition* applies; otherwise x is *false*"):

NOT q $\Leftrightarrow$ q *false*
p OR q $\Leftrightarrow$ p or q or both *true*
p AND q $\Leftrightarrow$ both p and q *true*

According to the rules of precedence (also see Section 7.1) OR has the least connective strength among the Boolean operators, AND is medium and NOT has the greatest strength. Hence the following applies:

p OR NOT q AND r = p OR ((NOT q) AND r)

The relational operations also apply to Boolean values because by definition *true > false*. The operators $>$, $<$, $>=$ and $<=$ are applied to Boolean values only in exceptional cases.

At this time we cannot do a lot with logical values. However, they become especially important in conditional statements. To assist in writing an executable program, we introduce two further procedures from our SIO interface to read and display logical values (TRUE and FALSE):

PROCEDURE GetBool(): BOOLEAN;   (*Reads a Boolean value*)
PROCEDURE PutBool(b: BOOLEAN);   (*Writes TRUE or FALSE*)

```
MODULE RelOps EXPORTS Main;              (*Relational operations, Sept. 12, 1993. LB*)

  IMPORT SIO;

  VAR
    i, j: INTEGER;
    greater, less, equal: BOOLEAN;
BEGIN                                                        (*Statement part*)
  SIO.PutText("Relational operations\nPlease enter two numbers: ");

  i:= SIO.GetInt();
  j:= SIO.GetInt();

  greater:= i > j;                                    (*greater is true if i > j*)
  less:= i < j;                                          (*less is true if i < j*)
  equal:= i = j;                                        (*equal is true if i = j*)

  SIO.PutInt(i); SIO.PutText(" > "); SIO.PutInt(j); SIO.PutText(" is ");
  SIO.PutBool(greater); SIO.Nl();

  SIO.PutInt(i); SIO.PutText(" < "); SIO.PutInt(j); SIO.PutText(" is ");
  SIO.PutBool(less); SIO.Nl();

  SIO.PutInt(i); SIO.PutText(" = "); SIO.PutInt(j); SIO.PutText(" is ");
  SIO.PutBool(equal); SIO.Nl();
END RelOps.
```

Example 4.5: *Relational operations*

GetBool and PutBool function like GetInt and PutInt; the only difference is that they handle logical instead of numeric values. With the help of this extension, we can develop a variant of Example 4.2 (Example 4.4).

Example 4.5 shows how to assign the results of relational operations to logical variables. However, it is not always necessary to assign the result of a relational operation to a variable. The above program can readily be shortened if we specify the relational operations directly as parameters of PutBool. (Since relational operations return Boolean values, they can occur wherever Boolean values or expressions are required.) Instead of SIO.PutBool(greater), we could write SIO.PutBool(i > j). A possible program execution could take the following form:

```
Relative operations
Please enter two numbers:   23 -5
23 >  -5 is TRUE
23 <  -5 is FALSE
23 =  -5 is FALSE
```

In Example 4.5 we declared both INTEGER and BOOLEAN variables. We used the Boolean variables to store results of relational operations. Different types cannot be mixed arbitrarily. Statements such as the following would be senseless:

```
i := j + greater;  equal := i;
```

We cannot add a number to a Boolean value and we cannot assign a number to a Boolean variable, etc. In programming languages with a strict type system, the compiler automatically detects such statements as semantic errors.

> A counterexample is the programming language C, which has no Boolean type, but permits logical operations with integers. The semantics are completely in the hands of the programmer, and if this human erroneously applies different semantics to the same variable, the compiler has no chance to detect this (because the logical variables are formally integers as well). Although no programming language can detect every senseless action (that would be nice), we should at least preclude those errors that can be detected.

4.3 Characters

Programs process not only numbers and logical values, but also character strings. Modula-3 offers two predefined data types for this purpose: TEXT and CHAR. We begin with the data type for individual characters, the type CHAR.

4.3.1 Range

The type CHAR designates a finite, ordered set of characters. In many respects, this set is similar to the integers. CHAR also represents an ordinal type (compare Section 4.1).

One difference is that the number of possible character values is usually much smaller than the possible integer values.

> There are normally 256 different character values. Those who know the binary representation of characters will immediately recognize that this reflects the number of different values that can be represented in a *byte*, or in 8 *bits*, because $2^8 = 256$.

The other important difference is that we do not interpret these values as numbers. Most of these are readable characters, such as upper-case and lower-case letters of the alphabet, digits and special characters on the

\n	line feed	\f	form feed
\t	tabulator	\r	carriage return
\'	apostrophe	\"	quotation mark
\\	backslash		

Table 4.6: *Escape sequences for special characters*

keyboard of a computer, e.g., . , ; !. Additional, nonprintable characters serve to control input/output devices, e.g., a special character for line feed.

> We have already introduced the line feed as text. All characters can be specified as (very short) text (see Section 4.4).

Which CHAR value corresponds to which character depends on the code system of the respective computer. Most computers (except IBM mainframes) use the ASCII code system [AU92]. In Modula-3, coding corresponds to the ISO Latin-1 code (an extension of the ASCII codes). Normally a programmer does not even need to know this. The language system handles the internal details of character coding.

Character literals can be defined with the help of the apostrophe ('). Any character (except the apostrophe character itself) can be specified between apostrophe characters.

> 'A' stands for capital A,
> 'z' for lower-case z,
> '@' for @ and
> '1' for the *character* 1.

The difference between the character '1' and the number 1 is important: The number 1 is of type INTEGER and can occur in arithmetic expressions. The character '1' is of type CHAR and can only be used as a character.

The above notation for character literals obviously works only for printable characters, and we cannot specify the apostrophe character itself. Nonprintable and other special characters must be specified via a detour, the *escape sequences*. An escape sequence consists of a *backslash* (\) followed by either a special character or a three-digit number. The special characters and their meanings are listed in Table 4.6.

> The carriage return character moves to the start position of the *current* line on the monitor or on the printer. The designation stems from times when computers were operated without monitors, but connected to electric typewriters.

To specify any special character, the \ can be followed by an octal number with exactly three digits [AU92] corresponding to the code value of the

```
        ⋮
    VAR i, j: INTEGER; ch: CHAR; b: BOOLEAN;

BEGIN
    i:= ORD('1');                    (*ordinal value of '1' (49) is assigned to i *)
    ch:= VAL(66, CHAR);        (*character with ordinal value 66 ('B') is assigned to ch *)
    j:= ORD(TRUE);                (*ordinal value of TRUE (1) is assigned to j *)
    b:= VAL(0, BOOLEAN);
                    (*b is assigned the Boolean value with ordinal value 0 (FALSE)*)
        ⋮
```

Example 4.7: *The standard functions ORD and VAL*

desired character (from the ISO code table). For example, '\012' stands for the carriage return (because the code value of carriage return $= 10_{10} = 12_8$), and '\061' indicates '1' (because the code value of '1' $= 49_{10} = 61_8$).

4.3.2 Operations

The usual arithmetic operations are not permitted on characters. However, because characters, similar to integers, represent an *ordinal type*, the relational operations (with the same syntax and semantics as for integers) are defined on characters.

Nevertheless, there is one difficulty: It is not self-evident which character is larger or smaller. Is 'A' greater or less than ';'? Is 'z' > 'Z', or vice versa? This could depend on the underlying code system, although we just stated that a programmer need not know it. Therefore it makes sense not to employ such relational operations without restriction in programs. However, we can be sure that the following conditions always apply:

$$'A' < 'B' < 'C' < \cdots 'X' < 'Y' < 'Z'$$
$$'a' < 'b' < 'c' < \cdots 'x' < 'y' < 'z'$$
$$'0' < '1' < '2' < \cdots '7' < '8' < '9'$$

Additional details regarding the order of characters can be taken from the ISO Latin-1 code table, but the authors dissuade from doing so. In all other cases it is best to avoid using the ordering of characters and at most comparing them for equality or inequality.

> As we will later see, we can define (unordered) sets of characters that facilitate the formation of groups or classes of characters, e.g., the set of control characters, the set of punctuation marks, etc. (see Section 8.3).

```
    ⋮
  CONST
    Conv = ORD('A') – ORD('a');        (*difference between ordinal values of 'A' and 'a' *)
  VAR
    ch: CHAR;

BEGIN
  ch:= SIO.GetChar();                  (*Reads a character and assigns it to ch *)
  ch:= VAL(ORD(ch) + Conv, CHAR);      (*Converts ch to upper case *)
  SIO.PutChar(ch);                     (*Outputs ch *)
    ⋮
```

Example 4.8: *Converting a lower-case letter*

Predefined functions

The predefined functions FIRST and LAST are also defined for type CHAR.
They return the character with the smallest and largest code number, respectively (normally these are special characters that the programmer seldom needs).

Likewise the predefined functions INC and DEC can be used as with numbers to compute the successor and predecessor, respectively, of a character. INC('B') returns 'C'; DEC('B') is 'A'. The result of DEC('A') depends on the character coding. We should avoid writing programs that depend on which character precedes 'A', 'a' or '0', and likewise with the successor of 'Z', etc. INC(LAST(CHAR)) and DEC(FIRST(CHAR)) produce an error.

Two additional predefined functions permit conversion between integers and characters. The function ORD requires a parameter of any ordinal type (in our case, type CHAR) and returns its *code value* – the *ordinal number* – of the character as an INTEGER number, e.g., ORD('1') = 49.

The function VAL is the inverse function of ORD. It takes an integer as parameter along with any ordinal type (in our case, type CHAR). The integer is interpreted as the code value of the specified type. The result is the corresponding value of the specified type, e.g., VAL(49, CHAR) = '1'.

Given that i is of type INTEGER and ch of type CHAR, the following always apply:

```
ORD(VAL(i, CHAR))   = i
VAL(ORD(ch), CHAR)) = ch.
```

Example 4.7 sets the value of i to the ordinal value of the character '1' (which is ASCII code 49, not 1). The value of ch is set to the character with ordinal value 66 (which is the letter 'B') in ASCII code. The example also shows how ORD and VAL can be used for another ordinal type (BOOLEAN).

For the input/output of individual characters we introduce two additional procedures of the interface SIO:

```
PROCEDURE GetChar(): CHAR;            (*Reads a character*)
PROCEDURE PutChar(ch: CHAR);          (*Outputs a character*)
```

GetChar reads a character and returns it as its function value. PutChar outputs the character in ch. Example 4.8 transforms a lower-case letter into upper case. (The code fragment does not test whether the character read is actually a lower-case letter.)

4.4 Texts

A text is a sequence of characters. Hence many programming languages do not offer the predefined type TEXT because corresponding type constructors permit specifying a character string from individual characters. However, Modula-3 includes the predefined type TEXT.

4.4.1 Range

A text consists of any number of characters (including none). The respective language environment constrains the maximum size, but this ceiling is normally so high that the restriction proves negligible.

Text literals can be specified between double quotation marks ("). A text literal can include any characters except the quotation mark (") and the backslash, which must be specified indirectly as escape sequences. A text literal must be contained on one line, but it may include the escape sequences for carriage return and line feed (see Table 4.6).

The following are examples of valid text literals:

```
"This is a Modula-3 text"
"\n"
"This text ends with a line feed\n"
"\"To thine own self be true\"\n"
"The above quote is from Shakespeare's Hamlet\n"
```

If we display these text literals on the monitor with SIO.PutText, we obtain:

```
This is a Modula-3 text
This text ends with a line feed
"To thine own self be true"
The above quote is from Shakespeare's Hamlet
```

By contrast, the following text literals are not valid:

```
"This is a Modula-3 text
and this is its continuation"
""Quote""
```

It is important to note the difference between text constants (of type TEXT) and character constants (of type CHAR):

```
CONST
   CharConst = 'A';
   TextConst = "A";
```

Both declarations are legal. TextConst declares a text of length 1, while CharConst declares a character. They have different types, and only the operations are restricted to those of the respective type. However, it is easy to convert between the types (see the following subsection).

4.4.2 Operations

For Modula-3 texts, the language specifies an *infix* operator (written directly between texts) as well as a number of operations in the form of the predefined interface Text. This interface is not part of the language itself, but it must be present with the same syntax and semantics in every environment.

The concatenation operator &

Concatenation means sequentially merging two character strings. This allows us to merge any number of texts to a single text. If we execute the program in Example 4.9, we obtain the output:

```
This is a Modula-3 text,
this is its continuation,

and this is its end.
```

Of the operations provided by the standard interface Text, Example 4.10 lists the most important. The complete interface is included in Appendix C.1.1.

Equal returns a logical *true* value if and only if the contents of two texts specified as parameters is the same (where upper- and lower-case letters are considered different). Length returns the length of a text (as the number of contained characters). GetChar allows extraction of a character at

```
MODULE Texts EXPORTS Main;          (*Concatenation, Sept. 15, 1993. LB*)

  IMPORT SIO;

  CONST
    LF = "\n";                      (*LF stands for line feed *)
    T1 = "This is a Modula–3 text,";
    T2 = "this is its continuation,";
    T3 = "and this is its end.";
    T4 = T1 & LF & T2 & LF & LF & T3 & LF;

BEGIN                               (*statement part *)
  SIO.PutText(T4);
END Texts.
```

Example 4.9: *A program with the concatenation operator*

```
INTERFACE Text;                     (*Copyright Digital Equipment Corporation *)
  ⋮
PROCEDURE Equal(t, u: T): BOOLEAN;
(*Returns TRUE if t and u have the same length and the same content. *)

PROCEDURE Length(t: T): CARDINAL;
(*Returns the number of characters in t. *)

PROCEDURE GetChar(t: T; i: CARDINAL): CHAR;
(*Returns the character at position i (where first character has position 0) in t.
  If i >= Length(t), a run-time error results. *)

PROCEDURE FromChar(ch: CHAR): T;
(*Returns a text consisting of the character ch. *)
  ⋮
END Text.
```

Example 4.10: *Excerpt from the Text interface*

position i in a text t (the valid range for i being [0 .. Length(t)-1]). FromChar transforms a character to a text.

Before we examine an example of the use of these functions, we need to add an important note. Of the relational operations, equality (=) and inequality (#) are also valid for texts. However, it might happen that the expressions text1 = text2 or text1 # text2 (assuming that text1 and text2 are of type TEXT) functions differently than we anticipate.

It is possible that text1 = text2 yields *false* (or text1 # text2 *true*) although the two character strings are equal. The Equal function of the Text interface always functions according to expectations. Therefore we should always use this function for the comparison of two texts.

> The reason for this curious behavior in text comparisons cannot be explained fully at this time. The type TEXT does not really represent texts, but pointers (*references*) to texts (see Section 11.5). The

```
MODULE TextComparison EXPORTS Main;              (*Text comparison, 11.05.94. LB*)

  IMPORT SIO, Text;

  CONST
    T1 = "This is a Modula–3 text";
    T2 = "his is a Modula–3 text";
  VAR
    text1, text2: TEXT;

BEGIN                                            (*statement part *)
  text1:= "T";
  text2:= text1 & T2;                            (*contents of text2: This is a Modula-3 text*)
  SIO.PutText(T1 & "\n");
  SIO.PutText(text2 & "\n");
  SIO.PutBool(T1 = text2); SIO.Nl();             (*outputs FALSE*)
  SIO.PutBool(Text.Equal(T1, text2)); SIO.Nl();  (*outputs TRUE*)
END TextComparison .
```

Example 4.11: *Text comparison*

relational operations (= and #) compare only these pointers, while the
Equal function compares the actual *contents* of the texts.

Example 4.11 makes this distinction clear. After the value assignment T1
and text2 reference two different character strings which are equal but not
the same. The expression T1 = text2 returns *false*, whereas Text.Equal(T1,
text2) yields *true*:

```
This is a Modula-3 text
This is a Modula-3 text
FALSE
TRUE
```

Now let us write a small program that presents the user with three
tasks. If the tasks are completed correctly, the program displays TRUE,
otherwise FALSE.
The tasks are:

- Input a text of a certain length.

- Input the same text again.

- Enter a text that ends with a certain character.

Example 4.12 lists the program. Note that in the third task EndChar must
be converted to type TEXT using Text.FromChar so that the concatenation

```
MODULE TextExercise EXPORTS Main;        (*Exercises with texts, Sept. 15, 1993. LB*)

  IMPORT SIO, Text;

  CONST
    EndChar = '.';                          (*end character for 3rd exercise*)
    Length   = 3;                           (*length of text in 1st exercise*)
    T1       = "Please enter a text of length";
    T2       = "Please_re–enter_the_same_text";
    T3       = "Please enter a text that ends with '";
    T4       = "' \n";

  VAR
    text: TEXT; b: BOOLEAN; ch: CHAR; len: INTEGER;
BEGIN                                        (*statement part*)
  SIO.PutText(T1);                           (*request a text of length ...*)
  SIO.PutInt(Length); SIO.NI();              (*"Length" (= 3)*)
  text := SIO.GetText();
  b := Text.Length(text) = Length;           (*b = TRUE if length of text is correct*)
  SIO.PutBool(b); SIO.NI();

  SIO.PutText(T2 & "\n");
  text := SIO.GetText();
  b := Text.Equal(text, T2);                 (*b = TRUE if text = T2*)
  SIO.PutBool(b); SIO.NI();

  SIO.PutText(T3 & Text.FromChar(EndChar) & T4);
  text := SIO.GetText();
  len := Text.Length(text);
  ch := Text.GetChar(text, len − 1);         (*ch is the last character*)
  b := ch = EndChar;                         (*b = TRUE if ch = EndChar*)
  SIO.PutBool(b); SIO.NI();
END TextExercise.
```

Example 4.12: The program gives the user exercises

```
    ⋮
  SIO.PutText(T3 & Text.FromChar(EndChar) & T4);
  text:= SIO.GetText();
  SIO.PutBool(Text.GetChar(text, Text.Length(text) − 1) = EndChar);
  SIO.NI();
    ⋮
```

Example 4.13: Abbreviation of the third exercise in Example 4.12

operator can merge it into a text. The expression T3 & EndChar & T4 would be incorrect because we cannot use a value of type CHAR directly as text.

We could have spared ourselves some variables and lines of code by passing the functions directly as parameter values. Example 4.12 represents an abbreviated form of the third task in Example 4.13.

The preferred solution is often a matter of taste. Shorter programs are often more comprehensible, but it is hard to say whether this is the case here. At any rate, note that we certainly could not have omitted the variable text, which stores the entered text. A solution such as the following is incorrect:

```
SIO.PutBool(Text.GetChar(SIO.GetText(),
    Text.Length(SIO.GetText()) −1) = EndChar);
```

The input is requested twice, although we only need it once.

In this case, if the user had entered a longer text the second time, the program would even crash because Text.GetChar would attempt to read from a position that does not exist in the first text.

4.5 Floating-point numbers

Real numbers play a very important role in mathematics. Therefore most programming languages provide them as a predefined type. However, representing real numbers in a computer creates additional difficulties.

Whole numbers are infinite only in size: Every whole number has a predecessor and a successor. The real numbers, we could say, are also infinite in their density (between any two real numbers there exists another real number). Whole numbers form a *denumerably infinite* set, while the set of real numbers is *nondenumerable* [Tru88]. In other words, the real numbers form a continuum.

A real number can contain an infinite number of digits. When we approximate a real number with a finite number of places after the decimal, then we must always consider the precision of our approximation when using such values. The approximated representation of real numbers in a computer is called *floating-point* representation.

Assume that we have a four-digit decimal floating-point-arithmetic. This means that the decimal point can "float" left or right, but we still have only four positions. The largest number that we can represent is 9999 and the smallest number is 0.001. The numbers 0.00011, 0.00012, 0.000111, 0.000112, etc. cannot be distinguished in our four-digit arithmetic. Nonrepresentable numbers are *rounded* to a representable number. This means that practically all computations with floating-point numbers are subject to *rounding errors*.

In floating-point representation a real number x is described with two whole numbers, the *exponent* and the *mantissa* [Wir73]:

$$x = mantissa * base^{exponent}$$

The values of base, mantissa and exponent depend on the respective computer system. The base is either 10 or a small power of 2. The dimension of the mantissa and the exponent determine the range and the precision of the representation. Typically many more places are reserved for the mantissa than for the exponent.

A normal form is defined by the following condition:

$$\frac{1}{base} \leq \frac{mantissa}{maximum\ mantissa} < 1$$

This condition assures that the floating point is always to the left of the first digit that is not zero in the mantissa. In this form the density of representatives in intervals of the real number axis declines exponentially with increasing x. For base 10, e.g., the interval 0.1 – 1 contains the same number of representatives as the interval 1000 – 10000.

A digital computer can only represent finite numbers and only with finite precision. Thus floating-point numbers in a computer differ significantly from real numbers in mathematics. The field of *numerics* deals with computation with floating-point numbers [IK66, YG66]. We can only compute with imprecise numbers if we integrate the imprecision in the computation. We must know exactly how far the results of a computation can deviate from the theoretical, precise value. (We could say that we must compute with particular precision using imprecise numbers.) This book does not treat numerics in detail, but only describes how floating-point numbers are declared and used in Modula-3.

4.5.1 Range

The range for floating-point numbers is both greater and more fine-grain than for integers. Modula-3 provides three predefined types (REAL, LONG-REAL and EXTENDED), which differ only in range and precision. The smallest range is for REAL, the largest for EXTENDED. The characteristic data of the individual types, such as the smallest and largest positive representable value, is stored in the in standard interfaces for each type (see Appendix C.1.4). The limits are symmetric to 0 (contrary to the integers).

Thus it suffices to specify the smallest and largest positive values. By smallest positive number we mean the smallest number x, such that 0 is separate and distinct from $0 + x$[1]. The limits depend on the language environment. In many language environments, e.g., the limits for LONGREAL and EXTENDED are the same.

4.5.2 Floating-point literals

Floating-point literals can be represented in the form of rational numbers with decimal points, optionally followed by an exponent part, interpreted as a power of ten.

Syntax of floating-point literals

$Number_{94}$ = $\cdots$ | $Digit_{98}$ { $Digit_{98}$ } "." $Digit_{98}$ { $Digit_{98}$ } [$Exponent_{95}$].
$Exponent_{95}$ = ("E" | "e" | "D" | "d" | "X" | "x") ["+" | "−"] $Digit_{98}$ { $Digit_{98}$ }.

A leading sign is not reflected here as part of the number because it is not part of the syntax of the number, but is part of an expression (see Section 7.1). The sign of the exponent is part of the number.

The exponent part begins with a letter E, D, or X, which specifies the type of the number. E stands for type REAL, D for LONGREAL (double precision), and X for EXTENDED.

The following are correct examples of floating-point numbers:

1.1	is of type REAL
1.1D0	the same value of type LONGREAL
1.1X0	the same value of type EXTENDED
1.5e2	type is REAL, value = 150
−1.5x+2	type is EXTENDED, value = −150
1.5E−3	type is REAL, value = 0.0015

The following are illegal examples of floating-point literals:

1	This is an integer.
1.	Digit must follow the decimal point.
1.1D	A digit must follow the exponent letter.
1.5 e2	A number must not contain a blank.
1.5e 2	A number must not contain a blank.

Table 4.14 shows typical values for the limits of representable values of floating-point types.

---

[1]This value usually refers to the normal form.

	MinPos	MaxPos
REAL	1.17549435E−38	3.40282347E +38
LONGREAL	2.2250738585072014D−308	1.79769313486623157D+308

Table 4.14: *Typical ranges for floating-point types*

4.5.3 Operations

Arithmetic operations

The usual arithmetic operations are predefined for floating-point numbers (Modula-3 notation is given in parentheses):

- addition (+)

- subtraction (−)

- multiplication (*)

- division (/)

The result of a floating-point expression is always a floating-point value. The + and − signs can also be used as unary operators. The + sign can be omitted (+x = x).

The rules of precedence (see Section 7.1) are defined as usual, with addition and subtraction having the least, multiplication and division medium, and the unary sign the greatest connective strength.

The semantics of the arithmetic, as might be expected, deviates from the usual semantics customary arithmetic.

Similar to integers, an *overflow* can occur if the result of a computation is too large (or too small in negative direction). Floating-point numbers can also produce an *underflow* if the absolute value of a result is so small that it cannot be represented.

The following rules apply for the basic operations [Wir73]:

1. *Commutativity of addition and multiplication*

   $$x + y = y + x$$
   $$x * y = y * x$$

   and if x >= y >= 0, then (x − y) + y = x

2. *Symmetry around 0*

   $$x − y = x + (−y) = −(y − x)$$
   $$(−x) * y = x * (−y) = −(x * y)$$
   $$(−x) / y = x / (−y) = −(x / y)$$

3. *Monotony*
   if $0 <= x <= a$ and $0 <= y <= b$,
   then the following always apply:

$$x + y <= a + b$$
$$x * y <= a * b$$
$$x - b <= a - y$$
$$x / b <= a / y$$

We do not discuss additional rules that derive from these [Wir73].

It is important to know that the associative and distributive laws do not always apply. Additive operations prove particularly hazardous. If we subtract nearly equal numbers from one another, the difference can become so small that it cannot be represented. Similar problems arise, e.g., when we add two very different numbers. The smaller number can fall under the precision limit of the larger number and thus be ignored in the addition. This effect is called *cancellation*. If we add the smaller number to the larger one ten times, the value of the larger number might not change. However, if we had first added ten times the smaller number, the sum could be large enough to change the larger number.

For the following example (based on [Wir73]) let us return to our four-digit floating-point arithmetic. The initial value for the floating-point numbers x, y and z are: $x = 8.800$, $y = 2.200$ and $z = -0.999$. This gives us the following results:

$$(x + y) + z = 11.00 + (-0.999) = 10.01$$
$$x + (y + z) = 8.800 + 1.201 \quad = 10.00$$

Division also demands caution. Division by a very small number (even an intermediate result in an expression) can cause an overflow. The language environment detects division by 0 and reports a run-time error.

Relational operations

Relational operations for floating-point numbers are similar to those for integers. The semantics demand some attention, however, especially for equality (and inequality).

A floating-point number stands for an infinite sequence of real numbers up to the next representable number. If two floating-point numbers are "equal", this only means that the difference between them is not larger than the smallest representable value. This means that we should avoid testing equality. Instead of $x = y$, it is always better to employ relational operations in the form $ABS(x - y) < \varepsilon$, whereby ε represents the necessary precision.

Built-in function	Direction	Note
FLOAT(i)	INTEGER $\rightarrow$ REAL	Converts an integer to a floating-point number. The value of the number is preserved.
FLOAT(r, LONGREAL)	REAL $\rightarrow$ LONGREAL	Converts a REAL number to a LONGREAL type. The value of the number is preserved.
ROUND(r)	REAL $\rightarrow$ INTEGER	Returns the integer closest to r.
TRUNC(r)	REAL $\rightarrow$ INTEGER	Truncates (cuts off) the digits after the decimal point.
FLOOR(r)	REAL $\rightarrow$ INTEGER	Returns the largest integer i such that $i \leq r$.
CEILING(r)	REAL $\rightarrow$ INTEGER	Returns the smallest integer i such that $i \geq r$.

Table 4.15: *Type conversions between reals and INTEGER*

Another – unexpected – phenomenon is that x <= y is not always the same as NOT (x > y).

Handling these and similar difficulties is one of the most important tasks of numerics. This field offers algorithms that accommodate these restrictions of the computers. We repeat the warning:

Computations with floating-point numbers demand knowledge of numerics.

Conversions

Modula-3 has predefined functions to convert floating-point numbers to integers and vice versa. Table 4.15 specifies the direction of type conversion and how the conversion is done. (Let i be of type INTEGER and r of type REAL). The function FLOAT can also convert between the different floating-point types (REAL, LONGREAL and EXTENDED) in all directions (Table 4.15 includes an example for the case REAL $\rightarrow$ LONGREAL).

There is obviously a significant difference between converting an integer to a floating-point number or vice versa. In the former case the value is preserved, while the latter generally sacrifices precision. Thus there are a number of functions for the latter conversion direction, allowing control over the rounding. Likewise there is a difference between converting a less precise floating-point representation to a more precise floating-point representation (which preserves the value) or vice versa (which can induce a loss of precision).

If r >= 0 then TRUNC(r) = FLOOR(r), and if r < 0 then TRUNC(r) = CEILING(r). The rounding border for ROUND is exactly in the middle, i.e., ROUND(0.5) = 1.

The following examples give an impression of the above functions:

CEILING(1.499E2) = 150   CEILING(−1.519E2) = −151
ROUND(1.499E2) = 150   ROUND(−1.519E2) = −152
TRUNC(1.499E2) = 149   TRUNC(−1.519E2) = −151
FLOOR(1.499E2) = 149   FLOOR(−1.519E2) = −152

Additional predefined functions such as FIRST, LAST and ABS are also defined for floating-point numbers. LAST returns the highest positive value an, and FIRST is simply −LAST.

ABS returns the absolute value of a floating-point number: ABS(r) = r if r >= 0; ABS(r) = −r if r < 0.

Mathematical functions

For floating-point numbers every language environment offers a large number of mathematical functions in the form of prefabricated interfaces. They frequently contain basic functions, such as square root and trigonometric functions. Many language environments also offer a great deal more, such as help for various numeric functions, for statistics, etc.

4.5.4   Input and output of floating-point numbers

To write example programs with floating-point numbers, we need to be able to read and output floating-point numbers. Here we use the following procedures from the SIO interface:

```
PROCEDURE GetReal(): REAL;                    (*Reads a floating-point number*)
PROCEDURE PutReal(r: REAL);                   (*Outputs a floating-point number *)
PROCEDURE GetLongReal(): LONGREAL;   (*Reads a long floating-point number*)
PROCEDURE PutLongReal(r: LONGREAL); (*Outputs a long floating-point number*)
```

The syntax of floating-point numbers that we input at the keyboard is more relaxed than that of Modula-3 literals: Whole numbers are also accepted and converted to floating-point numbers. Example 4.16 shows a program that reads, writes and converts floating-point numbers. A possible execution of the program could be the following:

```
MODULE Reals EXPORTS Main;                    (*Real operations, Sept. 15, 93. LB*)

  IMPORT SIO;

  VAR
    real: REAL;
BEGIN
  SIO.PutText("Range and conversion of floating–point numbers\n");
  SIO.PutText("MaxReal = "); SIO.PutReal(LAST(REAL));
  SIO.PutText(" MaxLongReal = "); SIO.PutLongReal(LAST(LONGREAL));

  SIO.PutText("\nPlease enter a floating–point number: ");
  real:= SIO.GetReal();                         (*the entered number is assigned to real*)

  SIO.PutText("ROUND("); SIO.PutReal(real); SIO.PutText(") = ");
  SIO.PutInt(ROUND(real)); SIO.NI();

  SIO.PutText("TRUNC("); SIO.PutReal(real); SIO.PutText(") = ");
  SIO.PutInt(TRUNC(real)); SIO.NI();

  SIO.PutText("FLOOR("); SIO.PutReal(real); SIO.PutText(") = ");
  SIO.PutInt(FLOOR(real)); SIO.NI();

  SIO.PutText("CEIL ("); SIO.PutReal(real); SIO.PutText(") = ");
  SIO.PutInt(CEILING(real)); SIO.NI();
END Reals.
```

Example 4.16: *Input / output and conversion of floating-point numbers*

```
Range and conversion of floating-point numbers
MaxReal = 3.402823E38 MaxLongReal = 1.797693D308
Please enter a floating-point number:  3.501
 ROUND(3.501)  = 4
 TRUNC(3.501)  = 3
 FLOOR(3.501)  = 3
 CEIL (3.501)  = 4
```

As our second example for floating-point numbers, we will solve a quadratic equation [Wir73]. Here we need functions for raising to powers and for taking the square root. Such functions are available in the interface Math of the Modula-3 language environment. For example, Math.pow(x, y) returns x^y, Math.sqrt(x) returns $\sqrt{x}$ for x > 0 (for x ≤ 0 Math.sqrt(x) always returns 0).

The solution to the quadratic equation

$$ax^2 + bx + c = 0$$

can be found with the familiar formula:

$$x_1 = \frac{-b + \sqrt{b^2 - 4ac}}{2a}, \quad x_2 = \frac{-b - \sqrt{b^2 - 4ac}}{2a}$$

```
MODULE Square EXPORTS Main;                           (*Sept. 15, 1993. LB*)

  IMPORT SIO, Math;

  CONST
    Two = 2.0D0;                                    (*2 as longreal constant*)
    Four= 4.0D0;                                    (*4 as longreal constant*)
  VAR
    a, b, c, d, e, f, x1, x2: LONGREAL;
BEGIN
  SIO.PutText("Quadratic equation\nPlease enter a, b, c: ");

  a:= SIO.GetLongReal();                                     (*input of a*)
  b:= SIO.GetLongReal();                                     (*input of b*)
  c:= SIO.GetLongReal();                                     (*input of c*)

  e:= Math.pow(b, Two) – Four*a*c;                      (*e:= b² – 4ac*)
  d:= Math.sqrt(e);                                     (*d:= √(b² – 4ac)*)
  f:= Two * a;                                               (*f:= 2a*)

  x1:= (–b + d) / f;
  x2:= (–b – d) / f;

  SIO.PutText("x1 = "); SIO.PutLongReal(x1); SIO.Nl();
  SIO.PutText("x2 = "); SIO.PutLongReal(x2); SIO.Nl();
END Square.
```

Example 4.17: *Solving a quadratic equation*

Example 4.17 shows the solution. The variables e, d and f, which serve
to store intermediate results, are particularly interesting. Their use not
only makes our program more comprehensible, but also faster, because we
carry out only once the (possibly extensive) computations that occur in the
formula repeatedly. The functions of the Math interface use data of type
LONGREAL; thus we use the corresponding LONGREAL procedures of the
SIO interface. The following is a possible execution of Example 4.17:

```
Quadratic equation
Please enter a, b, c:  2 10 3
x1 = -0.320550528229663
x2 = -4.6794494717703365
```

The solution in Example 4.17 has several weaknesses: For input values
where b^2-4ac becomes negative, it produces an incorrect result instead of
an error message. Furthermore, it does not test for a=0 and so accepts the
formula from familiar mathematics without criticism [Wir72]. For subtractions with very divergent or with nearly equal values, the cancelation effect
mentioned above can occur, making the result worthless. For example, if

the values of b^2 and $4ac$ are so far apart that within the representable precision $\sqrt{b^2 - 4ac} = \sqrt{b^2}$, then the one result is 0 and the other $-\frac{b}{a}$. This indicates that we could achieve much more precise results with other algorithms.

Chapter 5

Statements

The preceding chapter presented a number of data types. Regarding statements, however, we have only briefly considered the *assignment*, the *procedure call* and the *statement sequence* (compare Section 3.4.4). This chapter reviews assignments and sequences and then describes in detail the statements for branches and loops. Procedure invocation is handled later in combination with the declaration of procedures (see Section 9.2).

Later chapters introduce additional special statements as we need them.

5.1 The assignment

The assignment statement serves the purpose of assigning a value to a variable. Here we repeat the syntax of the assignment statement from Section 3.4.4:

Syntax of the assignment statement

$\text{AssignStmt}_{25} = \text{Expr}_{66} \; \text{":="} \; \text{Expr}_{66}.$

First the expression on the left side is evaluated, which determines the target address (the container for the value). In by far most cases this is simply the name of a variable. If the target address is not known in advance, then it can be determined at run time (e.g., see arrays in Section 8.1 or references in Section 11.5).

Then the expression on the right side is evaluated and its value is assigned to the target address. The original value of the variable on the left side is lost after the assignment.

The preceding chapter presented several examples of assignments. Here we show how the value of two variables, x and y, can be interchanged (or swapped). If we were to write x:= y and y:= x, we would overwrite one of

the original values, losing the value in x. Thus we must introduce an auxiliary variable as a temporary repository for one of the two values (thus
sometimes called a *triangular swap*):

```
VAR
  x, y, repository: INTEGER;
BEGIN
  ⋮
    repository := x;  x:= y;  y:= repository;
```

It would be easy to underrate the importance of the assignment statement at first glance; after all, it serves simply to copy some value from
one location to another. This makes it all the more surprising that – as
proven by extensive measurements – about half of all executed computer
commands are assignments [Tan90]. Thus the assignment statement has
fundamental importance, but does not suffice to express complex behavior.

5.2   Structured statements

This raises the question of what kinds of statements we need to express
complex algorithms. Assume the example of systematically escaping from
a labyrinth (Chapter 1.1). The statements were:

> "Go to the first possible branch. If it goes left, follow it. Other-
> wise continue straight. Keep going straight until you reach a
> T-junction and then take a right turn there.

> Repeat the whole procedure until you see light. If you reach a
> dead end, then turn around and continue as though the inter-
> ruption had not occurred."

What kinds of statements does this example contain? The whole description represents a *sequence* of statements. That is, first we must "go to
the first possible branch", and only then do we take the next step. However, this sequence does not suffice, for the statements are sometimes associated with *conditions*, such as "If [the branch] goes left, follow it". At
certain points the procedure presents *alternatives* or *branches*: Have we
already reached a "left branch"? If so, then we must turn left; otherwise
we continue straight. Conditions also control *repetitions*, or *loops*, in the
algorithm: "Keep going straight until you reach a T-junction". The sub-
steps need to be repeated until some *terminal condition* – "you reach a
T-junction" – is met.
Finally, the entire procedure represents a loop. All steps must be repeated, possibly even endlessly (for our procedure would never get us out

```
REPEAT
  go_to_branch
  IF no light yet THEN
    IF found left branch THEN
      go_left
    ELSE
      go_straight
    END
  END
  WHILE no light yet AND no T-junction found
    go_to_branch
  END
  IF no light yet THEN go_right END
UNTIL light seen
```

Example 5.1: *Procedure for escaping from a labyrinth*

of some labyrinths!). The repetition stops when the terminal condition – "you see light" – occurs.

The types of statements provided by structured imperative programming languages actually fall into these three categories:

- Sequence

- Loop

- Branch

Loops and branches collectively are called *structured statements*. They serve to bracket other statement sequences in order either to allow their repeated execution or to select a certain sequence thereof.

These types of statements can occur in any combination. For example, loops can contain further loops, branches can contain sequences, sequences can contain loops, etc. If structured statements contain statements, we call this *nesting* of statements. Such nesting should be reflected optically in the typed source code using indentation. Hence statements in a sequence appear in line vertically. In Example 5.1 we wrote the algorithm like structured statements and indented accordingly. Note that the global terminal condition – stop when you see light – must be checked after each step because it can apply after each movement. For example, if the terminal condition occurs after the first statement, go_to_branch, then none of the subsequent movement statements is executed, for all further steps first check whether the light condition has been met.

GoTos

Unstructured imperative programming languages usually provide a *GoTo statement* that permits expressing both loops and branches. This can take the following form: "If a>b then GoTo statement$_1$, else GoTo statement$_2$". Thus the conditional GoTo statement is very powerful, indeed too powerful. It enables a jump to any position in a program, e.g., into the middle of a loop or branch. This property makes the GoTo statement a source of errors because it encumbers reading the programmer's intended loops or branches from the spaghetti of GoTo statements. If we execute a statement sequence repeatedly, then it seldom makes sense to jump to some position within this sequence from the outside. Although an experienced programmer can avoid senseless jumps, it is far better if the programming language precludes such errors. Structured statements completely replace GoTos and also permit jumps only within a structured framework.

> *E. W. Dijkstra* [Dij68a] first warned of the danger of unrestricted Go-Tos. He did not stop at identifying the danger, but developed the concept of structured programming, which triggered a new epoch in programming.

Structured programming languages deliberately restrict programming to the above constructs because these constructs enable us to assure that statements always have a single entry point and a single exit. This applies not only to simple statements, but also to composite, complex statements. We can always rest assured that every statement has a well-defined starting point and end point; a jump to the middle is impossible.

This enables us to validate the correctness of the individual statements independently. For each statement, we can say which state what we expect *before* its execution, or which *preconditions* must apply. As a result, for each statement we can specify which *postconditions* will apply after execution of the statement. Thus we can validate the correctness of a statement independently. On assembly of statements to increasingly complex statements, we only need to validate the preconditions and postconditions. There is no danger of trespassing into a statement from outside it.

It is easy to see the advantage of validating the correctness of a component consisting of 10 to 50 lines of code compared to validating a complete program system consisting of hundreds of thousands of lines of code in which jumps can occur to arbitrary locations.

We do not explain validation methodology in detail here. Validation can involve methodical testing methods or formal methods. Proving the correctness of a program with purely formal methods is called *verification* [DFS88].

We must emphasize that restricting the form of statements alone does not suffice to master the complexity of larger programs. As long as all statements of a program share a common (global) state space, precise validation of a large program remains hopeless. Thus, as we have already addressed, we need to structure not only the statements but also the state space. In Modula-3 the most important structuring tool for the state space is the module, which we have already introduced briefly (see Chapter 10). However, at this point we will handle only the statements.

5.3 Sequence

Statements that must be executed one after the other form a *sequence*. We handled the syntax of the sequence (or statement sequence) with the introduction to the block concept:

Syntax of the statement sequence

$Stmts_{23} = [Stmt_{24} \{ ";" Stmt_{24} \} [";"]]$.

Modula-3 permits combining any number of statements, separated by semicolons, to a statement sequence. The statements in a sequence are executed in the order of their appearance. This does not require a separate example, as the programs presented so far all contained statement sequences.

5.4 Branches

Branches (or *selections*) bracket a set of statement sequences and, depending on certain circumstances, select exactly one of these sequences for execution. Modula-3 has two kinds of branches, the *If* statement and the *Case* statement.

5.4.1 If statement

The IF statement permits testing a sequence of conditions whose evaluation provides the basis for selecting the appropriate statement sequence (the
matching alternative).

To assign to the variable min the smaller of the values x and y (all of type INTEGER) in Modula-3, we can write the following:

    IF x < y THEN min := x ELSE min := y END;

The statement following the reserved word THEN executes if the evaluation of the condition x < y yields *true*. Otherwise (x < y yields *false*) the statement following ELSE executes.

Syntax of the If statement

$\text{IfStmt}_{31} = \text{"IF" Expr}_{66} \text{ "THEN" Stmts}_{23}$
$\quad\quad\quad \{ \text{"ELSIF" Expr}_{66} \text{ "THEN" Stmts}_{23} \} [\text{"ELSE" Stmts}_{23}] \text{"END"}.$

An IF statement generally takes the following form:

```
IF      b₁ THEN statement sequence₁
ELSIF b₂ THEN statement sequence₂
ELSIF b₃ THEN statement sequence₃
⋮
ELSIF bₙ THEN statement sequenceₙ
ELSE            statement sequence₀
END;
```

Each condition b_i is a Boolean expression (compare Section 4.2). They are evaluated sequentially until one returns the value *true*. If such a condition b_i is found, then the corresponding *statement sequence$_i$* executes, thus completing the IF statement (with the program continuing after the END of the IF statement). If no *true* condition is found and there is an ELSE clause, then the statement *sequence$_0$* after the reserved word ELSE executes. If no *true* condition is found and there is no ELSE clause, then no statement sequence is executed within the IF statement.

The following statement:

IF b_1 THEN *A*1 ELSIF b_2 THEN *A*2 ELSE *A*0 END

simply represents a short form of:

IF b_1 THEN *A*1 ELSE IF b_2 THEN *A*2 ELSE *A*0 END END

Since each new ELSE IF requires an additional END to terminate the nested IF statement, the compact form is preferable if we need to test more than one condition.

We can infer that if an IF statement contains more than one *true* condition, the *first* such condition triggers selection. This does not apply in all programming languages. Among the languages conceived for parallel processing, some treat multiple *true* conditions by *arbitrary* selection from among the statement sequences with *true* conditions (*guarded statements* by *Dijkstra* [Dij75], e.g., in SR [And91]). This introduces a certain *nondeterminism* into the execution of selection statements, which can be useful in nonsequential programs (see Chapter 16).

```
CONST
   Conv = ORD('A') – ORD('a');       (*difference between ordinal values of 'A' and 'a'*)
VAR
   ch: CHAR;
BEGIN
   ch:= SIO.GetChar();                (*reads a character and assigns it to ch*)
   IF (ch >= 'a') AND (ch <= 'z') THEN      (*value of ch is a lower-case letter*)
      ch:= VAL(ORD(ch) + Conv, CHAR);            (*converts to upper case*)
   END;
   SIO.PutChar(ch);                           (*outputs ch*)
   ⋮
```

Example 5.2: *Testing a condition with an If statement*

Example 4.8 showed how to transform lower-case letters into upper case. Let us extend this example with a test to assure that we apply the transformation only to lower-case letters. All other characters should produce no action (Example 5.2). This calls for an IF statement without an ELSE clause.

Assume that we want to determine the order of magnitude of the positive number x, to the thousands position:

```
IF x >= 0 THEN
   IF      x < 10    THEN SIO.PutText("one-digit")
   ELSIF x < 100   THEN SIO.PutText("two-digit")
   ELSIF x < 1000 THEN SIO.PutText("three-digit")
   ELSE                    SIO.PutText("at least four-digit")
   END; (*IF (x < 10)*)
ELSE
   SIO.PutText("negative")
END; (*IF x >= 0*)
```

This program fragment exploits the fact that the ELSIF conditions are evaluated sequentially; the tests are not independent. For example, if we exchange the ELSIF branches that test $x < 100$ and $x < 1000$, then the program would identify any number between 10 and 999 as three-digit. In this case three-digit would mean at most three digits rather than exactly three digits. We can eliminate this sequential dependency by always testing the full range, thus making the tests disjunct:

```
IF      (x >= 0)    AND (x < 10)     THEN SIO.PutText("one-digit")
ELSIF (x >= 10)   AND (x < 100)   THEN SIO.PutText("two-digit")
ELSIF (x >= 100) AND (x < 1000) THEN SIO.PutText("three-digit")
ELSIF (x >= 1000)                      THEN SIO.PutText("at least four-digit")
ELSE                                          SIO.PutText("negative")
END; (*IF (x >= 0) ···*)
```

```
MODULE Ifs1 EXPORTS Main;                              (*Sept. 20, 1993. LB*)

  IMPORT SIO;

  VAR i: INTEGER;

BEGIN                                                  (*statement part*)
  SIO.PutText( "Test of divisibility by 2 to 5\n" &
               "Please enter a number: ");
  i:= SIO.GetInt();
  SIO.PutText("Your number is divisible by ");

  IF
    ((i MOD 2) = 0) OR ((i MOD 3) = 0) OR((i MOD 4) = 0) OR ((i MOD 4) = 0)
  THEN                                        (*at least one of the conditions holds*)
    IF (i MOD 2) = 0 THEN SIO.PutInt(2) END;               (*divisible by 2*)
    IF (i MOD 3) = 0 THEN SIO.PutInt(3) END;               (*divisible by 3*)
    IF (i MOD 4) = 0 THEN SIO.PutInt(4) END;               (*divisible by 4*)
    IF (i MOD 5) = 0 THEN SIO.PutInt(5) END;               (*divisible by 5*)
  ELSE                                                  (*no condition holds*)
    SIO.PutText("none of the numbers from 2 to 5")
  END; (*IF (i MOD 2) = 0 ...*)
  SIO.Nl();
END Ifs1.
```

Example 5.3: *If statements nested to a depth of 1*

This variant permits every interchange of ELSIF branches, but at the price of more effort in constructing and evaluating the conditions.

In Modula-3 all structured statements have an easily recognizable start and an end (in the form of keywords); the end of a structured statement is not always so easy to recognize because most structured statements employ the same keyword (END). Thus we recommend commenting the end of a structured statement as in the examples above.

IF-ELSIF-ELSIF statements test all conditions until the first one is *true*. All subsequent ones are ignored. This essentially differs from putting the conditions in individual IF-THEN statements. To make this clear, let us write a program that reads a number and determines whether the number is divisible by 2, 3, 4 and/or 5 (Example 5.3). First we test whether any conditions can be fulfilled at all. If not, we output a corresponding message (in the ELSE branch). If any conditions can be fulfilled, then we test each condition individually. The simple IF-THEN statements are nested in the IF-THEN-ELSE statement.

The solution in Example 5.3 is correct, but not especially elegant because each condition is tested redundantly.

```
MODULE Haho EXPORTS Main;                              (*Sept. 20, 1993. LB*)

  IMPORT SIO;

  VAR
    ch: CHAR; i: CARDINAL;                             (*i: counter for position*)

BEGIN                                                  (*statement part*)
  SIO.PutText("Please enter a line beginning with 'Haho':\n");

  i:= 1;                                               (*1st character is at 1st position*)
  ch:= SIO.GetChar();                                  (*read 1st character*)

  IF (ch = 'H') OR (ch = 'h') THEN
    INC(i); ch:= SIO.GetChar();                        (*1st letter is H or h*)
    IF (ch = 'A') OR (ch = 'a') THEN
      INC(i); ch:= SIO.GetChar();                      (*2nd letter is A or a*)
      IF (ch = 'H') OR (ch = 'h') THEN
        INC(i); ch:= SIO.GetChar();                    (*3rd letter is H or h*)
        IF (ch = 'O') OR (ch = 'o') THEN
          INC(i); SIO.PutText("Correct\n");            (*4th letter is O or o*)
        END; (*IF (ch = 'O')...*)
      END; (*IF (ch = 'H')...*)
    END; (*IF (ch = 'A')...*)
  END; (*IF (ch = 'H')...*)
  IF i < 5 THEN                                        (*A difference was detected*)
    SIO.PutText("The position of the first deviation is ");
    SIO.PutInt(i); SIO.NI()
  END; (*IF i < 5*)

END Haho.
```

Example 5.4: *Repeatedly nested If statements*

One possible program flow is the following:

```
Test of divisibility by 2 to 5
Please enter a number:  30
Your number is divisible by 2 3 5
```

A series of conditions that are to be tested until one of them produces
false presents a different kind of problem. Here we offer another program
that reads a character string and tests whether it begins with "Haho", without case sensitivity, so that we accept "Haho", "haho", "HAHO" etc. We cannot use Text.Equal because this procedure is case sensitive. If a character
string does not begin with "Haho", then we output the first position where
the first deviation occurred. This requires nesting the individual IF-THEN
statements (see Example 5.4). The variable i always contains the position
of the next character. After each successful test of a character, i is incremented by one. For matching words, i ascends to 5, and for nonmatching

words it represents the first deviating position. The following is a possible program flow:

```
Please enter a line beginning with 'Haho'
haha
The position of the first deviation is 4
```

5.4.2 Case statement

The CASE statement computes an expression whose value determines the selection of a statement sequence from a set of statement sequences.

Menu input typical of many interactive programs could take the following form:

```
SIO.PutText("Choose one of the following: ");
SIO.PutText("(1) first, (2) second, (3) third menu item.");

CASE SIO.GetInt() OF
  1 => SIO.PutText("first menu item")
 |2 => SIO.PutText("second menu item")
 |3 => SIO.PutText("third menu item")
ELSE SIO.PutText("improper input")
END;
```

Rather than a computation, here the expression consists of the return value of the function SIO.GetInt. Depending on whether the user inputs 1, 2 or 3, the corresponding statement executes. If the user inputs any other number, the statement in the ELSE branch executes.

Syntax of the Case statement

$$CaseStmt_{27} = \text{"CASE" } Expr_{66} \text{ "OF" } [Case_{42}] \{ \text{ "|" } Case_{42} \}$$
$$[\text{ "ELSE" } Stmts_{23}] \text{ "END".}$$
$$Case_{42} = Labels_{43} \{ \text{ "," } Labels_{43} \} \text{ "=>" } Stmts_{23}.$$
$$Labels_{43} = ConstExpr_{65} [\text{ ".." } ConstExpr_{65}].$$

Thus a Case statement sequence generally takes the following form:

```
CASE expression OF
```
$$| \ List_1 => statement \ sequence_1$$
$$| \ List_2 => statement \ sequence_2$$
$$\vdots$$
$$| \ List_n => statement \ sequence_n$$
```
ELSE statement sequence₀
```
$$\text{ELSE } statement \ sequence_0$$
```
END (*CASE expression*)
```

The type of the expression must be an ordinal type (i.e., not REAL or TEXT). $List_i$ represents a list of individual values (in the form of constant expressions) or ranges. A range is specified as lower bound .. upper bound, whereby the bounds themselves are part of the range. The ELSE branch is optional. All values that occur in any of the CASE lists of a given CASE statement must be disjunct. The order of specification of the individual values or ranges, contrary to the IF-ELSIF-ELSIF statement, is arbitrary.

During execution of the Case statement the expression is evaluated first. If there exists a $List_i$ containing a matching value (of which there can be only one), then the corresponding *statement sequence$_i$* executes. If there is no such list and an ELSE branch was specified, then *statement sequence$_0$* executes.

If there is no list that contains the value and no ELSE branch, then a run-time error results. This is a significant difference compared to the IF statement. If there is no valid condition in an IF statement, then the statement has no effect apart from the evaluation of the condition itself. The CASE statement assumes an error if none of the lists contains the value of the CASE expression. In such cases it is always best to generate a run-time error. In this way the programmer can more easily localize and correct the error. If the program were to protract execution and possibly continue computations with erroneous data, the error would be more difficult to localize.

> For this reason we should consider the run-time error imposed by the language environment not as an irritation, but as an aid. Although a program crash proves frustrating, unfortunately it is usually our own fault.

As an example of a CASE statement, let us rewrite our program for the basic operations of integer arithmetic so that it selects only one operation specified by the user. DIV and MOD must be specified by their first letters (upper or lower case). Our first attempt is Example 5.5.

This solution represents a situation that unfortunately sometimes occurs in practice as well. It functions correctly for correct user input, but crashes if the user enters an incorrect operation character. Hence we can generally conclude that a CASE statement without an ELSE branch should only be used if every possible value of the CASE expression occurs in one of the CASE lists.

> The compiler outputs a warning when translating a CASE statement that does not cover all possible values: CASE statement does not handle all possible values. This makes it easy to find such dangerous CASE statements.

We can easily correct our error by inserting an ELSE branch (Example 5.6). This solution is still not correct because it returns the result k even in

```
MODULE Case EXPORTS Main;                              (*Sept. 20, 1993. LB*)

   IMPORT SIO;

   VAR
      i, j, k: INTEGER;                        (*i and j are the operands, k the result*)
      operator: CHAR;                          (*contains the entered operator "code"*)
BEGIN                                                      (*statement part*)
   SIO.PutText( "Basic arithmetic functions\n" &
                  "Please enter two numbers and an operator\n");

   i:= SIO.GetInt();
   j:= SIO.GetInt();
   operator:= SIO.GetChar();

   CASE operator OF
      | '+'    => k:= i + j;
      | '–'    => k:= i – j;
      | '*'    => k:= i * j;
      | 'D', 'd' => k:= i DIV j;
      | 'M', 'm'=> k:= i MOD j;
   END; (*CASE operator*)

   SIO.PutText("Result = "); SIO.PutInt(k); SIO.Nl();

END Case.
```

Example 5.5: *Case statement without Else branch (danger of run-time error)*

the event of a user error, although the value of k would then be undefined. We can attain a better solution using nested CASE statements (Example 5.7). The outer CASE statement filters out cases with erroneous input. The inner CASE statement no longer needs to handle errors, so that all possible values of the CASE expression are now covered in the CASE lists.

> This solution suffers from the repeated evaluation of expressions in a way similar to the flaw in Example 5.3. Similar considerations apply. Additionally, CASE statements with few cases – such as our outer CASE statement – should better be avoided.

Two possible executions of Example 5.7 (omitting the greeting text) follow:

```
23 34 .
Invalid operator
```

```
23 34 *
Result = 782
```

```
⋮
CASE operator OF
  | '+'    => k:= i + j;
  | '−'    => k:= i − j;
  | '*'    => k:= i * j;
  | 'D', 'd' => k:= i DIV j;
  | 'M', 'm'=> k:= i MOD j;
ELSE          SIO.PutText("Invalid operator\n");                    (*k remains undefined!*)
END; (*CASE operator*)
SIO.PutText("Result = "); SIO.PutInt(k); SIO.NI();
```

Example 5.6: Case statement with Else branch

```
⋮
CASE operator OF
  | '+', '−', '*' , 'D', 'd', 'M', 'm' =>                          (*if operator is correct*)
  CASE operator OF                                 (*now the list contains all possible values*)
    | '+'    => k:= i + j;
    | '−'    => k:= i − j;
    | '*'    => k:= i * j;
    | 'D', 'd'  => k:= i DIV j;
    | 'M', 'm' => k:= i MOD j;
  END; (*CASE operator*)
  SIO.PutText("Result = "); SIO.PutInt(k); SIO.NI();
ELSE                                    (*if the operator character was a typing error*)
  SIO.PutText("Invalid operator\n");
END;
```

Example 5.7: Case statements with error handling

```
⋮
IF      operator = '+'   THEN k:= i + j;
ELSIF  operator = '−'   THEN k:= i − j;
ELSIF  operator = '*'   THEN k:= i * j;
ELSIF  (operator = 'D') OR (operator = 'd') THEN k:= i DIV j;
ELSIF  (operator = 'M') OR (operator = 'm') THEN k:= i MOD j;
ELSE SIO.PutText("Invalid operator\n");
END; (*IF operator*)
⋮
```

Example 5.8: If replacing Case

```
⋮
CASE SIO.GetChar() OF
  | 'A' .. 'Z' => SIO.PutText("capital letter\n");
  | 'a' .. 'z' => SIO.PutText("lower–case letter\n");
  | '0' .. '9' => SIO.PutText("number\n");
ELSE            SIO.PutText("other\n");
END; (*CASE SIO.GetChar()*)
⋮
```

Example 5.9: Case statement with range lists

```
⋮
IF (SIO.GetChar() >= 'A') AND (SIO.GetChar() <= 'Z') THEN
  SIO.PutText("capital letter\n");
ELSIF (SIO.GetChar() >= 'a') AND (SIO.GetChar() <= 'z') THEN
(*On each invocation a new character is read - which we do not want!*)
⋮
```

Example 5.10: Case improperly replaced by If – side effect!

```
⋮
ch:= SIO.GetChar();
IF (ch >= 'A') AND (ch <= 'Z') THEN
  SIO.PutText("capital letter\n");
ELSIF (ch >= 'a') AND (ch <= 'z') THEN
  SIO.PutText("lower–case letter\n");
ELSIF (ch >= '0') AND (ch <= '9') THEN
  SIO.PutText("number\n");
ELSE
  SIO.PutText("other\n");
END; (*IF SIO.GetChar()*)
⋮
```

Example 5.11: Case replaced by If – side effect disabled

In the program fragment in Example 5.9 the CASE statement classifies the entered characters into categories and outputs a corresponding text. The invocation of SIO.GetChar is used directly as the CASE expression.

5.4.3   Equivalence of If and Case

IF statements can be transformed to CASE statements and vice versa. There are situations where either IF or CASE is absolutely preferable. Otherwise this is a matter of taste.

The CASE statement of Example 5.6 is easy to replace with an IF statement (Example 5.8).

Which variant we choose is a matter of taste here; however, the corresponding CASE statement is more readable. If the expression in the CASE statement is complicated and time consuming, then a CASE statement is more efficient because the expression is only computed once. If there are but a few cases to distinguish, then preference usually goes to an IF statement. If the CASE expression triggers a *side effect* (i.e., the expression not only returns a value, but also changes the state space), then the CASE statement cannot be replaced so easily with an IF statement. For example, if we naively convert the CASE statement in Example 5.9 one-to-one to an IF statement, this would simply be incorrect because we would invoke GetChar at each prompt (Example 5.10). Invoking GetChar causes a typical side effect: on each invocation the procedure reads a new character from the keyboard. The resulting program behaves differently from Example 5.9. We can easily disable this side effect by introducing an auxiliary variable (ch) (Example 5.11). The resulting IF construct is *equivalent* to the CASE version (although less efficient).

5.5 Loops

Loops (or *repetition statements*) repeat the statements that they bracket (the *loop body*). Either a loop is infinite or it ends on a certain condition, the *loop condition*. The role of a loop condition can be seen from two viewpoints. It is either the condition that controls whether the loop body is to be repeated, or the condition to terminate the repetition. In the first case we also call the loop condition *entry condition*; in the second case *termination condition*. For a given loop the following always applies: *termination condition = NOT entry condition*.

In some loops the loop body executes at least once, while in others the loop body might not execute at all. Modula-3 offers four types of loops that differ primarily in the specification of the loop condition

- While (Section 5.5.1)

- Repeat (Section 5.5.3)

- For (Section 5.5.4)

- Loop (Section 5.5.5)

5.5.1 While loop

This repetitive control structure evaluates the loop condition *before* executing the loop body. Take the example of integer division, with dividend divided by divisor, both of type CARDINAL. A naive algorithm might subtract dividend from divisor until no further subtraction is possible because divisor has become larger than dividend. The number of subtractions represents the result of integer division:

```
result := 0;
WHILE dividend > divisor DO
   INC(result); dividend := dividend – divisor
END;
```

As long as the condition dividend > divisor is *true*, the statements after the keyword DO are executed. The condition must be tested *before* execution of the statements because the divisor could be larger than the dividend from the start; the result of this integer division would be 0; it is computed correctly by the loop (because no computation is done at all). After the computation, the division remainder is contained in the variable dividend.

Syntax of the While loop

WhileStmt$_{40}$ = "WHILE" Expr$_{66}$ "DO" Stmts$_{23}$ "END" .

Expr$_{66}$ must be a Boolean expression. The WHILE loop executes as follows: First Expr$_{66}$ the loop condition is evaluated. If it is *true*, then the loop body (Stmts$_{23}$) is executed and then the condition is reevaluated. This is repeated until the condition is *false*. Then the WHILE statement terminates and the program resumes at the line after the END. At this location the loop condition is certainly *false*. If the condition is initially *false*, the loop body does not execute at all. On the other hand, if the condition never becomes *false*, then the loop body executes infinitely! It is the programmer's responsibility to assure that the loop condition is set to *false* at some point in the loop body. The WHILE statement only tests the condition, but does not set it.

As our first example of the WHILE statement, let us generalize Example 3.5 (page 47) such that the program computes the arithmetic mean of a number sequence of any length (Example 5.12). We need to be able to read any number of numbers in a loop, and the entry of a stop character indicates the end of the sequence. We will store the sum of the sequence in the variable sum. On each repetition of the loop we read a new number and increase the count of numbers n by 1 and sum by the value of the number. The termination condition is the entry of the stop character.

Note the initializations before the WHILE loop: To be able to use a counter in a loop, it must be set to a start value before the loop begins! We test for the stop character using the function SIO.LookAhead, which returns the next character in the input stream without removing it. Thus, e.g., if the next character is a digit, then the number is read with GetInt.

```
MODULE ArithMean EXPORTS Main;                              (*04.11.94. LB*)
(*The program computes the arithmetic mean of a series of numbers*)

   IMPORT SIO, Text;

   CONST
      Stop = '.';                                    (*terminates the input stream*)
   VAR
      x, n: INTEGER;                        (*x: current value, n: number of values*)
      sum: INTEGER;                           (*stores the sum of the input numbers*)
      mean: REAL;                              (*arithmetic mean is type REAL*)
BEGIN
   SIO.PutText( "Arithmetic mean of a series of numbers\n" &
            "Terminate input with " & Text.FromChar(Stop) & "\n");

   sum := 0;                                        (*sum initialized to 0*)
   n:= 0;                                           (*n initialized to 0*)

   WHILE SIO.LookAhead() # Stop DO    (*Termination condition: the stop character*)
      x:= SIO.GetInt();                           (*reads a number into x*)
      INC(sum, x);                                (*increments sum by x*)
      INC(n);                                     (*increments n by 1*)
   END; (*WHILE x # Stop*)

   IF n > 0 THEN
      mean:= FLOAT(sum) / FLOAT(n);
      SIO.PutText("Arithmetic mean = ");
      SIO.PutReal(mean); SIO.Nl()
   ELSE
      SIO.PutText("Empty input stream\n")
   END; (*IF n ¿ 0*)
END ArithMean.
```

Example 5.12: *Arithmetic mean of a series of numbers*

At the end of the loop we output the arithmetic mean as a REAL number because the sum divided by the count might not be divisible without a
remainder. One possible execution of the program (without the greeting)
might be the following:

```
-100 8 50 50 16 4 .
Arithmetic mean = 4.6666665
```

```
MODULE Euclid EXPORTS Main;                          (*20.09.93. LB*)
  IMPORT SIO;

  VAR
    a, b, x, y: CARDINAL;              (*a, b: input values; x, y: working variables*)
BEGIN                                                  (*statement part*)
  SIO.PutText("Euclidean algorithm\n Enter 2 positive numbers: ");

  a:= SIO.GetInt();                              (*first number assigned to a*)
  b:= SIO.GetInt();                              (*second number assigned to b*)

  x:= a; y:= b;                        (*x and y can be changed by the algorithm*)

  WHILE x # y DO
    IF x > y THEN x:= x – y ELSE y:= y – x END;
  END; (*WHILE x # y*)

  SIO.PutText("Greatest common divisor of ");
  SIO.PutInt(a); SIO.PutText(" and "); SIO.PutInt(b);
  SIO.PutText(" = "); SIO.PutInt(x); SIO.Nl();
END Euclid.
```

Example 5.13: *The Euclidean algorithm (without input validation)*

Euclidean algorithm

The next example features the famous algorithm of Euclid to find the greatest common divisor (GCD) of two positive numbers. The algorithm is specified as follows:

1. Compare the two numbers. If they are equal, the GCD is the same.

2. If the numbers are not equal, subtract the smaller number from the larger one and replace the larger number by the result of the substraction.

3. Continue at step 1.

The algorithm stops upon finding the GCD – at the latest when the numbers are both 1.

> The algorithm did not become famous without cause, for it represents one of the first algorithms ever. The geometric inspiration is quite obvious: The algorithm can be executed geometrically with relative ease.

With the help of a WHILE loop we can quite easily express the algorithm (let $x > 0$ and $y > 0$):

```
WHILE x # y DO
  IF x > y THEN x:= x – y ELSE y:= y – x END;
END; (*WHILE x # y*)
```

```
MODULE Euclid2 EXPORTS Main;                              (*17.05.94. LB*)

  IMPORT SIO;

  VAR
    a, b: INTEGER;                                         (*input values *)
    x, y: CARDINAL;                                   (*working variables *)
BEGIN                                                   (*statement part*)
  SIO.PutText("Euclidean algorithm\nEnter 2 positive numbers: ");

  a:= SIO.GetInt();
  WHILE a <= 0 DO
    SIO.PutText("Please enter a positive number: "); a:= SIO.GetInt();
  END; (*WHILE a < 0*)

  b:= SIO.GetInt();
  WHILE b <= 0 DO
    SIO.PutText("Please enter a positive number: "); b:= SIO.GetInt();
  END; (*WHILE b < 0*)

  x:= a; y:= b;                      (*x and y can be changed by the algorithm*)
  WHILE x # y DO
    IF x > y THEN x:= x − y ELSE y:= y − x END;
  END; (*WHILE x # y*)

  SIO.PutText("Greatest common divisor = "); SIO.PutInt(x); SIO.NI();
END Euclid2.
```

Example 5.14: *The Euclidean algorithm with controlled input*

In Example 5.13 the algorithm is embedded in a program. Since we know that the algorithm is defined for positive numbers, we declare the variables as type CARDINAL.

Program 5.13 has one shortcoming: If the user enters a negative number, the program crashes (at run time the language environment detects that we are attempting to assign a negative value to a variable of type CARDINAL). Even worse, if one of the entered numbers is zero, then the program falls into an *infinite loop*. For example, if the second entry is 0, then x is always decremented by 0; the termination condition is never met. Although negative numbers and zero are actually erroneous input, the punishment is too severe. We must always assume that an interactive user can make a mistake. In such cases we should request a new entry instead of letting the program crash. Program example 5.14 eliminates this shortcoming. After entry of each number, a WHILE loop requests input of a new number until a positive number is entered. If the number is correct from the start, this WHILE loop has no effect. Note that we had to change the type of the input variables a and b to INTEGER to prevent the program from still crashing on assignment of a possibly negative number.

The actual algorithm in Example 5.14 is surprisingly the smallest part of the program. This is also typical of larger program systems: The various management tasks (input/output, error handling, etc.) often require a much larger portion of the code than the actual computations.

5.5.2 Loop invariants

As another example we will develop an algorithm that multiplies two natural numbers using only addition and subtraction. The algorithm is actually quite simple: x * y is equivalent to x + x ⋯ + x (y times). We introduce two auxiliary variables: result to store the result and steps to count the number of steps (Example 5.15).

Example 5.15: *Multiplication using only addition and subtraction*

```
    ⋮
  result:= 0;
  step:= y;
  WHILE step > 0 DO
     result:= result + x; step:= step − 1;
  END; (*WHILE*)
    ⋮
```

Now we can pose the question: Can we be sure that this algorithm is correct? How can we be sure? If we attempt to test the algorithm for all possible numbers, then even the fastest computer in the world would require centuries. Even for such a simple case, exhaustive testing is impossible. We must find assurance in another way, i.e., with a more mathematical approach. Although we do not discuss formal *verification* [DFS88] in detail, we will show how to check the correctness of a loop semiformally. We use the following idea:

- We formulate the required result (call it Q) using predicate logic.

- We look for a condition that applies during the entire execution of the loop (an *invariant*). We can write this *loop invariant* (call it I) for the WHILE loop as follows (we put the invariant in parentheses {} to indicate that it is not directly part of the algorithm):

$$\{I\} \text{ WHILE } condition \text{ DO } statements \{I\} \text{ END}$$

- We look for a termination condition B such that the result Q ensues from $B \wedge I$ (written $B \wedge I \Rightarrow Q$). Note that the termination condition for the WHILE loop is the negation of the WHILE condition. The WHILE loop executes until the WHILE condition becomes *false*, or the termination condition becomes *true*.

- Now we can be sure that if our loop terminates at some time, then it must return the correct result. I applies for each iteration of the loop, B applies after the loop, and $B \wedge I$ imply the correct result. If we prove this for a given algorithm, then we have proven the *partial correctness* of the algorithm.

- Finally, we also show that the algorithm terminates. Then we have proven the *total correctness*.

Now let us try to apply this procedure to Example 5.15.

- The required result is easy to formulate:

$$Q : \text{result} = x * y.$$

- We find the invariant as follows: Before the first execution of the loop result = 0 and step = y. With each iteration result is increased by x and step is decreased by 1. The algorithm is defined for natural numbers; i.e., x and y must not be negative. Hence we can derive the additional requirement that step must not become negative (the loop body is only executed if step > 0). Thus the following condition always applies:

$$I : (\text{result} + (\text{step} * x) = x * y) \wedge (\text{step} >= 0)$$

- Furthermore, the following applies: If step = 0, then result = x * y. This gives us the termination condition

$$B : \text{step} = 0.$$

The WHILE condition thus becomes step # 0. We could have written the loop in the form WHILE step # 0 DO ⋯ END. Our variant is more robust because the loop is simply skipped if step erroneously receives a negative value.

- This already demonstrates the partial correctness. I is a valid invariant, and if B is *true* as well, then I becomes the result. For example, if y = 0 then the loop body is not executed – result = 0 is the correct answer.

- For the total correctness we must still prove that the loop actually terminates. Here we must show that we approach the termination condition with each iteration. In this case this means that steps > 0 must become *false* at some point. Since steps > 0 always applies at the start of the loop body and steps is reduced by 1 with each iteration, it must eventually become 0.

It would also be possible to find other algorithms that meet the same invariant and termination condition and yet are still different. [WG92, RW92] offer such an algorithm, which is somewhat more complicated, yet still more efficient (it requires less iterations) and fulfills the same conditions.

Assertions

Modula-3 allows specification of *assertions* at any location in a statement sequence. We can use assertions, e.g., to formulate loop invariants. Strictly speaking, this feature is not part of the language, just as the invariants are not part of the algorithm. Modula-3 permits assertions with the following syntax:

Assertion = "<*" "ASSERT" $Expr_{66}$ "*>" .

$Expr_{66}$ is a Boolean expression. If it is *true*, the program continues to run. If it is *false*, a run-time error is generated which terminates the program with an error message.

We could extend the program fragment in Example 5.15 so that we specify the loop invariant directly as an assertion (Example 5.16).

As language elements, assertions belong to the *pragmas*. Pragmas are used primarily to control the functioning of the compiler. Pragmas are always bracketed in the special symbols <* and *>. One pragma, e.g., allows disabling compiler warnings, while another permits linking program components that were written in another programming language (e.g., in C) (see Appendix B.8.5).

The observant reader might be wondering why we cannot test the assertion with an IF statement, as in Example 5.17. This would be possible. However, using assertions as pragmas indicates that testing the condition is not part of the algorithm, but belongs other dimensions: on the one hand to the documentation and simultaneously to the the improvement of security. Another advantage of specifying assertions in the form of pragmas is that they can be ignored by setting a compiler option. We can direct the compiler (with the option -A) to ignore all assertions (to handle them as comments). Thus a program might contain many assertions during its development phase. Once we are convinced that our program is correct, the assertions can simply be "compiled out"; then they only serve as comments, but no longer affect the size or execution speed of the compiled program. If we had chosen the version with the IF statement, we would have to manually remove the assertions in the final phase. Such obstacles would normally lead programmers to prefer to do without assertions, thus saving not only their own energy but also storage and CPU time. Naturally the loss is much greater for serious applications: Faulty programs result!

```
result := 0;
step := y;
<* ASSERT (result + (step * x) = x * y) *>
WHILE step > 0 DO
   result := result + x; step:= step − 1;
   <* ASSERT (result + (step * x) = x * y) *>
END; (*WHILE*)
```

Example 5.16: *Multiplication algorithm with assertion*

```
result:= 0;
step:= y;
WHILE step > 0 DO
   IF (result + (step * x) = x * y) THEN
      result:= result + x; step:= step − 1;
   ELSE
      SIO.PutText("ASSERTION ERROR — CAUTION!");
   END (*IF*)
END; (*WHILE*)
```

Example 5.17: *If statement instead of assertion (unfavorable)*

5.5.3 Repeat loop

This loop statement has its termination condition *after* the execution of the loop body.

The following algorithm determines whether the positive number candidate is a prime number. The variable i is initialized to 1 and then incremented by 1 in each iteration until either candidate can be divided by i without a remainder (hence not a prime number) or until the following applies:

$$i^2 > \text{candidate}$$

Variables i and candidate of the code fragment are of type CARDINAL:

```
i:= 1;
REPEAT
   i:= i + 1
UNTIL ((candidate MOD i) = 0) OR (i * i > candidate);
IF i * i > candidate THEN
   SIO.PutText("Prime number")
END;
```

The statement between the keywords REPEAT and UNTIL executes until the termination condition is fulfilled. An interesting aspect of this example is that the actual work is done in the evaluation of the termination condition, while the loop body itself simply consists of an addition.

```
MODULE Prim EXPORTS Main;                                    (*21.09.93. LB*)

  IMPORT SIO;

  VAR candidate, i: INTEGER;
BEGIN
  SIO.PutText("Prime number test\n");
  REPEAT
    SIO.PutText("Please enter a positive number; enter 0 to quit. ");
    candidate:= SIO.GetInt();
    IF candidate > 2 THEN
      i:= 1;
      REPEAT
        i:= i + 1
      UNTIL ((candidate MOD i) = 0) OR (i * i > candidate);
      IF (candidate MOD i) = 0 THEN SIO.PutText("Not a prime number\n")
      ELSE SIO.PutText("Prime number\n")
      END; (*IF (candidate MOD i) = 0 ...*)
    ELSIF candidate > 0 THEN
      SIO.PutText("Prime number\n")                          (*1 and 2 are prime*)
    END; (*IF candidate > 2*)
  UNTIL candidate <= 0;
END Prim.
```

Example 5.18: *Prime number testing with Repeat*

Syntax of the Repeat loop

$$\text{RepeatStmt}_{35} = \text{"REPEAT" Stmts}_{23} \text{"UNTIL" Expr}_{66}.$$

Expr_{66} (the condition) is a Boolean expression. First the loop body executes; then the condition is evaluated. If the condition is *false*, the loop body is repeated until the condition becomes *true*. This terminates the RE-PEAT statement, and execution resumes with the next statement.

Contrary to the WHILE statement, the loop body of the REPEAT statement always executes at least once (because the condition is tested only after the first iteration). Furthermore, a WHILE statement repeats as long as the condition is *true*, while a REPEAT statement executes as long as the condition is *false*. If the condition is never *true*, the loop body repeats infinitely. The REPEAT statement – similar to the WHILE statement – only tests the loop condition, but does not set it.

In Example 5.18 the prime number algorithm is imbedded in a program that enables us to use the algorithm repeatedly. The algorithm is embedded in an outer REPEAT loop that terminates the program on an entry ≤ 0.

Let us rewrite the multiplication algorithm of Example 5.15 using a REPEAT loop. The loop invariant remains intact; only the termination condition changes. In Example 5.19 we list the complete program source code. The program explicitly asks whether the user wants to use the algorithm

```
MODULE Mul EXPORTS Main;                                    (*21.09.93. LB*)

  IMPORT SIO;

  VAR
    x, y, result, step: INTEGER;
    stop: CHAR;                                         (*controls termination*)
BEGIN
  REPEAT
    SIO.PutText("Multiplication of two positive numbers: ");

    REPEAT
      x:= SIO.GetInt();
      IF x <= 0 THEN SIO.PutText("Enter a positive number: ") END;
    UNTIL x > 0;                        (*Reads until a positive number is entered*)
    REPEAT
      y:= SIO.GetInt();
      IF y <= 0 THEN SIO.PutText("Enter a positive number: ") END;
    UNTIL y > 0;                        (*Reads until a positive number is entered*)

    result:= 0;
    step:= y;
    REPEAT
      result:= result + x; step:= step − 1;
      <* ASSERT (result + (step * x) = x * y) *>
    UNTIL step = 0;

    SIO.PutText("x * y = "); SIO.PutInt(result); SIO.Nl();
    SIO.PutText("Do you want to continue ? y/n ");
    stop:= SIO.GetChar();
  UNTIL (stop = 'N') OR (stop = 'n');        (*on all other characters we continue*)
END Mul.
```

Example 5.19: *Multiplication and input control with Repeat*

again. The algorithm with the WHILE loop also functioned properly for y=0.
The variant with the REPEAT loop only functions correctly if y > 0. On y =
0 after the first iteration we would have step = - 1. We have now inserted
the test y > 0 into the entry component. In this case the WHILE variant is
better.

The following reflects a possible execution:

```
Multiplication of two positive numbers:   -3 2
Enter a positive number:   3
x * y = 6
Do you want to continue?  y/n n
```

5.5.4   For loop

This kind of loop is used in cases where the number of iterations is known in advance. For example, to write all numbers from 1 to 100 on the screen, we could simply write the following:

FOR i:= 1 TO 100 DO SIO.PutInt(i) END;

In this loop a (read-only) variable i is automatically declared and initialized to 1. Then the loop body (the statement after the keyword DO) executes, the variable automatically is incremented by 1, and the loop body executes again. This repeats until the variable becomes greater than 100. Let us examine this more precisely:

Syntax of the For loop

$ForStmt_{30}$ = "FOR" $Ident_{89}$ ":=" $Expr_{66}$ "TO" $Expr_{66}$
["BY" $Expr_{66}$] "DO" $Stmts_{23}$ "END".

The general form of a FOR statement is:

FOR id := *startValue* TO *endValue* BY *step* DO *statement sequence* END

$Ident_{89}$ represents the *control variable* (or *counter*). It is declared only through its occurrence in a FOR statement, and it disappears again after the statement. Its *scope* (see Section 9.1) is restricted to the loop body of the FOR statement. The three expressions ($Expr_{66}$) must be of an ordinal type (e.g., INTEGER or CHAR, but not REAL or TEXT).

The FOR statement executes as follows: First – and only once – the three expressions are evaluated. The first (after the := symbol) is the *start value* of the control variable, the second (after the keyword TO) is the *final value*, and the third (after BY) is the *step* for incrementing the control variable. On omission of the optional BY phrase, the *step* is set to 1.

> *Step* is always of type INTEGER, even if the control variable is, e.g., of type CHAR. The control variable is incremented as though the statement INC(*control variable, step*) concluded the loop.

With a positive step the loop runs incrementally; with a negative step it decrements. With step = 0 the loop is infinite.

The value of the control variable is set to the start value. For an incremental loop the statement tests whether the control variable ≤ the final value; for a decremental loop, whether the control variable ≥ the final value. If the corresponding condition is *true* the loop body executes. Next

the control variable is incremented by the step (which amounts to decre-
menting for a negative step) and everything repeats as long as the final
value is not exceeded. If the start value is greater than the final value at
the start of an incremental loop (or smaller for a decremental loop), then
the loop body does not execute at all.

The control variable is set internally only and cannot be modified by the
programmer (it is *read-only*).

The FOR loop – contrary to WHILE and REPEAT loops – assures that
the loop progresses toward the termination condition. Thus it is easy to
demonstrate that a FOR loop terminates: If step # 0, it always terminates
(assuming that all statements in the loop body terminate).

> Some programming languages (e.g., Modula-2) restrict the step to a
> constant expression. Then the compiler can always detect the case step
> = 0 and generates an error message on compilation. This guarantees
> that a *For* loop always terminates. Naturally the drawback of this
> solution is that the step cannot be computed at run time.

> In Modula-3 the FOR loop is defined especially cleanly. In many other,
> otherwise respectably defined programming languages, the FOR loop
> has two traps, due to the fact that the control variable is a normal
> variable:

> 1. Although it is strongly discouraged, the programmer can modify
>   the control variable within the loop. The consequences are un-
>   predictable. Take an example like the following:
>
>   FOR i:= 1 TO N DO i:= i – 1; ··· END;
>
>   This is obviously an infinite loop. Fortunately Modula-3 prohibits
>   such actions.
> 2. The value of the control variable is undefined after the loop. If
>   the programmer nevertheless makes some assumption about its
>   value, the compiler cannot detect this. What makes the situation
>   worse is that this value depends on the respective compiler. This
>   means that the program might run properly in one language en-
>   vironment but incorrectly in another. This problem cannot occur
>   in Modula-3 because the control variable no longer exists after
>   the loop.

As an example of a FOR loop, let us rewrite our multiplication exercise
once again:

```
result := 0;
FOR step := y TO 1 BY −1 DO result := result + x; END;
```

As expected, this algorithm is easiest to specify with the FOR loop because we know in advance that we need to add x to itself exactly y times. We no longer need to define the variable step; it can serve as control variable.

We could replace the decremental loop with an incremental one:

```
result := 0;
FOR step := 1 TO y DO result := result + x; END;
```

For our next example we will write a program that outputs every fifth number to 32. With a FOR loop the solution is a single line:

```
FOR i:= 1 TO 32 BY 5 DO SIO.PutInt(i) END;
```

This yields the following output:

```
1  6  11  16  21  26  31
```

We present additional examples of FOR loops after introducing arrays (Section 8.1).

5.5.5 Loop statement

The LOOP statement is an endless loop; however, departure is possible at any location using the EXIT statement.

Syntax of the Loop statement

$$\text{LoopStmt}_{33} = \text{"LOOP" Stmts}_{23} \text{ "END".}$$
$$\text{ExitStmt}_{28} = \text{"EXIT".}$$

The statements within LOOP statement are repeated until an EXIT statement is encountered. An EXIT causes immediate departure from the loop and continuation of program execution after the end of the respective loop. In nested loops the EXIT statement exits only the inner loop, i.e., the loop in which the EXIT appears.

> Taken precisely, EXIT raises the predefined *Exit exception* (see Section 15).

Although we present the EXIT statement in the context of the LOOP statement, it can occur in any loop. It can exit any loop. Use EXIT only as an emergency exit! This applies particularly for loops other than LOOP. You can exit a FOR, REPEAT or WHILE loop at any location with EXIT. However, the verification method using invariants applies only if all statements have only one entry point and one exit point.

| We highly recommend using the EXIT statement only in the context of a LOOP statement.

The EXIT statement violates our initial requirements because it permits departure from a loop at an arbitrary location. Although the LOOP statement still has only one exit point (at the END of the loop), the IF statement that typically contains the EXIT statement has at least two exit points.

```
LOOP
    ⋮
    IF x < 0 THEN EXIT ELSE DEC(x) END  (*Jumps to end if x < 0 *)
    ⋮
END (*LOOP*)
```

A LOOP statement can also have no exit point, which means that it does not terminate.

You might ask what necessitates programming infinite loops. In most cases infinite loops make no sense and are due to programming errors. However, there are exceptions, especially in the area of *parallel programming* (see Chapter 16), where infinite loops prove quite practical. Consider, e.g., our language environment, tirelessly waiting for our commands, or programs that send and receive messages around the clock in a communication network. For such cases it is quite appropriate to have a distinct language construct where the normal case is an infinite loop and termination (EXIT) is the exception. For normal sequential programs, however, the LOOP statement should be avoided!

Now let us write a program that can apply the Euclidean algorithm to any number of positive number pairs. The user can end the program by entering a number ≤ 0. On such an entry, we want the program to terminate immediately rather than prompting for the second number. For such purposes the LOOP statement makes expression somewhat easier than with other loops (Example 5.20). For the sake of completeness, we will rewrite the Euclidean algorithm using a LOOP statement. The following is a possible program execution:

```
Euclidean algorithm:   Enter pairs of numbers
3 6 12 28 0
Greatest common divisor = 3
Greatest common divisor = 4
End of Euclidean algorithm
```

In general LOOP statements that contain only a single EXIT statement at the beginning or end can always be replaced easily with a WHILE or

```
MODULE Loop EXPORTS Main;                                   (*18.05.94. LB*)

  IMPORT SIO;

  VAR
    a, b, x, y: INTEGER;              (*a, b: input value; x, y: working variables*)
BEGIN                                                    (*statement part*)
  SIO.PutText("Euclidean algorithm: Enter pairs of numbers\n");

  LOOP
    a:= SIO.GetInt();
    IF a <= 0 THEN EXIT END;              (*immediately exits the outer Loop*)

    b:= SIO.GetInt();
    IF b <= 0 THEN EXIT END;              (*immediately exits the outer Loop*)

    x:= a; y:= b;                              (*a and b are certainly > 0*)
    LOOP
      IF x > y THEN x:= x − y ELSIF y > x THEN y:= y − x ELSE EXIT END
    END; (*inner LOOP*)
    SIO.PutText("Greatest common divisor ="); SIO.PutInt(x); SIO.NI();
  END; (*outer LOOP*)

  SIO.PutText("End of Euclidean algorithm\n");
END Loop.
```

Example 5.20: *Input control and the Euclidean algorithm with Loop and Exit*

REPEAT statement. Exit points at various locations in a large outer loop
are easier to implement with a LOOP statement. Despite this seductive
power, we repeat our warning that the LOOP and EXIT statements should
be avoided so as not to encumber the verification of our programs unnecessarily.

5.5.6 Equivalence of the repetition statements

The most powerful repetition statement is obviously the LOOP statement.
Generally the LOOP statement cannot simply be replaced with the other
repetition statements (as is the case inversely). WHILE and REPEAT loops
are equally flexible; they can always be converted to one another easily.
The FOR loop offers the least flexibility and so can always be replaced easily
with other loops; nevertheless, it has particular advantages in processing
arrays (Section 8.1).

> Arrays are data structures consisting of similar elements and requir-
> ing that the number of elements be known before the the creation of an
> array. This is why FOR loops − which require knowing the number of
> steps in advance − usually provide an ideal tool for processing arrays.

```
VAR k: INTEGER;
BEGIN
  k:= 3;                                    (*Variable "k" outside the For loop*)
  FOR k:= 1 TO k * k BY k DO SIO.PutInt(k) END;
  SIO.PutInt(k);                  (*this is the outer k, not the control variable "k"!*)
  ⋮
```

Example 5.21: *Exotic For loop*

The following shows how to express WHILE and REPEAT statements using IF and LOOP statements:

WHILE *B* DO *A* END ≡ LOOP IF *B* THEN *A* ELSE EXIT END END

REPEAT *A* UNTIL *B* ≡ LOOP *A*; IF *B* THEN EXIT END END

Note that the EXIT statement occurs only once in each of these cases. WHILE and REPEAT statements can also be converted to one another easily:

WHILE *B* DO *A* END ≡ IF *B* THEN REPEAT *A* UNTIL NOT *B* END

REPEAT *A* UNTIL *B* ≡ *A*; WHILE NOT *B* DO *A* END

Now let us express the FOR loop using IF and WHILE statements (we omit exception handling here; refer to the complete specification in [Nel91]):

FOR id := *startValue* TO *endValue* BY *step* DO *A* END ≡

startValue, endValue and step are computed once and stored internally in pseudovariables (E and S). The variable id *can only be modified internally.*

id := *startValue*; E:= *endValue*; S:= *step*;
IF S >= 0 THEN
   WHILE id <= E DO *A*; INC(id, S) END (*increment id*)
ELSE
   WHILE id >= E DO *A*; INC(id, S) END (*decrement id*)
END (*IF S >= 0*)

On the basis of this definition we can correctly interpret the somewhat pathological program fragment in (Example 5.21). Outside the FOR loop the variable k has the value 3. Since the expressions are evaluated before execution of the loop, we have *startValue* = 1, *endValue* = 9 and *step* = 3. Within the loop body the k declared outside is invisible and the k used as control variable is a different variable! After the FOR loop the control variable k ceases to exist. The program fragment will produce the following output on the screen:

```
1  4  7  3
```

This example is not intended to say that the FOR loop should be used in this way. It should merely say that the behavior of the loop can be derived unambiguously from the definition even for this curious case – a property that not every language definition shares.

Chapter 6

User-defined simple types

Thus far we have used only predefined (built-in) types. We have declared constants and variables, but no types.

We have seen that assigning data to types brings many advantages. However, if we only had the predefined data types to work with, we could write only relatively simple programs. A particular strength of many programming languages (especially the Pascal family) is the possibility for the programmer to define custom types based on the predefined types using *type constructors*. This principle applies recursively, i.e., further types can derive from these custom (or user-defined) types.

Such custom types are normally defined using type declarations, with a name assigned by the user. This type name can then be used in variable declarations as a type name. Modula-3 even allows specifying a type directly in the variable declaration, which creates a nameless type. We will initially avoid this manner of implicit type declaration and explicitly declare all user-defined types.

This chapter introduces two simple user-defined types: the *enumeration* and the *subrange*.

6.1 Enumeration

In practice we often require a list of names (identifiers). For example, we might write a program that manages our classes. To assign designations to the classes, we might number them, e.g., Mathematics = 1, Software = 2, etc. However, it would be more elegant to use the designators Mathematics and Software themselves in a program. This is where enumerations come in. We define an enumeration by listing a sequence of identifiers.

```
TYPE
  Abc1    = {a, b, c};
  Abc2    = {a, b, c, d, e, f, g, h, i, j, k, l, m};
  Abc3    = {n, o, p, q, r, s, t, u, v, w, x, y, z};
  Friends = {Eleanor, Peter, Robert, Albert};
  Classes = {Software, Mathematics, English, Business};
  Empty   = {};
```

Example 6.1: *Declaration of enumerations*

Syntax of the enumeration

$$\text{EnumType}_{51} = "\{" [\text{IDList}_{87}] "\}".$$
$$\text{IDList}_{87} = \text{Ident}_{89} \{ "," \text{Ident}_{89} \}.$$

Thus an enumeration (EnumType_{51}) consists of a list (IDList_{87}) of identifiers (Ident_{89}) delimited by commas, all enclosed in braces. The values of an enumeration are exactly the listed identifiers. These identifiers form a set that is ordered by the sequence of their occurrence in the list. Enumerations are *ordinal types*. Given the enumeration:

$$\mathsf{T} = \{ identifier_1, identifier_2, \cdots, identifier_n \};$$

Thus $identifier_i < identifier_{i+1}$ holds for all $1 \le i \le n - 1$. Example 6.1 shows some enumerations. Note that an enumeration can be empty (as Empty in the example).

> What is the sense of an empty enumeration? Perhaps not much, but it can be used as a null value enumeration. The existence of a null value sometimes facilitates the general description of a problem. An empty enumeration could represent the list of classes for a college major that does not exist (yet).

The elements of an enumeration can be referenced with an expression of the form *Typname.identifier*. The identifier is *qualified* by the type name. Thus Friends.Eleanor, Abc1.a, Abc2.a, Abc3.n and Classes.Mathematics are all valid and distinct identifiers.

> You might find it annoying that we must write the type name before the identifier, analogous to having to write the number 1 as INTE-GER.1. In many other languages, such as Pascal and Modula-2, the identifiers in the list must be used without any qualification. The advantage of the Modula-3 solution is that it prevents *name conflicts*. A name conflict occurs when multiple identifiers with different meanings bear the same name (such as Abc1.a and Abc2.a). Such a name conflict can occur especially easily if we import an enumeration from another module and its values conflict with the identifiers of the importing module. In such a case we would have to rename our own identifier. This uncomfortable situation cannot occur in Modula-3.

Why do we need enumerations at all? An ordered set of identifiers could easily be simulated with the declaration of constants, e.g.:

```
CONST
  a = 0; b = 1; c = 2; d = 3; ···
  Peter = 0; Robert = 1; Albert = 2; Eleanor = 3;
  Software = 0; Mathematics = 1; English = 2; Business = 3;
```

It is easy to see how error-prone this method is. If we had erroneously written Albert = 1 instead of Albert = 2, then Albert and Robert would be equal. This error cannot occur with enumerations; the identifiers within a list are disjunct. What is more important, in the constant solution the identifiers represent normal INTEGER values. The relational operation Mathematics = Robert would return *true* which as a rule is quite ridiculous. Furthermore, we could incorporate these numbers in an arbitrary arithmetic operation; the compiler would compile c * Eleanor + English – Albert, although it makes no sense. Such operations are precluded with enumerations.

One important application of enumerations is to represent the states of a small state space. Enumerations often serve as the index range of an array (see Chapter 8.1). They have an inherent similarity to CASE statement (an enumeration defines a finite collection of values; a CASE statement selects from such). Thus enumerations can often be processed ideally with a CASE statement.

6.1.1 Predefined enumerations

In Modula-3 the types BOOLEAN and CHAR are declared as predefined enumeration types. This is important because this directly implies that both types specify an order. Type BOOLEAN is defined as {FALSE, TRUE}, thus FALSE < TRUE.

> The reserved identifiers TRUE and FALSE can be understood as synonymous for BOOLEAN.TRUE and BOOLEAN.FALSE. Since the identifiers are reserved, a name conflict is precluded.

The values of type CHAR are defined in the code table. We also do not qualify the values of type CHAR with the type name; instead, we use the notation that we already introduced for character literals (see Section 4.3).

6.1.2 Range

The range of an enumeration that is not predefined is specified by the programmer. The possible values of a variable in a given enumeration are exactly the identifiers specified in the list.

```
TYPE
   Days    = {Monday, Tuesday, Wednesday, Thursday,
              Friday, Saturday, Sunday};
   Classes = {Software, Mathematics, English, Business};
VAR
   day: Days;                                    (*stores the current day*)
   class: Classes;                               (*stores the current class*)
BEGIN                                            (*Enumerations*)
   ⋮
   IF (day = Days.Tuesday) AND (class = Classes.Mathematics) THEN
      SIO.PutText("Take along compass\n")        (*Tuesdays is geometry*)
   ELSIF (day < Days.Saturday) AND (class = Classes.English) THEN
      SIO.PutText("Take along dictionary\n")
   ELSIF day > Days.Friday THEN
      SIO.PutText("Enjoy rest, rehabilitation and recreation\n")
   END; (*IF day ...*)
```

Example 6.2: *Use of enumerations*

6.1.3   Operations

Relational operations

Relational operations are executed relative to the *ordinal number* of the
identifier. This number represents the position of the identifier in the declaration list, with the first identifier having ordinal number 0 (compare
type CHAR in Section 4.3). The ordinal numbers are normal non-negative
integers; hence the syntax and semantics of relational operations for enumerations is identical to that for integers. If the variable class is of type
Classes (see Example 6.1), then the test class < Classes.English for class
= Classes.Software or class = Classes.Mathematics returns *true*, otherwise
false.

In Example 6.2 we assume that the variables day and class contain a
correct value before they are tested.

Predefined functions

All predefined functions that apply to ordinal types also work for enumerations: If T is an enumeration, then

FIRST(T)   is the smallest element of type T
LAST(T)   is the largest element of type T
NUMBER(T) is the number of elements of type T

With the declarations of Example 6.2:

```
FIRST(Classes)     = Software
LAST(Classes)      = Business
NUMBER(Classes) = 4
```

Since enumerations are ordinal types, ORD and VAL (see Section 4.3.2) can also be used. If e is an enumeration variable or constant, then ORD(e) is the ordinal number of the current enumeration value. If o is the ordinal number of an enumeration value of enumeration T, then VAL(o, T) is the corresponding enumeration value. Therefore:

```
VAL(ORD(e), T) = e
```

For a particular value:

```
ORD(Classes.English) = 2, VAL(2, Classes) = Classes.English
```

Thus the ORD and VAL functions can be used to convert enumeration values to ordinal numbers and back. In a carefully designed program such conversions are seldom necessary, and if so, then usually for the input/output of enumeration elements.

We can determine the predecessor and successor of an enumeration value as follows:

```
INC(e), DEC(e)
```

This sets the value of e to the next (previous) identifier in the list. If the variable is class = Classes.English, then after INC(class) the value of class has changed to Classes.Business, and after DEC(class) the value of class is Classes.Mathematics. If the value of the parameter of INC or DEC is the value of LAST or FIRST of the enumeration, respectively, then the language environment generates a run-time error – as we would expect.

Input and output of enumeration elements

The identifiers of an enumeration are visible only within the program. We cannot simply input and output them. We must employ either corresponding texts or the ordinal numbers. Example 6.3 shows a module that converts ordinal numbers to enumeration elements and later transforms the enumeration elements to texts. We can often process an enumeration easily with the FOR statement, e.g., to output all ordinal values of an enumeration:

```
FOR day := FIRST(Days) TO LAST(Days) DO SIO.PutInt(ORD(day)) END
```

```
MODULE Enumerations EXPORTS Main;

  IMPORT SIO;

  TYPE
    Days = {Monday, Tuesday, Wednesday, Thursday,
            Friday, Saturday, Sunday};
  VAR
    day: Days; ord: INTEGER;

BEGIN                                                         (*Enumerations*)
  REPEAT                                      (*Reads until a valid ordinal number is input*)
    SIO.PutText("Please enter an ordinal number for a weekday: ");
    ord:= SIO.GetInt();
  UNTIL (ord >= ORD(FIRST(Days))) AND (ord <= ORD(LAST(Days)));

  day:= VAL(ord, Days);              (*Converts the ordinal number to a weekday*)

  CASE day OF
    | Days.Monday        => SIO.PutText("Monday\n");
    | Days.Tuesday       => SIO.PutText("Tuesday\n");
    | Days.Wednesday     => SIO.PutText("Wednesday\n");
    | Days.Thursday      => SIO.PutText("Thursday\n");
    | Days.Friday        => SIO.PutText("Friday\n");
    | Days.Saturday      => SIO.PutText("Saturday\n");
    | Days.Sunday        => SIO.PutText("Sunday\n");
  END; (*CASE*)

END Enumerations.
```

Example 6.3: *Input / output with enumeration*

6.2 Subranges

In many applications the values of certain variables fall within limits that
are known in advance. In representing the days of the months, for example,
we can be sure that the values must fall between 1 and 31. If a variable
that stores a day assumes the value 35, we can be certain that our program
contains an error (whereby we do not consider the *35th of May* by *Erich
Kästner*). It would be nice to have the language environment detect such
errors automatically. Thus we need a means to specify a restricted range.
This is the purpose of the *subrange*, which allows us to restrict the range of
an ordinal type. We call the original type that we want to restrict the *base
type*.

Subranges are not really distinct types. They are *subtypes* of the base
type (see Section 7.4).

Syntax of the subrange

SubrangeType$_{57}$ = "[" ConstExpr$_{65}$ ".." ConstExpr$_{65}$ "]".

```
TYPE
   SubR1       = [-1..16];                           (*base type: Integer *)
   SubR2       = [Abc2.a .. Abc2.f];                 (*base type: Abc2 *)
   SubR3       = [Abc3.p .. Abc3.x];                 (*base type: Abc3 *)
   Workdays    = [Days.Monday .. Days.Saturday];     (*base type: Days *)
   Weekend     = [Days.Saturday .. Days.Sunday];     (*base type: Days *)
   Weekdays    = [Days.Monday .. Days.Sunday];       (*base type: Days *)
   SingleValue = [1..1];                             (*base type: Integer *)
   Empty       = [1..0];                             (*base type: Integer *)
```

Example 6.4: *Declaration of subranges*

The two constant expressions (ConstExpr$_{65}$) serve as (inclusive) lower
and upper bounds. The two bounds must be of the same type. If the lower
bound is greater than the upper bound, we have an empty subrange.

> The empty subrange is similar to the empty enumeration. It proves
> useful as a *null value*.

Thus a subrange is written as:

Subrange = [lowerBound .. upperBound];

Example 6.4 shows some valid subrange declarations (in part with reference to the declarations in Examples 6.1 and 6.2).

Type SubR1 specifies a subrange of INTEGER. Variables of type SubR1
can take on values between −1 and 16. The values of a variable of type
SubR2 are defined between Abc2.a and Abc2.f, and for a variable of type
Workdays between Days.Monday and Days.Saturday. Type Weekday encompasses the entire range of type Days as defined in Example 6.3. Such a
subrange seldom makes sense, but is permissible. On the other hand, it
is not permissible to assign a variable of a subrange a value outside the
specified subrange. If the invalid value is a constant expression, the compiler will report the error at compile time. If the invalid value is a variable
expression, then the language environment detects the error only at run
time and generates a *run-time error*.

Let us declare the following variables:

```
VAR
   day: Days;                (*enumeration*)
   workday: Workdays;        (*subrange*)
   weekendDay: Weekend;      (*subrange*)
```

Note that the three types Days, Workdays and Weekend intersect on
Days.Saturday. All of the following statements are correct:

```
day := Days.Saturday;
workday := day;
weekendDay := day;
weekendDay := workday;
```

However, if the first statement were day := Days.Friday, then the last two statements would be invalid (and would produce run-time errors).

Are subranges really useful? If we already have the type INTEGER, why do we need another type to specify a subrange thereof? We could employ appropriate statements to test whether the value is in the desired range. This is true, although we might have to carry out this test quite often, and, more important, we might forget such a test. Yet if a subrange is defined once in the declaration, the test is always carried out automatically. The importance of subranges rests in improved program security.

If the application itself indicates that the value of a variable must lie within a certain subrange, then it makes sense to declare the variable as a subrange. Then the program is automatically interrupted on an erroneous assignment, and some faulty value cannot cascade through our program. Here again, this type of error handling proves useful only for localizing program errors. If the value of variables is determined interactively by the user, we must explicitly test the input. For example, if we prompt for a date, the program must not crash if the user inputs May 35, but must (politely) request another input.

In Example 6.5 we first output all possible values of the type WorkHours. The last assignment (workhour := hour) generates a run-time error because the value of hour is outside the range of WorkHours (hour = LAST(WorkHours) + 1). The inverse assignment (hour := workhour) can never go wrong because the range Hours fully encompasses WorkHours (also see Section 7.4).

6.2.1 Operations

A subrange allows exactly the same operations as its base type.

> This rule derives from the fact that subranges have a *subtype* relationship to their base type (see Section 7.4).

6.2.2 Predefined subranges

Predefined enumerations were introduced in (Section 6.1.1). There is also one predefined subrange. Type CARDINAL is actually defined as

```
TYPE
   CARDINAL = [0 .. LAST(INTEGER)]
```

```
   ⋮
TYPE
   WorkHours = [8 .. 18];                          (*working hours*)
   Hours      = [0 .. 24];                         (*hours in a day*)
VAR
   hour: Hours;
   workhour: WorkHours;

BEGIN
   FOR a:= FIRST(WorkHours) TO LAST(WorkHours) DO SIO.PutInt(a) END;
                                                        (*output all*)
   hour:= LAST(WorkHours);                              (*hour := 18*)
   workhour:= hour;                                 (*workhour := 18*)
   INC(hour);                                           (*hour := 19*)
   workhour:= hour;          (*run-time error because 19 is not in range [8 .. 18]*)
   ⋮
```

Example 6.5: *Range check with subranges*

Modula-2, the predecessor of Modula-3, defined type CARDINAL not as a subrange of INTEGER, but so as to exploit the entire word length of the hardware platform for the representation of a non-negative number. This meant double the range size (the sign bit was not wasted), for a 16-bit machine 2^{16} instead of 2^{15}. This advantage has become negligible with increasing word length (32- and 64-bit machines) in contrast to the drawback that the semantics of CARDINAL in Modula-2 was not clearly defined. Therefore in Modula-2 INTEGER and CARDINAL were assignment compatible but not expression compatible (see Section 7.1).

Chapter 7

Expressions and declarations

A major advantage of the type concept is that we cannot arbitrarily mix data of different types. This guards the integrity of the semantics of the data (we cannot add numbers to texts, use Boolean values in arithmetic expressions, etc.).

This chapter precisely specifies the rules for *compatibility* of different data types within an expression and in an assignment. However, first we need to describe precisely the syntax and semantics of expressions, declarations and assignments.

7.1 Expressions

Thus far we have used expressions rather intuitively. We all know the syntax and semantics of school arithmetic, and we have built on this knowledge. For example, we all know that expressions consist of *operands* and *operators*. In the expression a + b * c we have the operands a, b and c and the operators + and *.

However, we have already encountered some examples where both syntax and semantics deviate from the familiar. This section presents the syntax and semantics of expressions in Modula-3, to the extent that we already know the operand types and their operations (see Figure 7.1).

7.1.1 Syntax of expressions

In reading the syntax of expressions, we must note that the syntax alone does not suffice to distinguish valid expressions from invalid ones: expressions for all types are combined in a single syntax and mixed. Whether a *syntactically correct* expression is *valid* as well, can be determined at compile time or possibly even only at run time (see Section 7.6). For example, the "expression" 3.1415 AND NUMBER("hello") > LAST(14) is syntactically

$ConstExpr_{65}$ = $Expr_{66}$.
$Expr_{66}$ = $E1_{67}$ { "OR" $E1_{67}$ }.
$E1_{67}$ = $E2_{68}$ { "AND" $E2_{68}$ }.
$E2_{68}$ = { "NOT" } $E3_{69}$.
$E3_{69}$ = $E4_{70}$ { ("=" | "#" | "<" | "<=" | ">" | ">=" | "IN") $E4_{70}$ }.
$E4_{70}$ = $E5_{71}$ { ("+" | "–" | "&") $E5_{71}$ }.
$E5_{71}$ = $E6_{72}$ { ("*" | "/" | "DIV" | "MOD") $E6_{72}$ }.
$E6_{72}$ = {"+" | "–"} $E7_{73}$.
$E7_{73}$ = $E8_{74}$ { $Selector_{78}$ }.
$E8_{74}$ = $Ident_{89}$ | $Number_{94}$ | $CharLiteral_{91}$ | $TextLiteral_{92}$
                | $Constructor_{79}$ | "(" $Expr_{66}$ ")".
$Selector_{78}$ = "." $Ident_{89}$ | "^" | "[" $Expr_{66}$ { "," $Expr_{66}$ } "]"
                | "(" [$Actual_{47}$ { "," $Actual_{47}$ } ")".
$Constructor_{79}$ = $Type_{48}$ "{" [$SetCons_{80}$ | $RecordCons_{82}$ | $ArrayCons_{84}$] "}".
$\vdots$
$Ident_{89}$ = $Letter_{100}$ { $Letter_{100}$ | $Digit_{98}$ | "_" }.
$Letter_{100}$ = "A" | "B" | .. | "Z" | "a" | "b" | .. | "z".
$Digit_{98}$ = "0" | "1" | .. | "9".

Figure 7.1: *Syntax of expressions*

correct, although it is completely absurd (the parameters of the predefined functions are invalid, and AND applies only to Boolean expressions). However, we cannot determine this from the syntax.

The basic element of syntax is **expression operator expression**. Syntactic units $E1_{67}$ to $E6_{72}$ serve to produce the operators. With the help of $E7_{73}$, $E8_{74}$, $Selector_{78}$ and $Constructor_{79}$ the individual (sub)expressions are formed.

Let us begin bottom-up with $E8_{74}$. An expression can be a name (identifier), a literal, a $Constructor_{79}$ or an expression in parentheses. A Modula-3 *identifier* ($Ident_{89}$) is a sequence of letters and digits that must begin with a letter. An interesting feature is the use of the underscore ("_") within an identifier. This enables keeping longer identifiers readable (e.g., this_is_substantially_long) – although we should keep identifiers short but pregnant, and generally avoid the underscore. The syntax of number, character and text literals was covered in the introduction of the respective data types.

Let us go farther up in the syntax. An $E7_{73}$ is an $E8_{74}$, possibly followed by a series of selectors. This allows us to form the values of enumeration types: Weekday.Friday. These are called *qualified identifiers*. We will encounter other, similar selectors later to help us process arrays and procedure invocations and to access record and object fields.

An $E6_{72}$ is an $E7_{73}$ with an optional leading sign to represent negative numbers. Here Modula-3's syntax is quite generous and even allows using multiple leading signs (mathematically correct, but otherwise nonsensical). Expression $E5_{71}$ consists of one or more $E6_{72}$, joined by multiplicative operators. This means that, e.g., $-a * -b + c$ and $-a * -b + + - + c$ are valid expressions.

And so it continues to $Expr_{66}$, which consists of a $E1_{67}$ or of $E1_{67}$ expressions joined by OR operators. The syntax of a constant expression ($ConstExpr_{65}$) is the same as for $Expr_{66}$. However, it must be possible to evaluate all the corresponding operands at compile time. Thus a constant expression cannot contain variables (except as parameters of certain predefined functions, such as FIRST, LAST and NUMBER).

The syntax also expresses the rules of precedence (compare Section 2.4). The order of the syntactic rules exactly reflects the precedence rules; the weakest operator is OR (see $Expr_{66}$), and the strongest is the leading sign ($E6_{72}$). The *infix* operators (located between two operands) are left-associative; i.e., on equal priority they are evaluated from left to right. Thus, e.g., a * b * c is interpreted as $(ab)c$ rather than as $a(bc)$.

Parentheses have the highest priority (see $E8_{74}$). When we are unsure of the precedence, we should resort to parentheses. They often increase the readability of programs, and at no cost. Rather than a OR b < c OR d AND e, we should write a OR (b < c) OR (d AND e)

7.1.2 Evaluation of expressions

An expression defines a computation that results in either a value or a variable. In an assignment, e.g., the expression must yield a variable on the left side and a value on the right side (see Section 7.5). A simple expression consists of an identifier or a literal. More complex expressions are formed using the operators and constructors defined in the syntax.

An expression is evaluated recursively. Consider, e.g., the expression a + b. The operands a and b are themselves expressions, e.g., a = x * y and b = z DIV w. x, y, z and w are likewise expressions that again can contain operators and constructors. This continues until we arrive at simple expressions whose values are immediately available. The order of computation of operands in an operation is undefined except for OR and AND (see next section).

Caution: This comment does not refer to the precedence of operations, nor to whether they are left- or right-associative. Instead it is a matter of the order in which the operations are evaluated. Given an expression like a + b for computation, we cannot know whether a or b is evaluated first. Remember that a and b are expressions themselves.

The concrete semantics of expressions are handled with the respective data types (e.g., as the semantics of arithmetic and logical expressions was handled in Section 4). Here we complement the description of logical expressions in Section 4 with additional rules.

7.1.3 Evaluation of logical expressions

For OR and AND operations, the language definition requires *left-to-right* and *lazy evaluation*. The latter means that the second operand is evaluated only if the result of the expression is not fixed after evaluation of the first operand. For an OR expression, if the first operand yields *true*, or for an AND expression the first operand is *false* then the second operand is no longer relevant; evaluation can be terminated (and Modula-3 *does* end evaluation). The following pseudocode conveys this somewhat more formally (with p and q being logical expressions):

$$p \text{ AND } q \equiv \text{ IF NOT } p \text{ THEN FALSE ELSE } q \text{ END}$$
$$p \text{ OR } \quad q \equiv \text{ IF } p \text{ THEN TRUE ELSE } q \text{ END}$$

The following example shows the advantage of this rule:

IF (x # 0) AND ((y DIV x) = 10) THEN S1 ELSE S2 END;

If x = 0, then the first operand yields *false* and evaluation of the AND expression terminates immediately (since the result of the overall expression can only be *false*). Thus the second operand is not computed and the division by zero is not executed.

> Without this rule (as, e.g., in the programming language Pascal) y DIV x could be computed first, division by 0 would generate a run-time error.

In general, the laws of predicate logic apply for logical operations. The scope of these laws is restricted in Modula-3 through the above rules. In principle, e.g., the law of commutativity applies, yet we have just seen that (x # 0) AND ((y DIV x) = 10) is not the same as ((y DIV x) = 10) AND (x # 0). Another restriction can result if the logical values are computed by functions that have a side effect. The following AND expression is anything but commutative:

SIO.GetChar()='A' AND SIO.GetChar()='B'

Depending on what the user inputs first, the expression requires input of one or two letters. If we turn the expression around, the user must begin with "B" instead of "A" to make the whole expression *true*

Thus the following laws hold only if the logical expressions p, q and r can be evaluated in finite time without a run-time error or side effect:

1. *Commutativity:*

> p OR q = q OR p
> p AND q= q AND p

2. *Associativity:*

> $(p$ OR $q)$ OR r = p OR $(q$ OR $r)$
> $(p$ AND $q)$ AND r = p AND $(q$ AND $r)$

3. *Distributivity:*

> $(p$ AND $q)$ OR r = $(p$ OR $r)$ AND $(q$ OR $r)$
> $(p$ OR $q)$ AND r = $(p$ AND $r)$ OR $(q$ AND $r)$

4. *The de Morgan laws:*

> NOT $(p$ OR $q)$ = NOT p AND NOT q
> NOT $(p$ AND $q)$ = NOT p OR NOT q

7.2 Declarations

Declarations were introduced briefly in Section 3.4.4. We also employed declarations in almost all our examples. They serve to introduce new names for constants, variables and types. Now we will treat these three kinds of declarations more exactly. Later we will discover declarations for additional language elements.

Syntax of declarations

> Declaration$_{13}$ ="CONST" { ConstDecl$_{14}$ ";" }
> | "TYPE" { TypeDecl$_{15}$ ";" }
> | "VAR" { VariableDecl$_{17}$ ";" }

7.2.1 Constant declarations

> ConstDecl$_{14}$ = Ident$_{89}$ [":" Type$_{48}$] "=" ConstExpr$_{65}$.

A constant declaration (ConstDecl$_{14}$) firmly associates an identifier (on the left side of the equal sign) with a value (to the right of the equal sign). In other parts of the program, this identifier serves as a synonym for this value. The value is specified with a *constant expression*. The following are examples of constant declarations:

```
CONST
  A = 10;
  B = 2 * A;
  C = A + 5 * B;
  D = LAST(INTEGER) - C;
```

These declarations give us B = 20 and C = 110. Naturally we could have written C = 110 directly. The advantage in using expressions is that if A changes, then B and C change, too. The value of a constant can only be changed, of course, by editing and recompiling the program source code. D immediately demonstrates the advantage of formulating expressions.

Consider the following declarations:

```
TYPE
  Workdays        = [Days.Monday .. Days.Saturday];
CONST
  Worktime        = 8;                      (*hours of work per day*)
  Weekdays        = NUMBER(Workdays);       (*workdays in a week*)
  HoursPerWeek    = Weekdays * Worktime;    (*hours of work per week*)
```

The value of HoursPerWeek is 48. If we change the type declaration for Workdays to

```
TYPE
  Workdays = [Days.Monday .. Days.Friday];
```

then the value of HoursPerWeek (after recompilation) changes to 40.

The following example shows some non-arithmetic expressions:

```
CONST
  Ch1           = 'A';
  Ch2           = LAST(CHAR);
  B             = 'a' > 'A';
  Ext           = NUMBER(CHAR) > 256;
  CountryCode   = "01-";
  AreaCode      = "201-";
  Family        = CountryCode & AreaCode & "310-6588";
  Office        = CountryCode & AreaCode & "270-5509";
```

The value of Ch2 contains the last character in the character set. B is a Boolean constant; its value is *true* if character 'a' has a higher code than 'A'. Ext is also a Boolean constant; its value is *true* if type CHAR uses extended coding (more than 1 byte). Family and Office are text constants whose values are "01-201-310-6588" and "01-201-270-5509", respectively.

The syntax of constant expressions also shows that after the name of the constant, separated by a colon, we can explicitly declare a type. As we have seen, in general, the type of a constant derives from the expression on the right side of the equal sign. However, this is not always true. For a non-negative whole number, e.g., we cannot tell whether it is of type INTEGER or CARDINAL. However, in the following declaration the type is unambiguous:

```
CONST A : CARDINAL = 0;
```

In such a case the unambiguity does not help much; we can do as much with a CARDINAL zero as with an INTEGER zero. However, it can be advantageous to specify that this constant must have a value from the range of CARDINAL. The following example shows this more clearly:

```
CONST
    VacationPlanning: [1..12] = 7;          (*we plan our vacation*)
    ⋮
    VacationMonth: [1..12] = VacationPlanning + 1;
```

Both constants depict a month as a number between 1 and 12. But we have made an error here: If we change VacationPlanning to 12, VacationMonth is assigned an invalid number. The compiler detects this error because we have specified the valid range. A proper solution would be:

```
    VacationMonth: [1..12] = VacationPlanning MOD 12 + 1;
```

7.2.2 Type declarations

$$\text{TypeDecl}_{15} = \text{Ident}_{89} \ (\ "=" \ | \ "<:" \ ) \ \text{Type}_{48}.$$

The general forms of a type declaration are thus:

```
TYPE
    identifier = type;
    identifier <: type;
```

This binds an identifier to a type. This identifier can now be used anywhere in a program where a type can occur (such as in the optional part of the constant declaration). Later we will see how complex types can be constructed by the programmer (Sections 8.1 and 8.2).

The second form serves to define a type only partially as a subtype of another type. (This kind of type declaration is needed primarily in interfaces. We treat them in Section 7.4.)

7.2.3 Variable declarations

VariableDecl$_{17}$ = IDList$_{87}$ (":" Type$_{48}$ ":=" Expr$_{66}$ | ":" Type$_{48}$ |":=" Expr$_{66}$).
IDList$_{87}$ = Ident$_{89}$ { "," Ident$_{89}$}.

Closer consideration of the syntax of variable declarations reveals some new aspects. We have the following three variants:

```
a, b, c: type;
a, b, c: type := expression;
a, b, c  := expression;
```

We associate a list of identifiers with a type and possibly with an initial value as well. Thus far we have always used the first form. The other two forms allow us to *initialize* a variable on declaration.   The value of the expression is assigned to all variables in the identifier list (to the left of the colon). The initialization of all variables in a block (also see Section 9.1) occurs – in the order of the declarations – *before* the execution of the first statement of the statement part.

> Imagine these initializations as a series of assignments "hidden" in the keyword BEGIN.

```
VAR
   i, j : INTEGER := 1;
   b   : BOOLEAN := FALSE;
   t    : TEXT := "This is a text";
BEGIN (*statement part*)
```

At the first statement after BEGIN we have i = 1, j = 1, b = FALSE and t = "This is a text".

Note that a variable is initialized only once on declaration. If a variable is used in a loop nested within a loop such that the outer loop must repeatedly initialize its value for the inner loop, then initialization on declaration is the wrong approach!

The third form of variable declaration specifies only the initialization; the type is implicitly specified by the initial value. Implicit type specification can make the programmer uncertain about the type of a variable. Thus we will avoid the third form for the time.

The syntax also indicates that we can specify the type directly in the variable declaration. In this case the type is nameless. The following example demonstrates this.

```
VAR a, b, c: [1 .. 16];
```

We recommend avoiding this form for the time.

```
CONST
  N = 10;
TYPE
  T1 = [1 .. 10];                          (*equivalent to T2, T3, T4*)
  T2 = [1 .. N];                           (*equivalent to T1, T3, T4*)
  T3 = [1 .. 2 * 2 * 2 + 2];               (*equivalent to T1, T2, T4*)
  T4 = T1;                                 (*equivalent to T1, T2, T3*)
  T5 = {a, b, c};                                (*equivalent to T6*)
  T6 = {a, b, c};                                (*equivalent to T5*)
  T7 = {a, b, d};                     (*not equivalent to the other types*)
```

Example 7.2: *Equivalent types*

In fact, the following declaration would be almost silly:

VAR e, f, g: {Monday, Tuesday, Wednesday};

The components of an enumeration cannot even be accessed without a type name. A possibility to use the variables e, f, g at all is to additionally declare a named type with the same components, e.g.,

TYPE Days = {Monday, Tuesday, Wednesday};

due to structural equivalence (Section 7.3), this type is equivalent to the type of e, f and g.

Note also that the kinds of declarations that we suggested avoiding for the time do have their justification in certain cases where they appear in a restricted context and where their scope is small and comprehensible (Section 9.1).

7.3 Equivalence of types

Modula-3 employs *structural* equivalence of types. Two types are equivalent if their *expanding* results in the same type. Expanding means that all constant expressions are replaced by their values and all type names are replaced by their definitions. In Example 7.2 the types T1, T2, T3 and T4 are mutually equivalent. T5 is also equivalent to T6. T7 is not equivalent to any of the specified types.

Many programming languages, e.g., Pascal and Modula-2, employ *name equivalence*. Here types are equivalent only if they are explicitly declared as such. In Example 7.2 only T1 and T4 are name equivalent; all others are considered different types from this perspective.

7.4 Subtypes

Modula-3 supports a general concept of *subtyping*. We use the special symbol "<:" to specify the subtype relationship.

If Sub and Super are two types and the relationship Sub <: Super exists, then all values of Sub are also values of Super.

In this case Sub is a *subtype* of Super, and Super is the *supertype* of Sub. In Modula-3 a type can have any number of subtypes, but only one supertype. (There are programming languages where a type can have multiple supertypes.) The subtype relationship is often called the *Is-a* relationship: A value of a subtype *is* a value of its supertype. Given the relationship Workdays <: Weekdays, then all Workdays are Weekdays. The inverse need not apply; all days of the week are not workdays, thank goodness.

At the moment we can give only one example of the subtype relationship: The subrange types (Section 6.2) are actually not independent types, but subtypes of their base types. The following rules apply to subranges:

$$[u .. o] <: B \qquad \text{whereby B is the common base type of u and o}$$
$$[u .. o] <: [U .. O] \qquad \text{if } [u .. o] \text{ is a subset of } [U .. O]$$

For example, given the subrange

```
TYPE
  SubR1 = [3 .. 8];
  SubR2 = [0 .. 2];
```

we have the relationships Ub1 <: INTEGER and Ub2 <: INTEGER. Actually, all values of Ub1 and Ub2 are also values of INTEGER (but obviously not vice versa). What is the relationship between Ub1 and Ub2? Neither of the ranges is a subset of the other (indeed, they are disjunct); there is no subtype relationship between these two types. An assignment involving variables of types Ub1 and Ub2 is not permitted (see Section 7.5).

Take an example where the ranges overlap, e.g., the types Workdays and Weekend from Example 6.4. We have the following relationships:

```
Workdays <: Days
Weekend  <: Days
```

Workdays and Weekend are subtypes of the same base type, but do not share a subtype relationship to one another (neither range is a subset of the other). We can still make an assignment between variables of these types because the ranges overlap. However, such an assignment can produce an error if the assigned value is not in the range of the target variable. In general, the following holds: Variable of ordinal types whose ranges overlap can be assigned to one another (see Section 7.5).

Reflexivity and transitivity

The subtype relationship is *reflexive* and *transitive*. Formal stated:

$$T <: T$$
$$T <: U \wedge U <: V \Rightarrow T <: V$$

In words, every type is its own subtype and supertype. In addition, if type T is a subtype of U and U is a subtype of V, then T is also a subtype of V. For example, let T1 = [1 ..100], T2 = [10 .. 80] and T3 = [30 .. 50]. Then T3 <: T2 and T2 <: T1. This implies that T3 <: T1 – which is easy to see.

However, T <: U and U <: T does not imply that U and T are equal (see Section 7.4).

Operations on subtypes

All operations defined for a supertype are also defined for the subtype. This means that for operands of a subrange type all operations of the corresponding base type apply. For example, for operands of type T1 = [1 .. 100] we can employ all INTEGER operations.

In general it is possible to define *additional* operations for subtypes. We will employ this feature when we handle *object types* (see Section 13).

7.5 Assignment compatibility

We repeat the syntax of the assignment:

$$AssignStmt_{25} = Expr_{66} ":=" Expr_{66}.$$

The expression on the left side of the colon (often abbreviated *LHS* for *left-hand side* expression) must result in a variable. The expression on the right side (*RHS* for *right-hand-side* expression) returns a value. This value must be *assignment compatible* with the variable on the left side and be within its range.

You might wonder why the syntax specifies an expression on the left side rather than simply $Ident_{89}$. The meaning of the more general syntax will become clear stepwise as we become familiar with more complex LHS expressions (e.g., indexed array elements, Section 8.1).

When are assignments legal? An expression A of type R is *assignment compatible* with a variable var of type L (i.e., var := A is legal) if one of the following conditions applies:

1. R and L are equivalent (see Section 7.3), or

2. R <: L or

3. R and L are ordinal types that overlap in at least one value, and the value of A is in the range of L, or

4. L <: R and R is an *array type* or a *reference type* for which certain conditions apply (see Sections 8.1, 10, and 11).

Rule 1 is the simplest case: If the types are the same, then trivially any value of the one expression is a possible value of the other expression. Rule 4 is mentioned here for the sake of completeness and will be explained later.

Rule 2 expresses the fact that in the *subtype relationship* all values of the subtype are also values of the supertype (all Workdays are days, but not all Days are Workdays).

For Rules 2 and 3 we have already seen examples in the context of subranges (Section 6.2). If the variable workday is of type Workdays and day of type Days, then it is clear that the assignment day := workday cannot go wrong because all possible values of workday can also be values of day.

Violations of Rules 3 and 4 can be checked in part at compile time; otherwise they can only be tested at run time when the current values are known.

> In order to detect errors at run time, the compiler must make the necessary preparations. It generates control statements that check Rule 3 at run time. For example, if we assign a variable int of type IN-TEGER to a variable of type [1 .. 16], then at compile time the compiler cannot know whether the value of int falls in the subrange. However, the compiler can generate another command or commands to test this condition at run time (e.g., exactly before the assignment in question). Such tests represent additional overhead for the length and speed of programs, but this generally proves negligible given the speed of modern digital computers. Furthermore, most compilers allow removal of the test with a compiler option, in which case the compiled program becomes shorter and faster, but at the expense of run-time checks. We discourage removing the run-time checks in general. However, there are situations that demand the increased efficiency delivered by removing the run-time checks; such program components must be checked especially carefully by the developer.

7.6   Expression compatibility

With expressions of the form *operand$_1$ operator operand$_2$* we have a problem similar to that of assignment compatibility: What kinds of operands can we mix, and for which kinds is this impossible. For example, can we add INTEGER numbers to CARDINAL numbers? The rules of expression compatibility provide the answer.

In Modula-3 the operands of such expressions must share a common supertype (an exception is the IN operation; see Section 8.3). Before evaluation of the expression, the operands are converted to this common type. For types that have no subtype relationship with any other type (e.g., REAL), this means that both operands must be of the same type. However, CARDINAL <: INTEGER; therefore INTEGERs can be added to CARDINALs.

The following example is correct because addition of s1 and s2 takes place in the range of INTEGER:

```
VAR
    s1: [1 .. 2] := 2;
    s2: [3 .. 4] := 3;
    i:  INTEGER;
BEGIN
    i:= s1 + s2; (*type of the expression s1+s2 is INTEGER, value is 5*)
```

To combine operands of different types in an expression (e.g., mixing REALs and INTEGERs), we must employ the conversion functions (see Section 6). In Modula-3 expressions there is no *implicit* type conversion, but there is *explicit* type conversion. The lack of implicit type conversions helps to minimize programming errors.

> A number of programming languages offer implicit type conversion. The most spectacular example is *PL / 1*, where totally different operands can occur mixed in an expression. At first glance this seems like a comfortable feature, but it can invoke the most unexpected errors.

> Other languages (like Oberon-2 [WG92, RW92, Mös93]) define a regulated and sensibly restricted implicit type conversion (*type inclusion*). In Oberon-2 the numeric types form a hierarchy. The larger and more precise the range of a numeric type is, the higher it is in the hierarchy. Expressions with operands belonging to different numeric types are evaluated in the range of the hierarchically higher operand. For example, to add an INTEGER and a REAL number, the INTEGER is automatically converted to REAL.

Result type

The result type of an expression (usually called the type of the expression) with two operands is not necessarily the type of its operands. The results depends on the *operator*. Addition, for example, maps all INTEGER subranges onto a result of type INTEGER (even if both operands have the same subrange type). The relational operators (greater than, less than, etc.) map all permitted operand types onto the result type BOOLEAN. We discuss the result type of an operator with the introduction of the respective operator.

The rules of type equivalence together with the compatibility rules form the basic framework of the type system.

These rules regulate which expressions are valid and which assignment is permissible. This system of rules allows the compiler to report all impermissible expressions and assignments. This helps to automatically detect a number of programming errors and thus to significantly increase the security of programs.

Chapter 8

Composite static types

Thus far all data (constants and variables) seemed like our own personal acquaintances. We declared each one and assigned them individual values. This allows us to solve a number of tasks. Certainly we could solve more challenging tasks, for, as far as statements are concerned, we already have quite a powerful arsenal. With loop statements we can carry out unlimited (in principle infinite) computations. However, regarding data we are still quite behind: We cannot define *data collections* (or *data aggregates*) yet. Our data types so far were all *scalar*. A variable of a scalar type can contain only a single value at a given time.

With the help of type constructors we can create various aggregates. Without a computer we would use a table, a list or file cards to manage information. We need a table, for example, to record the daily sales of a business for every day of the year. A list could help us to describe the contents of a warehouse. We use file cards to collect heterogeneous information such as birth dates, addresses and employee salaries. In programs we can store tables in the form of arrays, file cards as records, and lists in the form of dynamic data structures (see in Section 11.5). In addition, programming languages provide us with sets, which are especially important in mathematics. Likewise arrays originally came to programming languages due to the need to represent mathematical vectors and matrices.

This chapter presents the *static* type constructors – arrays, records and sets. These types are static because their size is known in advance. This applies to most tables (e.g., we know how many days of the year we need to reserve for storage of sales) and for file cards. For the warehouse list this generally does not apply; Although we might know approximately how many articles we can store, the momentary number varies greatly, and we cannot specify an exact upper limit. Here we need *dynamic* data structures, which we will tackle later.

Computers are used primarily for storing and managing large amounts of data. We are frequently confronted with applications such as banking systems and reservation systems. They manage an enormous set of data in a *database*. This book does not cover database systems; we limit ourselves to the basic concepts for data structuring as provided by programming languages and on which database technology builds.

An introduction to databases can be found in [Ull82, Dat90], as well as in a wealth of other literature. It is interesting that in recent years *object-oriented databases* [KM94] have brought the concepts of programming languages and those of database technology closer.

8.1 Arrays

An array is an ordered collection of *elements* of the same type which can be accessed collectively as a whole. The elements are "numbered" – although not necessarily with numbers – and an element can be selected individually via this "number" (its *index*).

Without arrays, many programming tasks are impossible to solve. We cannot store the above sales table by declaring 365 individual variables (of type REAL). Instead, we would like to store 365 REAL numbers together and access them via the number of the day. Hence we could write:

```
TYPE
    Days = [1..365];
    Sales = ARRAY Days OF REAL;
VAR
    sales: Sales;
```

Now the variable **sales** can store 365 individual values. Days is the *index type* and corresponds to the columns in the table. This "column type" allows us to access the individual *elements* as follows:

```
sales[10]:= 105000.0;
```

This assigns a value to the tenth element of the array.

Syntax of the array type

$$\text{ArrayType}_{19} = \text{"ARRAY" [Type}_{18} \{ \text{","} \text{Type}_{48} \} \text{] "OF" Type}_{48}.$$

The type after the keyword OF is the *element type*; the others are the *index types*. Index types must be ordinal types (e.g., subrange or enumeration). Static arrays – whose size is specified on declaration – require specification of at least one index type. The number of indices reflects the number of *dimensions* of the array. The length of a static array can be computed at compile time.

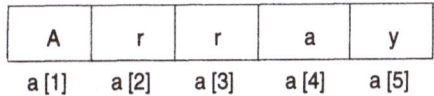

Figure 8.1: *Unidimensional array of characters*

```
    ⋮
TYPE
    Index = [1 .. 5];                                                    (*index type*)
    Array = ARRAY Index OF CHAR;                                         (*array type*)
VAR
    a: Array;                                           (*"a" can store 5 characters*)
BEGIN
    FOR i:= FIRST(Index) TO LAST(Index) DO a[i]:= SIO.GetChar() END;
    FOR i:= FIRST(Index) TO LAST(Index) DO SIO.PutChar(a[i]) END;
    ⋮
```

Example 8.2: *Accessing an array of characters*

8.1.1 Unidimensional arrays

Assume that IndexType is an ordinal type (e.g., [1 .. 10]), and ElementType is an arbitrary type. We can specify a *unidimensional* array as follows:

   TYPE A1 = ARRAY IndexType OF ElementType

Unidimensional arrays are often called *vectors* after their mathematical roots.

An element of an array can be accessed by *indexing* The index expression is written in square brackets after the name of the array variable. The expression must be assignment compatible with the index type. The value of the index expression determines the element to be selected. This allows the language environment to test whether the array has been indexed with an appropriate index value: If we attempt to access an array with index type [1..10] using the index value 11, we would produce an error because 11 is not contained in the index type.

> This *range check* is even more important in the context of array indices
> than for variables of a subrange type. If a variable has an erroneous
> value, that is bad enough. However, an incorrect index in an array
> additionally leads to accessing memory regions that do not belong to
> the array. This means that some other variable can be overwritten
> randomly – probably with fatal consequences for the program.

The type Array in Example 8.2 defines an array that consists of five elements of type CHAR. The first FOR loop assigns arbitrary characters to the elements of the array; the second FOR loop outputs the contents of the

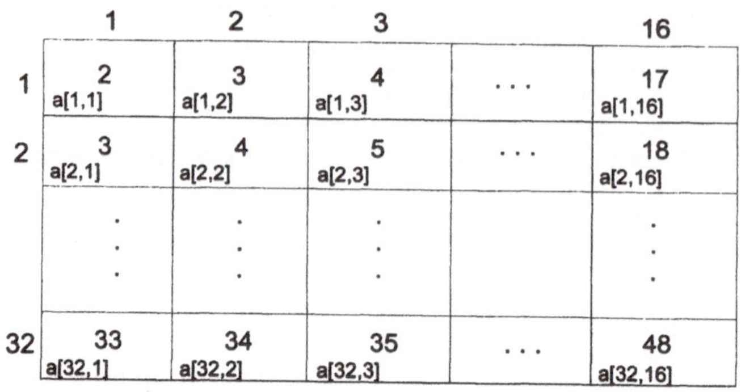

	1	2	3		16
1	2 a[1,1]	3 a[1,2]	4 a[1,3]	. . .	17 a[1,16]
2	3 a[2,1]	4 a[2,2]	5 a[2,3]	. . .	18 a[2,16]
	. . .	. . .	. . .		. . .
32	33 a[32,1]	34 a[32,2]	35 a[32,3]	. . .	48 a[32,16]

Figure 8.3: *Bidimensional array of Integers*

array. If we were to input the letters of the word "Array", the program would output the character sequence "Array" (Figure 8.1).

The example also demonstrates how naturally the FOR loop lends itself to processing arrays. With the help of the FIRST and LAST functions we can easily iterate through the array.

We could have written the FOR loop as follows:

```
FOR i:= 1 TO 5 DO a[i]:= SIO.GetChar() END
```

However, this solution has the drawback that changes in the index also necessitate changes in the loop. To extend index to [1 .. 100], we would also have to change the loop to FOR i:= 1 TO 100 DO ···. Such adaptation is undesirable; it is both work-intensive and error-prone. The solution in Example 8.2 requires no such adaptation: FIRST and LAST always return the current boundary values, thus restricting adaptation to a single location.

8.1.2 Multidimensional arrays

Arrays with more than one index are called *multidimensional* arrays. Bidimensional arrays have special importance because they are particularly suited to representing *matrices*. Figure 8.3 shows such a bidimensional array (in this case with values corresponding to the sum of row and column indices).

A bidimensional array type can be declared in two ways:

1. TYPE A2 = ARRAY Index1 OF ARRAY Index2 OF Element

2. TYPE A2 = ARRAY Index1, Index2 OF Element

```
    ⋮
TYPE
  Row     = [1 .. 32];                                (*row index*)
  Column = [1 .. 16];                                 (*column index*)
  Matrix  = ARRAY Row, Column OF INTEGER;              (*array type*)
VAR
  matrix: Matrix;                        (*"matrix" can store 32 × 16 numbers*)
BEGIN
  FOR i:= FIRST(Row) TO LAST(Row) DO
    FOR j:= FIRST(Column) TO LAST(Column) DO
      matrix[i, j]:= i + j;
    END; (*FOR j*)
  END; (*FOR i*)
    ⋮
```

Example 8.4: *Bidimensional array of Integers*

The first notation emphasizes that the element type of the first array is itself an array, while the second form more directly expresses the bidimensional character. We usually use the second notation. The first form is necessary if a bidimensional array is constructed as a unidimensional array of another *named* array (such as the type Plane in Example 8.5). Both notations can be generalized – as the syntax indicates – for arrays with any number of dimensions, and the two notations can even be mixed.

In a multidimensional array an element of the nth dimension can be accessed as follows:

a$[i_1]$ $[i_2]$ $\cdots$ $[i_n]$

The following simplified form is better:

a$[i_1, i_2, \cdots, i_n]$

The exact syntax for indexing is defined in the syntax for expressions (compare Section 7.1.1). Below we show the corresponding excerpt from the expression syntax.

Syntax for indexing arrays

E7$_{73}$ = E8$_{74}$ { Selector$_{78}$ }.
  ⋮
Selector$_{78}$ = "[" Expr$_{66}$ { "," Expr$_{66}$ } "]" | $\cdots$

Example 8.4 type Matrix defines a bidimensional array. Type Row defines the index type for rows and type Column for columns. The variable matrix stores in each element the sum of its index values (Figure 8.3).

Shape

Following the pattern of the bidimensional array, we can define arrays of any dimension. We term the element type of the "last" array the *base type* of the array. The *shape* of a multidimensional array is the sequence of the cardinality of its dimensions. A type that is not an array has an *empty* shape. In the following example A1, A2 and A3 have the same shape, but A4 has a different shape.

```
TYPE
  A1  = ARRAY [1 .. 2], [3 .. 5]      OF INTEGER;
  A2  = ARRAY [0 .. 1], [7 .. 9]      OF INTEGER;
  A3  = ARRAY ['A' .. 'B'], ['X .. 'Z'] OF INTEGER;
  A4  = ARRAY [0 .. 1], [6 .. 9]      OF INTEGER;
```

8.1.3   Array constructors

With the help of *array constructors* we can define array values. These are quite useful if we want to initialize an array on declaration.

The exact syntax is part of the syntax for expressions (see Figure 7.1, page 126):

Syntax of array constructors

$E8_{74}$ $\quad = \mathsf{Ident}_{89} \mid \mathsf{Number}_{94} \mid \mathsf{CharLiteral}_{91} \mid \mathsf{TextLiteral}_{92}$
$\quad\quad\quad\quad\quad \mid \mathsf{Constructor}_{79} \mid \text{"(" } \mathsf{Expr}_{66} \text{ ")"}.$
$\mathsf{Constructor}_{79} = \mathsf{Type}_{48} \text{ "\{" [} \mathsf{ArrayCons}_{84} \mid \cdots \text{] "\}"}.$
$\mathsf{ArrayCons}_{84} = \mathsf{Expr}_{66} \text{ \{"," } \mathsf{Expr}_{66} \text{ \} ["," ".."]}.$

In an $\mathsf{ArrayCons}_{84}$ we can specify a list of expressions that are assigned to the elements of the array sequentially. Specifying ".." causes all non-initialized elements to assume the value of the last expression (which is computed only once and not recomputed for each subsequent element). Array constructors can be assigned to array constants and array variables. If no ".." is specified, then the constructor must contain exactly as many elements as the array to which the constructor is assigned.

Example 8.5 demonstrates the use of multidimensional arrays and array constructors. A point in N-dimensional space can be represented in mathematics as a sequence of coordinates. In a program we use an array. Note, however, that the dimension of the array is something quite different from the dimensions of mathematical space. The N coordinates of a point can be stored in *one* array dimension.

Example 8.5 employs arrays to represent points in N-dimensional space. The origin of this space is a point whose coordinates are all 0. The example

```
CONST
  N = 3;
TYPE
  Point   = ARRAY [1..N] OF REAL;            (*point in N-dimensional space*)
  Plane   = ARRAY [1..2] OF Point;
CONST
  Origin      = Point {0.0, ..};             (*all elements set to 0.0*)
  XNorm       = Point {1.0, 0.0, ..};        (*all elements from 2nd set to 0.0 *)
  YNorm       = Point {0.0, 1.0, 0.0, ..};   (*all elements from 3rd set to 0.0*)
  XNormPlane= Plane {Origin, XNorm};
VAR
  aPlane:= Plane {Point{-1.0, 1.0, 0.0, ..}, Point{1.0, 1.0, 0.0, ..} };
```

Example 8.5: *Initialization of a bidimensional array*

shows how we declare the constant Origin of type Point. If all elements of the array are not the same, then the same notation still can be used to indicate that the elements starting at a certain position are all the same (see constants XNorm and YNorm in Example 8.5).

> This method even allows leaving the dimension of the space open: We can set the constant N to every value ≥ 3. After recompilation of the source code, the constants Origin, XNorm and YNorm are declared correctly again for the new space!

A polygon in N-dimensional space consists of a fixed number of points that we can represent as an array of points. A plane in Example 8.5 is a bidimensional array; a point is an array of coordinates; a plane an array of points.

The declaration of variable aPlane is also an example of omitting the explicit specification of the type of the variable and implicitly determining it through the initialization value (see Section 7.2.3). The array constructor makes this obvious anyway. On the other hand, we could justifiably consider the following declaration as "pompous"[1]:

aPlane: Plane := Plane{Point{-1.0,1.0,0.0, ..}, Point{1.0,1.0,0.0, ..} };

Example 8.6 defines a polygon consisting of M points. The variable circle is initialized such that it approximates a circle. To make the approximation more fine-grained, it suffices to increase M.

8.1.4 Operations on arrays

Assignment

Arrays can be assigned to one another if they have the same base type and the same shape (same number of elements in each dimension; see above,

---

[1]This designation for exaggerated formalism is used by Niklaus Wirth.

```
MODULE Array3 EXPORTS Main;
  IMPORT Math;                                (*Math exports mathematical functions*)

  CONST
    N = 3; M = 100;
  TYPE
    Point = ARRAY [1..N] OF LONGREAL;          (*point in N-dimensional space*)
    Polygon = ARRAY [1..M] OF Point;           (*polygon in N-dimensional space*)
  VAR
    circle: Polygon;                           (*use polygon to approximate circle*)
    radius: LONGREAL := 10.0D0; alpha: LONGREAL:= 0.0D0;
    step: LONGREAL:= 6.28D0 / FLOAT(NUMBER(Polygon), LONGREAL);
BEGIN
  FOR i:= FIRST(circle) TO LAST(circle) DO
    circle[i, 1]:= Math.sin(alpha)*radius;
    circle[i, 2]:= Math.cos(alpha)*radius;
    FOR j:= 3 TO N DO circle[i, j]:= 0.0D0 END;          (*circle in x/y plane*)
    alpha:= alpha+step;
  END;
  ⋮
```

Example 8.6: *Circle approximated by a polygon*

Section 8.1.2). This enables the assignment of the constant array Circuit to the variable triangle in Example 8.7.

Relational operations

Assignment-compatible arrays can be tested for (in)equality. Two arrays are equal if they have an equal number of elements and their elements are pairwise equal (see Example 8.7). No other relational operations are valid on arrays.

Predefined functions

The FIRST and LAST functions apply to array types as well as to variables of type array. They return the first and last value, respectively, of the index type of the array. For multidimensional arrays these function can be applied to each dimension individually. Thus we could have written Example 8.4 in the more general form of Example 8.8. The expression FIRST(matrix[FIRST(matrix)]) determines the first element in the second dimension. The index expression between the square brackets serves to select the second dimension; here we can use an arbitrary element of the first dimension. The expression FIRST(matrix[LAST(matrix)]), e.g., is equivalent to the previous one.

The function NUMBER can also be applied to arrays and returns the number of elements (of the first dimension of the array) (Example 8.8).

```
CONST
  N = 2;
TYPE
  Point       = ARRAY [1..N] OF REAL;
  Triangle    = ARRAY [1..3] OF Point;
  Cities      = {Vienna, Salzburg, Klagenfurt};
  CityTriangle = ARRAY Cities OF Point;
CONST
  Circuit = CityTriangle{Point{1.4, 2.5}, Point{4.5, 0.6}, Point{3.2, 3.2}};
VAR
  triangle: Triangle;
BEGIN
  triangle:= Circuit;                              (*assignment of arrays *)
  ⋮
  IF triangle # Circuit THEN                       (*comparison of arrays *)
  ⋮
```

Example 8.7: *Assignment and relational operations on arrays*

```
  ⋮
TYPE
  Line   = [1 .. 32];                              (*line index*)
  Column= [1 .. 16];                               (*column index*)
  Matrix = ARRAY Line, Column OF INTEGER;          (*array type*)
VAR
  matrix: Matrix;                          (*"matrix" can contain 32 × 16 numbers*)
BEGIN
  FOR i:= FIRST(matrix) TO LAST(matrix) DO                   (*from 1 to 32*)
    FOR j:= FIRST(matrix[FIRST(matrix)]) TO LAST(matrix[FIRST(matrix)]) DO
                                                            (*from 1 to 16*)
    matrix[i, j]:= i + j;
    END; (*FOR j*)
  END; (*FOR i*)
  SIO.PutInt(NUMBER(matrix));           (*number of elements in 1st dimension: 32*)
  SIO.PutInt(NUMBER(matrix[FIRST(matrix)]));   (*elements in 2nd dimension: 16*)
  ⋮
```

Example 8.8: *Predefined functions on multidimensional arrays*

The function SUBARRAY crops out part of an array. Its general form is:

    SUBARRAY(a: Array; from, count: CARDINAL)

The result of SUBARRAY is a *variable* whose type is array of the element type of a (if a is multidimensional, then SUBARRAY applies to the first dimension). Imagine this variable overlapping part of a. SUBARRAY thus returns part of the array itself, not a copy thereof.

The result contains count elements, whereby the first from elements of the original array remain untouched. For from = 0 the subarray is overlaid

```
    ⋮
TYPE
   Array1 = ARRAY [1 .. 100] OF INTEGER;
   Array2 = ARRAY [1..10] OF INTEGER;
VAR
   a1:= Array1{0, ..};              (*"a1" stores 100 numbers (all initialized to 0) *)
   a2:= Array2{1, ..};              (*"a2" stores only 10 numbers*)
BEGIN
(*copy a2 to a1 starting at index 11: *)
   SUBARRAY(a1, 10, NUMBER(a2)):= a2;
(*assign the first 10 elements of a1 to array a2: *)
   a2:= SUBARRAY(a1, 0, NUMBER(a2));
(*replace a1_11..a1_15: *)
   FOR i:= 0 TO 4 DO SUBARRAY(a1, 10, 5)[i]:= 3 * i END;
(*shifts 5 values from index 11 by 1 element: *)
   SUBARRAY(a1, 11, 5):= SUBARRAY(a1, 10, 5);
    ⋮
```

Example 8.9: *The use of the subarray function*

beginning at FIRST(a), for from = 1 from FIRST(a)+1, etc. SUBARRAY(a, 0, NUMBER(a)) overlays the complete subarray over the entire array a. The index type of the result is [0 .. count-1]. In Example 8.9 we see various uses of SUBARRAY: We can even assign overlapping ranges within an array to one another – the exact definition of SUBARRAY permits this (see Language Description B.2.3).

8.1.5 Example: Schedule

In Example 8.10 we set up a small class schedule for students. We define a matrix whose rows represent days and whose columns reflect the hours. (We optimistically assume that classes take place only Monday through Friday and only between 7:00 and 20:00 hours.) The two constant arrays DayNames and ClassNames contain text constants. First we initialize the schedule to the value None. Then we record several entries in the schedule and output the schedule for all mornings.

The output of the name of a class employs nested indexing: Class-Name[schedule[day, hour]]. The expression schedule[day, hour] – its type is Classes – indexes the array ClassNames, which contains the corresponding text.

> We neglected elegant formatting in our output. For a program intended for a broad market, this would be an important factor. For our example, an attractive table would be appropriate, with days as column headers and the hours labeling rows. To achieve this, we would have to reverse the order of the FOR loops because the variable schedule contains the days in its first dimension and the hours in its second.

```
MODULE ClassSchedule EXPORTS Main;                          (*27.05.94. LB*)

  IMPORT SIO;

  TYPE
    Days       = {Monday, Tuesday, Wednesday, Thursday, Friday};
    Hours      = [7..20];
    Morning    = [8..12];
    Classes    = {None, English, Software, Mathematics};
    Schedule   = ARRAY Days, Hours OF Classes;
  CONST
    DayNames  = ARRAY Days OF TEXT{
                    "Monday", "Tuesday", "Wednesday", "Thursday", "Friday"};
    ClassNames= ARRAY Classes OF TEXT{
                    "None", "English", "Software", "Mathematics"};

  VAR
    schedule: Schedule;                                 (*stores the schedule*)
BEGIN
  FOR day:= FIRST(Days) TO LAST(Days) DO
    FOR hour:= FIRST(Hours) TO LAST(Hours) DO
      schedule[day, hour]:= Classes.None;               (*initialize to None*)
    END; (*FOR hour*)
  END; (*FOR day*)

  FOR hour:= 8 TO 18 DO                                (*English nearly all day*)
    schedule[Days.Monday, hour]:= Classes.English;
  END; (*FOR hour*)

(*Software Tuesday to Friday at 10*)
  FOR day:= Days.Tuesday TO Days.Friday DO
    schedule[day, 10]:= Classes.Software;
  END; (*FOR day*)

  schedule[Days.Tuesday, 8]:= Classes.Mathematics;
  schedule[Days.Friday, 9]:= Classes.Mathematics;

(*print schedule for mornings *)
  FOR day:= FIRST(Days) TO LAST(Days) DO
    SIO.PutText(DayNames[day] & "\n");
    FOR hour:= FIRST(Morning) TO LAST(Morning) DO
      SIO.PutInt(hour);
      SIO.PutText(":" & ClassNames[schedule[day, hour]]);
    END; (*FOR hour*)
    SIO.Nl();
  END; (*FOR day*)
END ClassSchedule.
```

Example 8.10: Class schedule as bidimensional array

As reader you might object that you could produce such a schedule more efficiently on paper by hand, and that you do not need a computer for this. This is true. Example 8.10 was intended to demonstrate the basic data structures and several elementary operations. We still lack sufficient knowledge to produce a program that properly manages a schedule. For example, we would have to make a real schedule *persistent*; i.e., it must not simply disappear after execution of the program, as in Example 8.8 (see Chapter 14).

8.1.6 Linear search in an array

Next let us solve a classic problem in computer science: searching for an element in an array. It is easy to guess why searching is a classic problem. We store the information in our computers for a reason: We want to be able to use the stored information, and this means that we must be able to find it. Let us assume for now that the data are stored completely randomly in an array (i.e., there is no relationship between an element value and its position in the array – in contrast to a sorted array, where "smaller" elements appear before "larger" ones.) Thus to find a value, we must search the array linearly from the start, one element at a time.

First let us formulate the task precisely. Given an array a of INTEGERs with an index range between 1 and N and the target value x, we want to find the first occurrence of this value in a. The precondition is:

$$N > 0 \land (\exists j : 1 \le j \le N : a[j] = x)$$

In words, N must be positive, and the value x must occur in a. In addition, we implicitly assume that a, x and N do not change during the execution of the search procedure.

> The assumption that the target element actually occurs in the array is not so unrealistic: We can increment N by 1 and copy x to the last position. Then we always find x, and we know that if x is found at the last position, then it was not contained in the original array. This approach is called the *sentinel* method.

The program must fulfill the following postcondition:

$$a[i] = x \land (\forall j : 1 \le j < i : a[j] \ne x)$$

The first expression (before $\land$) states that x was found at position i; the second states that x occurs at no position with a smaller index. Let us derive the algorithm from this postcondition. We need a loop that linearly searches the entire array until the target element is found. The second expression of the postcondition can serve as our loop invariant, because this relationship must be preserved during the entire search. We will use the invariant I:

$$I : (\forall j : 1 \leq j < i : a[j] \neq x)$$

The first expression of the postcondition could serve as termination condition for the loop. We will use a WHILE loop with the following form (see Section 5.5):

$$\{I\} \text{ WHILE } condition \text{ DO } statements \ \{I\} \text{ END}$$

The WHILE condition will be the negation of the termination condition (i.e., $a[i] \neq x$). Now the body of the While loop is easy to see: We want to search the entire array linearly, so we need to increment the index by 1 in each iteration. The final algorithm becomes:

```
{precondition ≡ N > 0 ∧ (∃j : 1 ≤ j ≤ N : a[j] = x)}
i := 1;
{I}
WHILE a[i] ≠ x DO
    INC(i)
    {I}
END;
{I ∧ a[i] = x ≡ postcondition}
```

A detailed proof of the partial correctness of the above algorithm can be found in [DFS88]. It is easy to demonstrate termination (and thus the total correctness): Since we postulated $x \in a$, and since i searches the array linearly from the start, $a[i] \neq x$ cannot remain *true* forever, and the WHILE loop must terminate. Example 8.11 shows a corresponding solution in Modula-3.

In Example 8.12 we search a text array. In the first WHILE loop we read texts into array a, where we will later search. Since we might not completely fill the array, we use the variable last to store the index of the last valid value. If the Stop character is input at the start, then the search is not carried out at all (i <= last is never *true*). In the search we do not use a sentinel, thus complicating the termination condition.

The test of the termination condition relies on *lazy evaluation* (Section 7.1.3). If we exchange the two conditions, then we might try to access an element that does not exist.

```
    ⋮
    CONST
      N = 10;                                        (*number of elements in array*)
    TYPE
      Array = ARRAY [1..N+1] OF INTEGER;
                                          (*the position N+1 is reserved for the sentinel*)
    VAR
      a: Array;                                        (*the array to be searched*)
      x, i: INTEGER;                                   (*x contains the target value*)
    BEGIN                                              (*statement part*)
    (*... a and x are initialized appropiately ... *)
      a[LAST(a)]:= x;                                  (*sentinel at position N+1*)
      i:= FIRST(a);
      WHILE x # a[i] DO INC(i) END;
      IF i = LAST(a) THEN SIO.PutText("NOT found");
      ELSE SIO.PutText("Found at position: "); SIO.PutInt(i)
      END;
    ⋮
```

Example 8.11: *Linear search with sentinel*

The following reflects a possible execution of the program:

```
Please enter a text, or terminate input with .
Peter Paul Martha Julia Eleanor .
Search text := Julia
Found at position:   4
```

For large quantities of data, linear searching can become too prolonged. On the average, we have to search half of the array, and in the worst case all of it. If we order the data according to some principle, then we can employ much faster methods. Thanks to the alphabetic order of the telephone book, e.g., we can quickly find the corresponding first letter. If we are looking up the name *Newman*, then we open the telephone book approximately at the middle. If we happen to open to the letter K, then we do not continue to search in the first half, but only after K. On second try we might flip to P, and on the third attempt we might land at N. This is not linear searching. If we encounter persons of the same name, we might then have to continue with a linear search. We do not discuss improved search methods here, but refer the reader to a number of algorithms in the literature [Knu81, Sed93, Wir76].

8.1.7 Sorting an array

We have seen that the precondition for rapid searching is the existence of some order in the array. This means that we have to *sort* our data.

```
MODULE LinearSearch2 EXPORTS Main;                          (*1.12.94. LB*)

  IMPORT SIO, Text;

  CONST
    N = 128;                               (*maximum number of elements in array*)
    Stop = ".";                                       (*end of input stream*)
  TYPE
    Array = ARRAY [1..N] OF TEXT;
  VAR
    a: Array;                                   (*the array, in which to search*)
    x: TEXT;                                    (*current text or search text*)
    i, last: INTEGER;                             (*last: last valid index*)

BEGIN                                                    (*statement part*)
  SIO.PutText("Please enter a text, or terminate input with " & Stop & "\n");
  last:= FIRST(a) − 1; x:= SIO.GetText();
  WHILE NOT Text.Equal(x, Stop) AND (last < LAST(a)) DO
    INC(last); a[last]:= x; x:= SIO.GetText();
  END; (*WHILE NOT Text.Equal ...*)

  SIO.PutText("Search text := ");
  x:= SIO.GetText();                            (*x contains the search text*)

  i:= FIRST(a);
  WHILE (i <= last) AND NOT Text.Equal(a[i], x) DO INC(i) END;
  IF i > last THEN SIO.PutText("NOT found");
  ELSE SIO.PutText("Found at position: "); SIO.PutInt(i)
  END; (*IF i > last*)
  SIO.Nl();
END LinearSearch2.
```

Example 8.12: *Linear search without a sentinel*

How do we sort an array of texts? How would we sort texts if they were written on file cards? Perhaps the simplest method is the following: We find the (alphabetically) smallest element and swap it with the first element. This assures that the (new) first element is in the correct position. Next we repeat the procedure with the second, third, etc. element. This produces an increasingly long sorted sequence at the start of the array. After we have progressed to the next-to-the-last element, the last element must also be correctly positioned, i.e., the largest.

We can easily implement this algorithm with a nested FOR loop (Example 8.13). For input we use the same statements as in Example 8.12. The outer FOR loop iterates through the array from the first to the next-to-the-last element. The inner loop seeks the smallest element within the unsorted rest. To the variable min we always assign the index value of the smallest element (at the start we assume that a_i is the smallest). If we find an element $a_j < a_{min}$, then we set min to j. After each iteration of the inner loop we swap a_i with a_{min}. To compare texts, we use the Compare

```
  ⋮
TYPE
   Array = ARRAY [1..N] OF TEXT;
VAR
   a: Array;                                      (*the array in which to search*)
   x: TEXT;                                                   (*auxiliary variable*)
   last, min: INTEGER;                (*last: last valid index, min: current minimum*)
BEGIN
  ⋮
  FOR i:= FIRST(a) TO last – 1 DO
    min:= i;                                         (*index of smallest element*)
    FOR j:= i + 1 TO last DO
      IF Text.Compare(a[j], a[min]) = –1 THEN min:= j END;            (*IF aⱼ < aₘᵢₙ*)
    END; (*FOR j*)
    x:= a[min]; a[min]:= a[i]; a[i]:= x;                     (*swap aᵢ and aₘᵢₙ*)
  END; (*FOR i*)
  FOR i:= FIRST(a) TO last DO
    SIO.PutText(a[i] & ” ”);
  END; (*FOR i*)                                                (*outputs sorted array*)
  SIO.NI();
  ⋮
```

Example 8.13: *Sorting by selecting the smallest element*

procedure of the Text interface. If text1 and text2 are of type TEXT, then Compare(text1, text2) returns 0 if the content of text1 is equal to that of text2, −1 if text1 comes before text2 in lexical order ("less than"), or +1 if text1 comes after text2.

The following is a possible execution of the program:

```
Please enter a text, or terminate input with .
Peter Paul Ely Martha Julia Alma .
Alma Ely Julia Martha Paul Peter
```

This sorting algorithm is quite simple, but not particularly efficient. For n elements we would have to iterate through the array on the average $\frac{n^2}{2}$ times. For more efficient sorting algorithms, we refer the interested reader to the literature [Knu81, Sed93, Wir76].

8.2 Records

A record serves to combine components of different types. Such heterogeneous combination makes sense when the components are logically related. The components receive a symbolic name with which they can be accessed.

Access to such components is thus static; i.e., they are already known at compile time.

To collect information on the employees of a company, as on file cards, we can write as follows:

```
TYPE
   EmpData = RECORD
                    name, firstname: TEXT;
                    salary: REAL;
                END;
VAR
   employee: EmpData;
```

The variable employee can now be stored as a single value. All information on an employee can be accessed together via employee. We use selectors to access individual components. To initialize the variable, we can write as follows:

```
employee.name:= "Smith";
employee.firstname:= "Fred";
employee.salary:= 20000.0;
```

We could say that the components of a record become part of a larger context, but do not lose their individual attributes such as name and type. The components of an array, by contrast, are more uniform; they are all of the same type and are identified with indices (actually with a "number" or address). However, the indices of an array can be computed dynamically, while the names of the components of a record are static.

Syntax of record types

$$
\begin{aligned}
&\text{RecordType}_{54} = \text{"RECORD" Fields}_{59}\text{ "END".} \\
&\text{Fields}_{59} \qquad = [\text{Field}_{60}\ \{\ \text{";" Field}_{60}\ \}\ [\ \text{";"}\ ]\ ]\ . \\
&\text{Field}_{60} \qquad = \text{IDList}_{87}\ (\ \text{":" Type}_{48}\ |\ \text{":=" ConstExpr}_{65} \\
&\qquad\qquad\qquad\quad |\ \text{":" Type}_{48}\ \text{":=" ConstExpr}_{65}\ ).
\end{aligned}
$$

The general form of a record type is thus:

TYPE T = RECORD *field list* END

The list of fields is very similar to a variable declaration. This is not an accident, but actually the goal: In a record we combine declarations. Initialization of the fields on declaration is restricted to constant expressions. Initialization is carried out on creation of a variable of type record. Example 8.15 shows how points on a (bidimensional) screen can be represented

	x	y	color [red]	color [green]	color [blue]
q:	10	10	100	100	100

Figure 8.14: *Record with simple and composite fields*

```
  ⋮
TYPE
    Colors      = {red, green, blue};                              (*primary colors*)
    Intensity   = [0 .. 100];                                   (*intensity in percent*)
    ColorValues = ARRAY Colors OF Intensity;
    Point       = RECORD
                    x, y: INTEGER := 0;
                    color := ColorValues {0, ..};                          (*black*)
                  END; (*Point*)
VAR
    p: Point;                                       (*p.x = 0, p.y = 0, all p.color_i = 0*)
    q: Point;                                       (*q.x = 0, q.y = 0, all q.color_i = 0*)
BEGIN                                           (*q receives new coordinates and color*)
    q.x:= 10; q.y:= 10;                         (*q is shifted by 10 in both directions*)
    FOR f:= FIRST(Colors) TO LAST(Colors) DO q.color[f]:= 100 END;    (*q turns white*)
  ⋮
```

Example 8.15: *Record declaration*

in a graphic program. In this example a point has two coordinates and one color value each for three primary colors (red, green and blue). The coordinates are initialized to 0 and the color to black.

The reader should note the difference between the Point type in the array in Example 8.5 and the Point type used in Example 8.15: We use the record here because the number of point coordinates is fixed and additional information (the color) needs to be stored with each point.

8.2.1   Record selectors

The elements of a record are accessed via *qualified identifiers*. The field name must be preceded by the name of the variable to which the field belongs – separated by a period. To initialize coordinate x of variable q in Example 8.15 and Figure 8.14, we would write the following:

    q.x := 10

In the event of nested records, the entire *path* of field names must be specified (see, e.g., the expression poly[i].p2.x in Example 8.19). The syntax of access to record fields (like indexing of arrays) is defined in the expression syntax (see Selector$_{78}$ in Figure 7.1, page 126).

8.2.2 Record constructors

Record values can be defined with the help of *record constructors*. For the exact syntax, we repeat the relevant excerpt from the syntax of expressions:

Syntax

$\text{Constructor}_{79} = \text{Type}_{48} \; "\{" [\text{RecordCons}_{82} \mid \cdots] "\}".$
$\text{RecordCons}_{82} = \text{RecordElt}_{83} \{ "," \text{RecordElt}_{83} \}.$
$\text{RecordElt}_{83} = [\text{Ident}_{89} ":="] \text{Expr}_{66}.$

A record constructor defines a list of values to be assigned to the record fields. With the help of record constructors we can establish the value of record constants and record variables. For fields for which the type declaration did not define a value, a value must be specified in the constructor. Fields values that were given a value in their type declaration need not be defined in the constructor. Here the value of the type declaration is used. After the assignment of a constructor all fields of the target record receive a valid value. The values of the constructors can be specified *positionally* or *by name*.

1. *Positional specification*
   The values are assigned sequentially to the record fields: the first value to the first field, the second value to the second field, etc. If the list of values is shorter than the number of fields, then the specifications of the type declaration apply to the remaining fields. For example, if the type Point is declared as in Example 8.15, then

   Point{20, 30}

   defines a point with x = 20 and y = 30. The color value remains as specified in the type declaration.

2. *Specification by name*
   This specification is syntactically similar to a value assignment. The sequence of the specifications is arbitrary in this case. The fields for which no assignment is made assume their values from the type declaration. The following constructor defines the same point as above:

   Point{y:= 30, x:= 20}

3. *Mixed specification*
   For a mixed specification, the positional specifications must be made first. We suggest avoiding mixed specifications because they are generally hard to read.

```
 ⋮
TYPE
   Colors      = {red, green, blue};                          (*primary colors*)
   Intensity   = [0 .. 100];                                  (*intensity in percent*)
   ColorValues= ARRAY Colors OF Intensity;
   Point       = RECORD
                       x, y: INTEGER ;
                       color: ColorValues;
                  END; (*Point*)
CONST
   Black   = ColorValues {0, ..};           (*Intensity value minimal => black*)
   White   = ColorValues {100, ..};         (*Intensity value maximal => white*)
   Yellow  = ColorValues {100, 100, 0};          (*red and green make yellow*)
   Origin  = Point{x:= 0, y:= 0, color:= Black};         (*record constructor*)
VAR
   p: Point := Origin;
   q:= Point {x:= 10, y:= 10, color:= White};             (*record constructor*)
BEGIN
   p.x:= p.x + 10;                                     (*shift p toward x by 10*)
   p.y:= p.y + 15;                                     (*shift p toward y by 15*)
   p.color:= Yellow;                                  (*set color of p to yellow*)
 ⋮
```

Example 8.16: *Record types, constructors and selectors*

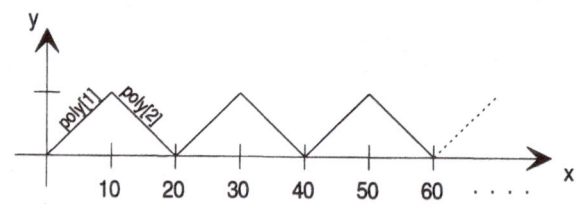

Figure 8.17: *A zigzag line stored in the variable "poly"*

poly [1]

	p1				p2				
x	y	color			x	y	color		
0	0	100	0	0	10	10	100	0	0

· · ·

Figure 8.18: *Array of records with various fields*

```
    ⋮
  CONST
    Red            = ColorValues {100, 0, 0};                    (*red color*)
    Step           = 10;
  TYPE
    Colors         = {red, green, blue};                        (*primary colors*)
    Intensity      = [0 .. 100];                                (*intensity in percent*)
    ColorValues    = ARRAY Colors OF Intensity;
    Point          = RECORD
                        x, y: INTEGER;
                        color: ColorValues := Red;
                     END; (*Point*)
    Line           = RECORD
                        p1, p2: Point;
                     END; (*Line*)
    Group          = ARRAY [1..16] OF Line;
  VAR
    p := Point{x:= 0, y:= 0};
    line := Line{p1:= p, p2:= Point{x:= Step, y:= Step}};
                          (*line joints point(0,0) with point(10,10) with a red line*)
    poly: Group;                          (*poly consists of a number of lines*)
    change: INTEGER := Step;              (*change of direction on Y axis*)
  BEGIN
    poly[FIRST(poly)]:= line;             (*poly[1] joins (0,0) with (10,10)*)
    FOR i:= FIRST(poly) + 1 TO LAST(poly) DO
      poly[i].p1:= poly[i − 1].p2;        (*poly[i].p1 takes p2 from predecessor*)
      poly[i].p2.x := poly[i − 1].p2.x + Step;      (*forward along X axis*)
      change:= − change;                  (*changes direction with each iteration*)
      poly[i].p2.y := poly[i − 1].p2.y + change;    (*up and down along Y axis*)
    END; (*FOR i*)
    ⋮
```

Example 8.19: *Nested records with constructors*

In Example 8.16 Black, White and Yellow are array constants whose values are set by array constructors. Origin is a record constant whose value is defined by a record constructor. Variables p and q are both of type Point. p is initialized to the value Origin, and q is initialized by a record constructor. In the statement part the attributes of the declared points can be changed as needed. Example 8.19 introduces lines and groups of lines in bidimensional space. A Line consists of two points. We define a group as an array of lines. The variable poly represents a red zigzag line (see Figure 8.17 and 8.18).

8.2.3   Operations with records

Assignment

Records can be assigned to one another if all their fields have the same names and types and have been declared in the same order in the record, which makes them *structurally equivalent* (see Section 7.3). In the following example R1 and R2 are equivalent, but different from R3 (the fields of R3 have the same types, but different names):

```
TYPE
    R1 = RECORD a: INTEGER; b: REAL END;
    R2 = RECORD a: INTEGER; b: REAL END;
    R3 = RECORD x: INTEGER; y: REAL END;
```

The initialization values belong to the record type. Thus the following types are different and thus not assignment compatible:

```
R4 = RECORD a: CARDINAL := 0 END;
R5 = RECORD a: CARDINAL END
```

On assignment between records, all fields of the *RHS* record (the right side of the assignment) are copied to the corresponding fields of the *LHS* record (on the left side).

Relational operations

Assignment compatible records can be tested for (in)equality. No other relational operation is permitted.

8.2.4   With statement

Before we examine a larger example, we introduce a new statement that allows us to use aliases for complex selectors that we need more than once. Thus we can make the source code more compact and readable – and we save some typing. Besides, it makes our programs more efficient because certain internal access computations associated with the selectors for record components and above all array indexing, only have to be carried out once.

Syntax of the With statement

$$\text{WithStmt}_{41} = \text{"WITH" Binding}_{46} \; \{ \; \text{","} \; \text{Binding}_{46} \; \} \; \text{"DO" Stmts}_{23} \; \text{"END".}$$
$$\text{Binding}_{46} = \text{Ident}_{89} \; \text{"="} \; \text{Expr}_{66}.$$

```
MODULE Students EXPORTS Main;                                    (*5.11.93. LB*)

  IMPORT SIO;
  CONST
    SubjectName = ARRAY Subjects OF TEXT {"English", "Software", "Mathematics"};
    MaxStudents = 300;                         (*maximum number of students*)
  TYPE
    Subjects   = {English, Software, Mathematics};
    Tests      = RECORD t1, t2: CARDINAL := 0 END;
    Student    = RECORD
                   name, firstName: TEXT := "";
                   studentNumber: CARDINAL := 0;
                   tests: ARRAY Subjects OF Tests;
                 END; (*Student*)
    Students   = ARRAY [1 .. MaxStudents] OF Student;
    StatData   = RECORD count, score: CARDINAL:= 0 END;        (*test statistics*)
    Statistics = ARRAY Subjects OF StatData;             (*statistics by subject*)
  VAR
    students: Students;                              (*stores all student data*)
    count: CARDINAL := 0;                        (*current number of records*)
    statistics:= Statistics{StatData{}, ..};    (*statistics of test results by subject*)
BEGIN
  SIO.PutText("Student Data Management\n");
                              (*initialize student data and the number of students*)
    ⋮
  FOR s:= 1 TO count DO                           (*upper boundary = current count*)
    WITH st = students[s] DO                              (*st is for students[s]*)
      IF st.studentNumber # 0 THEN                 (*no test without student number*)
        FOR f:= FIRST(Subjects) TO LAST(Subjects) DO
          WITH stat = statistics[f], t = st.tests[f] DO      (*t=students[s].tests[f]*)
            INC(stat.count, 2);                        (*exactly two tests per subject*)
            INC(stat.score, t.t1);                               (*add test 1*)
            INC(stat.score, t.t2);                               (*add test 2*)
          END; (*WITH stat, t*)
        END; (*FOR f*)
      END; (*IF st.studentNumber # 0*)
    END; (*WITH st = students[s]*)
  END; (*FOR s*)

  FOR f:= FIRST(Subjects) TO LAST(Subjects) DO
    SIO.PutText("Average for " & SubjectName[f] & " = ");
    SIO.PutReal(FLOAT(statistics[f].score) / FLOAT(statistics[f].count));
    SIO.Nl();
  END; (*FOR f*)
END Students.
```

Example 8.20: Output of test statistics

The general form of a WITH statement:

WITH *identifier = expression* DO *statement sequence* END

The identifier is declared via the WITH statement; its *scope* (see Section 9) extends to the END of the statement. The identifier is used as an abbreviation (nickname) for the expression. If the expression returns a value, then the identifier within the WITH statement stands for this value, and no new value can be assigned to the identifier (it is a read-only variable). If the expression yields a (read/write) variable, then the identifier is actually only another (shorter) name for the variable.

8.2.5   Example: Student data management

Let us develop a small student data management system: For each student, we want to store the name, first name and student number. For each class, the students must take exactly two tests (perhaps a too rigid assumption). The points scored on the tests are to be stored. Student who lack a valid (nonzero) student number are not considered in the assessment.

In Example 8.20 we assume that the student data has already been recorded. For larger and more complex data sets, we usually read the input data from a file (see Chapter 14) rather than from the keyboard. The data to be read must be tested for syntax (correct format) as well as semantics. The semantic test attempts to detect and reject senseless values. For a student number, e.g., we could require that all student numbers in the year 1995 begin with 95. Such a condition is easy to test.

Our program computes the mean of the test results within a subject. The initialization of the variable statistics was specified on declaration. This initialization must be moved to the statement part if we intend to use the variable repeatedly. For the subject-related statistics we must iterate through all the collected student data (the current number of students is stored on input in the variable count). For students with a valid student number, we increment the statistical counter. Note that we store the number of valid tests in the field count of the record StatData, which should not be confused with the variable count.

In processing the array students we did not use FIRST and LAST because we explicitly assume that the lower boundary of the array is always 1 (we need not consider the case that numbering of the students begins at -5 or 100). Assume that we input of the following data (here we use the European 1 (A) to 5 (F)):

FirstName	Name	StudentNo.	English	Software	Mathematics
Amelia	Smith	9400	2 5	3 4	4 5
Oscar	Small	9401	4 5	3 2	2 3
Julia	Jones	9402	4 1	3 2	3 4
Peter	Piper	0000	4 1	3 2	3 4

The program would give us the following output:

```
Average for English = 3.5
Average for Software = 2.8333333
Average for Mathematics = 3.5
```

8.3 Sets

Sets are generally very powerful constructs. Modula-3, like many other programming languages, restricts sets to those of ordinal types. We also limit our discussion to this view of sets.

Sets are an unordered collection of elements. Thus we cannot index the elements (there is no *i*th element). We can designate an element of a set only as itself. To read an element from an array, we specify its position (the index). With a set we proceed differently: We insert an element or test whether a certain element (that we already know) is *contained* in the set. As surprising as it may seem, this gives us a very powerful tool.

> Sets are closer to human memory than array storage is. People do not search in their memories as though they knew the position that contains the information, but did not know the contents. When people remember something, they already have the information. When people cannot remember something (such as the name of the medication against forgetfulness), they cannot iterate through a linear search of memory. The efforts that people make in such a case are quite mysterious. They seem to know something, but actually do not know it – a situation that has little to do with the storage of information in a computer.

A typical example of the use of sets in computer programs is the storage of switch values. To store in a variable the current position of the mouse keys of our computer, we could do the following:

```
TYPE
    Keys = {left, middle, right};
    Mouse = SET OF Keys;
VAR
    mouse: Mouse;
```

The pressed keys, but not the others, are contained in the set mouse. To initialize the variable mouse to "no key pressed", we can write:

mouse := Mouse{};

Thereby we assign to the variable an empty set of type Mouse. To add the middle mouse key (to any keys currently pressed), we write:

mouse := mouse + Mouse{Keys.Middle};

This joins the current set of pressed keys with the set containing only the element Keys.Middle. The following statement tests whether the middle key is pressed.

IF Keys.Middle IN mouse THEN (*middle mouse key pressed*) END;

The programming language SETL [S+86] builds fundamentally on sets. Many database languages also feature sets as "first-class-citizens", i.e., as full-fledged, unrestricted language construct. This means that we can define sets of any data type. Note that sets are one of the most basic mathematical constructs, and many other constructs can be expressed as special cases of sets. However, it is quite difficult to implement sets as full-fledged and efficient features.

Syntax of sets

SetType$_{56}$ = "SET" "OF" Type$_{48}$.

Type$_{48}$, the *base type* of sets, must be an ordinal type. The elements that are added to a set must be assignment compatible with this type.

8.3.1 Range

Since the base type itself represents a value set, the range of a set is a *power set* (a set of sets). This power set represents the set of all possible sets of the base type. If we create a set over the range [0..1], then the following values are contained in the range of the power set:

{} {0} {1} {0,1}

In words, the range encompasses the empty set, the sets containing either 0 or 1, and the set containing both elements.

Sets are unordered; thus the set {0,1} can also be written as {1,0}. An element can occur only once in a set: {0,1,1} is identical to {0,1}.

If the cardinality (number of possible values) of the base type is N, then the cardinality of the set formed therefrom is 2^N. This necessitates a restriction of the base type range. A set of type INTEGER, e.g., can never be represented fully. In general it makes sense to create sets of base types with modest cardinality.

For internal representation of sets we need at least one bit per element; this bit specifies whether the element is contained in the set. This simple representation would not be possible if sets were not so restricted. For example, if a SET OF RECORD ... were possible, then one bit per element would not suffice because the contents of the individual fields (or at least a pointer to them) would be necessary. However, with the help of user modules it is possible to design general and powerful sets (see Appendix A).

Even for a very thrifty representation we need 32 bits for a SET OF [1..32]. For the complete representation of SET OF INTEGER on a 32-bit computer we would need 2^{32} bits, or 512 Mbytes, of memory.

8.3.2 Set constructors

Set values can be defined with the help of set constructors.

Syntax

$$\text{Constructor}_{79} = \text{Type}_{48}\ ''\{''\ [\ \text{SetCons}_{80}\ |\ \cdots\ ]\ ''\}''.$$
$$\text{SetCons}_{80}\quad = \text{SetElt}_{81}\ \{\ '',''\ \text{SetElt}_{81}\ \}.$$
$$\text{SetElt}_{81}\quad = \text{Expr}_{66}\ [\ ''..''\ \text{Expr}_{66}\ ].$$

A set constructor lists values or ranges to be contained in the set. Example 8.21 demonstrates the use of set constructors. The constant All contains all elements in the range [1..16], Null is an empty set, and Several = {1,3,5,6,7,14,15,16}. The initialization of variable s (to {r1,11,r2}) is an example showing that a set constructor can also contain variable names.

8.3.3 Operations on sets

In addition to assignment, special set operations (analogous to the arithmetic operations) and relations are defined on sets.

Assignment

A set value can be assigned to a set variable if and only if their base types are equivalent. This means that only equivalent set types are assignment compatible.

In Example 8.22 the types Set1 and Set2 are *not* equivalent. Possible values of Set1 are {} {1} {2} {1, 2}, while for Set2 they are {} {2} {3} {2, 3}; therefore s1 and s2 are *not* assignment compatible.

```
TYPE
  Range = [1..16];
  Set    = SET OF Range;
CONST
  All      = Set{1..16};              (*contains all elements from 1 to 16*)
  Null     = Set{};                                            (*empty*)
  Several  = Set{1, 3, 5..7, 14..16};     (*contains: 1, 3, 5, 6, 7, 14, 15, 16*)
VAR
  r1: Range := 10; r2: Range := 12;
  s := Set{r1, 11, r2};                           (*s = Set{10,11,12}*)
```

Example 8.21: *Set constructors*

```
TYPE
  Set1 = SET OF [1..2];
  Set2 = SET OF [2..3];
VAR
  s1:= Set1{2}; s2:= Set2{2};
  ⋮
  s1:= s2;              (*impermissible, for Set1 is not compatible with Set2*)
```

Example 8.22: *Different set types*

Set operations

For sets, Modula-3 defines the operations listed in Table 8.24 (where S and T are operands of the same set type). The parentheses enclose the language's prescribed notation. Figure 8.23 visualizes the effect of the set operations for nondisjunct sets with the help of *Euler-Venn diagrams* [Tru88]. An Euler-Venn diagram represents sets as ovals. The set operations are depicted by shading. The diagram of S * T, e.g., shows the intersection (the set of all elements belonging to both sets) as shaded.

Example 8.25 shows several set operations.

Relations

For sets the usual relations are defined with the accustomed syntax and with semantics corresponding to set theory. In Table 8.26 S and T are operands of the same set type. The parentheses enclose the language's prescribed notation.

Example 8.27 shows how to output the contents of a set with the help of the IN relation.

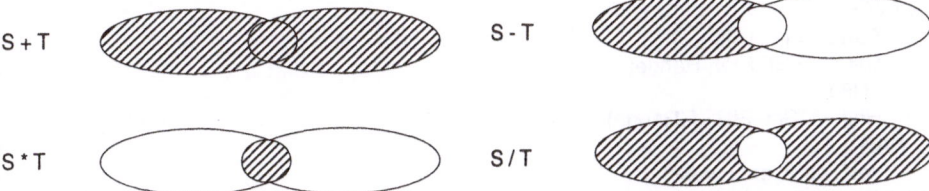

Figure 8.23: *Set operations depicted as Euler-Venn diagrams*

Union (+)	$S + T = \{x \mid (x \in S) \lor (x \in T)\}$ in words: $S + T$ is the set of all elements that occur in S or in T or in both sets.
Difference (−)	$S - T = \{x \mid (x \in S) \land (x \notin T)\}$ in words: $S - T$ is the set of all elements that occur in S but not in T.
Intersection (*)	$S * T = \{x \mid (x \in S) \land (x \in T)\}$ in words: $S * T$ is the set of all elements that occur both in S and in T.
Symmetric Difference (/)	$S/T = \{x \mid (x \in S \land x \notin T) \lor (x \in T \land x \notin S)\}$ in words: S/T is the set of all elements that occur in S or in T, but not in both

Table 8.24: *Set operations*

Equality (=)	$S = T$ true iff[2] S and T contain the same elements.
Inequality (#)	$S \neq T$ *iff* NOT$(S = T)$
Subset (<=)	$S <= T$ *iff* $\forall s \in S : s \in T$ iff all elements in S also occur in T
Proper Subset (<)	$S < T$ *iff* $(S <= T)$AND$(S\#T)$
Superset (>=)	$S >= T$ *iff* $T <= S$
Proper Superset (>)	$S > T$ *iff* $T < S$
Contained (IN)	e IN S *iff* $e \in S$ is *true* if element e is contained in set S. E must be assignment compatible with the base type of S. Note that the IN relation deviates from the other relations because it does not combine two operands of the same type.

[2]iff stands for "if and only if"

Table 8.26: *Set relations*

```
TYPE
   Range = [1..16];
   Set    = SET OF Range;
CONST
   Half =   Set{FIRST(Range)..LAST(Range) DIV 2};        (*1,2,3,4,5,6,7,8*)
VAR
   set1, set2, set3 := Set{};
BEGIN
  FOR e:= FIRST(Range) TO LAST(Range) BY 2 DO
     set1:= set1 + Set{e}
  END;                                                 (*set1 = 1,3,5,7,9,11,13,15*)
  set2:= Half – set1;                                       (*set2 = 2,4,6,8*)
  set1:= set1 – Half + set2;                          (*set1 = 2,4,6,8,9,11,13,15*)
  set3:= set1 * set2;                                       (*set3 = 2,4,6,8*)
  set3:= set1 + set2;                                 (*set3 = 2,4,6,8,9,11,13,15*)
  set3:= set1 / set2;                                      (*set3 = 9,11,13,15*)
  set3:= set1 – set2;                                      (*set3 = 9,11,13,15*)
```

Example 8.25: *Set operations*

```
FOR e:= FIRST(Range) TO LAST(Range) DO        (*over all possible elements *)
   IF e IN set3 THEN SIO.PutInt(e) END;              (*if present in set, output *)
END; (*FOR e*)
```

Example 8.27: *Outputting a set*

8.3.4 Example: Input of numbers

Let us write a program that reads an INTEGER. We will use SIO.GetChar, but not SIO.GetInt (Example 8.28). The number is a sequence of digits, possibly preceded by blanks or tabs; such leading white space is simply skipped. The sequence might also contain a leading sign. If no interpretable digit sequence is entered, an error message should be generated. We will keep statistics on any characters appearing after the digit sequence.

The program in Example 8.28 shows a very useful application of sets. As mentioned in Section 4.3, type CHAR does have a defined order, yet the current ordinal value of a character depends on the code table used. (Although this is also specified explicitly in Modula-3, it is still better to keep our program independent of code tables.)

```
MODULE Sets EXPORTS Main;                                        (*29.10.93. LB*)
  IMPORT SIO;
  TYPE
    CharacterSet = SET OF CHAR;                        (*set of all possible characters*)
  CONST
    Caps      = CharacterSet{'A' .. 'Z'};                      (*capital letters*)
    LowCase   = CharacterSet{'a' .. 'z'};                       (*lower case*)
    Letters   = Caps + LowCase;                                 (*all letters*)
    Digits    = CharacterSet{'0' .. '9'};                          (*digits*)
    Blanks    = CharacterSet{' ', '\t'};                      (*blanks & tabs*)
    Sign      = CharacterSet{'–', '+'};                       (*leading sign*)
    Stop      = '\n';
  VAR
    ch: CHAR; negative: BOOLEAN := FALSE;
    result: INTEGER := 0;                                          (*Result*)
    letters, digits, others: CARDINAL := 0;            (*counters for statistics*)
BEGIN
  SIO.PutText("Please enter a number\n");
  REPEAT ch:= SIO.GetChar() UNTIL NOT ch IN Blanks;    (*filters blanks and tabs*)
  IF ch IN Sign THEN
      negative:= ch = '–';                                      (*minus sign*)
      REPEAT ch:= SIO.GetChar() UNTIL NOT ch IN Blanks;  (*filters blanks & tabs *)
  END; (*IF ch IN Sign*)
  IF ch IN Digits THEN
      WHILE ch IN Digits DO                           (*reads the digits of the number*)
        result:= 10 * result + (ORD(ch) – ORD('0'));        (*ch is the last digit*)
        ch:= SIO.GetChar();                                  (*next character*)
      END;                              (*result is the unsigned value of the input number*)
      IF negative THEN result:= –result END;
      WHILE ch # Stop DO                              (*reads to stop character*)
          IF      ch IN Letters THEN INC(letters)
          ELSIF   ch IN Digits   THEN INC(digits)
          ELSE                         INC(others)
          END; (*IF ch IN*)
        ch:= SIO.GetChar();                                  (*next character*)
      END;                                (*all characters have been processed*)
      SIO.PutText("Input number = ");
      SIO.PutInt(result);
      SIO.PutText("\nStatistics on subsequent characters:\n");
      SIO.PutText("Letters = "); SIO.PutInt(letters);
      SIO.PutText(" Digits = "); SIO.PutInt(digits);
      SIO.PutText(" Others = "); SIO.PutInt(others);
      SIO.Nl();
  ELSE
      SIO.PutText("No interpretable number\n")
  END; (*ch IN Digits*)
END Sets.
```

Example 8.28: Reading a number using GetChar

8.4   Comparison of arrays, records and sets

Now we are familiar with all Modula-3 type constructors for defining static, composite types. Most imperative programming languages provide analogous constructors. In summary, let us compare the characteristics of these constructors

- *Size*
  All constructors are *static* in the sense that their size or the number of elements that they can accommodate is known in advance (at compile time). The special case of dynamic arrays is not considered at this point (see Section 11.2.3).

- *Element types*
  Arrays and sets are *homogeneous* structures. They store values of a single element type. Records are *heterogeneous* structures; they combine elements (components) of different types.

- *Access to elements*
  Access to record components is *static*; which component is selected in an expression is known at compile time. It is not possible to make computations at run time to determine which element will be accessed.

  Arrays are *dynamically* indexed: At run time we can compute which element to select.

  We cannot directly access the elements of a set. It is only possible to test whether an element is contained in the set.

- *Order of elements*
  The sequence of the components of a record and of an array are statically fixed. The index values of an array are ordered; there is a "first element" and a sequence of additional elements. The elements can be resorted dynamically by swapping their values. The elements of a set are not ordered; there is no "first element" in a set.

8.5   Packed data types

Packed data types serve to directly influence the internal representation of a data type. Usually the compiler employs an internal representation that is optimized primarily for speed of access (with respect to the underlying hardware architecture). However, sometimes we find it more important to optimize the use of storage, especially if we are processing a large amount of data, e.g., a very large array of records. Then we are no longer ambivalent about whether all bits are used optimally.

Packed data types are also employed when the format of the data is externally imposed (e.g., the format of incoming data for a communication channel). In such a case we can adapt the internal representation of our data directly to the external requirements.

A third application could be to drive a monochrome monitor directly from the main memory. In this case we manage a bidimensional array of BOOLEANs (e.g., *true* for black and *false* for white), whereby we must be sure that the Boolean value is represented in a single bit (which is usually not the case because in most computers bit addressing tends to be rather slow).

Syntax of packed data types

$$\text{PackedType}_{50} = \text{"BITS" ConstExpr}_{65} \text{ "FOR" Type}_{48}.$$

ConstExpr_{65} specifies the number of bits to be reserved for Type_{48}. A bidimensional array of bits could take the following form:

```
TYPE
    Bitmap = ARRAY Index, Index2 OF BITS 1 FOR BOOLEAN
```

Or the format of a network package could look like this:

```
TYPE
    Packet = RECORD
        addr: BITS 8 FOR [0..255];                    (*an 8-bit address*)
        number1, number2: BITS 3 FOR [0..7];          (*two 3-bit counters*)
        controlBits: ARRAY [0..1] OF BITS 1 FOR BOOLEAN;        (*2 bits*)
        info: ARRAY [3..128] OF BITS 8 FOR [0..255];       (*125-byte info*)
    END; (*Packet*)
```

The compiler is allowed to restrict the specification of bits. For example, it is not likely that a compiler on a machine with 32-bit word length would permit a type such as Int33 = BITS 33 FOR INTEGER.

The following applies for packed types and their unpacked versions:

$$\text{BITS n FOR T} <: \text{T} \ \wedge \ \text{T} <: \text{BITS n FOR T}$$

A type and its packed version are mutual subtypes; they are assignment compatible, and still not the same. The purpose of this rule is easy to perceive. Packed data types are represented differently in storage (normally more compactly) from normal types. However, they can be converted to each other and are thus assignment compatible. Formal variable parameters of an unpacked type cannot be passed as actual parameters to variables of the same type in packed version (this requires type identity; see Section 9.3.2).

The examples also show that packed data types are important only in advanced system-level programming, which is not the subject of this book. They also require precise knowledge of the internal representation of various data types. We mention them here for the sake of completeness and do not use them any more.

Chapter 9

Structuring algorithms

The previous chapter remedied a deficit in data structuring. Now we can define powerful data structures, data aggregates. With the help of structured statements we are capable of programming complex computations. But now let us critically examine the overall structure of our programs.

Our programs so far consisted of a main module, which itself consists of a block. In this block we first have all declarations in any order. A statement sequence of any length follows the keyword BEGIN. As long as the entire program expresses a single algorithm, there is no objection to this structure. However, if we assemble a large number of algorithms to a program – as usually is the case in practice – then there is a need to combine related declarations and statements to a syntactic unit. In addition, we want to be able to reuse algorithms. This necessitates managing algorithms as *named* units.

First we will more closely examine *blocks*, which do not immediately solve this problem. Still, they represent an important step toward *procedures*, which as named blocks represent invokable algorithms, and which we will discuss next.

9.1 Block structure

A block is the scope of a series of declarations. Thus far we had only one block per main module, so the scope of all names was accordingly the whole module. Many declarations (e.g., variables) are relevant only locally; they are needed for only a few statements. With the help of nested blocks we can restrict the definition of such local declarations to exactly the necessary scope.

Syntactically a block is a $Stmt_{24}$. Blocks can occur wherever statements are allowed. A block in a statement sequence is executed as soon as the preceding statement has been completed (see Section 5.3). Thus blocks do not change the control structure of the statements. The control structure continues to be determined by the static source code: The statement part of a block, like any other statement, is executed at its position in the source code.

This concept stems from the language *Algol-60*, which dates back to the 1960s.

Scope of identifiers

A block is the *scope* for identifiers, i.e., for names. Blocks can be nested to any depth. An identifier is defined, or *visible*, from the beginning to the end of the block in which it is declared. This also encompasses all nested blocks – unless the same name is *redeclared* in the nested block. Let us examine the code for a triangular swap (compare Section 5.1, page 84):

```
VAR x, y: INTEGER;
BEGIN
   x:= 1; y:= 2;
   VAR repos:= x;              (*repository needed only for the swap*)
   BEGIN
      x:= y; y:= repos;
   END (*inner block*)
(*...*)
END; (*outer block*)
```

Variables x and y are defined in both blos. Variable repos, needed exclusively for the swap, is defined only in the inner block.

Figure 9.1 depicts three blocks. The module block (also called *global block*) contains two nested blocks. The figure shows what happens when a name is redefined in an inner block that has already been declared in an outer block (variable x). In this case the redeclared identifier *eclipses* the one in the enclosing block, making the outer variable *invisible* in the inner block. In Figure 9.1 both the identifiers local are visible only in their own blocks (they are *local* to their blocks). Outside their blocks they are undefined. This means that variable local in the first block has nothing to do with the variable in the second block that happens to bear the same name. This is analogous to two persons named Smith living in the same building but in different apartments. The identifiers global and x, declared in the global block, are defined in the entire module. However, in the first block, identifier x is redeclared. This eclipses the global x in this inner block. (When we speak of "castle" and "king" in chess, these terms have a meaning different from the usual; in the local *context* of chess, a castle is not a large building!)

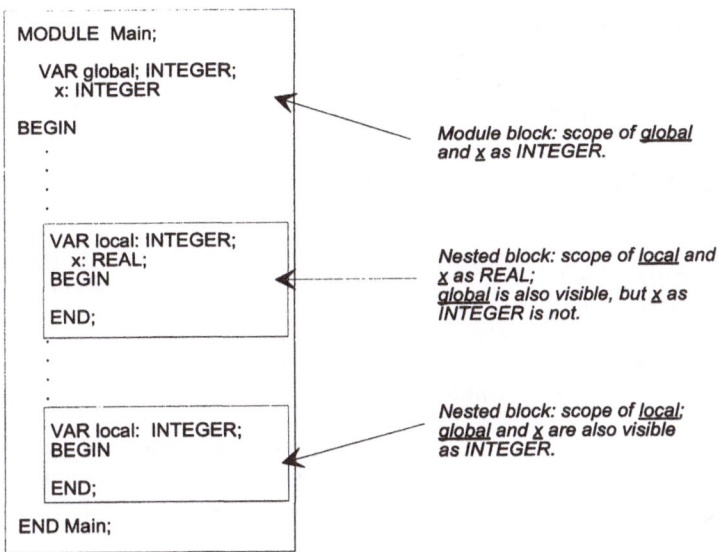

Figure 9.1: *Blocks*

Lifetime of variables

Blocks regulate not only the scope of identifiers but also the *lifetime* of variables. A variable's life begins on *activation* of the block (when control reaches the block's BEGIN) in which the variable is declared. Storage for local variables is allocated only at run time, when the block is executed. After the end of the block the variables vanish; their storage is deallocated. The lifetime of variables that are global to a main module is the duration of execution of the whole program. (We introduce data that outlive the duration of program execution in Chapter 14.)

> The declarations in local blocks can also encompass types and constants. Here we do not speak of lifetime because these constructs, in contrast to variables, are static in nature and do not change during program execution.

Syntax of blocks

$Block_{12}$ = {$Declaration_{13}$ }"BEGIN" $Stmts_{23}$ "END".
$Stmt_{24}$ = $Block_{12}$ | $\cdots$.

Thus a block consists of declarations and a statement sequence. However, a statement can be a block itself. This recursion in the syntax expresses that blocks can be nested. Blocks define the rules that determine the *visibility* of identifiers and the *lifetime* of variables.

```
MODULE GCD EXPORTS Main;                                    (*3.12.93. LB*)

  IMPORT SIO;

  VAR a, b, res: CARDINAL;
BEGIN
  a := SIO.GetInt();
  b := SIO.GetInt();

  VAR                                              (*start of block*)
    x: CARDINAL := a;        (*x is "born" and is initialized to the value of a*)
    y: CARDINAL := b;        (*y is "born" and is initialized to the value of b*)
  BEGIN                              (*x and y can be modified by the algorithm*)
    WHILE x # y DO
     IF x > y THEN x := x – y ELSE y := y – x END;
    END;
    res := x;                    (*copies the result to the global variable res*)
  END;                               (*end of nested block, x und y disappear*)

  SIO.PutInt(res);
END GCD.
```

Example 9.2: *Nested blocks*

As an example we will re-implement the already familiar algorithm of
Euclid (Example 5.13 from page 100). To be able to use this algorithm in
a larger context, we need to make a copy of the variables whose greatest
common divisor we calculate. Thus we can prevent the algorithm from
destroying the original values, which we might need later. For this purpose,
Example 5.13 declares two additional global variables, (x and y), which
can then be modified in the algorithm. Variables x and y are only of *local*
importance for the computation, however. Thus it would be advisable to
restrict their scope and lifetime to their actual application. We can achieve
exactly that with a block (Example 9.2). Variables x and y are declared only
in the inner block. When program execution enters the block (reaches the
block's BEGIN), storage is allocated for these variables; when we exit the
block (reach the block's END) this storage is deallocated again, so that both
variables disappear. We store the result in the global variable res.

Blocks also conceal a trap! In the above example, if we had erroneously
declared the variable res in the enclosed block, then this new incarnation
of res would temporarily eclipse the global declaration (Example 9.3). The
result would be assigned to the local res, and the global variable res would
never receive the GCD. The underlying cause of this error is that our program communicates with its environment only through global variables. It
reads the input data from global variables and stores the result in a global
variable as well.

```
VAR
   a, b, res: CARDINAL;
BEGIN
   ⋮
   VAR                                              (*start of block*)
      x: CARDINAL := a; y: CARDINAL := b;
      res: CARDINAL;                        (*res is erroneously redeclared*)
   BEGIN
      WHILE x # y DO
         IF x > y THEN x:= x – y ELSE y:= y – x END;
      END;
         res:= x;                    (*result stored in LOCAL (!) variable res*)
      END;                         (*end of block: local res disappears*)
   ⋮
```

Example 9.3: *Error: block stores result in local variable*

9.2 Procedures and functions

Blocks alone do not suffice to allow us to assemble programs from smaller parts. We need to complement the concept. First, we need to be able to *name* blocks in order to be able to *activate* them repeatedly at different locations. Second, the transfer of input and output values should not occur via ad hoc copying of global variables to local ones and vice versa, but through a well-defined mechanism – *parameter passing*. These concepts are available in most imperative programming languages in the form of *procedures* and *functions*, and they are so basic that the imperative programming languages are often called *procedure-oriented*.

In practice, procedures serve to solve a subproblem of a program and to provide this solution to the rest of the program. We have already used some built-in procedures and functions such as INC and ROUND. We have also repeatedly employed the procedures of the module SIO. In this section we will learn how to define our own procedures and functions.

Mathematical functions

In Section 3.4 we noted that the concept of functions in computer science closely resembles that of mathematics. In mathematics we write $y = f(x)$. That is, y is the value that results when we apply the function f to x. We also say that f is a *mapping* of the domain of x onto the range of y. If there are multiple parameters, then we must take the Cartesian product of all parameter types. If $z = f(x, y)$, then f is the mapping of all pairs (x, y) (with x and y from the respective domains) onto the range of z. Naturally the definition of f is not repeated with each application; we specify it once and thereafter "know" it (compare the trigonometric functions that are frequently used in geometry).

Functions are implemented in many programming languages through the construct *procedure* or *function*. They have names and can be parameterized. We can understand them completely in the sense of their mathematical definition. They map the parameter types onto the result type. However, there are also significant differences between theoretical functions and practical, executable procedures: Procedures take time to execute; they can even run endlessly (if they contain an endless loop), or they can crash and thus never reach their normal end. Furthermore, a procedure can have *side effects* (compare Section 9.3.4) in addition to its actual computation (such as reading from the keyboard buffer, if it contains an invocation of SIO.GetChar(), thus changing the state of the keyboard buffer; two "identical" invocations of SIO.GetChar() do not return the same results!).

Procedures and functions in Modula-3

Procedures in Modula-3 are *named, parameterized blocks*. Syntactically, functions are a special case of procedures, which is why they are often called *function procedures*. Procedures that return a value as their result (in the sense that $\sin(\pi)$ returns the value 0) are called *functions*. In the following we speak generally of procedures unless we need to emphasize this difference. We employ the expression *pure procedures* (or *proper procedure*)to emphasize that a procedure is *not* a function.

Formal and actual parameters

First let us examine Example 9.4. The Euclidean algorithm is now defined as a function procedure named Euclid. The procedure must first be *declared*; this specifies its name, the *formal parameters* and a block. The formal parameters serve as place holders for various parameter values within the block that defines the algorithm. The list of formal parameters, enclosed in parentheses, is specified after the procedure name. In Example 9.4 x and y are formal parameters of type CARDINAL. This defines the procedure for arbitrary CARDINAL values. The type of the result (also CARDINAL) is specified after a colon at the end of the parameter list. The value of the result is returned with the RETURN statement.

A procedure declaration, like all other declarations, is only the static explanation of a structure. Declaration does not activate the statements of the block. Activation occurs through a *procedure call* (or *procedure invocation*). The assignment res:= Euclid(a, b) effects the evaluation of the expression on the right side, the statement part of the Euclidean algorithm.The

```
VAR
   a, b: CARDINAL;                         (*a and b will be actual parameters*)
   res: CARDINAL;                          (*res will store the result*)

   PROCEDURE Euclid(x, y: CARDINAL): CARDINAL =      (*Procedure signature*)
   BEGIN
      WHILE x # y DO
         IF x > y THEN x:= x – y ELSE y:= y – x END;
      END;
      RETURN x                             (*return result as function value*)
   END Euclid;
   ⋮
BEGIN                   (*statement part of a block in which the declaration is defined*)
   ⋮
                                                   (*a and b are set*)
   res:= Euclid(a, b);        (*function invocation with actual parameters a and b*)
   ⋮
```

Example 9.4: *Function procedure*

formal parameters x and y are *replaced* by the values of the corresponding *actual parameters* a and b. Finally, the result is stored in the variable res.

9.2.1 Procedure declaration

Procedures are *declared* once. Here we specify the exact algorithm for which the procedure stands. This is similar to mathematics: The sine function was defined once, and this allows us to use it illimitably often.

A procedure declaration resembles that of a constant: The declaration establishes a fixed bond between a name and a block (instead of a literal). As we will soon see (Section 9.7), we can also declare *procedure types* and thus variables of a procedure type.

> Many programming languages allow only the definition of procedure constants. Thus these languages do not distinguish procedure constants, types and variables, as they offer only procedures. The availability of procedure types and procedure variables raises the expressive power of a programming language significantly.

A procedure declaration consists of a *procedure head* and a *procedure body*. The procedure head consists of the procedure name and the *signature*. The signature contains the list of formal parameters, and for a function the return type as well. For formal parameters we specify their name, type, *passing mode* and *default value* (see Sections 9.3 and 9.5).

The scope of a formal parameter is the block of the procedure in whose signature it is defined. The identifiers of the formal parameters are invisible outside this procedure.

The procedure body consists of a block that defines the actual algorithm of the procedure. This algorithm is executed when the procedure is *called.*

Syntax of procedure declarations

$Declaration_{13}$ $= ProcedureHead_{18}$ ["=" $Block_{12}$ $Ident_{89}$] ";" | $\cdots$.
$ProcedureHead_{18}$ = "PROCEDURE" $Ident_{89}$ $Signature_{19}$.
$Signature_{19}$ = "(" $Formals_{20}$ ")" [":" $Type_{48}$] ["RAISES" $Raises_{22}$].
$Formals_{20}$ = [$Formal_{21}$ { ";" $Formal_{21}$ } [";"]].
$Formal_{21}$ = ["VALUE" | "VAR" | "READONLY"]
                   $IDList_{87}$ ":" $Type_{48}$ | $IDList_{87}$ ":=" $ConstExpr_{65}$ |
                   $IDList_{87}$ ":" $Type_{48}$ ":=" $ConstExpr_{65}$.

The syntax of declaration of procedure constants is a refinement of the already specified declaration syntax (Section 3.4.4). The procedure body can be omitted – but this is permitted only in INTERFACES (see Section 10).

A pure procedure declaration takes the following general form (whereby *formal parameter$_i$* stands for a parameter's name, type, passing mode and default value, joined in the syntactical unit $Formal_{21}$):

PROCEDURE *Name(formal parameter$_1$; $\cdots$ formal parameter$_n$)* =
    local declarations
BEGIN
    statement sequence
END *Name*;

The identifier after the keyword PROCEDURE and after the END of the procedure block must be the same; this serves as the name of the procedure. The general form of a function procedure is:

PROCEDURE *Name(formal Par$_1$; $\cdots$ formal Par$_n$): return type* =
    local declarations
BEGIN
    statement sequence;
    RETURN *return value*
END *Name*;

Syntactically, functions differ from pure procedures in that their signature specifies a *return type* . This can be any type except an open array (see Section 11.2.3). It is written after the formal parameter list, separated by a colon. Functions must contain at least one RETURN statement that specifies the result, i.e., the return value of the function. The *return value* is an expression of type *return type*.

The syntax indicates that the list of formal parameters can be empty. The declaration of a parameterless procedure takes the following form: PROCEDURE *Name*() = ⋯ END *Name*. A parameterless procedure is still more powerful than a simple block because it has a *name* and can thus be invoked repeatedly.

> You might wonder whether the empty parentheses after the name are absolutely necessary. They are necessary because we must distinguish a procedure declaration (or a procedure call) from a procedure identifier. A procedure identifier without parentheses stands for a procedure constant or for a procedure variable; a procedure identifier with parentheses is a procedure declaration or call.

The RAISES clause in the signature is treated in Chapter 15. All other elements of the signature are handled in detail in the following sections of this chapter.

9.2.2 Procedure invocation

We invoke a procedure by using the procedure name in our program. The actual parameters are specified in parentheses after the name. The invocation of a pure procedure is a *statement* (the call statement). By contrast, a function is invoked in the evaluation of an *expression* (compare Section 7.1.1) of which it is an operand.

Syntax of the procedure call

$\text{CallStmt}_{26} = \text{Expr}_{66} \ ''('' \ [\ \text{Actual}_{47} \ \{ \ '',''\ \text{Actual}_{47} \ \} \ ] \ '')''.$

$\vdots$

$\text{E7}_{73} \qquad = \text{E8}_{74} \ \{ \ \text{Selector}_{78} \ \}.$
$\text{E8}_{74} \qquad = \text{Ident}_{89} \ | \ \cdots$
$\text{Selector}_{78} = ''('' \ [\ \text{Actual}_{47} \ \{ \ '',''\ \text{Actual}_{47} \ \} \ ] \ '')'' \ | \ \cdots .$
$\text{Actual}_{47} \quad = [\ \text{Ident}_{89} \ '':='' \ ] \ \text{Expr}_{66} \ | \ \text{Type}_{48}.$

The Expr_{66} in the call statement (CallStmt_{26}) must finally yield an identifier (of the procedure constant or variable to be invoked). A function call is always an expression; the procedure name derives from E8_{74} and the list of actual parameters in this case as Selector_{78}. For both kinds of invocation, the actual parameters are specified in the same way.

The general form of the procedure call is:

procedure name(*actual parameter*$_1$, ⋯ *actual parameter*$_n$)

The procedure call causes the *activation* of the block of the invoked procedure: The formal parameters are replaced by the corresponding actual parameter (Sections 9.3 and 9.5 explain how). The local data of the procedure block are created; i.e., storage space is allocated for them. Control then passes from the location of the procedure call to the statement part of the activated block (after the BEGIN of the invoked procedure).

The invocation of a parameterless procedure takes the form: *procedure name*() (e.g., SIO.GetChar()).

> The empty parentheses are necessary for the same reason as with the declaration.

End of a procedure execution

A procedure terminates when it reaches either its END or a RETURN statement. A RETURN statement immediately ends execution of the procedure. On termination of a procedure all its local variables disappear (their storage is deallocated).

Syntax of the Return statement

ReturnStmt$_{36}$ = "RETURN" [Expr$_{66}$].

Function procedures *must* terminate with a RETURN statement because this specifies the return value. Pure procedures can also be terminated with RETURN, yet we recommend *avoiding* this practice! This makes the procedure a block with multiple exits. This significantly complicates validating such blocks compared to procedures with a single exit. For a function we also recommend a *single* RETURN statement as the last statement of the block. Recursive functions often have multiple exits; the advice does not apply here (see Section 12).

After termination of an invoked procedure, control flow continues at the location after the procedure call.

Invocation chain

A procedure can call another procedure, which can call a further procedure, etc. This produces a chain of procedure calls. The last member of the chain is the procedure that is active; the others are *suspended* (see Figure 9.5). A suspended procedure continues execution after the return of control from the procedure it invoked; it has not completed its work. Therefore all its local variables are still "alive"; the block defining the algorithm of the procedure has not terminated.

The local data regions of invoked procedures are allocated sequentially, and only the last one can be accessed. On a return from a procedure call, the last data region is deallocated, and the next data region becomes accessible. This corresponds to a desktop on which the last files to be deposited

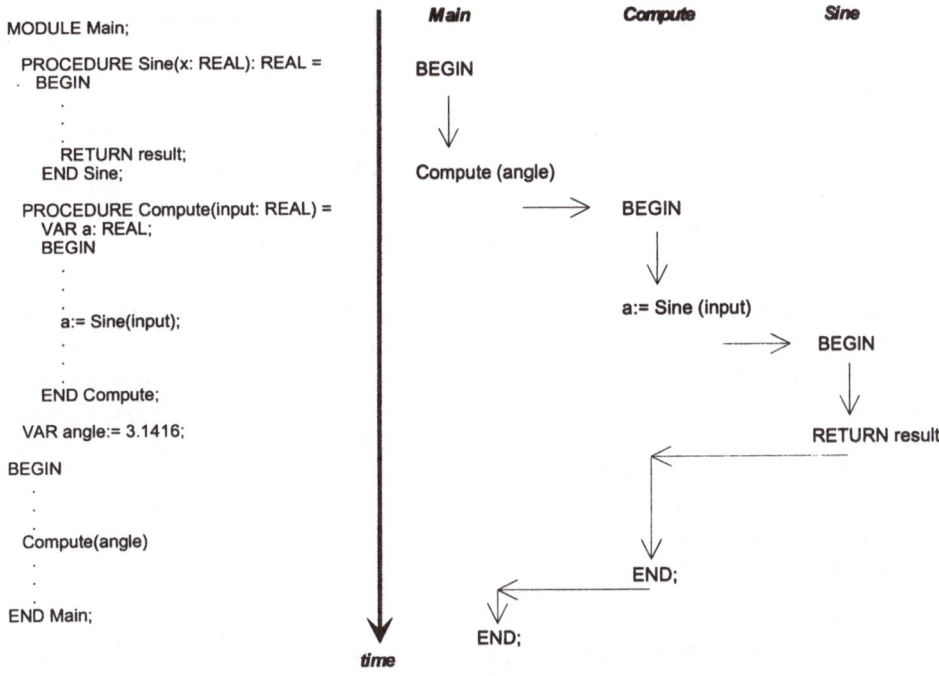

```
MODULE Main;

  PROCEDURE Sine(x: REAL): REAL =
  . BEGIN
      .
      .
      .
    RETURN result;
  END Sine;
  PROCEDURE Compute(input: REAL) =
      VAR a: REAL;
      BEGIN
      .
      .
    a:= Sine(input);
      .
      .
  END Compute;
  VAR angle:= 3.1416;
BEGIN
  .
  .
  Compute(angle)
  .
  .
END Main;
```

Figure 9.5: *Program branches via procedure calls*

are processed first. Such storage structure is called a *stack*. The local data of the procedures (including parameters) are normally stored according to the stack principle, in the *invocation stack*.

We see that procedures (in contrast to simple blocks) can change the control flow of a program. The statements of a procedure are executed only on invocation, and through multiple invocations they can be executed repeatedly. The entire dynamic flow of a program becomes harder to follow. Therefore it is important that we be certain of the correctness of individual procedures and that we clearly specify their semantics. Then we can view a procedure call as a single complex statement whose correctness has been verified (or at least tested) and whose semantics is known.

9.3 Modes of parameter passing

What kinds of parameter passing do we need? We have seen that we can communicate between blocks via variables of the enclosing block. But we have also seen that this is unclear and error-prone. The concept of the procedure makes it possible to regulate this communication much better. With

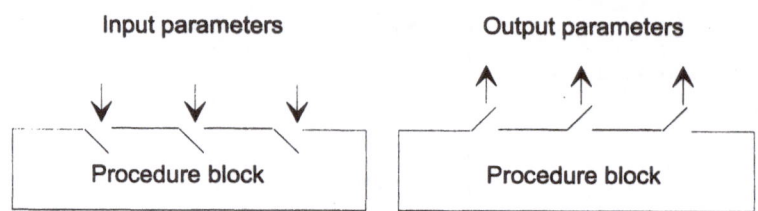

Figure 9.6: *The most important kinds of parameters*

the specification of the parameters in the signature, we provide the door to the procedure and so regulate communication. The parameter type corresponds to the size of the door: A Boolean door is very tiny, allowing only *true* and *false* as values. A door of type INTEGER has a normal size, and for RECORD or ARRAY parameters we need a veritable gate. By specifying the mode of parameter passing, we regulate the direction of communication. Some doors open only in one direction, either as entries or exits, while others open in both directions. We categorize the parameter passing modes exactly according to this metaphor (Figure 9.6):

- *Input parameters*
  These parameters provide a procedure with input values. The actual parameter of an input parameter must be an expression that is evaluated directly before the procedure call and is assigned as initial value of the corresponding formal parameter. Thus far our examples have used only this kind of parameter.

- *Output parameters*
  With this kind of parameter a procedure can return a result to the invoking procedure. Its value is undefined at the time of the procedure call; it receives a value within the invoked procedure. The value assigned to the output parameter in the invoked procedure is also accessible in the context of the invoking procedure.

- *Input/output parameters*
  These parameters combine both of the above attributes: They receive a well-defined input value from the invoking procedure and a well-defined output value from the invoked procedure. Input/output parameters are like industrial products that pass through different stations in their processing: Each station receives the product in some state and modifies this state accordingly.

Modula-3 provides modes of parameter passing – as in most procedural programming languages – with a somewhat different categorization (Figure 9.7) that rely greatly on their technical implementation of parameter passing; these are discussed in the following sections.

Some programming languages (e.g., Ada) define the kinds of parameters exactly in the above categories.

9.3.1 Value parameter

We use value parameters to implement input parameters. In the list of formal parameters of a procedure declaration we can write the keyword VALUE before a value parameter. For this kind of parameter passing, we can also omit the keyword since this is the default (see Section 9.5).

Consider a value parameter to be a local variable that receives its initial value from the invoking procedure. The actual parameter is an *expression* whose type must be *assignment compatible* with the formal parameter. This value appears in the formal parameter as soon as the procedure begins to execute. The invoked procedure can then modify the formal parameter at will; changes remain local to the invoked procedure.

We can imagine this as follows (Figure 9.7): If the actual parameter for a value parameter is a variable, then we pass a copy of the contents of the container (the "drawer"). The invoked procedure can do with it what it wants; the original contents are not touched.

9.3.2 Variable parameters

Variable parameters implement input/output parameters. In the procedure declaration we write the keyword VAR before the formal variable parameter.

For a variable parameter the actual parameter must be a (writeable) *variable* of the *same* type. On invocation, the formal parameter is replaced by a *reference* to this variable. This makes the actual parameter directly accessible in the invoked procedure. Every modification of the formal parameter is immediately effective in the actual parameter.

Metaphorically, the invoking procedure allows the invoked procedure access to the container, the "drawer", of the actual parameter. Through the formal parameter the invoked procedure can directly access the drawer of the actual parameter. Therefore every modification immediately affects the actual parameter.

A pure output parameter would mean that the invoking procedure allows access to the drawer, but first removes all valuables (for the invoked procedure, the contents are undefined). A procedure signature does not unambiguously reveal whether a variable parameter is used only as output parameter. This can lead to semantic errors if, e.g., the invoking procedure fails to provide an initial value for an input/output

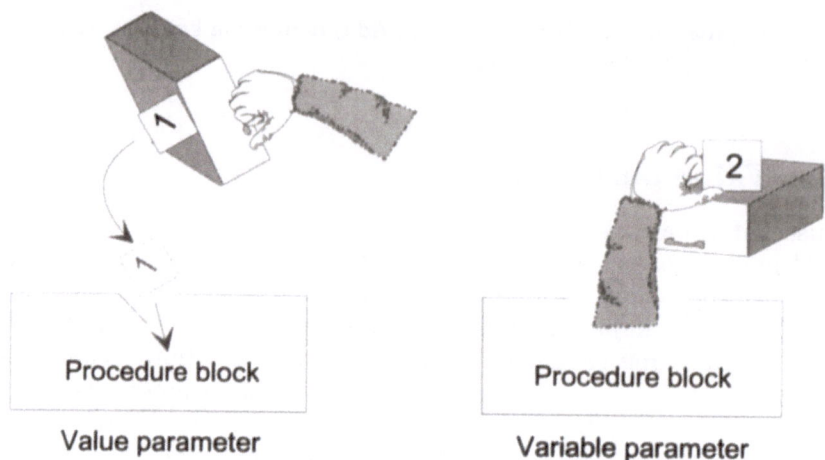

Figure 9.7: *Value and variable parameters*

parameter. This problem can be avoided by careful documentation (e.g., as commentary in the signature).

We should also be careful never to use variable parameters for pure input parameters. This would be like handing over our whole wallet at the cash register instead of just paying the appropriate amount. Given boundless trust, this can work well, but in general it is better not to go this route.

9.3.3   Read-only parameters

We employ read-only parameters for large input parameters. If we want to pass a whole "cabinet" with numerous "drawers", (composite parameters such as arrays and records), then copying the entire contents is quite time-consuming. Therefore we prefer to allow the invoked procedure to look directly into the drawer, but not to modify anything. Here we write the keyword READONLY before the corresponding formal parameters in the procedure declaration.

On invocation a read-only parameter receives an actual initial value – like a value parameter. Within the invoked procedure this value can only be read. A read-only parameter, similar to a variable parameter, is usually replaced by a reference to the actual parameter. However, since no modification is permitted, operations within the invoked procedure have no access to the actual parameter.

Whether the replacement of a read-only parameter occurs as value or as reference depends on the actual parameter. If the actual parameter is a variable, then it is passed as with a variable parameter, as a reference to the variable. Otherwise the read-only parameter behaves like a value parameter.

We must keep in mind this parameter passing technique; otherwise we can easily fall in a trap: For example, a procedure might have two parameters, one read-only input parameter and one output parameter that is declared as a variable parameter. If we pass the same variable to the input parameter as to the output parameter, then the procedure writes to the variable that it simultaneously reads as input – which can have unforeseeable consequences. If the input parameter were declared as a value parameter, there would be no problem in passing the same variable for both parameters – the input parameter is only read as a local copy. See the example of matrix multiplication (Section 9.3.5).

9.3.4 Information transfer via global variables

The same applies for blocks of procedure declarations as for nested blocks in the statement part: All identifiers declared in the enclosing blocks are *visible* (unless we have redeclared the identifier). In procedures we can access variables of outer blocks just as in other nested blocks. In Example 9.2 the nested block accesses the variables a, b and res of the outer block. Likewise the procedure Euclid in Example 9.4 could access these variables. We call this *accessing global variables*. Modifying a global variable causes a *side effect* – the procedure modifies not only its variable parameters, but also additional variables.

Although we theoretically could implement input/output parameters as global access, this is usually poor practice:

- Our procedures are no longer building blocks with fixed input and output because now they depend on additional variables. A basic requirement of structured programming (Section 3.1) was to create building blocks whose correctness can be checked independently of others.

  Procedures that access global data cannot be reused anywhere except in the context where they are declared (for the global variables are only there).

- The readability of programs declines significantly because the procedure signature alone no longer indicates the inputs and outputs of the procedure.

- Two identical invocations of the same procedure generally lead to different results.

For these reasons, information transfer via global variables between an invoking procedure and an invoked procedure should be avoided. But why is it permitted at all? There are cases where access to global variables is actually necessary, namely to represent the hidden state space of a module – the invoking procedure does not know these variables. We will see examples in Section 10.

9.3.5   Comparing the kinds of parameters

Euclidean algorithm with procedures

Example 9.8 presents the Euclidean algorithm in a program. All logically distinct subtasks are in separate procedures. The familiar function Euclid has two value parameters of type CARDINAL and returns a CARDINAL value. The actual parameters no longer have to be stored in local variables to protect the original values from destruction, as in Example 9.2. Passing value parameters has the same effect.

Functions return only a single value. Therefore we did not define the procedure Input, which reads a pair of numbers, as a function. We return the two numbers as variable parameters. Naturally, we could have defined a function that returns one number and then called it twice, or we could have chosen a record as the function value, in the form:

```
TYPE Result = RECORD x, y: INTEGER END;
PROCEDURE Input(): Result = · · ·
```

In this case the solution would not have been justified because it is more complex and there is no reason to combine the variables in a record.

We could have chosen the following pathological solution:

```
PROCEDURE Input(VAR x: CARDINAL): CARDINAL =
```

Here the first number is returned as a variable parameter, the second as a function value. The unsuitability of this asymmetrical solution should be obvious. If we need to return more than one value, then all result values should be defined as variable parameters.

We generally recommend equipping functions only with value parameters!

The procedure Output handles the output of the result, whose value it receives as a value parameter. The parameterless function Terminate tests whether the program should be terminated (i.e., whether the user inputs a character that is not a digit). Note that SIO.LookAhead waits until some character is available in the input stream.

The parameterless procedure Compute combines the control over input and output as well as the computation of the GCD. Note that thanks to this procedure our module no longer contains any global variables. Thus we

```
MODULE Procedures EXPORTS Main;                          (*3.12.93. LB*)

  IMPORT SIO;

  PROCEDURE Euclid(x, y: CARDINAL): CARDINAL =    (*function, value parameters*)
  BEGIN
    WHILE x # y DO
      IF x > y THEN x:= x – y ELSE y:= y – x END;
    END;
    RETURN x                     (*return greatest common divisor as function value*)
  END Euclid;

  PROCEDURE Input(VAR x, y: CARDINAL) =         (*procedure with VAR parameters*)
  BEGIN
    x:= SIO.GetInt(); y:= SIO.GetInt();                   (*return values in x and y*)
  END Input;

  PROCEDURE Output(res: CARDINAL) =           (*procedure with value parameters*)
  BEGIN
    SIO.PutText("Greatest common divisor = ");
    SIO.PutInt(res); SIO.NI();                             (*output value of res*)
  END Output;

  PROCEDURE Terminate(): BOOLEAN =               (*parameterless function*)
  CONST Digits = SET OF CHAR{'0' .. '9'};
  BEGIN
    RETURN NOT (SIO.LookAhead() IN Digits);              (*TRUE if not a digit*)
  END Terminate;

  PROCEDURE Compute() =                           (*parameterless procedure*)
  VAR a, b: CARDINAL;                                (*a and b for input values*)
  BEGIN
    Input(a, b);            (*after invocation, a and b contain the entered numbers*)
    Output(Euclid(a, b));          (*value from Euclid as actual paramter for Output*)
  END Compute;

BEGIN                                        (*statement part of module block*)
  SIO.PutText("Greatest common divisor using Euclidean method\n" &
              "Please enter a pair of numbers, or anything else to quit\n");
  REPEAT Compute() UNTIL Terminate()
END Procedures.
```

Example 9.8: *Procedures and functions with various parameters*

handle all the communication between procedures via parameter passing. The scopes are all small and distinct. The statement part of the module is very simple: Apart from outputting a greeting, it contains only a loop that controls the repetition of computation.

Matrix multiplication

Example 9.9 implements the initialization and multiplication of matrices. The procedure Init returns an initialized array (with rather arbitrary values) in a variable parameter. The matrix looks like this:

$$\begin{pmatrix} 2 & 3 & 4 & 5 \\ 3 & 4 & 5 & 6 \\ 4 & 5 & 6 & 7 \\ 5 & 6 & 7 & 8 \end{pmatrix}$$

The procedure Init is called twice to initialize arrays a and b. We could have defined Init as a function with the signature:

PROCEDURE Init(): Matrix =

In this case, however, the use of a variable parameter is more efficient (the function variant would need to copy the entire matrix from the local data region of Init to the invoking procedure).

Procedure Mul receives the arrays to be multiplied via the read-only parameters x and y and returns the result in variable parameter z. The elements of z are computed according to the usual rules of matrix multiplication:

$$z_{i,j} = \sum_{k=1}^{N} x_{i,k} \, y_{k,j}$$

Through the use of FIRST and LAST, the procedure is kept so general that it can be used not only for $N \times N$ matrices. However, it does not test whether the fundamental prerequisite of matrix multiplication is fulfilled: (Lines(x) = Lines(z) ∧ Columns(x) = Lines(y) ∧ Columns(y) = Columns(z)). The interested reader can extend the procedure Mul accordingly. The result is output with the imported procedure MatrixIO.WriteMatrix(r):

```
54    68    82    96
68    86   104   122
82   104   126   148
96   122   148   174
```

Read-only parameters conceal a trap! If we invoke a procedure using the same variable as actual parameter for both a read-only and a variable parameter, the result is unpredictable. The reason is referential substitution. Normally this does not cause an error because the compiler assures that a read-only parameter is not modified. But if the same variable in the invoking procedure serves as actual parameter for a variable parameter, then the compiler is tricked:

```
MODULE MatrixMult EXPORTS Main;                              (*27.10.93. LB*)

  IMPORT MatrixIO;

  CONST
    N    = 4;
  TYPE
    Matrix = ARRAY [1 .. N], [1 .. N] OF INTEGER;

  VAR
    a, b, r: Matrix;                     (*r: result; a and b to be multiplied*)

  PROCEDURE Init(VAR x: Matrix) =                        (*initializes x*)
  BEGIN
    FOR i:= FIRST(x) TO LAST(x) DO
      FOR j:= FIRST(x[FIRST(x)]) TO LAST(x[FIRST(x)]) DO
        x[i, j]:= i + j;                                      (*x_{i, j} = i + j*)
      END;
    END;
  END Init;

  PROCEDURE Mul (READONLY x, y: Matrix; VAR z: Matrix) =
  BEGIN
    FOR i:= FIRST(z) TO LAST(z) DO                                  (*rows*)
      FOR j:= FIRST(z[FIRST(z)]) TO LAST(z[FIRST(z)]) DO        (*columns*)
        WITH sum = z[i, j] DO                   (*sum is short for z[i, j]*)
          sum:= 0;
          FOR k:= FIRST(y) TO LAST(y) DO                (*row_i × column_j*)
            INC(sum, x[i, k] * y[k, j]);       (*z_{i, j} = \sum_k x_{i, k} * y_{k, j}*)
          END; (*FOR k*)
        END; (*WITH sum = z[i, j]*)
      END; (*FOR i*)
    END; (*FOR j*)
  END Mul;

BEGIN                                                   (*statement part*)
  Init(a); Init(b);
  Mul(a, b, r);                                             (*r:= a * b*)
  MatrixIO.WriteMatrix(r);
END MatrixMult.
```

Example 9.9: Procedures with complex parameters

The procedure views the same variable through two "windows"; through one it is read-only, but through the other modifiable.

Assume that we write the following on invocation:

  Mul(a, b, b)

This is an error because b would serve as both read-only and variable parameter.

Parameters x and y could have been value parameters, but this would diminish the efficiency of the program. This can be necessary, however, if we want to transfer the result of the multiplication to array b (or a). The invocation Mul(a, b, b) would only be correct if were to change the signature of procedure Mul accordingly:

  PROCEDURE Mul (x, y: Matrix; VAR z: Matrix)

Another programming error ensues if we specify the input parameters as variable parameters:

  PROCEDURE Mul (VAR x, y, z: Matrix)

In this case the invocation Mul(a, b, b) would also lead to unpredictable results. The original invocation Mul(a, b, r) would continue to work, but we must consider the signature incorrect at any rate.

9.4   Identifying the procedures

A question arises: How do we decide which subtasks "earn" their own procedure? For example, does it make sense to write such tiny procedures as Input or Terminate in Example 9.8? Invoking a procedure does involve some overhead; parameter passing, invocation and return all cost time and storage. Would numerous small procedures not encumber our program?

We generally recommend deciding less on the basis of the absolute size of the logical task. The procedure Input is certainly quite simple; in this specific case we could have integrated the two statements directly into the procedure Compute. However, it is clear that input, computation and output are decidedly different tasks. Thus we prefer to distinguish them syntactically. This becomes especially clear if we want to modify the program later. For example, if we decide to extend the input procedure to assure that Input returns only positive numbers, then we could carry out this modification *locally* in this procedure. All other parts of the program, including all invocations of Input, remain untouched. This is a very important advantage.

As always, we can exaggerate this decomposition into procedures. A program in which most procedures consist of 1-2 lines is certainly extreme.

The early recognition of logically different subtasks is a characteristic of good design. Very large procedures are unfavorable at any rate, yet overly small procedures should not be the rule either. The deciding criterion should be the internal logic of the problem.

9.5   Name, type and default value of a parameter

Declaring the name and type of a formal parameter closely resembles a variable declaration. As the syntax shows, formal parameters can be initialized on declaration; in this context we call the initial value the *default value*.

> The term default is used in various contexts in computer science and elsewhere. The general meaning can be explained in the context of medication prescriptions. A package often bears the instruction: "If not otherwise prescribed by the doctor, take ..." What follows is the default value in the sense of computer science.

The default value of a formal parameter applies if a procedure call fails to specify a corresponding actual parameter. In this case the default value substitutes for the missing actual parameter. If the corresponding actual parameter is specified, the default value has no effect. Default values are not permitted for variable parameters.

> This restriction makes sense: A variable parameter takes effect in the context of the invoking procedure, and in the procedure declaration we cannot make general assumptions about the invoking procedure. As with medication that must be administered by the doctor, the default "If not otherwise prescribed by the doctor, take ..." makes no sense.

Identifiers of the same type (and same default value) can be combined in a list, similar to variable declaration. Variable parameters require specification of a type. For other kinds of parameters, either type or default can be omitted, but not both. If type is omitted, the type of the parameter is derived from the default value. If both are specified, then the default value must be in the range of the type. We suggest avoiding implicit type specification (i.e., omitting type specification) here as with variable declarations!

Actual parameters

The general form of a procedure call is:

P(*actual Parameter$_1$,* $\cdots$ *actual parameter$_n$*)

P stands for a procedure expression – normally the name of a procedure constant or procedure variable. The actual parameters are a list of expressions separated by commas (Section 9.2.2). The list can be empty, but the parentheses must always be specified. Similar to a record constructor (see Section 8.2.2), the actual parameters can be specified *positionally* or *by name*.

- *Positional specification*
  For positional specification the actual parameters replace the formal ones one by one: the first actual parameter replaces the first formal parameter, the second actual parameter replaces the second formal parameter, etc. (as we have passed all parameters thus far). The list of actual parameters can be shorter than that of the formal parameters, in which case the remaining actual parameters must have a corresponding default value.

- *Specification by name*
  The specification of actual parameters by name syntactically resembles an assignment. The sequence of specification is not relevant. The formal parameters without a specified value must have a corresponding default value.

- *Mixed specification*
  Mixing the above two kinds of specification requires specifying the positional parameters first. We generally recommend avoiding mixed specification!

The general pattern for invocation is:

$$Name(actual_1, actual_2, \cdots)$$

or

$$Name(formal_1 := actual_1, formal_2 := actual_2, \cdots)$$

The following invocations are equivalent and all match the signature of the Euclid procedure of Example 9.4:

Euclid(a, b) $\equiv$ Euclid(x:= a, y:= b) $\equiv$ Euclid(y:= b, x:= a)

9.6   Eval statement

For functions that have a side effect, it might be that we want to invoke only the side effect and not the result. Thus for various systems we often find outputs like this: "Press any key" (e.g., after insertion of the wrong diskette, the system waits until the disk is replaced). The program does not care *what* the user inputs, but only *whether* a (any) key has been pressed.

For the above, not infrequent case, Modula-3 provides the EVAL statement. It evaluates the subsequent expression (normally a function call) and discards the result.

Syntax of the Eval statement

$EvalStmt_{29}$ = "EVAL" $Expr_{66}$.

We can implement the above example in Modula-3 as follows:

⋮
```
SIO.PutText("Press any key to continue");
EVAL SIO.GetChar();              (*waits until a key is pressed*)
```
⋮

Example 9.10 is program 5.5 (page 94), in which primitive calculator functions entered at the keyboard can be computed, re-implemented here with the help of procedures. The procedure GetOperation handles input of the operands and the operator. It contains two nested procedures. Skip skips any whitespace (blanks, tabs, linefeeds). Op reads the operator. If the input begins with a non-numeric character or if the operator is typed improperly, the program terminates.

9.7 Procedure types

Procedures can also be defined as types. Procedure types allow us to define variables of a procedure type. Then we can assign various actual procedures to a procedure variable. This allows us to bind an algorithm *dynamically* to a name. This becomes quite exciting when we use *parameters* of procedure types, which means that we can pass a complete algorithm to a procedure. We define procedure types with a signature.

Syntax of procedure types

$Type_{48}$ = $ProcedureType_{53}$ | $\cdots$
$ProcedureType_{53}$ = "PROCEDURE" $Signature_{19}$.

9.7.1 Operations with procedures

Assignment

An expression of a procedure type can be assigned – in accordance with the usual rules of assignment – to a procedure variable if the value of the expression is in the range of the type of the variable.

```
MODULE Operations EXPORTS Main;                              (*13.12.94. LB*)
  IMPORT SIO;
  TYPE Op = {Add, Sub, Mul, Div, Mod, Halt};        (*arithmetic operations + Halt*)

  PROCEDURE GetOperation(VAR x, y: INTEGER; VAR op: Op) =    (*reads operation*)
  CONST Digit = SET OF CHAR{'0' .. '9'};                     (*set of digits*)

    PROCEDURE Skip() =                                    (*skips whitespace*)
    CONST Blanks = SET OF CHAR{' ', '\t', '\n'};              (*whitespace*)
    BEGIN
      WHILE SIO.LookAhead() IN Blanks DO EVAL SIO.GetChar() END
    END Skip;

    PROCEDURE GetOp(): Op =             (*reads and converts operator character*)
    BEGIN
      Skip();
      CASE SIO.GetChar() OF
        | '+' => op:= Op.Add; | '–' => op:= Op.Sub; | '*' => op:= Op.Mul;
        | 'D', 'd' => op:= Op.Div; | 'M', 'm' => op:= Op.Mod;
      ELSE op:= Op.Halt;
      END; (*CASE operator*)
      RETURN op
    END GetOp;

  BEGIN                                                       (*GetOperation*)
    Skip();
    IF NOT (SIO.LookAhead() IN Digit) THEN
      op:= Op.Halt;                       (*input does not begin with digit => Halt*)
    ELSE
      x:= SIO.GetInt(); op:= GetOp(); y:= SIO.GetInt();          (*read operation*)
    END; (*IF NOT ...*)
  END GetOperation;

  VAR x, y, z: INTEGER; op: Op;
BEGIN
  SIO.PutText("Arithmetic operations in the form x op y\n");
  REPEAT
    GetOperation(x, y, op);
    IF op # Op.Halt THEN
      CASE op OF
        | Op.Add => z:= x + y; | Op.Sub => z:= x – y; | Op.Mul => z:= x * y;
        | Op.Div => z:= x DIV y; | Op.Mod => z:= x MOD y;
      END; (*CASE op*)
      SIO.PutText(" = "); SIO.PutInt(z, 1); SIO.Nl();
    END; (*IF op*)
  UNTIL op = Op.Halt;
END Operations.
```

Example 9.10: Simple calculator functions

```
   ⋮
TYPE Proc = PROCEDURE (t: TEXT := "I am more equal\n");

  PROCEDURE P (t: TEXT := "I am even more equal\n") =
  BEGIN
    SIO.PutText(t);
  END P;

VAR a: Proc;

BEGIN
  a:= P;                       (*P has a type different from a, but is assignabe to a*)
  IF a = P THEN SIO.PutText("The two are equal\n") END;        (*a = P is TRUE*)
  a();                                           (*outputs "I am more equal"*)
  P();                                      (*outputs "I am even more equal"*)
   ⋮
```

Example 9.11: *Relationship of default, type and value*

Before enumerating the rules of assignment compatibility, let us introduce the predefined constant NIL, whose type is compatible with any procedure type and whose value means "no procedure". Beyond procedures, NIL is also defined on reference (pointer) types (see Chapter 11).

An expression of a procedure type PE can be assigned to a procedure variable pv if either PE = NIL or the following conditions apply:

- The number of parameters of PE and pv is equal, and the corresponding parameters have the same type and are passed in the same way. Note that the name and default value of the parameters need not agree.

- Both have the same result type or no result type.

- The set of exceptions generated by PE is a subset of the set of exceptions of pv (see Section 15).

If these rules are fulfilled, we say that type PE is *covered* by the type of variable pv. More simply stated, if the signatures of two procedure types are the same, then they are equivalent and thus assignment compatible. If they contain different parameter names and/or default values, then they are not equivalent, but still assignment compatible. Parameter names and default values have no influence on the *value* of a procedure. In Example 9.11 a and P are not of the same type because they have different default values; nevertheless, they are assignment compatible. After the assignment a:= P they are equal, yet the respective default values are determined by the respective signatures. The program outputs the following text:

```
The two are equal
I am more equal
I am even more equal
```

Procedure constants that are assigned to a procedure variable must be global; i.e., they cannot be nested in any block. The reason that a local procedure cannot be assigned to a procedure variable is a matter of principle: If a nested procedure could be assigned to a variable, then the invocation of this procedure might escape the scope (e.g., via a global variable or a variable parameter in the enclosing procedure). This would enable invoking a local procedure outside its context, which must not be permitted.

Relational operations

Assignment compatible procedures can be tested for (in)equality. No other relational operations are permitted on procedures.

Procedure parameters

As an example, let us assume that we want to apply various procedures (or functions) to each element of a set. We can write a very general procedure (Process) that iterates through all elements of the set and applies the procedure specified as parameter to all elements (Example 9.12). The formal parameter of Process is of type PROCEDURE. We can inject even more dynamics if the actual parameter is not a procedure constant but a procedure variable. We can always write the same invocation, Process(s, p), and, depending on the actual value of p, a broad spectrum of different computations could be carried out. The output of the above program would be:

```
    2    4    6    8   10
 -10   -8   -6   -4   -2
```

```
MODULE ProcVar EXPORTS Main;                                    (*10.12.93. LB*)

  IMPORT SIO;

  TYPE
    Range   = [ −10..10 ];
    Set     = SET OF Range;
    Apply   = PROCEDURE (elem: Range);

  PROCEDURE Positive(e: Range) =
  BEGIN                                        (*processes positive elements*)
    IF e > 0 THEN SIO.PutInt(e) END;           (*ignores nonpositive elements*)
  END Positive;

  PROCEDURE Negative(e: Range) =
  BEGIN                                        (*processes negative elements*)
    IF e < 0 THEN SIO.PutInt(e) END;           (*ignores non-negative elements*)
  END Negative;

  PROCEDURE Process(s: Set; apply: Apply) =
  BEGIN                                         (*iterates through entire set*)
    IF apply # NIL THEN               (*applying Nil procedure has no effect*)
      FOR r:= FIRST(Range) TO LAST(Range) DO
        IF r IN s THEN apply(r) END             (*calls apply for each element*)
      END; (*FOR r*)
      SIO.Nl();
    END; (*IF apply # NIL*)
  END Process;

  PROCEDURE Init(VAR s: Set)=
  BEGIN                                        (*fills set with initial values*)
    s:= Set{};
    FOR r:= FIRST(Range) TO LAST(Range) BY 2 DO
      s:= s + Set{r};               (*s becomes the set{-10,-8,-6,-4,-2,2 ,4 ,6 ,8,10}*)
    END; (*FOR r*)
  END Init;

  VAR
    s: Set;                         (*the set that is processed in various ways*)
    p: Apply := Positive;           (*variable p set to procedure Positive*)
BEGIN
  Init(s);
  REPEAT
    Process(s, p);                  (*In 1st iteration, invokes Positive, in 2nd Negative*)
    IF p = Positive THEN p:= Negative ELSE p:= NIL END;
  UNTIL p = NIL;
END ProcVar.
```

Example 9.12: Formal and actual procedure parameters

Chapter 10

Modules

Before we begin with this chapter, let us take an excursion into the world of home stereo systems: In the 1950s and 1960s high-end high fidelity devices were usually built into cabinets. The turntable was operated from above, and the controls for the radio and for volume and tone were at the front (or also at the top). Loudspeakers were built in underneath and at the sides. The complete stereo system was a unit. Meanwhile this approach has been forsaken almost completely. High-quality systems now consist of a number of separate components; CD player, amplifier, tuner and speakers each have their own housing. The components are connected via cables that transmit the audio information. The advantages are obvious: The buyer can individually configure a system according to price and quality criteria. If a component breaks down (e.g., the tuner), it can be repaired individually while the rest of the system remains functional. Furthermore, the individual components are better because specialists have concentrated on designing each specialized solution.

Why have manufacturers not always specialized in the production of components? Beyond marketing considerations, there is another problem: The components must work together, must be *compatible*. The plugs of the cables must fit into the input/output sockets of the components, the electrical currents produced by the components must be handled by the amplifier, etc. To make this all possible, standards evolved over time; today we can normally integrate a newly purchased component into an existing system without any problems.

> This modularization continues within the components, and not only with stereo components. Similarly, producers of other electronic products build these from prefabricated, purchased subcomponents. Such devices are no longer repaired if they break down; the service technician localizes the problem and replaces the defective component.

We are not that far along yet in computer science. We do have a multitude of standards, especially in the area of communication between computers

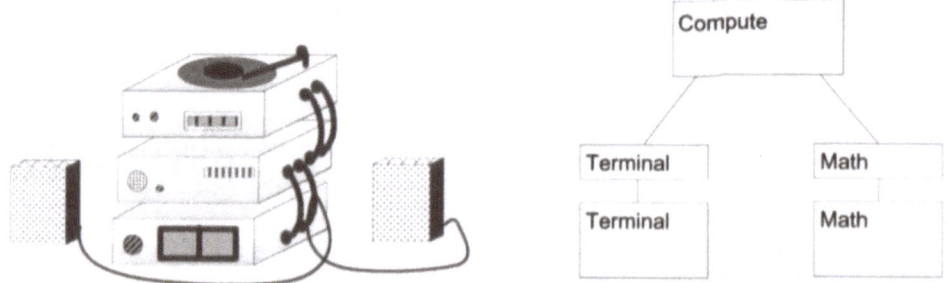

Figure 10.1: *Components of a stereo systems and modules*

(e.g., ISO/OSI) and programming languages themselves (e.g., *ANSI* standards for Pascal, C and Cobol). However, the inner structure of typical application programs remains inaccessible from the outside and is so completely interwoven that we have no chance of using components from old programs in order to build new ones (just as was the case with the old integrated stereo system). Still, we are working hard in this area, and one of the results has been the *module concept*. A module corresponds roughly to such a component of a stereo system. It is an enclosed functional unit that solves part of the overall task. To provide its functionality to the rest of the system, each module has at least one interface to the outside. This corresponds roughly to the sockets on the back of a stereo component.

Since computer programs generally consist of many more components than a stereo system, we have reached the limits of our analogy. We will see that program modules offer much more than simply dividing the problem into subtasks. Thus far each of our programs has consisted of a single module. With modules, we can decompose larger programs into parts that pose smaller problems and that we compose (under the control of the compiler) into a program.

- *Modules have an interface.*
  Only things that appear in the *interface* are available to the *clients* of a module. Everything else is invisible to the client, i.e., syntactically inaccessible.

- *Modules have a memory.*
  Contrary to local variables of procedures, the variables declared within modules retain their values during the entire program execution. We can simply use variables that are global to the module in order to store states, but restrict the difficulties created by global variables (see Section 9.3.4) to a small scope because these variables are not accessible from outside the module.

- *The usage of modules can be checked.*
  It is quite difficult to involve multiple programmers in a project. All the team members' work must be synthesized, which demands difficult coordination (setting up and upholding conditions as prerequisites for modification of common data structures, etc.). Here the compiler can help by assuring at least that all variables are used in accordance with their types, that the parameters of a procedure invocation match the procedure, and that everything used has been defined.

- *Modularization reveals dependencies between program parts.*
  The interface of a module must be *imported* explicitly by its client. This facilitates understanding the static dependencies between program components.

- *Modules are reusable.*
  Certain parts of typical computer programs are as similar as two hairs on your head. This applies, e.g., for procedures for screen output. Rather than reinventing such procedures, we want to produce them once – in generalized form – and then reuse them. In modules we can collect such "independent" procedures. We can package solutions needed by multiple projects in module collections (or *libraries*), and from there they can be incorporated into various programs.

We have already used such libraries: The modules Math and Text are part of the Modula-3 standard library[1] provided by the language environment. The module SIO was developed by the authors of this book to provide simple input and output.

The goal is to develop new programs by assembling components from a collection of existing modules – as with a stereo system. Furthermore, we need to be able to exchange program components (just as with a stereo system) to adapt the program to changing requirements.

Information hiding

Type constructors let us structure the data that a program processes. Procedures allow us to decompose larger algorithms to smaller, more manageable tasks and to make parts of algorithms reusable. Modules collect related algorithms (or procedures) *and* data structures. This makes modules more than a simple collection of procedures because modules also have an internal state; i.e., they can "remember" things between procedure invocations. The interface of the module assures that clients have all necessary information to control the functionality of the module; clients have no other form of access to the state of a module. This is *information hiding*. Both

---

[1]This library was authored by the developers of Modula-3 [HKMN94, Nel91].

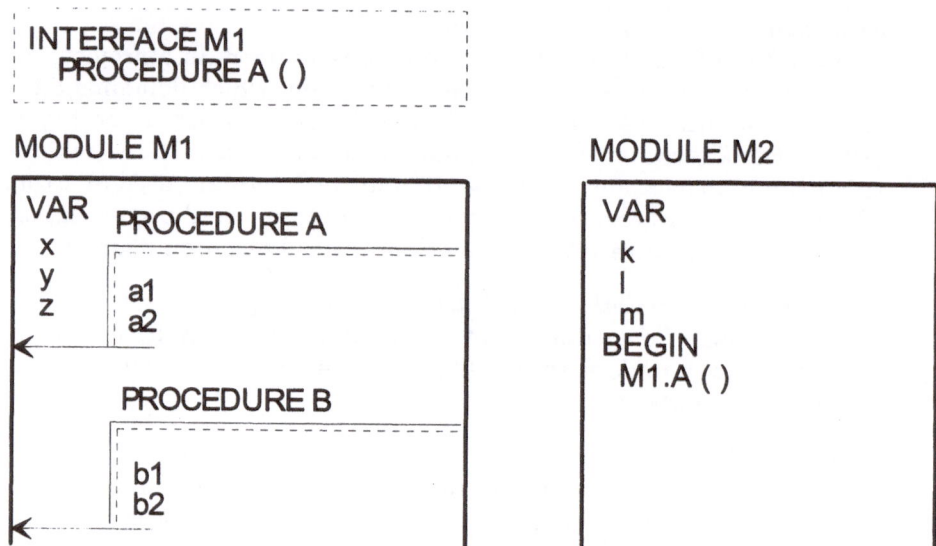

Figure 10.2: *Visibility within and across module boundaries*

algorithms and data are provided to the client not directly, but only in part, insofar as necessary, via the interface. This has nothing to do with keeping secrets or with privacy of data. Instead, it precludes errors that occur when a client, deliberately or not, writes algorithms that depend on the inner structure of the imported module. If this inner structure changes later, then this has unpredictable consequences for the client and leads to problems that we can avoid as follows: As long as we do not modify the interface of a module, we can change and improve the internal structure of the module.

State space

We term the current value of a variable its state, and the possible values of all variables collectively are the *state space* of the program. Initializations and assignments change the state space. Variables declared within a procedure, i.e., *local variables*, do not change the *global state space*. The state space of a procedure, however, consists of its local state space *and* the environment in which it is defined (the block in which it is declared; see Section 9.1). The structuring of the state space with the procedure concept resembles one-way mirrored walls; we cannot look into the procedure, except through the specially provided door of parameter passing, but we can look out and see the environment. Even more, we can change or even destroy this state space by modifying global variables.

The module concept is comparatively stronger. It allows us to subdivide the global state space. The enclosing walls of modules are sealed inasmuch as only those components of a module that are specified in its interface can be accessed by its clients. Data that are not exported cannot be modified, deliberately or accidentally, by clients – they are not visible (*information hiding*). Figure 10.2 illustrates this situation: A module *M2* must use a procedure exported by *M1* to modify the state of *M1*. The state variables x, y, z themselves are *invisible* to *M2*. State changes can occur only via the commonly agreed interface.

Division of labor and server modules

Almost always a program must solve numerous tasks that sometimes are scarcely related to one another. Thus it must have a user interface that, like a filter, assures that the program receives only input data that it can process. A program frequently has a component that handles the storage of results on a disk to make them *persistent*. In addition, results must be brought into human-readable form and then output to the screen or printer. And last but not least, the processing part itself contains various components. Figure 10.3 shows an example of the structure of a program for statistics computations. It encompasses components for collecting the data to be evaluated, for controlling the computations (input of the commands for evaluation), for the computations themselves, and for graphical display of the results. These components can be quite independent (in that they do not use each other's services – they process the same common data base). On the other hand, screen, printer, database and mathematical functions are more general *server modules* (or simply *servers*) that handle the interaction of the application with the user, printer and hard disk. They do not need (nor should they) any knowledge of the details of the application. These server modules can also be used in other applications.

It is very important to solve such distinct subproblems in separate modules, for programs are not simply written once and then preserved for all time. A modular program is easier to adapt to changed requirements. Assume that some years after purchasing our program, the user acquires a new printer. We could be asked to adapt the program to the new printer. If we have structured our program well, then we only need to exchange *one* module. In the whole software system the printer is never accessed directly. We only access the printer via procedures in the interface of the printer module. If we change the printer, this module must be adapted or exchanged. There is no need to modify the programs that use the printer. The prerequisite is a well-designed printer interface that does not require modification for this adaptation.

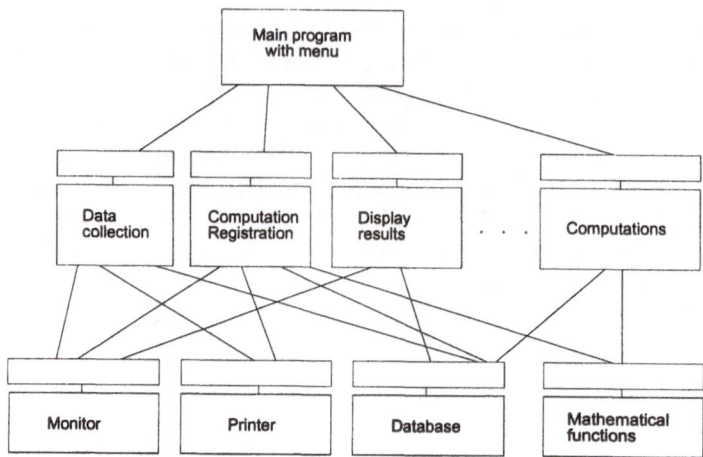

Figure 10.3: *The components of a statistics program*

If we have structured our system well in modules, then this facilitates *maintenance* to correct errors or extend functionality. Such components can be *reused* in other projects. A poorly modularized system thus becomes significantly more expensive to develop and maintain than one that consists of distinct modules with minimal interdependence. This chapter presents modules as they can be developed in Modula-3.

> The module was introduced into programming languages rather late. With Mesa [MMS79] and the popular Modula-2 [Wir82], the module concept, also used by Modula-3, began to prevail. The languages C and Fortran have always offered separate compilation of program components, but in these languages the programmer is responsible for avoiding name conflicts and for ensuring the proper invocation of the separately compiled components. Other languages, particularly Cobol, lack features for structuring algorithms and simply build a program from multiple, independently executable subprograms that invoke one another. Modula-2 provides an interface for each module, which the compiler monitors. The name scopes in a module itself are protected and distinct from other modules.

10.1   Structure

A module usually consists of an interface and an implementation. For the clients of the module, the interface makes everything visible that is necessary in order to use the module: the type declarations, the identifiers and the signatures of the procedures that the module provides. We say that the module *exports* these declarations. Everything else, i.e., the code of the procedures, the necessary internal variables, etc., belong to the *implementation*, which represents the realization of the interface and is not visible to client modules.

10.1.1 Interface

An interface resembles the modules that we already know. Instead of the keyword MODULE, they begin with INTERFACE, followed by the name and the declaration part. The interface terminates with END, the interface name and a period:

Syntax

$$\text{Interface}_2 = [\ \text{"UNSAFE"}\ ]\ \text{"INTERFACE"}\ \text{Ident}_{89}\ \text{";"}\ \{\ \text{Import}_{10}\ \}$$
$$\{\ \text{Declaration}_{13}\ \}\ \text{"END"}\ \text{Ident}_{89}\ \text{"."}.$$

In contrast to modules, an interface contains no block, i.e., no statement part. It can contain type, constant, variable and procedure declarations:

- *Type declarations*
  Type declarations in the interface permit the client of a module to declare variables of a type that the module can process. Hence the types of the parameters of the exported procedures must also be exported in all cases (unless they are predefined types).

- *Procedure declarations*
  Only the name and signature of a procedure may appear in the interface. This suffices to allow clients to invoke the procedure; they know the procedure's name and its parameter list.

- *Constant and variable declarations*
  Variables declared in the interface can be read and written both by the implementor of the interface and by its clients. Thus they are global variables whose scope extends beyond the module. Constants can be made accessible to clients in a similar way.

  Variables are seldom exported. It is almost always better to export one procedure that returns the value of the variable and another that permits setting the variable's value. The variable itself remains part of the hidden state of the module. This allows the module to better control access to the variables, e.g., in order to check conditions to assure that the variable was set at an appropriate time and with a sensible value.

```
INTERFACE Interface;

  CONST
    Constant = 1;                                          (*exported Constant *)
  TYPE
    Type = RECORD a, b: INTEGER END;                        (*exported type *)
PROCEDURE Procedure(par1: INTEGER; VAR par2: Type);
(*exported procedure; uses Type, also exported *)

END Interface.
```

Example 10.4: *The interface of a module*

Figure 10.4 shows an example of an interface that exports a type Type, a constant Constant and a procedure Procedure. Since the procedure has a parameter of type RECORD, this type *must* also be exported – the compiler requires this, and a client could not use the procedure otherwise.

The keyword UNSAFE designates an *unsafe interface*. Unsafe interfaces and modules permit additional language elements and disable certain checks on the part of the compiler and the language environment. Particularly in the area of system programming, this is sometimes necessary. Unsafe languages elements are often language-environment specific; also, they can produce errors that cannot occur in normal modules. Therefore unsafe modules and interfaces must be designated as such. We do not treat this subject here, but Appendix B.7 describes unsafe modules in detail.

10.1.2 Implementation

Most of the components of the syntax of an implementation module are already familiar:

Syntax

$Module_3$ = ["UNSAFE"] "MODULE" $Ident_{89}$ ["EXPORTS" $IDList_{87}$]
            ";" { $Import_{10}$ } $Block_{12}$
$Ident_{89}$ ".".

Similar to unsafe interfaces, here the keyword UNSAFE designates unsafe modules (see Section 10.1.1 and Appendix B.7).

An implementation module of an interface must export the interface using the EXPORTS statement after the name of the module. We have encountered this statement thus far only as the special case EXPORTS Main. The implementation module that exports the interface Main is the main module. The interface Main is not used by any other module. Main is a

```
MODULE Implementation EXPORTS Interface;

  VAR state: Type;

  PROCEDURE Procedure(par1: INTEGER; VAR par2: Type) =
    BEGIN
        par2.a:= state.a;                    (*reads hidden inner state *)
        par2.b:= Constant + par1;            (*visible declaration from interface! *)
    END Procedure;

BEGIN                                        (*statement part of module *)
  state.a:= 0;
  state.b:= 0;
END Implementation.
```

Example 10.5: *The implementation of the interface*

feature of the language environment. Only the main module stands alone and can be launched as a program from the language environment.

The EXPORTS statement can be omitted, in which case the module is the implementation for the interface of the same name.

We can export multiple interfaces, thereby creating multiple entries to the module. This allows us, e.g., to separate write operations (which change data) from read operations. Then we provide the interface for the write operations only to privileged clients, while the read operations are generally accessible. All identifiers declared in these multiple interfaces must be distinct. There is an exception to this rule: procedure names can occur in multiple interfaces of a module. This allows us to set default values of parameters of a procedure differently in the read interface from those in the write interface. On the other hand, several modules can export the same interface. This enables distributing the implementation of a complex server with a simple interface across multiple implementation modules. The compiler and linker check whether exactly one implementation (in one of the implementation modules) corresponds to each exported procedure.

In any case, all declarations of the interfaces are visible to the exporting modules. Example 10.5 shows an implementation of the interface for Example 10.4: Because the interface becomes part of the module through the EXPORTS statement, the type name Type and the constant Constant can be used directly. The implementation of Procedure is specified here.

The statement part of an implementation module handles initializations; it is executed only once at the start of the program. The initialization sequence for modules is always imported modules before importing modules. Thus during the initialization of a module it can always employ the services of imported modules: the latter are already initialized and so functional. *Cyclical imports* (module A imports an interface from module B and vice versa) mean that we cannot rely on the sequence (which becomes random). However, such mutual dependencies are normally a sign of poor module structure. Cyclical import of interfaces is forbidden.

10.1.3   Compilation units

Both interface and implementation can be spread across multiple source code files. It is even possible that a module consists of only an interface – if it exports only type declarations and no procedures. Each source code file forms a (*compilation unit*) that can be processed by itself by the compiler.

> Since Modula-3 permits multiple implementation modules for an interface, the term "module" becomes somewhat fuzzy: It is either a functional unit of a program – with interfaces and implementations collectively – or a Modula-3 MODULE, i.e., a compilation unit. In Modula-2 the interfaces are also called "modules" (*definition module*), but we do not use the term in this way. To distinguish between functional unit and compilation unit, we use the term "implementation module".

10.2   Using modules

A module that employs the services of another module must explicitly *import* the other's interface using the IMPORT statement. Thereby it imports the declarations that it needs before declaring its own local identifiers (which are invisible to clients). The compiler thus has all the information it needs to test whether the client uses the imported modules properly (e.g., whether the variables and expressions passed as parameters to an imported procedure each have the right type). In accordance with the principle of information hiding, the compiler checks only the interface of the imported module. The implementation need not even be available!

The IMPORT statement either lists only the names of the imported modules or completely specifies all identifiers of the procedures, constants, types and variables that we want to use from an imported module.

Syntax

$$\text{Import}_{10} \quad = \text{"FROM" Ident}_{89} \text{ "IMPORT" IDList}_{87} \text{ ";"}$$
$$\qquad\qquad\quad | \text{ "IMPORT" ImportItem}_{11} \text{ \{ "," ImportItem}_{11} \text{ \} ";".}$$
$$\text{ImportItem}_{11} = \text{Ident}_{89} \text{ [AS Ident}_{89} \text{].}$$

Normally we import an interface as a whole. An example that we have already used is

```
IMPORT SIO;
```

To use a name from the imported module, we write the interface name as qualifier before it:

SIO.PutText("Use imported procedure!");

However, we can also import individual names of an interface, which we then use without qualification:

FROM SIO IMPORT PutText;
⋮
PutText("Use imported procedure!");

This notation is shorter and has the advantage of indicating exactly what each client imports from a server. However, it also has drawbacks: Examining the procedure call does not reveal where PutText is defined (imported or in this module). In addition, name clashes can result from different modules using the same name. For example, PutText is exported by a number of modules that deal with input/output. If we always prefix the name of the interface from which the procedure stems, then we achieve clarity about which PutText is intended in each case. This also prevents name clashes if a module needs to import procedures named PutText from several modules simultaneously.

We can also import modules under an alias: With this version of the IMPORT statement we always import the module as a whole and under a different name. Instead of just specifying the module name after the keyword IMPORT, we write *module* AS *newName*.

IMPORT SIO AS Out;
⋮
Out.PutText("Use imported procedure!");

Thus we can abbreviate names of epic length (such as IntegerToIntegerTable from the Modula-3 library) to make the source code more compact (and to save tedious typing). The construct also helps to quickly exchange modules: For testing purposes we might want to replace one module with another that generates additional information which is relevant only for the program developer. We could use this alternative module with a single code change – and reverse the change again later.

The different versions of the IMPORT statement can also be mixed. It is possible to import an entire module and additionally to import individual components explicitly from the same module. Example 10.6 shows how the example interface is imported and how its exported elements are used.

In the remainder of this chapter, we examine more closely the use of the module concept.The possibility to organize software systems in mod-

```
MODULE Client EXPORTS Main;                                    (*CW*)

  IMPORT Interface;                    (*importing the exported declarations *)

VAR
  a: Interface.Type;                          (*using the imported Type *)
BEGIN
  Interface.Procedure(Interface.Constant, a);    (*invoke imported procedure *)
END Client.
```

Example 10.6: *Usage of* Interface

ules (with corresponding interfaces) can be used in various forms to design software systems:

- Structuring the data space

- Type creation

- Development of toolkits

10.2.1 Structuring the data space

Modules have a *state*; they can contain data that "live" throughout the entire execution of the program.

Data capsules

If the state space of a software system is structured in such a way that the states of a server module can only be accessed through its own exported functions and procedures, but never through direct access or modification of variables, then we call this a data capsule.

A piggy bank[2] is a perfect, very simple example of the separation of state spaces through information hiding. We can insert money, but never know how much is there. It is also not possible to remove money from the piggy bank, to exchange coins, or to cheat in any way. The only other permissible operation is smashing the piggy bank. However, if we carry out this operation, we have our money again, but no piggy bank.

Based on this description, we propose the interface PiggyBank in Example 10.7. It encompasses only the procedure Deposit, which takes the deposited cash amount as parameter, and the function procedure Smash, which returns the contents of the piggy bank.

The module Saving (Example 10.8) can now use this interface. It permits depositing any amount of money. In a loop the user is prompted for the amount of deposit. This is hardly elegant, but to keep the program

---

[2]This example was used by Prof. Rossak in an introductory lecture.

```
INTERFACE PiggyBank;                                              (*RM*)

PROCEDURE Deposit(cash: CARDINAL);
PROCEDURE Smash(): CARDINAL;

END PiggyBank.
```

Example 10.7: *The interface of a "piggy bank"*

```
MODULE Saving EXPORTS Main;                                       (*RM*)

FROM PiggyBank IMPORT Deposit, Smash;
FROM SIO IMPORT GetInt, PutInt, PutText, NI;

VAR cash: INTEGER;

BEGIN                                                        (*Saving *)
  PutText("Amount of deposit (negative smashes the piggy bank): \n");
  REPEAT
    cash := GetInt();
    IF cash >= 0 THEN
      Deposit(cash)
    ELSE
      PutText("The smashed piggy bank contained $");
      PutInt(Smash());
      NI()
    END;
  UNTIL cash < 0
END Saving.
```

Example 10.8: *Using the piggy bank*

simple, entering a negative amount smashes the piggy bank. Observe that neither does the client module Saving know nor does the interface give any clue how the piggy bank collects the deposited money. To reveal this secret, we would have to read the implementation module of the piggy bank (in Example 10.9).

In the implementation module we find the bodies of both the procedures Deposit and Smash. In addition, the implementation module has variable contents, which represents the encapsulated state of the piggy bank and is not visible in this form to the outside. Smash sets the contents of the piggy bank to a negative value (which is senseless for a piggy bank). Deposit checks each time whether the piggy bank is okay. The ASSERT pragma (see Appendix B.8.5) assures that the condition "piggy bank still okay" is met (if not, the ASSERT terminates the program with a run-time error). Once the piggy bank has been smashed, it cannot be restored. Any further invocation of either procedure causes program termination. What the ASSERT pragma does in Deposit corresponds to the initialization of the local variable oldContents in Smash – it fails because of the assignment of a negative

```
MODULE PiggyBank;                                              (*RM / CW*)

VAR contents: INTEGER;                              (*state of the piggy bank *)

PROCEDURE Deposit(cash: CARDINAL) =
(*changes the state of the piggy bank *)
   BEGIN
      <*ASSERT contents >= 0*>                   (*piggy bank still okay? *)
      contents := contents + cash
   END Deposit;

PROCEDURE Smash(): CARDINAL =
   VAR oldContents: CARDINAL := contents;     (*contents before smashing *)
   BEGIN
      contents := –1;
      RETURN oldContents                            (*smash piggy bank *)
   END Smash;

BEGIN
   contents := 0                          (*initialization of state variables in body *)
END PiggyBank.
```

Example 10.9: *The implementation of the piggy bank*

value to a CARDINAL type, also producing a run-time error.

Deposit always adds to contents; Smash assumes that some contents exist. Where are the contents actually defined? For simple state spaces – as with our piggy bank – we can couple initialization with the variable declaration by writing:

```
VAR contents: CARDINAL := 0;
```

More commonly, initializations of the local state space takes place in the statement part of the data capsule. This statement part is executed at the start of the program. Once this initialization has been completed, the module "lives" only through the invocation of its procedures from the client module.

The importance of structuring the data space by division into several state spaces in multiple modules is related primarily to the security it affords in the event of modifications. We need not fear accidentally changing a variable that is still needed elsewhere for other purposes. Thereby we can drastically reduce the need to check which variables are accessible in which situation and thus have to be watched during programming.

10.2.2 Type creation

A type consists of a data representation and the operations defined on it. Chapter 8 introduced various possibilities for defining new types. So what is new here?

With the type constructors provided by the programming language, we can define the kinds of data types that the language designers foresaw for us. We can combine a number of predefined, built-in types to larger structures in arrays, records and sets. The access operations on these data types are likewise predefined. The data types themselves are programming types of the language that have no semantics governing their use. What happens if our application includes line sequences (polygons) that represent graphical objects, series of temperature measurements or information on the water depth of a lake at different locations? We can manage the data of all three categories with arrays and/or records, perhaps even using arrays with identical structures. However, usage within the program would be quite different.

Coordinates, temperatures and water depths are all represented as REAL values. For a sequence of temperature measurements, we might be interested in the mean and the deviation – which would be totally irrelevant information for coordinate values. Water depth is a function of the location, whereas temperature measurements at a location are a function of time. Although the data representation might (by chance) be identical, the operations are quite different; therefore measurement sequences and polygons are quite different types. Thus it would make sense to define an application-specific type for for each of these three categories. This is where the module concept comes in.

Computations with fractions

As an example of the definition of data types, let us now define a type for the rational numbers (call it *Fraction*). Modula-3 provides only INTEGER and REAL types, but we can have fractions if we need them.

Let us consider the representation of fractions independently of their implementation, on paper. A horizontal line separates the numerator at the top from the denominator beneath it:

$$\frac{numerator}{denominator}$$

Actually, a fraction is a number pair *(numerator, denominator)* for which the basic arithmetic operations

addition, subtraction, multiplication and division

```
INTERFACE Fraction;                                                          (*RM*)
(*defines the data type for rational numbers *)

  TYPE T = RECORD
               num : INTEGER;
               den : INTEGER;
           END;

  PROCEDURE Init     (VAR fraction: T; num: INTEGER; den: INTEGER := 1);
  PROCEDURE Plus   (x, y : T) : T;                                           (*x + y *)
  PROCEDURE Minus (x, y : T) : T;                                            (*x − y *)
  PROCEDURE Times (x, y : T) : T;                                            (*x * y *)
  PROCEDURE Divide (x, y : T) : T;                                           (*x / y *)

  PROCEDURE Numerator      (x : T): INTEGER;         (*returns the numerator of x *)
  PROCEDURE Denominator  (x : T): INTEGER;         (*returns the denominator of x *)
END Fraction.
```

Example 10.10: *Interface for fraction computations*

are defined. For the sake of simplicity, we ignore additional operations such
as reduction.

> The interested reader should implement reduction with the help of the
> Euclidean algorithm (see Example 9.4 on page 179).

To implement fractions, we need an interface that provides such number
pairs as a type along with its associated operations.

From the interface Fraction we export primarily the type T, which provides the number pair *(numerator, denominator)* as a record. Furthermore,
we export procedures to manipulate such T records.

> Normally the name of the central type defined in a module in a Modula-
> 3 program is simply called T. Programs that uphold this convention
> then import the module as a whole (with IMPORT module;) and access
> the type accordingly as module.T. This convention emphasizes that a
> type must be seen collectively with its data representation and the
> operations defined thereon. The same idea is followed in assigning
> names to the operation procedures: The Name Plus itself has little ex-
> pressive power (*What* are we adding?) – only the module name lends
> it this expressive power (Fraction.Plus).

But how can a client of Fraction create examples (*instances*) of fractions?
It can declare variables of type Fraction.T. However, these need to have initial values. This is the job of the procedure Init. In addition, after manipulation of a Fraction, whatever its implementation, we need to be able to output it. We achieve this by defining the function procedures Numerator and
Denominator, which return the numerator or denominator, respectively, of

```
MODULE Fractions EXPORTS Main;                                      (*RM*)

IMPORT Fraction;
FROM SIO IMPORT PutInt, Nl;

VAR a, b, c, d: Fraction.T;          (*declaration of variables of type Fraction.T*)

BEGIN                                                          (*Fractions*)
(*Initialization of Fraction variables*)
    Fraction.Init(a, 3, 4);                                          (*3/4*)
    Fraction.Init(b, 1, 4);                                          (*1/4*)
    Fraction.Init(c, 1);                                             (*1*)

    d := Fraction.Plus(a, b);                                   (*3/4 + 1/4*)
    PutInt(Fraction.Numerator(d)); PutInt(Fraction.Denominator(d)); Nl();

    d := Fraction.Plus(b, c);                                   (*1/4 + 1*)
    PutInt(Fraction.Numerator(d)); PutInt(Fraction.Denominator(d)); Nl()
END Fractions.
```

Example 10.11: *Fraction arithmetic*

a fraction as INTEGER. Hence we need no special procedures, e.g., to display fractions on the screen; we already have server modules to output the standard types.

The module Fractions uses the type defined in the interface Fraction. Since we import Fraction as a whole, we must always qualify the components of the interface using the interface name, i.e., Fraction. For the sake of simplicity, we have initialized the fractions a, b, and c with constants. Naturally we could have employed read operations here instead.

Now let us examine the implementation module of the data type Fraction (Example 10.12). The implementations of the individual operations require no explanation. The implementation module knows and uses the actual realization of the type T for fractions; therefore the corresponding record components are accessed directly by the parameters of the procedures.

In fact, in this version even the client knows the representation of a fraction as a record. The type, including its internal componentwise representation, was exported in the interface. However, we did not access the fields of the record in the client module. Therefore this representation can be changed later. Indeed only the implementation module of Fraction needs to know this representation; the client can manipulate fractions only with the help of exported procedures. Through the use of opaque data types, described in Section 11.4.1, such "self-control" of the client is no longer necessary. The realization of the type no longer appears in the interface.

Note furthermore that modules that implement data types usually have an empty body. The initialization of the instances of the created data type are left up to the client.

```
MODULE Fraction;                                                              (*RM*)

PROCEDURE Init (VAR fraction: T; num, den: INTEGER) =
  BEGIN                                                      (*initialization of a fraction *)
    fraction.num := num; fraction.den := den
  END Init;

PROCEDURE Plus (x, y: T) : T =                            (*adds fractions (no reduction) *)
  VAR sum : T;
  BEGIN
    IF x.den # y.den THEN
      x.num := x.num * y.den; y.num := y.num * x.den;
      sum.den := x.den * y.den
    ELSE sum.den := x.den
    END;
    sum.num := x.num + y.num;
    RETURN sum
  END Plus;

PROCEDURE Minus(x, y : T) : T =                                  (*subtracts fractions *)
  BEGIN                                                (*internally uses module services *)
    y.num := - y.num;
    RETURN Plus(x, y)
  END Minus;

PROCEDURE Times (x, y : T) : T =                    (*multiplies fractions (no reduction) *)
  VAR prod : T;
  BEGIN
    prod.num := x.num * y.num; prod.den := x.den * y.den;
    RETURN prod
  END Times;

PROCEDURE Divide(x, y : T) : T =                                     (*divides fractions *)
  VAR inv: T;
  BEGIN
    inv.num := y.den; inv.den := y.num;
    RETURN Times(x, inv)
  END Divide;

PROCEDURE Numerator (x: T): INTEGER =                 (*returns numerator of fraction *)
  BEGIN
    RETURN x.num
  END Numerator;

PROCEDURE Denominator (x: T): INTEGER =            (*returns denominator of fraction *)
  BEGIN
    RETURN x.den
  END Denominator;

BEGIN                                                                   (*empty body *)
END Fraction.
```

Example 10.12: Implementation of fraction arithmetic

```
INTERFACE Polygon;                                                  (*CW*)

  TYPE
    Point = RECORD x, y: LONGREAL END;            (*coordinates in mm *)
    T = ARRAY OF Point;

PROCEDURE Shift(VAR p: T; dx, dy: LONGREAL);
(*move a Polygon along axes *)

PROCEDURE Center(READONLY p: T): Point;
(*compute center of gravity (mean of x- and y-coordinates) *)

PROCEDURE Rotate(VAR p: T; c: Point; a: LONGREAL);
(*rotate Polygon around Point c with angle a (in radiants) *)

END Polygon.
```

Example 10.13: *The interface of the Polygon module*

10.2.3   Creating toolboxes

A collection of functionally independent, but semantically related procedures is called a *toolbox*. Examples include collections of search or sorting procedures or functions that control input/output operations.

Toolkits only partly exploit the structuring possibilities of the module concept because toolkits manage only a set of procedures, but no data. Still, they are an important aid for keeping order in a complex software system.

10.3   An example with graphic elements

We close this chapter with another example to illuminate the various aspects of modules. We will develop two small components of a system for manipulation of graphic elements. Our task is to represent and manipulate two-dimensional objects of the real world (such as a technical drawing) in a program, with the goal of processing them on screen (although we do not go into detail on screen input/output here).

1. *Graphic elements*
   A technical designer might use a ruler, a curve template and a compass to construct various lines of the design object. Theoretically, however, a ruler alone could suffice. Curves and arcs can be assembled from numerous short straight segments. These segments only need to be sufficiently short to meet any requirements for precision.

   We will employ precisely this approach for the internal representation of all line segments. We store only straight line segments by storing the coordinates of all corners. This structure is called a *polygon* (compare the polygons defined differently in Section 8.1).

```
MODULE Graphic EXPORTS Main;                                              (*CW*)

  IMPORT Polygon, Viewport, Math;

  CONST Deg45 = FLOAT(Math.Pi, LONGREAL)/4.0d0;                           (*45° *)

  VAR rectangle: ARRAY [1..4] OF Polygon.Point;
    center: Polygon.Point;
  BEGIN
(*We have a graphic monitor with 1200 × 800 pixels and want
  to be able to store undistorted standard letter-size pages (8.5×11 inches).
  The page height should extend across the total height of the screen. *)
    Viewport.Proportion(1200, 800);
                                          (*compute width for undistorted display *)
    Viewport.Set(x:= 0.0d0, y:= 0.0d0, height:= 11.0d0);

(*Coordinates of a rectangle on a 8.5×11 page: *)
    rectangle[1].x:= 10.0d0;     rectangle[1].y:= 10.0d0;
    rectangle[2].x:= 20.0d0;     rectangle[2].y:= 10.0d0;
    rectangle[3].x:= 20.0d0;     rectangle[3].y:= 20.0d0;
    rectangle[4].x:= 10.0d0;     rectangle[4].y:= 20.0d0;

(*Invoke operations: *)
    center:= Polygon.Center(rectangle);
    Polygon.Shift(rectangle, 5.0d0,5.0d0);
    Polygon.Rotate(rectangle, center, Deg45);
  END Graphic.
```

Example 10.14: *Polygon operations*

2. *Operations*

As operations for processing drawings on screen, we have chosen shifting and rotation of elements. Other operations that we do not handle here include enlarging, mirroring, decomposing and composing elements of polygons. However, we do facilitate such extensions by providing an auxiliary operation, the computation of the center. Once we know the center, enlarging and mirroring are easy to solve in a manner similar to shifting and rotation.

Example 10.13 shows our Modula-3 realization of polygons. Polygons are arrays of Point records. The module defines the type Polygon.T and the operations thereon.

The open array parameter (see Section 11.2.3) of the procedures assure that we can process polygons of any length. The client stores the polygons of required length as variables of type ARRAY ⋯ OF Polygon.Point (see Example 10.14).

We omit operations for initializing and reading polygons. The client must declare variables of type ARRAY ⋯ OF Polygon.Point and initialize them directly. To read the points of a polygon, the client accesses elements of the array directly as well. In this respect the module fails to completely meet our requirements for data type definitions because these basic operations are left to the client. Therefore we can consider the module to be a toolbox that provides algorithms for the manipulation of special arrays.

Finally, Example 10.15 lists the implementation of the operations. The interested reader should explore whether the manipulations of the coordinates of the polygons really produce the desired effects.

Interface Viewport (Example 10.16) shows a very simple data capsule in its pure form. The state space of this module consists of a viewport definition.

To be able to display the polygons from module Polygon (Example 10.13) on screen, we need to map the coordinate system of the real world from which the polygons stem, onto the pixel coordinates of the screen. Hence we define the *viewport*, which is a rectangle in the world coordinate system that just barely fits onto the screen.

The coordinates of the viewports can be reset and read. The procedure Viewport.Set precludes nonsensical entries for viewport coordinates (see Example 10.17). In our example the ASSERT pragma (see in Appendix B.8.5) assures that the conditions specified in the interface as comments are upheld (if not, then ASSERT halts the program with a run-time error). However, Viewport.Set can do more than just transfer the values from outside to the state space of the module: To achieve undistorted representations, the width/height proportion of the viewports must correspond to that of the graphic monitor. With Viewport.Proportion the width/height proportion of the graphic monitor can be set comfortably; we only have to specify the pixels displayed in x and y directions.

Viewport.Proportion is an example of how the module concept helps to decouple the interface to the outside from the implementation. Viewport.Proportion *translates* the parameters to an internal representation (the variable proportion as LONGREAL), visible only *within* the module Viewport.

Viewport.Set can use information on the size proportions of the graphic monitor to compute from either of the parameters width or height the other parameter. Instead of the second parameter we simply pass Viewport.Undistorted. The ASSERT pragma again assures that at least one of the two parameters has a sensible value.

```
MODULE Polygon;                                                               (*CW*)

  IMPORT Math;

  PROCEDURE Shift(VAR p: T; dx, dy: LONGREAL) =
    BEGIN
      FOR i:= FIRST(p) TO LAST(p) DO
        p[i].x:= p[i].x + dx; p[i].y:= p[i].y + dy;
      END; (*FOR i*)
    END Shift;

  PROCEDURE Center(READONLY p: T): Point =
    VAR sumX, sumY:= 0.0d0; result: Point;
    BEGIN
      FOR i:= FIRST(p) TO LAST(p) DO
        sumX:= sumX + p[i].x; sumY:= sumY + p[i].y;
      END (*FOR i*);
      WITH n = FLOAT(NUMBER(p), LONGREAL) DO
        result.x:= sumX / n;
        result.y:= sumY / n;
      END; (*WITH n*)
      RETURN result;
    END Center;

  PROCEDURE Rotate(VAR p: T; c: Point; a: LONGREAL) =              (*a in radiants *)
    VAR a2, length: LONGREAL;
    BEGIN
      FOR i:= FIRST(p) TO LAST(p) DO
        WITH px = p[i].x, py = p[i].y DO
                        (*length of line between point of rotation and target position *)
          length:= Math.sqrt((px–c.x)*(px–c.x) + (py–c.y)*(py–c.y));
                                   (*angle between center-to-target line and x-axis *)
          IF length # 0.0d0 THEN
            IF px–c.x < 0.0d0 THEN
              a2:= Math.acos(–(py–c.y)/length) + a + FLOAT(Math.Pi, LONGREAL)
            ELSE
              a2:= Math.asin((py–c.y)/length) + a
            END; (*IF*)
                        (*new point results from length and a2 via cos und sin laws *)
            p[i].x:= Math.cos(a2)*length+c.x;
            p[i].y:= Math.sin(a2)*length+c.y;
          END; (*IF length*)
        END; (*WITH px*)
      END; (*FOR i*)
    END Rotate;

BEGIN                                          (*statement part of module is empty *)
END Polygon.
```

Example 10.15: Implementation of polygon operations

```
INTERFACE Viewport;                                                    (*CW*)

  CONST Undistorted = 0.0d0;

PROCEDURE Set( x, y: LONGREAL:= 0.0d0;
                     width, height: LONGREAL:= Undistorted);
(*Set sets this excerpt from the real world that is to be
   displayed on the screen. x, y is the left top corner in world coordinates;
   width is the dimension of the window along the x-axis and
   height along the y-axis.
   width and height must be > 0; one of the two parameters can be set to Undistorted;
   its value will then be computed with Proportion. *)

PROCEDURE Get(VAR x, y, width, height: LONGREAL);
(*read the viewport coordinates *)

PROCEDURE Proportion(width: CARDINAL:= 640; depth: CARDINAL:= 480);
(*set the proportion width/depth of width to height of the graphic window *)

END Viewport.
```

Example 10.16: *A data capsule: specifying the viewports*

10.4 Modularization

We have seen that we can decompose programs into modules. However, the module concept of the programming language alone by far does not suffice to reach our goal of modular program development. We must exercise extreme care to design modules and their interfaces so that we achieve small, interchangeable components – modules – that have strictly delineated functionality. We have learned the concepts of *data capsules*, *user-defined* data types and *toolkits* (which build on the module concept). The following comments should help in deciding what should be combined in modules:

- *Keep the interface small!*
  We gain flexibility with smaller units. Modules often offer too much functionality and have too many prerequisites to be able to work. Let us go back to our stereo system analogy. Professional devices separate the amplifier into preamplifier, equalizer (to generate and regulate the sound) and power amplifier (to generate the necessary power). The power amplifier must be adapted to the speakers, the preamplifier to the sound source. The equalizer does not always provide the required additional functionality that we want to introduce. The more the conditions around an amplifier can change, the more we depend on splitting up the functionality, because producers cannot offer an integrated device to cover every situation.

```
MODULE Viewport;                                                    (*CW*)

VAR
  vx, vy, vwidth, vheight: LONGREAL:= 0.0d0;        (*Viewport in world coordinates *)
  proportion: LONGREAL:= 640.0d0/480.0d0;           (*proportion width/hight of monitor *)

  PROCEDURE Set(x, y, width, height: LONGREAL) =
    BEGIN
      <*ASSERT NOT (width = height AND width = Undistorted) AND
                  NOT (width # Undistorted AND width < 0.0d0) AND
                  NOT (height # Undistorted AND height < 0.0d0) *>
      vx:= x;
      vy:= y;
      IF width = Undistorted
         THEN vwidth:= height*proportion
         ELSE vwidth:= width
      END;
      IF height = Undistorted
         THEN vheight:= width/proportion
         ELSE vheight:= height
      END
    END Set;

  PROCEDURE Get(VAR x, y, width, height: LONGREAL) =
    BEGIN
      x:= vx; y:= vy; width:= vwidth; height:= vheight;
    END Get;

  PROCEDURE Proportion (width: CARDINAL:= 640; depth: CARDINAL:= 480) =
    BEGIN
      proportion:= FLOAT(width, LONGREAL) / FLOAT(depth, LONGREAL);
    END Proportion;

BEGIN                              (*initialization of state space in variable declarations *)
END Viewport.
```

Example 10.17: *Implementation of the viewport definition*

- *Separate functionality!*
  From the requirement of narrow interfaces we directly derive the
  next: A module should solve only one subproblem. This significantly
  facilitates modification and reuse in other programs.

  Programming novices often make the error of including the formatting of the results of a computation in the module that handles the
  computation. The computation might be controllable via a clean, narrow interface – but when aspects such as screen formatting or error
  handling are handled in the same module, this restricts its reusability. To use the computations in a new program, we also have to import
  the screen output (which might or might not work there).

This problem often arises in error handling. Serious errors cause a message on screen, while a "normal" unsuccessful termination is returned as a status and handled by the client. This might be rather practical for the invoking module (it is freed of bothersome work), but it has serious drawbacks: This gives us a module that depends on its connection to a certain terminal, although otherwise it has nothing at all to do with the monitor and keyboard. Such dependency seriously encumbers the reuse of such a module in another context (which, in fact, was one of the declared advantages of modularization). And, what is worse, this blurs the functionality of the module. The client relies on error handling occurring in part in the module. If we modify such a module, we must find all the locations in the clients where *no* error handling occurs — and these can be very difficult to localize. How to treat errors that we do not want to handle immediately is covered in Section 15.

Our philosophy should be to have narrow interfaces that provide only what is *absolutely necessary* for *one* subtask. Large collective modules that solve multiple tasks unnecessarily encumber modifications of a software system. It is important to keep modules free of dependencies that have nothing to do with the task. On the other hand, modules can become too small, so that a client always needs multiple servers for a single task. This also impedes comprehensibility and modifiability because it causes numerous dependencies across module boundaries.

In the design of a program, if we always keep in mind the reusability of components, then we might come closer to real modular programming.

Chapter 11

Dynamic data structures

We can categorize the data types discussed so far as follows:

- Predefined scalar data types, such as INTEGER, REAL and CHAR that are built into the language environment

- User-defined scalar data types, such as enumerations and subranges

- User-defined composite data types, such as records, arrays and sets

These are all *static data structures* in the sense that their structure and storage requirements must be specified when the program is coded. For arrays, however, this size can vary within the limits prescribed by the language environment. Arrays also have a certain *dynamic* aspect due to the indexed access to its elements. If we want to manage a large amount of data in main memory, then initially arrays are our only option. However, arrays also suffer from the restriction of static size and structure.

Static data structures are difficult and inefficient to adapt to many problems. Example 8.20 (page 161) began to sketch a student data management system. Our underlying data structure was an array of records (the variable students). As long as we construct this data structure only once and then iterate through it repeatedly, this array structure proves adequate – apart from the inconvenient aspect that we must define the maximum number of students in advance. What happens if the number of students changes over time, as is the case in a real university? Some students leave the university and new ones arrive. The behavior of the whole system is *dynamic*. Again and again, new records must be created and old ones need to be retired. The size of the data set and the connections between the records change continuously. Such dynamism of data proves quite typical of practical problems.

This chapter presents *dynamic data structures*. We call data structures dynamic if both their size and their structure can change at *run time*. Dynamic structure does not imply arbitrary changes; naturally, we provide

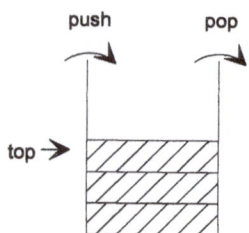

Figure 11.1: *Stack storage*

a certain basic structure. However, this structure must be able to adapt flexibly to the data (more in Section 11.5).

Many programs must process any amount of data. Clearly, real computers can process only as much data as their available memory permits. When we say "any amount", we mean "restricted only by available storage". Nevertheless, even programs like these hold only part of the overall amount of data that they process in main memory; the remaining data are on some *background storage* medium (usually the hard disk). In this chapter we limit discussion to data structures that are stored in main memory (which can also include *virtual memory* [Tan92]).

For managing dynamic data structures, Modula-3 provides the concept of *references*, or *pointers*. Before we discuss pointers, let us examine to what extent we can express dynamism with already familiar languages constructs – particularly with arrays – within prescribed quantitative limits.

11.1   Dynamism in static data structures

Here we introduce *stacks* and *queues* as data structures that – within the bounds of an array – can store any number of data elements. Then we will see how to process the elements of an array with explicit storage of links rather than with index arithmetic.

11.1.1   Implementation of stacks as arrays

Stacks, or *last-in, first-out* (LIFO) queues, are structures that are open at one end (top) and closed at the other (bottom). New elements are added at the top of the stack, and they are removed again from this same end (Figure 11.1). The last element added is the first to be removed.

The stack metaphor for this storage structure alludes to a stack of trays or plates in a cafeteria, where customers take clean trays and plates from the top of each stack and employees return clean trays and plates to the top of the corresponding stack[1].

> Stacks are not completely new here. In Section 9.2.2 we mentioned that the data regions of procedures are ordered according to the stack principle.

First we define the operations associated with stacks. If we store the contents of a stack in an array info and the variable top always points to the top element of the stack (top is 0 when the stack is empty; otherwise top is the index of the top element on the stack), then we can specify the following operations (ET is the element type that is stored in the stack):

- push(elem: ET):
  INC(top); info[top] := elem;

- pop(): ET:
  If top # 0 then: DEC(top); *Return* info[top+1]

- empty(): BOOLEAN:
  Return top = 0

However, this defines an infinite stack, which is certainly a fine abstraction, but impossible to implement. Therefore we introduce the operation Full, which returns *true* if the stack is full. To implement the stack as an independent data capsule, we can declare an interface like the one in Example 11.2. A client of the stack need not know how large the stack really is; it suffices to assure that we do not try to remove something from an empty stack or to append something to a full stack (Example 11.4). In program StackUser, if we enter a series of numbers, the program will accept input until the stack is full. Then the program returns the numbers in *reverse* order – which should not be a surprise.

We can implement stacks as arrays for which we make practically no use of the array's direct access feature (Example 11.3). Instead, we let the stack grow form an initial position and maintain an additional information element (top), which indicates the position in the array of the topmost element. In the implementation we employ no explicit test of the boundary conditions (push on a full or pop on an empty stack). If these are not observed by the client, the value of top exceeds the array's index range; then the run-time system of the language environment prevents any attempt to reference nonexistent array elements, and the program terminates with a run-time error.

---

[1] This cafeteria analogy also provides some of the vocabulary of stacks. With a spring-loaded rack for plates, the top plates maintains the same height, regardless of how many plates the rack contains. When we add a plate, we *push* the stack down; when we remove a plate, we thereby *pop* the next plate up. See Figure 11.31

```
INTERFACE Stack;                                                    (*14.07.94 RM, LB*)

  TYPE ET = INTEGER;                                                    (*element type*)

  PROCEDURE Push(elem : ET);                              (*adds element to top of stack*)
  PROCEDURE Pop(): ET;                               (*removes and returns top element*)
  PROCEDURE Empty(): BOOLEAN;                          (*returns true if stack is empty*)
  PROCEDURE Full(): BOOLEAN;                             (*returns true if stack is full*)

END Stack.
```

Example 11.2: Interface definition of a stack

```
MODULE Stack;                                                       (*14.07.94 RM, LB*)
  CONST
    Max = 16;                                  (*maximum number of elements on stack*)
  TYPE
    S    = RECORD
             info: ARRAY [1 .. Max] OF ET;
             top: CARDINAL := 0;                              (*initialize stack to empty*)
           END; (*S*)

  VAR stack: S;                                                     (*instance of stack*)

  PROCEDURE Push(elem:ET) =
  BEGIN
    INC(stack.top); stack.info[stack.top]:= elem
  END Push;

  PROCEDURE Pop(): ET =
  BEGIN
    DEC(stack.top); RETURN stack.info[stack.top + 1]
  END Pop;

  PROCEDURE Empty(): BOOLEAN =
  BEGIN
    RETURN stack.top = 0
  END Empty;

  PROCEDURE Full(): BOOLEAN =
  BEGIN
    RETURN stack.top = Max
  END Full;
BEGIN
END Stack.
```

Example 11.3: Implementation of a stack

```
MODULE StackUser EXPORTS Main;                          (*14.02.95. LB*)

  FROM Stack IMPORT Push, Pop, Empty, Full;
  FROM SIO IMPORT GetInt, PutInt, PutText, Nl;

BEGIN
  PutText("Stack User. Please enter numbers:\n");
  WHILE NOT Full() DO
    Push(GetInt())                              (*add entered number to stack*)
  END;
  WHILE NOT Empty() DO
    PutInt(Pop())                        (*remove number from stack and return it*)
  END;
  Nl();
END StackUser.
```

Example 11.4: *Client of a stack*

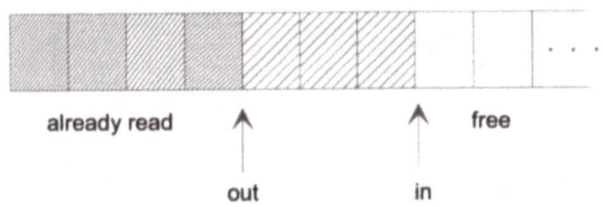

Figure 11.5: *An "infinite" FIFO queue*

11.1.2 FIFO queues in arrays

We retain our assumption that we know the maximum number of elements that we need to manage, but we forsake the "unfair" assumption of "last come, first served"; instead we consider a "fair" queue like at a British bus stop, a *first-in, first-out* (*FIFO*) queue. We define the operations in the form of an interface (Example 11.7) and employ the element type TEXT.

For the implementation we can initially pose the following considerations (see Figure 11.5):

• We need a write pointer (in) that indicates the position where a new element can be added.

• Analogously, we need a read pointer (out) that indicates where the next element can be removed.

• in ≥ out must always hold; the read pointer must never exceed the write pointer.

• in = out means that the FIFO queue is empty.

```
INTERFACE Fifo;                                              (*14.07.94 RM, LB*)

   TYPE ET = TEXT;                                                (*element type*)

   PROCEDURE Enqueue(elem:ET);                              (*adds element to end*)
   PROCEDURE Dequeue(): ET;                      (*removes and returns first element*)
   PROCEDURE Empty(): BOOLEAN;                       (*returns true if queue is empty*)
   PROCEDURE Full(): BOOLEAN;                          (*returns true if queue is full*)

END Fifo.
```

Example 11.7: Interface definition of a queue

```
MODULE Fifo;                                                 (*14.07.94 RM, LB*)

   CONST Max = 16;                   (*Maximum number of elements in FIFO queue*)
   TYPE
     Fifo = RECORD
             info: ARRAY [0 .. Max – 1] OF ET;
             in, out, n: CARDINAL := 0;
           END; (*Fifo*)

   VAR w: Fifo;                                              (*contains FIFO queue*)

   PROCEDURE Enqueue(elem:ET) =
   BEGIN
     w.info[w.in]:= elem;                                   (*stores new element*)
     w.in:= (w.in + 1) MOD Max;                     (*increments in-pointer in ring*)
     INC(w.n);                             (*increments number of stored elements*)
   END Enqueue;

   PROCEDURE Dequeue(): ET =
   VAR e: ET;
   BEGIN
     e:= w.info[w.out];                                  (*removes oldest element*)
     w.out:= (w.out + 1) MOD Max;                   (*increments out-pointer in ring*)
     DEC(w.n);                             (*decrements number of stored elements*)
     RETURN e;                                         (*returns the read element*)
   END Dequeue;

   PROCEDURE Empty(): BOOLEAN =
   BEGIN
     RETURN w.n = 0;
   END Empty;

   PROCEDURE Full(): BOOLEAN =
   BEGIN
     RETURN w.n = Max
   END Full;
BEGIN
END Fifo.
```

Example 11.8: Implementation of a queue

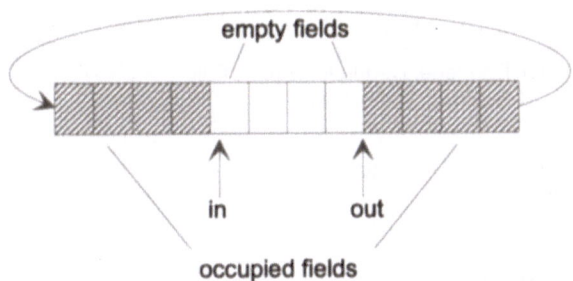

Figure 11.6: *FIFO queue implemented as a ring*

This works well as long as we do not insert more than the maximum number of elements. If elements are subsequently both inserted and removed, then the group of elements that are still in the queue slowly rises – in the direction of higher indices. When the in index reaches the last element of the array, this does not mean that the array is full. At the other end of the array, at the smaller index values, there are meanwhile free places that we can use now. We can use these places either by shifting the queue element-by-element back to the start of the array, or more elegantly by letting our read and write pointers gently glide across the array boundaries. We can achieve the latter by viewing our array not as a linear structure, but as a circular structure in which the first address directly succeeds the last address (Figure 11.6). Rather than simply incrementing the pointer by one position, we carry out addition in the residue class determined by the size of the array [Tru88].

For addition within the residual class defined by the array size N, we use the modulo operation MOD. The expression (i + 1) MOD N always produces a number in the range [0 .. N − 1]. For i = N −1, (i + 1) MOD N = 0. Thus the value of the expression demonstrates circular behavior: the largest value is followed by the smallest.

However, the ring structure produces a conflict with the considerations above:

- It is still true that the read pointer must not overtake the write pointer, but this does not mean that in ≥ out always applies. If the write pointer has begun again at the start, then in ≤ out (as in Figure 11.6).

- in = out no longer means that the queue is empty. If the write pointer catches up to the read pointer from behind (it must not pass!), then in = out, although the queue is presently full.

Therefore we introduce a counter that stores the number of elements, producing the solution in Example 11.8. Example 11.9 shows a client.

```
MODULE FifoUser EXPORTS Main;                              (*14.07.94. LB*)

  FROM Fifo IMPORT Enqueue, Dequeue, Empty, Full;
  FROM SIO IMPORT GetText, PutText, NI;

BEGIN
  PutText("FIFO User. Please enter texts:\n");
  WHILE NOT Full() DO
    Enqueue(GetText())
  END;
  WHILE NOT Empty() DO
    PutText(Dequeue() & " ")
  END;
  NI();
END FifoUser.
```

Example 11.9: *Client of a queue*

```
CONST
  MaxStudent = 32;                      (*maximum number of students in class*)
  TYPE
    Index     = [1 .. MaxStudent];
    Student   = RECORD
                      lastname, firstname: TEXT;
                  END; (*Student*)
  VAR
    class: ARRAY Index OF Student;
    next: Index := 1;
```

Example 11.10: *Student data structures*

What happens if we try to stuff more elements into the queue than space allows? This implementation does not raise a run-time error; instead, the oldest elements are simply *overwritten* by the newer ones. Section 16 introduces a variant of the FIFO queue that in such a case forces the industrious producer to *wait*.

11.1.3 Example: Rotating shifts

The example of a circular queue finds many applications. Here we use it to organize rotating work shifts. A number of elements are to be selected sequentially, with no element being selected a second time until all others have had their turn.

Shifting window

The students in a high school class could organize the task of cleaning the blackboard so that the job rotates from one student to the next, and a given student, after completing the job, takes a turn again only after all other

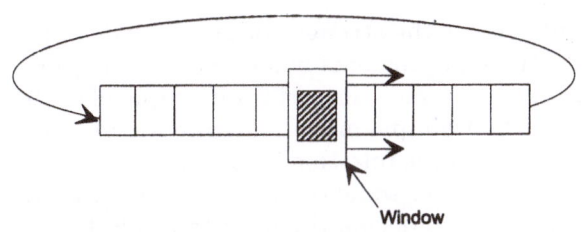

Figure 11.11: *A shiftable window*

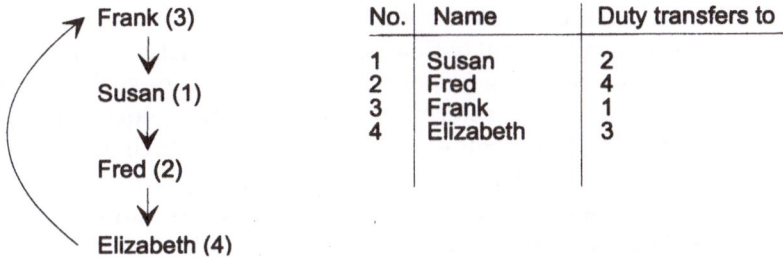

Figure 11.12: *Blackboard duty schedule: Graph and representation as array*

students have taken their next turns. Example 11.10 shows the possible data structures. Similar to our ring management above, the next student to serve as board cleaner results from residual class computation:

next := (next MOD MaxStudent) + 1

Here we employ the technique of circular closed arrays to implement a *shiftable window* on this array (see Figure 11.11). The window is shifted one position to the right each time (toward higher index values) and marks the next student. Once the maximum index value is reached, the window is reset to the beginning.

11.1.4 Explicit address management with pointers

All our examples so far have shown that the array is an ideal data structure if the following conditions hold true:

1. The number of elements is known in advance, or at least reliably predictable.

2. The number of elements changes little or not at all at run time.

3. The indexes of the elements to be processed can be *computed* with an arithmetic expression.

The last point reflects the strength of arrays. They provide comfortable and efficient solutions to problems where we can *compute* which elements to select and process. The most important example of such problems is matrix computations. Our simple modulo arithmetic to compute the rotation of blackboard duty also falls into this category.

Let us assume that after some time the students find this strict schema too boring. They prefer to decide themselves the order of succession, naturally upholding the principle of fairness. The students propose a graph that assures that all students take their turns, but in an arbitrary order. The left side of Figure 11.12 shows such a schedule.

The students promise that when they are currently doing duty, they will remind their successor of impending duty. To store such a structure, each student must contain a reference to the respective successor. For this reference, we use the index value, i.e., the position, which amounts to the address of the successor. We call such a reference a *pointer*. The student record must be extended to include such a pointer (Example 11.13). The procedure Init initializes the array class. For the sake of simplicity, we initialize the array statically. Note that the boundaries of the constant array FirstNames result from the initialization values. Type Index interprets the number of names in FirstNames as the upper array boundary. Both the names in the class (we use only first names) and the schedule are coded statically according to Figure 11.12.

> The interested reader should consider how to handle the initialization interactively. For example, in one iteration through the array, all names could be read, and a second iteration could prompt for the names of each successor.

The procedure Iterate moves through the array along the chain of duty. Instead of using the modulo function, we determine the next student with the value of the next field. The successor within the array is no longer computed arithmetically, but determined, independently of the physical position of the element, by an additional field in the element record. Note the fundamental difference between Init and Iterate. Init processes class as an array, from FIRST to LAST, or with fixed indices. Iterate processes the array with the help of an additional path that is determined by the linking of the values of the field next in the respective data record. The window that marks the next student with duty must "jump". The "target address" of the jump is indicated in the field next (see the right part of Figure 11.12). Procedure Iterate assumes that the duty chain forms a ring that contains all index values exactly once. If this assumption does not apply, then the procedure exhibits erroneous behavior. The output of Example 11.13 is:

```
Susan => Fred => Elizabeth => Frank =>
```

```
MODULE Students EXPORTS Main;                                    (*15.07.94 LB *)

  IMPORT SIO;
  CONST                                                       (*list of students *)
    FirstNames = ARRAY OF TEXT{"Susan", "Fred", "Frank", "Elizabeth"};
  TYPE
    Index      = [1 .. NUMBER(FirstNames)];               (*index type for class*)
    Student    = RECORD
                   firstname, lastname: TEXT := "";
                   next: Index;                                (*pointer to next*)
                 END; (*Student*)
    Class      = ARRAY Index OF Student;               (*array of student data*)
  VAR
    class: Class;                                 (*stores student data of class*)

  PROCEDURE Init(VAR cl: Class) =
  BEGIN
    FOR v:= FIRST(Index) TO LAST(Index) DO cl[v].firstname:= FirstNames[v−1] END;
    cl[1].next:= 2;                                     (*Fred follows Susan*)
    cl[2].next:= 4;                                     (*Elizabeth follows Fred*)
    cl[4].next:= 3;                                     (*Frank follows Elizabeth*)
    cl[3].next:= 1;                                     (*Susan follows Frank*)
  END Init;

  PROCEDURE Iterate(READONLY cl: Class) =
  VAR next: Index := FIRST(Index);                     (*iteration begins at index 1*)
  BEGIN
    REPEAT
      SIO.PutText(cl[next].firstname & " => ");            (*output first name*)
      next:= cl[next].next;                             (*next student in schedule*)
    UNTIL next = FIRST(Index);                            (*circle is complete*)
    SIO.NI();
  END Iterate;
BEGIN
  Init(class);
  Iterate(class);
END Students.
```

Example 11.13: *Student data structures linked by pointers*

This solution adds flexibility. However, the price of this flexibility is the added storage required for this next-duty pointer to the next logical successor and the drawback that we can no longer simply compute whose turn is on the fifth or the 57th day. To determine this, we have to iterate through the chain of successors.

With this increased flexibility we also lose security. Where the shifting window made it easy to see that we cover the whole array (all students), the explicit passing of duty requires us to first prove that we reach all students.

```
MODULE StudentList EXPORTS Main;                                    (*15.07.94 LB *)

  IMPORT SIO;

  TYPE
    StudentRef = REF Student;                            (*reference to student record*)
    Student    = RECORD
                    lastname, firstname: TEXT := "";
                    next: StudentRef;                              (*points to next*)
                 END; (*Student*)
  VAR
    class: StudentRef := NIL;                     (*points to start of student list*)

  PROCEDURE Init(VAR head: StudentRef) =
  VAR new: StudentRef;
  BEGIN
    SIO.PutText("Enter names in reverse order of schedule; terminate with "EOF"\n");
    WHILE NOT SIO.End() DO                       (*End() is TRUE if "EOF" is read*)
      new:= NEW(StudentRef);              (*student record created, address in new*)
      new.firstname:= SIO.GetText();          (*firstname set in student record*)
      new.next:= head;                      (*new record points to previous head*)
      head:= new;                               (*new record is at start of list*)
    END; (*WHILE*)
  END Init;

  PROCEDURE Iterate(head: StudentRef) =
  BEGIN
    WHILE head # NIL DO
      SIO.PutText(head.fistname & " => ");                      (*output first name*)
      head:= head.next;                        (*sets next student in schedule*)
    END; (*WHILE*)
    SIO.Nl();
  END Iterate;

BEGIN
  Init(class);
  Iterate(class);
END StudentList.
```

Example 11.14: *Linked list with references, elements appended at the front*

11.1.5 Address management by the system

In the above example we imposed a structure – a *list* that contains the
sequence of blackboard duty – over the array structure. Here we added the
field (next) to the student record, which enabled *indirect* index computation.
Would it not be simpler and more efficient if the programming language
supported the construction of such a structure as a list? For this purpose,
Modula-3 provides a type constructor for pointers (references) along with
the corresponding operations. Before the detailed explanation in Section
11.2, we present the basic idea and an introductory example.

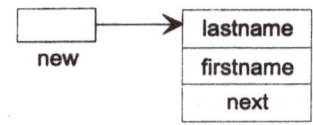

Figure 11.15: *Effect of New*

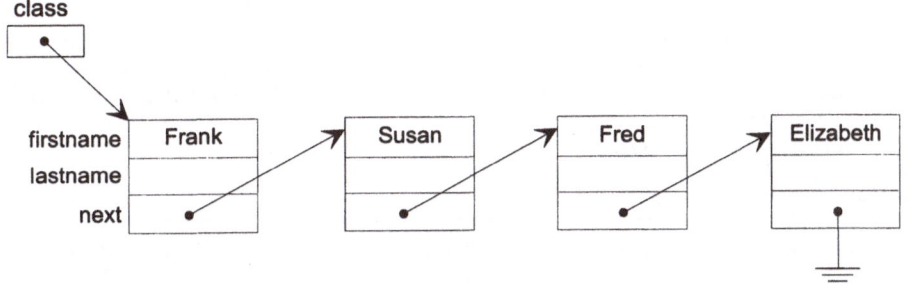

Figure 11.16: *Student list built with references*

We can create a pointer to any type by preceding the type with the keyword REF. The original type is called the *referenced type*. Thus in Example 11.14 the type StudentRef is a *reference* to the record type Student. The reference to the next element (field next) and the variable class are also of type StudentRef.

The variable class is initialized with the value NIL. The NIL value can be assigned to any pointer variable; it means that the pointer points nowhere (we have encountered the NIL value already in procedures, with a similar meaning). Note that if we forget to initialize a pointer, its value can be *undefined*. But if a pointer variable has the value NIL, then its value is certainly *defined*. This distinction is very important because the value NIL can be tested and thus always leads to well-defined behavior. (Even if the programmer forgets, at least the language environment notices the operation that attempts to follow a NIL pointer). An uninitialized pointer, on the other hand, can produce undefined behavior. Therefore the Modula-3 language environment automatically initializes pointer variables to NIL. Still, it is better not to rely on this and to explicitly initialize our variables.

A fundamental operation on a pointer variable is the invocation of the predefined function NEW. It requires a pointer type as parameter. Invoking NEW effects the following:

- Memory appropriate to the size required for the referenced type is allocated somewhere in the system memory region.

- The address of this memory is returned as function value.

```
PROCEDURE Init(VAR head: StudentRef) =
VAR new, last: StudentRef;
BEGIN
  SIO.PutText("Enter names according to schedule; terminate with "EOF"\n");
  WHILE NOT SIO.End() DO
    new:= NEW(StudentRef);              (*create student record; address in new*)
    new.lastname:= SIO.GetText();             (*name set in student record*)
    new.next:= NIL;                                  (*add new to end*)

    IF head = NIL THEN                         (*add to head of empty list*)
      head:= new; last:= new;                 (*both point to only element*)
    ELSE                                   (*add to end of non-empty list*)
      last.next:= new; last:= new;
    END; (*IF head = NIL*)
  END; (*WHILE*)
END Init;
```

Example 11.17: *Linked list with references, elements are added at end*

The statement new := NEW(StudentRef) creates a new student record and assigns its address to the variable new (Figure 11.15). Thereafter we can use the pointer variable to reference the elements of the referenced type. The expression new.firstname designates the field firstname of the record to which new points.

The Init procedure in Example 11.14 builds a data structure that consists of a chain of student records. Input is controlled using the Boolean function SIO.End(): It returns *true* if it encounters an "End-Of-File" signal[2]. The head, or root, of the record chain is stored in the variable class (Figure 11.16). A new record is always added at the head of the *list*. This is why we iterate through the records in reverse order. We can easily change this by adding new elements at the end rather than at the beginning of the list. We store the pointer to the last element added in the variable last. The new element is always added at the position last.next (Example 11.17).

Compared to the procedure of the same name in Example 11.13, Iterate has become simpler. It is also robust: it can even be invoked with an empty student list, in which case it does nothing.

What has improved over our array solution? First, we have eliminated the constant MaxStudent. We no longer need any assumptions about the number of students – the program remains the same for two or for 2000 students. A less obvious advantage is that pointers allow us to easily add new students to the list and remove others. We examine *list structures* in more detail in Section 11.5.1.

---

[2]On a Unix keyboard this is the key combination Ctrl+D and on MS-DOS PCs this is Ctrl+Z.

11.2 Dynamic data in Modula-3

A pointer, or reference, is either NIL or it points to some (usually nameless) region of memory in which a value of a certain type is stored.

Syntax of the pointer type

RefType$_{55}$ = ["UNTRACED"] [Brand$_{58}$] "REF" Type$_{48}$.
Brand$_{58}$ = "BRANDED" [ConstExpr$_{65}$].

UNTRACED is explained in Section 11.2.1 and BRANDED in Section 11.4.1.

In Modula-3, reference types are bound to another type, the *referenced* type. A reference contains an address, but this address is always of data whose type is already known at compile time. Why is this important? If a pointer were to reference data whose type were unknown at compile time, then the compiler could not check whether the referenced element actually exists. Then we might easily encounter the error that our search for an unknown address produces a pointer to data of another type.

> Imagine that you want to buy an ice cream, open a door labeled "Ice Cream Shop", and find yourself in an office supply store, or perhaps on an unknown island such as Jules Verne's "L'ile mysterieuse". Type binding guarantees that a pointer always references data of a known element.

11.2.1 Allocation and deallocation

Until this chapter, we have allocated memory for our data by means of variable declarations. Data that are global to a module are created at the start of the module. Thus these are often called *static data*. Data declared locally to an enclosed block are created automatically on entry into the block and are destroyed on leaving the block. These are often called *semidynamic data*. Data that are created (allocated) and then destroyed (deallocated) on demand are called *dynamic data*. Allocation in Modula-3 occurs *explicitly* (with the function NEW), while deallocation occurs *implicitly*, i.e., automatically (see below).

Observe that we are now speaking of static and dynamic data in another context than before. Here it is not a matter of the structure and size of a data type, but of creating data by allocating memory for them. It makes sense to store the anchor, or root, of a dynamic data structure (e.g., of a list) statically, i.e., in a module variable (such as the variable class in Example 11.14). This is the normal case. As many advantages as dynamic data structures have, we do need one fixed point (like the pulleys of *Archimedes*).

```
    ⋮
TYPE
  StudentRef = REF Student;                    (*Ref type bound to type Student*)
  Student    = RECORD
                  catalogNo: INTEGER;
                  firstname, lastname: TEXT;
               END; (*Student*)

  VAR ref1, ref2: StudentRef;
BEGIN
  ref1:= NEW(StudentRef);                    (*create data record with address in ref1*)

  ref1.catalogNo:= 1;                             (*set fields of new data record*)
  ref1.firstname:= "Peter"; ref1.lastname:= "Tall";

  ref2:= NEW(StudentRef, catalogNo:= 2,
             firstname:= "Julie", lastname:= "Short");
                                             (*data record created and initialized*)

  ref2:= ref1;       (*ref2 now points to first record; thus second cannot be referenced*)

  ref1:= NIL;                        (*first record can still be referenced with ref2*)
  ref2:= NIL;                              (*now 2nd record is also inaccessible*)
    ⋮
```

Example 11.18: *Allocating and deallocating memory for dynamic data*

Allocation

We can create an example of a referenced data type with the predefined function NEW. The signature of NEW is:

    NEW(referenced type, · · ·);

The first parameter is obligatory. If the type is a reference to a record type, then optional initializations of record fields can follow. They must be specified by name; no positional initialization is permitted here. If the referenced type is an open array, then the size of the open dimensions must be specified here (see Section 11.2.3).

As we have seen, NEW has two effects:

1. It allocates memory for data of the referenced type (creates a new data container), which is actually a side effect.

2. It returns a pointer to the allocated memory.

Example 11.18 shows how to create and use dynamic data. First a record is created and its address is assigned to ref1. Then the fields of

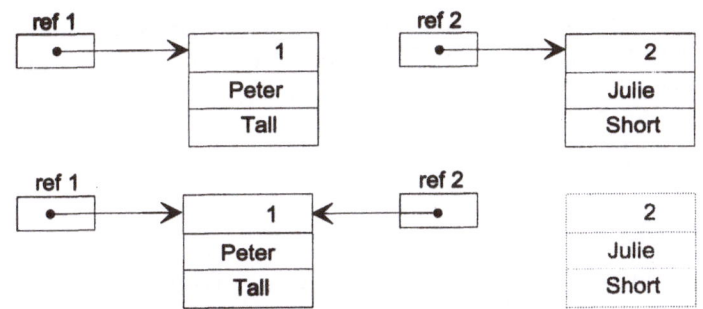

Figure 11.19: *Effect of the pointer assignment ref2 := ref1*

the referenced type are set. On allocation of the next record, (referenced by ref2) we initialize the fields with the optional parameters of NEW.

> The reader might wonder how this mysterious, system-internal alloca-
> tion of memory works. A language environment that provides dynamic
> data must have its own *memory management* – linked to the operating
> system of the computer. This memory management requests blocks of
> free memory from the operating system. Memory management also
> handles blocks that become free, either returning them to the oper-
> ating system or keeping them in reserve to cover later requests from
> the program. The organization of the free memory region from which
> NEW allocates space for variables is called the *heap* because this data
> region lacks regular structure and grows in accordance with require-
> ments. The name alludes to a data structure [Sed93] that is used often
> (but not always) for managing free memory.

Reference assignment and relational operations

The normal rules of assignment apply to assignments to references. However, note that the value of a reference is an address. The assignment ref2
:= ref1 in Example 11.18 does *not* mean that the data fields of the first
record are copied to those of the second. Instead, the statement causes ref2
to point to the same record as ref1 (Figure 11.19). Thus the record to which
ref2 previously pointed becomes inaccessible (no other pointer references
it). After the assignment ref1 := NIL, the first record can still be referenced
with ref2. After ref2 := NIL the first record also becomes inaccessible.

Similar considerations apply to relational operations on references (tests
for equality and inequality are permitted). If two references are equal, this
means that they point to the same record. If they are unequal, then they
point to different records, which still might have the same contents. Section 4.4 showed that comparing texts can prove curious: Texts that we consider "equal" are unequal. Therefore we mentioned the function Text.Equal,

which always behaves "correctly". Now we can clarify this phenomenon: In Modula-3 TEXT is a reference. Thus if we compare two variables of type TEXT, they might reference two different text examples that have the same content. But the function Text.Equal always compares the contents of referenced texts – which can be arduous.

Dereferencing

We access allocated data by *dereferencing*. Thus far we have always achieved this by specifying the reference variable, but this does not always work. The syntax of dereferencing is part of the syntax of expressions (see Section 7.1.1). If r is a variable of a reference type, then r^ stands for whatever r references. We say "r dereferenced". If the ^operator (the *dereferencing operator*) is followed by further selectors (a "[" for indexing or a "." for access to a record field), then we can omit the ^operator. This makes the following statements equivalent:

```
ref1^.firstname := "Peter";
ref1.firstname := "Peter";
```

> This abbreviation is particularly important when accessing fields of objects, as Section 13 will show. To emphasize the presence of a pointer, it is often useful to write the ^operator.

The ^operator is requisite if we are accessing the referenced data as a whole. For example, to assign the entire record referenced by ref1 to a variable of record type Student, we could write:

```
VAR
    student: Student;                    (*student is a record*)
    ref1: REF Student;                   (*ref1 points to a record *)
BEGIN
    (*copy record to which ref1 points to the variable student*)
    student := ref1^;
```

Note that this assignment is not a pointer assignment; ref1^ designates the referenced data rather than the pointer. It copies the whole record to which ref1 points to the variable student.

Deallocation

References are normally controlled by the run-time system of the language environment; we call such pointers *traced references*. If previously referenced data become inaccessible at some point (because all referencing pointers are reassigned or set to NIL), then their allocated memory is automatically deallocated by the language environment and so freed for other use. This part of the run-time system is called the *garbage collector*. In Modula-3, deallocation of dynamic memory occurs *implicitly*; the programmer need not (indeed cannot) handle it.

Many programming languages (and their environments) lack garbage collection. In this case it is the job of the programmer to release unused memory. This can lead to two errors. The programmer can forget to deallocate, which leads to inflated memory consumption, even of all available memory. On the other hand, the programmer can release memory that is still referenced by a pointer somewhere else in the program. If such a *dangling pointer* is used later, then it can reference a region of memory that meanwhile has been reallocated. This leads to unpredictable behavior (at best a program crash). Systems with garbage collection preclude such errors.

Automatic deallocation of memory can be undesirable in certain cases, especially in system programming, such as within an operating system. Certain systems programs require *explicit* control over the release of dynamic data as well (just consider the garbage collector itself, which can also be written in Modula-3). For pointers not controlled by the garbage collector (*untraced reference*), the language provides the keyword UNTRACED. Untraced references are not disposed of automatically, but only explicitly with the predefined DISPOSE function. However, DISPOSE can only be used in *unsafe modules* (see Section 10.1.1 and Appendix B.7) because it can cause dangling pointers.

11.2.2 Operations with references

Let us summarize the operations on references:

1. Allocation with NEW.

2. Dereferencing to access the referenced data.

3. Testing for equality or inequality. Any other relational operation makes no sense in safe modules. System programs can also test controlled references in unsafe modules for greater than or less than. How to interpret the result depends strongly on the architecture of the computer and its memory management.

4. Assignment with the usual rules of assignment compatibility. Section 11.3 (on subtyping) treats assignment in more detail.

11.2.3   Open (dynamic) arrays

In Section 8.1 we termed array types whose index ranges are specified at compile time *static* arrays. However, Modula-3 permits us to delay specification of the size of individual dimensions until run time. We call such arrays *open* or *dynamic* arrays. Note that their structure remains a "normal" array structure; only their size is dynamic. The size is specified only *once*, at run time, and from then on nothing changes.

Array syntax allows us to leave the type of the index undefined, or *open*, in the declaration of an array type, e.g.:

```
TYPE
  Vector = ARRAY OF REAL;
  Matrix = ARRAY OF ARRAY OF INTEGER;
```

An open array can only be used in certain contexts:

1. as formal parameter

2. as referenced type

3. as element type of another array

4. as type in an array constructor

This means, e.g., that we cannot declare a variable of type Matrix, but we can declare a variaable of type REF Matrix. Open arrays can be created *only* with a reference, thus only with the help of NEW. We must supply as parameters the sizes of the open dimensions sequentially, for example:

```
VAR
  n: INTEGER := SIO.GetInt();                          (*reads size*)
  m: INTEGER := SIO.GetInt();               (*size of second dimension*)
  vector := NEW(REF Vector, n);            (*creates vector with n elements*)
  matrix := NEW(REF Matrix, n, m);            (*creates (n×m) matrix*)
```

If an open dimension acquires size n at run time, then its index type is [0 .. n-1] (a subrange of INTEGER). Example 11.20 stores student data in an array whose size is determined only at run time. Student data are read and output. We can use the WITH statement to dereference class[i] to abbreviate and accelerate its performance (the expression class[i] is computed only once). Here again, we can use the built-in FIRST and LAST functions. Note that its argument must be of type array (rather than a pointer type to an array type); therefore we must write class^.

```
MODULE DynArr EXPORTS Main;                          (*15.015.94. LB*)

  FROM SIO IMPORT PutText, PutInt, GetInt, GetText;

TYPE
  Class    = REF ARRAY OF Student;
  Student  = RECORD
                  catalogNo: INTEGER;
                  firstname, lastname: TEXT;
             END; (*Student*)

  VAR class: Class; n: CARDINAL;

BEGIN
  PutText("Enter the number of students and their names\n");
  n:= GetInt();                                  (*read number of students*)
  class:= NEW(Class, n);                         (*array of students created*)
  FOR i:= FIRST(class^) TO LAST(class^) DO
     WITH cl = class[i] DO
       cl.catalogNo:= i;
       cl.firstname:= GetText(); cl.lastname:= GetText();
     END; (*WITH cl*)
  END; (*FOR i*)
  FOR i:= FIRST(class^) TO LAST(class^) DO
     WITH cl = class[i] DO
       PutInt(cl.catalogNo); PutText(": ");
       PutText(cl.firstname & " " & cl.lastname & "\n");
     END; (*WITH cl*)
  END; (*FOR i*)
END DynArr.
```

Example 11.20: *Allocation and usage of an open array*

11.2.4 Arrays of references

We can enhance the dynamics of Example 11.20 by storing references to
student data in the array rather than the data themselves. This particularly makes sense if the records are very large (often the case in practice).
If we want to reorder the data (e.g., sort by name), we can sort the array
of pointers without needing to move the voluminous data itself. Here the
pointer functions as a sort of *surrogate*.

> Such a solution is not entirely for free: We must explicitly allocate
> storage for the referenced data, and access becomes one step more in-
> direct. Therefore we recommend arrays of pointers only for really large
> records.

Example 11.21 is a modification of the program in Example 11.20.
Class is no longer an array of students, but an array of student references (the fact that Class is itself an open array plays no role in this context). Accordingly, the student records must be created explicitly. Other-

```
MODULE DynDyn EXPORTS Main;                              (*15.015.94. LB*)

  FROM SIO IMPORT PutText, PutInt, GetInt, GetText;

  TYPE
    Class    = REF ARRAY OF REF Student;
    Student  = RECORD
                 catalogNo: INTEGER;
                 firstname, lastname: TEXT;
               END; (*Student*)

  VAR class: Class; n: CARDINAL;
BEGIN
  PutText("Enter the number of students and their names\n");
  n:= GetInt();                                         (*read number of students*)
  class:= NEW(Class, n);                                (*array of students created*)
  FOR i:= FIRST(class^) TO LAST(class^) DO
    WITH cl = class[i] DO
      cl:= NEW(REF Student);                            (*student record created*)
      cl.catalogNo:= i;
      cl.firstname:= GetText(); cl.lastname:= GetText();
    END; (*WITH cl*)
  END; (*FOR i*)
  FOR i:= FIRST(class^) TO LAST(class^) DO
    WITH cl = class[i] DO
      PutInt(cl.catalogNo); PutText(": ");
      PutText(cl.firstname & " " & cl.lastname & "\n");
    END; (*WITH cl*)
  END; (*FOR i*)
END DynDyn.
```

Example 11.21: *(Open) array of pointers*

wise, the program quite resembles Example 11.20. Expressions such as
class[i].catalogNo now mean something different because class no longer
designates a student record, but a pointer to such. More precisely, we could
write class^[i]^.catalogNo. However, since the semantics of the first notation is unambiguous from the declarations, Modula-3 permits the shorter
notation.

11.3 Subtypes

Before we continue discussing operations with references, let us examine
the *subtype concept* of Modula-3 in more detail. This concept takes on new
dimensions in combination with references. We complete our discussion of
the concept in the context of *objects* in Chapter 13.

   The basic principle was already introduced in Section 7.4: Given the
two types Sub and Super with the relation Sub <: Super, all values of Sub

are also values of Super. The subtype relation is *reflexive* and *transitive*.

For many types, Modula-3 defines concrete subtype rules. (We already saw those for subranges in Section 7.4).

11.3.1 Subtype rule for references

```
NULL <: REF T <: REFANY
NULL <: UNTRACED REF T <: ADDRESS
```

In words, all traced references are subtypes of type REFANY (and all untraced references are subtypes of ADDRESS). Thus REFANY (or ADDRESS) is the supertype, the root, of all reference types. NULL is a subtype of all references. The only value in its range is NIL. This means that every reference type contains NIL. Thus we can assign NIL to any reference variable.

Simulated genericity

Recall the rules of assignment compatibility in Section 7.5 on page 135. Rule 2 (R <: L) states that the type of the right side of an assignment must be a subtype of the left side. In the case of references, this opens immense flexibility. We can assign any reference to a variable of type REFANY. As we know, for value parameters the actual parameter must be *assignment compatible* with the formal parameter. Thus if we define a procedure with formal parameters of type REFANY, we can invoke this procedure with actual parameters of any reference type. This allows us to create procedures that work with different types. This is a specialized and restricted implementation of the concept of *genericity*.

A component (e.g., a module or a procedure) is *generic* if its services are type-independent, but still type-safe. The most common solution is to provide the component with type parameters which are then made concrete on use. For this purpose Modula-3 provides the *generic module*, which can be parameterized with module names (see Appendix B.5.4). The use of REFANY parameters amounts to a "cheap" imitation of genericity – although it works only for reference types. An example is given in Section 11.4.3.

Assignment of a supertype value

Rule 4 of the assignment compatibility rules (Section 7.5, page 136), states that in the case of references and arrays a value of a supertype can be assigned to a variable of a subtype if certain conditions are met. What are these conditions? Take the program excerpt in Example 11.22. It is clear that we can assign r2 to the variable any without problems because Student <: REFANY. The statements r1 := any and adr := any can be legal – according

```
TYPE
  Student = REF RECORD lastname, firstname: TEXT END;
  Address= REF RECORD street: TEXT; number: CARDINAL END;
VAR
  r1: Student;
  r2 := NEW(Student, firstname:= "Julie", lastname:= "Tall");
  adr := NEW(Address, street:= "Washington", number:= 21);
  any: REFANY;
BEGIN
  any:= r2;                         (*always safe assignment*)
  r1:= any;              (*legal because type of any = Student*)
  adr:= any;                        (*produces run-time error*)
```

Example 11.22: *Assignment of a supertype with a run-time error*

to Rule 4. In the first case the assignment can be carried out because any contains a value of type Student, which is assignment compatible with r1. This is not the case with the second assignment (adr := any). any still points to student data, and these cannot be assigned to a variable of type address. Thus this statement produces a run-time error.

The example allows us to derive the general condition in Rule 4: A value of a supertype Super can be assigned to a variable of a subtype Sub if it falls in the range of Sub. This condition can be tested at run time.

We can formulate this condition in a different way. We can say that after the assignment any := r2 the variable any has changed not only its value but also its type. Its *actual type* (or *dynamic type*) has changed from REFANY to Student. We also distinguish between the declared (static) and the actual type. The actual type of the expression on the right side of the assignment must always be assignment compatible with the declared type of the variable on the left side (the actual type of the variable is irrelevant since it is overwritten by the assignment).

Rule 4 is closely related to Rule 3, which relates to subranges. We can assign a value of type Day to a variable of type Workday if and only if the value falls in the range of workdays.

Additional examples of assignment between different but compatible types are presented in the context of objects (Section 13).

11.3.2   Subtype rule for arrays

Array type Sub is a subtype of array type Super if they have the same number of dimensions, if they share the same base type (element type in the last dimension), and if for each dimension either both are open arrays or Sub is fixed (fixed number of elements) and Super open, or both are fixed and have the same number of elements. Thus an open dimension is always a supertype of a corresponding fixed dimension. In Example 11.23 the fol-

```
TYPE
   FixedMatrix   = ARRAY [1 .. 100], [1 .. 100] OF REAL;
   FixedVector   = ARRAY [1 .. 100] OF REAL;
   SmallVector   = ARRAY [1 .. 50] OF REAL;
   Matrix        = ARRAY OF ARRAY OF REAL;
   Vector        = ARRAY OF REAL;
VAR
   v: REF Vector := NEW(REF Vector, 100);
   m: REF Matrix := NEW(REF Matrix, 100, 100);
   fv: FixedVector; sv: SmallVector; fm: FixedMatrix;
BEGIN
   v^:= fv;
   m^:= fm;
   fv:= v^;
   fm:= m^;
   v^:= sv;                              (*run-time error due to different structure*)
```

Example 11.23: *Assignment compatibility of arrays*

lowing apply: FixedMatrix <: Matrix, FixedVector <: Vector and SmallVector
<: Vector.

Assignment compatibility of arrays

Rules 2 and 4 apply for assignment compatibility of arrays (Section 7.5 on
page 136), but they are always restricted by an additional rule: Assignment
compatible arrays must have the same shape. Therefore the assignment
v^:= sv in Example 11.23 produces a run-time error. The other assignments
are legal.

11.4 Abstract and encapsulated data types

Let us summarize what a data type entails (also see Section 10.2.2):

- *Range*
  The range determines the values contained in the type. Values can
  certainly occur in multiple types.

- *Operations*
  These specify what can be done with the values. Additional operations
  are not permitted. For built-in numeric types the language provides
  assignment, arithmetic operations and relational operations. For our
  custom-defined types, we provide operations such as push and pop for
  our stack.

The specification of the range and the operations as well as any additional conditions suffices to exactly define a data type. Most programming languages, including Modula-3, provide no means for complete *specification* of a data type. To define a new type, we specify its range and operations in an interface. The exact specification results later from the implementation of the procedures. Consider, e.g., a date type: We cannot directly specify that the value of the days in January range to 31, but in February they usually only go to 28. For the operations, we can only specify the signatures; everything else can only be recorded in comments.

> Indeed there are programming languages (e.g., *Eiffel* [Mey89]) that offer more than Modula-3 in this respect. On the other hand, there are *specification languages* (such as *Z* [PST91]) whose explicit goal is to serve as a specification tool. There are also specification languages that are more or less integrated into a programming language environment (e.g., *Larch* in C and Modula-3 [GH93]).

Another problem is that until now we could not prevent clients of the type from applying operations that were not intended (compare Example 10.10 on page 216).

Abstract data types solve these problems. They have the following features:

- They have a name.

- The operations are completely enumerated (including initialization).

- The semantics of the operations is also fully specified (e.g., in an algebraic form).

- Their data are accessible only through the specified operations. This is achieved by hiding the actual structures of the data.

With the help of the name, individual *examples* (also called *instances*) of the abstract data type can be declared. These are variables whose range corresponds to the abstract type.

If the specification of the semantics is missing, then we speak of *encapsulated data types*. In practice, this distinction is often neglected.

11.4.1 Opaque data types

The principle of information hiding, where a module hides its data from its clients, is already familiar (Section 10.2.1). This allows us to prevent an erroneous client from destroying the data. This principle guarantees

```
INTERFACE FractionType;                              (*19.12.94. RM, LB*)
(*defines the data type of rational numbers *)

   TYPE T <: REFANY;            (*T is a subtype of Refany; its structure is hidden*)

   PROCEDURE Create       (z: INTEGER; n: INTEGER := 1): T;
   PROCEDURE Plus         (x, y : T) : T;                        (*x + y *)
   PROCEDURE Minus        (x, y : T) : T;                        (*x – y *)
   PROCEDURE Mult         (x, y : T) : T;                        (*x * y *)
   PROCEDURE Divide       (x, y : T) : T;                        (*x : y *)
   PROCEDURE Numerator    (x : T): INTEGER;
   PROCEDURE Denominator  (x : T): INTEGER;
END FractionType.
```

Example 11.24: *Fraction as encapsulated data type*

increased security through regulation of the *scope*. Hidden variables are *invisible* to clients.

Now we introduce something new: Instead of variables (the data itself), the *structure* of the data – wholly or in part – can be hidden. Clients can create any number of instances of the respective type in *their own* scopes. Access to these instances is restricted because the client only partially knows the structure.

An undisciplined client could directly access the fields of a variable of type Fraction.T in Example 10.10 (page 216). This would not be possible if the client knew only the operations and not the data fields. This would force the client to use only the operations declared in the interface.

This is where the concept of opaque types comes in. The idea is as follows: We publish the type name (e.g., T) and declare that T is a subtype of another type. This additional type is either a predefined type (e.g., REFANY) or the public part of the type (e.g., called Public). The opaque part of a type must naturally be revealed somewhere. This *revelation* is best done in a scope that is closed to the client.

As an example we will re-implement the module Fraction as an encapsulated data type. In Example 10.10 the interface exposed the inner structure of the fraction type. Example 11.24 shows the new interface. Type T is now declared as a subtype of REFANY. We changed the name of the procedure Init to Create. The procedure Create first creates a new instance of type FractionType.T, then initializes its fields, and finally returns the reference to the instance as a function value. Otherwise the interface is the same as in Example 10.10.

The client (Example 11.25) can now generate any number of fractions with the help of the Create function. The rest of the client remains unchanged. The most important change is that the client can no longer access the data fields of the fractions. The client has all instances of the numbers

```
MODULE FractionClient EXPORTS Main;                          (*19.12.94. RM, LB*)

  FROM FractionType IMPORT T, Create, Plus, Numerator, Denominator;
  FROM SIO IMPORT PutInt, PutText, Nl;

VAR a, b, c, d: T;                   (*declaration of variables of type FractionType.T*)

BEGIN                                                        (*Fractions *)
(*initialization of fraction variables: *)
  a:= Create(3, 4);                                          (*3/4*)
  b:= Create(1, 4);                                          (*1/4*)
  c:= Create(1);                                             (*1*)

  d := Plus(a, b);                                           (*3/4 + 1/4*)
  PutInt(Numerator(d)); PutText("/");
  PutInt(Denominator(d), 1); Nl();

  d := Plus(b, c);                                           (*1/4 + 1*)
  PutInt(Numerator(d)); PutText("/");
  PutInt(Denominator(d), 1); Nl();
END FractionClient.
```

Example 11.25: *Client of encapsulated data type FractionType.T*

available, but can access them only through the procedures defined in interface FractionType.

However, this statement is not quite accurate! Assignment and relational operations (test for equality) always apply to all references. For instance, in Example 11.25 we could write IF a = b THEN ···. In the client, however, we cannot write a.num := 1.

To explain how opaque data types are implemented, we first need to examine the term *revelation* more closely.

11.4.2 Revelation

A revelation reveals, within a certain scope, parts of a type that were undefined until then. Revelations can occur only in interfaces or in the outer block of implementation modules.

Syntax the revelation declaration

> Declaration$_{13}$ = ··· | "REVEAL" Ident$_{89}$ ("=" | "<:") Type$_{48}$.

There are two kinds of revelation: partial and complete. For an opaque type we can specify any number of partial and exactly one complete revelation.

A complete revelation takes the following form:

> REVEAL T = type expression

```
MODULE FractionType;                                         (*19.12.94. RM, LB*)

  REVEAL T =   BRANDED REF RECORD                       (*opaque structure of T*)
                 num, den: INTEGER
               END;

PROCEDURE Create (x: INTEGER; y: INTEGER := 1): T =
  BEGIN                                            (*creates and initializes a fraction*)
    RETURN NEW(T, num:= x, den:= y);         (*creates and initializes an instance of T*)
  END Create;

PROCEDURE Plus (x, y: T) : T =                       (*adds fractions (no reduction)*)
  VAR sum := NEW(T);                                      (*returns result in sum*)
  BEGIN
    IF x.den # y.den THEN
      x.num := x.num * y.den;
      y.num := y.num * x.den;
      sum.den := x.den * y.den
    ELSE
      sum.den := x.den
    END;
    sum.num := x.num + y.num;
    RETURN sum
  END Plus;

PROCEDURE Minus(x, y : T) : T =                             (*subtracts fractions*)
  BEGIN                                        (*internally already uses services of this module*)
    y.num := − y.num;
    RETURN Plus(x, y)
  END Minus;
  ⋮
```

Example 11.26: *Revelation of an opaque data type*

T must be an opaque type. type expression must not be a simple type
name, but must actually define a type. The revelation states that type
expression is the concrete type of opaque type T. If T is a subtype of any
type S, then type expression <: S must also apply.

> This condition is checked by the language environment. Since rev-
> elations are defined across module boundaries, it can generally be
> checked only at link time.

A complete revelation exposes the internal structure of T. It is (normally) specified in an implementation module (see Example 11.26). The
outer type constructor of type expression must be a *branded reference* type.
The specification BRANDED marks a type to distinguish it from all other
types. This suppresses structural type equivalence (compare Section 7.3).
The optional ConstExpr$_{65}$ after the keyword BRANDED must be a text
constant; if specified, this text unambiguously identies the type. If it is

not specified, then the system generates an internal identification that is unique during a program execution.

> Explicit branding particularly makes sense when variables of a BRANDED type can outlive the lifetime of the whole program execution (are persistent).

It is easy to understand why the revelation of opaque types must be distinguished from all other types. Otherwise it might happen that a client – e.g., by pure chance – defines a type that has exactly the same structure as the opaque type. Now if the client – again by chance – employs this type instead of the opaque type, this suddenly grants access to the fields that should be opaque. As improbable as such a double chance might be, it must be explicitly precluded. The branding mechanism prevents this problem because it allows the compiler to detect the incorrect assignment in this case, and the client cannot employ the structurally equivalent type instead of the branded opaque type.

The declaration from Example 11.26 reveals the internal structure of T:

REVEAL T = BRANDED REF RECORD num, den: INTEGER END

It is known only in the scope of this implementation module; clients have no access to the fields num and den. Because the type has a brand, it is *not equivalent* to any other type declared as REF RECORD num, den: INTEGER END.

Opaque data types (except objects; see Section 13) can be created only where their inner structure is known, i.e., in the scope of the complete revelation. This restriction is understandable since NEW cannot simply allocate memory for an unknown record.

The partial revelation expresses only that a type is a subtype of another type. We use partial revelations – normally – in interfaces. They can reveal a little more information about an opaque type without exposing its final structure. The form of a partial revelation is:

REVEAL T <: type

type can be any type. The s of an opaque type must be linearly ordered via the subtype relation; i.e., the following must apply:

REVEAL type <: $type_1$ $\land$ REVEAL type <: $type_2$ $\Rightarrow$
$type_1$ <: $type_2$ $\lor$ $type_2$ <: $type_1$

This additional language element provides the expressive features to hide not only algorithms but also type definitions in server modules.

11.4.3 An abstract and a generic stack

The stack in Example 11.2 (page 230) has the following shortcomings:

1. It consists of a single stack example.

2. The type of the elements is fixed (INTEGER).

3. The maximum size of the stack is preset.

Now let us design a stack that corrects these drawbacks. Our stack must have the following properties (see Example 11.28):

1. *Encapsulation*
It exports an opaque type and the operations thereon. The client can create any number of stacks and use them with complete type security. In short, we will redesign the stack as an encapsulated data type.

2. *Genericity*
The stack must handle data of various (although not completely arbitrary) types. It uses simulated genericity by using REFANY (see 11.3.1). We can store data of any pointer type on the stack in Example 11.28 (see Example 11.27).

3. *Arbitrary size*
We remove the Full operation from the interface. We feign an infinite stack in the hope that the client will not store so many elements that total memory is exhausted. We could explicitly test this condition, but for the sake of simplicity we omit the test, which is language environment dependent.

Example 11.28 shows the corresponding interface. It exports the opaque type T and the element type ET. All procedures receive a parameter that determines the actual stack (compare Example 11.2, page 230). We receive a new, empty stack with the procedure Create.

Example 11.27 demonstrates the usage of the abstract and generic stack. Two stacks are defined; stackFraction will store rational numbers; stackComplex, complex numbers. Both stacks are initialized on declaration to NIL (i.e., empty). Since both numeric types are defined as references to records, they are assignment compatible with REFANY. The output of Example 11.27 looks like this:

```
1/4 1/3 1/2 1/1
4:6 3:4.5 2:3 1:1.5
```

```
MODULE StacksClient EXPORTS Main;                                          (*LB *)

  IMPORT Stacks;
  IMPORT FractionType;
  FROM Stacks IMPORT Push, Pop, Empty;
  FROM SIO IMPORT PutInt, PutText, Nl, PutReal, PutChar;

  TYPE Complex = REF RECORD r, i: REAL END;

VAR
  stackFraction: Stacks.T:= Stacks.Create();
  stackComplex : Stacks.T:= Stacks.Create();

  c: Complex; f: FractionType.T;
BEGIN
  PutText("Stacks Client\n");
  FOR i:= 1 TO 4 DO
    Push(stackFraction, FractionType.Create(1, i));                 (*stores numbers 1/i *)
  END;
  FOR i:= 1 TO 4 DO
    Push(stackComplex, NEW(Complex, r:= FLOAT(i), i:= 1.5 * FLOAT(i)));
  END;
  WHILE NOT Empty(stackFraction) DO
    f:= Pop(stackFraction);
    PutInt(FractionType.Numerator(f)); PutText("/"); PutInt(FractionType.Denominator(f), 1);
  END;
  Nl();
  WHILE NOT Empty(stackComplex) DO
    c:= Pop(stackComplex);
    PutReal(c.r); PutChar(':'); PutReal(c.i);PutText(" ");
  END;
  Nl();
END StacksClient.
```

Example 11.27: *Client of an abstract generic stack*

Note that here we have achieved flexibility in part at the cost of security. The system can test that we store only references on this stack; however, it cannot test whether we store correct references. If we accidentally put complex numbers on stackFraction, the system could not detect the error. With "real" genericity we could correct this deficit; this would mean that we would use the element type as a formal parameter of the encapsulated data type and that on declaration of the variables we could specify their concrete, actual type. In this case the compiler could certainly detect whether we are putting complex numbers on the fractions stack, or vice versa.

How can we store something other than references (e.g., INTEGERS) on the stack in Example 11.28? This is possible only via a detour, namely a pointer to INTEGER. We could declare the following type: Int = REF INTEGER. Such a solution is obviously not really satisfying because now we

```
INTERFACE Stacks;                                         (*14.07.94 RM, LB*)

  TYPE
    T <: REFANY;                                          (*type of stack*)
    ET = REFANY;                                          (*type of elements*)

  PROCEDURE Create(): T;                      (*creates and intializes a new stack*)

  PROCEDURE Push(VAR stack: T; elem: ET);             (*adds element to stack*)
  PROCEDURE Pop(VAR stack: T): ET;
                    (*removes and returns top element, or NIL for empty stack*)
  PROCEDURE Empty(stack: T): BOOLEAN;           (*returns TRUE for empty stack*)

END Stacks.
```

Example 11.28: Interface of an abstract generic stack

```
MODULE Stacks;                                            (*14.07.94 RM, LB*)

  REVEAL
    T = BRANDED REF RECORD
          info: ET; next: T;
        END; (*T*)

  PROCEDURE Create(): T =
  BEGIN
    RETURN NIL;                              (*a new, empty stack is simply Nil *)
  END Create;

  PROCEDURE Push(VAR stack: T; elem:ET) =
  VAR new: T := NEW(T, info:= elem, next:= stack);            (*create element*)
  BEGIN
    stack:= new                                           (*add element at top*)
  END Push;

  PROCEDURE Pop(VAR stack: T): ET =
  VAR first: ET := NIL;                        (*Pop returns Nil for empty stack*)
  BEGIN
    IF stack # NIL THEN
      first:= stack.info;                      (*copy info from first element*)
      stack:= stack.next;                              (*remove first element*)
    END; (*IF stack # NIL*)
    RETURN first;
  END Pop;

  PROCEDURE Empty(stack: T): BOOLEAN =
  BEGIN
    RETURN stack = NIL
  END Empty;

BEGIN
END Stacks.
```

Example 11.29: Implementation of an abstract generic stack

can access the value of a number only indirectly. This is less efficient than direct access, and the readability of the program suffers.

Example 11.29 shows the implementation of the stack. The procedure Push creates a new stack element and adds it to the front. The elements are initialized on invocation of NEW. The function Pop removes and returns the first element; for an empty stack it returns NIL.

11.4.4   Rules for the design of encapsulated data types

From the examples above we can derive the general rules for the design of encapsulated data types in Modula-3:

1. *Module for type design*
   We define an interface which specifies the type name and the operations defined on it (in the form of procedure signatures). All procedure signatures must contain a parameter of the given type. It is advisable to offer an explicit procedure for the creation of elements of the encapsulated type. This procedure can also *initialize* the data fields of the opaque type.

2. *Opaque type*
   The type whose name is declared in the interface must be *opaque*; the details are revealed elsewhere (with a REVEAL declaration), normally in the implementation part. However, since Modula-3 also permits partial revelation, it is possible that the revelation might be distributed across multiple modules. Thus we could specify $type_1$ as a subtype of $type_2$, which again is a subtype of $type_3$, etc. The purpose is to show more and more of the structure of the type – but not everything. Finally, there must be exactly one *complete* revelation (with the = sign). This must be marked as BRANDED so that no client can "steal" the type by chance.

3. *Hidden procedure body*
   The bodies of the procedures listed in the interface are hidden in the implementation part. The clients must not make any explicit and also should not make any implicit assumptions about the implementations.

Although this last requirement is important, it is difficult to maintain. If the author of the client module knows the implementation of the opaque procedure bodies, then certain properties of the implementation can all too readily – perhaps unconsciously – find their way into the usage of the operations. Only a formal specification can protect us to some extent, but even there can be no guarantee against unconscious assumptions.

11.5 Dynamic structures

Let us summarize and enhance our knowledge of dynamic data structures.

We use dynamic data structures because we want to manage any number of elements connected arbitrarily. The concept of pointer types provides all that we need, and it is in fact more powerful than necessary. With pointers, we can dynamically construct arbitrary, "wild" data structures. However, this would be just as dangerous as jumping around within a program (which we banished in Section 5, and which Modula-3 does not permit at all). Actually, some authors designate the pointer as the Goto statement of data structures. Therefore we must restrict ourselves to well-defined dynamic data structures.

The names of statically created variables give them an unambiguous reference point. Naturally, to manage any number of dynamically created elements, we cannot assign an endless number of names, especially not dynamically. A record that we create dynamically with NEW has no name itself. References allow us to access a nameless variable via its address. The reference variable "knows" the memory location just as with static data the variable identifier knows the memory location. To prevent confusion of these addresses by the programmer, they are hidden. We can only work through the entire structure as with the thread of Ariadne, starting with the name of the first data element, and we must take the utmost care that we do not lose grasp of our thread!

We achieve a dynamic structure by linking unnamed variables. The variables are all records of the same type, each has a field whose contents point to the next variable in the structure. We need only a single pointer to the first unnamed variable, stored in a static named variable. By sequentially reading the field that points to the next record, we can move on to read or modify the entire structure. This structure is called a *list* (see 11.5.1).

Naturally multiple chains of pointers can ensue from one information node. Likewise such a chain can emanate from each element of an array of references. A general network of branches from nodes can be used to represent various *graphs* [Tru88]. If such branches are restricted accordingly, the result is a tree, discussed in Section 12.2.1. Lists, trees and graphs occur in many forms. In general, however, they are well-studied and well-understood structures. They can help us avoid the dangers mentioned above. References are necessary to achieve dynamic data structures. However, we must always very carefully design dynamic data structures and that we make them no more "dynamic" than really necessary!

> Some programming languages (e.g., Lisp [M+62] and Orca [Bal90]) directly support certain dynamic data structures, such as lists and graphs; then we can do without explicit pointers.

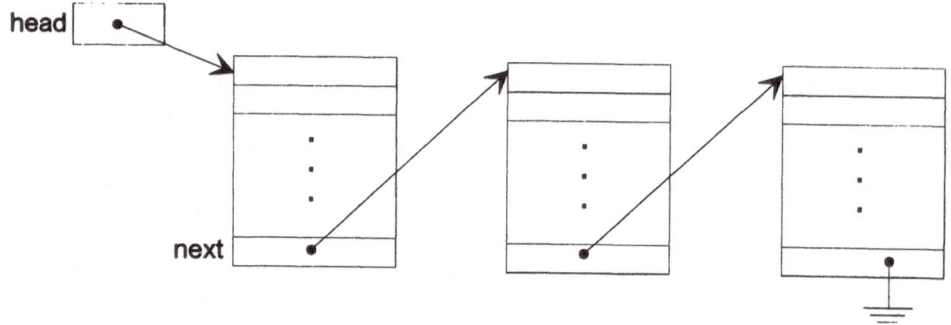

Figure 11.30: *Singly linked list*

11.5.1   Lists

In a singly linked linear list we connect a number of records of a fixed, but otherwise arbitrary record type. Our record might look like this:

```
TYPE RT = REF RECORD
                lastname, firstname: TEXT;
                age: CARDINAL;
                next: RT;
            END
```

The type RT contains a field itself that is of type RT and points to the *next* element (of type RT) in the list. This field allows us to construct an arbitrary list of records. The start (head) of such a chain is a simple variable of type RT (Figure 11.30). The end of the chain is a record whose pointer field contains the value NIL. We can interpret this as the last element pointing to an adjoining empty list.

Note that this recursive type structure is possible only because RT is a reference type. A static record type T = RECORD ⋯ n: T END is illegal – this type would have to contain infinite memory. Appendix B.4 specifies the exact rules for when type structures are permitted that contain themselves.

This brings us to the following basic structure for singly linked lists: Each list consists of the empty list, or of an element that is followed by a (possibly empty) list. Based on this recursive definition of a list, we can now define additional *invariants*.

> The considerations for proving the correctness of dynamic – and thus in principle unlimited – data structures are quite similar to those that we proposed in establishing loop invariants (see Section 5.5.2) – in principle likewise unlimited.

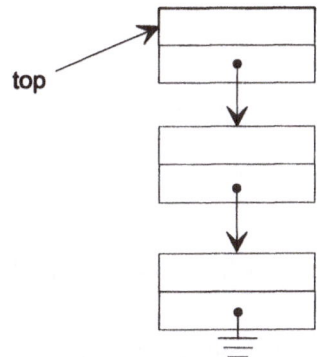

Figure 11.31: *Stack constructed with pointers*

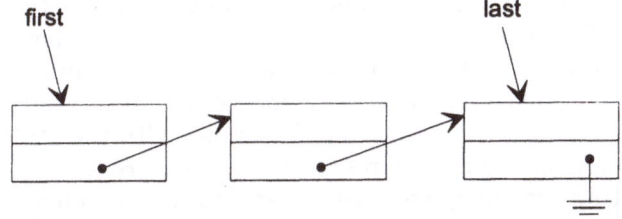

Figure 11.32: *Queue constructed with pointers*

Such a list invariant could take the following form: For every list operation it must hold that before its execution a (possibly empty) list existed and after its execution a (possibly empty) list must exist again. We can use this recursive structure later for simple formulations of recursive algorithms (see Section 12.1.5). For the time we limit ourselves to the iterative processing of lists, which is generally more efficient anyway.

11.5.2 Kinds of lists

Our first, intuitively designed example of references (Example 11.14) was related to the stack (Figure 11.31). We were dissatisfied with it because it stored students in reverse order (normal for stacks). The simplicity of a dynamic stack stems from its execution of operations basically only on the (current) top stack element. For example, head := head.next would remove the top element. Iterating through an entire stack structure is possible only by sequentially removing the elements (which destroys the stack).

A somewhat more powerful list structure is the *queue* (Figure 11.32). We use queues in Example 11.17 to store student data in the correct order. We can implement a queue with the help of a pointer to the start (first) and one to the end (last) of the queue. In an empty queue first and last are set

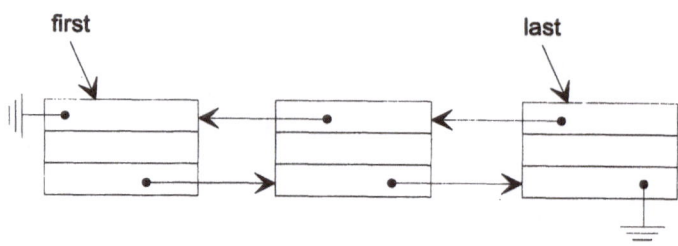

Figure 11.33: *Doubly linked list*

to NIL. When we add the first element to an empty queue, both pointers reference this new element. Once the queue is no longer empty, inserting a new element means setting the successor field of the last element added (to which last points) to the new element and then also setting last to this new element. Thereby we achieve a structure in which first points to the first and last to the last element. The first element points to the second, the next-to-the-last to the last, and the last to NIL. In this situation we can easily remove the first element from the queue with the statement first := first.next. Removing the last element of the queue requires more complex actions: Starting with first, we must iterate through all elements.

As another basic data structure, we introduce the *doubly linked list*. This structure allows insertion and removal at both ends with only a single access each. To enable double linking, we again need two pointers, first and last (or one pointer and circular linking). In addition, each element requires a forward and a backward pointer for double linking.

We often use lists to implement *sorted lists*. Structurally a sorted list corresponds to a singly linked list. On the level of data declaration it does not differ from a stack-like list. However, the operations differ. Insertion must incorporate the sorting criterion. Searching means iterating through the list until either the element is found or the "next element" according to the search criterion is already "greater" than the target.

11.5.3 Singly linked, sorted linear list

We define a singly linked, sorted list of INTEGER values as an encapsulated data type. In interface 11.34 we define type T with the basic operations Insert and Remove. Insert inserts an element into the list. In parameter found, Remove returns *false* if and only if the list contains no element with the specified value. Otherwise it removes the first occurrence of such an element.

The procedure type Action has a parameter of type INTEGER. Iterate invokes action for all elements sequentially and passes the stored value as actual parameter. In Example 11.14 we first constructed the list of stu-

```
INTERFACE Intlist;                                          (*16.07.94. RM, LB*)

  TYPE
    T <: REFANY;
    Action = PROCEDURE(value: INTEGER);

PROCEDURE Create(): T;
(*returns a new, empty list *)

PROCEDURE Insert(VAR list: T; value: INTEGER);
(*inserts new element in list and maintains order *)

PROCEDURE Remove(VAR list: T; value: INTEGER; VAR found: BOOLEAN);
(*deletes (first) element with value from sorted list,
  or returns false in found if the element was not found *)

PROCEDURE Iterate(list: T; action: Action);
(*applies action to all elements (with key value as parameter) *)

END Intlist.
```

Example 11.34: *Interface for sorted lists*

dents and then output it. We could have defined another procedure in the interface (Output). However, if we want to keep the interface of the list general, then such a procedure is too specialized (compare Chapter 10). It must handle the concrete form of the output, which has nothing to do with the list. Therefore we prefer to introduce the procedure Iterate, which takes a processing procedure as parameter. This processing procedure (the action) is then invoked by the list module for all list elements. The concrete form of the output is left up to the clients. Additional auxiliary procedures, such as Search, should also be considered.

It is up to the implementor of an encapsulated data type to determine how to actually order the individual elements in the list, as long as Iterate presents the elements in the correct order. It is usually simpler, however, to consider the desired sequence when inserting. The advantage is that this facilitates searching for an element. In particular, in the case of a fruitless search, we do not need to iterate to the end of the whole structure, but can terminate once we find a value that, with respect to the target, would violate the sorting order. We still need to clarify what happens if we encounter identical values in regard to our sorting order. Let us just assume that in this case the later arrival is inserted later in the list.

The basic algorithm for construction and insertion consists of finding the insertion position and inserting there. The graphical representation, as in Figure 11.35, with elements in boxes and pointers as arrows to them, proves an immense help in designing and understanding algorithms for dynamic data structures.

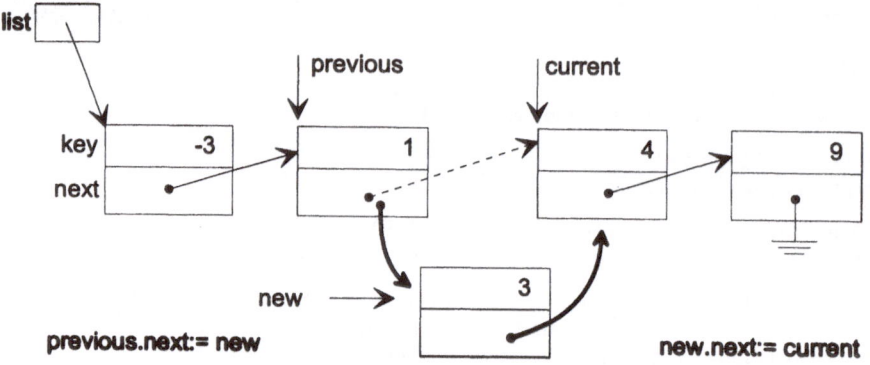

Figure 11.35: *Insertion of the element "3" in a sorted list*

In *pseudocode* (a sort of source code where we simply replace the missing details with textual description) the algorithm could take the following form:

```
(*Find insertion position:*)
    auxPointer := head
    WHILE auxPointer.key <= new.key DO
        revise auxPointer to next
    END
(*insert:*)
    connect to predecessor of auxPointer
```

Before implementing it in Modula-3, we need to refine this algorithm. For the sake of simplicity, we assumed the general case. In specific cases we need to consider that the action "connect to predecessor" depends on whether there is a predecessor; this is not the case in an empty list. Therefore we must either handle special cases or assure from the start for the lifetime of the data structure that the list is never empty.

It is quite simple to assure that a list is never empty. Before the first and after the last element, we insert marks that have unreal key values (e.g., the names "aaaaaa" and "zzzzzz" for lexicographic sorting). On insertion and removal, the marks do not disturb the algorithm. The marks behave like "normal" elements that are never referenced. On initializing the list, we must assure that we create the marks. However, this complicates the test of whether the list is empty.

To remove a record we must again either add a test on empty or assure that the list can never be empty. The removal operation could take

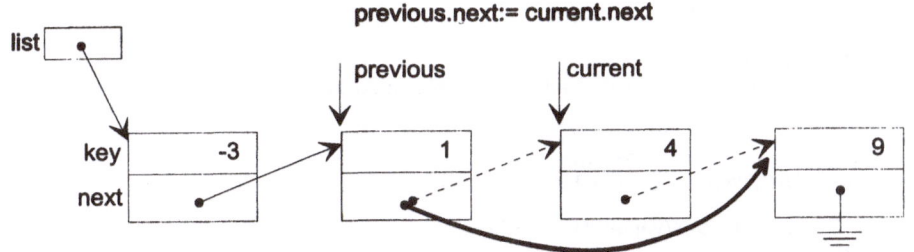

Figure 11.36: *Removing the element "4" from a sorted list*

place by manipulating the predecessor of the element to be removed (see Figure 11.36). Therefore with each search step we access not the element itself, but its predecessor. We check its predecessor pointer (previous) to determine whether the predecessor is the target value to be removed. An alternative to this procedure would be to do a normal search, but to have the delete pointer trail the search pointer by one element (as in Example 11.38).

The sorting criterion in Example 11.38 is the value of a key. The element with the smallest key value is at the head of the list, the second-smallest key value is the second, etc.

In our example list we can accommodate "any" number of INTEGER values. In practice we usually store large records in a list, and these contain one or more keys by which the list can be sorted.

A client (Example 11.37) can declare any number of instances of type Intlist.T (Example 11.37 has only one instance, the variable list). It must be created and initialized with Intlist.Create. The client of the sorted INTEGER list can add any number of numbers to the list, display the entire list, and remove individual elements. The client must handle outputting individual elements. The procedure Output implements this function. It is passed as a parameter to Iterate and then, through the list, can access every element.

> Normally the invocation chain goes from client to the server. The client that is higher in the module hierarchy invokes the services of the server. We often call an invocation that goes from the server to the client an *upcall* because its direction is opposite, i.e., "upward" in the module hierarchy.

In the input control part of the program, elements to be inserted receive preferential treatment. When we enter a number, it is inserted. All other actions are bound to single-character commands. D displays the list; R n removes the element with key value n.

```
MODULE ListUser EXPORTS Main;

  IMPORT Intlist;
  FROM SIO IMPORT PutText, PutInt, GetInt, Nl, LookAhead, GetChar;

  VAR
    list: Intlist.T := Intlist.Create();
    lines: CARDINAL := 0; ch: CHAR;

  PROCEDURE Output(value: INTEGER) =
  BEGIN
    PutInt(value);
    lines:= (lines + 1) MOD 16;
    IF lines = 0 THEN Nl() END;                        (*after 16 values, start new line*)
  END Output;

BEGIN                                                              (*ListUser*)
  PutText("ListUser\n" &
    "Enter a number to insert, R number to remove, D for display, Q to quit\n");
  REPEAT
    ch:= LookAhead();
    CASE ch OF
      | '0' .. '9', '+', '–' => Intlist.Insert(list, GetInt());
      | 'R', 'r' => EVAL GetChar();                    (*skip command character*)
              VAR found: BOOLEAN;
              BEGIN
                Intlist.Remove(list, GetInt(), found);
                IF NOT found THEN PutText("False\n") END;
              END;
      | 'D', 'd'=> EVAL GetChar();                     (*skip command character *)
              Intlist.Iterate(list, Output);
              lines:= 0; Nl();                         (*reinitialize line counter*)
    ELSE
      EVAL GetChar();                                  (*skip everything else*)
    END; (*CASE ch*)
  UNTIL (ch = 'Q') OR (ch = 'q');
END ListUser.
```

Example 11.37: *Client of the sorted list*

A possible program execution (without greeting text) could take the following form:

```
5 3 7 -4 12 0 1 D R 3 D
-4  0  1  3  5  7  12
-4  0  1  5  7  12
```

Example 11.38 shows the implementation. On insertion and removal, we use the variables current and previous to iterate through the list so that previous always points to the element before the current element. Thus on both insertion and removal we can always carry out the corresponding pointer operations. The implementation of Insert shows that when keys are equal, the latecomer is inserted after those of the same value that came earlier (the WHILE statement continues to search if key values are equal).

Example 11.38: *Implementation of sorted lists*

```
MODULE Intlist;                                                (*16.07.94. RM, LB*)

  REVEAL                                      (*reveal inner structure of T*)
    T = BRANDED REF RECORD
          key: INTEGER;                                           (*key value*)
          next: T := NIL;                             (*pointer to next element*)
        END; (*T*)

  PROCEDURE Insert(VAR list: T; value:INTEGER) =
  VAR current, previous: T;
    new: T := NEW(T, key:= value);                        (*create new element*)
  BEGIN
    IF list = NIL THEN list:= new                            (*first element*)
    ELSIF value < list.key THEN                         (*insert at beginning*)
      new.next:= list; list:= new;
    ELSE                                             (*find position for insertion*)
      current:= list; previous:= current;
      WHILE (current # NIL) AND (current.key <= value) DO
        previous:= current; current:= current.next;       (*previous hobbles after*)
      END;                       (*after the loop previous points to the insertion point*)
      new.next:= current;                    (*current = NIL if insertion point is the end*)
      previous.next:= new;                                (*insert new element*)
    END; (*IF list = NIL*)
  END Insert;

  PROCEDURE Remove(VAR list: T; value:INTEGER; VAR found: BOOLEAN) =
  VAR current, previous: T;
  BEGIN
    IF list = NIL THEN found:= FALSE
    ELSE                                                    (*start search*)
      current:= list; previous:= current;
      WHILE (current # NIL) AND (current.key # value) DO
        previous:= current; current:= current.next;       (*previous hobbles after*)
      END;            (*holds: current = NIL or current.key = value, but not both*)
      IF current = NIL THEN
        found:= FALSE                                       (*value not found*)
      ELSE
        found:= TRUE;                                         (*value found*)
        IF current = list THEN list:= current.next    (*element found at beginning*)
        ELSE previous.next:= current.next
        END;
      END; (*IF current = NIL*)
    END; (*IF list = NIL*)
  END Remove;
```

```
PROCEDURE Create(): T =
BEGIN
  RETURN NIL;                          (*creation is trivial; empty list is NIL*)
END Create;

PROCEDURE Iterate(list: T; action: Action) =
BEGIN
  WHILE list # NIL DO
    action(list.key); list:= list.next;
  END;
END Iterate;

BEGIN                                                        (*Intlist *)
END Intlist.
```

Chapter 12

Recursion

Did you ever stand between two mirrors? If the two mirrors are about the same size and approximately parallel, you can see yourself from both the front and the back. Even more, in the background of your back view is the other mirror with the front view. And the front mirror reflects not only your face but also the mirror behind you, which in turn reflects your back as well as the reflection of your reflection in the front mirror, which in turn reflects everything. Assuming that the mirrors are of good quality, this creates the illusion of being in an infinitely deep hallway in which you appear endlessly often and ever smaller until you fade into darkness. How could we describe this more simply? You see an image that contains itself. The distance between the two mirrors causes the image within the image to continue to shrink. It also contains the edge of the mirror, which itself does not reflect; therefore it was not actually reflected infinitely.

We also see this phenomenon in the self-portraits of several painters who depicted themselves in the act of painting; however, in the painting they were not painting just any subject, but the very picture that they were painting at that time. Thus the painting must depict the painter and, again, the picture itself. Naturally the included picture is also smaller than the actual self-portrait, usually so much smaller that after three or four such steps the contained self-portrait no longer reflects detail and so degenerates to a line sketch, thereby terminating the recursion.

What do such physical phenomena and artistic frivolity have to do with computer science? A great deal. Recursive procedures and functions – which contain invocations of themselves – provide some of the most powerful means part known for representing algorithms. They are just as powerful as the Turing machine described in the introduction (Section 1.1.3).

We have encountered a recursive definition already in Chapter 2. We defined the natural numbers as follows:

NaturalNumber = Digit | Digit NaturalNumber .

Here the left side of the definition is a component of the right side. Why is this not a circular definition? We provided for the following:

- We had a nonrecursive exit.

- The part that contained the left side (the recursive alternative) also contained another component (here Digit) that ensured that the natural number on the left side would be longer than that on the right side. (We can represent the number 56 as Digit NaturalNumber, whereby Digit = 5 and NaturalNumber = Digit = 6.)

Both these conditions are necessary to ensure that a recursive definition is well-founded. Every recursive definition must consist of at least two components, (at least) one of them recursive and (at least) one nonrecursive.

1. In addition to its actually recursive part, the recursive alternative contains another part that ensures that applying the definition produces a residual recursive part of ever diminishing size, so that finally a (or the) nonrecursive alternative applies.

2. The nonrecursive alternatives can be resolved directly (without further branching). Because they are often simple, we term this the *trivial case*.

It is difficult to prove that a substitution process converges to a nonrecursive case. In the definition of a natural number the leading digit fulfilled this condition.

In the following we show how to employ recursion to program elegant algorithms and powerful data structures. Note that this does not require any new Modula-3 language elements: the procedure concept suffices to formulate recursive algorithms. The concept of references suffices for recursive data structures, which in turn are best processed by recursive algorithms.

Many older programming languages such as Basic, Fortran and Cobol do not support recursive programming. This encumbers problem solving in some domains so much that writing certain software (e.g., for program translation, pattern recognition and expert systems) prove practically insurmountable in these languages. Other programming languages, including Lisp and Prolog, feature recursion as a primary structuring element. Modula-3 takes an intermediate position, offering recursion alongside other structuring elements.

12.1 Recursive algorithms

12.1.1 Fundamentals of recursive programming

Why, from a syntactic viewpoint, can we write recursive procedures at all? The name of a procedure is visible within its block; therefore we can invoke the procedure itself just as any other procedure. This opens quite some possibilities.

To assure the correctness and termination of a recursive program, we must abide by the rules presented above. Every recursive program contains at least one nonrecursive alternative (possibly empty), and if the recursive alternative is selected, we must assure that preceding (and possibly subsequent) steps eventually lead us into the nonrecursive branch.

Thus recursive procedures are structured according to the following pattern:

```
PROCEDURE Rek (···) ··· =
   BEGIN
      ⋮
      IF ··· THEN Rek (···) END;
      ⋮
   END Rek;
```

A classic example of recursive algorithms is the definition of *factorial*:

$$n! = n(n-1)!$$
$$0! = 1$$

We can map this definition directly onto the procedure Factorial (Example 12.1).

Let us examine the invocation Factorial(4). First the condition n = 0 is *false*, so the procedure begins to compute the expression n * Factorial(n-1); for our specific values this is 4 * Factorial(3). The expression contains the function call Factorial(3); the function is thus invoked again, this time with n = 3. The next invocation continues with Factorial(2), and so on until the invocation Factorial(0). Now the function returns the value 1. This means that evaluation of the expression 1 * Factorial(0) can be completed, returning 1. This invocation stems from the evaluation of the expression (2 * Factorial(1)), which yields 2 * 1, and so on until the first expression, 4 * Factorial(3), returns 4 * 3 * 2 = 24.

However, we could also compute the factorial iteratively using the following formula:

$$n! = \begin{cases} \displaystyle\prod_{i=1}^{n} i & \text{for } n \geq 1 \\[2ex] 1 & \text{for } n = 0 \end{cases}$$

```
PROCEDURE Factorial (n: CARDINAL): CARDINAL =
  BEGIN
    IF n = 0 THEN RETURN 1                          (*trivial case *)
    ELSE RETURN n * Factorial(n–1)                  (*recursive branch *)
    END (*IF*)
  END Factorial;
```

Example 12.1: *Recursive computation of the factorial n!*

The corresponding iterative program segment is:

```
VAR fact: CARDINAL := 1;
BEGIN
  FOR i := 1 TO n DO fact := fact * i END;
END
```

Another example of a recursive definition or a recursive algorithm is the computation of the nth power of x:

$$x^n = x x^{n-1}$$
$$x^0 = 1$$

Here, too, we are more familiar with the corresponding iterative formulation:

$$x^n = \begin{cases} \displaystyle\prod_{i=1}^{n} x & \text{for } n \geq 1 \\[2em] 1 & \text{for } n = 0 \end{cases}$$

All these recursive algorithms might be elegant. Still, the corresponding iterative algorithms seem more familiar and thus simpler. What, then, is the actual value of recursion?

Let us try to understand the procedure Reverse in Example 12.2. What does Reverse really do? We maintain that it inverts a character string of any length. A possible execution of the program could be:

```
Please enter a character string:
Blanks are characters, too!
!oot ,sretcarahc era sknalB
```

How does this program succeed with only a single variable of the very simple type CHAR? The secret is in the stack of the run-time system of the language environment. As we learned in the introduction of the procedure concept, each procedure call requires storing the local variables, the actual parameters and the return address for resuming execution after the invocation. Naturally this also applies for the recursive invocation of

```
MODULE TextReversal EXPORTS Main;                           (*18.07.94. RM; LB*)

  FROM SIO IMPORT GetChar, PutChar, PutText;

PROCEDURE Reverse() =
  VAR ch : CHAR;
  BEGIN
    ch := GetChar();
    IF ch # '\n' THEN
      Reverse();
      PutChar(ch)
    END
  END Reverse;

BEGIN                                                       (*TextReversal*)
   PutText("Please enter a character string:\n");
   Reverse();
END TextReversal .
```

Example 12.2: *Text reversal*

a procedure as well. Thus after Reverse reads "B" and detects that it is
not the return character, we move into the THEN branch, where we rescue
all local information onto the stack before the next invocation of Reverse.
When this recursive invocation (and all the recursive calls stemming from
it) have been processed, control is returned (as after every procedure call)
to the invoking environment. The subsequent statement outputs the contents of the local variable ch, which has been rescued onto the stack for
each recursive invocation. The reversal of the word results because each
invoked Reverse procedure itself invoked Reverse recursively between the
read and output operations. The return character entered after the last
printable character neither invokes a new procedure call nor generates output. In fact, viewed statically, it does nothing at all! This represents the
trivial case and ensures a nonrecursive invocation of Reverse. This breaks
the recursion chain, and the procedure call of Reverse that accepted the
last character before the return character (here the character "!") can print
its local variable ch and then pass control to its invoking environment.

Fibonacci numbers

Every recursive solution has an equivalent iterative solution. In many
cases, however, the recursive solution is easier to formulate and its correctness is easier to check. On the other hand, the iterative solution often
enjoys the advantage of greater efficiency, both in terms of the time associated with the administrative overhead of a procedure call and because,
as the following example will show, indiscriminate application of recursion
can lead to unnecessary recomputation of already available results.

top of stack

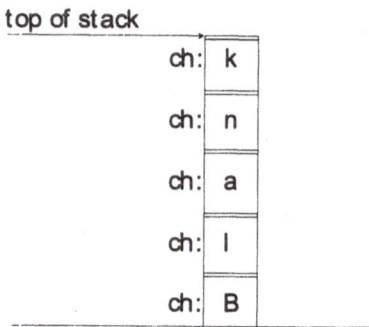

Figure 12.3: *Invocation stack of* Reverse *after entry of "Blank"*

An example of a problem that can be solved quite easily, yet quite inefficiently with a recursive approach is the computation of *Fibonacci* numbers.
Fibonacci numbers were introduced by the monk and mathematician Fibonacci in 13th century to describe biological processes (e.g., the reproduc-
tion of rabbits). Fibonacci numbers are defined with a recursive formula:

$$\text{fib}(n) = \text{fib}(n-1) + \text{fib}(n-2) \qquad \text{where } \text{fib}(0) = 1, \text{fib}(1) = 1.$$

This formula shows that the recursion extends over two steps. The next
respective Fibonacci number is the sum of its two immediate Fibonacci
predecessors. (The biological assumption is that females of two generations
are fertile). Thus we need two initial values or nonrecursive definitions for
the trivial cases: fib(0) = 1 (we begin with one pair) and fib(1) = 1 (the
initial pair gave birth to another pair in period 1; in period 2 – fib(2) – both
pairs can bear young.)

A recursive solution for the computation of Fibonacci numbers is quite
simple. We only need to transform the mathematical definition to Modula-3
syntax to obtain the solution given in procedure Fibonacci (Example 12.4).
But consider the execution sequence of this procedure for a call with the
parameter 5. Fibonacci(5) invokes Fibonacci(4) and Fibonacci(3). Then
Fibonacci(4) invokes Fibonacci(3) and Fibonacci(2). This makes the second invocation of Fibonacci(3). Since each of these evaluations invokes Fi-
bonacci(2) and Fibonacci(1), Fibonacci(2) is invoked three times in all. The
execution tree of Fibonacci(5) is depicted in Figure 12.5.

These recomputations of values that have already been computed elsewhere do not constitute a general characteristic of recursive programming;
instead, they result from the *functional* style employed here. However, this
style is closely related to recursive programming.

```
PROCEDURE Fibonacci(n : CARDINAL) : CARDINAL =
  BEGIN                                              (*Fibonacci *)
    IF n <= 1 THEN RETURN 1                          (*n = 0 or n = 1*)
    ELSE RETURN Fibonacci(n−1) + Fibonacci(n−2)
    END (*IF *)
  END Fibonacci;
```

Example 12.4: *Procedure to compute Fibonacci numbers*

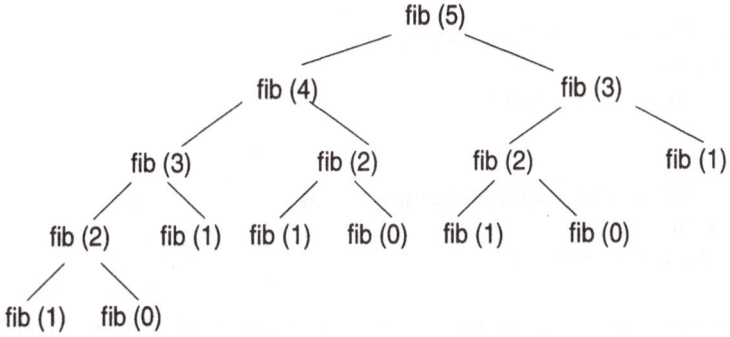

Figure 12.5: *The recursion tree generated by Fibonacci(5)*

The reader should attempt to design and program an iterative solution
to compute Fibonacci numbers and then compare this to the recursive
solution. The iterative solution is likewise simple and consists primarily of a FOR loop in which we add the last two values generated. We
have to be much more careful than with the recursive solution to ensure that in computing fib(n) we replace the value of fib(n-2), but not
of fib(n-1).

It would certainly be a mistake to conclude from this example that a recursive solution is fundamentally inefficient, memory-consuming and slow.
In many cases, unlike in this example, its efficiency differs little from the
iterative solution, and any loss of efficiency is more than compensated for
by greater comprehensibility of program correctness and the reduced writing overhead. Thus we should always consider whether the first solution
that comes to mind – be it recursive or nonrecursive – is the appropriate solution for the specific task, for the data volume to be processed, and for the
frequency of execution of the program. If we consider the overall costs of a
program over its life cycle, including the cost of possible errors, then we are
more likely to choose a recursive over a nonrecursive solution than if we
simply count how many procedure calls are associated with the recursive
solution.

End recursion

Since recursion represents a popular means for problem-solving especially in the field of *artificial intelligence* (*AI*), the AI community has studied the question of efficiency of recursive solutions and found forms that can be programmed recursively – such as in *Lisp* [M⁺62] – but that are automatically transformed to an iterative solution. This is easily possible with *tail recursion*.

```
PROCEDURE TailRecursion (n: ···, ···) : ··· =
  BEGIN
    IF trivialCase THEN ···
    ELSE
      ⋮
      RETURN TailRecursion(n-1, ···)
    END (*IF*)
  END TailRecursion;
```

By tail recursion we mean a form of recursion where no other action is necessary (except returning control to the invoking environment) after the recursive invocation, and the last recursive invocation returns the desired result. Our function Factorial in Example 12.1 belongs to this group.

12.1.2 Using recursion

We can employ recursion as an implementation method whenever the problem is recursive in nature. There are two possibilities:

1. Not only does the algorithm apply to the problem as a whole, but also the problem can be decomposed and the algorithm again can be applied to these smaller parts. The Fibonacci numbers serve as such an example (all mathematical sequences and series can principally be computed in this way). The same applies to sorting problems: If we can sort a large array, then naturally we must be able to sort two smaller ones. Thus if we can split the array such that the one half contains all the smaller elements (as yet unsorted) while the other half contains the larger ones, then we can apply the sorting algorithm recursively to each half (see Section 12.1.3).

2. Data structures are defined recursively. Consider lists (Section 11.5.1). A list consists of a node and a pointer to a successor, which in turn represents a list. If an algorithm works for the list as a whole, then it must also work for the list represented by the successor (see Section 12.1.5).

Another important example is a *syntax parser*, which is a program to process input that has complex syntax. Every compiler requires a parser. Since the syntax is usually defined recursively, a recursively structured parser is easier to build. Consider the expression syntax: an addition has two operands, each of which is itself an expression.

To design or to understand a recursive algorithm, as with proofs, you can find help in complete induction [Tru88]:

1. Find the recursive case. Here we assume that the problem is of arbitrary size. We attempt to separate one part such that the decomposition produces one or more subproblems whose basic structure is equivalent to the original problem description, but which have a narrower scope, or a lesser order (e.g., $\prod_{i=1}^{n} i = (\prod_{i=1}^{n-1} i)i$).

2. Define the end condition. That is, find the special case that can be solved immediately without recursion (e.g., $\prod_{i=1}^{1} i = 1$).

3. Test the convergence of the solution. Here we must first test whether the recursion we located in the first step actually reduces the magnitude of the problem. In addition, we must test whether this reduction ensures that we always reach the nonrecursive case, as found in the second step.

The reader should now attempt to use this approach to find the error in the following procedure, which claims for a given n to compute the sum of all odd numbers $\leq n$:

Example 12.6: *Erroneous recursive procedure*

```
PROCEDURE FauxPas(n: CARDINAL): CARDINAL =
  BEGIN
    IF n = 1 THEN RETURN 1
    ELSE RETURN n + FauxPas(n–2)
    END
  END FauxPas;
```

Unfortunately, this approach does not always help with recursive data structures. Sometimes we need multiple *indirect recursion*; here procedures do not invoke themselves, but are invoked by an invoked procedure. The syntax parser for an arithmetic expression does not invoke itself, but is invoked for each operand of the expression. We can only understand such invocation structures if we have understood the recursion in the data structure. Then for each procedure involved we must determine independently that it has a nonrecursive part or invokes another procedure that has a nonrecursive part.

Error detection

To help us gain an initial understanding of a simple recursive procedure, we can carry out a manual simulation. This helps us to understand what occurs in the computer (how the invocation stack is built up and reduced, etc.). However, this approach exceeds our capacities as soon as the procedure becomes a bit more complex. Thus we must concentrate on understanding whether and how the recursion converges.

How can we find an error in a procedure that seems to be correct to the best of our knowledge, but that runs infinitely (or terminates with some incomprehensible error message, such as when the system reports that all memory has been consumed)?

To determine exactly what the procedure does, it helps to insert test output commands at critical locations. Such critical points certainly include the start of the procedure and before each recursive invocation. In particular, we need to cover each recursive and nonrecursive branches of the procedure. Stopping the program at each such point (e.g., with EVAL SIO.GetChar) allows us to follow the invocations exactly. The following output data usually prove helpful:

- The parameter values on each invocation

- The values that determine which branch the procedure selects

- Possibly the level of recursion

To reflect the level of recursion, we need an additional parameter (e.g., level: CARDINAL). Each recursive invocation then increments this parameter (level + 1).

In any case, of course, we must ensure that, after localizing the error, we remove not only the test output but also the recursion level parameter. (Otherwise someone reading our procedure or its environment could waste valuable time puzzling over the function of this left-over test code.) Even better, the languages environment might provide automatic support for inserting test expressions in our program and later removing or deactivating them.

We have addressed methods for error localization only sketchily. The ideas by no means apply only to recursive algorithms, but here it is often particularly difficult to follow program flow. Many language environments provide *debuggers* (derived from the term *bug* for a program error). These allow stepwise execution of programs and interactive display of program states. For many programmers, debuggers have earned a reputation for delaying error localization because they tend to be employed before an erroneous program has been thought through exactly. Sommerville provides insight into methodical error localization in [Som92].

12.1.3 Quicksort

In Section 8.1, Example 8.13, we saw a simple sorting procedure with the drawback that the algorithm's overhead rises quadratically with an increasing number of elements. The analysis of the efficiency of algorithms is a very important subject with a multitude of available literature, e.g., [Knu81, Sed93, Wir76], but we do not discuss efficiency here. We only show one of the most famous sorting procedures, developed by C. A. R. Hoare. Because of its excellent speed (in most cases), it is called *Quicksort*.

The Quicksort algorithm is a classic example of recursion. It builds on the *divide-and-conquer* principle. The basic idea is that we decompose a problem recursively into subproblems until it becomes trivial. The Quicksort algorithm divides an array to be sorted into two parts, whereby all elements of one part are smaller than those of the other. These parts are themselves decomposed until the magnitude of the problem, here the size of the array to be sorted, becomes so small that sorting becomes trivial. The algorithm is described as follows:

1. Take any element x, e.g., the element in the middle.

2. Approach the middle from both sides. If you find an element on the left that is greater and on the right one that is smaller than x, then swap the two. This assures that we move both elements closer to their final positions.

3. Repeat the above step until you reach the middle.

4. Apply the above algorithm recursively to the left and right halves of the array until the array becomes trivial.

In the first three steps the array is *partitioned*. Afterwards it consists of two parts: the left part contains all elements that are smaller than x, the right side all those larger. Example 12.7 shows an implementation.

The excellent performance of the algorithm stems from the partitioning phase, where elements often "leap" across larger distances, directly putting them close to their final positions. Consider the following sequence:

    10 25 13 85 3 -2 4 7 77 1

First the element a[4], i.e. 3, is selected. The first partitioning swaps the following pairs: (10, 1) (25, -2) and (13, 3). In the new order all elements to the left of 3 are smaller, those to the right of three are larger than 3: 1 -2 3 85 13 25 4 7 77 10. The array is *not sorted yet*. We need to apply partitioning to all subarrays. For subarrays of size 2, naturally, partitioning produces complete sorting of the subarray. The number of iterations through the

```
PROCEDURE Quicksort(VAR a: ARRAY OF ElemType; left, right: CARDINAL) =
VAR i, j: INTEGER; x, w: ElemType;
BEGIN
(*Partitioning:*)
    i:= left;                                          (*i iterates upwards from left*)
    j:= right;                                         (*j iterates down from right*)
    x:= a[(left + right) DIV 2];                       (*x is the middle element*)
    REPEAT
        WHILE a[i] < x DO INC(i) END;                  (*skip elements < x in left part*)
        WHILE a[j] > x DO DEC(j) END;                  (*skip elements > x in right part*)
        IF i <= j THEN
            w:= a[i]; a[i]:= a[j]; a[j]:= w;                      (*swap a[i] and a[j]*)
            INC(i); DEC(j);
        END; (*IF i <= j*)
    UNTIL i > j;
(*recursive application of partitioning to subarrays:*)
    IF left < j THEN Quicksort(a, left, j) END;
    IF i < right THEN Quicksort(a, i, right) END;
END Quicksort;
```

Example 12.7: *Quicksort*

array rises logarithmically rather than quadratically with respect to array size. A more precise analysis can be found in the literature cited above.

We would add one programming note on Example 12.7: The procedure is parameterized with an open array, so that it can be employed without changes for an array of any size. Therefore on the first invocation of Quicksort we specify the actual values for left and right as follows:

Quicksort(array, 0, NUMBER(array)-1)

Using FIRST and LAST here would be wrong because the formal parameter a is an open array that is always indexed from 0. The index boundaries of array are thus lost within the procedure.

12.1.4   The Towers of Hanoi

The game Towers of Hanoi provides an interesting exercise. We have three "towers", i.e., three posts: Start, Finish and Temp. The Start post holds a number of disks of different sizes, sorted by size with the largest at the bottom. The task is to transfer the disks to Finish so that they are stacked there in the same order. We can move only *one* disk at a time, and no disk can ever be placed on a smaller one. The post Temp serves as temporary storage. We have no other help. The initial situation with four disks looks like this:

```
Start    Finish    Temp
  |        |         |
 ===       |         |
=====      |         |
=======    |         |
=========  |         |
```

This task seems to be a clear case for recursion. We want to decompose the problem until it reduces to moving a single disk (*divide-and-conquer*). Our first goal is to transfer all except the bottom disk onto the temporary post, making use of the Finish post and preserving the order so that no disk ever rests on a smaller one. Then we can transfer the largest disk to Finish. This reduces the problem by one disk. Then Temp and Finish swap roles, and we can repeat the procedure for the next largest disk. The strategy of the solution for n disks looks like this:

- n = 0: Do nothing – trivial case.

- n > 0:

  1. Transfer tower of size n-1 from Start to Temp (by means of Finish).
  2. Move disk from Start to Finish – its correct position
  3. Transfer tower of size n-1 from Temp to Finish (by means of Start).

The program is shown in Example 12.8. The actual solution rests in the simple recursive procedure Tower. Everything else, the cumbersome data structures and the long procedures, only serve to *display* the problem on screen.

> This is another example showing that the "peripherals" often cost more overhead than the actual solution to a problem. Naturally, we could have settled for a much simpler solution – such as outputting a number with each step. However, this would have unchallenging, and certainly boring.

Example 12.8: *The Towers of Hanoi*

```
MODULE Hanoi EXPORTS Main;                                        (*18.07.94*)

  FROM SIO IMPORT PutChar, GetChar, Nl;

  CONST
    Height    = 4;
  TYPE
    Post      = {Start, Finish, Temp};
    State     = RECORD
                    top: [0..Height] := 0;
                    disks:= ARRAY [1..Height] OF [0..Height] {0, ..}
                END; (*State*)
  VAR
    posts: ARRAY Post OF State;

  PROCEDURE Line(num: CARDINAL; pattern: CHAR := ' ') =
  BEGIN
    WHILE num > 0 DO PutChar(pattern); DEC(num) END;
  END Line;

  PROCEDURE Disk(d: [0..Height]) =
  BEGIN
    IF d = 0 THEN                                                 (*empty disk*)
      Line(Height); Line(1, '|'); Line(Height);
    ELSE                                                     (*draw disk pattern*)
      Line(Height–d); Line(3 + 2*(d–1), '='); Line(Height–d);
    END;
  END Disk;

  PROCEDURE Display() =
  BEGIN
    FOR p:= FIRST(posts) TO LAST(posts) DO Disk(0) END; Nl();
    FOR line:= Height TO 1 BY –1 DO
      FOR p:= FIRST(posts) TO LAST(posts) DO
        Disk(posts[p].disks[line]);
      END;
      Nl();
    END;
    Nl(); EVAL GetChar();
  END Display;

  PROCEDURE Transfer(from, to: Post) =
  BEGIN
    WITH f = posts[from], t = posts[to] DO
      INC(t.top);
      t.disks[t.top]:= f.disks[f.top];
      f.disks[f.top]:= 0;
      DEC(f.top);
    END; (*WITH f, t*)
  END Transfer;
```

```
PROCEDURE Tower(height:[0..Height] ; from, to, between: Post) =
BEGIN
  IF height > 0 THEN
    Tower(height − 1, from, between, to);
    Transfer(from, to); Display();
    Tower(height − 1, between, to, from);
  END;
END Tower;

BEGIN                                              (*main programm Hanoi*)
  posts[Post.Start].top:= Height;
  FOR h:= 1 TO Height DO
    posts[Post.Start].disks[h]:= Height − (h − 1)
  END;
  Display();
  Tower(Height, Post.Start, Post.Finish, Post.Temp);
END Hanoi.
```

The program halts after each step (by means of EVAL GetChar()). We resume execution by pressing the return key. After the first iteration we have the following output:

The following is the last output:

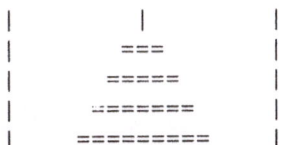

12.1.5 Recursive list management

In Section 11 we saw that lists are fundamentally recursive. Each list consists of a first element and a rest, which is itself a (smaller) list. Nevertheless, we handled our first list management iteratively. However, we might expect that lists with recursive procedures are easier to process. Let us transform the procedures of the iterative solution (Example 11.38 on page 269). Naturally we maintain the same interface and clients, changing only the implementation.

First we must find the nonrecursive cases. All procedures share a collective trivial case, the empty list. In addition, we have the case where

```
MODULE RecList;                                                    (*16.07.94. RM, LB*)

  REVEAL                                              (*Inner structure of T revealed*)
    T = BRANDED REF RECORD
        key: INTEGER;                                                     (*keyword*)
        next: T := NIL;                                        (*pointer to next element*)
      END; (*T*)

  PROCEDURE Create(): T =
  BEGIN
    RETURN NIL;
  END Create;

  PROCEDURE Insert(VAR list: T; value:INTEGER) =
  VAR new: T;                                                            (*new node*)
  BEGIN
    IF list = NIL THEN list:= NEW(T, key := value)
    ELSIF value < list.key THEN
      new := NEW(T, key := value);
      new.next := list;
      list := new;
    ELSE                                              (*seek position for insertion*)
      Insert(list.next, value);
    END; (*IF list = NIL*)
  END Insert;

  PROCEDURE Remove(VAR list:T; value:INTEGER; VAR found:BOOLEAN) =
  BEGIN
    IF list = NIL THEN                                                   (*empty list*)
      found := FALSE
    ELSIF value = list.key THEN
      found := TRUE;
      list := list.next
    ELSE
      Remove(list.next, value, found);
    END;
  END Remove;

  PROCEDURE Iterate(list:T; action:Action) =
  BEGIN
    IF list # NIL THEN
      action(list.key); Iterate(list.next, action);
    END;
  END Iterate;
BEGIN                                                                    (*RecList*)
END RecList.
```

Example 12.9: Sorted list with recursive procedures

we locate the position for insertion or the element to be deleted. Then we have nothing more to do than to reduce the list until it becomes a trivial case. We achieve this by recursively invoking the procedure with the actual parameter values list.next. This results in the (actually stunningly simple) solutions in Example 12.9. The entire iterative parts of the procedures in Example 11.38 have been reduced to single recursive invocations. Note that list is a variable parameter. On first invocation, the variable containing the pointer to the head of the list is passed to it. On the following recursive invocations, the next field of the previous element is passed, pointing to the next element in the list. Thus from the viewpoint of the procedure, the list grows smaller by one element with each step, and insertion and deletion always occur at the head of the current list.

The transformation from Iterate to a recursive function is easy – but the iterative form might be even simpler.

12.2   Recursive data structures

Lists already provide one example of processing recursive data structures with recursive procedures. In this section we delve deeper into the application of the recursion principle to data structures. The prototype of such recursive data structures is the *tree*.

12.2.1   Trees

Linear lists are dynamic: within the physical limitations of our computer's memory, we can form chains of any length, linking any number of information nodes. This is the list's greatest advantage over the array. At the same time, this is its drawback: What if a list really does contain tens of thousands, or even hundreds of thousands of elements (absolutely realistic numbers in practice)? Then sequential iteration through a linear list can take unacceptably long. Thus we need other dynamic *structures* that, although they might be more complex, can be searched more quickly and better serve large amounts of data.

The basic idea is that we must multiply link the information nodes somehow; we are not satisfied with the simple relations predecessor and successor, but need something more. If we connect the *nodes* freely with one another (we call the links *edges*, then we have a general *graph*, which plays an important role both in mathematics and in computer science [Tru88, Sed93]. Because increased freedom has its price, we begin with some restrictions. One important subclass of graphs is *trees*. A tree is a graph in which every node except for the *root* has exactly one predecessor (*parent*). The root has no predecessor. Each node can have any number of

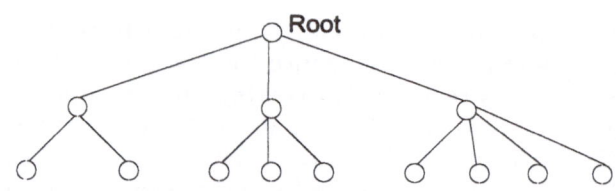

Figure 12.10: *A general tree as an acyclic graph*

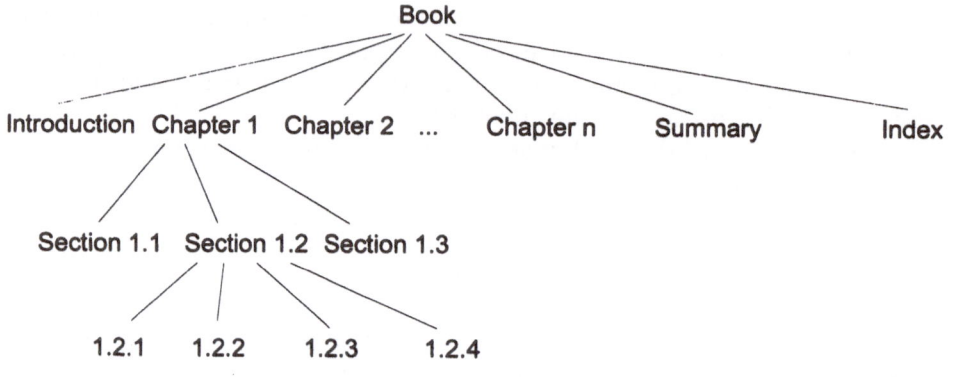

Figure 12.11: *Structure of a book*

successors (*children*). A tree is always *acyclic*; i.e., it contains no links that contain the same node repeatedly (no topological cycles).

The most frequent representation of trees is depicted in Figure 12.10. This treelike representation also reveals the origin of the name tree. This similarity is based on the fact that the branching structure of a natural tree – apart from seldom exceptions usually induced by external influences – is also acyclic.

> Note that in Figure 12.10 the root is at the top. Mathematicians and computer scientists apparently share a tendency to turn matters on their heads.

In programs, we implement trees using pointers. Pointers reference one node from another, which makes trees *directed graphs*; every edge has one direction. Furthermore, we have one unambiguous entry point into a data structure consisting of such pointers: the pointer that we statically declare in the program that employs this data structure. Continuing our botanical metaphor, we call this entry point the *root*, while nodes without a successor are called *leaves*. (The analogy has its problems, but since nature cannot defend itself against such analogies, we adhere to this terminology. We trust that the tree spirits will forgive us.)

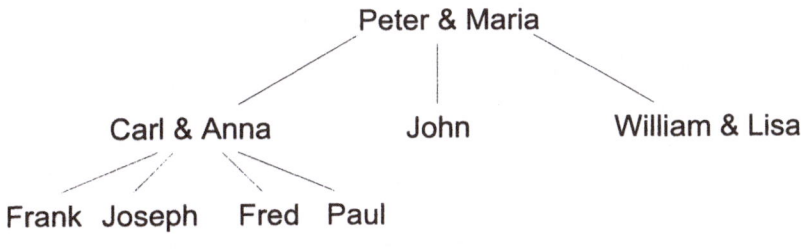

Figure 12.12: *A family tree*

Now let us consider how we could design such a tree. Obviously each node must contain information to allow us to reach its successors. Furthermore, a node should contain some kind of signpost information that tells us when we have reached our goal and when we must visit another immediate successor node. This suggests implementing a node as a record and entering the edges as fields of type REF RECORD · · · in this record.

This definition defines any node. Thus in principle it applies for the root, for an inner node and for leaves. The only difference is that the root lacks a predecessor and the leaves have no successors, while inner nodes have exactly one predecessor and at least one successor. The structure of a book serves as one example of a tree (Figure 12.11).

Family trees

Consider the family tree beginning with Peter and Maria in Figure 12.12. Family trees have strongly influenced the terminology of trees as data structures. Hence we call the node "Peter & Maria" the *parent* of "John", while "John" and "William & Lisa" are *children* of "Peter & Maria". This sounds less curious if we express it more precisely: The node designated as "John" is the child node of the node designated as "Peter & Maria". Furthermore, "John" and "William & Lisa" are *sibling* nodes.

Note that, because the graph is acyclic, each node's parent is determined unambiguously. On the other hand, a given parent node generally has multiple children. Clearly, each child node represents the root of an entire subtree. Thus the recursive definition really is justified. Note also that in our trees we forbid incestuous relations, thereby precluding violations of the acyclic condition of the tree structure.

Paths

A *path* in a graph is a sequence of edges starting at one node and leading to some end node. Accordingly the *path length* is the number of edges on a

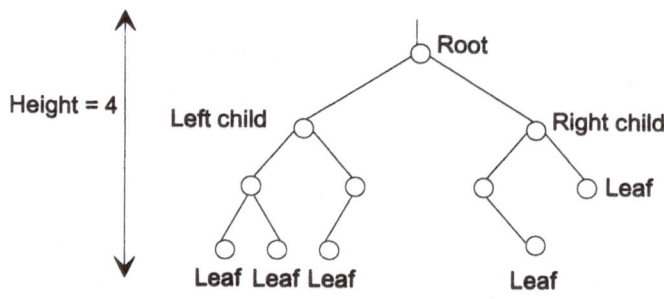

Figure 12.13: *A binary tree*

path, which corresponds to the number of successor nodes along the path from the first node. The number of nodes on the longest path starting at the root is the *height* of the tree. The height of an empty tree is 0; the height of a tree consisting of only a root is 1.

12.2.2   Binary trees and search trees

A *binary tree*, the simplest form of tree (Figure 12.13), has at most two successors for each node. We can best implement such a binary tree using records whose successors left and right point to the respective left and right subtrees. However, let us approach this solution gradually.

Search methods and implicit trees

Assume that we have a sequence of records stored in an array of fixed length. These records describe articles that we have in stock, where each article is uniquely identified by an article number. The articles are stored in the array in ascending order of article number. However, since these article numbers were assigned according to some ingenious system, article 1374 need not by any means be at position 1374. (Indeed, we do not even have that many articles.) We can only be assured that all articles with smaller article numbers fall before article 1374 and all with larger article numbers fall afterward. How can we search quickly and efficiently?

Certainly, searching the array from the first position to the correct one is not ideal. In the case of a nonexistent article, our search would always stop at the last position. Indeed, we do not read the telephone book from front to back to find the entry for "Zorro". We open the book somewhere close to where we expect to find the name and then move stepwise forward or back, usually in decreasing increments, until we find the correct page.

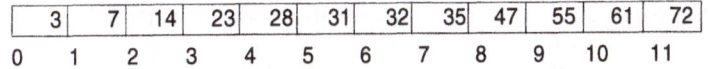

Figure 12.14: *Binary search in an array*

We can formalize this procedure in the following algorithm (in pseudocode):

```
WHILE search element not found DO
    divide and test partition element
    IF search element = partition element THEN
        found
    ELSIF  search element < partition element THEN
        search before partition element
    ELSE  (*search element > partition element*)
        search after partition element
    END (*IF search element = partition element*)
END (*WHILE*)
```

This leaves the following questions to be answered:

- Do we want to formulate the algorithm iteratively or recursively?

- Do we have information that can help us decide where to partition?

For the sake of simplicity, let us answer the first question in favor of a recursive solution. We must answer the second question in the negative; in such a case we can demonstrate that halving the search field proves best. Thus we select the element in the middle of the field still to be searched as our partition element. Let us try this using the data in Figure 12.14 by searching for some values. The program in Example 12.15 employs this principle.

In Example 12.15, we do not use an array of nodes that contain key values as well as other data fields, such as:

TYPE Node = RECORD key: INTEGER; data ···END

Instead, we declare an array of integers. However, such an integer can serve as a key for a record of any complexity, serving as the criterion for sorting and searching.

The procedure Search returns the index value of the element found. If the element is not found, it returns a value (MaxInd) outside the index range ([0..MaxInd - 1]).

```
PROCEDURE Search( READONLY arr: ARRAY [0 .. MaxInd – 1] OF INTEGER;
                  left, right: [0 .. MaxInd – 1];
                  argument: INTEGER): [0..MaxInd] =
VAR middle := left + (right – left) DIV 2;
BEGIN                                                    (*binary search *)
  IF argument = arr[middle] THEN RETURN middle                 (*found*)
  ELSIF argument < arr[middle] THEN              (*search in left half*)
    IF left < middle
      THEN RETURN Search(arr, left, middle – 1, argument)
      ELSE RETURN MaxInd          (*left boundary reaches middle: not found*)
    END (*IF left < middle*)
  ELSE                                            (*search in right half*)
    IF middle < right
      THEN RETURN Search(arr, middle + 1, right, argument)
      ELSE RETURN MaxInd          (*middle reaches right boundary: not found*)
    END (*IF middle < right*)
  END (*IF argument = arr[middle]*)
END Search;
```

Example 12.15: *Binary search*

First we check at index 5; from there, depending on the target value, we move on left or right, thereby reaching index position 2 or 8. From there we continue our search according to the procedure. Thus the recursive algorithm always follows a prescribed path through our data structure. Each element is viewed as a watershed: its value determines whether we continue searching right or left.

We could elevate this observation to a principle. For the search algorithm we obtain the structure in Figure 12.16. Obviously we see a tree evolving. The indices in Figure 12.16 have lost importance. We could replace them with pointers by storing with the key a corresponding pointer to the respective left and right successors. This tree indicates that we need at most four search steps (the height of the tree) to find any element (or establish its non-existence).

12.2.3 Binary search trees

We define a *binary search tree* (or *ordered binary tree*, Figure 12.17) as a binary tree where for each of its nodes all elements in the left subtree are smaller than the node itself, and all elements in the right subtree are greater than or equal to the node itself:

> *For all nodes of the tree we require that:*
> *– all keys in the left subtree < key in node* ∧
> *– all keys in the right ≥ key in node*

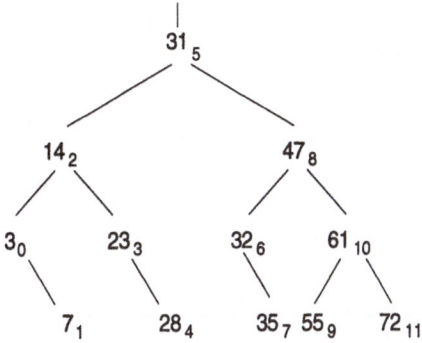

Figure 12.16: *Search path depicted as a tree*

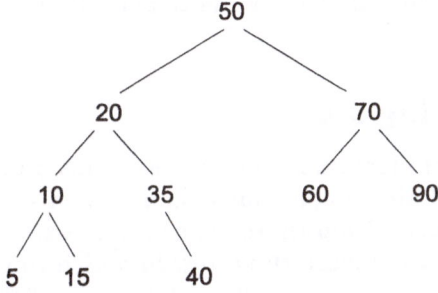

Figure 12.17: *A binary search tree*

By this definition any duplicates are inserted in the right subtree. Note that we achieve an equivalent definition if we insert duplicates in the left subtree, i.e., if we change the $<$ sign in the first line of the definition to $\leq$ and the $\geq$ sign in the second line to $>$.

During our search for a value in the tree, if we have opted for the left subtree, then we can be assured that all values in the right subtree are too large. This definition ensures that we can find the target value (or determine that it is not present) in relatively few steps – for n nodes approximately $\log_2 n$ steps.

Implementation forms

Now how can we implement search trees? Although arrays present one possibility, let us turn to the classical implementation of binary search trees. As in Example 12.18, this form uses references. Since we need no external access to any element except the root, it suffices to statically declare a single variable of type Tree in the program. The rest of the tree is a dynamic data structure like those we encountered with lists; the only difference is that the tree structure spreads out in two dimensions, making the data structure somewhat more complex.

Example 12.18: *Search tree as dynamic data structure*

```
TYPE
  Tree = REF RECORD
              info: INTEGER;
              left, right: Tree;
          END; (*Tree*)
VAR myTree: Tree;
```

Here the field info represents any information that contains some key value, or, more precisely, a key function. In Section 13.4.4 we will see means of representation that allow us to actually store complex information in a search tree.

12.2.4   Traversing a tree

Instead of individual elements, sometimes we need to process a tree as a whole, e.g., to output all elements on screen. For this purpose we obviously must begin at the root. From there we can process the left and right subtrees. However, we can choose the order in which to process the tree: We can process the data stored in the root *before* we visit the subtrees, *between* our visits to the left and right subtrees, or *after* visiting both subtrees. In each subtree we do recursively the same as in the root. Another decision is whether to first traverse left or right (or alternately left and right, but we omit this case). This makes a total of three basic strategies for *tree traversal* with two variants for each. We select the appropriate strategy to suit our problem domain.

The three traversal strategies (in the following pseudocode we use the names of the strategies as the names for the recursive traversal procedures) are:

- *Preorder*: Visit root first

```
visit root;                 visit root;
Preorder(leftSubtree);      Preorder(rightSubtree);
Preorder(rightSubtree);     Preorder(leftSubtree);
```

- *Inorder*: Visit root between subtrees

```
Inorder(leftSubtree);       Inorder(rightSubtree);
visit root;                 visit root;
Inorder(rightSubtree);      Inorder(leftSubtree);
```

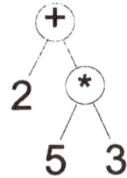

Figure 12.19: *The tree of an arithmetic expression*

- *Postorder*: Visit root last

    Postorder(leftSubtree);   Postorder(rightSubtree);
    Postorder(rightSubtree); Postorder(leftSubtree);
    visit root;   visit root;

If we traverse the search tree in Figure 12.17 (left first), we obtain the following order of visitation:

    Preorder: 50, 20, 10, 5, 15, 35, 40, 70, 60, 90.
    Inorder: 5, 10, 15, 20, 35, 40, 50, 60, 70, 90.
    Postorder: 5, 15, 10, 40, 35, 20, 60, 90, 70, 50.

One obvious application of inorder emerges: outputting the entire search tree as a sorted sequence.

For searching, we most often use the preorder strategy: Is the target element in the root? If not, continue searching to the left or right. Preorder and postorder strategies become more comprehensible if we consider the tree that emanates from the operators and numbers of an arithmetic expression (Figure 12.19). In this type of tree the leaves are always numeric values and the other nodes are always operators. Output in inorder 2 + 5 * 3 does not specify whether to compute (2 + 5) * 3 or 2 + (5 * 3).

Preorder output (+ 2 * 5 3) contains this information. It corresponds to functional notation. If we had the functions Plus and Times, we could write Plus(2, Times(5, 3)), the function names leading, the operators trailing as parameters.

Output in postorder corresponds to *RPN* (*reverse Polish notation*), as employed by some calculators: 2 5 3 * +. This processing strategy accommodates how a computer works. First we need all the parameters of an operation. When an operator is processed, the parameters are simply taken from the stack. In this case, we would stack 2, 5 and 3. Then the * sign indicates multiplication of the top two elements on the stack and pushing the result onto the stack. The + sign functions similarly, giving us the result 17 on the stack.

```
INTERFACE BinTree;                                      (*05.07.94. CW, LB*)

TYPE
  Direction = {Left, Right};                            (*traversal direction*)
  Order    = {Pre, In, Post};                           (*traversal strategy*)
  Action   = PROCEDURE (e: ElemT; depth: INTEGER);

  T        <: REFANY;                                    (*hidden tree type*)
  ElemT  = INTEGER;                                      (*element type*)

PROCEDURE Create(): T;
(*Initializes new instance of tree*)

PROCEDURE Search(tree: T; e: ElemT): BOOLEAN;
(*searches for an element e in tree. Returns true if present, else false*)

PROCEDURE Insert(VAR tree: T; e: ElemT);
(*Inserts e in tree*)

PROCEDURE Delete(VAR tree: T; e: ElemT): BOOLEAN;
(*Deletes an element e in tree. Returns true if present, else false*)

PROCEDURE Traverse(tree: T;                              (*Traverses tree*)
                   action: Action;                       (*Applies Action to each node*)
                   order := Order.In;                    (*default*)
                   direction := Direction.Right);
END BinTree.
```

Example 12.20: *Interface of the binary search tree*

12.2.5   Implementation of the binary search tree

In this section we implement a binary search tree as encapsulated data type (see the INTERFACE in Example 12.20). The procedure Traverse is somewhat unconventional: Parameters make it possible to select the strategy and the traversal direction. These parameters have default values. Traverse expects a procedure parameter of type Action. Then on traversal action is invoked for each node. The client of the interface can thus carry out various actions, e.g., printing the nodes (hence the whole tree).

Many actions require knowing the level of the current node. The level of the root is 0, of its children 1. The maximum level in a tree is termed its *height* or *depth*; the *level* of a node corresponds to the *path length* from the root to that node; compare Section 12.2.1.

The client in Example 12.21 reads the keys of a tree from a file and stores the result in a file (see Section 14 and Appendix C.3.3). The client's output of the tree is largely formatted: the root is at the far left, the levels are represented as tabs, the right subtree is at the top, and the left subtree is at the bottom. (If we turn the printout by 90 degrees, we have the usual graph representation.) The default values of the procedure Traverse (inorder, right to left) support this simple output. The output of the tree in

```
MODULE BinUser EXPORTS Main;                              (*21.07.94. LB*)

  IMPORT SIO, SF, BinTree;

VAR
  in: SIO.Reader := SF.OpenRead("dat");                (*Input in file "dat"*)
  out: SIO.Writer := SF.OpenWrite();           (*User specifies output file*)
  tree: BinTree.T := BinTree.Create();

  PROCEDURE Print(x: BinTree.ElemT; depth: INTEGER) =
  BEGIN
    FOR i:= 0 TO depth – 1 DO SIO.PutText(" ", out) END;
    SIO.PutInt(x, 3, out); SIO.Nl(out);
  END Print;

BEGIN                                                        (*BinUser*)
  WHILE NOT SIO.End(in) DO
    BinTree.Insert(tree, SIO.GetInt(in));
  END;
  BinTree.Traverse(tree, Print);
  SIO.PutText("\n\n", out);

  SIO.PutText("Enter the key of the node to be deleted\n");
  WHILE NOT SIO.End() DO
    IF BinTree.Delete(tree, SIO.GetInt()) THEN                  (*found*)
      BinTree.Traverse(tree, Print); SIO.PutText("\n\n", out);
    ELSE                                                     (*not found*)
      SIO.PutText("\nNot found\n")
    END; (*IF found*)
  END; (*WHILE NOT SIO.End()*)
  SF.CloseWrite(out);              (*Ouput file becomes persistent on closing*)
END BinUser.
```

Example 12.21: *Client of the binary search tree*

Figure 12.17 would be:

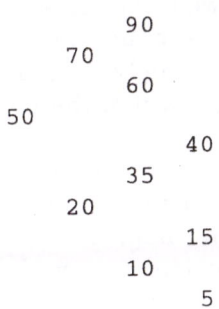

```
              90
        70
              60
  50
                  40
            35
        20
                  15
            10
                5
```

The client in Example 12.22 tries all traversal parameters. For inorder it outputs a tree; otherwise it outputs a sequence of numbers. The output of the same tree (see Figure 12.17) with traversal direction left to right (default is right to left) would be:

```
                    5
            10
                    15
        20
            35
                    40
    50
            60
        70
            90
```

As regards the implementation, we assume that trees are sufficiently recursive to formulate the algorithms for searching, insertion, deletion and traversal recursively. The iterative solutions are also easy to find, yet the simplicity of the recursive algorithms is more convincing than for lists.

The trivial case is an empty tree. All algorithms (similar to with lists) are based on the idea of decomposing the tree – naturally not literally, but from the viewpoint of the respective procedure – until it becomes trivial, i.e., empty.

The algorithm for *searching* can thus be formulated as follows:

```
IF empty THEN not present
ELSE
    IF     key < root key THEN search in left subtree
    ELSIF key > root key THEN search in right subtree
    ELSE found
    END (*IF key ···*)
END (*IF empty*)
```

Naturally the root changes with each traversal until we reach either an empty tree (not found) or the subtree whose root contains the target key.

The algorithm for insertion is almost as easy. Here we apply the same recursive principle to reach the position (certainly a leaf) where the new node must be inserted (see Example 12.24).

Deletion is a more difficult task. Here it does not suffice to simply find the target node. If this node is a leaf, it can be deleted immediately (Figure 12.23 a). However, if it is any other node, then its parent must take over the child's subtree (otherwise we literally dismantle our tree by pruning branches (subtrees), which we must avoid).

If the target node has only one subtree, the matter is still simple: with the pointer that pointed to the target, the parent of the target node can take over the target's subtree (Figure 12.23 b). However, if the target node has two subtrees, then we have complications: with one pointer, the parent

```
MODULE Traversal EXPORTS Main;                           (*22.07.94. LB*)

  IMPORT SIO, SF, BinTree, Text;

VAR
  in: SIO.Reader := SF.OpenRead(prompt:= "Input file for tree: ");
  out: SIO.Writer := SF.OpenWrite(prompt:= "Output file for traversal: ");
  tree: BinTree.T := BinTree.Create();
  print: BinTree.Action;

  PROCEDURE PrintTree(x: BinTree.ElemT; level: INTEGER) =
  BEGIN
    FOR i:= 0 TO level–1 DO SIO.PutText(" ", out) END;
    SIO.PutInt(x, 3, out); SIO.Nl(out);
  END PrintTree;

  PROCEDURE PrintSequence(x: BinTree.ElemT; level: INTEGER) =
  BEGIN
    SIO.PutInt(x, 1, out); SIO.PutText(", ", out);
  END PrintSequence;

BEGIN                                                      (*Traversal*)
  WHILE NOT SIO.End(in) DO
    BinTree.Insert(tree, SIO.GetInt(in));
  END; (*WHILE NOT SIO.End(in)*)

  FOR o:= FIRST(BinTree.Order) TO LAST(BinTree.Order) DO
    FOR d:= FIRST(BinTree.Direction) TO LAST (BinTree.Direction) DO
      IF o = BinTree.Order.In THEN
        print:= PrintTree                    (*prints elements in tree format*)
      ELSE
        print:= PrintSequence                 (*prints elements in sequence*)
      END; (*IF o*)

      BinTree.Traverse(tree, print, o, d);                  (*traverses*)

      SIO.PutText("\n\n", out);
    END; (*FOR d*)
  END; (*FOR o*)

  SF.CloseWrite(out);
END Traversal.
```

Example 12.22: *Client traverses the search tree in various ways*

cannot assume two subtrees. Therefore the endangered subtrees must receive a new root in such a way that the order relation defining a search tree is upheld. Thus either the largest node of the left subtree or the smallest node of the right subtree must substitute as the new root to replace the target node (Figure 12.23 c). Note that removing this "replacement node" is always simple because one of its successors must be empty (otherwise it would not be the largest or smallest.

(a)

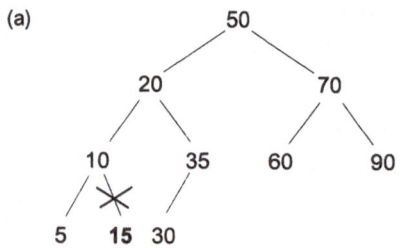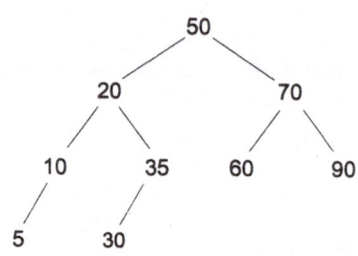

(b)

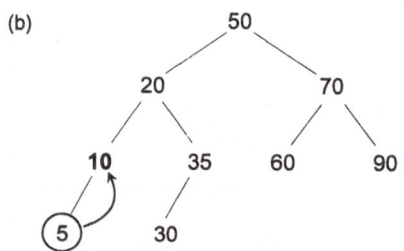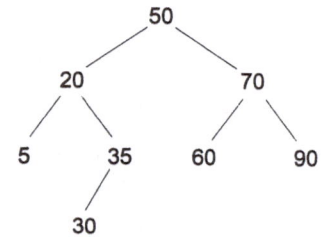

(c)

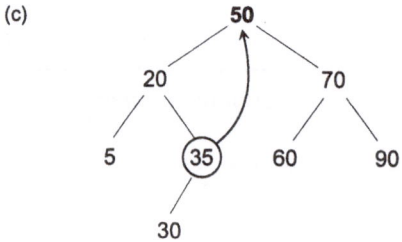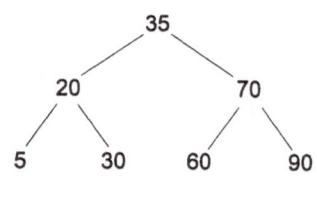

Figure 12.23: *Deletion of nodes 15, 10 and 50*

The procedure Delete in Example 12.24 demonstrates the implementation of the deletion operation. If the target node has two subtrees ((tree.left # NIL) ∧ (tree.right # NIL)), then this invokes the procedure LeftLargest. It finds the largest element in the left subtree and uses it to replace the target node.

Example 12.24: *Implementation of a binary search tree*

```
MODULE BinTree;                          (*05.07.94. CW, LB*) (*Binary Tree*)

  REVEAL
    T = BRANDED REF RECORD
          key: ElemT;
          left, right: T := NIL;
        END; (*T*)

  PROCEDURE Create(): T =
  BEGIN
    RETURN NIL                           (*An empty tree is simply "Nil"'*)
  END Create;

  PROCEDURE Search(tree: T; e: ElemT): BOOLEAN =
  BEGIN
    IF tree = NIL THEN RETURN FALSE
    ELSIF tree.key = e THEN RETURN TRUE
    ELSIF e < tree.key THEN RETURN Search(tree.left, e)
    ELSE RETURN Search(tree.right, e)
    END; (*IF tree...*)
  END Search;

  PROCEDURE Traverse(tree: T; action: Action;
                  order := Order.In; direction := Direction.Right) =

    PROCEDURE PreL(x: T; depth: INTEGER) =
    BEGIN
      IF x # NIL THEN
        action(x.key, depth);
        PreL(x.left, depth + 1);
        PreL(x.right, depth + 1);
      END; (*IF x # NIL*)
    END PreL;

    PROCEDURE PreR(x: T; depth: INTEGER) =
    BEGIN
      IF x # NIL THEN
        action(x.key, depth);
        PreR(x.right, depth + 1);
        PreR(x.left, depth + 1);
      END; (*IF x # NIL*)
    END PreR;
```

```
PROCEDURE InL(x: T; depth: INTEGER) =
BEGIN
  IF x # NIL THEN
    InL(x.left, depth + 1);
    action(x.key, depth);
    InL(x.right, depth + 1);
  END; (*IF x # NIL*)
END InL;

PROCEDURE InR(x: T; depth: INTEGER) =
BEGIN
  IF x # NIL THEN
    InR(x.right, depth + 1);
    action(x.key, depth);
    InR(x.left, depth + 1);
  END; (*IF x # NIL*)
END InR;

PROCEDURE PostL(x: T; depth: INTEGER) =
BEGIN
  IF x # NIL THEN
    PostL(x.left, depth + 1);
    PostL(x.right, depth + 1);
    action(x.key, depth);
  END; (*IF x # NIL*)
END PostL;

PROCEDURE PostR(x: T; depth: INTEGER) =
BEGIN
  IF x # NIL THEN
    PostR(x.right, depth + 1);
    PostR(x.left, depth + 1);
    action(x.key, depth);
  END; (*IF x # NIL*)
END PostR;

BEGIN                                                      (*Traverse*)
  IF direction = Direction.Left THEN
    CASE order OF
      | Order.Pre    => PreL(tree, 0);
      | Order.In     => InL(tree, 0);
      | Order.Post   => PostL(tree, 0);
    END (*CASE order*)
  ELSE                                          (*direction = Direction.Right*)
    CASE order OF
      | Order.Pre    => PreR(tree, 0);
      | Order.In     => InR(tree, 0);
      | Order.Post   => PostR(tree, 0);
    END (*CASE order*)
  END (*IF direction*)
END Traverse;
```

```
PROCEDURE Delete(VAR tree: T; e: ElemT): BOOLEAN =

  PROCEDURE LeftLargest(VAR x: T) =
  VAR y: T;
  BEGIN
    IF x.right = NIL THEN                        (*x points to largest element left*)
      y:= tree;                                  (*y now points to target node*)
      tree:= x;                                  (*tree assumes the largest node to the left*)
      x:= x.left;                                (*Largest node left replaced by its left subtree*)
      tree.left:= y.left;                        (*tree assumes subtrees ...*)
      tree.right:= y.right;                      (*... of deleted node*)
    ELSE                                         (*Largest element left not found*)
      LeftLargest(x.right)                       (*Continue search to the right*)
    END;
  END LeftLargest;

BEGIN
  IF tree = NIL THEN RETURN FALSE
  ELSIF e < tree.key THEN RETURN Delete(tree.left, e)
  ELSIF e > tree.key THEN RETURN Delete(tree.right, e)
  ELSE                                           (*found*)
    IF tree.left = NIL THEN tree:= tree.right;
    ELSIF tree.right = NIL THEN tree:= tree.left;
    ELSE                                         (*Target node has two nonempty subtrees*)
      LeftLargest(tree.left)                     (*Search in left subtree*)
    END; (*IF tree.left...*)
    RETURN TRUE
  END; (*IF tree...*)
END Delete;

PROCEDURE Insert(VAR tree: T; e: ElemT) =
BEGIN
  IF tree = NIL THEN tree:= NEW(T, key:= e);
  ELSIF e < tree.key THEN Insert(tree.left, e)
  ELSE Insert(tree.right, e)
  END; (*IF tree...*)
END Insert;

BEGIN
END BinTree.
```

Chapter 13

Objects

Many view the concept of *object orientation* as the culmination of traditional, structured programming concepts (many of which we have already come to know in this book), while many see it as something totally new. Both views are legitimate. First we introduce object orientation as a completely new concept, and then we embed it in the already familiar world of Modula-3.

13.1   Object-oriented modeling

Behind object orientation there is a certain view of how to *model* part of reality.

> Permit us a philosophical comment right at the start. In computer science we often say that we map a part of *reality* onto a *model*. We should be aware that we cannot find reality without an observer. When I say that this is the real world, then my statement, my observation, is part of it. This does not mean that the world is unreal or subjective, but only that the respective observer's complete world view is also part of that world. For example, we have good reason to assume that the world of a two-year-old child differs significantly from that of a forty-year-old adult, whereby obviously neither of the two need be more or less real. The fundamental difference between the "real" world and some modeled world seems to be that in the "real" world our view is *unconscious*, while in modeling we attempt to assume some *conscious* view. The process of thinking itself remains unconscious in modeling as well, but the basic concepts on which we build our model are conscious.

Object-oriented modeling takes the following view: The (modeled) world consists of a set of objects that represent self-contained units. They know

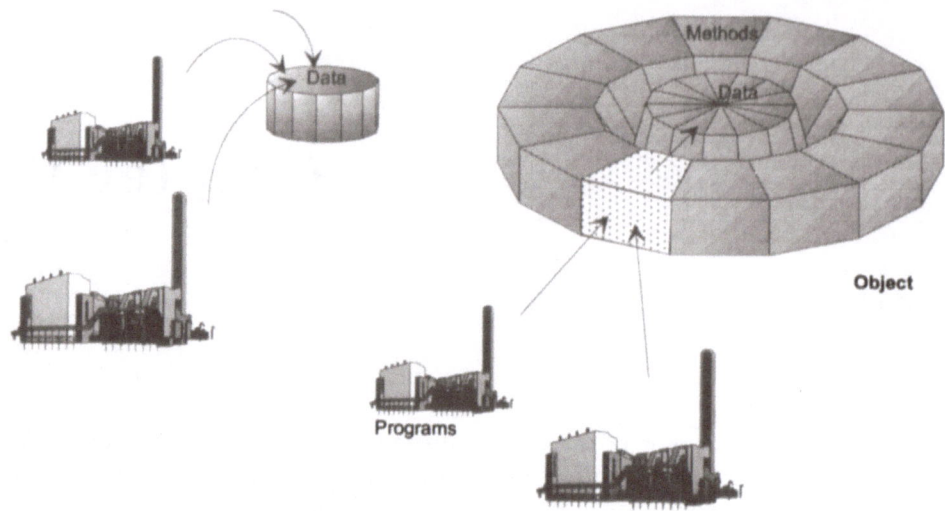

Figure 13.1: *Objects*

their own microworld where their states are stored in *fields* and their possible behavior patterns in *methods* (Figure 13.1). Objects can communicate with the outside world, i.e., with other objects, by sending and receiving *messages*. These objects are classified so that all objects of the same kind belong to one *class* (i.e., they have the same type).

> This kind of modeling proves quite useful for a number of technical problems. If we apply them to human domains, we have a particularly gloomy view of society: all individuals are classified strictly according to attributes, but are self-contained and encapsulated, and communicate with the outside world only via exactly specified, existing channels.

To access such an object, we must send it a message, which can contain parameters. In object orientation, the procedure that processes a given message is called a *method* and is invisible to the outside, just as the object's data is hidden. The answer is returned in the form of a message. This is the only way to access an object. The messages and their parameters are specified in advance. Thus an object equates to a data capsule (see Section 10.2.1), with the difference that we can create any number of objects of a given type, but can have only one – *the* – data capsule. With the introduction of encapsulated data types (Section 11.4), we gained the ability to repeatedly create encapsulated data, but we still had to provide the operations separately from the data.

However, the real advance of objects over data capsules and encapsulated data types is *extensibility*, enabled by the combination of data and

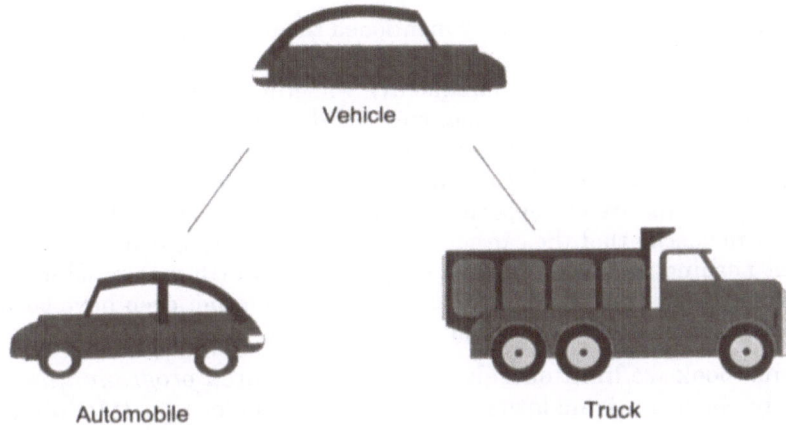

Figure 13.2: *Class hierarchy of vehicles*

the methods that process them. From existing object definitions we can derive new ones by specifying, "Take this definition and add the following data fields and the following methods". This forms a *subclass* of the original class, or *superclass*.

Subclasses have an *Is-a relationship* to their superclass: each object of a subclass *is* likewise an object of the corresponding superclass.

If we take the class Vehicles, we can derive the classes Cars and Trucks (see Figure 13.2). We can say that every car (passenger vehicle) or truck (cargo vehicle) *is* a vehicle (but not inversely, for not every vehicle is a car). Extensibility is a great advantage. For a system of classes, we can continue to add subclasses, making a system with new, additional features, without sacrificing the original features. This also enables us to delay certain decisions. Over time, the class of cars can be extended with various subclasses and thus specialized (e.g., cars for city traffic, cars for difficult terrain, etc.): they all remain cars and *inherit* all the features of a car.

A particular advantage of object-oriented modeling is its handling of *complexity*. Everything in this book so far has been moving in this direction. We have acquired ever more powerful language tools to better *structure* our solutions. Our efforts have taken two directions: on the one hand, we enhanced our data structures; on the other hand, our control structures. In the concept of *encapsulated data type* we combined these directions. Object orientation refines and extends this concept.

Object-oriented modeling encompasses a large part of the *life cycle* of a software project. It includes methods for object-oriented analysis (*OOA*), design (*OOD*) and implementation [RBP+91]. Object-oriented modeling has strongly affected and modified perceptions of the life cycle [Mey89].

In the introduction we briefly mentioned the *top-down* and *bottom-up* methods of system development. In the object-oriented view it is easier to *change* one's orientation frequently: sometimes the developer views the whole from the top; sometimes the details of individual components take precedence. In particular, it is easier to build *semifinished systems* that are complemented continually. Here semifinished does not mean that we develop cars with only two wheels at first, but that we can specify that the car has an engine with certain features, without needing to have a finished engine ready. Furthermore, later we can add a subclass for electric cars, which might not even have been foreseen when the information system was developed.

In this book we limit ourselves to object-oriented *programming*, which primarily concerns translation of an existing model to a (Modula-3) program.

Object orientation is certainly quite fashionable nowadays. Therefore there is an overwhelming amount of literature on the subject and nearly as many opinions on exactly what object orientation is and what it is not. We cannot engage in this discussion here; we attempt to present the concepts that seem to command a broad consensus. However, the reader should not be too surprised to encounter differing perceptions on this subject. (For additional reading, we recommend [Mey89], [RBP+91], [KM94] and [Mös93].)

13.2   Object-oriented programming

In object-oriented programming objects consist of a set of *object fields* (also called *instance variables*), which define the state space of the object and *methods* , which describe the behavior of the object. Objects have a type, and individual objects are *instances* of this type. Objects are *classified* according to their class membership. Many languages, including Modula-3, have an absolute root class to which all objects belong per definition.

The term class is used in differing ways. (We can even observe something of a "war between the classes".) Some see a class as the type, i.e., the *schema*, of an object group, while others mean concrete collections of objects (of compatible type). The first view tends to fall in the domain of programming languages, while the second is common in database fields. Here, by class we mean simply the type of the objects, but we do want to call attention to this important difference in terminology.

13.2.1   Encapsulation

The object concept, as already pointed out, is a further development of the concept of abstract data types; thus encapsulation is naturally a funda-

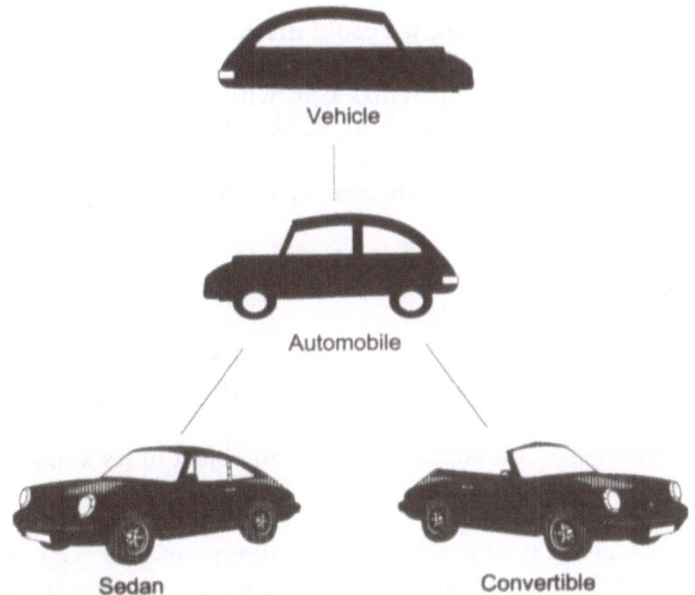

Figure 13.3: *Class* Car *serves as abstract superclass*

mental feature of classes. In a strict sense, a class interface should contain
only messages (more precisely, the signatures of messages, i.e., their names
and parameter lists); the fields must be hidden. Nevertheless, many object-
oriented programming languages do permit direct access to the fields of an
object.

Classes (object types) have a dual role: they have *clients* on the one
hand and *heirs* (subclasses) on the other. Clients use the services of a class,
or have a *uses* relationship. The client of a class Car can use cars in accordance with the interface. For clients, a restricted view usually suffices;
they normally see only part of the class interface.

The heirs (subclasses) inherit and extend the features of their superclass. They have an *is-a* relationship to the superclass (a car *is* a vehicle; a
convertible *is* a car). They need more knowledge of the inner structure of
the superclass than does the client. Hence a class must normally present a
somewhat more detailed interface for its subclasses than for its clients.

13.2.2 Inheritance

A subclass *inherits* all features of its superclass and can extend the superclass. Thus subclasses normally extend the set of fields and methods of the
superclass. Inheritance proves especially suited to *specialization* of a more
general class. A car is a specialization of vehicles; a convertible could be

a specialization of a car. Here we could discuss which is the more general case, a sedan with a hard roof or a convertible. To resolve this conflict, we can define an *abstract superclass* Car, which simply serves to allow us to derive *concrete subclasses*, such as Sedan and Convertible (Figure 13.3). With the help of inheritance, we can produce a *hierarchy* of classes. The subclass relationship corresponds exactly to the subtype relationship that we already know.

13.2.3 Polymorphism

We call variables that can take on various forms (that is, that can have different types) *polymorphous*. Procedures with polymorphous parameters are called *polymorphous procedures*.

Because an object of a subclass *is* also an object of its superclass, wherever an object of the superclass can be used, we can use an object of a subclass instead – but not inversely! Thus we can assign to any variable or parameter of a given type a value of any subtype of this type. This makes the object variables or parameters *polymorphous*. An object variable can change its type at run time. We can assign a Truck instance to a Vehicle variable. Note that it is not the object instance that changes its type, but the variable that can contain references to various object instances. We call the actual type the *dynamic type* and the declared type the *static type*. Assignment is not permitted between objects if the dynamic type of the right-hand expression is neither a subtype nor a supertype of the declared type of the left-hand expression. To this extent polymorphism is restricted: Vehicle variables cannot be assigned to Person objects. Simply stated, assignments are possible only along the type hierarchy that begins at the declared type.

Methods are polymorphous procedures: they can be applied to any object of a class hierarchy. For example, once we have defined a method to determine the speed of vehicles, it can be applied to cars, trucks and convertibles. Polymorphism in object-oriented languages is restricted to types within a class hierarchy. (For more on polymorphism in general, see [Mey89, CW87].)

13.2.4 Dynamic binding

A polymorphous procedure can be applied to objects of various classes (within the same class hierarchy). Often we need to adapt an algorithm more or less to accommodate the specific subclass. Therefore we can *override* methods of a superclass in its subclasses. Overriding means exchanging the algorithm of a method. If a truck's acceleration is different from that of a sedan (trucks record speed in a logbook), then the subclasses Truck and Sedan can override the method to determine speed. The new method is invoked by the same message, but does something different, depending on whether the message was sent to a Sedan or a Truck object. The *dynamic binding* mechanism guarantees that – depending on which subclass an object belongs to – the correct method is always applied. An algorithm that determines the speed of different vehicles simply sends an object the "set speed" message. Which method is actually invoked depends on the type of the object. Thus the methods are not statically bound at compile time, but dynamically at run time, when actual class membership is available.

13.2.5 Object-oriented applications

The spectrum of object-oriented applications is growing daily. In addition to object-oriented programming languages, e.g., object-oriented database systems [KM94] are ever more widespread. The first object-oriented application domain of all was *simulation*. The first application was implemented in the programming language *Simula-67* [DDH72], which was the first object-oriented programming language. In simulation we attempt to imitate the static structure and the dynamic behavior of some microcosm. We can develop simulations of a queue at a bank or of a production process. In such a simulation we can represent the individual machines and workpieces to be processed as objects. Each has its own state space and behavior. In terms of both space and time, each has a relatively independent existence. At times they need to exchange messages and *synchronize* their flow (see Section 16). Particularly this application domain puts inheritance to good use: there are typically abstract object superclasses (e.g., all tools, all machines, all queues, etc.) with certain commonalities; concrete object classes can be derived from these superclasses (e.g., the queue for a certain kind of machine for a specific kind of workpiece).

Another widespread application domain is object-oriented user interfaces. The actual dissemination of object-oriented concepts can be attributed to the success of the language *Smalltalk* [GR83] and menu-driven user interfaces, which were both developed at the end of the 1970s at the *Xerox Palo Alto Research Center* (*Xerox PARC*); this is why books on object-oriented programming even today most often use the example of user interfaces. The basic idea is that the user can *select* an object on the screen and then sends it a message, thus triggering some action (e.g., deletion, copying, etc.). The user first selects the object and then adds action. This action can be object-specific (more precisely, class-specific); i.e., the action of a subclass can be a refinement or specialization of an action of a superclass. (By contrast, in the procedural way of thinking, the action – the procedure – is always the focus and can be applied to various objects.)

This idea, together with the concepts of encapsulation, inheritance and polymorphism, has a very significant feature: *identical* actions are executed by *the same* program code (*code sharing*), and for *similar* actions only the deviating parts are processed by additional code. The major improvement here is by no means only that programs become shorter (which is also the case). Even before object-oriented programming, a very important quality attribute of a user interface was consistency, whereby the same or similar services should not be presented in different ways. The user should be able to learn certain conventions quickly, e.g., deletion with the delete key, selection with the left mouse button. It is unacceptable to require different actions on a case-by-case basis. Before object orientation these features were achieved by introducing very strict conventions for the development of a software product; programmers abided by these conventions to varying degrees. The object-oriented approach goes to the core of the problem: if all delete operations are executed by the same code, then deletion will always present the same appearance to the user. If certain subclasses require some modification of the deletion operation from the superclass, then at least the common parts are processed by the same code, and only the class-specific aspects are handled by the subclass. Polymorphous procedures can process variants of classes, and new variants can be added later without modifying existing code.

This should not give the impression that object orientation is a panacea for all programming problems. For example, it is not easy to design a thoroughly object-oriented user interface, that is, to find an adequate hierarchy of abstract classes. The following sections should make this clearer.

In the following we show how the basic concepts presented above (and some additional ones) find expression in Modula-3.

13.3   Object types in Modula-3

We have already mentioned the similarity of subclass and subtype relationships. Naturally this is no coincidence: Modula-3's subtype concept was deliberately so designed. We need absolutely no new language elements in order to meet the first requirement of object-oriented programming – encapsulation. The Modula-3 implementations of encapsulated data types presented in Section 11.4 (e.g., the encapsulated stack type in Example 11.28) are based on *subtyping* and *hidden data types*. However, this does not suffice to describe inheritance, polymorphism and dynamic binding. Here Modula-3 offers a new type constructor (**OBJECT**), which provides all significant object features.

13.3.1 Declaration of object types

Modula-3 objects are instances of object types (classes), which consist of *fields* (also called *instance variables* or *attributes*) and *methods*.

Syntax of object types

$\text{ObjectType}_{52} = [\text{ TypeName}_{85} \mid \text{ObjectType}_{52}][\text{ Brand}_{58}]$
"OBJECT" Fields_{59}
["METHODS" Methods_{61}]
["OVERRIDES" Overrides_{63}] "END".
Methods_{61} = [Method_{62} { ";" Method_{62} } [";"]].
Method_{62} = Ident_{89} Signature_{19} [":=" ConstExpr_{65}].
Overrides_{63} = [Override_{64} { ";" Override_{64} } [";"]].
Override_{64} = Ident_{89} ":=" ConstExpr_{65}.

The typical form of an object type declaration is:

```
TYPE Object = Super OBJECT
            fields
            METHODS
            methods
            OVERRIDES
            overridden methods
            END
```

Object is a subtype of Super. If we omit the supertype – which the syntax allows – Object would be a subtype of the predefined type ROOT, the root of all classes. Object inherits all attributes and methods from Super. This means that each instance of Object contains fields and methods of the same name as those in Super. Let us formulate an abstract vehicle class:

```
Vehicle = OBJECT
    position: RECORD x, y: REAL END;          (*coordinates*)
    speed: REAL;                              (*current speed*)
    load: REAL;                               (*weight of load in kg*)
METHODS
    newPos(x, y: REAL);                       (*set position*)
    setSpeed(mph: REAL);                      (*set speed*)
    loadFreight(kg: REAL);                    (*add to load*)
    unloadFreight(kg: REAL);                  (*subtract from load*)
END;
```

Thus our vehicles have position and speed and store the weight of their load. The fields are defined in a similar way as in records (see Section 8.2).

The method declarations specify the possible messages that the object class understands, along with their parameters. We can extend this vehicle class to an abstract car by additionally storing the number of passengers:

```
Car = Vehicle OBJECT
     passengers: [0..9]:= 0;                    (*number of passengers*)
   METHODS
     getIn(number: [1..9]);                         (*add to passengers*)
     getOut(number: [1..9]);               (*subtract from passengers*)
   END;
```

At some point the methods must be set to concrete procedures; otherwise they are NIL. We can write:

```
   ⋮
   METHODS
     getIn(number: [1..9]):= GetIn;
   ⋮
```

Thus the method named getIn is set directly to the procedure GetIn in the object declaration. This procedure thereby *implements* the method and must accept as its first parameter the current object (see Section 13.3.3).

A subtype developer who is quite satisfied with the object Car but who cannot use the method for setting speed (for cars that feature cruise control) can use the OVERRIDES clause to specify a custom method:

```
   SpecialCar = Car OBJECT
     OVERRIDES
       setSpeed:= SetCruiseControl;
     END;
```

This creates another subclass that is identical to class Car except that it has a different setSpeed method. Observe that here we only reference names; the message signature has already been defined in the superclass.

13.3.2 Implementation of objects

Objects in Modula-3 are always references. They are implemented internally as pointers to special records. In addition to the object fields, these records also have a pointer to a method table (see Figure 13.4). The internal representation of a subtype is exactly the same; only the list of fields and methods can be extended. It is clear that a method written for objects of type Vehicle can also process objects of type Car because Cars have the

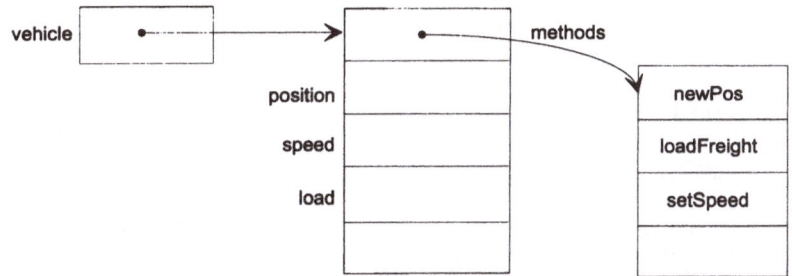

Figure 13.4: *Schema of the implementation of objects*

same structure, and their extension does not matter. All fields that the vehicle method requires are present in Cars with the same type at the same position in the record. The method does not access the extending fields (in fact, we could say that it is not even "aware" of their existence). Extending the class with new methods works analogously.

Subtyping simply copies all methods of the supertype into the new method table. We have seen that they can be used likewise for the new type. Only overridden methods are not copied. They are entered anew in the table at the corresponding position.

Dynamic binding of methods to the current object results because each method is looked up *in the object itself*. Sending the message setSpeed invokes the procedure that is entered at the corresponding position in the method table of the current object. For practical reasons, the method table is stored statically with the type (for objects of the same type, the methods are always the same). However, the pointer to the method table must be stored in each object.

13.3.3   Implementation of methods

Example 13.5 shows the implementation of a stack object. The type Stack contains the field top, which points to the stack. The stack is structured as a list of Nodes. The methods that define the operations on the stack are *implemented* as ordinary procedures. Apart from the first parameter, the signature of such a procedure must *cover* the signature of the method which it implements. That is, apart from parameter names, the default values and the raises set (see Chapter 15), the parameters and the return type must be *identical* if we omit the first parameter of the procedure. The first parameter identifies the current object, i.e., the *receiver*, to whom the message is sent. If the type of the object is T, then the type of the receiver must be a supertype of T (normally T itself). This parameter must be a value parameter (which prevents a method from destroying its receiver).

```
MODULE StackObj EXPORTS Main;                           (*24.01.95. LB*)

  TYPE
    ET    = INTEGER;                                    (*Type of elements*)
    Stack = OBJECT
              top: Node := NIL;                         (*points to stack*)
            METHODS
              push(elem:ET):= Push;                     (*Push implements push*)
              pop() :ET:= Pop;                          (*Pop implements pop*)
              empty(): BOOLEAN:= Empty;                 (*Empty implements empty*)
            END; (*Stack*)
    Node  = REF RECORD info: ET; next: Node END;

  PROCEDURE Push(stack: Stack; elem:ET) =               (*stack: receiver object (self)*)
  VAR new: Node := NEW(Node, info:= elem);              (*Element instantiate*)
  BEGIN
    new.next:= stack.top;
    stack.top:= new;                                    (*new element added to top*)
  END Push;

  PROCEDURE Pop(stack: Stack): ET =                     (*stack: receiver object (self)*)
  VAR first: ET;
  BEGIN
    first:= stack.top.info;                             (*Info copied from first element*)
    stack.top:= stack.top.next;                         (*first element removed*)
    RETURN first
  END Pop;

  PROCEDURE Empty(stack: Stack): BOOLEAN =              (*stack: receiver object (self)*)
  BEGIN
    RETURN stack.top = NIL
  END Empty;

VAR
  stack1, stack2: Stack := NEW(Stack);                  (*2 stack objects created*)
  i1, i2: INTEGER;
BEGIN
  stack1.push(2);                                       (*2 pushed onto stack1*)
  stack2.push(6);                                       (*6 pushed onto stack2*)
  i1:= stack1.pop();                                    (*pop element from stack1*)
  i2:= stack2.pop();                                    (*pop element from stack2*)
END StackObj.
```

Example 13.5: *Stack implemented as object type*

With this parameter the object identifies *itself* within the implementing procedure. Therefore this parameter is often called *self*. (In many programming languages SELF is a keyword; Modula-3 leaves the naming to the programmer.)

13.3.4 Accessing object components

As with record types, the fields and methods of an object type are accessed with qualified identifiers. We can read and write to fields and invoke methods. For example, if o is an object variable with a field f and a method m, then the field can be accessed as o.f and the method can be invoked as o.m(*actual parameters*).

In Example 13.5 we declare two Stack objects and create them with NEW. The created objects can then be accessed through their methods.

In the terminology we have used thus far we need to replace the expression *method invocation* with *message passing*. We say that we send message m to object o; o is the *receiver* of the message. The expression method invocation reflects the most common implementation: methods are implemented as procedures (not only in Modula-3), and sending a message to an object amounts to a procedure invocation. However, we must be aware that the concept of message passing differs from that of procedure invocation. This difference finds expression in the syntax: the form of a procedure invocation is P(o, *actual parameters*), which means that the same procedure can be applied to various objects; the form of a corresponding method call is o.m(*actual parameters*), which means that the method corresponding to the dynamic type of o is applied. The most important difference is that the procedure invocation is *statically* bound, while a method call is *dynamically* bound. Thus the procedure invocation P(o, *actual parameters*) employs the same algorithm, whereas o.m(*actual parameters*) can harbor any of various algorithms, depending on the current class of o.

In Example 13.5 we could have written Push(stack1,2) instead of stack1.push(2). The difference will become obvious later when we handle encapsulation, inheritance, polymorphism and dynamic binding.

The syntax indicates a difference between the (already mentioned) procedural and the object-oriented ways of thinking: In procedural programming languages (such as Pascal, Modula-2, C and Fortran) the algorithm is the focus. We develop an algorithm and invoke it with various parameters. The object to be processed is itself a parameter. First comes the "verb" (what is to be done), then the "object" (what is to be processed). In object-oriented programming languages (such as Modula-3, Eiffel, Oberon-2 and C++) the focus is on the object; what is to be done with it follows.

13.3.5 Creating objects

As we mentioned above, Modula-3 objects are always references to unnamed "special records". Thus objects must be instantiated with the predefined NEW function. Here the fields of the object can be set to values other than the default values (compare creating references to Record types, Section 11.2.1). Invoking

>   car := NEW(Car, passengers := 1)

creates a new Car object and sets the passengers field.

A specialty of Modula-3 permits creating objects of an unnamed subtype, with very similar syntax. We could have created an instance of type SpecialCar, as defined on page 314 as follows:

>   myCar := NEW(Car, setSpeed := setCruiseControl)

This amounts to a short form of:

>   myCar := NEW(Car OBJECT OVERRIDES setSpeed := SetCruiseControl)

On creation of a new object with NEW, its fields are created as well. The methods of a given class are the same for every object of the class; hence they only need to be physically created once. This does not conflict with inheritance or with the ability to override methods in a subclass. Thus methods belong to the whole class and so to the type. Therefore the methods can also be invoked via their type name. If O is an object type and m is a method thereof, then O.m invokes this method. Methods are invoked in this way on a *supercall* (see page 323).

An assignment between objects is subject to the rules of assignment compatibility (Sections 7.5 and 11.3). For assignment between objects, *reference semantics* apply. That is, if o1 and o2 are assignment compatible objects, then after the assignment o1:= o2 the object o1 references the same set of fields and methods as o2.

Objects cannot be dereferenced. In order to duplicate the set of fields, we would have to copy the fields individually (o1.f1:= o2.f1; o1.f2:= o2.f2; etc.). Methods cannot and need not be copied.

13.3.6 Subtyping rules for objects

We are already familiar with most subtyping rules. For objects, the following additional rules are defined:

>   ROOT <: REFANY
>   UNTRACED ROOT <: ADDRESS
>   NULL <: T OBJECT ··· END <: T <: ROOT

These definitions indicate that all objects are references. All traced objects are subtypes of ROOT, the root of all object types. The type NULL is a subtype of every object type, so that every object can assume the value NIL.

As with references that are not objects, objects are automatically managed by the *garbage collector*, so that storage for *traced* object instances to which there is no reference is automatically deallocated. Untraced object types are subtypes of UNTRACED ROOT, and their storage must be deallocated explicitly (with the DISPOSE procedure, which is permitted only in unsafe modules (see Appendix B.7)).

13.4 Encapsulation of object types

Thus far we have encountered objects only in their completely exposed form. However, we cannot present objects to clients in this way; this would violate the principle of information hiding. It would be quite senseless on the one hand to show clients the method getIn and on the other hand to allow free access to the passengers field. Yet we already know all language elements needed to enable encapsulation of Modula-3 objects in the sense of object-oriented programming. Now let us put them together.

Let us transform the example of the piggy bank in Section 10.2.1 to a piggy bank object (Example 13.7). We will implement the piggy bank object as an encapsulated data type. We can omit the procedures Deposit and Smash since the corresponding methods (deposit and smash) are now integral parts of type T. No assignments follow the method signatures, so that they are initialized to NIL. The implementation of these methods is *deferred* [Mey89]; they must be overridden by a subtype (which is done most simply in a separate implementation module).

The method smash can disable the piggy bank object, but cannot dispose of it (as by setting it to NIL) because the receiver parameter must always be a value parameter. The client must dispose of an object. (Objects are also created by clients.)

Creation and initialization of encapsulated objects

In Section 11.4 we expressly recommended that the interface of an encapsulated data type always include a procedure that creates and initializes instances of a hidden type. The implementation of this procedure should be in the implementation module, where the declaration of the type is fully revealed. Indeed, the latter is necessary because "ordinary" pointers (non-objects) can only be created in the scope of their full revelation.

The interface of the piggy bank object (Example 13.7) had no Create procedure, but instead an init method. We deferred creation to the client (Example 13.6). This is possible because objects can be created even if their type is hidden. But why does it make sense to separate creation and initialization of objects? The answer is in inheritance. Along a type hierarchy

```
MODULE PiggyBank EXPORTS Main;                              (*22.06.94. RM, LB*)

  IMPORT PiggyObj;
  FROM SIO IMPORT PutText, PutInt, GetInt, Nl;
TYPE
  PiggyBanks = ARRAY [0 .. 1] OF PiggyObj.T;
VAR
  sty: PiggyBanks;                                          (*sty of piggy banks*)
  amount, index: INTEGER;
  active := NUMBER(PiggyBanks);                 (*number of intact piggy banks*)
BEGIN                                                          (*PiggyBank2*)
  PutText("Piggy bank:\n" &
          "Positive amount is deposited; negative amount smashes bank.\n" &
          "Odd amounts go in piggy bank 1; even amounts go in piggy bank 0.\n");

  FOR s:= FIRST(sty) TO LAST(sty) DO
    sty[s]:= NEW(PiggyObj.T).init();                (*create and initialize object)*)
  END;

  WHILE active > 0 DO
    amount:= GetInt();
    index:= ABS(amount) MOD NUMBER(sty);
    IF amount >= 0 THEN                                           (*deposit*)
      IF sty[index] # NIL THEN sty[index].deposit(amount) END
    ELSE                                                           (*smash*)
      PutText("Contents of piggy bank–"); PutInt(index, 1);
      PutInt(sty[index].smash(), 6); Nl();
      sty[index]:= NIL;                              (*object actually destroyed*)
      DEC(active);                          (*reduce number of intact piggy banks*)
    END; (*IF amount >= 0*)
  END; (*WHILE active > 0 smash all piggy banks*)
END PiggyBank.
```

Example 13.6: *Usage of the piggy bank object type*

each subtype can add new fields to the inherited ones. The farther down the hierarchy a subtype is, the more "heavyweight" it becomes. We must create an object where it is heaviest, where no further subtypes are added, normally at the client level. The hidden fields still need to be initialized by their owner. Therefore, for each object that is defined in an interface, we provide an init method. In trivial cases where all fields are initialized with constant values, we can omit the init method (in the case of the piggy bank, we could have spared ourselves the init method for this reason).

Immediately after creation of an object, the client must invoke the object's init method. Before this method initializes the fields that are visible to it, it can invoke the init method of its supertype, which can invoke its supertype's method, and so on. In this way initialization can progress through to the root type (see also the redefinition of methods in Section 13.4.3). In

```
INTERFACE PiggyObj;                                    (*22.06.94. RM, LB*)

   TYPE
      T      <: Public;
      Public = OBJECT
                METHODS
                   init(): T;
                   deposit(cash: CARDINAL);            (*deposit cash*)
                   smash(): CARDINAL;      (*return contents and block piggy bank*)
                END; (*Public*)
END PiggyObj.
```

Example 13.7: Interface of the piggy bank object type

```
MODULE PiggyObj;                                       (*22.06.94. RM, LB*)

   REVEAL
      T = Public BRANDED OBJECT
            contents: INTEGER;
         OVERRIDES
            init:= Init;
            deposit:= Deposit;
            smash:= Smash;
         END; (*T*)

   PROCEDURE Init(t: T): T =
   BEGIN
      t.contents:= 0;
      RETURN t
   END Init;

   PROCEDURE Deposit(t: T; amount: CARDINAL) =
   BEGIN
      <* ASSERT t.contents >= 0 *>           (*error in smashed piggy bank*)
      INC(t.contents, amount);
   END Deposit;

   PROCEDURE Smash(t: T): CARDINAL =
   VAR s: CARDINAL := t.contents;            (*record piggy bank contents*)
   BEGIN
      t.contents:= −1;                       (*piggy bank is disabled*)
      RETURN s
   END Smash;

BEGIN
END PiggyObj.
```

Example 13.8: Implementation of the piggy bank object type

adherence to a widespread convention, the init method usually has a signature like a function with a return type T. As its result init returns the object to be initialized. Since the init method can only be applied to an object already created (with NEW), a pure procedure signature would suffice; we already know the object to be initialized. However, the function form has two advantages:

1. The client can invoke the init method directly on declaration, e.g.,

   ```
   VAR sp := NEW(PiggyObj.T).init();
   ```

   If init were defined as a pure procedure, then the client would have to write:

   ```
   VAR sp := NEW(PiggyObj.T);
   BEGIN
     sp.init();
   ⋮
   ```

   The former notation has the advantage that the invocation of the init method is less often forgotten, which avoids a frequent and unpleasant error.

2. A possible failure of an initialization can be signaled with the return value NIL. This allows immediately undoing the instantiation.

A sty full of piggy bank objects

The client module (Example 13.6) shows how the objects are created and initialized, how their methods are invoked, and how they are finally disposed of. The following is a possible execution of the program in Example 13.6 (without greeting):

```
1 2 3 4 5 6 7 8 9 10 -1 -2
Contents of piggy bank-1 25
Contents of piggy bank-0 30
```

In the implementation of the piggy bank object type (Example 13.8), the methods defined in the interface are overridden by a concrete implementation. Note that init allows us to "repair" a "smashed" piggy bank object.

13.4.1 Inheritance

Now let us extend our piggy bank so that it accepts only deposits of valid coins; we will call our extension a coin bank. Invalid amounts are not accepted, and the coin bank is intelligent enough to record the sum of invalid amounts. We can implement this kind of coin bank as a specialization of our piggy bank. It requires an additional method to calculate the sum of invalid amounts, and we must adapt the method deposit accordingly (Example 13.9 and 13.10). The interface introduces the constant Valid, which defines the set of valid coins. The type CoinBank.T is a subtype of Piggy-Obj.T. Therefore the coin bank contains all fields and methods of a piggy bank. The hidden field contents is also present, although not directly accessible. The modified specification of the method deposit is in the form of a comment. The method missed is new.

The implementation in Example 13.10 overrides deposit with a new procedure that calls the deposit method of the superclass (PiggyObj.T) for valid amounts (the supermethod is designated by explicit specification of its type name). Invocation of a method of a superclass is called a *supercall*. Note that we must pass the receiver object as the first parameter in order to invoke a method via its type name. To invoke the (parameterless) method m "normally" via an object o of type T, we write o.m(). However, for a supercall we write T.m(o). A supercall is actually a procedure invocation: we thereby circumvent dynamic binding and directly invoke the procedure that implements the method m in type T. The method missed returns the sum of invalid amounts, which is stored in a new, hidden field.

The usage of a coin bank very much resembles that of a piggy bank. Example 13.11 has an instance of a coin bank. Note that it is important that we explicitly specified the type (CoinBank.T) in the declaration of the variable bank. If we had only written VAR bank := NEW(CoinBank.T).init(), then the static type of the variable bank would derive from the declared return type of init(), i.e., PiggyObj.T. In this case the method invocation bank.missed() would not be possible because a PiggyObj.T object does not recognize this method – although in principle the *dynamic type* of bank would permit this. This example shows that it really is advisable to always explicitly specify the type (except in trivial cases).

The declaration of the variable bank in Example 13.11 poses another question. Here we assign an object of subtype CoinBank.T a value of its supertype (the return type PiggyObj.T of init). Section 11.3 showed that this is permissible if the value on the right side of the assignment is in the range of the type on the left side. Is this condition met? We can only answer this question by precisely following the execution of the above assignment. The invocation of NEW(CoinBank.T) creates a (nameless) object of type Coin-Bank.T. We send this object the init message (we invoke its init method),

```
INTERFACE CoinBank;                                    (*22.06.94. RM, LB*)

  IMPORT PiggyObj;

  CONST
    Valid = SET OF [1 .. 20] {1, 2, 5, 10, 20};              (*valid coins*)
  TYPE
    T <: Public;                                     (*subtype of PiggyObj.T*)
    Public = PiggyObj.T OBJECT
            METHODS                          (*deposit accepts only valid coins*)
              missed(): CARDINAL;                  (*sum of invalid amounts*)
            END; (*Public*)
END CoinBank.
```

Example 13.9: Coin bank object type is a subtype of PiggyObj.T

```
MODULE CoinBank;                                       (*22.06.94. RM, LB*)

  IMPORT PiggyObj;

  REVEAL
    T = Public BRANDED OBJECT
          invalidAmount: CARDINAL := 0;                  (*additional field*)
        OVERRIDES
          missed := Missed;
          deposit:= Deposit;
        END; (*T*)

  PROCEDURE Deposit(bank: T; sum: CARDINAL) =
  BEGIN
    IF sum IN Valid THEN
      PiggyObj.T.deposit(bank, sum)          (*method of superclass (supercall)*)
    ELSE
      INC(bank.invalidAmount, sum);
    END;
  END Deposit;

  PROCEDURE Missed(bank: T) : CARDINAL =
  BEGIN
    RETURN bank.invalidAmount
  END Missed;

BEGIN                                                       (*CoinBank*)
END CoinBank.
```

Example 13.10: Implementation of the coin bank object type

which returns the same object. The type of the object instance remains
CoinBank.T. Thus the actual return value of init is of type CoinBank.T. Thus
the assignment is correct.

```
IMPORT CoinBank;

VAR
  bank: CoinBank.T := NEW(CoinBank.T).init();          (*create & initialize*)
  sum, contents, missed: INTEGER;

BEGIN
  ⋮
    IF sum >= 0 THEN                                              (*deposit*)
      bank.deposit(sum)                                   (*sum for deposit*)
    ELSE                                                            (*smash*)
      missed:= bank.missed();                    (*first removes missed coins*)
      contents:= bank.smash();              (*removes contents of coin bank*)
  ⋮
```

Example 13.11: *Usage of subclass* CoinBank

13.4.2 Polymorphism and dynamic binding

In the above example we developed first the class of piggy banks and then its subclass, the class of coin banks. Thus every coin bank *is* a piggy bank, but a specialized one. Thus we can use polymorphous variables and procedures. To really exploit this feature, we need some new language constructs that will help us to determine the dynamic type of an object or to access an object according to its dynamic type. NARROW and ISTYPE are built-in functions; TYPECASE is a new statement. The dynamic type of a reference variable can be tested only at run time if its static type is a traced reference type or an object type (even untraced).

Narrow

The signature of NARROW is:

    NARROW(x: Reference; T: ReferenceType): T

Note that the second parameter of NARROW is a type (such a signature is not permitted for user-defined procedures in Modula-3). The type must be a traced reference type or an object type. NARROW tests whether x is contained in type T. If not, it generates a run-time error. If so, x is returned unchanged, but no longer with its original static type, but as a T object. NARROW is typically used in cases where T is a subtype of the static type of x (hence the name: it restricts the type range to the subtype). Assume the following declarations (P1 and P2 are procedures and are not specified further):

```
TYPE
   Super = OBJECT METHODS          m1() := P1 END;
   Sub   = Super OBJECT METHODS m2() := P2 END;
VAR
   super := NEW(Super);
   sub   := NEW(Sub);
```

super has a method (m1); sub has inherited this method and has the additional method m2. The following method invocations and assignments are no problem:

```
super.m1();
sub.m1();
sub.m2();
super := sub;              (*Dynamic type of super becomes Sub*)
```

The last statement assigned sub to super. Thus the dynamic type of super changes to Sub; in other words, super later points to a Sub object. The method m2 can also be applied to super. However, the compiler does not permit the invocation super.m2() because the declared (static) type of super is Super, which does not recognize the method m2. The NARROW function can help in this situation:

```
NARROW(super, Sub).m2();
```

With the NARROW function we maintain that an object (super) is contained in the specified type (Sub) and thus the additional fields and methods (m2) are present. For this reason the compiler permits the above assignment: the programmer assumes liability that the object actually is contained in the type. If this assertion is false (e.g., if the assignment super := sub is missing), then NARROW produces a run-time error.

Istype

Situations can occur (especially in polymorphous functions) where we do not know the dynamic type of a variable or a parameter. In such cases NARROW is too strict; it generates a run-time error if the dynamic type is unsuitable. Here it would be better if we could test the dynamic type at run time. For this purpose Modula-3 provides ISTYPE and TYPECASE. The signature of ISTYPE is:

```
ISTYPE(x: Reference; T: ReferenceType): BOOLEAN
```

ISTYPE returns *true* if and only if x is contained in type T. The type must be a traced reference type or an object type. In the above example

```
ISTYPE(super, Sub)
```

would return *false* before the assignment super := sub, but afterwards *true*.

Typecase

ISTYPE allows us to formulate conditional statements. To allow testing the *type* of an expression analogously to testing the *value* of an expression, Modula-3 provides the TYPECASE statement. Its syntax closely resembles that of the CASE statement; the major difference is that the values of the CASE marks must be types.

Syntax

$$\text{TCaseStmt}_{37} = \text{"TYPECASE" Expr}_{66} \text{"OF" [Tcase}_{45}\text{]}$$
$$\{ \text{"|" Tcase}_{45} \} \text{ ["ELSE" Stmts}_{23}\text{] "END".}$$
$$\text{Tcase}_{45} \quad = \text{Type}_{48} \{ \text{"," Type}_{48} \} \text{ ["(" Ident}_{89}\text{ ")"] "=>" Stmts}_{23}.$$

The general form of a TYPECASE statement is:

TYPECASE *expression* OF
| *type_1* (*auxiliary variable_1*) => *statement_1*
⋮
| *type_n* (*auxiliary variable_n*) => *statement_n*
ELSE *statement_0*
END

The type of the expression must be a traced reference type or an object type. All *type_i* must be subtypes of this type. The ELSE branch and the auxiliary variables are optional. The scope of *auxiliary variable_i* is *statement_i*. Types that have no auxiliary variables and select the same statement can be combined in a list. Therefore we can write the following:

| *type_i* => *statement*
⋮
| *type_k* => *statement*

in shorter form as follows:

type_i, ⋯ *type_k* => *statement*

The TYPECASE statement executes as follows: First the expression is computed. If the result is contained in several of the enumerated types, then the alternative is selected that appears first (*type_i* with the smallest *i*). This means that in the TYPECASE statement we must consider the order of the alternatives. If *type_1* <: *type_2* <: *type_3*, then in the TYPECASE statement *type_1* should appear first. If *type_3* were to appear first, then this alternative would snatch all objects of types *type_1* to *type_3*. This means that type NULL should only appear as first and type ROOT only as last alternative.

Despite its syntactic resemblance, the TYPECASE statement differs significantly from the CASE statement: Not only does it evaluate types instead of values, it is also sensitive to the order of alternatives. Since the latter is not true of the CASE statement, in this aspect TYPECASE resembles the IF-ELSIF statement more.

The type of the *auxiliary variable$_i$* (if present) is *type$_i$*; it is initialized with the value of the expression. If the expression is contained in none of the listed types, then the ELSE branch is executed if available; otherwise a run-time error is generated.

For the equivalence of TYPECASE and IF statements with ISTYPE tests, similar considerations apply as for the equivalence of CASE and IF statements (Section 5.4.3). Usually they can be transformed back and forth without difficulty; however, we do need to watch for any side effects.

Example 13.12 declares instances of both a piggy bank and a coin bank. The procedures Deposit and Withdraw are polymorphous. Each has a formal parameter of type PiggyObj.T. According to the rules of assignment compatibility, any subtypes are permitted as actual parameters, including coin banks. The procedure Deposit first invokes the method deposit. The mechanism of dynamic binding assures the selection of the unrestricted deposit method for piggy bank objects, but the restricted one for coin bank objects. In this procedure let us generate an error message in the event of an invalid deposit attempt for a coin bank. Hence we test the dynamic type of the parameter s with ISTYPE. The procedure Withdraw employs TYPE-CASE (although it could just as well use ISTYPE) to determine the dynamic type of parameter p. If the type is CoinBank.T, we can invoke the method missed. Note the order: if we exchange the two alternatives, then TYPE-CASE would always execute alternative PiggyObj.T.

A possible execution of Example 13.12 (without greeting) is the following:

```
1 2 3 4 5 6 7 8 9 10 -1
Invalid amount for coin bank = 3
Invalid amount for coin bank = 4
Contents of piggy bank = 40
Invalid attempts = 7 Contents of coin bank = 8
```

13.4.3 Generalization

Let us develop a savings account which permits more flexibility than a piggy bank. We want to allow any number of deposits and withdrawals and to be able to query the account balance. We will not consider the computation of interest here.

The question is, can we define such a savings account as a specialization or extension of the piggy bank? The method deposit can be used for making deposits. But the method smash creates some problems: it destroys the

```
MODULE BankPoly EXPORTS Main;                              (*27.06.94. LB*)

  IMPORT PiggyObj, CoinBank;
  FROM SIO IMPORT PutText, PutInt, GetInt, Nl;

  PROCEDURE Deposit(p: PiggyObj.T; amount: CARDINAL) =
  BEGIN
    p.deposit(amount);              (*the correct method is selected automatically*)
    IF ISTYPE(p, CoinBank.T)              (*tests whether p is of type CoinBank.T*)
       AND NOT amount IN CoinBank.Valid    (*and whether the amount is invalid*)
    THEN
      PutText("Invalid amount for coin bank = "); PutInt(amount); Nl();
    END; (*IF ISTYPE(p, CoinBank.T)...*)
  END Deposit;

  PROCEDURE Withdraw(p: PiggyObj.T) =
  VAR t: TEXT;
  BEGIN
    TYPECASE p OF                            (*tests the dynamic type of p*)
    | CoinBank.T(c) => t:= "coin";                              (*coin bank*)
                       PutText("Invalid attempts = ");
                       PutInt(c.missed());     (*c designates p as coin bank object*)
                       PutText(" ");
    | PiggyObj.T    => t:= "piggy";                            (*piggy bank*)
    END; (*TYPECASE p*)
    PutText("Contents of " & t & " bank" & " = ");
    PutInt(p.smash());                          (*smash was not overridden*)
    Nl();
  END Withdraw;

VAR
  coin: CoinBank.T := NEW(CoinBank.T).init();    (*creation & initialization*)
  piggy: PiggyObj.T := NEW(PiggyObj.T).init();   (*creation & initialization*)
  amount: INTEGER;

BEGIN
  PutText("CoinBank accepts only valid coins.\n" &
    "Positive amounts are deposited; negativ amount smashes bank.\n" &
    "Amounts < 6 go to coin bank, others to piggy bank.\n");
  REPEAT
    amount:= GetInt();
    IF amount >= 0 THEN                                          (*deposit*)
      IF amount < 6 THEN Deposit(coin, amount) ELSE Deposit(piggy, amount) END;
    ELSE                                                          (*smash*)
      Withdraw(piggy); Withdraw(coin);
    END; (*IF amount >= 0*)
  UNTIL amount < 0;
END BankPoly.
```

Example 13.12: Polymorphous procedures

```
INTERFACE Saving;                                          (*25.06.94. LB*)
   CONST
     Max = 1.0e10;                                         (*suffices for now*)
   TYPE
     T <: Public;
     Public = OBJECT
              METHODS
                init (initialBalance: REAL := 0.0;    (*0 ≤ initialBalance ≤ maxBalance*)
                      maxBalance: REAL := Max;           (*0 ≤ maxBalance ≤ Max*)
                      maxDeficit: REAL := 0.0): T;        (*0 ≤ maxDeficit ≤ Max*)

                balance(): REAL;                       (*returns account balance*)

                transact(amount: REAL): BOOLEAN;
                 (*maxDeficit ≤ amount + balance ≤ maxBalance; balance is invisible! *)
                          (*Returns TRUE if and only if the transaction succeeds*)
              END; (*Public*)
END Saving.
```

Example 13.13: *Generalized superclass for saving*

piggy bank. This method is certainly not suitable for checking the balance
of a savings account. This brings us to a typical problem of object-oriented
programming: we can specialize a class only if it is general enough, which
does not apply for the class PiggyBank. Now we have the following possibilities: we fully reveal the internal structure so that the heirs can use
the fields in other ways, or each time we request our account balance we
destroy our "piggy bank" and generate a new one. However, we choose yet
another approach that is often unavoidable: we redesign our class hierarchy.

> This experience could bring some readers to reject object-oriented pro-
> gramming because the promised flexibility seems to falter. We want to
> warn against premature resignation just as much as exaggerated eu-
> phoria. Object-orientation has many merits, but we need to learn how
> to use them properly. Generalizing a superclass whose first design was
> too specialized is part of the daily work of an object-oriented program-
> mer. The situation is more delicate: A superclass that is much too
> general is also of no value. If everything is generic, if all design deci-
> sions are deferred, then this is just as bad as decisions made too early
> and too rigidly. We are left with the old wisdom of finding the golden
> middle.

The class of the "generalized piggy bank" should be formulated such
that both savings accounts and piggy banks can be derived as special-
izations thereof. Our first decision is to change the type of the deposits
from INTEGER to REAL (Example 13.13). This means that we can handle
amounts in cents and we can easily add interest computation later.

```
MODULE Client EXPORTS Main;                                    (*22.06.94. LB*)

    IMPORT Saving;
    FROM SIO IMPORT PutText, PutReal, GetReal, LookAhead, GetChar, Nl;

VAR
    sp: Saving.T := NEW(Saving.T).init(initialBalance:= 200.0, maxDeficit:= 100.0);
    ch: CHAR;

BEGIN                                                              (*Client*)
    PutText("Savings transactions\n" &
        "Press numbers for transactions, B for balance, Q to quit\n");
    REPEAT
        ch:= LookAhead();                  (*tests first character without removing it*)
        CASE ch OF
          | '0' .. '9', '+', '–' =>                                       (*number*)
                IF NOT sp.transact(GetReal()) THEN PutText("Error\n") END;
          | 'B', 'b', 'Q', 'q' =>                              (*balance or quit*)
                PutText("Account balanace = "); PutReal(sp.balance()); Nl();
                EVAL GetChar();                          (*moves reader position*)
        ELSE                         (*character is neither number nor command*)
            EVAL GetChar();                                         (*read on*)
        END; (*CASE ch*)
    UNTIL (ch = 'Q') OR (ch = 'q');
END Client.
```

Example 13.14: *A client of class* Saving

We define an init method with a number of parameters with default values. The permitted ranges for the parameters are given as comments. We define two other methods: transact and balance. transact permits both deposits and withdrawals; the leading sign of the amount determines the direction of the transaction. The comment specifies the valid range of the amount. Since the field status is invisible to clients, the method balance returns the current account balance.

Example 13.14 shows a client of the interface Saving; the implementation is in Example 13.15. The client can make transactions on the account and request the account balance. A possible execution of Example 13.14 (without greeting) could be:

```
10 20 -15 22 q
Account balance = 237
```

The implementation of the init method provides no protection against improper invocation. The conditions of the correct initialization are specified in the interface as comments. The reader should consider how to make init robust with respect to incorrect invocation. The method transact tests whether the requested transaction is permissible. Note that the

```
MODULE Saving;                                              (*22.06.94. LB*)

  REVEAL
    T = Public BRANDED OBJECT
         status: REAL;                          (*current account balance*)
         max: REAL;                                   (*maximum balance*)
         min: REAL;                                    (*minimum balance*)
      OVERRIDES
         init:= Init;
         transact:= Transact;
         balance:= Balance;
      END; (*T*)

  PROCEDURE Init(self: T; initialBalance: REAL := 0.0;
                 maxBalance: REAL := Max;
                 maxDeficit: REAL := 0.0): T =
  BEGIN
    self.status:= initialBalance;
    self.max:= maxBalance;                (*initially max must not be negative*)
    self.min:= –maxDeficit;               (*initially min must not be positive*)
    RETURN self;
  END Init;

  PROCEDURE Transact(self: T; amount: REAL): BOOLEAN =
  BEGIN
    IF amount >= 0.0 AND amount <= self.max – self.status OR
       amount < 0.0 AND amount >= self.min – self.status
    THEN                                         (*deposit or withdrawal*)
      self.status:= self.status + amount;
      RETURN TRUE
    ELSE                                      (*transaction not permitted*)
      RETURN FALSE
    END; (*IF amount >= 0.0...*)
  END Transact;

  PROCEDURE Balance(self: T): REAL =
  BEGIN
    RETURN self.status
  END Balance;

BEGIN
END Saving.
```

Example 13.15: *Implementation of class* Saving

tests are formulated not in the form self.status + amount <= self.max, but
in the equivalent form amount <= (self.max - self.status). This prevents an
overflow in the event that self.status + amount > LAST(REAL) (although few
of us are threatened by this danger).

With the help of the generalized type Saving.T, we can define the various subtypes. For example, a piggy bank type would have to override

```
INTERFACE SavingsAccount;                                    (*01.07.94. LB*)

  IMPORT Saving;

  TYPE
    T       <: Public;
    Public =  Saving.T OBJECT                    (*T is a subtype of Saving.T*)
              METHODS
                  oldBalance(): REAL;            (*returns previous balance*)
              END; (*Public*)

END SavingsAccount.
```

Example 13.16: SavingsAcct.T is a subtype of Saving.T

```
MODULE SavingsAccount;                                       (*01.07.94. LB*)

  IMPORT Saving;

  REVEAL
    T = Public BRANDED OBJECT
          previous: REAL;                        (*stores previous balance*)
        OVERRIDES
          init:= Init;
          oldBalance:= OldBalance;
        END; (*T*)

  PROCEDURE Init(self: T; initialBalance, maxBalance, maxDeficit: REAL): Saving.T =
  BEGIN
     EVAL Saving.T.init(self, initialBalance, maxBalance, maxDeficit);        (*supercall*)
     self.previous:= self.balance();   (*fields of super class already initialized*)
     RETURN self                                  (*returns self as Saving.T*)
  END Init;

  PROCEDURE OldBalance(self: T): REAL =
  VAR p: REAL := self.previous;                   (*copy previous balance*)
  BEGIN
     self.previous:= self.balance();     (*set previous balance to new balance*)
     RETURN p
  END OldBalance;

BEGIN
END SavingsAccount.
```

Example 13.17: Implementation of the savings account

the methods transact and balance such that negative transactions (with-drawals) are ignored and the first request for the account balance blocks all further transactions. We could achieve a blockage, for example, by reinitializing the Saving object with sp.init(0.0, 0.0, 0.0). This blocks all further transactions on the account, as with smashing a piggy bank. We gain the additional advantage that on an attempt to deposit to a blocked account,

```
   IMPORT SavingsAccount;
VAR
   acct: SavingsAccount.T := NEW(SavingsAccount.T).init(maxDeficit:= 300.0);
   amount, oldBalance, balance: REAL; success: BOOLEAN;
BEGIN                                                                             (*Saving*)
   ⋮
   success:= acct.transact(amount);                                (*amount transacted*)
   ⋮
   oldBalance:= acct.oldBalance();
   balance:= acct.balance();
```

Example 13.18: *Client of the savings account*

the transact method returns *false* instead of generating a run-time error. Requesting the account balance is not blocked (balance always returns 0), but we could achieve this by overriding the method.

To model a savings account with various balances and interest computations would be no problem now. However, let us make things easier: let us define a savings account with one additional feature, requesting the previous balance. We could invoke this method once a week to determine how much we have spent in that week. This request should then set the previous balance to the new one. In the interface we need only a single additional method, oldBalance (Example 13.16).

In the implementation we still need a hidden field that stores the previous account balance (Example 13.17). On each request, this field is set to the new account balance. We also have to override init because the field previous must also be initialized, since the fields of Saving.T were initialized by a supercall. The client is shown in Example 13.18.

Redefinition of methods and fields

Now let us construct a coin bank using the class Saving; our coin bank should accept only valid coins. How can we achieve this? We can develop a new method that accepts only amounts contained in a tailored enumeration type, e.g.:

```
   TYPE
      Coins = {Penny, Nickel, Dime, Quarter, Half, Dollar};
      CoinBank = Saving.T OBJECT
         METHODS
            depositCoins(amount: Coins);
         END;
```

This solution has the drawback that, although the method depositCoins accepts only valid coins, the inherited method transact is still present, and

```
INTERFACE CoinSaver;                                      (*02.07.94. LB*)
  IMPORT Saving;
  TYPE
    T       <: Public;
    Coins   = {Penny, Nickel, Dime, Quarter, Half, Dollar, Invalid};
    Valid   = [Coins.Penny .. Coins.Dollar];
    Public  = Saving.T OBJECT
              METHODS
                 transact(amount: Valid): BOOLEAN;        (*redefined!*)
              END; (*Public*)

  PROCEDURE Coin(t: TEXT): Coins;              (*auxiliary procedure*)
  (*tests whether t is a coin name. Returns coin value (possibly Invalid)*)
END CoinSaver.
```

Example 13.19: *CoinSaver redefines the method* transact

an undisciplined client could still deposit any amount. Another possibility is to override transact so that it always returns *false* for invalid amounts. This is an improvement, but not quite what we want. We want a coin bank that simply recognizes nothing but coins. Here we must modify the signature of the method transact, which is not permitted in overriding. Thus we must *redefine* the method so that it has the same name but a different signature. Modula-3 permits redefinition of both methods and fields (in the latter case, e.g., we can define the same name with a different type).

The redefinition of a method (or of a field) resembles the case where we redefine a name within a nested block. The new name eclipses the old.

In redefining a name in a subtype, however, we can still access the eclipsed name with the NARROW statement. This is a rather unusual use of NARROW: instead of restricting the type to a subtype, we access the supertype (in this case "broaden" would be a more descriptive name).

Example 13.19 shows the interface of the new coin bank (we will call it coin saver); Example 13.20 shows the implementation, and Example 13.21 shows a client. These examples demonstrate the use of a supertype and its derivatives. Depending on the amount and the type of the input (numeric or text), the deposit goes into either the piggy bank or the coin bank, or the *general saver* (from the superclass Saver).

The module CoinSaver provides an auxiliary procedure that tests whether a text contains a valid coin name. If so, it converts the text to the corresponding coin value; otherwise it returns Coins.Invalid. Unambiguous abbreviations are permitted (e.g., the character string "Di" identifies the dime; "D" alone is rejected because it could also designate a dollar coin). This auxiliary procedure facilitates the client's input of coins. A possible

```
MODULE CoinSaver;                                        (*02.07.94. LB*)
  IMPORT Saving, Text;
  REVEAL
    T = Public BRANDED OBJECT
        OVERRIDES
          transact:= Transact;
        END; (*T*)

  PROCEDURE Transact(self: T; amount: Valid): BOOLEAN =
  VAR number: REAL;
  BEGIN
    CASE amount OF
      | Coins.Penny   => number:= 1.0;
      | Coins.Nickel  => number:= 5.0;
      | Coins.Dime    => number:= 10.0;
      | Coins.Quarter => number:= 20.0;
      | Coins.Half    => number:= 50.0;
      | Coins.Dollar  => number:= 100.0;
    END; (*CASE amount*)
    RETURN NARROW(self, Saving.T).transact(number);      (*transact from Saving*)
  END Transact;

  PROCEDURE Coin(t: TEXT): Coins =
  CONST V = ARRAY Valid OF TEXT
          {"Penny", "Nickel", "Dime", "Quarter", "Half", "Dollar"};
  VAR coin: Valid; found := 0; c := FIRST(Coins);
  BEGIN                                          (*Reads coin (possibly abbreviated)*)
    WHILE (c <= LAST(Valid)) AND (found < 2) DO
      IF Text.Equal(t, Text.Sub(V[c], 0, Text.Length(t))) THEN
        coin:= c; INC(found);
      END; (*IF Text.Equal(t, ...*)
      INC(c);
    END; (*WHILE c*)
    IF found = 1 THEN RETURN coin ELSE RETURN Coins.Invalid END;
  END Coin;

BEGIN                                                    (*CoinSaver*)
END CoinSaver.
```

Example 13.20: *The implementation overrides the redefined method*

execution of Example 13.21 (greeting text omitted) could be:

```
1 2 5 300 500 D Dollar Dime Penny q
D is not a valid coin
Total in coin saver = 111
Total in savings account = 8
Total in general saver = 800
```

We can summarize the difference between overriding and redefining as
follows: Overriding a method leaves its name and signature untouched;

```
MODULE PolyClient EXPORTS Main;                                    (*02.07.94. LB*)
  IMPORT CoinSaver, SavingsAccount, Saving;
  FROM SIO IMPORT GetReal, PutReal, LookAhead, GetText, PutText, GetChar, Nl;

  PROCEDURE Output(s: Saving.T) =
  VAR t: TEXT;
  BEGIN
    TYPECASE s OF                                            (*tests dynamic type of s*)
    | CoinSaver.T      => t:= "coin saver";
    | SavingsAccount.T=> t:= "savings account";
    | Saving.T         => t:= "general saver";
    END; (*TYPECASE s*)
    PutText("Total in " & t & " = "); PutReal(s.balance()); Nl();
  END Output;

CONST
  Numbers = SET OF CHAR {'0' .. '9', '+', '–'};
  Blanks = SET OF CHAR {' ', '\t', '\n'};
VAR
  saver: CoinSaver.T := NEW(CoinSaver.T).init();
  acct: SavingsAccount.T := NEW(SavingsAccount.T).init();
  sav: Saving.T := NEW(Saving.T).init();
  coin: CoinSaver.Coins; amount: REAL; ch: CHAR; t: TEXT;
BEGIN                                                              (*PolyClient*)
  PutText("Amount<100 –> savings account; amount>=100 –> general saver/Q=quit:\n");
  REPEAT
    ch:= LookAhead();                                        (*check next character*)
    IF (ch = 'q') OR (ch = 'Q') THEN                         (*quit*)
      Output(saver); Output(acct); Output(sav);
    ELSE
      IF ch IN Numbers THEN                                  (*number*)
        amount:= GetReal();
        IF amount < 100.0 THEN                           (*amount to savings account*)
          EVAL acct.transact(amount)                         (*no error control*)
        ELSE                                             (*amount to general saver*)
          EVAL sav.transact(amount)                          (*no error control*)
        END; (*IF amount < 100.0*)
      ELSIF ch IN Blanks THEN EVAL GetChar();                (*skip blanks*)
      ELSE                                             (*text – amount to coin saver*)
        REPEAT
          t:= GetText(); coin:= CoinSaver.Coin(t);
          IF coin = CoinSaver.Coins.Invalid THEN
            PutText(t & " is not a valid coin\n")
          END;
        UNTIL coin # CoinSaver.Coins.Invalid;
        EVAL saver.transact(coin)                            (*no error control*)
      END; (*IF ch IN Numbers*)
    END; (*IF ch = ...*)
  UNTIL (ch = 'q') OR (ch = 'Q');
END PolyClient.
```

Example 13.21: Client of CoinSaver, SavingsAcct and Saving

there is actually only *one* method with different forms, and dynamic binding assures that the correct variant is found. Redefining gives the subtype a completely new method, but with the same name as in the supertype. This means that redefinition breaks the chain of dynamic binding.

Assume that we had overridden the method balance in the coin saver. Then within the polymorphous procedure Output of Example 13.21, for coin bank objects the overridden method would be selected (due to dynamic binding). But if we had *redefined* balance (e.g., such that it returns a coin array such as balance(): ARRAY Valid OF CARDINAL) then the call s.balance in the procedure Output would *not* find this method; instead it would find the method that corresponds to the declared type of the parameter s (i.e., Saving.T), which is the supermethod. Naturally this is correct, since the new method has a different signature – what should PutReal do with a value of the coin array? We can invoke the new method either with a variable of the redefining type (or its subtypes), e.g., saver.balance(), or with NARROW (NARROW(s, CoinSaver.T).balance()).

The redefinition of methods and fields can make a program quite incomprehensible; therefore it should be used with extreme caution! However, there are two cases where redefinition proves quite useful or even indispensable:

1. It can be useful to redefine the init method with a different signature. On the one hand, this allows us to change the return type of the init method to the type of the actual subtype. In Example 13.9, if we had redefined the init method with the signature init(): CoinBank.T, then the declarations VAR bank: CoinBank.T := NEW(CoinBank.T).init() and VAR bank := NEW(CoinBank.T).init() would be equivalent. In this case redefinition contributes to the comprehensibility of our program. On the other hand, it is often necessary to provide the init method in a subtype with new parameters that were not needed in the supertype. Since the init method is normally invoked only once in the life cycle of an object, forfeiting dynamic binding here is no real loss.

2. Sometimes we employ redefinition without knowing it, when we redefine an invisible method of a hidden type by chance. In this case we have not lost anything because the invisible method was inaccessible anyway.

We must advise that we have not yet achieved our goal in our example. We can still circumvent our coin saver: with the following statement, the client (Example 13.21) could still access the supermethod and deposit an arbitrary amount in the coin saver:

EVAL NARROW(saver, Saving.T).transact(amount)

```
INTERFACE Tree;                          (*21.01.95 CW, LB*) (*root class Tree*)

  TYPE
    Direction = {Ascend, Descend};                  (*ascending or descending*)
    Order     = {Pre, In, Post};                       (*traversal strategy*)
    Action    = PROCEDURE (e: REFANY; depth: INTEGER);    (*action at node*)

    Compare = PROCEDURE (d1, d2: REFANY): [-1 .. 1];       (*order relation*)
              (*Compare the contents (or key values) to which d1 and d2 point*)
                        (*Result: 0 if d1 = d2; -1 if d1 < d2; 1 if d1 > d2*)

    ElemT = REFANY;

    T = OBJECT
        METHODS
          init(compare: Compare): T;        (*initialization sets order relation*)
          search (e: ElemT): ElemT;              (*searches for element like e*)
                                             (*returns e if found, else NIL*)
          insert (e: ElemT);                         (*inserts e in tree*)
                             (*multiple insertions of an are element possible*)
          delete (e: ElemT): ElemT;             (*deletes element like e*)
                                             (*returns e if deleted, else NIL*)
          traverse ( action: Action;                (*action at each node*)
                     order := Order.In;               (*traversal strategy*)
                     direction := Direction.Ascend);  (*traversal direction*)
        END; (*T*)
END Tree.
```

Example 13.22: *Interface of the root class* Tree

However, this is only possible if the client also imports the interface Saving, which would not be necessary otherwise. If a client imports only the interface CoinSaver, then there is no possibility to deposit anything but a valid coin in the coin saver. This should demonstrate that we should never import unnecessary interfaces. Better compilers output a warning if names or interfaces are not used. We should observe these warnings; unused components can cause someone reading our program much pondering.

13.4.4   The tree class hierarchy

Using a larger example, we will now show how to build a class hierarchy. Section 12.2.1 introduced trees. This section describes how to define a class hierarchy that permits us to handle various kinds of nodes and trees.

The root class

Our very first task is to find a root class containing exactly the fields and methods that all imaginable heirs and clients share. How well we succeed in finding such a root class depends in part on how well we can predict

all future subclasses. This is relatively easy for common problems such
as trees. For larger problems with which we are less familiar, it becomes
improbable that we can find the root class on first try. In such cases we
have to develop the root class in several steps.

In the case of trees, we can say that the methods search, insert, delete
and traverse certainly apply for all kinds of trees. First they are all deferred, since their implementation depends on the kind of tree (binary
tree, B-tree, AVL-tree, etc.; see [Knu81, Sed93, Wir76]). Therefore these
methods should not be implemented, but only declared, in the root class.
Naturally we do need to establish the semantics, at least in the from of
comments, in the root class already.

Genericity

So far, so good! We also want to keep our abstract tree *generic*. In this case,
this means that it should remain independent of both the kind of tree and
the type of the nodes. It would be easiest if we could provide the encapsulated data type with a type parameter. Although Modula-3 has no type
parameter, it does offer the possibility to specify module parameters (see
Appendix B.5.4). If we adhere to the convention that the type name of an
encapsulated data type is always T, then we can have a type parameter in
the form ModuleName.T. Hence we can define the interface of the root class
as a generic interface with a formal module parameter (call it Element).
The type of the nodes would then be Element.T. The module Element then
requires concrete actual parameter modules.

However, we will take a different approach. We will *simulate* genericity
through subtyping (similar to Section 11.4.3, Example 11.29). Therefore
as element type for the root class we initially choose the root of all pointer
types: REFANY. In the clients that define the various node types, we will
replace this type with corresponding subtypes.

This decision does not complete our work. Normally some order is defined on a tree. The concrete choice of the order relation depends on the
type of the nodes, which only the respective clients or heirs know. Until
now we have simply known the type of the node (e.g., ElemT = INTEGER),
so that the order relation was clear. For example, we know exactly how to
compare two INTEGERs. If we had chosen the solution with a generic module, we would have to require that every variant of Element must also provide a Compare procedure to compare two elements (of the type Element.T).
For our simulated genericity we choose the solution requiring that the comparison procedure must be specified as a parameter in the init method. This
gives us the basics of the interface of the root class (Example 13.22).

Naturally the interface quite resembles that in Example 12.20. One
difference is that ElemT is no longer an INTEGER but a REFANY. In a nar-

```
INTERFACE BinaryTree;                              (*06.07.94. CW, LB*)

  IMPORT Tree;
  TYPE T <: Tree.T;                          (*T is a subtype of Tree.T*)

END BinaryTree.
```

Example 13.23: Client interface of a binary tree

row sense, this has nothing to do with object orientation: the concept of genericity is *orthogonal* to object orientation (i.e., they are independent).

> There are programming languages that feature genericity, but are not object-oriented, such as the original definition of Ada.

The other difference is that this interface is more abstract than that in Example 12.20. Because the central type is an OBJECT, not only the concrete implementation but also the possibility of subclasses is deferred. There is no implementation module Tree. All methods are deferred and must be overridden in subclasses.

Subclass of binary trees

As the first subclass of the root class Tree, let us define the most important kind of tree, the binary tree. We know how to construct a binary tree from Section 12.2.2. The question is only what should appear in the interface. The first suggestion is: actually nothing; the interface Tree already contains everything that a client needs. The data structure that defines the left and right branches could be hidden in the implementation part.

However, if we decide to go that route, then we might not be able to derive a subclass of binary trees. *AVL-trees* [Wir76], e.g., are binary trees for which a restriction applies to the height of the subtrees of each node (the height of the left and right subtrees of any node must not differ by more than 1). This produces nicely *balanced* trees, which generally makes searching significantly faster than in an unbalanced tree. To be able to implement an AVL-tree (fairly sensibly), we need access to the underlying structure of the binary tree. This leads us to the following decision: for binary trees we will specify two interfaces: one for clients and the other for future subclasses.

> Aside from naming conventions, the Modula-3 language environment provides no support for distinguishing these interfaces. The accepted Modula-3 convention is to name the client interface after the problem (e.g., BinaryTree); the name of the interface that reveals the internal representation of the data structure ends with "Rep" (e.g., BinTreeRep). Administrative measures can be taken in the respective operating system to assure that only authorized modules can access Reps.

```
Persons:
        Wanda
Peter
                Paul
                        Martha
                                Bob
        Bob

Books:
                134
                        38
        38
                13
12
        2
```

Figure 13.25: *Output of BinaryClient*

Example 13.23 shows the client interface. Here we export the new type. The client need not know any more about binary trees than that they exist; hence everything else is hidden.

Clients of the binary tree class

Example 13.24 shows a client of this interface. The module imports only BinaryTree. It need not and should not import BinTreeRep! Naturally the programmer must be familiar with the interface Tree to know the method names and signatures. However, only BinaryTree needs to be imported.

We define the two types (Person and Book). The key of a person record is a text (the name); the key of a book record is a number (catalog number). In both cases, additional information is collected in the info field. The client anticipates an input file in which names and catalog numbers appear pairwise (we neglect other information). We store the person records in personTree and the book records in bookTree.

For each key type we must specify the respective comparison procedure, (CompareNumber or CompareName). (Here we simply rely on the Integer and Text interfaces provided by the language environment; these abide by the same conventions for the return value as the method compare). For each type we also specify the action to be executed on traversal. Here we define the common procedure Output, which works for both types. However, we could have written separate output procedures for names and catalog numbers. The procedure Output also shows an example of the use of level parameters.

The client creates the person and book records and stores them in the corresponding trees. Finally, both trees are output with the root node at the

```
MODULE BinaryClient EXPORTS Main;                          (*06.07.94 LB *)
  IMPORT SIO, SF, BinaryTree, Text, Integer;
TYPE
  Person = REF RECORD name: TEXT; info: REFANY END;
  Book   = REF RECORD catalogNumber: CARDINAL; info: REFANY END;

VAR
  in: SIO.Reader := SF.OpenRead();              (*in must contain name / number pairs*)
  personTree: BinaryTree.T := NEW(BinaryTree.T).init(CompareName);
  bookTree: BinaryTree.T := NEW(BinaryTree.T).init(CompareNumber);
  person: Person; book: Book;

  PROCEDURE CompareNumber(e1, e2: REFANY): [–1 .. 1] =
  BEGIN
    WITH i1 = NARROW(e1, Book).catalogNumber,
         i2 = NARROW(e2, Book).catalogNumber DO
      RETURN Integer.Compare(i1, i2)     (*integer comparison from standard library*)
    END
  END CompareNumber;

  PROCEDURE CompareName(e1, e2: REFANY): [–1 .. 1] =
  BEGIN
    WITH t1 = NARROW(e1, Person).name,
         t2 = NARROW(e2, Person).name DO
      RETURN Text.Compare(t1, t2)        (*text comparison from standard library*)
    END
  END CompareName;

  PROCEDURE Output(x: REFANY; level: INTEGER) =
  BEGIN
    FOR i:= 0 TO level–1 DO SIO.PutText(" ") END;
    IF ISTYPE(x, Book) THEN
      SIO.PutInt(NARROW(x, Book).catalogNumber, 3); SIO.Nl();
    ELSE
      SIO.PutText(NARROW(x, Person).name & " "); SIO.Nl();
    END;
  END Output;

BEGIN                                                      (*BinaryClient*)
  WHILE NOT SIO.End(in) DO
    person:= NEW(Person); person.name:= SIO.GetText(in);
    personTree.insert(person);                             (*construct person tree*)
    book:= NEW(Book); book.catalogNumber:= SIO.GetInt(in);
    bookTree.insert(book);                                 (*construct book tree*)
  END; (*WHILE NOT SIO.End*)
  SIO.PutText("Persons:"); SIO.Nl();
  personTree.traverse(Output);                             (*output person tree*)
  SIO.Nl(); SIO.PutText("Books:"); SIO.Nl();
  bookTree.traverse(Output);                               (*output book tree*)
END BinaryClient.
```

Example 13.24: Client of the binary tree interface

```
INTERFACE BinTreeRep;                                    (*06.07.94.  CW, LB*)

  IMPORT Tree, BinaryTree;

  REVEAL
    BinaryTree.T <: Public;
  TYPE
    Public = Tree.T OBJECT                   (*public for subclasses (<: Tree.T)*)
      root: NodeT:= NIL;                              (*root of binary tree*)
      compare: Tree.Compare;                          (*compare function*)
    END; (*Public*)

    NodeT = OBJECT                                        (*type of node*)
      left, right: NodeT := NIL;                 (*pointer to child nodes*)
      info: REFANY := NIL;
    END; (*NodeT*)

END BinTreeRep.
```

Example 13.26: *Subclass interface of the binary tree*

left, then each level indented by several blanks. Assume that the input file contains the following entries: Peter 12 Bob 38 Paul 134 Wanda 2 Martha 13 Bob 38. Figure 13.25 shows the output of the program.

13.4.5   Subclasses of binary trees

Example 13.26 shows the BinTreeRep interface, which reveals the data structures required by a subclass. The declaration of BinaryTree.T is an example of a partial revelation (compare Section 11.4).

The root of the tree is no longer stored with the client, which now has only a reference to the overall structure, the object instance itself. Therefore we store the root in a field root pointing to a node type that contains the usual pointers left and right along with any other information. We could have defined the node type as a REF RECORD ···; however, this would prevent deriving a subclass from the node type. We might not want to derive a subclass – at the moment we do not know. In such a case it is always better to choose the more general solution, i.e., the object type: for an object type we need not define a subclass; for a record type we cannot.

The types still do not have to be specified fully here; they are completed in the implementation module. Since the algorithms of a binary tree are already familiar (Section 12.2.1, Example 12.24), we show only the interesting parts of the implementation (Example 13.27). Due to the root field, the implementation of Search, Insert and Delete have become somewhat more complicated (we show only Insert). We must start our recursion not at tree, but at tree.root. Therefore the procedures themselves are not recursive, but they invoke a nested recursive procedure. The tests in the

```
MODULE BinaryTree EXPORTS BinaryTree, BinTreeRep;
  IMPORT Tree;
  REVEAL
    T = Public BRANDED OBJECT
        OVERRIDES
            init:= Init;
            search:= Search;
            delete:= Delete;
            insert:= Insert;
            traverse:= Traverse;
        END; (*T*)

PROCEDURE Init(tree: T; compare: Tree.Compare): Tree.T =
    BEGIN
        tree.root:= NIL; tree.compare:= compare;
        RETURN tree;
    END Init;
    ⋮
PROCEDURE Insert(tree: T; e: Tree.ElemT) =

    PROCEDURE InsertElem(VAR node: NodeT; new: Tree.ElemT) =
        BEGIN
        IF node = NIL THEN
            node:= NEW(NodeT, info:= new)
        ELSIF tree.compare(node.info, new) > 0 THEN    (*new < node.info*)
            InsertElem(node.left, new)
        ELSE                                           (*new >= node.info*)
            InsertElem(node.right, new)
        END;
        END InsertElem;

    BEGIN                                              (*Insert*)
        InsertElem(tree.root, e)
    END Insert;
    ⋮
BEGIN
END BinaryTree.
```

Example 13.27: *Structure of the binary tree implementation*

node for the direction to continue searching are executed with the compare procedure, which must be specified in the initialization procedure.

The subclasses of binary trees are easy to add to the interface Bin-TreeRep. To implement an AVL-tree, we need an additional interface to allow creation of AVL-trees (Example 13.29). This quite resembles the client interface of BinaryTree. The AVLTreeRep interface is quite simple (Example 13.30); all we need is an additional field in each node that expresses the degree of balancedness of a tree (see [Wir76]).

The client of the AVL-tree is practically identical to a client of the binary tree; it must only import the tree type AVLTree instead of BinaryTree. In

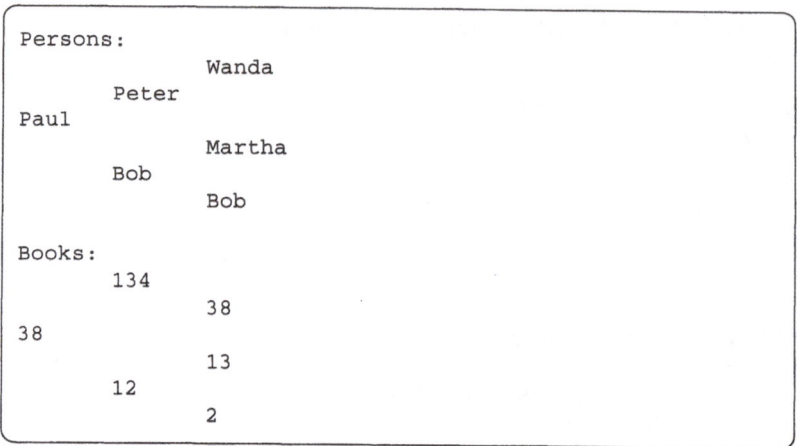

```
Persons:
                    Wanda
          Peter
Paul
                    Martha
          Bob
                    Bob

Books:
          134
                    38
38
                    13
          12
                    2
```

Figure 13.28: *Output of a balanced tree*

the module in Example 13.24, if we replace BinaryTree with AVLTree, then
our names and catalog numbers are stored in a balanced AVL-tree instead
of an ordinary tree. For the same input as before (Peter 12 Bob 38 Paul
134 Wanda 2 Martha 13 Bob 38), this program generates more aesthetic,
balanced trees (Figure 13.28).

Since the implementation of insert and delete for an AVL-tree is somewhat complicated, we show only the basic structure of the implementation
module (Example 13.31). The interested reader can find the detailed algorithm in [Wir76] and a complete Modula-3 implementation in the software
package included with this book.

```
INTERFACE AVLTree;                                    (*08.07.94. CW, LB*)

  IMPORT BinaryTree;
  TYPE T <: BinaryTree.T;              (*T is a subtype of BinaryTree.T *)

END AVLTree.
```

Example 13.29: Client interface of an AVL tree

```
INTERFACE AVLTreeRep;                                 (*06.07.94. CW, LB*)

  IMPORT BinTreeRep;
  TYPE
    NodeT = BinTreeRep.NodeT OBJECT          (*public for subclasses*)
      balance: [-1 .. 1];                    (*degree of balancedness*)
    END; (*NodeT*)

END AVLTreeRep.
```

Example 13.30: Subclass interface of an AVL tree

```
MODULE AVLTree EXPORTS AVLTree, AVLTreeRep;           (*08.07.94. CW*)

  IMPORT BinaryTree, BinTreeRep;

  REVEAL
    T = BinaryTree.T BRANDED OBJECT
        OVERRIDES
          delete:= Delete;
          insert:= Insert;
        END;

  PROCEDURE Insert(tree: T; e: REFANY) =
  ⋮
  PROCEDURE Delete(tree: T; e: REFANY): REFANY =
  ⋮
BEGIN
END AVLTree.
```

Example 13.31: Implementation of an AVL tree

Chapter 14

Persistent data structures

All programs that we have written thus far suffer from a serious flaw: we cannot terminate them without losing all our data. We developed refined structures to allocate memory for our data elegantly and efficiently. But as soon as the program terminates – or in the event of a power failure – we lose all data. In the main memory of our computer, all data are *temporary*; they can only be accessed by a running program and require the power supply of the computer. For this reason practically all computers are equipped with storage media that can retain data even without a continuous power supply. We call these hard disks or diskettes – collectively *background storage*. We must store our data on such background storage to allow them to survive the end of the program. We call such nontemporary data *persistent*.

In most language environments, the only way to transfer data from main memory to background storage is by way of the operating system. The operating system stores them in *files* on the hard disk or other storage medium. Later we can request that the operating system restore access from our program to a certain file. This chapter deals with this mechanism.

Databases

In files we normally store only data structures that can be transferred from background storage to main memory or vice versa in a single step. If the data structures to be managed are very complex and larger than available main memory can store, e.g., the customer and product file of a large company, then this mechanism no longer suffices. Then we use special *database systems* that not only store the data but also provide long-range data management. They feature interactive ad hoc data queries; i.e., we can retrieve data without having to write a program. In addition, database systems offer *data security*: they can handle the crash of a program without suffering a loss of data. Also, they feature regular data backup on multiple

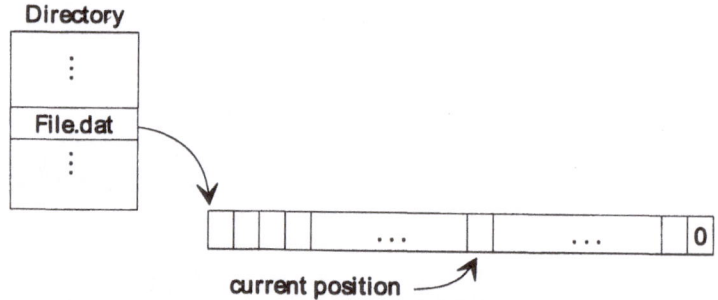

Figure 14.1: *Data structure of a file in the operating system*

media to prevent data loss due to hardware failure. The structure and use of such databases is a separate and important field of computer science [Ull82, Dat90]. In this book we treat only the storage of smaller amounts of data in individual files.

14.1 Files

From the viewpoint of the computer operating system, a file is a sequence of information units (usually bytes). Special *drivers* (operating system programs) transfer such a sequence to a suitable *device*, the background storage [FI85]. This allows the data to survive even a power shutoff. To assure that the file can be found later, the operating system stores a *directory* on the same device, containing an entry with the name of the file and the position of the data on the device.

This means that to make data persistent, we must transform them into a sequence of characters (bytes) and write it to a file. To read persistent data, we must read and interpret a sequence of characters from a file.

14.1.1 Accessing files

There are two fundamental modes for reading or writing files: *sequential* and *direct*. Reading a file sequentially transfers the data like music from an audio cassette: from start to finish, one after the other, without the option to skip parts or to begin somewhere in the middle. Direct access more closely resembles playing an individual song from a CD: reading begins at the specified start position; during reading a jump can be made to a different position in the file to continue reading there. The comparison is similar for writing a file.

The difference between these modes hinges on the possibility of explicit positioning. For such positioning, the operating system maintains a pointer for each file it processes, to manage the current read/write position (see Figure 14.1). After each character is read/written, this pointer is incremented. For direct access, this pointer is explicitly set by the user program.

14.1.2 Access functions

As a rule, programs never process files directly, but employ operating system functions.

- *Open or create a file*
  This function opens a named file for reading or creates a file for writing. To open a file, the operating system first reads the directory of the device, and then, via the file name, determines the physical position of the data (Figure 14.1). On opening, the current read/write position is set to the beginning of the file. Opening a file for writing deletes any existing data. If the named file does not exist, the operating system creates a new, empty file.

  Two additional functions allow changing the contents of a file: open for appending and for read/write. In the former case, the new data is simply written at the end of the existing file. In this case, on opening, the write position is set after the last character of the file. Opening a file as read/write allows both read and write operations and provides functions to set the file position (see below).

- *Read from a file, write to a file*
  The read functions read the contents of a file; the write functions modify the contents. Every read or write operation references the current read/write position. After reading or writing, the pointer position is incremented.

- *Test for end of file*
  Reading past the *end of file* (*EOF*) is an error; therefore the language environment provides a function to test whether EOF has been reached. Writing beyond EOF extends the file.

- *Set read/write position*
  For devices that support random access, the operating system provides a function to allow setting the read/write pointer explicitly from a program. This allows reading or modifying part of a file without touching the rest.

- *Closing a file*
  To assure the persistency of all changes to a file, (i.e., by writing them

to the device), the file must be closed (due to file buffering in main memory; see Section 14.2.1).

However, even after finishing reading a file, it should on principle be closed. Figure 14.1 shows that some data structures are necessary to handle files. Their memory should always be deallocated after they are no longer needed; closing a file does this deallocation.

14.1.3   Files and main memory

For the programmer, both files and main memory serve as storage media for data. However, they differ significantly:

	Main memory	*Files*
Access	type-safe	untyped
	fast	slow
Capacity	limited space	much space
Longevity	temporary	persistent

For the programmer, the greatest difference is that we access main memory with variables whose types are supported by the compiler. We process data in files only indirectly by invoking functions of the language environment. The compiler handles mapping the values of variables onto the structure of main memory; we do not notice this. For files, the programmer is responsible for handling this mapping (although with the support of the language environment). Other differences primarily concern the physical properties of the media, which make the one or the other more suitable, depending on our tasks.

14.1.4   File types

Most operating systems do write typeless data to a file (actually, they know only one type, the character), yet they distinguish several data types. The type of a file determines what kind of data can be stored in the file. Frequently operating systems distinguish between *binary files* and *text files*. Text files store information in human-readable form; thus we must format all data. To access files that are processed only by programs requires no reformatting. Here we store the data directly as they are stored in main memory. This is not only faster – we omit formatting – but also more compact. We store such data in binary files.

Other examples of file types include *executable programs* and *directories*. Finally, other input/output devices are handled as files with special file types. For the programmer, reading from the keyboard and writing to the screen or printer behaves just like reading from or writing to a file in background storage.

Most mainframe operating systems also offer additional access methods as file types [Tan92]. Depending on whether we read or write the data characterwise or recordwise, we must select the appropriate access method. For *recordwise access* to a file we exchange a certain number of characters with the device determined by a fixed *record length*. We can adjust the record length so that it exactly matches our data unit (e.g., a person record). The current position then becomes a record number.

14.2 Files in Modula-3

Modula-3 itself provides no language constructs to handle files. As in most other programming languages, this does not mean that we have to communicate directly with the operating system: the Modula-3 language environment provides the objects and procedures that take care of the details of invoking operating system functions for us.

> Older programming languages (including Pascal [Wir71]) support file handling in the language. The advantages of automatic data conversion between variables in main memory and data in files are counterbalanced by drawbacks: either the details of the programming language develop a greater dependency on the respective operating system, or the language supports only a small part of the features that the operating system provides. The former often leads to a multitude of dialects of the language that offer constructs customized to the respective operating system. If the language offers too few features, then the programmer resorts to direct communication with the operating system and only employs the language constructs partially. Both are unsatisfactory and result in programs that are hard to port to other platforms. Therefore file management is usually taken out of the realm of the programming language and placed in standard libraries, where adaptations to the respective operating system are easier to carry out than in the compiler. Additional machine-dependent libraries provide the programmer with further functions of the respective platform.

14.2.1 Input and output streams

The Modula-3 language environment provides input and output streams for file access. These are defined in the standard library, where they are called *reader* and *writer*. These are objects that can be associated with a file on initialization. It is also possible to associate an output stream with a monitor or printer or an input stream with an input device such as a keyboard.

```
MODULE ReadFile EXPORTS Main;

 IMPORT Rd, FileRd, SIO, SF;

 CONST FileName = "input.dat";

 VAR rd: Rd.T;                                    (*reader object *)
   t: TEXT;
 BEGIN
   IF SF.FileExists(FileName) THEN
     rd:= FileRd.Open(FileName);                  (*establish link to file *)
     WHILE NOT Rd.EOF(rd) DO                       (*check for end of file *)
       t:= Rd.GetLine(rd);                         (*read to end of line *)
       SIO.PutText(t); SIO.NI();
     END;
     Rd.Close(rd)                                 (*close file *)
   END (*IF*)
 END ReadFile.
```

Example 14.2: *Displaying the file* input.dat *on screen*

Assume that the background storage contains a file named input.dat. The following statement associates an input stream with this file:

```
VAR rd: Rd.T;
BEGIN
  rd := FileRd.Open("input.dat");
    ⋮
```

rd is the object that represents the input stream. The procedure FileRd.Open[1] initializes the input stream and associates it with the file. We use rd only as a pointer to the file. To read from the file, we can write either:

```
t:= Rd.GetLine(rd);
```

or:

```
c:= Rd.GetChar(rd);
```

GetLine reads the file to the next end-of-line character and assigns the data to the variable t of type TEXT. GetChar reads only a single character from the file. The following tests whether the end of file has been reached:

```
Rd.EOF(rd)
```

---

[1]In earlier version 2 of the Modula-3 standard library, the functionality of the modules FileRd and FileWr was contained in the module FileStream.

```
MODULE WriteFile EXPORTS Main;

  IMPORT Wr, FileWr;

  CONST FileName = "output.dat";

  VAR wr: Wr.T;                                    (*writer object *)
  BEGIN
    wr:= FileWr.Open(FileName);                    (*establish link to file *)
    Wr.PutText(wr, "first line\n");                (*output to file *)
    Wr.PutText(wr, "2\n");
    Wr.PutText(wr, "—-End—-\n");
    Wr.Close(wr)                                    (*close file *)
  END WriteFile.
```

Example 14.3: *Writing the file "output.dat"*

Reading a file almost always occurs in a WHILE loop, as shown in Example 14.2; this example shows a program that reads the contents of a text file input.dat and displays it on screen.

Before reading a file, it is usually necessary to test whether the file is even accessible. Example 14.2 uses the function SF.FileExits for this purpose. It returns *true* if the file is readable. The module SF (*simple files*) contains some utility functions that make frequently needed file handling functions simpler than the more flexible but more complicated functions of the library (see Appendix C.3.4).

Writing a file works analogously: we associate an output stream with a background storage file. The file need not exist; it is created automatically. If it exists, then it is overwritten and its old contents are lost. Wr.PutText or Wr.PutChar writes the file. Example 14.3 shows how to write a file output.dat with three text lines.

The interfaces to modules Rd and Wr are in Appendices C.3.1 and C.3.2. These are *abstract modules* in that they only define the behavior of input and output streams. The procedures in these modules invoke methods that all input or output streams must have. Rd.T and Wr.T objects contain these methods only as empty shells. It is the responsibility of anyone who implements subtypes of Rd.T and Wr.T to breathe life into these methods. The modules FileRd and FileWr implement such subtypes. They behave like Rd.T or Wr.T, and they possess the necessary methods to read/write files via operating system services. In this way the Modula-3 library determines a concept for reading and writing physical media and assures uniformity. We can write to monitors, printers or files in the same way. Even communication between programs is possible with special input and output streams (we can connect streams to channels; see Section 16.5.4). Table 14.4 shows the names of some input/output devices along with the modules that implement the corresponding input and output stream objects.

Read/write files	FileRd/FileWr
Write to screen	Stdio: pre-initialized output stream stdout
Read keyboard	Stdio: pre-initialized input stream stdin
Write to printer	Depends on operating system; usually via FileWr with a special file name

Table 14.4: *Modules that implement input/output streams*

To describe the various characteristics of different media, they are assigned certain attributes. These can be queried and affect the functionality of several procedures in Rd and Wr:

- *Seekable*
  The procedure Seek enables changing the read/write position of an open file in background storage. Not all streams are seekable (keyboard and screen are not). This attribute can be tested with the function procedure Seekable. The current position can be queried with Index.

- *Intermittent*
  Some input streams cannot constantly provide new data (although the "end" of the stream has not been reached); invoking Rd.GetChar for an intermittent input stream blocks the program until new data are ready. The keyboard is an example of such a stream: while the user is considering what to enter, the program must wait. This attribute can be tested with Rd.Intermittent.

- *Buffered*
  Often data are not written to an output stream immediately in order to improve the speed of transfer. Writing to a hard disk, e.g., takes just as long for a whole block of data as for an individual byte. Therefore the data are kept in main memory in a *buffer* and actually written only when they amount to a whole block. Typical block sizes for hard disks are 512, 1024 or 4096 bytes.

  This means that we must take care that the program does not terminate before the buffer has been written. Wr.Flush explicitly writes, or *flushes*, the buffer (before it is full), thus making the data persistent. Wr.Close automatically flushes the buffer.

  Whether there is a buffer between a program and the output stream can be tested with Wr.Buffered. For an unbuffered output stream, on each invocation of a write function the invoking program must wait until the data have been physically stored. An input stream must always be buffered because the data are provided with the speed of

```
PROCEDURE PutRealArray(wr: Wr.T; READONLY r: ARRAY OF REAL) =
  BEGIN
    FOR i:= FIRST(r) TO LAST(r) DO
      Wr.PutText(wr, Fmt.Int(i) & " " & Fmt.Real(r[i]) & "\n");        (*index value *)
    END; (*FOR*)
  END PutRealArray;
```

Example 14.5: *Storing a* REAL *array* (initial version)

the device (or the user's typing speed), which might be faster than the program can read. The input buffer functions as a circular queue (compare Section 11.1.2): if the program is faster than the device (i.e., the buffer is empty), then the program must wait. If the input device is faster, then the data in the buffer are collected in the buffer. If the buffer is full, the input device must be delayed.

As documented in Appendices C.3.1 and C.3.2, input and output streams provide other information and functions. We do not treat these in detail here. The reader/writer concept is described in greater detail in [Nel91].

14.2.2 Fmt and Scan

Both Rd and Wr contain only procedures to read and write characters (type TEXT is a character sequence). These modules handle the *transfer* of raw data. To store numbers or Boolean values, we first need to *format* them; i.e., to transform them into a form that Wr can process we need to convert the values into their TEXT representations (e.g., the Boolean value *true* to the TEXT value "TRUE"). Inversely, reading requires converting the text back to its respective type. We speak of *scanning* the text to obtain our data. Using text files consumes more storage space for the file (see Section 14.1.4), but has the advantage that the file contents are readable by humans.

The modules Fmt and Scan convert the basic types to TEXT and vice versa. Appendices C.2.1 and C.2.2 show these modules. Example 14.5 writes an array of REAL numbers as index/value pairs to a pre-initialized output stream.

Example 14.6 reads this array from a pre-initialized input stream. It amounts to the mirror image of PutRealArray in Example 14.5. The procedure contains awkward expressions because it cannot anticipate how many characters (digits) either the array index or the value will have. The procedure thus exploits the fact that we store the indices and values as follows:

index blank value EOL

The procedure first reads the input stream to the next end-of-line character (EOL) and transfers the data to the TEXT variable t. Then it seeks the

```
PROCEDURE GetRealArray(rd: Rd.T; VAR r: ARRAY OF REAL) =
  VAR i, delimiter: CARDINAL; t: TEXT;
  BEGIN
    WHILE NOT Rd.EOF(rd) DO
      t:= Rd.GetLine(rd);
      delimiter:= Text.FindChar(t, ' ');              (*between index and value *)
      i:= Scan.Int(Text.Sub(t, 0, delimiter));                    (*convert index *)
      r[i]:= Scan.Real(Text.Sub(t, delimiter+1, Text.Length(t)-delimiter-1));   (*value *)
    END; (*WHILE*)
  END GetRealArray;
```

Example 14.6: *Reading a* REAL *array* (initial version)

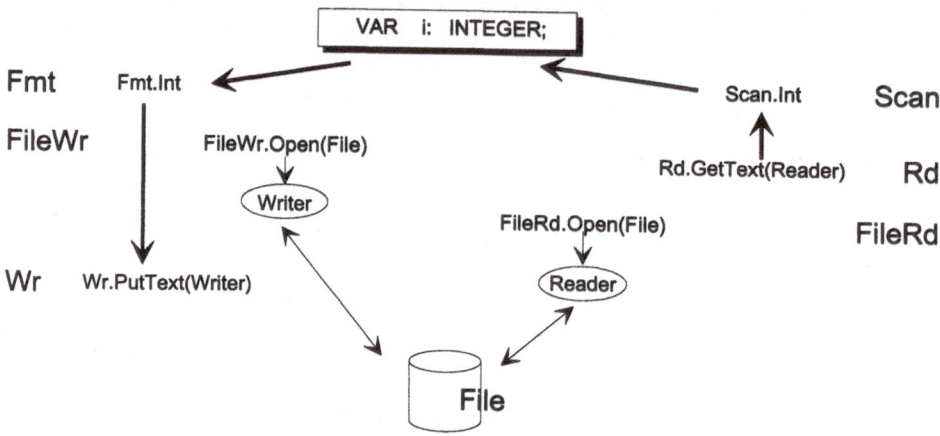

Figure 14.7: *Reading and writing an integer variable*

blank that separates the index from the value and converts the first part of t to an integer, then the rest to a real number.

> The procedure Text.FindChar(t, c) searches TEXT variable t for the character c and returns the position of its first occurrence from the start of t as a cardinal number. If there is no such character, then the procedure returns −1. Positions of characters in texts begin at 0.

> The procedure Text.Sub(t, p, l) has three parameters: a TEXT variable t, and a position p and a length l as cardinal values. Starting at position p, it extracts from t a number l of characters and returns them as TEXT.

GetRealArray is somewhat sensitive. The file must contain exactly the data that the procedure anticipates; e.g., it must not contain additional blanks. Furthermore, the size of the array in the file must correspond exactly to the parameter array r.

Figure 14.7 summarizes which modules are involved in reading and writing an INTEGER variable.

```
CONST NumbLength = 10;
  ⋮
PROCEDURE PutRealArray(wr: Wr.T; READONLY r: ARRAY OF REAL) =
  BEGIN
    FOR i:= FIRST(r) TO LAST(r) DO              (*write with fixed length *)
      Wr.PutText(wr, Fmt.Pad(Fmt.Int(i), NumbLength) &
                     Fmt.Pad(Fmt.Real(r[i]), NumbLength) &"\n");
    END; (*FOR*)
  END PutRealArray;
  ⋮
PROCEDURE GetRealArray(rd: Rd.T; VAR r: ARRAY OF REAL) =
  VAR i: CARDINAL;
  BEGIN
    WHILE NOT Rd.EOF(rd) DO
      i:= Scan.Int(Rd.GetText(rd, NumbLength));         (*convert index*)
      r[i]:= Scan.Real(Rd.GetText(rd, NumbLength));     (*convert value*)
      EVAL Rd.GetLine(rd);                                 (*skip EOL*)
    END; (*WHILE*)
  END GetRealArray;
```

Example 14.8: *Reading and writing with fixed file format* (2nd version)

Fixed file formats

GetRealArray is so complicated because it must accommodate digit sequences of various lengths. If we assume that the input file itself was produced by a program, then we can extend the list of preconditions for the proper functioning of GetRealArray: we simply require that all numbers in the file have a fixed number of characters. We can achieve this for all numbers with leading zeros or blanks (Scan.GetInt handles both easily); naturally the number of characters per number must be large enough to represent the largest possible number. Example 14.8 shows the procedures PutRealArray and GetRealArray for writing and reading a file with fixed column format. PutRealArray employs the function Fmt.Pad to assure the required column width. GetRealArray can now assume a fixed file structure:

(10 characters for index) (10 characters for value) EOL

We no longer need a delimiter (blank). However, memory requirements rise considerably and can amount to a multiple of that in our earlier version (consider a file consisting of 90% zero values).

Error handling

We sacrifice a great deal of security when we read data structures from files: files lie outside the realm of the program and cannot be tested by the compiler. If our program depends on the presence of data structures in files, then we must test whether the file exists and whether its contents are correct. The former is rather simple (before initializing the input stream, we test the existence of the file). However, we can only test the correctness of the contents if, on each access to file and on each scan of a character sequence, we test whether the operation was successful. This can make programs quite unreadable (GetRealArray alone has three such operations around which IF statements would have to entwine; compare Example 15.1 on page 372).

Modula-3 supports the concept of *exception handling*, which allows shifting error handling (Chapter 15). All operations on input and output streams are tested by the procedures in Rd, Wr, Fmt and Scan. In exceptional situations, these procedures generate *exceptions*, which terminate execution of the procedure and must be handled by one of the procedures in the invocation chain (see Chapter 15). Exceptional situations include reading past the end of file or attempting to write to a device that is full and cannot accept more data; for the module Scan, e.g., it is exceptional to find a letter in a TEXT representing a number.

14.2.3   Simple-IO

We already know Fmt and Scan, which handle the necessary conversions between the flat data structure of an operating system file and our type-bound data. At the language environment level, conversion and reading/writing are strictly separated. This has the advantage that we need not change read/write operations to store a variable with a newly defined type: we only need to re-implement the corresponding conversion procedures that transform the type into a character sequence and back.

In our programs this argument bears less weight because we generally want one procedure to store a variable and one to read it. The module SIO shows how such procedures are written and how they process human input.

> The authors developed SIO for this book. The module offers very simple keyboard input and screen output (as we have used it so far), yet it also serves as an example of general input/output processing.

Since we can also associate an input stream with the keyboard instead of a file, it makes sense to develop read procedures such that they can read not only from existing files but also keyboard input. However, we cannot expect the user to enter numbers with leading zeros and a fixed number of digits.

> Our first version of GetRealArray in Example 14.6 can handle numbers of different lengths. However, it functions only with a certain file

structure (number, blank, number, EOL). If the user types a tabulator instead of a blank, nothing works because the procedure cannot find the start of the next number.

Appendix C.3.3 shows the complete interface of SIO. The predefined numeric types (except EXTENDED) and TEXT and BOOLEAN each have a procedure that reads a value from the input stream and one that writes a value to the output stream. In contrast to the read procedures we have seen so far, the SIO.Get··· procedures (except SIO.GetChar) handle input much more tolerantly: first they skip all *blanks* (including all tabulators and EOL characters, collectively called *white space*). As soon as they encounter a printable character, they read on to the next whitespace and interpret the contents. This makes these procedures suitable for user input at the keyboard. SIO.GetChar just reads and returns the next character. All other read procedures in SIO skip the first character that cannot be part of the value being read (normally a blank). SIO.TermChar returns the value of this delimiter character.

We can "look ahead" to see a character that has not been read yet by reading it with SIO.LookAhead, thereby returning it to the input stream. This procedure can be implemented with Rd.UngetChar. Input streams are always buffered; the buffer enables returning characters to the input stream. The function Available returns *true* if there are unread characters available in the respective buffer.

The functions Length and Seek have been assumed by module Rd. End corresponds to Rd.EOF. Example 14.9 shows the procedures GetRealArray and PutRealArray, which now use SIO: in particular, reading can be expressed much more convincingly with such procedures.

Implementation of SIO

The Simple-IO procedures have default values for input and output streams; we have not used or showed them so far. If the parameter rd or wr is omitted (or passes a NIL pointer), then these procedures read from the keyboard or write to the screen. As additional convenience, the input of numeric values can be repeated: if the user types a character string that cannot be interpreted as a number (e.g., because it contains letters), then the procedure outputs an error message, and input must be repeated. Naturally, this only works when reading from the keyboard. If the procedures read something uninterpretable from a file, then they generate an exception. Example 14.10 shows the implementation of the procedures SIO.GetInt and SIO.PutInt. The declaration RAISES {Error} means that the function can generate an exception (see Chapter 15).

All procedures that write to output streams empty the write buffer with each operation (see Section 14.2.1) when we write to the screen.

```
PROCEDURE PutRealArray(wr: Wr.T; READONLY r: ARRAY OF REAL) =
  BEGIN
    FOR i:= FIRST(r) TO LAST(r) DO
      SIO.PutInt(i, 10, wr);                              (*index on writer *)
      SIO.PutChar(' ', wr);                        (*whitespace as delimiter *)
      SIO.PutReal(r[i], wr);                          (*real value to writer *)
      SIO.Nl(wr);                                  (*whitespace as delimiter *)
    END; (*FOR*)
  END PutRealArray;

PROCEDURE GetRealArray(rd: Rd.T; VAR r: ARRAY OF REAL) =
  VAR i: CARDINAL;
  BEGIN
    WHILE NOT SIO.End(rd) DO
      i:= SIO.GetInt(rd);                                    (*read index *)
      r[i]:= SIO.GetReal(rd);                                (*read value *)
    END; (*WHILE*)
  END GetRealArray;
```

Example 14.9: *Reading and writing with Simple-IO* (3rd version)

Treating screen output as a file produces a somewhat pathological effect that also buffers screen output, although this does not yield an improvement in processing speed. Therefore programmers must always be sure to empty the screen output buffer to assure the timely display of the contents. When we use Simple-IO, we can ignore this.

Scanning input streams with Lex

The read procedures of Simple-IO employ the library module Lex. This module provides procedures for reading and interpreting characters from an input stream. Lex.Skip is used to skip whitespace in the input stream. Lex.Int reads all characters that could be part of an integer and terminates at the first character that is not a digit. If the first character that Lex.Int reads is not a digit, then the procedure generates the exception Lex.Error. SIO.GetInt handles the exception and repeats the read operation (only if it was read from the keyboard). Exceptions are explained in Chapter 15.

14.3 Persistent variables

Often we need files only to store our data structures. Here, when the program terminates, we want to avoid losing the values that one or more variables reference. We want to make the *variables* persistent; therefore we write them to a background storage file – not because we value the file. There are other cases: a text editor generates a file that is processed by completely different programs (e.g., a compiler).

```
MODULE SIO;                                                      (*10.05.94. LB*)
  :
TYPE
  Kind = {Integer, Real, LongReal, Boolean}
  :
PROCEDURE GetInt(rd: Reader := NIL): INTEGER RAISES {Error} =
  VAR i: INTEGER; count: CARDINAL := MaxError;          (*MaxError = 3 *)
  BEGIN
    IF rd = NIL THEN rd:= Stdio.stdin END;
    LOOP
      TRY
        IF End(rd) THEN RAISE Error END;
        Lex.Skip(rd);
        i:= Lex.Int(rd);
        EXIT
      EXCEPT
        Lex.Error, Rd.Failure, FloatMode.Trap =>
          FormatError(rd, Kind.Integer, count);     (*handles input format errors *)
      END; (*TRY*)
    END; (*LOOP*)
    ConsumeNext(rd);                       (*consumes and saves following dilimiter *)
    RETURN i;
  END GetInt;

PROCEDURE PutInt(i: INTEGER; length:= 3; wr: Writer := NIL) =
  BEGIN
    IF wr = NIL THEN wr:= Stdio.stdout END;
    Wr.PutText(wr, Fmt.Pad(Fmt.Int(i), length));
    IF wr = Stdio.stdout THEN Wr.Flush(wr) END;
  END PutInt;
  :
```

Example 14.10: *Part of the implementation of Simple-IO*

In this section we want to discuss *persistent variables*. Thus far we have encountered only variables whose lifetime extends at most over the duration of execution of a program (the state space of the modules; see Section 10.2.1). However, we could extend the hierarchy of state spaces – auxiliary variables of a nested block, local variables of a procedure, global variables of a module – by one level, one state space, that is accessible to multiple programs and outlives the execution of individual programs. (Similar ideas have been realized in database-oriented programming languages [KMP+83, KM94, SM92]). We call this the *external state space*.

What is necessary to support persistent variables? Before the program executes, the current values of persistent variables must be read from a database; i.e., the program assumes part of the external state space. While the program executes, these variables are treated as normal variables. However, before the program terminates, the values in the database must be updated to the last values of the program variables; this updates the external state space.

    PERSISTENTVAR max: INTEGER

Unfortunately, the Modula-3 compiler cannot handle such declarations. Still, we can easily envision it. In the following we explain a concept for attaining these semantics with the help of objects.

14.3.1   Implementation

We write the values of persistent variables to a global text file. This file is global in the sense that multiple programs can store their variables in the same file. However, we store not only the value but also the associated identifier. We give this file the somewhat inflated name "database of persistent variables"[2]. With the launching of each program that employs persistent variables, there is a check whether the identifiers associated with the variables already have values stored in the database. If so, then these values are used for initializing the variables that are declared as persistent. The structure of the database is quite simple, consisting of lines in the following form:

   identifier : value EOL

The value can be surrounded by whitespace. Such a database could also be created and maintained with a text editor.

    We store persistent variables in objects that have a setup method to seek a value in the database. If this method is invoked immediately on declaration of variables, then we have the desired effect of automatic initialization with the current value of the persistent variables:

    VAR max:= NEW(Persistent.Integer, key:="max").setup()

As the database identifier for a variable, we simply use the name of the variable. Since the compiler does not support persistent variables, the programmer must assure that their values are updated in the database before the program terminates. The final statement in the program (preferably protected in a TRY-FINALLY statement; see Section 15.3) is the invocation of an operation that updates the value of all persistent variables in the database:

    Persistent.End()

---

[2]In the version introduced here, this file has little in common with a database. Here it serves as a place holder for a much larger, more complex system that would represent the external state space in a realistic application [BEW94].

```
  TRY                          (*Persistent.End must be invoked in any case *)
    Persistent.Start("test.db");

(*Persistent variables *)
  VAR
    i := NEW(Persistent.Integer, key := "int").setup();
    r := NEW(Persistent.Real, key := "real").setup();
    t := NEW(Persistent.Text, key := "text").setup();
  BEGIN
    SIO.PutText("int: ");   SIO.PutInt(i.val);   SIO.Nl();
    SIO.PutText("real: ");  SIO.PutReal(r.val);SIO.Nl();
    SIO.PutText("text: ");  SIO.PutText(t.val); SIO.Nl();

(*Access to variable via val field *)
    INC(i.val);
    r.val := r.val + 1.0;
    t.val := t.val & ".";
  END;

(*Update database *)
  FINALLY
    Persistent.End()
  END;
```

Example 14.11: *Use of persistent variables*

The setup method enters all persistent variables in a list that is then processed by the End procedure. Example 14.11 shows a program that modifies
an INTEGER, a REAL and a TEXT variable on each invocation.

> Be aware that we still lack some aspects of a realistic solution for the
> implementation sketched here: For the time, we ignore the problem
> that multiple programs can, in some overlapping order, read the value
> of a persistent variable and then update its value (only the last value
> holds). We assume that only a single program is running that could
> change the external state space. We would also need a mechanism
> that guarantees that only one program can change a given persistent
> variable at a certain time.

> Furthermore, we would need a well-conceived naming scheme for data-
> base identifiers (the keys) of persistent variables: various producers of
> service modules would have to reach agreement to avoid accidentally
> using the same identifier for quite different persistent variables, which
> could then overwrite one another. We do not deal with this problem
> here.

Example 14.12 shows the interface of the module Persistent. The type
Persistent.T is the supertype for all objects that manage persistent variables. Essentially, this object contains the setup method that seeks the

```
INTERFACE Persistent;                                                    (*CW*)

  IMPORT Rd, Wr, Lex;

  CONST
    DefaultPersistentDB = "/software/lib/m3PersDB/persistentDB";
    DefaultPersistentRefany = "/software/lib/m3PersDB/persistentRefany.";

  TYPE T <: Public;
    Integer <: PublicInteger;
    Char <: PublicChar;
    Boolean <: PublicBoolean;
    Real <: PublicReal;
    Text <: PublicText;
    Refany <: PublicRefany;

    Public = OBJECT key: TEXT
      METHODS setup() RAISES {Lex.Error} END;
    PublicInteger = T OBJECT val:= 0
      METHODS setup(): Integer RAISES {Lex.Error} END;
    PublicChar = T OBJECT val:= VAL(0, CHAR)
      METHODS setup(): Char RAISES {Lex.Error} END;
    PublicBoolean = T OBJECT val:= FALSE
      METHODS setup(): Boolean RAISES {Lex.Error} END;
    PublicReal = T OBJECT val:= 0.0
      METHODS setup(): Real RAISES {Lex.Error} END;
    PublicText = T OBJECT val:= ""
      METHODS setup(): Text RAISES {Lex.Error} END;
    PublicRefany = T OBJECT val: REFANY:= NIL
      METHODS setup(): Refany RAISES {Lex.Error} END;

  PROCEDURE End() RAISES {Wr.Failure};

  PROCEDURE Start( persistentDB:= DefaultPersistentDB;
                    persistentRefany:= DefaultPersistentRefany)
    RAISES {Rd.Failure};
END Persistent.
```

Example 14.12: *Simulation of persistent variables*

database value matching the key. Example 14.13 reveals the type Persistent.T. The value is stored as a TEXT value and is converted to the respective type with an internal method textToVal. The setup method invokes the method textToVal on reading the database. valToText is invoked by Persistent.End before updating the database.

The attribute val exists only for subtypes of Persistent.T (Persistent. Integer, e.g., has an INTEGER attribute val). These subtypes must override the two type-dependent conversion methods textToVal and valToText with the conversion procedures that they need.

```
INTERFACE PersistentRep;                                       (*CW*)

IMPORT Persistent, Lex;

REVEAL
   Persistent.T = Persistent.Public BRANDED OBJECT
                 textVal: TEXT;
              METHODS
                 valToText ();
                 textToVal () RAISES {Lex.Error};
              OVERRIDES
                 setup := Setup;
              END;

PROCEDURE Setup (self: Persistent.T) RAISES {Lex.Error};

END PersistentRep.
```

Example 14.13: *Revelation of Persistent.T*

Pickles

The module Persistent can also store persistent variables of type REFANY. Note that it is critical to store not only a pointer but also the data which it references! Here the Modula-3 standard library offers a comfortable feature: the module Pickle (also called Pkl in older library versions) [Nel91]; the following is its simplified interface:

```
INTERFACE Pickle;

IMPORT Rd, Wr;

PROCEDURE Write(wr: Wr.T; ref: REFANY);
PROCEDURE Read(rd: Rd.T): REFANY;

END Pickle.
```

Pickle.Write writes all data that are accessible via the pointer ref to an output stream. Pickle.Read reads data from an input stream and reconstructs them in main memory to match the structure that was written with Pickle.Write. These procedures allow implementing the type Persistent.Refany just as easily as other types of the interface Persistent.

For the interested reader, we present an excerpt from the implementation of the module Persistent (Example 14.14). The excerpt contains the part that handles the INTEGER subtype of Persistent.T. The other subtypes function analogously.

Example 14.14: *Part of the implementation of the module* **Persistent**

```
MODULE Persistent EXPORTS Persistent, PersistentRep;

IMPORT SIO, SF, Fmt, Lex, Scan, Rd, Wr, TextTextTbl, RefList, Pickle;
FROM Text IMPORT Equal, FindChar, GetChar;
    ⋮
REVEAL
  Integer = PublicInteger BRANDED OBJECT          (*revelation of persistent integer*)
                OVERRIDES
                    setup := IntSetup;            (*install type-dependent methods*)
                    valToText := IntvalToText;
                    textToVal := TextToIntval
                END;
    ⋮
PROCEDURE Setup (self: T) RAISES {Lex.Error} =
  VAR value: TEXT;
  BEGIN
(*enter in list of all persistent variables*)
    persVars := RefList.Cons(self, persVars);

(*first read text string belonging to self.key*)
    IF persValues.get(self.key, value) THEN
      self.textVal := value;                             (*store text string*)
      self.textToVal();                    (*convert text string to respective type*)
    END;
  END Setup;
    ⋮
PROCEDURE IntSetup (self: Integer): Integer RAISES {Lex.Error} =
  BEGIN
    NARROW(self, T).setup();                    (*start overridden method*)
    RETURN self;
  END IntSetup;
    ⋮
PROCEDURE IntvalToText (self: Integer) =
  BEGIN                          (*type-dependent conversion for integer values →TEXT *)
    self.textVal := Fmt.Int(self.val);
  END IntvalToText;
    ⋮
PROCEDURE TextToIntval (self: Integer) RAISES {Lex.Error} =
  BEGIN                          (*type-dependent conversion for integer values TEXT →*)
    self.val := Scan.Int(self.textVal);
  END TextToIntval;
(***********************)
(*Persistent database *)
(***********************)

CONST
  PrintableChars = Lex.Blanks + Lex.NonBlanks
                    + SET OF CHAR{VAL(128, CHAR).. LAST(CHAR)};
```

```
(*global data*)
VAR
  dbName, pklDataPrefix: TEXT;              (*database name and prefix for Pickle files*)
  persValues := NEW(TextTextTbl.T);              (*hash table Persvarnames to values*)
  persVars: RefList.T := NIL;                    (*list of names of pers. variables*)

PROCEDURE ReadDB (dbName: TEXT) RAISES {Rd.Failure} =
  VAR
    rd: Rd.T;
    name, value: TEXT;
  BEGIN
    TRY
      IF SF.FileExists(dbName) THEN             (*no values without database file*)
        rd := SF.OpenRead(dbName);
        Lex.Skip(rd);
(*Read database file completely: *)
        WHILE NOT Rd.EOF(rd) DO
          name := Lex.Scan(rd, Lex.NonBlanks – SET OF CHAR{':'});
          EVAL SIO.GetChar(rd);                             (*skip : *)
          Lex.Skip(rd);
(*Read value (can be enclosed in quotes) *)
          IF NOT Rd.EOF(rd) AND SIO.LookAhead(rd) = '"' THEN
            EVAL SIO.GetChar(rd);                           (*skip " *)
            value := Lex.Scan(rd, PrintableChars – SET OF CHAR{'"'});
            EVAL SIO.GetChar(rd);                        (*skip second " *)
          ELSE
            value := Lex.Scan(rd, PrintableChars – Lex.Blanks);
          END;
          Lex.Skip(rd);
(*Enter key / value pair in hash table *)
          EVAL persValues.put(name, value);
        END;
      END;
      Rd.Close(rd);
(*Unexpected end of file and Lex error converted to Rd.Failure: *)
    EXCEPT
      Rd.EndOfFile=>
        RAISE Rd.Failure(AtomList.List1(
          Atom.FromText("unexpected EOF in persDB "& dbName)));
    | Lex.Error=>
        RAISE Rd.Failure(
          AtomList.List1(Atom.FromText("formatting error in persDB " & dbName)));
    END;
  END ReadDB;
```

```
PROCEDURE WriteDB (dbName: TEXT) RAISES {Wr.Failure} =
  VAR
    wr:= SF.OpenWrite(dbName, overwrite:= TRUE);
    name, value: TEXT; iter:= persValues.iterate();
  BEGIN
(*Read hash table and write to database file *)
    WHILE iter.next(name, value) DO
      IF Equal(value, "") OR
        FindChar(value, '\t')>=0 OR FindChar(value, ' ')>= 0
      THEN                                    (*value contains whitespace *)
        Wr.PutText (wr, name & ": \"" & value & "\"\n");
      ELSE
        Wr.PutText (wr, name & ": " & value & "\n");
      END;
    END;
    Wr.Close (wr);
  END WriteDB;

(***********************)
(*Setup / Write Database *)
(***********************)


PROCEDURE Start( persistentDB:= DefaultPersistentDB;
                 persistentRefany:= DefaultPersistentRefany)
  RAISES {Rd.Failure}=
  BEGIN
    dbName:= persistentDB; pklDataPrefix:= persistentRefany;
    ReadDB(dbName);
  END Start;

PROCEDURE End() RAISES {Wr.Failure} =
  VAR var: T;
  BEGIN
    WHILE persVars # NIL DO
      var:= NARROW(persVars.head, T);
      var.valToText();
      EVAL persValues.put(var.key, var.textVal);       (*replace old or write new*)
      persVars:= persVars.tail;
    END;
    WriteDB(dbName);
  END End;

BEGIN
  TRY
    Start();                                  (*read database (with default name) *)
  EXCEPT Rd.Failure(err)=>
    SIO.PutText("\nPersistent: "& RdUtils.FailureText(err) & "\n");
    <*ASSERT FALSE*>                          (*generate run-time error*)
  END;
END Persistent.
```

Chapter 15

Exception handling

Thus far we have concentrated on writing programs as correctly as possible. However, each program is embedded in a larger context and must communicate with its environment. We make a number of assumptions about the environment (indeed, we incorporate these assumptions into our programs) that must apply in order for our program to work at all: input data must be present, there must be space on the hard disk for writing results, numeric values must be in certain valid ranges, etc. However, certainly some exception situations arise where these assumptions do *not* apply. The program must handle these situations also, without crashing or producing erroneous results. In addition, we could design the program so that it tests all possible errors in every situation. However, this strategy would prove quite involved and unnatural.

> John Searle pondered about the nature of *common sense knowledge*, saying: "Every morning when I enter my office, I assume that there is no abyss behind the door. But do I really make this assumption? Obviously not: I simply enter. Still, if there were an abyss behind the door, I would nevertheless react to it." We can construe this abyss as an *exception situation*. It is clear that we must also behave correctly in such exception situations.

Instead of testing for each action whether it was completed successfully, let us make provisions for exceptional cases. These provisions will only be activated if an exception actually occurs; otherwise they do not encumber normal program flow. Therefore this kind of exception handling makes programs both more comprehensible and more efficient.

15.1   Exceptions in a program

Exceptions are program states that are not anticipated under normal conditions of program execution. For this reason we prefer not to make their

```
  ⋮
VAR
  rd1, rd2: Rd.T;
  error: BOOLEAN;
  values1, values2: ARRAY [1..10] OF REAL;
BEGIN
(*Open files *)
  IF SF.FileExists(File1) THEN                              (*Does file exist? *)
    rd1:= SF.OpenRead(File1);
    IF SF.FileExists(File2) THEN
      rd2:= SF.OpenRead(File2);
      GetRealArray(rd1, values1, error);          (*error indicates success or failure *)
      IF error THEN SIO.PutText("Input file has wrong format"); SIO.Nl()
      ELSE
        GetRealArray(rd2, values1, error);
        IF error THEN SIO.PutText("Input file has wrong format"); SIO.Nl()
        ELSE                                 (*process only if input was successful *)
          Process(values1, values2);
  ⋮
      END (*IF error*)
    END (*IF error*)
    ELSE
      SIO.PutText(File2 & " cannot be read"); SIO.Nl();
      error:= TRUE;
    END (*IF FileExists*)
  ELSE
    SIO.PutText(File1 & " cannot be read"); SIO.Nl();
    error:= TRUE;
  END (*IF FileExists*)
  ⋮
```

Example 15.1: *Error handling without exceptions*

handling part of the algorithm. If we read a series of INTEGER values from a file, we do not want to be bothered with testing whether the input contains non-numeric characters; we could not do anything with these anyway, and we would need to terminate program execution. If several files are to be read, then it can be quite bothersome to test before each operation whether an error has already occurred.

The code fragment in Example 15.1 shows the situation. The program consists of repeatedly nested IF statements and uses a variable error. Distributed throughout the program are tests of the success of operations. All this has nothing to do with the actual algorithm; indeed, this encumbers understanding the algorithm.

The concept of exception handling enables us to develop algorithms as though everything would go well. If an error occurs, then we say that an exception situation has occurred: we generate an exception. Then, since the

```
EXCEPTION FileError(TEXT);                (*declaration of exception conditions *)
    ⋮
VAR rd1, rd2: Rd.T;
   values1, values2: ARRAY [1..10] OF REAL;
BEGIN
   TRY
(*Does file exist? *)
      IF NOT SF.FileExists(File1) THEN RAISE FileError(File1) END;
      IF NOT SF.FileExists(File2) THEN RAISE FileError(File2) END;

(*Read file *)
      rd1:= SF.OpenRead(File1);
      rd2:= SF.OpenRead(File2);
      GetRealArray(rd1, values1);
      GetRealArray(rd2, values2);

(*Process file *)
      Process(values1, values2);
    ⋮
   EXCEPT
   | FileError(fname)=>
       SIO.PutText(fname &" cannot be read"); SIO.Nl();
   | SIO.Error=>
       SIO.PutText("Input file has wrong format"); SIO.Nl();
   END; (*TRY-EXCEPT*)
    ⋮
```

Example 15.2: *Error handling with exceptions*

algorithm can no longer function properly, we terminate normal execution. The program branches to *handlers*, which then react to the situation.

Example 15.2 shows a program fragment that does the same as the fragment in Example 15.1, but handles exception errors with exceptions. The statements where exceptions can occur are *guarded* with a TRY-EXCEPT statement (see Section 15.2.4). This amounts to a bracketing of the statements. If an error occurs (which still must be detected), then a RAISE statement *generates* an exception. This terminates execution of the statements between TRY and EXCEPT. Similar to a CASE statement, the EX-CEPT branch tests which exception has occurred. If there was no exception, then the EXCEPT branch is not executed. Just as in Example 15.1, Example 15.2 tests the existence of the input files. However, the second version is formulated more clearly because error handling is distinct form the actual algorithm.

Naturally, exception situations are often detected by server modules on the system level: the hard disk might produce a read error while reading a file (perhaps due to dust at that position); this is recognized by the procedure that invoked the operating system service to read the file and that was

```
PROCEDURE GetRealArray(rd: Rd.T; VAR r: ARRAY OF REAL)
   RAISES {SIO.Error} =                                      (*delegates SIO.Error *)

   VAR
     i: CARDINAL;
   BEGIN
     WHILE NOT SIO.End(rd) DO
       i:= SIO.GetInt(rd);                            (*read index: SIO.Error can occur *)
       r[i]:= SIO.GetReal(rd);                        (*read value: SIO.Error can occur *)
     END; (*WHILE*)
   END GetRealArray;
```

Example 15.3: *Delegation of exceptions*

notified by the server module of the failure of the read operation. However, this procedure cannot really handle the exception. Such a service procedure to read data from files cannot know what effect the lack of these data means to the invoking application. The file could contain important configuration data without which the program cannot execute. Perhaps the data can be retrieved elsewhere. Thus, on occurrence of an exception, the procedure terminates and reports the situation to the invoking procedure. For the invoking procedure, this has the same effect as a RAISE statement: its algorithm is also terminated. It either also delegates the exception condition to its invoking procedure, or it *handles* it in the TRY-EXCEPT statement that invoked the procedure. In Example 15.2 the procedure GetRealArray does not handle the exception generated in SIO module, but delegates them (see also Example 15.3). The situation is finally handled in the procedure that invoked GetRealArray. After the exception is handled, the exception condition is reset and the program continues normal execution after the corresponding TRY-EXCEPT statement.

To indicate that a procedure should not handle an exception situation but only delegate it, we enter the name of the exception in a list after the keyword RAISES. Example 15.3 shows the procedure GetRealArray (familiar from Chapter 14), where we have now specified delegation of exceptions.

> Many programming languages provide no (usable) exception mechanism. This tends to produce programs that are either slower and less comprehensible due to numerous explicit error tests, or – what can be worse – error situations are not handled with adequate care.

> Other programming languages with exception handling permit error handling to ignore the exception and to resume program execution at the point where the exception occurred. Modula-3 does not permit resumption. If the procedure that generated the exception is left during the search for a handler, then there is no way back. However, careful planning of exception handling lets us always achieve the desired effects.

15.2 Exception handling in Modula-3

15.2.1 Exceptions, run-time errors, programming errors

Not every error that hinders a program from functioning is an exception situation in the sense of this chapter. We term errors made by the programmer *programming errors*: due to an incorrect algorithm or an erroneous structure, the program fails to meet specifications. Exception handling does not allow us to manage this kind of error; only careful problem analysis and program planning combined with careful verification and testing can avoid such errors. In addition, we distinguish *run-time errors* and *exceptions*:

- *Run-time errors*
  These are due to a programming error and are detected by the run-time system of the language environment. Run-time errors can be seen as predefined exceptions generated by the language environment in certain situations. Examples of run-time errors include accessing an array element with an index beyond the index range, assigning a negative value to a CARDINAL variable, dereferencing a NIL pointer, and an overflow in REAL arithmetic.

  > None of the three available Modula-3 language environments allows intercepting exception situations detected by the run-time system. Run-time errors always cause program termination.

- *Exceptions*
  We speak of exceptions in the context of an error situation detected by a program itself (rather than by the underlying language environment, operating system or hardware). On detection of such an error situation, the program explicitly *generates* an exception. This need not occur directly in a procedure written by the programmer, but can frequently occur in a module of the Modula-3 library.

As sketched here, the border between *run-time errors* and *exceptions* is less a conceptual one and more a matter of implementation. Whether a certain situation can be handled by the program as an exception or demands immediate program termination as a run-time error (see Appendix C.1.6) depends on the compiler and the language environment.

Modula-3 provides explicit language constructs for declaring, raising and handling exceptions. The Modula-3 library predefines a number of exceptions, and we can add definitions of others. There are two basic operations on exceptions: *raising* and *handling*. An exception is raised by a RAISE statement and intercepted and handled by a TRY-EXCEPT statement.

15.2.2   Declaration of exceptions

Exceptions are identified via their names. An exception declaration takes
the following form:

Declaration$_{13}$ = $\cdots$ |"EXCEPTION" { ExceptionDecl$_{16}$ ";" } | $\cdots$
ExceptionDecl$_{16}$ = Ident$_{89}$ ["(" Type$_{48}$ ")"].

The identifier Ident$_{89}$ is the name of the exception. An exception can
have a parameter whose type is specified on declaration of the exception.
For example, the SIO interface defines the parameterless exception Error
(see Appendix C.3.3 on page 542). This enables clients of the module to
access the exceptions that the procedures of the module generate. Example
15.2 handles SIO.Error in its TRY-EXCEPT statement.

Exporting the EXCEPTION declaration in an interface allows clients to
raise the exception themselves.

15.2.3   Generation of exceptions

An exception is raised by a RAISE statement:

RaiseStmt$_{34}$ = "RAISE" QualID$_{86}$ ["(" Expr$_{66}$ ")"].

Expr$_{66}$ computes the parameters of the exception. Its type was specified
on declaration of the exception. Parameterless exceptions omit this expression along with the parentheses. The RAISE statement raises an exception
and thereby begins the search for a corresponding handler.

15.2.4   Exception handling

To handle exceptions, we bracket the statement sequence in which a given
exception could occur within a TRY-EXCEPT statement and specify a list of
handlers. A handler is simply a statement sequence. The syntax of the
TRY-EXCEPT statement is:

TryXptStmt$_{38}$ = "TRY" Stmts$_{23}$ "EXCEPT" [Handler$_{44}$] { "|" Handler$_{44}$ }
                ["ELSE" Stmts$_{23}$] "END".
Handler$_{44}$ = QualID$_{86}$ { "," QualID$_{86}$ } ["(" Ident$_{89}$ ")"] "=>" Stmts$_{23}$.

This enables writing statements that generally take the following form:

```
TRY
    guarded statements
EXCEPT
| exception₁(parameter₁) => handler₁
⋮
| exceptionₙ(parameterₙ) => handlerₙ
ELSE handler₀
END
```

The TRY-EXCEPT statement executes as follows:

1. If no exception occurs in the guarded statements, then they execute as though there were no enclosing TRY-EXCEPT statement. After execution of the statements, program execution resumes after the END of the TRY-EXCEPT statement.

2. If an exception does occur in the guarded statements, then the statement sequence terminates and control passes to the EXCEPT branch. If $exception_i$ occurred, then the variable $parameter_i$ is set to the value of the expression of the parameter of the RAISE statement, and execution resumes at $handler_i$. $handler_i$ is a statement sequence; it is also the scope of the variable $parameter_i$. The type of this variable is the same as was specified on declaration of the exception.

   Thus the exception was handled. The exception condition no longer applies, and program execution continues after the END of the TRY-EXCEPT statement.

3. However, if an exception occurs in the guarded statements and it does not appear in the list, then $handler_0$ of the ELSE branch executes, the exception condition is reset, and execution resumes after the TRY-EXCEPT statement.

   If there is no ELSE branch (i.e., the TRY-EXCEPT statement fails to provide a handler), then either the exception is delegated or the program terminates with a run-time error (see Section 15.2.5).

Exceptions that occur in the handler are not guarded. We can intercept such exceptions if we write the TRY-EXCEPT statement as a guarded statement of a further TRY-EXCEPT statement.

15.2.5 Delegating exceptions

If we do not handle an exception in a procedure, but only want to inform the invoking procedure of the occurrence of an exception condition, then we must specify this in the procedure declaration. The complete syntax of procedure signatures is:

$\text{ProcedureHead}_{18} = \text{"PROCEDURE" Ident}_{89} \text{ Signature}_{19}.$
$\text{Signature}_{19} \quad = \text{"(" Formals}_{20} \text{ ")" [":" Type}_{48} \text{] ["RAISES" Raises}_{22} \text{]}.$
$\text{Raises}_{22} \quad = \text{"\{" [QualID}_{86} \text{ \{ "," QualID}_{86} \text{ \}] "\}"}.$

Hence the RAISES set represents a second exit from the procedure: either the procedure terminates normally and returns any data in variable parameters or as return value, or it generates an exception, which has the same effect in the invoking procedure as an explicit RAISE statement:

```
PROCEDURE Action1                  PROCEDURE Action2()
   (VAR error: BOOLEAN) =             RAISES {exception}=
BEGIN                              BEGIN
   ⋮                                  ⋮
   IF error condition THEN            IF error condition THEN
      error := TRUE;                     RAISE exception;
   END;                               END;
   ⋮                                  ⋮
   END Action1;                       END Action2;
⋮                                  ⋮

Action1(error);                    Action2();
IF error THEN RAISE exception;     ⋮
⋮
```

Action1 and Action2 in the above pseudocode both test for the occurrence of an exception condition. Action1 reports the exception condition with a Boolean variable, Action2 with an exception. The explicit RAISE statement and the delegated exception have the same effect: the procedure that invoked Action1/2 terminates and the search for a handler begins.

This can occur across multiple levels of the invocation chain. Whenever an exception occurs in a procedure (whether via a RAISE statement or in an invoked procedure that delegates handling), it is delegated if, first, there is no handler in the procedure itself (see Section 15.2.4) and, second, if its name appears in the RAISES set of the procedure. If an exception that cannot be delegated occurs outside a TRY-EXCEPT statement or if the EXCEPT branch has neither a handler nor an ELSE, then the program terminates with a run-time error.

Now let us describe completely the search for a handler:

1. If the exception occurs in a statement guarded by a TRY-EXCEPT statement and a handler or an ELSE branch exists there, then con-

trol passes to the handler, the exception condition is reset, and program execution continues after the TRY-EXCEPT statement (see Section 15.2.4).

2. If the exception occurs in a statement guarded by a TRY-EXCEPT statement and neither a corresponding handler nor an ELSE branch exists there, then the procedure terminates and, if its name appears in the RAISES set of the procedure, the exception condition is delegated.

3. If the exception does not occur in a guarded statement, then the procedure terminates and, if its name appears in the RAISES set of the procedure, the exception condition is delegated.

4. If the exception can be neither handled nor delegated, then program execution terminates with a run-time error.

If an exception was delegated, then the same search for a handler begins anew. Exceptions frequently pass through a whole sequence up the invocation chain. Example 15.3 shows how the exception SIO.Error is only delegated. SIO.Error occurs when one of the two procedures SIO.GetInt or SIO.GetReal reads a character string that cannot be interpreted as a number (see Example 14.10, page 363). GetRealArray does not handle this error. The semantics of the problem for GetRealArray are such that the array cannot be read completely; for this procedure there is no handling for this problem. Instead of raising an exception itself, GetRealArray simply delegates the exception and lets the invoking procedure handle it (in Example 15.2 it is "handled" simply with an error message). In Section 15.4 we discuss planning exception handling for larger programs so that exception situations are always handled where sufficient information is available on the effects of the problem.

15.3 Delaying exception handling

The occurrence of an exception causes the immediate termination of the current procedure and all other procedures in the invocation chain that propagate the exception. However, for many algorithms, simply termining execution and propagating the exception condition is not acceptable error handling. For example, the Modula-3 compiler creates temporary files that can become quite large, but are relevant only during compilation. These files should be deleted – even if an exception condition occurs during compilation.

In environments where multiple programs share a computer system, reliable cleanup is very important after program execution. A program must temporarily reserve a given service so that it is not disturbed by competing programs. Outputting to a printer is such a service that obviously can be used by only one program at a time; other jobs must wait (Chapter 16 discusses such synchronization problems in detail). Naturally this also means that each program must release the resource when finished. If an exception occurs in a printing program *after* the reservation of the printer, then in any event the printer must be released again before the printing program is terminated – otherwise the printer would remain blocked. In a more general sense, the following sequence occurs frequently in software systems:

> *Reserve resource*
> *Process*
> *Release resource*

Delegating exceptions in the *processing* part is obviously impossible; it would terminate the total algorithm and leave the resources blocked. Therefore we guard such statements with the TRY-FINALLY statement:

> *Reserve resource*
> TRY
>   *Process*
> FINALLY
>   *Release resource*
> END;

Delegation of the exception is delayed by this statement: after the occurrence of the exception, the guarded statements (between the keywords TRY and FINALLY) abort, the part after FINALLY executes, and then the search for a handler for the exception begins. The FINALLY branch *always* executes, even if no exception occurs.

If the only exception that can occur during processing is Error, then the TRY-FINALLY statement corresponds to the following TRY-EXCEPT statement:

> *Reserve resource*
> TRY
>   *Process*
> EXCEPT
>   Error=> *Release resource*; RAISE Error
> END;
> *Release resource*

```
PROCEDURE IntegerCopy() RAISES {SIO.Error} =
  VAR
    in:= SF.OpenRead();                          (*opens input file *)
    out:= SF.OpenWrite();                        (*opens output file *)
    count: CARDINAL:= 0;              (*counts successfully read values *)
  BEGIN
    TRY
      WHILE NOT SIO.End(in) DO
        SIO.PutInt(SIO.GetInt(in), 6, out);
        IF SIO.TermChar(in) = '\n' THEN SIO.NI(out) END;
        INC(count);
      END; (*WHILE*)
    FINALLY                                    (*always close files *)
      SIO.PutInt(count);
      SIO.PutText(" values copied"); SIO.NI();
      SF.CloseRead(in); SF.CloseWrite(out);
    END; (*TRY FINALLY*)
  END IntegerCopy;
BEGIN
  SIO.PutText("File copy program\n");
  TRY
    IntegerCopy();
  EXCEPT                             (*any exception handling after closing *)
    SIO.Error => SIO.PutText("!Error!\n");
  END;
```

Example 15.4: *Delaying exceptions: the file is always closed*

If any of multiple exceptions could occur, then the code *"Release resource"* would have to be duplicated further. A solution with an ELSE branch is impossible because then we lose information about which exception occurred. This demonstrates that the problem of delaying exception handling with the TRY-EXCEPT statement can only be solved with code duplication and that the TRY-FINALLY statement proves to be a great advantage here.

> The same distinction between run-time errors and exceptions, as described in Section 15.2.4, applies for the TRY-FINALLY statement: depending on the implementation of the language environment, run-time errors cause *immediate* program termination (without processing the FINALLY branch first), while exceptions always invoke the FINALLY branch.

> The authors are convinced that this is a shortcoming of the current Modula-3 environments. Here the distinction between exceptions and run-time errors makes no sense; resources should *always* be released regardless of this distinction.

Syntax of the TRY-FINALLY statement

$TryFinStmt_{39}$ = "TRY" $Stmts_{23}$ "FINALLY" $Stmts_{23}$ "END".

Example 15.4 demonstrates the delay of exceptions. The procedure IntegerCopy opens a file for reading and one for writing and copies integer values from one file to the other. If an exception occurs (e.g., if the input file contains a non-numeric character), then both files are properly closed before the procedure terminates; i.e., all data that had already been copied into the output file before the error occurred are stored. If the input file is difficult to reach (e.g., a modem transfer), then this behavior is desirable. When the operation restarts, only the missing data need to be copied (although our example lacks a mechanism for automatic resumption).

15.4   Strategies for exception handling

The importance of exception handling becomes clear only in larger systems, which require us to plan carefully the strategy for various exception situations. In particular, we need a structure of *responsibilities*.

Exception handling needs to be planned into the system architecture. In a properly designed system, each module handles a clearly defined task. In the definition of module duties, the responsibilities for error situations must also be specified.

In determining the strategy for exception handling, we encounter a fundamental contradiction. Assume that an exception interrupts a long invocation chain that crosses module boundaries. If we handle the exception locally (i.e., in the procedure where the situation was detected), this simplifies our program structure. However, at this location we know almost nothing about the application that initiated the invocation chain. Only the highest level of invocation best knows the consequences of the exception on program execution. To handle the exceptions there, we must propagate them through the entire invocation chain. Although this complicates the program structure somewhat, the exception mechanism of the language does ease such delegation considerably.

In general we must take care to handle immediately those exceptions that need no knowledge about the application. Other exceptions that cannot be handled locally should be propagated upwards until the responsible level handles them. Thus for each procedure definition we must choose from the following possibilities:

- *Handling without exceptions*
  Naturally not every exception situation must be handled as an exception. Many problems can be intercepted more simply with IF state-

ments, with propagation of the information via a return value or variable parameter.

- *Procedures with local exception handling*
  After the invocation of a procedure with local exception handling, the program always has a normal state (i.e., no exception condition applies). The procedure must have handled every problem, or it terminated the action and thus restored a normal state.

- *Complete delegation of exception conditions*
  Procedures have two tasks: if they terminate normally, then they leave a valid program state; if this is not possible, they terminate with an exception that the invoking procedure must handle.

- *Partial handling of exception conditions*
  Procedures with partial handling appear quite frequently in service modules. They detect an exception that they cannot handle. However, before they terminate, they ensure that the state of the server remains consistent. Often the service procedure then generates a new exception with its own name, declared in the service module. The client thus remains capsuled off from the module (information hiding), but is informed of the failure of the operation.

In the course of the invocation chain, all these possibilities could occur. Consider one final example. On storage of a text in a word processor, we might encounter the following invocation chain (starting at the bottom): in writing a character, a procedure of the language environment determines that the capacity of the hard disk has been exhausted and generates a corresponding exception. The procedure that stores the entire text in a loop delegates this exception upwards. The exported procedure for storing a document handles this exception by generating an appropriate error message. This procedure generates its own, new exception and passes the error message as parameter. The menu function of the main program handles this exception by outputting the error message. No exception is propagated further.

Chapter 16

Parallel programming

Thus far we have always (implicitly) assumed that the statements of a statement sequence execute one after the other. Programs consisting of such statement sequences are termed *sequential*. However, in practice some problems are difficult or impossible to solve with a sequential program. Here we can resort to *parallel programming*, which is actually the more general view: sequential programs can be viewed a special (although very important) case of parallel programs.

> We might feel a bit like Orgon in Moliere's *Tartuffe* as he first heard of poetry and discovered that his whole life long he had been speaking in prose. Even so, we find that we have been writing sequential programs until now. This fact becomes interesting only because we now know that there is something else – parallel programs.

16.1 Motivation for parallelism

Better utilization of existing resources

Parallelism was first introduced in the 1960s, motivated by the fact that input/output consume by orders of magnitude more time than internal operations. Although input/output has become faster since then, the same applies to internal operations; hence the relationship has remained much the same. While one program is waiting for input/output, it makes sense to let another program do something useful. When input/output in the former program is finished, then the latter can be *interrupted*, and the former program can be continued. The concept of *interruption* has significantly improved the *throughput* (number of programs processed per unit of time) of computers while simultaneously introducing new problems. One problem was that a program can be interrupted almost unnoticed and continued later. As we shall see, this is not always easy.

Assume that your work is interrupted because the computer beeps: an
e-mail has arrived. While you read the e-mail, someone knocks and
enters your office: here we already have the second level of interruption. Now, if the telephone starts ringing as well, then we have the
third level of nesting. We must handle each interruption individually
and then return to the previous task. Clearly an interruption cannot
take effect at any arbitrary time: sometimes it has to wait.

Modern computers also employ parallelism to better manage their *resources* when the application programs themselves are sequential. This
requires that such parallelism be fully *transparent* for user programs; in
fact, the authors of user programs should not even need to be aware of the
parallelism.

Transparent parallelism has many applications. Most *operating systems* share the computer among several programs such that while one program is waiting for input/output, another program carries out computation.

Likewise the hardware level employs much parallelism. All newer processors, e.g., employ *pipelining*: various phases of the execution of instructions (such as loading an instruction, decoding an instruction, loading
operands, etc.) can overlap. While one command is being decoded, the next
can be loaded, and so on. The *superscalar* processors, which are finding
ever increasing application, can even start multiple instructions simultaneously.

Inherently parallel applications

Consider a flight reservation system. Passengers at various counters
around the world can make reservations for the same flight. All these reservations must be processed through the same software system. A customer
in Klagenfurt would be quite unhappy to have to wait while a passenger in
San Francisco books. A ticketing system must process these jobs simultaneously, in *parallel*.

This example points out a fundamental difficulty of parallel programming: What happens if a passenger in Klagenfurt and one in San Francisco
want to book the same flight, which has only one seat available? Clearly
one of the two must win. In any case, we must avoid selling the same
seat twice. We can readily imagine the following: First Klagenfurt checks
whether there is a seat available. Shortly thereafter the query arrives from
San Francisco and also finds the seat available. On the basis of this information, both locations reserve the seat. Because this must never happen,
the methods of parallel programming provide solutions to avoid such conflicts.

We could identify many applications that are inherently parallel: all
systems that simultaneously serve multiple customers (banks, warehouses,

etc.); systems that control airplanes, ships, train stations, etc.; telecommunications systems that operate (possibly huge) networks of telephone and computer connections and that must simultaneously assure a large number of connections.

Accelerating algorithms

Some algorithms can be formulated as both sequential and parallel, yet processing them on even the fastest sequential computer takes too long. What "too long" means depends on the problem. Consider the weather forecast: to be able to compute an accurate forecast requires numerous computations. Yet what good is a perfect forecast if we deliver the results too late? A program that uses Wednesday's data to compute Thursday's weather forecast, but delivers the forecast on Friday, is not quite what we had in mind.

In such a case we can take one of two approaches: either we improve our model so that it requires less computation, or we accelerate the computer. The former approach is more economical in the long run and also intellectually more challenging. In practice the second approach is often preferred. The computer industry invests a great deal to make computers ever faster. However, accelerating the classical von Neumann machines (see Section 1.2) has reached physical limits. This phenomenon, called the *von Neumann bottleneck*, is imposed by the von Neumann architecture. Although John von Neumann addressed the possibility of parallel processing already in the 1950s, the von Neumann architecture is fundamentally sequential: the arithmetic and logic unit (ALU) reads and interprets the instructions in main memory sequentially.

> Today's top processors operate at over 200 MHz; i.e., they take less than five nanoseconds (10^{-9} seconds) to execute an operation (e.g., an addition). There is good reason to believe that there is not much room for improvement.
>
> The reader might wonder whether there is a need to accelerate further. The question is justified, but cannot be discussed here in detail. Parallel computers are becoming more widespread, and parallelism will gain in importance in the future.

At this time parallelism seems to represent the only possibility to significantly accelerate computers. This includes transparent parallelism hidden in the computer architecture or the lower levels of the operating system, as well as *explicit* parallelism, which enables the programmer to express algorithms in parallel form and map them onto a parallel architecture.

16.2   Parallel programs

Parallel programs can best be expressed as a collection of *cooperating sequential processes*.

| A *process* is a virtual processor that executes its instructions sequentially and has its own state space.

A process is thus an *active* element. We can imagine that each process has its own (real or virtual) processor (its own engine). A process executes its sequential statements parallel to other processes. Here we are not interested in fully independent processes, but in ones that communicate with one another.

> When two computers do different things in two different rooms, we could speak of parallel processes, but this would be of no particular interest. The situation becomes interesting when there is some connection between the two.

A process can *synchronize* its execution with that of other processes; i.e., processes can wait for one another. As needed, they can also *communicate* with one another by exchanging data via *shared variables* or via *communication channels* using *messages*.

A related collection of processes forms a *parallel program*. In general, we do not know which statements of the individual processes overlap. Usually we cannot make any assumptions about the temporal execution of individual processes.

If the processes actually do have their own physical processors, then we speak of *truly parallel processes*. If the processes run on a single processor, hence only virtually have their own processors, then we speak of *quasi-parallel processes* or *concurrent processes*.

Both cases require a mechanism that handles synchronization and communication. This mechanism is usually in the form of a *scheduler* that coordinates execution of the processes. The scheduler for quasi-parallel processes must also implement the virtual processors, thus assuring that the processes run (quasi) as though each had its own processor.

| For the development of parallel programs, the same rules apply, regardless of whether the processes are truly parallel or quasi-parallel.

Validating the correctness of a parallel program should be independent of whether the program is truly parallel or quasi-parallel. Therefore in this chapter we use the term *parallelism* unless we need to emphasize the distinction.

In the light of efficiency considerations, the difference becomes significant. A quasi-parallel program is generally *slower* than an equivalent sequential program. Nevertheless, the development of such programs makes sense if no equivalent sequential program can be found or if the sequential variant would be too complicated. A truly parallel program *can* (but need not) prove faster than an equivalent sequential program. Synchronization restricts the degree of parallelism. Every (sensible) parallel program has sequential components; if the sequential share is quite large, then parallelism can yield little acceleration. In addition, communication can slow down parallelism. If the processes spend more time waiting for messages than in processing them, then parallelism cannot help much. With an awkward design, the truly parallel variant (executed on a number of independent processors) can actually become slower than its sequential counterpart. In many designs, efficiency considerations can be decisive.

In the following, we concentrate on the fundamental concepts that are independent of the kind of parallelism. The following ground rule applies for all parallel programs:

The verification of a parallel program must preclude any assumptions about the absolute or relative speed of the involved processes.

> A very intriguing area of computer science, *real-time programming*, deals with problems that require considering the execution time of a program. Consider, e.g., an *on-line* control (on-line meaning that the computer participates directly in the controlled process, e.g., the security system of a power plant). Here events occur to which the computer *must* react within specified time limits. In real-time systems it does not suffice to simply deliver correct results; the timing must also be correct. These assumptions about the timing of execution make verification more difficult by posing additional requirements. We do not discuss the problems of real-time systems.

Lightweight and heavyweight processes

Processes are often classified as *heavyweight* or *lightweight* processes. Heavyweight processes have their own state space (*address space*), while several lightweight processes share a global state space. Heavyweight processes could be running on different computers that share communication channels. Lightweight processes are generally on the same computer and can communicate via shared variables. Switching between lightweight processes is a relatively inexpensive action. When heavyweight processes share a computer, switching becomes more difficult (and more expensive). Lightweight processes are often called *threads* (from thread of control); we will usually use this terminology.

> The best-known example of heavyweight processes are those of the *Unix* operating system (most larger operating systems have similar processes). Unix processes each occupy their own address space (in

virtual memory) and are quite independent of one another, apart from the fact that they use the same resources, under the management of the operating system. They can also communicate, although their communication is quite awkward.

Unix processes within a processor are quasi-parallel. Given a supply of Unix computers, several processes can run truly parallel, while others are quasi-parallel. Thus we can write parallel programs that execute in quasi-parallel as well as in truly parallel mode or even mixed.

16.3   Threads in Modula-3

Modula-3 supports the concept of parallel threads. A sequential Modula-3-program consists of a single thread (the *main thread*). It is possible to create additional threads that are all executed in quasi-parallel mode. Threads can either run in an endless loop or terminate. Once the main thread terminates, this ends all threads generated by it.

16.3.1   Schedulers of Modula-3 environments

The existing language environments feature schedulers only for quasi-parallel threads. The scheduler embedded in the *run-time system* manages allocation of the processor to the threads. In principle, the allocation strategy (*scheduling*) can be quite different in various environments. We generally assume that the strategy is *fair*; i.e., if a thread is ready to run, it will get its turn and need not wait endlessly for the processor. The scheduler of most Modula-3 language environments employs *time slice scheduling*. A thread cannot monopolize the processor for longer than the specified time slice (e.g., 50 msec). When a time slice expires, execution of the thread is interrupted and the processor is allocated to another thread; this reallocation of resources from one process by the scheduler is called *pre-emption*. The waiting threads are generally managed with a ring-shaped closed structure; the scheduler switches from one thread to another along the ring. In this way the scheduler can assure that no waiting thread must wait endlessly for the processor.

> For technical reasons, the Modula-3 scheduler currently running on DOSPCs is non-pre-emptive and thus cannot fulfill the condition of fairness. If a thread does not relinquish control, it can monopolize the processor. Hence the threads themselves must be fair and from time to time relinquish the processor on behalf of others.
>
> If the threads use any form of synchronization (Section 16.4.4), then the scheduler automatically handles this relinquishing of the processor, for synchronization always occurs via the scheduler. If they re-

quire no synchronization, then they must periodically relinquish control explicitly using the Scheduler.Yield[1] procedure. If all processes behave fairly in this way, then fair scheduling can be achieved.

16.3.2 Creating threads

The Modula-3 language environment provides the interface Thread in the collection of standard interfaces (Appendix C.1.2 on page 527).

Fork

The procedure Fork creates a new thread and returns a new instance of Thread.T.

> TYPE Closure = OBJECT METHODS apply(): REFANY END;
>
> PROCEDURE Fork (cl: Closure): T;

The new thread is executed (quasi-)parallel to the creating thread. Fork accepts as parameter a *closure*, whose type must be a subtype of Thread.Closure. The type Thread.Closure first defines an empty closure; the corresponding subtype must fill the closure. In particular, the apply method must be overridden with the procedure that is to be executed by the newly created thread. The signature of apply is kept very general; it has no parameter and returns a function value of type REFANY. If we want a different signature, we must extend the Closure accordingly (see Example 16.4).

The statements in threads are implemented by the procedure that overrides the apply method in the thread closure. This is quite an ordinary procedure. We could say that threads are procedures that are launched not by invocation but by Fork. This is why it makes sense for Modula-3 to provide not a separate language construct but only a special interface for threads.

The invocation of Thread.Fork effects the following:

- Fork instructs the scheduler to start the procedure specified in the closure parameter as a new thread and returns a value of type Thread.T, which identifies the new thread.

- Thereby the statements of the apply procedure are executed in parallel with the invoking procedure.

---

[1] In the old version of the Modula-3 library the procedure is exported by the module Thread.

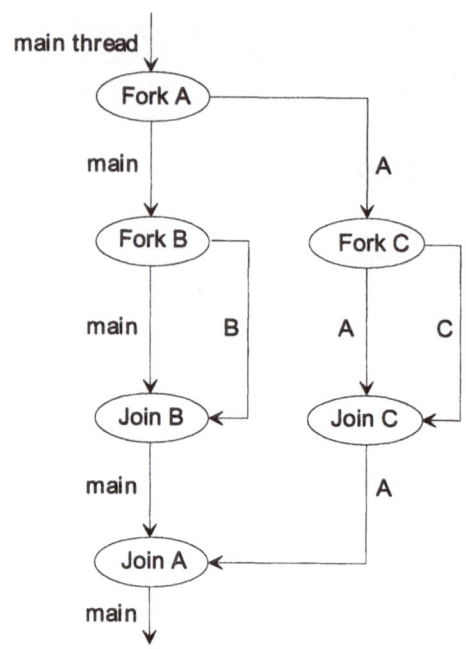

Figure 16.1: *Forking and joining threads*

Join

We can join two threads with a Join invocation.

PROCEDURE Join (thread: T): REFANY;

Thread.Join expects a parameter of type Thread.T, which identifies the thread that the invoking thread is to join. If the identified thread has not finished its work, the thread invoking Join must wait. After the Join the two threads are merged to a single control flow (see Figure 16.1). Thread.Join returns the return value of the procedure executed by apply.

Shared data

Modula-3 threads share an address space. Like all other procedures, a procedure launched as a thread can access the module's global variables in their common scope. They can also create dynamic data whose root is stored in a global variable. Multiple threads can access global variables and dynamic data collectively (and simultaneously). This can cause conflicts (see Section 16.4).

```
    ⋮
IMPORT Thread, Lists, SIO, SF;

VAR
    thread: Thread.T;                                    (*Thread instance*)
    cl := NEW(Thread.Closure, apply:= Start);            (*Closure instance*)
    list1, list2: Lists.T;                               (*two lists*)

PROCEDURE Start(self: Thread.Closure): REFANY =
BEGIN
    RETURN Lists.Get(SF.OpenRead("in1"));                (*reads a list from "in1"*)
END Start;

BEGIN
    thread:= Thread.Fork(cl);                            (*creates a thread; launches Start*)
    list2:= Lists.Get(SF.OpenRead("in2"));               (*reads list from "in2"*)
    list1:= Thread.Join(thread);                         (*waits for thread; stores its result*)
    ⋮
```

Example 16.2: *Reading two lists in parallel*

Private data

The procedures started as threads can invoke other procedures and thus
initiate an arbitrary invocation chain. Local data regions of an invocation
chain are created according to the stack principle (see Section 9.2.2).

If threads are to exist in parallel, we must ensure that they all can
process their invocation chains. The resulting local data regions must be
inaccessible for other threads. Thus Fork always creates a new invocation
stack for the local data regions of a new thread.

We can launch the same procedure repeatedly with Fork (see Example
16.5). The created threads all execute the same statements, but have their
own local data and so different states; thus the execution of the statements
of each thread is determined individually by its state space.

Examples of Fork and Join

Example 16.2 reads two lists from two files (in1 and in2) (quasi-)simul-
taneously. Two threads enable parallel reading. The variable cl is created,
and the function Start implements the apply method. Start returns a list.
The interface Lists (not specified further here) provides the procedures Get
and Put to read or output a list. The first statement of the program assigns
to the variable thread the value returned by Fork. The invocation of Fork
creates a thread that executes Start, i.e., reads the list from in1. The main
thread continues to run in parallel and simultaneously reads the second
list from in2 into the variable list2. With a Join, it waits for the result of the
other thread. Afterwards we have only the main thread.

```
PROCEDURE Max(a, b: INTEGER): INTEGER =          (*maximum of two numbers*)
BEGIN
  IF a > b THEN RETURN a ELSE RETURN b END
END Max;

VAR
  a: ARRAY [1..4] OF INTEGER;                              (*stores the data*)
  max: INTEGER;                              (*max stores the maximum of all a[i]*)
BEGIN
  max:= Max(Max(a[1], a[2]), Max(a[3], a[4]));          (*maximum of four numbers*)
```

Example 16.3: Maximum of four numbers (sequentially)

```
 ⋮
TYPE
  Closure = Thread.Closure OBJECT
            a, b, result: INTEGER;              (*parameters and result in Closure*)
            OVERRIDES
            apply:= Start
          END; (*Closure*)
VAR
  cl := NEW(Closure);
  thread: Thread.T;
  a: ARRAY [1..4] OF INTEGER;                              (*stores data*)
  max: INTEGER;                              (*max stores maximum of all a[i]*)

  PROCEDURE Start(cl: Closure): REFANY =                   (*invokes Max*)
  BEGIN
    cl.result:= Max(cl.a, cl.b);                  (*result stored in Closure*)
    RETURN NIL                                    (*return value not used*)
  END Start;
BEGIN
  cl.a:= a[1]; cl.b:= a[2];                      (*parameters set in Closure*)
  thread:= Thread.Fork(cl);         (*created thread starts; computes Max(a[1], a[2])*)
  max:= Max(a[3], a[4]);              (*main thread computes maximum of rest*)
  EVAL Thread.Join(thread);                      (*partial results available*)
  max:= Max(max, cl.result);                      (*final result computed*)
```

Example 16.4: Maximum of four numbers in parallel

The next two examples compute the maximum of four numbers. Example 16.3 shows a sequential solution; Example 16.4, a parallel solution. The parallel solution computes the maximum of a[1] and a[2] in parallel to the computation of the maximum of a[3] and a[4]; the parameters and the return value are stored in the closure. The same Max procedure is also invoked in the parallel version. The return value of the apply method is not used.

```
MODULE NThreads EXPORTS Main;

  IMPORT Thread, SIO;
  FROM Scheduler IMPORT Yield;

  CONST
    N = 10;
  TYPE
    Threads = [1..N];
    Closure = Thread.Closure OBJECT
                        id: Threads;               (*identifies thread*)
                 OVERRIDES
                        apply:= PrintId;
                 END; (*Closure*)

  PROCEDURE PrintId(cl: Closure): REFANY =
  BEGIN
    REPEAT
      SIO.PutInt(cl.id);
      IF cl.id = LAST(Threads) THEN SIO.Nl() END;
      Yield();                                     (*yields to other threads*)
    UNTIL SIO.Available();
    RETURN NIL;                                    (*return value not used*)
  END PrintId;

  PROCEDURE Fork() =
  BEGIN
    FOR i:= FIRST(Threads) TO LAST(Threads) – 1 DO
      EVAL Thread.Fork(NEW(Closure, id:= i))       (*N-1 threads are generated*)
    END;
    EVAL PrintId(NEW(Closure, id:= LAST(Threads)));  (*N-th thread = main*)
  END Fork;

BEGIN
  Fork();                                          (*start all threads*)
END NThreads.
```

Example 16.5: *N threads, explicit assignment with Yield*

Example 16.5 creates N threads. Each thread receives its own identifier (id). In a loop, they output their identifiers until any key is pressed
on the keyboard. SIO.Available does not block the invoking thread (as does
SIO.GetChar), but always returns immediately and returns *true* if and only
if input data are present (i.e., if a key has been pressed). Once a key is
pressed, the thread that is occupying the processor at that moment terminates and returns to its invoking procedure (Fork). After this invocation
there are no further statements and the whole parallel program terminates.

Note that the last thread is not started with Thread.Fork but as a procedure. This makes the Nth thread the main thread. If we had started the

Nth thread with Thread.Fork as well, then the main thread would terminate immediately after the invocation of Fork – and with it all others. To
avoid this, we would have to find some artificial way to hinder the main
thread.

The invocation of Yield serves to voluntarily relinquish the processor to
the other ready threads. This allows us to modify the system's scheduling
strategy; all threads repeatedly offer the others the possibility to output
their data.

Synchronization and communication

All examples so far made the (implicit) assumption that the processes are
independent of one another. As long as this is true, parallel programming
remains rather simple. While you read a book, numerous other people can
read other books; you do not need to know anything about it (as in reading
two lists from two different files). On the other hand, a group of students
could also be taking notes in their own notebooks simultaneously from a
blackboard. Problems could arise if they write at different speeds and the
blackboard is to be erased; the erasing should wait until all are finished.

Reading a book together at different speeds can cause difficulties in
turning pages (for young people of different sexes reading the same book
together can have severe consequences anyway, as we see in Dante's *Divine
Comedy* and Goethe's *Wahlverwandschaften*). It becomes more difficult if
another person wants to write in your notebook. We could arrange, e.g.,
that each person writes one page and then hands the notebook to the other.
This makes writing a single page *atomic*; for all other processes, an atomic
action in a process appears as an indivisible unit. Although it can carry out
multiple state transitions internally, these must be invisible to other processes. Viewed from outside, we can speak of the state of an atomic action
before and *after*, but there is no *in between*.

When processes produce data for or consume data from one another,
they must *communicate* (e.g., by having one person write on the blackboard and the others reading the text). These processes must also coordinate their work – *synchronize* (e.g., because only *one* may write on the
blackboard). Using Join is one simple way to synchronize; thereby one
thread waits for another to end. Synchronization becomes more interesting when the processes (or threads) access common *resources*. This can
be quite innocuous (such as reading a common blackboard), but more exact synchronization might be necessary in other cases (as in writing in a
shared notebook).

Shared resources can be accessed via *shared variables* or via *message
passing*. Lightweight processes usually (but not necessarily) employ the
former kind of communication; heavyweight processes, the latter.

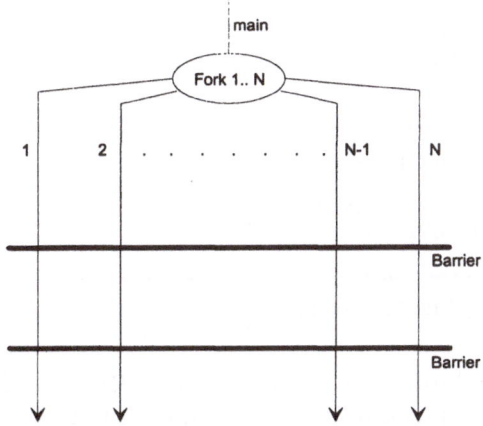

Figure 16.6: *Synchronization with barriers*

16.4 Shared variables

Communication between processes is innocuous as long as shared variables are only read. If a shared variable is modified, we have a conflict. For example, if two threads simultaneously write to a shared variable, we could have a nonsensical result. Assume, e.g., that two threads write to the shared variable r: RECORD a, b: INTEGER END. $thread_1$ writes r.a:= 1; r.b:= 2, $thread_2$ writes r.b:= 3; r.a:= 4. The actual sequence of the commands is: r.a:= 1; r.b:= 3; r.b:= 2; r.a:= 4. The result is: r.a=4, r.b=2. This result ensued from the combination of the two threads, yet neither of the two threads wanted to store these data in r. Such cases must be avoided. The following sections deal with this problem.

16.4.1 Data-parallel algorithms

In data-parallel algorithms, multiple processes process a shared array. The algorithm itself must ensure that the processes do not write to the same location simultaneously (thereby creating nonsensical data). Generally a process is permitted to read a location that is being written by another process. In such cases we must ensure that the reading process waits until the writing process is finished, so that no semifinished data are read.

To synchronize multiple processes, we often employ *synchronization with barriers*. Join can join only two threads, but this irrevocably, for afterwards there is but a single thread. *Barriers* represent significantly more powerful tools. A barrier can synchronize the control flow of any number of processes (threads): they wait for each other at the barrier. The processes

```
INTERFACE Barrier;                                                    (*11.10.93. LB*)
(*A join on a barrier blocks num-1 invoking threads.
 On the numth invocation all threads are released and the barrier is reinitialized.*)

  TYPE
    T <: Public;
    Public = MUTEX OBJECT METHODS join() END;

PROCEDURE Create(num: [1..LAST(CARDINAL)]): T;
(*Creates a new barrier initialized to num.*)
END Barrier.
```

Example 16.7: *Barrier interface*

are not destroyed, but remain active: when the last thread reaches the
barrier, all threads continue in parallel until the next barrier (see Figure
16.6).

Example 16.7 shows an interface that defines a barrier. Create creates
and initializes a new barrier. The number of threads that meet at a barrier
must be at least 1, but to make sense would be greater than 1. Example
16.8 demonstrates the use of barriers for a matrix multiplication (see also
sequential matrix multiplication in Example 9.9). For each element in the
result matrix, we create a thread that computes this element *independently*
of the other elements. Note that the threads read some of the same data,
but modify only their respective elements. With barrier.join() each thread
waits for the others. The main thread can use the same barrier to wait for
the others. Afterwards all threads continue to run in parallel.

> We must note again that for all our demonstrated algorithms, in prin-
> ciple it does not matter whether they are executed truly parallel or
> quasi-parallel. From the view of practice, however, data-parallel algo-
> rithms are only relevant with true parallelism, where they can achieve
> speed improvements. The example of matrix multiplication clarifies
> this. Assume a, b and r all have dimension $N \times N$, and the computa-
> tion of an element (DotProduct) requires a time of T time units, then
> execution time for sequential multiplication is $N^2 \times T$. If parallel mul-
> tiplication executes on a parallel computer whose processors have fast
> access to shared memory and which has at least N^2 processors, then
> we need only a time of T and a bit of management time at the start
> and end until all threads have joined at the barrier. If the parallel
> computer has less processors, then the algorithm requires more time.

As our next example of data-parallelism, we will compute the *prefix* of
a vector (array) [And91]. The prefix of vector a is a vector *sum* whose ith
element is $sum_i = \sum_{j=first(a)}^{i} a_j$. For $a = (1, 2, 3, 4, 5, 6, 7, 8)$ we have $sum =
(1, 3, 6, 10, 15, 21, 28, 36)$. The sequential solution is shown in Example 16.9;
a parallel solution, in Example 16.10. The idea of the parallel algorithm is

```
   ⋮
TYPE
  Matrix   = ARRAY OF ARRAY OF INTEGER;
  Closure = Thread.Closure OBJECT
               row, col: INTEGER;
             OVERRIDES
               apply:= StartMul
             END; (*Closure*)

VAR
  a, b, r: REF Matrix;                                    (*r:= a × b*)
  barrier: Barrier.T; num: CARDINAL;         (*num: start value of barrier*)

PROCEDURE InitMatrices(VAR a, b: REF Matrix) =           (*initializes a and b*)
   ⋮
PROCEDURE DotProduct(row, col: INTEGER;
   READONLY a, b: Matrix): INTEGER =     (*computes an element in result matrix*)
VAR sum: INTEGER := 0;
BEGIN
  FOR i:= FIRST(b) TO LAST(b) DO INC(sum, a[row, i] * b[i, col]) END;
  RETURN sum
END DotProduct;

PROCEDURE StartMul(cl: Closure): REFANY =
BEGIN
  r[cl.row, cl.col]:= DotProduct(cl.row, cl.col, a^, b^);     (*computes 1 element*)
  barrier.join();                              (*waits until all threads are ready*)
  RETURN NIL                             (*return value of apply is not needed*)
END StartMul;

PROCEDURE Fork() =                          (*creates thread for each result element*)
BEGIN
  FOR i:= FIRST(r^) TO LAST(r^) DO
    FOR j:= FIRST(r[0]) TO LAST(r[0]) DO
      EVAL Thread.Fork(NEW(Closure, row:= i, col:= j));
    END;
  END;
END Fork;

BEGIN
  InitMatrices(a, b);                         (*loads a und b with initial values*)
  r:= NEW(REF Matrix, NUMBER(a^), NUMBER(b[0]));           (*allocates r*)
  num:= NUMBER(r^) * NUMBER(r[0]) + 1;       (*number of result elements + 1*)
  barrier:= Barrier.Create(num);             (*creates and initializes barrier*)
  Fork();                              (*thread created for each element in result*)
  barrier.join();                            (*main thread waits for result*)
   ⋮
```

Example 16.8: Matrix multiplication with barriers

```
  ⋮
TYPE
   Vector = ARRAY OF INTEGER;
  ⋮
PROCEDURE Pref(a: REF Vector; VAR sum: REF Vector) =
BEGIN
   sum := NEW(REF Vector, NUMBER(aˆ));
   sum[FIRST(sumˆ)]:= a[FIRST(aˆ)];
   FOR i:= FIRST(sumˆ)+1 TO LAST(sumˆ) DO sum[i]:= sum[i–1] + a[i] END;
END Pref;
```

Example 16.9: *Prefix of an array – sequential*

to add, in each iteration, a left neighbor two iterations away; this neighbor has meanwhile accumulated the sum of its left neighbors. Thus in $\log_2(n)$ steps we compute the prefix.

16.4.2   Critical regions and mutual exclusion

Data-parallelism implies a certain kind of synchronization. If the parallel processes are to modify the shared variables freely, then we must explicitly ensure the consistency of the variables. We addressed this problem already in the reservation of seats on a flight. Assume that two processes simultaneously execute the following statement (where avail is the number of free seats):

IF avail > 0 THEN DEC(avail)
ELSE . . . (*no more seats available*) END

On a typical computer this statement is translated into corresponding machine code:

```
        LOAD    avail,R0        (*load avail into register R0*)
        CMP     R0              (*compare R0 to 0*)
        BLE     L1              (*jump to L1 if avail <= 0*)
        DECR    R0              (*decrement R0 by 1*)
        STORE   R0,avail        (*store new value*)
          ⋮
L1      . . .                   (*no more seats available*)
```

For every computer, we can assume that access to individual storage cells is atomic (hence parallel processes cannot simultaneously access a storage cell). Therefore the load and store instructions cannot conflict. However, the parallel processes all have their own set of registers (at least virtually). Hence the two processes might each read the value of avail into their respective R0 registers, simultaneously decrement these registers, and then

```
TYPE
   Vector = ARRAY OF INTEGER;
   Cl = Thread.Closure OBJECT
            id: CARDINAL;                                      (*identifies a thread**)
         OVERRIDES
            apply:= ApplyPref                                  (*thread algorithm*)
         END;

VAR
   barrier, stop: Barrier.T;                                   (*stop is used at end*)
   a, sum, old: REF Vector;                                    (*sum[i]:= a[i] + a[i-1] + ...*)
   n: CARDINAL;                                                (*number of elements*)
   ⋮
PROCEDURE Pref(i: INTEGER) =                                   (*algorithm for threads*)
VAR d: INTEGER := 1;                                           (*distance to next neighbor*)
BEGIN
   sum[i]:= a[i];
   barrier.join();                                             (*now all threads can begin*)
   WHILE d < n DO
      old[i]:= sum[i];                                         (*copy of current sum value*)
      barrier.join();                                          (*in each iteration, wait for others*)
      IF (i – d) >= FIRST(old^) THEN INC(sum[i], old[i–d]) END;
      barrier.join();                                          (*in each iteration, wait for others*)
      d:= 2 * d;                                               (*double distance*)
   END; (*WHILE d < n*)
   stop.join();                                                (*at end, all join in main thread*)
END Pref;

PROCEDURE ApplyPref(cl: Cl): REFANY =
BEGIN
   Pref(cl.id); RETURN NIL
END ApplyPref;

PROCEDURE Fork() =
BEGIN
   FOR i:= FIRST(a^) TO LAST(a^) DO
      EVAL Thread.Fork(NEW(Cl, id:= i))                        (*a thread for all elements*)
   END;
END Fork;

BEGIN
   Init(a, n);                                                 (*loads initial value of a and sets n*)
   barrier:= Barrier.Create(n);                                (*used in computation*)
   stop:= Barrier.Create(n+1);                                 (*controls termination*)
   Fork();                                                     (*starts threads for prefix computation*)
   stop.join();                                                (*at end, all join in main thread*)
   ⋮
```

Example 16.10: Prefix of an array – parallel

each write the new value back to avail. Regardless of which process wins the race, the result will be incorrect, for avail will have been decremented by 1 rather than 2.

Regions where shared variables can be modified by multiple processes are called *critical regions*. We require that only a single process can be in a critical region at a time. If one process is in the critical region, all other processes are prevented from entering. This property is called *mutual exclusion*. In other words, in a critical region, parallelism is disabled and the processes are sequentialized. In the flight reservation example, the process that represents the first passenger would have to exclude the second process until the first reservation is complete.

We can define the use of critical regions with the following steps:

1. Entry into critical region

2. Access to critical data

3. Exit from critical region

4. Execute remaining algorithm

The following conditions apply:

- *Mutual exclusion*
  At most one process is in the critical region.

- *No deadlock*
  If multiple processes need to enter a critical region, then one of them will actually succeed in doing so. The processes must not impede each other, as when the processes circularly wait for each other (a *deadlock* situation).

- *No unnecessary waiting*
  Processes outside the critical region must not prevent others from entering the critical region (not even by terminating).

- *No endless delay*
  When a process wants to enter the critical region, it must succeed in a finite number of tries. This means that in time all processes will be able to enter the critical region.

16.4.3   Type Mutex and the Lock statement

For the implementation of critical regions that meet the above conditions, Modula-3 provides the data type MUTEX and the LOCK statement. MUTEX is an object type. A LOCK statement can be executed on a MUTEX variable, thus defining a critical region with mutual exclusion. A LOCK statement has the following general form (where mu is of type MUTEX and S stands for an arbitrary statement sequence):

LOCK mu DO S END

The semantics of the LOCK statement correspond exactly to the above conditions. At a given time, only one thread can be in the statement part of a LOCK statement. If multiple threads try to enter simultaneously, then the first one gets through and the others are put in a *wait state* (their path is *blocked* – hence the name *lock*). When a thread exits (when it reaches the END of the LOCK statement), the next thread can enter (the first waiting thread is switched from waiting to ready). If a thread generates an exception in the critical region, then it is forced to exit the critical region. Thus an erroneous thread cannot hinder the others from entering the critical region at some time. The following pseudocode explains the semantics of the LOCK statement:

Thread.Acquire(mu); TRY S FINALLY Thread.Release(mu) END

Thread.Acquire implements the entry into and Thread.Release the exit from the critical region. The exit takes place even if an exception occurs within S.

These statements could also be written by the programmer. The procedures Acquire and Release are actually provided by the Thread interface (see Appendix C.1.2). However, programs are more secure if everything is handled automatically by the LOCK statement.

Consider a case where a thread executes the following code pattern:

```
LOOP
    ⋮
    LOCK mutex DO
        statements ···
        IF termination condition THEN EXIT END
    END; (*LOCK*)
    ⋮
END; (*LOOP*)
```

The EXIT statement has a feature that we have not discussed yet: In addition to the jump to the end of the loop, it generates an EXIT exception. This exception is intercepted by the hidden TRY-FINALLY statement of the LOCK statement, and mutex is unlocked. This allows the next thread to enter. Likewise the RETURN statement generates a RETURN exception before actually leaving the procedure.

Example 16.11 shows a very simplified algorithm for the flight reservation. The LOCK statement ensures that the field avail is a protected critical

```
    ⋮
TYPE
   Flight = MUTEX OBJECT                        (*Flight is a subtype of Mutex*)
                avail: CARDINAL;                   (*number of available seats*)
                ...                                            (*other fields*)
             END; (*Flight*)
    ⋮
PROCEDURE Reserve(flight: Flight): BOOLEAN =
BEGIN
     LOCK flight DO                                (*start of critical region*)
       IF flight.avail > 0 THEN DEC(flight.avail); RETURN TRUE
       ELSE RETURN FALSE
       END; (*IF*)
     END;                                            (*end of critical region*)
END Reserve;
    ⋮
```

Example 16.11: *Reservations protected by Lock*

region. It is important that common access (both reading and updating avail) be protected with LOCK. The following solution would be wrong:

IF flight.avail > 0 THEN LOCK DEC(flight.avail) END; RETURN TRUE END

Without LOCK before reading, two threads might execute the IF statement simultaneously, which would enable an erroneous reservation.

> What is particularly bothersome about such errors is that they can remain undetected for a long time. While the concepts of parallel programming were not yet mature, many such programs evolved that produced seldom, mysterious errors. Nowadays the methods for avoiding such errors are well-known. Our discussion treats only a part of them.

Conditional synchronization

Critical regions afford only limited possibilities for synchronization. Consider the very frequent case where a number of parallel *producers* generate data that are processed by a number of parallel *consumers*. For example, a mainframe anticipates input data from many terminals and redirects them to many applications such as editors, databases, etc. In such a case we use one (or more) buffers where the data are stored temporarily to compensate for the differences in speed between various processes. In the optimal case the buffer is always about half full, i.e., a producer always has room to deliver new data and a consumer always finds certain data. The state of the buffer must be kept consistent; therefore the buffer must be updated within a critical region. Problems begin when the buffer deviates too far in one direction or the other from half full. For example, assume that the buffer is full and a producer needs to deliver data. To test the state of the buffer, the producer must enter the critical region. Within the critical region the producer determines that data cannot be delivered. What should be done? Here we would want the producer to wait until a consumer removes data and thereby makes room. This would require the producer to leave the critical region and to re-enter as soon as the anticipated condition is fulfilled. This is where the concept of *conditional synchronization* comes in.

Many tools have been proposed that implement both mutual exclusion and conditional synchronization [And91]. We handle only the two most important: *monitors* and *semaphores*.

16.4.4 Monitor

Monitors were proposed by C. A. R. Hoare[Hoa74]. They integrate the above concepts with the concept of data capsules into a programming language. As Hoare proposed them, monitors have the following features:

- Monitors are abstract data types that reveal only their operations. Mutual exclusion is ensured on these operations (also called monitor procedures). This means that at most one process can be within a monitor.

- Within monitors we can use the type *condition*. Two basic operations are defined on a condition variable c: wait(c) and signal(c). The underlying idea is the following: A process must explicitly test the state of the monitor to determine whether conditions are fulfilled for the process's task. If so, the process carries out its task; if not, it goes into a wait state and temporarily leaves the monitor. This enables other processes to enter; these might change the state space so that the anticipated conditions are fulfilled. Processes waiting on such a condition must be awakened from their dormant state by an explicit signal from another process. The semantics of operations according to Hoare is as follows:

    - wait(c)
    The invocation of wait causes the invoking process to temporarily leave the monitor and to enter a queue.

    - signal(c)
    If at least one process is waiting for condition c, then the invocation of signal(c) removes the first waiting process from the queue, puts it in a ready state, and restarts it without delay. This means that no other process can enter the monitor between the waking and the starting of the dormant process because this process

could reverse the condition. The process invoking signal must leave the monitor (for mutual exclusion). If the signal(c) invocation is at the end of a monitor procedure (which is often the case), then fulfillment of the last condition is trivial.

If signal(c) is invoked while there is no process in the queue for c, then signal has no effect.

Modula-3 supports the concept of monitors with a somewhat modified semantics with the following features:

- There is no explicit monitor type; with the help of modules, monitors can be formulated as encapsulated data types. This has the drawback that mutual exclusion is not ensured automatically on monitor procedures; instead, the programmer must employ LOCKs. Another disadvantage is that the compiler cannot check whether condition variables are used only within monitors. The advantage of this approach is that mutual exclusion can be controlled at a finer level. Frequently a monitor procedure need not only process critical regions but also handle much additional work (with its local variables). Here mutual exclusion is not required and unnecessarily reduces the degree of parallelism.

- The condition type and the corresponding operations are provided by the Thread interface.

  - The semantics of Wait matches the classical definition by Hoare, with the exception that here the MUTEX variable that holds the lock must be specified explicitly.

  - The semantics of Signal is somewhat more relaxed. The awakened process need not continue execution immediately. It is also possible for another thread to enter the critical region and modify the condition. Therefore the awakened process must test the condition again. If the condition has become *false* meanwhile, then the process must wait again. Theoretically, this could leave a process rotating forever in such a loop (the phenomenon is called *starvation*). However, this is quite improbable. The advantage of this approach is increased flexibility; in particular, it is easy to produce a BROADCAST operation that wakes *all* processes waiting for a condition. The original strict semantics of signal precludes a BROADCAST operation because we can only restart one process without delay. However, after finishing its work, this process can send a signal that wakes the next, and so on.

```
INTERFACE Buffer;                                              (*15.10.93. LB*)
  TYPE
    T      <: Public;
    Data  =  INTEGER;

    Public = MUTEX OBJECT
             METHODS
                init(size: CARDINAL := 64): T;          (*invoke at start!*)
                get(): Data;                   (*blocked when buffer is empty*)
                put(data: Data);                (*blocked when buffer is full*)
             END; (*Public*)
END Buffer.
```

Example 16.12: *Interface of a buffer*

Example 16.12 shows the definition of an encapsulated data type Buffer.T. A Buffer must be initialized (with a certain size); thereafter the operations get and put can be used in any order. Buffer ensures that get waits when the buffer is empty and that put waits when the buffer is full, until the condition of the operation is fulfilled.

Example 16.13 demonstrates the use of Buffer. A number of threads produce data (for the sake of simplicity, their own thread identifiers) that are read and processed by a consumer. The consumer halts when it reads the Stop character (first it outputs statistics on the traffic). Afterwards Join of the main thread resumes and the whole program terminates.

Example 16.14 shows the implementation of the buffer, which is organized as a *circular buffer* (see Section 11).

> We could have set the fields in, out and n to 0 on declaration. However, if we want to re-initialize the variable of type Buffer.T repeatedly – with various buffer sizes – then we must place all initializations in the init method. The other fields cannot be set on type declaration anyway because they do not receive a constant value.

The condition variables nonFull and nonEmpty control the dynamic behavior of the system. When the buffer is full, the producers must wait for nonFull; when the buffer is empty, the consumers must wait for nonEmpty. After each successful put, nonEmpty can be signaled; after every successful get, nonFull.

> Instead of Thread.Signal, we can use Thread.Broadcast to remove from the queue all threads waiting for a condition. In this case it brings us no advantage because a put can only place one element in the buffer that can be taken by a get. In fact, this solution signals more than necessary. A signal is actually only necessary when a buffer was empty

```
MODULE BufUser EXPORTS Main;                                (*15.10.93. LB*)

  IMPORT Buffer, SIO, Thread;
  FROM Scheduler IMPORT Yield;

  CONST Stop = LAST(CARDINAL);                      (*signals end of transfer*)
  TYPE
    Producers  = [1..6];                                      (*producers*)
    ClProd     = Thread.Closure OBJECT
                     id: CARDINAL                        (*thread identifier*)
                   OVERRIDES
                     apply:= Producer                   (*thread algorithm*)
                   END;
  VAR buffer := NEW(Buffer.T).init();            (*create and initialize buffer*)

  PROCEDURE Producer(cl: ClProd): REFANY =
  VAR id: CARDINAL := cl.id;
  BEGIN
    REPEAT
      buffer.put(id); Yield();              (*yield resource to other processes*)
    UNTIL SIO.Available();                   (*terminates when a key is pressed*)
    buffer.put(Stop);                           (*signals end of transfer*)
    RETURN NIL;
  END Producer;

  PROCEDURE Consumer(cl: Thread.Closure): REFANY =
  VAR i: INTEGER; statistics := ARRAY Producers OF INTEGER {0, ..};
    ⋮
    PROCEDURE PutStatistics() =                          (*output statistics*)
    ⋮
  BEGIN
    REPEAT
      i:= buffer.get(); IF i # Stop THEN INC(statistics[i]) END;
    UNTIL i = Stop;                       (*i = Stop => consumer terminates*)
    PutStatistics();                                  (*output statistics*)
    RETURN NIL;
  END Consumer;
BEGIN
  FOR i:= FIRST(Producers) TO LAST (Producers) DO
    EVAL Thread.Fork(NEW(ClProd, id:= i));                  (*create producer*)
  END; (*FOR*)
  EVAL Thread.Join(Thread.Fork(NEW(Thread.Closure, apply:= Consumer)));
END BufUser.
```

Example 16.13: Communication via a buffer

```
MODULE Buffer;                                              (*15.10.93. LB*)
  IMPORT Thread;
  REVEAL
    T =      Public BRANDED OBJECT
                in, out, n: CARDINAL;          (*for circular buffer management*)
                nonEmpty, nonFull: Thread.Condition;        (*change signals*)
                data: REF ARRAY OF Data;                   (*buffer contents*)
             OVERRIDES
                init:= Init;
                get:= Get;
                put:= Put;
             END; (*Public*)

  PROCEDURE Init(t: T; size: CARDINAL := 64): T =
  BEGIN
    t.in:= 0; t.out:= 0; t.n:= 0;
    t.data:= NEW(REF ARRAY OF Data, size);
    t.nonEmpty:= NEW(Thread.Condition); t.nonFull:= NEW(Thread.Condition);
    RETURN t
  END Init;

  PROCEDURE Get(buffer: T): Data =
  VAR d: Data;
  BEGIN
    LOCK buffer DO
      WITH N = NUMBER(buffer.data^) DO
        WHILE buffer.n = 0 DO Thread.Wait(buffer, buffer.nonEmpty) END;
        <*ASSERT buffer.n > 0*>           (*here the buffer is definitely not empty*)
        d:= buffer.data[buffer.out];                       (*read from buffer*)
        buffer.out:= (buffer.out + 1) MOD N; DEC(buffer.n);
      END; (*WITH N*)
    END; (*LOCK buffer*)
    Thread.Signal(buffer.nonFull);            (*wakes a possibly waiting producer*)
    RETURN d;
  END Get;

  PROCEDURE Put(buffer: T; data: Data) =
  BEGIN
    LOCK buffer DO
      WITH N = NUMBER(buffer.data^) DO
        WHILE buffer.n = N DO Thread.Wait(buffer, buffer.nonFull) END;
        <*ASSERT buffer.n < N*>            (*here the buffer is definitely not full*)
        buffer.data[buffer.in]:= data;                  (*new element into buffer*)
        buffer.in:= (buffer.in + 1) MOD N; INC(buffer.n);
      END; (*WITH N*)
    END; (*LOCK buffer;*)
    Thread.Signal(buffer.nonEmpty);          (*wakes a possibly waiting consumer*)
  END Put;

BEGIN
END Buffer.
```

Example 16.14: Buffer implementation with a monitor

```
MODULE Barrier;                                              (*11.10.93. LB*)

  IMPORT Thread;

  REVEAL T = Public BRANDED OBJECT
                    n, count: INTEGER;
                    cond: Thread.Condition;
                  OVERRIDES
                    join:= Join;
                  END;

  PROCEDURE Create(num: [1..LAST(CARDINAL)]): T =
  BEGIN
    RETURN NEW(T, n:= num − 1, count:= num − 1, cond:= NEW(Thread.Condition));
  END Create;

  PROCEDURE Join(b: T) =
  BEGIN
    LOCK b DO
      IF b.count > 0 THEN
        DEC(b.count);
        Thread.Wait(b, b.cond);          (*waits until nth thread arrives*)
      ELSE                               (*all n threads have joined*)
        b.count:= b.n;                   (*count reset to n*)
        Thread.Broadcast(b.cond)         (*advance all threads*)
      END; (*IF b.count*)
    END; (*LOCK b*)
  END Join;

BEGIN
END Barrier.
```

Example 16.15: *Barrier implementation with a monitor*

or full before the signal. Dummy signals do not affect the correctness of the program, but they do dampen the efficiency. Thus, e.g., we could replace the line

Thread.Signal(buffer.nonFull)

with the following:

IF buffer.n = N-1 THEN Thread.Signal(buffer.nonFull) END

This branch should occur within the LOCK statement.

Note that the buffer-empty and buffer-full conditions must be tested in a loop. With the original strict signal semantics, an IF statement would suffice because we can be sure that no other process can change the condition. Thus we could have replaced the WHILE loops around the invocation

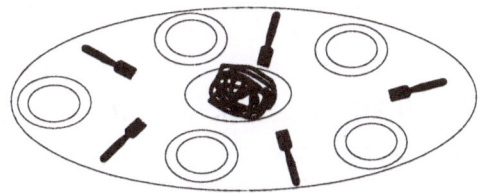

Figure 16.16: *The table of the dining philosophers*

of Wait with two IF branches. The corresponding IF statement in the Get procedure could be:

    IF buffer.n = 0 THEN Thread.Wait(buffer, buffer.nonEmpty) END

Example 16.15 shows the implementation of barriers with the help of monitors.

The dining philosophers

Our last example of monitors is Dijkstra's famous example of the dining philosophers [Dij68b]. Five philosophers are sitting at a table; in front of each philosopher is a plate and to the left of it a fork (Figure 16.16). The philosophers are either lost in thought or they are hungry and want to eat. However, the spaghetti in the middle of the table are so extremely long that a philosopher requires two forks to serve them.

What happens if two neighboring philosophers become hungry at the same time? Assume that both first reach for the left fork, then both for the right fork. One of the philosophers will fail because his right fork has already been picked up by the other philosopher. What is worse, if all philosophers become hungry at the same time and all reach for their respective left forks, then ... . Each philosopher would have to wait until his neighbor puts down his fork, but since all are waiting, all remain hungry. This is a typical resource allocation problem. We have less resources than necessary; therefore, unless we manage them carefully, a deadlock can occur.

The deadlock occurs here because a number of processes – by way of a number of resources – are circularly waiting for one another. There are a number of methods for avoiding or resolving deadlock [Tan92], but we cannot treat them in detail here. In this example the solution is not difficult: when he becomes hungry, a philosopher must first ensure – within a critical region – that both left and right forks are free. If this is the case, he must reserve them both in the same critical region. Example 16.17 shows the interface, Example 16.18 the implementation of an appropriate "fork management" system. The array avail contains for each philosopher the

412

16. Parallel programming

```
INTERFACE Fork;                                              (*10.03.94. LB*)

  CONST N = 5;                                    (*number of philosophers*)

  PROCEDURE PickUp(id: INTEGER);   (*blocked until invoking philosopher can eat*)

  PROCEDURE PutDown(id: INTEGER);                      (*put down fork*)
END Fork.
```

Example 16.17: Fork interface

```
MODULE Fork;                                                 (*10.03.94. LB*)

  IMPORT Thread;

  VAR
    mutex:= NEW(MUTEX);                         (*used for critical region*)
    avail:= ARRAY [0..N−1] OF [0..2] {2, ..};   (*avail[i] available forks for Phil_i*)
    available:= NEW(Thread.Condition);   (*signals that 2 forks are available*)

  PROCEDURE PickUp(id: INTEGER) =
  BEGIN
    LOCK mutex DO
      WHILE avail[id] # 2 DO Thread.Wait(mutex, available) END;
      DEC(avail[(id − 1) MOD N]); DEC(avail[(id + 1) MOD N]);
    END; (*LOCK*)
  END PickUp;

  PROCEDURE PutDown(id: INTEGER) =
  BEGIN
    LOCK mutex DO
      INC(avail[(id − 1) MOD N]); INC(avail[(id + 1) MOD N]);
      Thread.Broadcast(available);
    END; (*LOCK*)
  END PutDown;

BEGIN
END Fork.
```

Example 16.18: Fork implementation as monitor

number of free forks. The ith philosopher may eat if avail[i] = 2; otherwise he must wait for the signal available. When a fork is laid down, all (both) possibly waiting philosophers are notified with Thread.Broadcast. The expressions (id - 1) MOD N and (id + 1) MOD N compute the index of the left and right neighbors, respectively.

The solution in Example 16.18 does preclude deadlock, but it is not quite correct yet. We could encounter a scenario where two non-neighboring philosophers alternatingly eat. Then the philosopher between them never gets to eat because he never has two free forks (here the term *starvation* is quite literal). We could solve the problem easily by providing separate

```
MODULE Philosophers EXPORTS Main;                              (*LB*)

  IMPORT Thread, Fork,

  CONST
    N = Fork.N;                          (*number of philosopher processes*)
  TYPE
    Closure = Thread.Closure OBJECT
                  id: CARDINAL;
               OVERRIDES
                  apply:= Start
               END;
  VAR
    cls: ARRAY [0..N–1] OF Closure;

  PROCEDURE Philosopher(id: INTEGER) =
  BEGIN
    LOOP
      Think(id);
      Fork.PickUp(id);
      Eat(id);
      Fork.PutDown(id);
    END
  END Philosopher;

  PROCEDURE Start(self: Closure): REFANY =
  BEGIN
    Philosopher(self.id); RETURN NIL
  END Start;
    ⋮
BEGIN                                          (*dining philosophers*)
  FOR i:= 0 TO N–1 DO cls[i]:= NEW(Closure, id:= i) END;
  FOR i:= 0 TO N–1 DO EVAL Thread.Fork(cls[i]) END;     (*N threads started*)
```

Example 16.19: *Implementation of the dining philosophers*

rooms for thinking and for eating. No more than four philosophers may enter the dining room, and after eating they must leave the room. Thereby no one can be excluded permanently if we have a FIFO queue at the door.

Example 16.19 demonstrates the behavior of the philosophers, whereby the procedures Eat and Think and the program as a whole are not elaborated.

16.4.5 Semaphores

No discussion of parallelism can omit semaphores; they were the first methodical approach to the solution of the problems of mutual exclusion and conditional synchronization, and their use is widespread even today [And91]. Semaphores were introduced by Dijkstra [Dij68b].

The idea of the semaphore comes from a railway metaphor: Assume a railway station with five tracks, allowing up to five trains to be in the station area simultaneously. Thereafter the semaphore must be switched to block further trains until one or more trains have left the station again. The semaphore value is the current number of trains that can still enter the station.

We define semaphores as abstract data types with an INTEGER value, to which we assign an initial value (I) (in our example, the number of tracks). Two *atomic* operations, *P(s)* and *V(s)*, are defined on a semaphore s. *P* stands for testing and *V* for leaving (they actually stand for the corresponding Dutch words assigned by Dijkstra, himself from Holland). The number of successfully completed *P* or *V* operations is designated as n_P and n_V (where n_P could be the number of trains that entered the station and n_V the number that have left the station). $n_P \leq n_V + I$ always holds. The total number of trains that have ever entered the station can be larger than the number that have left by at most the number of tracks. The semaphore value is defined as $s = I + n_V - n_P$. Thus a semaphore has the invariant $s \geq 0$.

We can best express the semantics of P and V with the following pseudocode:

- *P(s)*: *wait until s > 0; s:= s – 1*

- *V(s)*: *s:= s + 1*

Semaphores enable expression of both mutual exclusion and conditional synchronization. For mutual exclusion we must use a semaphore with the initial value 1 (a *binary semaphore*).

With the semaphore invariant defined as above, we remain unprotected against a subtle error: the occurrence of false leave signals. For example, if an error caused three more *V* operations than necessary, the semaphore would allow a total of 8 trains to enter the station, which would be quite undesirable. We can protect against such an error with a more stringent invariant, i.e., $0 \leq s \leq I$. For implementation reasons, this is often omitted. The stricter semantics usually applies to binary semaphores, e.g., $0 \leq s \leq 1$. In this case we can best represent the semaphore value as BOOLEAN; the *V* operation sets the value to *true*. Thus false *V* sequences have no effect because they do not change the semaphore value (*true* remains *true*, regardless how often it is set).

Although Modula-3 does not provide semaphores, they are easy to implement. Example 16.20 shows an interface and Example 16.21 an implementation (corresponding to the general, less stringent semantics).

Example 16.22 shows a re-implementation of the buffer with semaphores. The interface and usage of the module Buffer remain unchanged!

```
INTERFACE Semaphore;                                      (*10.03.94. LB*)

  TYPE
    T <: Public;
    Public = MUTEX OBJECT
             METHODS
                 init(i: CARDINAL := 1): T;
                 P();
                 V();
             END;
END Semaphore.
```

Example 16.20: Semaphore interface

```
MODULE Semaphore;                                         (*10.03.94. LB*)

  IMPORT Thread;

  REVEAL
    T = Public BRANDED OBJECT
          s: CARDINAL;                      (*initial value of semaphore*)
          w: Thread.Condition;                               (*queue*)
        OVERRIDES
          init:= Init;
          P:= Test;
          V:= Leave;
        END; (*T*)

  PROCEDURE Init(sem: T; i: CARDINAL := 1): T =
  BEGIN
    sem.s:= i; sem.w:= NEW(Thread.Condition);
    RETURN sem;
  END Init;

  PROCEDURE Test(sem: T) =
  BEGIN
    LOCK sem DO
      WHILE sem.s = 0 DO Thread.Wait(sem, sem.w) END; DEC(sem.s);
    END; (*LOCK*)
  END Test;

  PROCEDURE Leave(sem: T) =
  BEGIN
    LOCK sem DO
      INC(sem.s); Thread.Signal(sem.w);
    END; (*LOCK*)
  END Leave;

BEGIN
END Semaphore.
```

Example 16.21: Semaphore implementation

```
MODULE Buffer;                                              (*10.03.94 LB*)
  IMPORT Semaphore;
  REVEAL
    T = Public BRANDED OBJECT
          in, out: CARDINAL;              (*for circular buffer management*)
          empty, full, mutex: Semaphore.T;
          data: REF ARRAY OF Data;                      (*buffer contents*)
        OVERRIDES
          init:= Init;
          get:= Get;
          put:= Put;
        END; (*Public*)

  PROCEDURE Init(t: T; size: CARDINAL := 64): T =
  BEGIN
    t.in:= 0; t.out:= 0;
    t.data:= NEW(REF ARRAY OF Data, size);
    t.empty:= NEW(Semaphore.T).init(size);        (*number of empty positions*)
    t.full:= NEW(Semaphore.T).init(0);            (*number of filled positions*)
    t.mutex:= NEW(Semaphore.T).init(1);           (*mutex is a binary semaphore*)
    RETURN t
  END Init;

  PROCEDURE Get(buffer: T): Data =
  VAR d: Data;
  BEGIN
    buffer.full.P();                  (*blocks if the buffer is empty (no filled position)*)
    buffer.mutex.P();                                  (*enter critical region*)
    d:= buffer.data[buffer.out];                          (*read from buffer*)
    buffer.out:= (buffer.out + 1) MOD NUMBER(buffer.data^);
    buffer.mutex.V();                                  (*leave critical region*)
    buffer.empty.V();               (*increment number of empty positions*)
    RETURN d;
  END Get;

  PROCEDURE Put(buffer: T; data: Data) =
  BEGIN
    buffer.empty.P();                 (*blocks if buffer is full (no empty position)*)
    buffer.mutex.P();                                  (*enter critical region*)
    buffer.data[buffer.in]:= data;                    (*new element into buffer*)
    buffer.in:= (buffer.in + 1) MOD NUMBER(buffer.data^);
    buffer.mutex.V();                                  (*leave critical region*)
    buffer.full.V();                 (*increment number of filled positions*)
  END Put;

BEGIN
END Buffer.
```

Example 16.22: Implementation of the buffer with semaphores

The number of elements is stored in semaphores: full stores the number of filled positions (starting at 0) in the buffer; empty, the number of empty positions (starting with the total buffer size). The field n from the solution in Example 16.14 becomes extraneous. Mutual exclusion is ensured by the semaphore mutex. The procedures Get and Put are largely symmetrical in this solution as well. First the state of the buffer is tested (Get tests for full, Put for empty positions). If the buffer state is correct, the thread that invoked Get or Put can enter the critical region (protected by mutex). Note that the sequence of the P operations is relevant: if Get were to first contain buffer.mutex.P() and then buffer.full.P(), then an empty buffer would cause deadlock because mutex would block any further thread (including a producer that could effect the desired state transition). The sequence of the V operations is almost irrelevant: reversing them would not cause an error.

> Our solution has the advantage that after buffer.mutex.V() a waiting thread can enter immediately. We could improve this solution by observing that Get and Put never access the same position in the buffer and that Get uses only buffer.out and Put uses only buffer.in. They always access disjunct parts of the shared variables. Thus we can protect Get and Put with different mutex semaphores and so can permit simultaneous reading and writing.

Perhaps you noticed from the above specifications that the operations P and Thread.Wait, as well as V and Thread.Signal are very similar. However, there is a significant difference: a semaphore stores a state, while a condition does not. A V increments the semaphore value even if no corresponding P was executed; by contrast, a Thread.Signal has no effect if no thread is waiting for the condition. Thus it is correct for the semaphore version of Get to start with simply buffer.full.P(). If a producer has already put something in the buffer, then the value of full is certainly greater than 0, so that the consumer (the thread invoking Get) can continue immediately. In the monitor version, however, Get must first explicitly test the number of filled positions. If Get were to start with an analogous statement Thread.Wait(buffer, buffer.nonEmpty), this could cause Get to wait endlessly. If all producers were there earlier and sent their signals into empty space, then the consumer can wait endlessly. However, if a producer comes later, the consumer is awakened. Such a solution would behave quite unpredictably: depending on timing, it would behave correctly sometimes and erroneously at other times. This must be avoided in any case in parallel programming.

These considerations show that the condition type is more primitive and basic than the semaphore. Thus semaphores can easily be implemented with monitors, while the reverse is quite cumbersome (although possible). Monitors have the additional advantage that they combine the idea of encapsulation with synchronization.

16.5   Message passing

We explained communication via shared variables with the analogy of reading a shared blackboard or writing in a shared notebook. By contrast, the model of message passing resembles communication by telephone and mail. Communication occurs via *channels*. We usually identify our partner by identifying the channel (similar to a telephone number or house address). Then we communicate by sending and receiving messages. It can be shown that the two communication models are equally powerful: either can fully simulate the other.

Message passing is certainly simpler and more basic because it makes less assumptions. This model corresponds directly to the frequent case where the linked computers have no shared memory (as in computer networks and with many of today's common parallel computers). The drawback of this model is the difficulty in writing correct programs with message passing (just as it is more difficult to write correct programs in an assembly language than in a higher programming language). Therefore many approaches have hidden the underlying message traffic under an additional layer that emulates the presence of shared variables [Bal90]. Naturally, such an additional layer should be *efficient*; thus there have been approaches to implement them directly in the hardware. The inverse case, using shared variables to simulate message passing, only makes sense in special cases. Such a special case exists when we want to study concepts of the message passing model on a single computer, as in the following examples. Message communication can run *synchronously* or *asynchronously*.

16.5.1   Client/server model

Most applications of message passing build on the client/server model [And91]. In this model a server provides public services; numerous clients can employ these services as needed. A file server, e.g., provides data for use by multiple programs on different computers; a printer server manages a central printer, etc. We have parallelism because the clients are mutually independent and the server must handle them all simultaneously in such a way that each client has the impression of exclusive use of the server.

A basic problem of this model is that the clients must find the server to be able to utilize its channels. This usually requires an additional server, a *name server* whose name and channels are known to all participants. Servers must be registered with the name server to make their services publicly available. Via the name server, the clients can establish connections to other servers (through the name of the specific server) and so receive the necessary communication channels.

16.5.2 Synchronous message communication

In synchronous communication, first a *rendezvous* is arranged and then communication flows – as with telephoning. Synchronization occurs before each message passing (between polite people, a whole telephone conversation elapses synchronously, one speaking while the other listens). Modula-3 does not directly support this model; programming languages that directly support synchronous communication include *Ada* and *Occam*. The theoretical foundations of such languages were laid by Hoare, among others, in the language *CSP* [Hoa85].

Remote procedure call

A special case of synchronous communication is the *remote procedure call* (*RPC*) [Nel81]. Here a procedure invocation takes place on computer A, but the execution of the procedure body takes place on another computer B. Ideally, from the viewpoint of the invoking procedure, there should be no difference between local and remote procedures.

Most Modula-3 language environments support this concept with *network objects*[2], whose methods can be invoked by processes in a different address space (possibly on a physically different computer) [BNOW94]. The invocation of a remote method is just as type-safe as a local invocation.

Implementing the RPC concept is not easy. For an ordinary procedure invocation we implicitly assume that the invoking procedure crashes when the invoked procedure crashes. For a remote procedure invocation, the crash of one of the two procedures is quite possible. If the invoked procedure (the *server*) crashes, then the invoking procedure is hung in a procedure invocation that fails to return control. If the invoking procedure (the *client*) crashes, we have an orphaned procedure body that cannot return control to the invoking procedure. For the solution to these problems, we find numerous proposals in the literature [Nel81, And91].

16.5.3 Asynchronous message communication

Asynchronous communication resembles correspondence by mail, where the messages are simply sent and the reply can come at some later time (if at all). Asynchronous communication is the more general case; synchronous communication is easy to simulate with the asynchronous model (the inverse is also easily possible with the availability of threads).

---

[2]The MS-DOS Modula-3 language environments do not contain the network object.

```
INTERFACE Channel;                                      (*11.03.94. LB*)

  TYPE
    Message = REFANY;

    T <: Public;
    Public = MUTEX OBJECT
             METHODS
                init(): T;
                send(message: Message);        (*sends message via channel*)
                receive(): Message;            (*receives message via channel*)
             END;

END Channel.
```

Example 16.23: *Interface of a channel*

16.5.4 Channels

The communication medium for message passing is the channel. Example 16.23 shows the interface of the abstract data type Channel. Processes can send and receive messages via the channels. The type of a message can be any reference. This allows sending data structures of any complexity through a channel.

Example 16.24 demonstrates such processes. The module ChanUser in Example 16.24 resembles the module BufUser in Example 16.13. This is no accident: communication via a buffer corresponds approximately to message passing. The concrete type of the message is a reference to a record that contains an identifier and a time stamp from the sender. The receiver prints this time stamp (the procedure PrintTime is not elaborated).

> Here we have neglected the aspects of the name server: the channel is simply declared as a global variable. However, the participating processes do not write directly to this channel, but only use it as a transmission medium.

Example 16.25 demonstrates an implementation of Channel. The implementation is based on shared memory. However, it is possible to modify the implementation – maintaining the same interface – so that send and receive are mapped onto real communication channels, e.g., of a computer network.

> Implementing the transmission of complex data structures is not quite trivial. If we transmitted only the reference, as in Example 16.25, this would be useless because the receiver would not find the referenced data in its own memory. However, Pickles (see Section 14.3.1) facilitates such an implementation. Just as "pickled" data can be stored in a file and read from there again, it can be sent and received on a network.

```
MODULE ChanUser EXPORTS Main;                           (*12.03.94. LB*)

  IMPORT Channel, SIO, Thread, Time;

  CONST
    Stop = NIL;                                 (*signal end of transmission*)

  TYPE
    Message = REF RECORD
                  id: CARDINAL; time: Time.T
               END;

  VAR
    channel := NEW(Channel.T).init();            (*create and initialize channel*)

  PROCEDURE Producer(cl: Thread.Closure): REFANY =
  VAR message := NEW(Message, id:= 1);             (*the field id is set only once*)
  BEGIN
    REPEAT
      message.time:= Time.Now();       (*the field time contains the sender's timestamp*)
      channel.send(message);                             (*send message*)
      Thread.Pause(0.5D0);                                (*wait briefly*)
    UNTIL SIO.Available();                     (*terminate when any key is pressed*)
    channel.send(Stop);                        (*signal end of transmission*)
    RETURN NIL;
  END Producer;

  PROCEDURE PrintTime(time: Time.T) =
    ⋮
  PROCEDURE Consumer(cl: Thread.Closure): REFANY =
  VAR message: Message;
  BEGIN
    REPEAT
      message:= channel.receive();                       (*receive message*)
      IF message # Stop THEN PrintTime(message.time) END;
    UNTIL message = Stop;                      (*Stop => consumer terminates*)
    RETURN NIL;
  END Consumer;
BEGIN
  EVAL Thread.Fork(NEW(Thread.Closure, apply:= Producer));
  EVAL Thread.Join(Thread.Fork(NEW(Thread.Closure, apply:= Consumer)));
  SIO.PutText("Stopped\n");
END ChanUser.
```

Example 16.24: Communication via a channel

```
MODULE Channel;                                                        (*11.03.94. LB*)

  IMPORT Thread;

  REVEAL
    T = Public BRANDED OBJECT
          empty: BOOLEAN;                     (*channel state: false if message present*)
          message: Message;                   (*channel stores a single message*)
          wait: Thread.Condition;
        OVERRIDES
          init := Init;
          send := Send;
          receive := Receive;
        END;

  PROCEDURE Init(chan: T): T =
  BEGIN
    chan.empty:= TRUE; chan.wait:= NEW(Thread.Condition);
    RETURN chan
  END Init;

  PROCEDURE Send(chan: T; message: Message) =
  BEGIN
    LOCK chan DO
      WHILE NOT chan.empty DO Thread.Wait(chan, chan.wait) END;
      chan.message:= message;                       (*copy message to channel*)
      chan.empty:= FALSE;                           (*message present in channel*)
      Thread.Signal(chan.wait);                     (*wake possibly waiting receiver*)
    END; (*LOCK*)
  END Send;

  PROCEDURE Receive(chan: T): Message =
  VAR message: Message;
  BEGIN
    LOCK chan DO
      WHILE chan.empty DO Thread.Wait(chan, chan.wait) END;
      message:= chan.message;                       (*read message from channel*)
      chan.empty:= TRUE;                            (*no message in channel*)
      Thread.Signal(chan.wait);                     (*wake possibly waiting receiver*)
    END; (*LOCK*)
    RETURN message;
  END Receive;
BEGIN
END Channel.
```

Example 16.25: Implementation of a message channel

The implemented channel can store only one message. If the channel is occupied by a previous message, the sender is blocked until a receiver fetches the message. If the channel buffer is empty, then the sender can continue execution after depositing the message. Thus the channel functions asynchronously, although, due to its low buffer capacity, it resembles a synchronous channel. If the channel had a larger buffer capacity, then its asynchronous nature would be more obvious.

Conclusion

In the course of studying, readers of this book might have been confronted with the following questions: Why should we learn programming at all? And if so, then why in Modula-3? In conclusion, we attempt to answer these questions.

Why programming?

Today many computer scientists and those who apply computer science believe that programming is a matter of secondary importance: the truly important phases of software development are analysis, specification and design; programming just adds the nuts and bolts.

In the early days of the computer age, many viewed programming as an art. Accordingly the programmer's job enjoyed high esteem. As software systems grew ever larger and more complex, the intuitive art of programming no longer sufficed. The importance of the preparatory phases increasingly won recognition. In the battle against the traditional view, many expressed opinions were polemic and somewhat exaggerated. Thereby programming lost its primary role.

We are convinced that it is high time for reconciliation in this area and for the recognition of the importance of all phases of software development as equal. Clearly, without a good analysis, a software project is doomed to failure from the start. However, it should also be clear that in the end software is produced by programmers. If they are poorly trained or unmotivated, this renders even the best analysis worthless.

In a lecture in March 1995 at the University of Klagenfurt, Niklaus Wirth analyzed the phenomenon of software chaos. He challenged that the ever rising complexity of software is not necessary, and indeed that it is bound to the loss of certain engineering qualities, such as an appreciation of efficiency and simplicity. We consider it the duty of every computer scientist to learn to program cleanly and *with style* – even if a later career might involve little programming.

Why Modula-3?

If the role of programming is seen as secondary, then the choice of a programming language often drops to tertiary importance. Naturally the programming language is only a tool. In most other areas of life, the importance of good tools is widely recognized. In the domain of software, the selection of a programming language normally involves considering nothing more than general availability. This leads to preserving antiquated programming languages. Today's most-used programming languages (such as C, Fortran and Cobol) are all more than twenty years old (Cobol and Fortan almost forty). Their greatest weakness is their security mechanisms: they afford only very restricted static controls.

We chose Modula-3 for this book because the language integrates the knowledge accumulated over the last twenty years in the area of language design in a clean and elegant manner. Although we do not maintain that this applies only to Modula-3, the number of such programming languages is not excessive. At any rate, it is important that the first programming language that a computer scientist learns – so to say, the native language – have these attributes.

Niklaus Wirth addressed the responsibility of universities in this matter. If the universities chase *after* practice instead of publicizing new developments, then the hope for any improvement in the chaotic software situation shall be in vain.

If we have succeeded in contributing to such an improvement, then our work has been worth the effort. We wish the reader lots of fun in programming in Modula-3.

Appendix A

A small database

So far we have developed many small programs, but we have not solved any more extensive tasks. Now we will attack a larger, cohesive example. Although our solution still contains many simplifications, it does represent a nontrivial program. We challenge the reader to extend the program according to needs and taste.

As regards methodology, space limitations require us to undertake drastic simplifications. We must skip the phases of the life cycle introduced in Chapter 1.1 and attempt to reach the program stage relatively quickly. However, we will discuss requirements and solution ideas in advance and describe them clearly. The source code of our solution is listed starting at page 443. We recommend that the reader, after reading the following considerations, delve into the details of the program.

A.1 The task

Let us implement a management system for audio CDs. You might wonder why we restrict ourselves to CDs. Why don't we include our vinyl and sheet music? Why not build a general management system that can handle any objects, including CDs? Naturally we could do that. However, we would get bogged down in detail and would never finish. Instead, we prefer to concentrate initially on a well-defined, restricted task, the CD management system.

What do we expect our CD management system to do? We can best define its tasks in terms of the *queries* that we would pose to the system. Take some example questions:

- Which CDs do I have?

- By which composers do I have at least one CD?

- Which artists perform on my CDs?

- Which Mozart CDs do I have?

- Which CDs do I have with violin concerts by Bach?

- Which CDs do I have with Yehudi Menuhin?

The answers to the first three questions are lists of CDs, composers and performers, respectively. The answers to the other questions are subsets of the set of CDs. An operation that yields a subset of a set on the basis of specified criteria (such as the name of a composer or an instrument) is called a *selection*. Naturally, we can pose much more complex questions: "Are there CDs on which Bruno Walter directs Mozart and plays Schubert on piano?" Or: "Is the average price of Mozart CDs greater than for CDs by Béla Bartók?" Before we set our fantasy free, let us concentrate on the simpler questions above. However, the system should not preclude later refinement. We want to store our data in objects and find an object model that applies independently of the specific query and that can be extended later.

A.2   The object model

Let us begin to define our object model. First we need a *schema* that describes the *object types* and their *relationships*. We have the following object categories:

- CDs

- Works

- Composers

- Performers

A CD should have an identifier such as "Bach Concerts" or "Mozart Chamber Music". We can use this identifier to classify the CDs. Works have a title, e.g., "The William Tell Overture". To enable easily distinguishing CDs, we require that the concatenation of the CD identifier with all titles of works on the CD must be unique. If we have Mozart's "Trio Divertimento, K. 563" as the sole work on each of two CDs, then we must change one of the two CD identifiers, e.g., to "Mozart Chamber Music 2".

Both composers and performers are persons, so it might make sense to define a common superclass Person. This neglects the reality that an orchestra or choir consists of more than a single person. We can designate a person by last name and first name. Groups of persons, such as an orchestra, also have a name, but no first name.

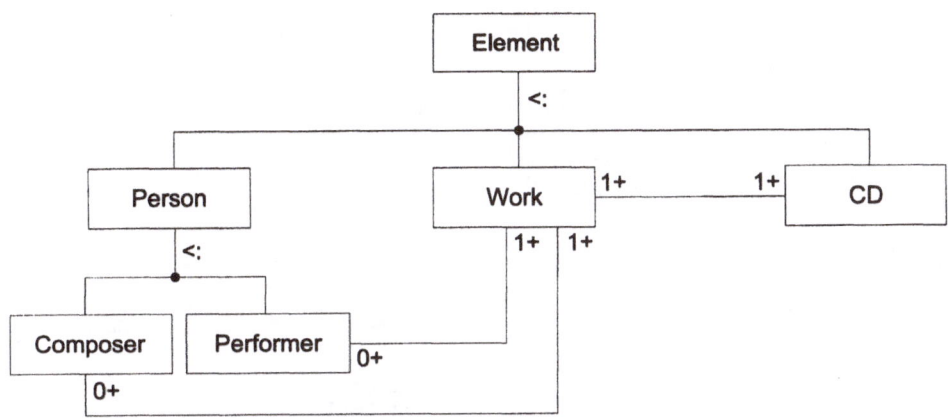

Figure A.1: *Relationships between the object types*

All objects should have methods to read and display them.

The next important question regards the *relationships* between the basic types:

- CDs contain works

- Works have composers and performing artists.

We could maintain that the relationship to works can be quite different for composers and performers: the composer remains the same, while the performer can vary. If we were managing sheet music, there would be no performer. Thus we could link performers to CDs rather than to works. Despite this objection, we retain the above relationships: they are quite simple and usually describe the situation well. However, these considerations do show that establishing an object model (or data model) is definitely a *creative process* during which we make decisions that might not be so clear at first, yet are of great importance to the realization of the system.

Now we can graphically represent the desired structure (see Figure A.1). We expressed the subtype relationship with the Modula-3 symbol (<:). The relationship where objects of one class contain objects of another is expressed with a connecting line between the corresponding boxes. The specification 0+ or 1+ refers to the cardinality of the relationship. The specification 1+ at both ends of the connecting line between work and CD indicates that a CD contains at least one work and a work must be present on at least one CD (otherwise it is irrelevant for our system). The specification 0+ on the connecting line between work and composer indicates that a work can have multiple composers, or possibly none (where the composer is unknown or uninteresting).

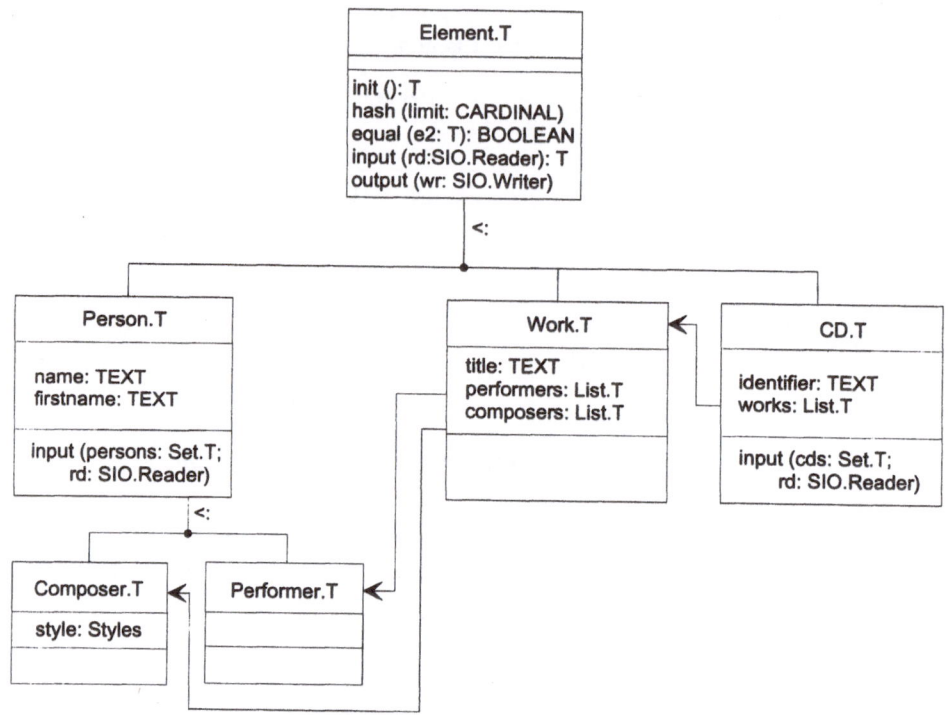

Figure A.2: *Detailed object model*

Figure A.1 depicts all classes we have defined so far as subclasses of the base type (Element). This base type collects all attributes and methods that all objects of the system share. For all objects, we require an unambiguous identification (often called *oid* for *object identifier*). This lets us determine whether two objects are *equal* or *identical* (one and the same). Two objects of the same type are equal if all their attributes have the same value. Two objects are identical if they are equal and they share the same object identifier. This distinction can be quite useful. Consider two persons named John Smith but living at different addresses. Assuming that all persons are represented as objects having the attributes name and address, the objects for the two John Smiths are neither equal nor identical. If the two parties move into the same house, their objects become equal but not identical. Elements need to have such an unambiguous identification.

Figure A.2 shows the object model in more detail. Each box has three parts: the first contains the name of the object types, the second the attributes (object fields), and the third the methods. A part can be empty. The figure includes two types that we have not defined yet, List.T and Set.T. We are familiar with lists and sets, and the definitions of these types follows later. For the time it suffices to know that they can store arbitrary objects; i.e., Set.T sets are not restricted to ordinal types.

We will use lists to store smaller data collections, such as the works on a CD or the composers of a work. For larger data collections, lists are much too inefficient, so we will use sets instead (see Section A.5.2).

Our most important set is the set of all CDs. It must contain all relevant data. To make checking data input simpler and faster (see input strategy, Section A.4.1), we additionally introduce the set of all composers and the set of all performers.

Figure A.2 maps the relationship *contains* onto lists. In our original schema we did not specify whether we can explicitly store a relationship in both directions. For example, we can map the relationship between CDs and works onto two lists: a CD contains a list of works and a work has a list of CDs on which it appears. However, for reasons of *consistency*, we choose the simpler variant: we store relationships in only one direction and so avoid *redundant representation*. Although this approach can slow down certain queries, our model is much clearer and thriftier with memory. In particular, it is easier to keep the lists free of contradiction, i.e., to guard their consistency. For example, to delete a CD, it suffices to delete it from the set of CDs. Since we do not store lists of CDs on which a work appears, we need not bother to delete the CD from each list of CDs for each respective work that the CD contains; in general, such redundant representation would encumber the preservation of consistency.

A CD contains a list of works. A work contains a list of composers and a list of performers. Composers and performers are persons. Composers also have a style. We use no other attributes for performers.

A.3 Interfaces of the object model

From our schema we can derive our interfaces directly. Despite comments, the semantics of the operations is often imprecise. In case of doubt, we will have to examine the corresponding implementation. In practice this is often unacceptable. However, this appendix seeks to encourage the reader to peruse the source code. All interfaces describe an encapsulated data type with possible additional services. Corresponding to our convention, the main type in each interface is always called T.

A.3.1 Interface of the base object

The interface Elem (page 443) defines the supertype of all objects that we manage. On initialization, each object of type Elem.T receives a unique identification. The method equal returns *true* if and only if two elements have the same identifier. The method hash returns a mapping of the identifier onto the range [0 .. limit]. We use the methods equal and hash in the implementation of object sets.

The type Elem.T defines additional methods for inputting and outputting an element.

The Interface Elem affords a number of types that the other modules can use. The type Compare defines a relational procedure for two elements. Procedures of this type serve as sorting functions for generic lists.

The type Action defines a closure around an action that can be applied to an element. Instead of an Elem.T-object, naturally we can use an object of any subtype. We will use this closure to apply an action to all elements of a list or of a set. The method action must be overridden with a corresponding procedure. The closure provides an environment for the procedure (similar to our THREAD closures in Chapter 16).

The type Selector is a closure around a Boolean function that can be applied to an element. We will use it to select elements from a list or a set if the method select evaluates to *true*. This method must be overridden with an appropriate function procedure.

A.3.2   The specific interfaces

The interfaces Person, Composer, Work and CD (starting on page 443) define the interfaces specific to the CD management system. They were derived directly from Figure A.2 and should be self-explanatory.

The only point that still might need some explanation is the redefinition of the method input. The types Person.T and CD.T redefine this method with an additional parameter of type Set.T. For technical reasons, this parameter cannot be specified in the superclass (Elem.T): this would cause the mutual import of the interfaces Elem and Set (pages 443, 444), which is not permitted. The set parameter contains a reference to the set in which the input procedures can search for an already existing object. New objects of a given class are added to this set. However, this parameter need not be specified (the default is NIL), allowing us to switch off this convenience service. To make this clearer, we define our user interface in the following section.

A.4 User interface

Our goal for the user interface is to enable the user to do the following:

1. Input new CDs.

2. Remove existing CDs.

3. Make queries.

Due to space considerations, we do not require a graphic user interface[1].

A.4.1 Input strategy

The input must meet the following requirements:

- It must be possible to input data either interactively form the keyboard or by reading a properly prepared file. We must provide the interactive user with a certain measure of convenience and protection against user errors. For input files, we can set up relatively strict rules.

- The basic input unit is the CD. Inputting a CD occurs in two steps:

   1. Input a CD identifier.
   2. Input the works. If we already have a CD with this identifier and the same work titles, then the interactive user is asked whether this CD is really new (e.g., a different performer is possible). If so, then a different CD identifier must be input (otherwise the CD is not entered in the database). For input from a file, such a CD is considered as already existing and is not added to the set of CDs.

- Inputting a work requires the following steps:

   1. Input the title.
   2. Input the composers.
   3. Input the performers.

- Inputting composers and performers occurs as follows:

   1. Input the last name.

---

[1] However, reimplementing the user interface as a graphical one should be possible; see the programs accompanying the book (Appendix D).

2. If the person is in the database, then the user views a suggestion for the first name(s). The user can confirm this or enter a new first name (such as Carl Philipp Emanuel if the name Bach does not mean Johann Sebastian Bach).

3. For composers we will also input the style (in the case of interactive input the style will be requested only for new composers).

- For the interactive user, we want to alleviate the job of inputting by accepting shorthand notation for data that are already known to the system (assuming that the abbreviation is unambiguous). Input will not be case sensitive.

- The structure of input is to be adapted primarily to the requirements of the interactive user. Therefore we define the following extremely simple input structure, where the user can answer each question in two ways:

  1. With new input (such as the first name of a composer)

  2. With a default input that is always activated in the same way (e.g., with the return key): The meaning of the default value depends on the context, but can be described generally as "no further input for this component". An empty title of a work, e.g., means that the CD contains no further works; an empty CD identifier indicates that we want to terminate CD input.

The interactive input of a CD takes the following form (where Johann Sebastian Bach is already in the database):

```
CD identifier:   Bach Oratorium
 Title of work:   Passion Music according to St. Matthew
   Composer(s)  =>
     Person's name:   Bach
Johann Sebastian Bach
Do the first names match?   "Return"
     Person's name:   "Return"
   Performer(s)  =>
     Person's name:   van Egmond
   First names:   Piet
     Person's name:   Utrecht Symphony Orchestra
   First names:   "Return"
     Person's name:   "Return"
 Title of work:   "Return"
CD identifier:
```

The above input could be prepared in a file as follows (where lines beginning with a period (".") are considered default input; comments can be
added to make the file easily readable):

```
Bach Oratorium
Passion Music according to St.Matthew
Bach
Johann Sebastian
baroque
.   End Composers
van Egmond
Piet
Utrecht Symphony Orchestra

.   End performers
.   End works
```

Note that a simple and consistent input strategy can save the user a lot of
frustration. This is not meant to say that we could not define a much more
comfortable input system than what we have just described. The reader
should feel free to improve the example in this direction!

A.4.2 Output

Output will be in the form of formatted, sorted lists. CD lists are sorted
alphabetically and lists within a CD chronologically according to the order
of input (usually the same as on the CD). For each output it should be
possible to redirect data to a file. The above CD should be output as follows:

```
Bach Oratorium
Passion Music according to St.Matthew
Johann Sebastian Bach (baroque)
Piet van Egmond, Utrecht Symphony Orchestra
```

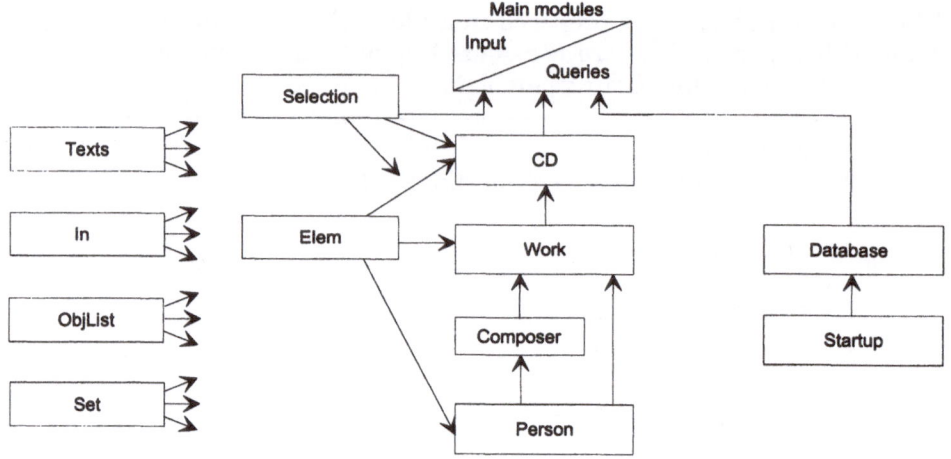

Figure A.3: *The module structure*

A.5   Implementation

The building blocks of our implementation will be modules. The architecture is determined by the following considerations:

- The *applications* of the system are specified as main modules. We define two prefabricated applications: one for input and one for frequent queries. For additional queries, additional applications can be developed.

- The types of the object model form a module hierarchy. This results on the one hand from the type hierarchy and on the other hand from the relationships between the types.

- The data are stored in persistent sets.

- Several auxiliary modules are available, e.g., to handle frequent selections, for command input, for menu output, etc.

This produces a module structure (Figure A.3). The arrows indicate the direction of import; the importing module is always the one to which the arrow points. Elem is imported by all modules of the object model. The auxiliary modules, such as Selection, Texts and In, can be imported wherever needed. The same applies for ObjList and Set. Set is classified primarily under the Database module, but it can be imported everywhere.

During implementation we have to take care which services build on which others. Thus far we have progressed top-down: we began with basic requirements and made them more concrete. Now we will invert the game: we must compose the system bottom-up. The services that are visible to the user build on internal services. This is similar to building a house: the drafts consider primarily the requirements and the environment. Here the facade might be of particular importance. However, it is advisable to begin construction with the foundation rather than the roof.

A.5.1 Persistent sets

Our task is a typical database application. Databases are designed for storing data and their relationships and for providing the data for various queries. We could end our design now and refer the reader to a familiar database system that would help to solve the task. But if we stay with our idea of solving the task with Modula-3 (which is certainly advisable as an example of programming in Modula-3), then we still have the following alternatives: either we link our Modula-3 environment to an existing database system, or we build one. For the first alternative we would have to develop a corresponding Modula-3 interface (we can link external programs with the help of the EXTERNAL pragma (see Appendix B.8.5)). Since our task is relatively simple, we will attempt our own solution.

Chapter 14 introduced persistent variables. We postulated that we want to store our data in sets of objects. If we make these sets persistent, then we have the basic functionality of a database system – storing and providing data long-range. Naturally, we must not forget that database systems offer much more: tools to ensure data consistency, simultaneous access for multiple users, and transactions [KM94], to name a few. However, we will settle for persistent sets (and call ours a poor man's database system).

The Database interface

The interface Database (page 445) exports three persistent sets: for CDs, composers and performers. To prevent involuntary destruction of our persistent data, the variables themselves are hidden. We export only functions that return the corresponding sets (more precisely, references to them).

To launch the database (by loading the persistent variables), we must invoke Persistent.Startup. We place this invocation in a separate module (Startup, pages 446 and 461), which we import in module Database (page 461). The Startup interface is empty; the import simply causes the loading of the implementation and the execution of its body.

A.5.2   Sets

Interface Set (page 444) shows the definition of the abstract data type Set.T. Sets of type Set.T are an unordered collection of any kind of objects.

In the initialization of a set (init), we can provide a (hint) on how large we estimate the set. This specification helps the implementation to find an efficient solution. If we seriously underestimate (i.e., by orders of magnitude), then it will become relatively slow; if we seriously overestimate it, then we squander memory.

The method insert inserts an element in the set if it is not already contained; delete removes an element if it is contained. The operation in tests whether an element is contained in a set. The method pick selects an arbitrary element from the set, or returns NIL if the set is empty. apply iterates through the entire set and applies the action procedure specified in parameter a to each element. Observe that by definition sets are unordered, and therefore the sequence in which apply progresses is undefined. exists returns an element for which the selection function (s.select) evaluates to *true* or NIL if no such element exists. The select method returns the subset on whose elements the selection function evaluates to *true*; if no selection criterion is specified (s = NIL), all elements are selected, thus creating a copy. Note that set.exists(s) is a short form of set.select(s).pick(). The method sort creates a sorted list from a set. The usual set operations (union, intersection, etc.) have the same semantics as described in Section 8.3.

The implementation (module Set, page 453) employs a *hash table*. For a complete description of hashing, refer to, e.g., [Knu81, Sed93, Wir76]; we limit ourselves to the bare necessities here. A *hash function* maps a domain of any kind (in our case, the object identifiers) onto a predefined range (in our case, spanned by the size of the hash table). The simplest hash function is value MOD limit. We implement the hash table as an array of lists.

The hash function maps the oid onto an index of the hash table. If we attempt to insert an existing object into a set or if we test whether it is contained in the set, the hash function gives us the index of the list in which the object could be. On insertion, we must insert the element in this list; on searching, we search in the same. If the number of elements is about the same as the size of the hash table, (computed from the hint parameter of the init method), then we have a good chance that the lists will be quite short. With a uniform distribution of the object identifiers, all hash values are equally probable. If our set grows orders of magnitude beyond our estimate, the lists become relatively long; in this case we can copy our entire hash table into a new, larger hash table (but this is not implemented in module Set). The advantage of using a hash table compared to lists is that we have many small lists instead of one large one, and we can very quickly find the right list. The remainder of the Set implementation should be clear from the source code.

A.5.3 Object lists

The interface ObjList (page 445) defines the list operations. In init we can specify a comparison function (compare). If compare is specified, the list is sorted accordingly; otherwise (compare = NIL) the list retains its chronological nature: elements are added at the end and removed from the beginning. We insert elements with insert and remove them with delete; delete returns the removed element, or NIL if no such element could be removed.

In addition to the usual list operations, ObjList.T contains operations that we have defined on sets. The apply method is applied sequentially to all elements. select returns a list with elements for which the selection criterion (s.select) evaluates to *true*. If there is no selection function (s = NIL), select creates a copy. The semantics of exists is also similar to that for sets. The method equal compares two lists. If the comparison function (compare) is specified, it is used in the comparison; otherwise the list elements are simply tested for reference equality. Given a positive result, in the first case the lists are equal with respect to the explicit comparison criterion; in the second case the list elements are identical. The implementation of lists is specified in module ObjList (page 457).

A.5.4 Auxiliary modules

Auxiliary modules are available to all other modules. The module In (page 446, 466) exports two Boolean functions that indicate whether input will be interactive or from a file and whether to use a text as default input (see Section A.4.1).

The module Texts (page 446, 461) provides procedures for various text conversions and searching as well as for inputting a command from a command menu. For example, Texts.Part tests whether the first of two text parameters is shorthand for the second. This operation is not case sensitive, and blanks are ignored. All text input uses this procedure. Texts.Search tests whether a text is shorthand for a text of a text list. Texts.CommandIn reads a command from a menu list.

A.5.5 Selections

We can carry out any kind of selection on our data by defining a corresponding selection closure. The most important and most frequent selections are provided in module Selection (page 446, 460). The selection closure (Selector) contains all parameters that we need for the provided selections. The field kind describes the kind of selection: e.g., CD identifier, composer name, etc. The parameter t contains the target text value (most selections search for a text), e.g., the target CD identifier or composer name. If we search for a style (e.g., all CDs by Romantic composers), then we need the parameter style. There are many examples of how to apply selections in various programs, e.g., in module Queries (page 466); therefore we present only a small example here. For the selection of all CDs whose titles begin with "viol", we have the following implementation:

```
VAR
   selector := NEW(Selection.Selector, kind:= Selection.Kind.Title, t:= "viol");
   viol: Set.T;
BEGIN
   viol:= Database.CDs().select(selector);                      (*selects works for viol...*)
   ⋮
```

The implementation of selections (page 460) consists in essence of a single recursive function which selects the appropriate measures on the basis of the actual parameter (whose supertype is Elem.T) and the chosen kind of selection. The above selection of titles beginning with "viol" executes as follows: The select method applies the selection function (page 460) to each element – here to every CD. The function Select is invoked with parameters of type CD.T; it determines that the chosen kind of selection is Title, so the selection must be forwarded to the list of works. Thus Select invokes the select method for works. Here the same selector is specified (s), inducing a recursive invocation of the Select function, which is now applied to each work in the list works. Thereby the type of the actual parameter is work.T. The work title can now be checked easily and the corresponding Boolean value is returned. However, we are not interested in the individual works; with this function we always select whole CDs. Therefore we apply the size method to the results of the works list selection. If it returns a positive number, then the selection by work titles for the specified CD ends with *true*, otherwise with *false*.

For selections by composers and performers, the depth of recursion goes one deeper, along the lists composers and performers for each work. The surprising compactness and power of the Select function is based on the fact that we have defined the selection operation with the same syntax and very similar semantics for both sets and lists.

A.5.6 Implementation modules of the object model

We have already discussed the interfaces of the object model. The implementations consist primarily of the implementations of the in and out methods. The out method is usually trivial. The module work (page 449) shows an example of how to use the action closure to output the continuation of a list, delimited by commas (e.g., Jascha Heifetz, Gregor Piatigorsky, William Primrose).

Implementing the input methods is significantly more complex. The tasks of the in method are to read relevant values for the respective type (e.g., for a composer, the name and style), to insert the object in the corresponding set (e.g., set of composers), and to return a value. The return value is determined as follows:

1. For new objects (as yet unknown to the database), the initial value, i.e., the value of the receiver of the in method, is returned.

2. If the object whose input is being processed is found in the database, then it is retrieved and returned as return value.

3. The value NIL is returned if there is no input.

The implementations of the input methods are based on our input strategy (Section A.4.1); they handle the services defined in that strategy. For example, if a composer or a performer is found in the corresponding file (where the file itself is a parameter of the in method), then the first names are suggested. For the input of works, we do not need such a help: although we can anticipate that someone might have many Mozart CDs, it is unlikely that these include twenty versions of "Eine kleine Nachtmusik". This justifies repeated typing. On the input of a CD, we have a great deal to test. According to our object model, CDs with an empty list of works should not be accepted. The concatenation of the CD identifier with each work title must be unique; we must test this condition here as well.

The input method may generate the Elem.Error exception anywhere. The exception is propagated up to the application (module Input, see below). Each module complements the text parameter of the exception with its own error message. The application can output this text, whereby the user knows the exact location of the errors. The user can terminate input of an element at any time with the end-of-file key (control-Z or control-D). After the output of an error message, the application can continue without problems.

A.5.7 Input

Inputting is implemented in the procedure Input.Add (page 463). The procedure provides a simple loop for inputting CDs and also handles input errors. For example, if we press the end-of-file key while inputting a work, we obtain the following error message:

```
Error during input->CDIn->WorkIn
```

The module Input enables deleting elements from the sets of CDs, composers or performers. The following must be observed: Since deletion from a database is a delicate matter, it can only be done interactively and with explicit confirmation. The user enters the short form of elements (e.g., the CD identifier); the corresponding CDs are selected to an alphabetically sorted list (candidates). The elements of this list are displayed one after the other for the user, who must confirm the deletion of each element.

Deletion does not ensure the consistency of the sets CDs, Composers and Performers. This means that if we delete all CDs by Brahms, Brahms still remains in set of composers. Likewise, if we delete Yehudi Menuhin from the set of performers, we retain his CDs nevertheless (and queries will find them). This sounds unacceptable at first, but it is not as bad as it seems. The relevant information resides in the set CDs, while the other two sets only serve to accelerate input control. We could redefine the semantics of these two sets as follows: they contain all composers and performers for whom we ever entered a CD; we should never delete anything from them except erroneous entries. However, the reader should consider how we could implement consistent management of the three sets. A simple solution would be to make the sets of composers and performers nonpersistent and to generate these sets anew at certain times, such as on launching the application. In our case, this solution would suffice.

When the user quits the input module, the system (procedure Save) asks whether changes should be saved. This is an additional security measure.

A.5.8   Queries

We have developed the entire system for the purpose of making queries. The module Queries (page 466) contains a collection of the most important queries. This module builds on the services of the module Selection (page 446, 460), which handles the difficult part of the work. The module Queries needs to handle only inputting the commands, setting the kind of selection and outputting the results.

The core of the module consist of two lines in the procedure Search:

```
cds:= Database.CDs().select(selector); (*selects from CDs*)
SortedOutput(cds, CD.Compare, wr);   (*CDs in alphabetical order*)
```

A.6   Interfaces

```
INTERFACE Elem;                                              (*23.02.95. LB *)
  IMPORT SIO;
  EXCEPTION Error(TEXT);                                  (*signals input error*)
  TYPE
    T        <: Public;               (*all elements must be subtype of Elem.T*)
    Public   = OBJECT
                METHODS
                  init(): T;                     (*init must be invoked as first operation!*)
                  hash(limit: CARDINAL): CARDINAL;        (*hash value in [0..limit]*)
                  equal(e2: T): BOOLEAN;          (*true if self and e2 are identical*)
                  input(rd: SIO.Reader := NIL): T RAISES {Error};      (*for reading*)
                  output(wr: SIO.Writer := NIL);                      (*for output*)
                END; (*Public*)

    Compare = PROCEDURE(e1, e2: T): [–1 .. 1];   (*-1: e1 < e2; 0: e1 = e2; 1: e1 > e2*)
    Action  = OBJECT
                METHODS                          (*closure for actions on elements*)
                  action(e: T)                     (*can be applied to an element*)
                END; (*Action*)
    Selector = OBJECT                          (*closure for selection on elements*)
                METHODS
                  select(e: T): BOOLEAN                      (*if true: e is selected*)
                END; (*Selector*)
END Elem.
```

```
INTERFACE Person;                                            (*22.02.95. LB *)
  IMPORT Elem, Set, SIO;
  TYPE
    T        <: Public;
    Public   = Elem.T OBJECT
                  name, firstname: TEXT:= "";                      (*can be empty*)
                METHODS
                  input(persons: Set.T := NIL;                     (*in redefined!*)
                    rd: SIO.Reader := NIL): T RAISES {Elem.Error};
                END;
    PROCEDURE Compare(e1, e2: Elem.T): [–1 .. 1];   (*comparison criterion: name*)
END Person.
```

```
INTERFACE Composer;                                              (*22.02.95. LB *)
  IMPORT Person;
  TYPE
    Style    =  {old, baroque, classical, romantic, modern, none};
    T        <: Public;
    Public   =  Person.T OBJECT
                    style := Style.none;              (*style initialized to "none"*)
                END;
  CONST
    StyleText = ARRAY [Style.old .. Style.modern] OF TEXT
                  {"old", "baroque", "classical", "romantic", "modern"};
  END Composer.
```

```
INTERFACE Work;                                                  (*22.02.95. LB *)
  IMPORT Elem, ObjList;
  TYPE
    T        <: Public;
    Public   =  Elem.T OBJECT
                    title: TEXT := "";                          (*title of work*)
                    composers: ObjList.T;                  (*list of composers*)
                    performers: ObjList.T;                 (*list of performers*)
                END; (*Public*)
  PROCEDURE Compare(e1, e2: Elem.T): [–1 .. 1];   (*comparison criterion: work title*)
END Work.
```

```
INTERFACE CD;                                                    (*25.03.95. LB*)
  IMPORT Elem, Set, ObjList, SIO;
  TYPE
    T        <: Public;
    Public   =  Elem.T OBJECT
                    identifier: TEXT := "";                     (*CD identifier*)
                    works: ObjList.T;                      (*list of works on CD*)
                METHODS
                    input(cds: Set.T := NIL;                   (*input: redefined!*)
                        rd: SIO.Reader := NIL): T RAISES {Elem.Error};
                END; (*Public*)
  PROCEDURE Compare(e1, e2: Elem.T): [–1 .. 1];               (*criterion: identifier*)
END CD.
```

```
INTERFACE Set;                                              (*23.03.95. LB, KHE *)
  IMPORT Elem, ObjList;
  CONST
    MinSize = 128;                                  (*minimum size of hash table*)
  TYPE
    T        <Public;
    Public   = OBJECT METHODS
                    init(hint: CARDINAL := MinSize): T;       (*must be 1st operation!*)
```

```
                insert(x: Elem.T);                    (*inserts x if it does not already exist*)
                delete(x: Elem.T);                              (*removes x if present*)
                in(x: Elem.T): BOOLEAN;                           (*true if x is in set*)
                size(): CARDINAL;                          (*number of elements in set*)
                pick(): Elem.T;                 (*returns arbitrary element of set or NIL*)
                apply(a: Elem.Action);                       (*applies a to all elements*)
                exists(s: Elem.Selector): Elem.T;
                          (*returns an element e such that s.select(e) is true, else NIL*)
                select(s: Elem.Selector): T;
                          (*returns the set whose elements s.select evaluates as true*)
                              (*if s = NIL, all are selected: generates a copy*)
                equal(set2: T): BOOLEAN;
                          (*true if size und all elements of two sets are equal*)
                union(set2 : T) : T;                                  (*self ∨ set2*)
                intersection(set2 : T) : T;                           (*self ∧ set2*)
                difference(set2 : T) : T;                             (*self - set2*)
                sort(compare: Elem.Compare): ObjList.T;
                              (*from a set, creates a list sorted by compare*)
            END; (*Public*)
END Set.
```

```
INTERFACE ObjList;                                         (*23.02.95. LB*)
  IMPORT Elem;
  TYPE
     T        <: Public;
     Public  =  OBJECT
                METHODS
                init(compare: Elem.Compare): T;              (*compare: sort criterion*)
                              (*if compare = NIL, elements sorted chronologically*)
                insert(elem: Elem.T);                           (*inserts keeping order*)
                delete(elem: Elem.T): Elem.T;                  (*removes elem, if present*)
                size(): CARDINAL;                          (*number of elements of list *)
                equal(list2: T; compare: Elem.Compare): BOOLEAN;
                          (*compares two lists for equality or identity of elements*)
                              (*equality tested if compare # NIL*)
                apply(a: Elem.Action);                       (*apply a to each element*)
                select(s: Elem.Selector): T;
                          (*returns a list for whose elements s.select evaluates true*)
                              (*if s = NIL, all elements selected; copy created*)
                exists(s: Elem.Selector): Elem.T;
                       (*returns an element for which s.select evaluates true, else NIL*)
            END; (*Public*)
END ObjList.
```

```
INTERFACE Database;                (*Exports the sets of the database. 08.03.95. LB*)
  IMPORT Set;
  PROCEDURE CDs(): Set.T;                                      (*set of all CDs*)
  PROCEDURE Composers(): Set.T;                             (*set of all composers*)
  PROCEDURE Performers(): Set.T;                           (*set of all performers*)
END Database.
```

```
INTERFACE Startup;              (*Exports nothing: its body must execute. 10.04.95. LB*)
END Startup.
```

```
INTERFACE Selection;            (*Auxiliary module for frequent selections. 08.04.95. LB*)
    IMPORT Elem, Composer;
    TYPE
      Kind       =   {Identifier, Title, Name, Comp, Style, Perf};        (*kind of selection*)
                                      (*selected by CD identifier, work title, person name,*)
                                            (*composer name, style, performer name*)
      Selector   <: SelPub;
      SelPub     =   Elem.Selector OBJECT
                        kind: Kind;                                (*Kind of Selection*)
                        t: TEXT;                         (*required by most selections*)
                        style: Composer.Style;                   (*for selection by style*)
                     END; (*SelPub*)
END Selection.
```

```
INTERFACE Texts;   (*Auxiliary module for text and command handling. 22.03.95. LB*)

    PROCEDURE Convert(text: TEXT): TEXT;
                            (*converts lower case to upper case and filters out blanks*)
    PROCEDURE Part(t1, t2: TEXT): BOOLEAN;
                            (*returns true if Convert(t1) is a substring of Convert(t2)*)
    PROCEDURE Search(text: TEXT; in: ARRAY OF TEXT): INTEGER;
                       (*returns position of first occurrence of text in in, or -1 if not found*)
    PROCEDURE CommandIn(READONLY menu: ARRAY OF TEXT): INTEGER;
        (*reads command from menu; returns index of command, or < 0, on default line*)

END Texts.
```

```
INTERFACE In;                   (*Auxiliary module for input handling 28.03.95. LB*)
    IMPORT SIO;

    CONST Delimiter = '.';

    PROCEDURE Interactive(rd: SIO.Reader): BOOLEAN;
                                         (*returns true if standard input used*)
    PROCEDURE Default(t: TEXT): BOOLEAN;
                            (*default text is empty, or begins with delimiter*)
END In.
```

A.7 Implementation modules

```
MODULE Elem;                                                    (*23.02.95. LB *)
    IMPORT Persistent, Startup;          (*Startup imported because of uniqueNumber!*)
    REVEAL
      T = Public BRANDED OBJECT
            objectID: CARDINAL := 0;                    (*0 for uninitialized objects*)
          OVERRIDES
            init:= Init;
            hash:= Hash;
            equal:= Equal;
          END; (*T*)
VAR
    uniqueNumber:= NEW(Persistent.Integer, key:= "Elem.uniqueNumber", val:= 0).setup();

    PROCEDURE Init(t: T): T =
    BEGIN
      INC(uniqueNumber.val);
      t.objectID:= uniqueNumber.val;                   (*objectID ist unique and > 0*)
      RETURN t
    END Init;

    PROCEDURE Equal(e1, e2: T): BOOLEAN =
    BEGIN
      <* ASSERT e1.objectID > 0 AND e2.objectID > 0 *>
      RETURN e1.objectID = e2.objectID
    END Equal;

    PROCEDURE Hash(e: T; limit: CARDINAL): CARDINAL =
    BEGIN
      <* ASSERT e.objectID > 0 *>
      RETURN e.objectID MOD limit
    END Hash;

BEGIN
END Elem.
```

```
MODULE Person;
    IMPORT Elem, Text, Set, SIO, In, Selection;
    FROM SIO IMPORT GetLine, PutText;

    REVEAL
      T = Public BRANDED OBJECT
          OVERRIDES
            input:= PersonInput;
            output:= PersonOutput;
          END; (*T*)

    PROCEDURE Compare(e1, e2: Elem.T): [-1 .. 1] =              (*compares last names*)
    BEGIN
      RETURN Text.Compare(NARROW(e1, T).name, NARROW(e2, T).name)
    END Compare;
```

```
  PROCEDURE PersonInput(p: T; persons: Set.T := NIL;              (*reads person data*)
           rd: SIO.Reader := NIL ): T RAISES {Elem.Error} =
VAR name: TEXT; found: T := NIL;
    selector := NEW(Selection.Selector, kind:= Selection.Kind.Name);
  BEGIN
    IF In.Interactive(rd) THEN PutText(" Person's name: ") END;
    TRY
      name:= GetLine(rd);
      IF NOT In.Default(name) THEN
        p.name:= name;
        selector.t:= name;
        IF persons # NIL THEN found:= persons.exists(selector) END;
        IF found # NIL THEN                          (*person already in set persons*)
          IF In.Interactive(rd) THEN
            PersonOutput(found); PutText("\n Do the first names match? ")
          END; (*IF In.Interactive(rd)*)
          name:= GetLine(rd);                                  (*read first name(s)*)
          selector.t:= selector.t & name;            (*search text: complete name*)
          found:= persons.exists(selector);                        (*search again*)
          IF In.Default(name) OR (found # NIL) THEN
            p:= found                     (*default or found again: return old value*)
          ELSE p.firstname:= name;                             (*new first name*)
          END; (*IF In.Default...*)
        ELSE                                (*person not found: request first name*)
          IF In.Interactive(rd) THEN PutText(" Firstnames: ") END;
          p.firstname:= GetLine(rd);
        END; (*IF found # NIL*)
        IF persons # NIL THEN persons.insert(p) END;      (*effective only if p # found*)
      ELSE p:= NIL                       (*p = NIL indicates empty input for person*)
      END; (*IF NOT In.Default(name)*)
      RETURN p;
    EXCEPT
      SIO.Error => RAISE Elem.Error("PersonInput")
    END; (*TRY*)
  END PersonInput;

  PROCEDURE PersonOutput(p: T; wr: SIO.Writer := NIL) =      (*outputs person data*)
  BEGIN
    PutText(p.firstname & " " & p.name, wr);
  END PersonOutput;
BEGIN
END Person.
```

```
MODULE Composer;                                          (*22.03.95. LB*)
  IMPORT Elem, Person, SIO, Set, In, Texts;
  REVEAL
    T       = Public BRANDED OBJECT
              OVERRIDES
                input:= ComposerInput;
                output:= ComposerOutput;
              END; (*T*)
```

```
PROCEDURE ComposerInput(k: T; composers: Set.T := NIL;
          rd: SIO.Reader := NIL): Person.T RAISES {Elem.Error} =
VAR t: TEXT; found: INTEGER;
   k2: T := k;                              (*k2 contains original value of k*)
BEGIN
  TRY
    k:= Person.T.input(k, composers, rd);              (*supercall: reads person data*)
    IF k # NIL THEN
      IF In.Interactive(rd) THEN
        IF k = k2 THEN                       (*k = k2: Composer is new; enter style*)
          SIO.PutText(" Style: ");
          found:= Texts.CommandIn(StyleText);
          IF found >= 0 THEN k.style:= VAL(found, Style) END;
        END; (*IF k = k2 *)
      ELSE                                 (*if not interactive, read style from file*)
        t:= SIO.GetLine(rd);
        IF NOT In.Default(t) THEN
          found:= Texts.Search(t, StyleText);          (*seek input in StyleText*)
          IF found >= 0 THEN k.style:= VAL(found, Style) END;
        END;(*IF NOT In.Default(t)*)
      END; (*IF In.Interactive(rd)*)
    END; (*IF k # NIL...*)
    RETURN k;
  EXCEPT
  | SIO.Error => RAISE Elem.Error("ComposerInput");
  | Elem.Error(text) => RAISE Elem.Error("ComposerInput->" & text);
  END; (*TRY*)
END ComposerInput;

PROCEDURE ComposerOutput(k: T; wr: SIO.Writer := NIL) =
BEGIN
  Person.T.output(k, wr);                        (*Supercall: output person data*)
  IF k.style # Style.none THEN
    SIO.PutText(" (" & StyleText[k.style] & ") ", wr)
  END; (*IF k.style*)
END ComposerOutput;

BEGIN
END Composer.
```

```
MODULE Work;                                        (*20.03.95. LB*)
  IMPORT Elem, Composer, Person, SIO, Database, ObjList, Text, In;
  REVEAL
    T        = Public BRANDED OBJECT
              OVERRIDES
                init:= Init;
                input:= WorkInput;
                output:= WorkOutput;
              END; (*T*)
```

```
PROCEDURE Init(work: T): Elem.T =
BEGIN
  work:= Elem.T.init(work);                        (*supercall: initializes Elem object*)
  work.composers:= NEW(ObjList.T).init(NIL);    (*list sorted chronologically by input*)
  work.performers:= NEW(ObjList.T).init(NIL);       (*list sorted chronologically*)
  RETURN work
END Init;

PROCEDURE Compare(e1, e2: Elem.T): [–1 .. 1] =              (*compares work titles*)
BEGIN
  RETURN Text.Compare(NARROW(e1, T).title, NARROW(e2, T).title)
END Compare;

PROCEDURE WorkInput(work: T; rd: SIO.Reader := NIL): Elem.T
                    RAISES {Elem.Error} =
VAR t: TEXT; c: Composer.T; p: Person.T;
BEGIN
  TRY
    IF In.Interactive(rd) THEN SIO.PutText(" Title of work: ") END;
    t:= SIO.GetLine(rd);                                    (*reads title*)
    IF NOT In.Default(t) THEN
      work.title:= t;
      IF In.Interactive(rd) THEN SIO.PutLine(" Composer(s) => ") END;
      REPEAT                                     (*reads list of composers*)
        c:= NEW(Composer.T).init();
        c:= c.input(Database.Composers(), rd);           (*reads composer data*)
        IF c # NIL THEN work.composers.insert(c) END;
      UNTIL c = NIL;
      IF In.Interactive(rd) THEN SIO.PutLine(" Performer(s) => ") END;
      REPEAT                                     (*reads list of performers*)
        p:= NEW(Person.T).init();
        p:= p.input(Database.Performers(), rd);          (*reads performer data*)
        IF p # NIL THEN work.performers.insert(p) END;
      UNTIL p = NIL;
    ELSE work:= NIL
    END; (*IF NOT In.Default(t)*)
    RETURN work
  EXCEPT
  | SIO.Error => RAISE Elem.Error("WorkInput");
  | Elem.Error(text) => RAISE Elem.Error("WorkInput–>" & text);
  END; (*TRY*)
END WorkInput;

TYPE
  Action = Elem.Action OBJECT                   (*closure for the action output*)
              enumeration,                      (*controls output of list of names*)
              nonempty: BOOLEAN;                (*suppresses unnecessary blank lines*)
              w: SIO.Writer := NIL
            OVERRIDES
              action:= Output;                  (*output action for list elements*)
            END; (*Action*)
```

```
    PROCEDURE Output(a: Action; e: Elem.T) =                    (*outputs person*)
    BEGIN
        a.nonempty:= TRUE;                              (*set only for non-empty lines*)
        IF a.enumeration THEN SIO.PutText(", ", a.w) ELSE a.enumeration:= TRUE END;
        e.output(a.w);
    END Output;

    PROCEDURE WorkOutput(work: T; wr: SIO.Writer := NIL) =
    VAR output := NEW(Action, w:= wr);                  (*example of closure for output*)
    BEGIN
        SIO.PutLine(work.title, wr);
        output.enumeration:= FALSE; output.nonempty:= FALSE;
        work.composers.apply(output);                   (*applies output to list of composers*)
        IF output.nonempty THEN SIO.Nl(wr) END;         (*no line feed for empty list*)
        output.enumeration:= FALSE; output.nonempty:= FALSE;
        work.performers.apply(output);                  (*applies output to list of performers*)
        IF output.nonempty THEN SIO.Nl(wr) END;         (*no line feed for empty list*)
    END WorkOutput;

BEGIN
END Work.
```

```
MODULE CD;                                                      (*20.03.95. LB*)
    IMPORT SIO, Set, Work, Elem, Text, ObjList, In;
    REVEAL
        T        = Public BRANDED OBJECT
                    OVERRIDES
                        init:= Init;
                        input:= CDInput;
                        output:= CDOutput;
                    END; (*T*)

    PROCEDURE Init(cd: T): Elem.T =
    BEGIN
        cd:= Elem.T.init(cd);                           (*supercall: initializes element data*)
        cd.works:= NEW(ObjList.T).init(NIL);            (*chronological list of works*)
        RETURN cd
    END Init;

    PROCEDURE Compare(e1, e2: Elem.T): [-1 .. 1] =      (*compares CD identifiers*)
    BEGIN
        RETURN Text.Compare(NARROW(e1, T).identifier, NARROW(e2, T).identifier)
    END Compare;

    TYPE TitleSel = Elem.Selector OBJECT cd: T OVERRIDES select:= TW END;
                                                        (*closure for selection of similar CDs*)

    PROCEDURE TW(s: TitleSel; e: Elem.T): BOOLEAN =
                                        (*compares CD identifier and titles in list of works*)
    BEGIN
        RETURN Text.Equal(s.cd.identifier, NARROW(e, T).identifier) AND
                NARROW(e, T).works.equal(s.cd.works, Work.Compare)
    END TW;
```

```
    PROCEDURE CDInput(cd: T; cds: Set.T := NIL;                    (*reads and inserts CD*)
                      rd: SIO.Reader := NIL): T RAISES {Elem.Error} =
    VAR work: Work.T; identifier: TEXT;
        selector:= NEW(TitleSel);                       (*to find CDs with same list of works*)
        existentCD: T;                      (*CD with same identifier and same list of works*)
    BEGIN
      TRY
        IF In.Interactive(rd) THEN SIO.PutText("CD identifier: ") END;
        identifier:= SIO.GetLine(rd);                                  (*reads CD identifier*)
        IF NOT In.Default(identifier) THEN                          (*default ends input*)
          cd.identifier:= identifier;
          REPEAT                                            (*reads all works for CD*)
            work:= NEW(Work.T).init();
            work:= work.input(rd);                              (*reads data for work*)
            IF work # NIL THEN cd.works.insert(work) END;
          UNTIL work = NIL;
          IF cd.works.size() > 0 THEN               (*CDs without works are not recorded!*)
            IF cds # NIL THEN                          (*search for CD with same titles*)
              selector.cd:= cd;
              existentCD:= cds.exists(selector);           (*compare identifier and title*)
              IF existentCD = NIL THEN cds.insert(cd);         (*does not exist: insert*)
              ELSIF In.Interactive(rd) THEN                    (*if already exists: ask user*)
                REPEAT
                  SIO.PutLine("CD with same identifier and same titles already exists.");
                  existentCD.output();
                  SIO.PutLine("If this is a new CD, please provide a new identifier: ");
                  identifier:= SIO.GetLine(rd);
                  IF NOT In.Default(identifier) THEN
                    cd.identifier:= identifier;
                    existentCD:= cds.exists(selector);             (*now unambiguous?*)
                  END; (*IF NOT In.Default*)
                UNTIL (existentCD = NIL) OR In.Default(identifier);
                IF existentCD = NIL THEN cds.insert(cd) END;   (*unambiguous: insert*)
              END; (*IF In.Interactive*)
            END (*IF cds # NIL*)
          ELSE cd:= NIL;                               (*CD without works is not permitted*)
          END; (*IF cd.works.size() > 0*)
        ELSE cd:= NIL                                         (*terminate CD input*)
        END; (*IF NOT In.Default*)
        RETURN cd
      EXCEPT
      | SIO.Error => RAISE Elem.Error("CDInput");
      | Elem.Error(text) => RAISE Elem.Error("CDInput->" & text);
      END; (*TRY*)
    END CDInput;

    TYPE Action = Elem.Action OBJECT w: SIO.Writer := NIL END;

    PROCEDURE Output(a: Action; e: Elem.T) =                        (*output work*)
    BEGIN
      e.output(a.w);
    END Output;
```

```
PROCEDURE CDOutput(cd: T; wr: SIO.Writer := NIL) =                    (*output CD*)
VAR output := NEW(Action, action:= Output, w:= wr);
BEGIN
  SIO.PutLine(cd.identifier, wr);
  cd.works.apply(output);
  SIO.PutLine("————————————————————————————————", wr);
END CDOutput;

BEGIN
END CD.
```

```
MODULE Set;                                                      (*23.02.95. LB, KHE *)

  IMPORT Elem, ObjList;

  TYPE
    Node = REF RECORD                                              (*node in list*)
                next: Node := NIL;
                e: Elem.T;
            END; (*node*)
  REVEAL
    T     = Public BRANDED OBJECT
                a: REF ARRAY OF Node;                              (*hash table*)
                num : CARDINAL;                             (*number of elements*)
            OVERRIDES
                init:= Init;
                in:= In;
                insert:= Insert;
                delete:= Delete;
                equal:= Equal;
                size:= Size;
                pick:= Pick;
                apply:= Apply;
                exists:= Exists;
                select:= Selection;
                union := Union;
                intersection:= Intersection;
                difference:= Difference;
                sort:= Sort;
            END; (*Set.T*)
  PROCEDURE Init(self: T; hint: CARDINAL := MinSize): T =
  BEGIN
    self.a:= NEW(REF ARRAY OF Node, MAX(hint, MinSize));
                                     (*minimum hash table size is MinSize*)
    FOR i:= FIRST(self.a^) TO LAST(self.a^) DO self.a[i]:= NIL END;
    self.num:= 0;
    RETURN self
  END Init;
```

```
PROCEDURE In(self: T; x: Elem.T): BOOLEAN =        (*true if x is contained in self*)
VAR cur: Node;                                                (*current node*)
BEGIN
  cur:= self.a[x.hash(NUMBER(self.aˆ))];                  (*hash index picks desired list*)
  WHILE cur # NIL AND NOT x.equal(cur.e) DO cur:= cur.next END;   (*search in list*)
  RETURN (cur # NIL)
END In;

PROCEDURE Insert (self : T; x : Elem.T) =
                                        (*inserts x in self if not already present*)
VAR cur: Node;                                                (*current node*)
BEGIN
  WITH head = self.a[x.hash(NUMBER(self.aˆ))] DO               (*hash index*)
    cur:= head;
    WHILE cur # NIL AND NOT x.equal(cur.e) DO cur:= cur.next END;
    IF cur = NIL THEN                         (*if not present: insert at front*)
      head:= NEW(Node, next:= head, e:= x); INC(self.num);
    END (*IF cur = NIL*)
  END (*WITH head*)
END Insert;

PROCEDURE Delete (self: T; x: Elem.T) =                    (*deletes x if present*)
VAR cur, prev: Node;
BEGIN
  IF x # NIL THEN                             (*nothing to remove in empty list*)
    WITH head = self.a [x.hash(NUMBER(self.aˆ))] DO             (*hash index*)
      cur:= head; prev:= NIL;
      WHILE cur # NIL AND NOT x.equal(cur.e) DO
        prev:= cur; cur:= cur.next
      END; (*WHILE cur*)
      IF cur # NIL THEN                              (*if found: remove*)
        IF prev = NIL THEN head:= cur.next ELSE prev.next:= cur.next END;
        DEC(self.num);
      END (*IF cur*)
    END (*WITH head*)
  END (*IF x # NIL*)
END Delete;

PROCEDURE Size (self: T): CARDINAL =              (*number of elements in set*)
BEGIN
  RETURN self.num
END Size;

PROCEDURE Apply(self: T; a: Elem.Action) =        (*apply a.action to all elements*)
VAR cur: Node;                                                (*current node*)
BEGIN
  IF self.num > 0 THEN
    FOR b:= FIRST(self.aˆ) TO LAST(self.aˆ) DO
      cur:= self.a [b];
      WHILE cur # NIL DO a.action(cur.e); cur:= cur.next END      (*applies action*)
    END (*FOR b*)
  END (*IF self.num > 0*)
END Apply;
```

```
PROCEDURE Equal (self: T; set2: T): BOOLEAN =
              (*true if number of elements and all elements of self and set2 are equal*)
VAR cur: Node;                                                    (*current node*)
  size: CARDINAL := 0;
BEGIN
  IF self.num = set2.num THEN                    (*if number equal, compare elements*)
    FOR b:= FIRST (self.a^) TO LAST (self.a^) DO
      cur:= self.a[b];
      WHILE (cur # NIL) DO
        IF NOT set2.in(cur.e) THEN RETURN FALSE END;
        INC (size); cur:= cur.next
      END (*WHILE cur*)
    END; (*FOR b*)
    RETURN size = self.num
  ELSE
    RETURN FALSE
  END (*IF self.num*)
END Equal;

PROCEDURE Exists(self : T; s: Elem.Selector): Elem.T =
    (*returns an e for which s.select(e) is true, or NIL (if no such element is present)*)
VAR cur: Node;                                                    (*current node*)
BEGIN
  IF s = NIL THEN RETURN self.pick()                          (*take any element*)
  ELSE
    IF self.num > 0 THEN
      FOR b:= FIRST(self.a^) TO LAST(self.a^) DO
        cur:= self.a[b];
        WHILE cur # NIL DO
          IF s.select(cur.e) THEN RETURN cur.e END;           (*select an element*)
          cur:= cur.next
        END; (*WHILE cur*)
      END; (*FOR b*)
    END; (*IF self.num > 0*)
    RETURN NIL
  END; (*IF s = NIL*)
END Exists;

PROCEDURE Pick(self : T) : Elem.T =
                            (*returns an arbitrary element, or NIL for empty set*)
VAR cur: Node;
  i:= FIRST(self.a^);
BEGIN
  IF self.num = 0 THEN RETURN NIL
  ELSE
    REPEAT cur:= self.a[i]; INC(i) UNTIL cur # NIL;
    RETURN cur.e
  END (*IF self.num = 0*)
END Pick;
```

```
PROCEDURE Selection(self : T; s: Elem.Selector): T =
                    (*returns the set of elements e for which s.select(e) evaluates true*)
VAR cur: Node;                                                        (*current node*)
    res: T := NEW(T).init(self.num);                                 (*res: result set*)
BEGIN
  IF s = NIL THEN Add(res, self)                          (*if s = NIL, create copy*)
  ELSE
    IF self.num > 0 THEN
      FOR b:= FIRST(self.a^) TO LAST(self.a^) DO
        cur:= self.a[b];
        WHILE cur # NIL DO
          IF s.select(cur.e) THEN res.insert(cur.e) END;
          cur:= cur.next
        END (*WHILE cur*)
      END (*FOR b*)
    END (*IF self.num ¿ 0*)
  END; (*IF f = NIL*)
  RETURN res
END Selection;

PROCEDURE Add(self : T; set2 : T) =               (*inserts all elements of set2 in self*)
VAR obj: Node;
BEGIN
  IF set2.num > 0 THEN                             (*empty set need not be added*)
    FOR b:= FIRST(set2.a^) TO LAST(set2.a^) DO
      obj:= set2.a[b];
      WHILE obj # NIL DO
        self.insert(obj.e); obj:= obj.next
      END (*WHILE obj*)
    END (*FOR b*)
  END (*IF set2*)
END Add;

PROCEDURE Difference(self : T; set2 : T) : T =                       (*self - set2*)
VAR res: T := NEW(T).init(self.num); obj: Node;
BEGIN
  IF self # set2 THEN
    FOR b:= FIRST(self.a^) TO LAST(self.a^) DO
      obj:= self.a[b];
      WHILE obj # NIL DO
        IF NOT set2.in(obj.e) THEN res.insert(obj.e) END;
        obj:=obj.next
      END (*WHILE obj*)
    END (*FOR b*)
  END; (*IF self*)
  RETURN res
END Difference;
```

```
PROCEDURE Intersection(self : T; set2 : T): T =                    (*self ∧ set2*)
VAR res: T := NEW(T).init(MIN(self.num, set2.num)); obj: Node;
BEGIN
  IF self = set2 THEN Add(res, self)
  ELSE
    FOR b:= FIRST(self.a^) TO LAST(self.a^) DO
      obj:= self.a[b];
      WHILE obj # NIL DO
        IF set2.in(obj.e) THEN res.insert(obj.e) END;
        obj:=obj.next
      END (*WHILE obj*)
    END (*FOR b*)
  END; (*IF self = set2*)
  RETURN res
END Intersection;

PROCEDURE Union(self : T; set2 : T) : T =                          (*self ∨ set2*)
VAR res: T := NEW(T).init(self.num + set2.num + (MinSize DIV 2));
BEGIN
  Add(res, self); Add(res, set2); RETURN res
END Union;

PROCEDURE Sort(self: T; compare: Elem.Compare): ObjList.T =
                            (*from set self, creates a list sorted by compare*)
VAR list: ObjList.T:= NEW(ObjList.T).init(compare); obj: Node;
BEGIN
  IF self.num > 0 THEN
    FOR b:= FIRST(self.a^) TO LAST(self.a^) DO
      obj:= self.a[b];
      WHILE obj # NIL DO
        list.insert(obj.e); obj:=obj.next         (*insertion in list ensures sorting*)
      END (*WHILE obj*)
    END (*FOR b*)
  END; (*IF self*)
  RETURN list
END Sort;

BEGIN
END Set.
```

```
MODULE ObjList;                                                  (*23.02.95. LB*)

  IMPORT Elem;

  REVEAL                                            (*inner structure of T revealed*)
    T = Public BRANDED OBJECT
          head: Node := NIL;                                    (*head of list*)
          compare: Elem.Compare := NIL;                       (*order function*)
          num: CARDINAL := 0;                            (*number of elements*)
```

```
   OVERRIDES
     init:= Init;
     insert:= Insert;
     delete:= Delete;
     equal:= Equal;
     apply:= Apply;
     select:= Select;
     exists:= Exists;
     size:= Size;
   END; (*T*)

TYPE
  Node = REF RECORD
            e: Elem.T;
            next: Node := NIL;
          END; (*node*)

PROCEDURE Init(list: T; compare: Elem.Compare): T =
BEGIN
  list.head:= NIL; list.compare:= compare; list.num:= 0;
  RETURN list;
END Init;

PROCEDURE Insert(list: T; elem: Elem.T) =                  (*inserts keeping order*)
VAR new: Node := NEW(Node, e:= elem);                        (*create new node*)

  PROCEDURE I(VAR x: Node) =
  BEGIN
    IF x = NIL THEN x:= new; INC(list.num);                      (*insert at head*)
    ELSIF list.compare # NIL AND list.compare(elem, x.e) = -1 THEN
      new.next:= x; x:= new; INC(list.num);             (*insert at correct position*)
    ELSE I(x.next);                                 (*continue searching recursively*)
    END; (*IF x = NIL*)
  END I;

BEGIN I(list.head)
END Insert;

PROCEDURE Delete(list: T; elem: Elem.T): Elem.T =
                              (*delete and return elem if present, else return NIL*)

  PROCEDURE D(VAR x: Node): Elem.T =
  VAR e: Elem.T;
  BEGIN
    IF x = NIL THEN RETURN NIL                              (*element not present*)
    ELSIF (list.compare = NIL) OR (list.compare(elem, x.e) = 0) THEN
      e:= x.e; x:= x.next; DEC(list.num); RETURN e              (*found and deleted*)
    ELSE RETURN D(x.next)                           (*continue searching recursively*)
    END; (*IF x = NIL*)
  END D;

BEGIN RETURN D(list.head)
END Delete;
```

```
PROCEDURE Equal(list: T; list2: T; compare: Elem.Compare): BOOLEAN =
                              (*compares two lists for equality or identity of elements*)
VAR x: Node := list.head; y: Node := list2.head;
BEGIN
   WHILE (x # NIL) AND (y # NIL) AND
      (((compare = NIL) AND (x.e = y.e)) OR           (*equal references*)
      ((compare # NIL) AND (compare(x.e, y.e) = 0))) DO   (*equal by criterion*)
         x:= x.next; y:= y.next;
   END;
      RETURN (x = NIL) AND (y = NIL)            (*both lists exhausted: equal*)
END Equal;

PROCEDURE Exists(list: T; s: Elem.Selector): Elem.T =      (*selects one element*)
VAR x: Node := list.head;
BEGIN
   IF s = NIL THEN RETURN x.e         (*no selection criterion: return first element*)
   ELSE
      WHILE (x # NIL) AND (NOT s.select(x.e)) DO x:= x.next END;
      IF x = NIL THEN RETURN NIL ELSE RETURN x.e END;
   END; (*IF s = NIL*)
END Exists;

PROCEDURE Select(list: T; s: Elem.Selector): T =               (*select sublist*)
VAR x: Node := list.head; res: T := NEW(T).init(list.compare);
BEGIN
   WHILE x # NIL DO
      IF (s = NIL) OR s.select(x.e) THEN
         res.insert(x.e)             (*if selection criterion fulfilled or not specified*)
      END;
      x:= x.next;
   END; (*WHILE x*)
   RETURN res
END Select;

PROCEDURE Apply(list: T; a: Elem.Action) =      (*applies a.action to all elements*)
VAR x: Node := list.head;
BEGIN
   WHILE x # NIL DO
      a.action(x.e); x:= x.next
   END;
END Apply;

PROCEDURE Size(list: T): CARDINAL =                        (*length of list*)
BEGIN
   RETURN list.num
END Size;

BEGIN                                                    (*ObjList *)
END ObjList.
```

```
MODULE Selection;                                                    (*08.04.95. LB*)

   IMPORT Elem, Person, Composer, Work, CD, Texts;

   REVEAL
     Selector = SelPub BRANDED OBJECT OVERRIDES select:= Select END;

   PROCEDURE CheckName(t: TEXT; p: Person.T): BOOLEAN =
                      (*checks names in both formats: firstname lastname and vice versa*)
   BEGIN
     RETURN Texts.Part(t, p.name & p.firstname) OR Texts.Part(t, p.firstname & p.name)
   END CheckName;

   PROCEDURE Select(s: Selector; e: Elem.T): BOOLEAN =       (*various selections*)
   BEGIN
     TYPECASE e OF
       | CD.T(cd) =>                       (* kinds of selection: by identifier or by works*)
           IF s.kind = Kind.Identifier THEN
              RETURN Texts.Part(s.t, cd.identifier);             (*check identifier*)
           ELSE                              (*continue search in list of works*)
              RETURN cd.works.select(s).size() > 0;
                          (*returns true if at least one element in the list is selected*)
           END; (*IF s.kind = Kind.Identifier*)
       | Work.T(work) =>             (*kinds of selection: by title, composers, performers*)
           CASE s.kind OF
           | Kind.Title =>
              RETURN Texts.Part(s.t, work.title);                (*check work title*)
           | Kind.Comp, Kind.Style =>           (*continue search in list of composers*)
              RETURN work.composers.select(s).size() > 0;
                          (*returns true if at least one element in the list was selected*)
           | Kind.Perf =>                        (*continue search in list of performers*)
              RETURN work.performers.select(s).size() > 0;
                          (*returns true if at least one element in the list was selected*)
           ELSE RETURN FALSE                    (*return false for unexpected kind*)
           END; (*CASE s.kind*)
       | Composer.T(composer) =>             (*kinds of selection: by style or name*)
           IF s.kind = Kind.Style THEN
              RETURN s.style = composer.style
           ELSE
              RETURN CheckName(s.t, composer);         (*check composer names*)
           END; (*IF s.kind = Kind.Style*)
       | Person.T(person) =>                 (*kind of selection: by performer name*)
           RETURN CheckName(s.t, person);              (*check names*)
       ELSE RETURN FALSE                       (*return false for unexpected kind*)
     END; (*TYPECASE e OF*)
   END Select;

BEGIN
END Selection.
```

```
MODULE Database;                                              (*08.03.95. LB*)

  IMPORT Persistent. Set, Startup;               (*Startup must be imported!*)
  VAR
    cds:= NEW(Persistent.Refany,
          key:= "Database.cds", val:= NEW(Set.T).init(500)).setup();
    composers:= NEW(Persistent.Refany,
          key:= "Database.composers", val:= NEW(Set.T).init(500)).setup();
    performers:= NEW(Persistent.Refany,
          key:= "Database.performers", val:= NEW(Set.T).init(1000)).setup();

  PROCEDURE CDs(): Set.T =
  BEGIN
    RETURN cds.val
  END CDs;

  PROCEDURE Composers(): Set.T =
  BEGIN
    RETURN composers.val
  END Composers;

  PROCEDURE Performers(): Set.T =
  BEGIN
    RETURN performers.val
  END Performers;

BEGIN
END Database.
```

```
MODULE Startup;                                              (*15.03.95. LB*)
  IMPORT Persistent;
BEGIN
  Persistent.Start("DB", "DB");            (*read persistent variables from DB*)
END Startup.
```

```
MODULE Texts;       (*Auxiliary module for text and command handling. 29.03.05. LB*)

  FROM Text IMPORT Equal, Length, Sub, FromChar, GetChar;
  IMPORT In, SIO;

  PROCEDURE MenuOutput(READONLY menu: ARRAY OF TEXT) =
  CONST Sep = " / ";
  BEGIN
    FOR i:= FIRST(menu) TO LAST(menu) DO
      IF (i + 1) MOD 6 = 0 THEN SIO.Nl() END;     (*new line after 6 commands*)
      SIO.PutText(menu[i] & Sep);
    END;
  END MenuOutput;
```

```
PROCEDURE CommandIn(READONLY menu: ARRAY OF TEXT;): INTEGER =
                    (*outputs menu and reads unambiguous short command from menu*)
VAR line: TEXT; index: INTEGER;
BEGIN
  TRY
    REPEAT                            (*outputs menu until correct selection or default*)
      MenuOutput(menu);
      line:= SIO.GetLine();
      IF In.Default(line) THEN index:= −1
      ELSE
        index:= Search(line, menu);
        IF index < 0 THEN SIO.PutLine("unknown or ambiguous") END;
      END; (*IF In.Default(line)*)
    UNTIL In.Default(line) OR (index >= 0);
    RETURN index;
  EXCEPT SIO.Error => SIO.PutLine("error in Command.Input"); RETURN −1
  END; (*TRY*)
END CommandIn;

PROCEDURE Convert(t: TEXT): TEXT =
                        (*converts lower case to upper case and filters out blanks*)
CONST Code = ORD('A') − ORD('a');              (*difference upper - lower case*)
  Lower = SET OF CHAR{'a' .. 'z'}; Blanks = SET OF CHAR{' ', '\t'};
VAR t2: TEXT := ""; ch: CHAR;
BEGIN
  FOR i:= 0 TO Length(t) − 1 DO
    ch:= GetChar(t, i);
    IF ch IN Lower THEN                          (*convert lower to upper case*)
      t2:= t2 & FromChar(VAL(ORD(ch) + Code, CHAR));
    ELSIF NOT (ch IN Blanks) THEN                (*filter out blanks*)
      t2:= t2 & FromChar(ch);
    END; (*IF (ch IN Lower)*)
  END; (*FOR i*)
  RETURN t2
END Convert;

PROCEDURE Search(text: TEXT; in: ARRAY OF TEXT;): INTEGER =
              (*if text is found exactly once in in: returns its index, else returns -1*)
VAR index:= 0; found := 0; position: INTEGER;
BEGIN
  text:= Convert(text);                    (*convert letters in text and in to upper case*)
  FOR i:= FIRST(in) TO LAST(in) DO in[i]:= Convert(in[i]) END;
  WHILE (index < NUMBER(in)) AND (found < 2) DO
    IF Part(text, in[index]) THEN position:= index; INC(found) END;
    INC(index);
  END; (*WHILE (index...*)
  IF found = 1 THEN RETURN position ELSE RETURN − 1 END;
END Search;
```

```
PROCEDURE Part(t1, t2: TEXT): BOOLEAN =              (*true if t1 is part of t2*)
BEGIN
  t1:= Convert(t1); t2:= Convert(t2);
  RETURN Equal(t1, Sub(t2, 0, Length(t1)))
END Part;
BEGIN
END Texts.
```

```
MODULE Input EXPORTS Main;                            (*30.03.95. LB*)
  IMPORT Persistent, Database, Elem, ObjList, Text, Selection,
    CD, Person, SIO, SF, In, Set, Texts;
  FROM SIO IMPORT Reader, Writer, GetLine, PutText, PutLine, PutInt, Nl;

  PROCEDURE Add() =                                   (*add new CDs to CD set*)
  VAR cd: CD.T; rd: Reader := SF.OpenRead();
  BEGIN
    TRY                       (*on input error, procedure returns after error message*)
      TRY                         (*file should be closed even in case of error*)
        REPEAT                             (*reads a series of CDs*)
          cd:= NEW(CD.T).init();
          cd:= cd.input(Database.CDs(), rd);    (*reads CD data and adds to database*)
        UNTIL cd = NIL;
      FINALLY SF.CloseRead(rd);
      END; (*TRY*)
    EXCEPT
    | SIO.Error =>         IF cd # NIL THEN Database.CDs().delete(cd) END;
                          PutLine("\nError in adding CD");
    | Elem.Error(text) => IF cd # NIL THEN Database.CDs().delete(cd) END;
                          PutLine("\nError in adding CD->" & text);
    END; (*TRY*)
  END Add;

  TYPE
    DeleteAction = Elem.Action OBJECT                 (*closure around delete action*)
                    cdset: Set.T;
                  OVERRIDES
                    action:= Delete;
                  END; (*DeleteAction*)

  PROCEDURE Delete(a: DeleteAction; e: Elem.T) =      (*interactive delete action*)
  VAR t: TEXT;
  BEGIN
    TRY                       (*on input error, procedure returns after error message*)
      e.output();                             (*display CD or composer or performer*)
      PutText(" Do you really want to delete? yes/no ");
      t:= GetLine();
      IF NOT In.Default(t) AND Texts.Part(t, "yes") THEN
        a.cdset.delete(e); PutLine(" -!- deleted -!- ");
      END; (*IF NOT In.Default...*)
    EXCEPT SIO.Error => SIO.PutLine("\nError during deletion")
    END; (*TRY*)
  END Delete;
```

```
PROCEDURE FileDelete() =                              (*deletion from persistent set*)
TYPE CDset = {CDs, Comp, Perf};
CONST Menu = ARRAY CDset OF TEXT{"CDs", "Composers", "Performers"};
VAR t: TEXT; index: INTEGER;
  candidates: ObjList.T;                              (*candidates for deletion*)
  cdset: Set.T;                                       (*set from which to delete*)
  cmp: Elem.Compare;           (*comparison function to sort candidates for deletion*)
  selector := NEW(Selection.Selector);               (*selects candidates for deletion*)
  output := NEW(OutputAction);
  delete := NEW(DeleteAction);
BEGIN
  TRY                          (*on input error, procedure returns after error message*)
    REPEAT
      SIO.PutText("Delete from set ");
      index:= Texts.CommandIn(Menu);
      IF index >= 0 THEN                              (*valid command*)
        PutText("What is to be deleted (! for all)? ");
        t:= GetLine(); selector.t:= t;                (*search text specified*)
        IF NOT In.Default(t) THEN                     (*set delete parameter*)
          CASE VAL(index, CDset) OF
          | CDset.CDs => cdset:= Database.CDs();
              cmp:= CD.Compare;
              selector.kind:= Selection.Kind.Identifier;
          | CDset.Comp => cdset:= Database.Composers();
              cmp:= Person.Compare;
              selector.kind:= Selection.Kind.Comp;
          | CDset.Perf => cdset:= Database.Performers();
              cmp:= Person.Compare;
              selector.kind:= Selection.Kind.Perf;
          END; (*CASE VAL(index, CDset)*)
          IF Text.Equal(t, "!") THEN                  (*entire set suggested for deletion*)
            candidates:= cdset.sort(cmp);
          ELSE                                        (*candidates are selected*)
            candidates:= cdset.select(selector).sort(cmp);
          END; (*IF Text.Equal*)
          PutInt(candidates.size());
          PutLine(" Candidates for deletion:");
          IF candidates.size() > 0 THEN
            candidates.apply(output);                 (*display candidates for deletion*)
            delete.cdset:= cdset;                     (*set action parameter*)
            candidates.apply(delete);                 (*apply delete action*)
          END; (*IF candidates.size() ¿ 0*)
        END; (*IF NOT In.Default*)
      END; (*IF index >= 0*)
    UNTIL (index < 0) OR In.Default(t) ;
  EXCEPT
  | SIO.Error => PutLine("\nError during deletion");
  | Elem.Error(text) => PutLine("\nError during deletion->" & text);
  END; (*TRY*)
END FileDelete;
```

```
TYPE
  OutputAction = Elem.Action OBJECT
                    w: Writer := NIL;
                    OVERRIDES
                    action:= Output;
                    END; (*OutputAction*)

PROCEDURE Output(a: OutputAction; e: Elem.T) =              (*applied to every CD*)
BEGIN
  e.output(a.w); Nl(a.w);
END Output;

PROCEDURE SortedOutput (cdset: Set.T; cmp: Elem.Compare;
                    wr: Writer := NIL) =              (*outputs sorted set*)
VAR list: ObjList.T; output:= NEW(OutputAction, w:= wr);
BEGIN
  TRY                                      (*close file even in case of error*)
    list:= cdset.sort(cmp);
    list.apply(output);
    PutText("Total number: ", wr); PutInt(cdset.size(), 1, wr);
    PutLine("\n————————————————————————————", wr);
  FINALLY SF.CloseWrite(wr);
  END; (*TRY*)
END SortedOutput;

PROCEDURE CommandInput() =              (*reads and interprets user commands*)
TYPE Commands = {Input, Delete, Output};
CONST CommandMenu = ARRAY Commands OF TEXT {"Input", "Delete", "Output"};
VAR commandIndex: INTEGER;
BEGIN
  REPEAT
    commandIndex:= Texts.CommandIn(CommandMenu);
    IF commandIndex >= 0 THEN
      CASE VAL(commandIndex, Commands) OF
      | Commands.Input   => Add()                      (*enter new CDs*)
      | Commands.Delete => FileDelete()                (*delete from a set*)
      | Commands.Output =>                             (*output set of CDs*)
            SortedOutput(Database.CDs(), CD.Compare, SF.OpenWrite())
      END; (*CASE VAL(commandIndex, Command)*)
    END; (*IF commandIndex*)
  UNTIL commandIndex < 0;
  PutLine("End of data entry —- thanks!");
END CommandInput;

PROCEDURE Save() =
  VAR t: TEXT;
BEGIN
  REPEAT                           (*user decides whether to save – no default!*)
    SIO.PutLine("Save changes? yes/no");
    t:= SIO.GetLine();
  UNTIL (Texts.Part(t, "no") OR Texts.Part(t, "yes")) AND NOT In.Default(t);
  IF Texts.Part(t, "yes") THEN Persistent.End() END;
END Save;
```

```
BEGIN
  CommandInput();                              (*read and execute command*)
  Save();                                      (*make any changes permanent*)
END Input.
```

```
MODULE In;                    (*Auxiliary module for input handling 28.03.95. LB*)
  IMPORT SIO, Stdio, Text;

  PROCEDURE Interactive(rd: SIO.Reader): BOOLEAN =      (*true for standard input*)
    BEGIN    RETURN (rd = NIL) OR (rd = Stdio.stdin)
    END Interactive;

  PROCEDURE Default(t: TEXT): BOOLEAN =                      (*true for default text*)
    BEGIN    RETURN (Text.Length(t) = 0) OR (Text.GetChar(t, 0) = Delimiter)
    END Default;

BEGIN
END In.
```

```
MODULE Queries EXPORTS Main;                                       (*29.03.95. LB*)

  IMPORT Composer, Database, CD, Person, ObjList,
         SIO, SF, Set, In, Elem, Texts, Selection;

  TYPE OutputAction = Elem.Action OBJECT w: SIO.Writer := NIL END;

  PROCEDURE Output(a: OutputAction; e: Elem.T) =                (*applied to every CD*)
    BEGIN    e.output(a.w); SIO.Nl(a.w);
    END Output;

  PROCEDURE SortedOutput(cdset: Set.T; cmp: Elem.Compare; wr: SIO.Writer) =
  VAR list: ObjList.T; output:= NEW(OutputAction, w:= wr, action:= Output);
  BEGIN
    list:= cdset.sort(cmp);
    list.apply(output);
    SIO.PutText("Total number: ", wr);
    SIO.PutInt(list.size(), 1, wr); SIO.Nl(wr);
  END SortedOutput;

  PROCEDURE All(command: Global; wr: SIO.Writer:= NIL) =        (*output whole sets*)
  VAR cdset: Set.T; cmp: Elem.Compare;
  BEGIN
    CASE command OF
    | Commands.CDs            => cdset:= Database.CDs();
                                 cmp:= CD.Compare;
    | Commands.Composers      => cdset:= Database.Composers();
                                 cmp:= Person.Compare;
    | Commands.Performers     => cdset:= Database.Performers();
                                 cmp:= Person.Compare;
    END; (*CASE command*)
    SortedOutput(cdset, cmp, wr);
  END All;
```

```
PROCEDURE Search(command: Seek; wr: SIO.Writer:= NIL) =        (*start selections*)
CONST Menu = ARRAY Seek OF TEXT {"CD Identifier", "Title",
        "Composer Name", "Style", "Performer Name"};
VAR t: TEXT; cds: Set.T; index: INTEGER; style := Composer.Style.none;
  selector := NEW(Selection.Selector);
BEGIN
  SIO.PutText(Menu[command] & ": ");
  IF command = Commands.S_Style THEN                          (*selection by style*)
    index:= Texts.CommandIn(Composer.StyleText);                   (*read style*)
    IF index >= 0 THEN style:= VAL(index, Composer.Style) END
  ELSE                                    (*other selections: all selected by text*)
    t:= SIO.GetLine();
    IF In.Default(t) THEN index:= −1
    ELSE selector.t:= t; index:= 0               (*set search text; set index non-negative*)
    END; (*IF Input.Default(t)*)
  END; (*IF command = Commands.S_Style*)
  IF index >= 0 THEN                               (*valid command specified*)
    CASE command OF
    | Commands.S_Identifier =>                          (*select by CD identifier*)
        selector.kind:= Selection.Kind.Identifier;
    | Commands.S_Work =>                                  (*select by work title*)
        selector.kind:= Selection.Kind.Title;
    | Commands.S_Composer =>                          (*select by composer name*)
        selector.kind:= Selection.Kind.Comp;
    | Commands.S_Style =>                             (*select by composer style*)
        selector.kind:= Selection.Kind.Style; selector.style:= style;
    | Commands.S_Performers =>                         (*select by performer name*)
        selector.kind:= Selection.Kind.Perf;
    END; (*CASE command*)
    cds:= Database.CDs().select(selector);                  (*select from CDs*)
    SortedOutput(cds, CD.Compare, wr);       (*output CDs sorted alphabetically*)
  END; (*IF index ¿= 0*)
END Search;

TYPE
  Commands = {CDs, Composers, Performers, NewFile,
              S_Identifier, S_Work, S_Composer, S_Style, S_Performers};
  Seek      = [Commands.S_Identifier .. Commands.S_Performers];
  Global    = [Commands.CDs .. Commands.Performers];
CONST
  Menu = ARRAY Commands OF TEXT
          {"CDs", "Composers", "Performers", "NewFile",
           "S_Identifier", "S_Work", "S_Composer", "S_Style", "S_Performers"};
```

```
  PROCEDURE CommandInput() =                          (*read user commands*)
  VAR wr: SIO.Writer := NIL;
    command: Commands; index: INTEGER;
  BEGIN
    REPEAT
      index:= Texts.CommandIn(Menu);
      IF index >= 0 THEN
        command:= VAL(index, Commands);
        CASE command OF
        | Commands.CDs .. Commands.Performers        => All(command, wr);
        | Commands.S_Identifier .. Commands.S_Performers => Search(command, wr);
        | Commands.NewFile                           =>        (*change file*)
            SF.CloseWrite(wr); wr:= SF.OpenWrite();
        END; (*CASE command*)
      END; (*IF index>= 0*)
    UNTIL index < 0;
    SF.CloseWrite(wr);
  END CommandInput;

BEGIN
  CommandInput()
END Queries.
```

Appendix B

Language Definition[1]

B.1 Definitions

A Modula-3 program specifies a computation that acts on a sequence of digital components called *locations*. A *variable* is a set of locations that represents a mathematical value according to a convention determined by the variable's *type*. If a value can be represented by some variable of type T, then we say that the value is a *member* of T and T *contains* the value.

An *identifier* is a symbol declared as a name for a variable, type, procedure, etc. The region of the program over which a declaration applies is called the *scope* of the declaration. Scopes can be nested. The meaning of an identifier is determined by the smallest enclosing scope in which the identifier is declared.

An *expression* specifies a computation that produces a value or variable. Expressions that produce variables are called *designators*. A designator can denote either a variable or the value of that variable, depending on the context. Some designators are *readonly*, which means that they cannot be used in contexts that might change the value of the variable. A designator that is not readonly is called *writable*. Expressions whose values can be determined statically are called *constant expressions*; they are never designators.

A *static error* is an error that the implementation must detect before program execution. Violations of the language definition are static errors unless they are explicitly classified as runtime errors.

A *checked runtime error* is an error that the implementation must detect and report at runtime. The method for reporting such errors is implementation-dependent. (If the implementation maps them into exceptions, then a program could handle these exceptions and continue.)

An *unchecked runtime error* is an error that is not guaranteed to be detected, and can cause the subsequent behavior of the computation to be arbitrary. Unchecked runtime errors can occur only in unsafe modules.

---

[1]This appendix is copyright by Digital Equipment Corporation and appears here with their permission.

B.2   Types

Modula-3 uses structural equivalence, instead of the name equivalence of
Modula-2. Two types are the same if their definitions become the same
when expanded; that is, when all constant expressions are replaced by their
values and all type names are replaced by their definitions. In the case of
recursive types, the expansion is the infinite limit of the partial expansions.
A type expression is generally allowed wherever a type is required.

A type is *empty* if it contains no values. For example, [1..0] is an empty
type. Empty types can be used to build non-empty types (for example, SET
OF [1..0], which is not empty because it contains the empty set). It is a
static error to declare a variable of an empty type.

Every expression has a statically-determined type, which contains every value that the expression can produce. The type of a designator is the
type of the variable it produces.

Assignability and type compatibility are defined in terms of a single
syntactically specified subtype relation with the property that if T is a subtype of U, then every member of T is a member of U. The subtype relation
is reflexive and transitive.

Every expression has a unique type, but a value can be a member of
many types. For example, the value 6 is a member of both [0..9] and INTE-
GER. It would be ambiguous to talk about "the type of a value". Thus the
phrase "type of x" means "type of the expression x", while "x is a member of
T" means "the value of x is a member of T".

However, there is one sense in which a value can be said to have a type:
every object or traced reference value includes a code for a type, called
the *allocated type* of the reference value. The allocated type is tested by
TYPECASE (Section ($\rightarrow$*B.3.18, p. 492*)).

B.2.1   Ordinal types

There are three kinds of ordinal types: enumerations, subranges, and IN-
TEGER. An enumeration type is declared like this:

TYPE T = {$id_1, id_2, \cdots, id_n$}

where the *id*'s are distinct identifiers. The type T is an ordered set of n
values; the expression T.id_i denotes the i'th value of the type in increasing
order. The empty enumeration { } is allowed.

Integers and enumeration elements are collectively called *ordinal values*. The *base type* of an ordinal value v is INTEGER if v is an integer,
otherwise it is the unique enumeration type that contains v.

A subrange type is declared like this:

    TYPE T = [Lo..Hi]

where Lo and Hi are two ordinal values with the same base type, called the base type of the subrange. The values of T are all the values from Lo to Hi inclusive. Lo and Hi must be constant expressions ($\rightarrow$*B.6.15, p. 516*). If Lo exceeds Hi, the subrange is empty.

The operators ORD and VAL convert between enumerations and integers. The operators FIRST, LAST, and NUMBER applied to an ordinal type return the first element, last element, and number of elements, respectively (Section B.6.13, page 514).

Here are the predeclared ordinal types:

INTEGER	All integers represented by the implementation
CARDINAL	The subrange [0..LAST(INTEGER)]
BOOLEAN	The enumeration {FALSE, TRUE}
CHAR	An enumeration containing at least 256 elements

The first 256 elements of type CHAR represent characters in the ISO-Latin-1 code, which is an extension of ASCII. The language does not specify the names of the elements of the CHAR enumeration. The syntax for character literals is in Section B.6.5, page 508. FALSE and TRUE are predeclared synonyms for BOOLEAN.FALSE and BOOLEAN.TRUE.

Each distinct enumeration type introduces a new collection of values, but a subrange type reuses the values from the underlying type. For example:

    TYPE
        T1 = {A, B, C};
        T2 = {A, B, C};
        U1 = [T1.A..T1.C];
        U2 = [T1.A..T2.C]; (* *sic* *)
        V = {A, B}

T1 and T2 are the same type, since they have the same expanded definition. In particular, T1.C = T2.C and therefore U1 and U2 are also the same type. But the types T1 and U1 are distinct, although they contain the same values, because the expanded definition of T1 is an enumeration while the expanded definition of U1 is a subrange. The type V is a third type whose values V.A and V.B are not related to the values T1.A and T1.B.

B.2.2 Floating-point types

There are three floating point types, which in order of increasing range and precision are REAL, LONGREAL, and EXTENDED. The properties of these types are specified by required interfaces in Section C.1.5, page 530.

B.2.3 Arrays

An *array* is an indexed collection of component variables, called the *elements* of the array. The indexes are the values of an ordinal type, called the *index type* of the array. The elements all have the same size and the same type, called the *element type* of the array.

There are two kinds of array types, *fixed* and *open*. The length of a fixed array is determined at compile time. The length of an open array type is determined at runtime, when it is allocated or bound. The length cannot be changed thereafter.

The *shape* of a multi-dimensional array is the sequence of its lengths in each dimension. More precisely, the shape of an array is its length followed by the shape of any of its elements; the shape of a non-array is the empty sequence.

Arrays are assignable if they have the same element type and shape. If either the source or target of the assignment is an open array, a runtime shape check is required.

A fixed array type declaration has the form:

TYPE T = ARRAY Index OF Element

where Index is an ordinal type and Element is any type other than an open array type. The values of type T are arrays whose element type is Element and whose length is the number of elements of the type Index.

If a has type T, then a[i] designates the element of a whose position corresponds to the position of i in Index. For example, consider the declarations:

VAR a := ARRAY [1..3] OF REAL {1.0, 2.0, 3.0};
VAR b: ARRAY [-1..1] OF REAL := a;

Now a = b is TRUE; yet a[1] = 1.0 while b[1] = 3.0. The interpretation of indexes is determined by an array's type, not its value; the assignment b := a changes b's value, not its type. (This example uses variable initialization, ($\rightarrow$B.4.3, p. 495), and array constructors, ($\rightarrow$B.6.8, p. 508).

An expression of the form:

ARRAY $Index_1, \cdots, Index_n$ OF Element

is shorthand for:

ARRAY $Index_1$ OF $\cdots$ OF ARRAY $Index_n$ OF Element

This shorthand is eliminated from the expanded type definition used to define structural equivalence. An expression of the form a[$i_1, \cdots, i_n$] is shorthand for a[i_1]$\cdots$[i_n].

An open array type declaration has the form:

TYPE T = ARRAY OF Element

where Element is any type. The values of T are arrays whose element type is Element and whose length is arbitrary. The index type of an open array is the integer subrange [0..n-1], where n is the length of the array.

An open array type can be used only as the type of a formal parameter, the referent of a reference type, the element type of another open array type, or as the type in an array constructor.

B.2.4 Records

A *record* is a sequence of named variables, called the *fields* of the record. Different fields can have different types. The name and type of each field is statically determined by the record's type. The expression r.f designates the field named f in the record r.

A record type declaration has the form:

TYPE T = RECORD FieldList END

where FieldList is a list of field declarations, each of which has the form:

fieldName: Type := default

where fieldName is an identifier, Type is any non-empty type other than an open array type, and default is a constant expression. The field names must be distinct. A record is a member of T if it has fields with the given names and types, in the given order, and no other fields. Empty records are allowed.

The constant default is a default value used when a record is constructed ($\rightarrow$*B.6.8, p. 509*) or allocated ($\rightarrow$*B.6.9, p. 509*). Either ":= default" or ": Type" can be omitted, but not both. If Type is omitted, it is taken to be the type of default. If both are present, the value of default must be a member of Type.

When a series of fields shares the same type and default, any fieldName can be a list of identifiers separated by commas. Such a list is shorthand for a list in which the type and default are repeated for each identifier. That is:

$f_1, \cdots, f_m$: Type := default

is shorthand for:

f_1: Type := default; $\cdots$; f_m: Type := default

This shorthand is eliminated from the expanded definition of the type. The default values are included.

B.2.5 Packed types

A declaration of a packed type has the form:

TYPE T = BITS n FOR Base

where Base is a type and n is an integer-valued constant expression. The values of type T are the same as the values of type Base, but variables of type T that occur in records, objects, or arrays will occupy exactly n bits and be packed adjacent to the preceding field or element. For example, a variable of type

ARRAY [0..255] OF BITS 1 FOR BOOLEAN

is an array of 256 booleans, each of which occupies one bit of storage.

The values allowed for n are implementation-dependent. An illegal value for n is a static error. The legality of a packed type can depend on its context; for example, an implementation could prohibit packed integers from spanning word boundaries.

B.2.6 Sets

A *set* is a collection of values taken from some ordinal type (→*B.2.1, p. 470*). A set type declaration has the form:

TYPE T = SET OF Base

where Base is an ordinal type. The values of T are all sets whose elements have type Base. For example, a variable whose type is SET OF[0..1] can assume the following values:

{}   {0}   {1}   {0,1}

Implementations are expected to use the same representation for a SET OF T as for an ARRAY T OF BITS 1 FOR BOOLEAN. Hence, programmers should expect SET OF [0..1023] to be practical, but not SET OF INTEGER.

B.2.7 References

A *reference* value is either NIL or the address of a variable, called the referent. A reference type is either *traced* or *untraced*. When all traced references to a piece of allocated storage are gone, the implementation reclaims the storage. Two reference types are of the same *reference class* if they are both traced or both untraced. A general type is traced if it is a traced reference type, a record type any of whose field types is traced, an array type whose element type is traced, or a packed type whose underlying unpacked type is traced.

A declaration for a traced reference type has the form:

TYPE T = REF Type

where Type is any type. The values of T are traced references to variables of type Type, which is called the *referent type* of T.
A declaration for an untraced reference type has the form:

TYPE T = UNTRACED REF Type

where Type is any untraced[2] type. The values of T are the untraced references to variables of type Type.

In both the traced and untraced cases, the keyword REF can optionally be preceded by "BRANDED b" where b is a text constant called the *brand*. Brands distinguish types that would otherwise be the same; they have no other semantic effect. All brands in a program must be distinct. If BRANDED is present and b is absent, the implementation automatically supplies a unique value for b. Explicit brands are useful for persistent data storage.

The following reference types are predeclared:

REFANY	Contains all traced references
ADDRESS	Contains all untraced references
NULL	Contains only NIL

The TYPECASE statement (→*B.3.18, p. 492*) can be used to test the referent type of a REFANY or object, but there is no such test for an ADDRESS.

B.2.8 Procedures

A *procedure* is either NIL or a triple consisting of:

- the *body*, which is a statement (→*B.3, p. 482*),

- the *signature*, which specifies the procedure's formal arguments, result type, and raises set (the set of exceptions that the procedure can raise),

- the *environment*, which is the scope with respect to which variable names in the body will be interpreted (*see also B.4, p. 494*).

A procedure that returns a result is called a *function procedure*; a procedure that does not return a result is called a *proper procedure*. A *top-level* procedure is a procedure declared in the outermost scope of a module. Any other procedure is a *local* procedure.

---

[2]This restriction is lifted in unsafe modules (→*B.5.6, p. 503*).

A local procedure can be passed as a parameter but not assigned, since in a stack implementation a local procedure becomes invalid when the frame for the procedure containing it is popped.

A *procedure constant* is an identifier declared as a procedure. (As opposed to a procedure variable, which is a variable declared with a procedure type.)

A procedure type declaration has the form:

TYPE T = PROCEDURE sig

where sig is a signature specification, which has the form:

$(formal_1; \cdots ; formal_n)$: R RAISES S

where

- Each *formal$_i$* is a formal parameter declaration, as described below.

- R is the result type, which can be any type but an open array type. The ": R" can be omitted, making the signature that of a proper procedure.

- S is the raises set, which is either an explicit set of exceptions with the syntax $\{E_1, \cdots, E_n\}$, or the symbol ANY representing the set of all exceptions. If " RAISES S" is omitted, "RAISES {}" is assumed.

A formal parameter declaration has the form

Mode Name: Type := Default

where

- Mode is a parameter mode, which can be VALUE, VAR, or READONLY. If Mode is omitted, it defaults to VALUE.

- Name is an identifier that names the parameter. The parameter names must be distinct.

- Type is the type of the parameter.

- Default is a constant expression, the default value for the parameter. If Mode is VAR, ":= Default" must be omitted, otherwise either ":= Default" or " : Type" can be omitted, but not both. If Type is omitted, it is taken to be the type of Default. If both are present, the value of Default must be a member of Type.

When a series of parameters share the same mode, type, and default, *name$_i$* can be a list of identifiers separated by commas. Such a list is shorthand for a list in which the mode, type, and default are repeated for each identifier. That is:

Mode $v_1, \cdots, v_n$: Type := Default

is shorthand for:

Mode v_1: Type := Default; $\cdots$; Mode v_n: Type := Default

This shorthand is eliminated from the expanded definition of the type. The default values are included.

A procedure value P is a member of the type T if it is NIL or its signature is *covered* by the signature of T, where *signature$_1$* covers *signature$_2$* if:

- They have the same number of parameters, and corresponding parameters have the same type and mode.

- They have the same result type, or neither has a result type.

- The raises set of *signature$_1$* contains the raises set of *signature$_2$*.

The parameter names and defaults affect the type of a procedure, but not its value. For example, consider the declarations:

```
PROCEDURE P(txt: TEXT := "P") =
  BEGIN
    Wr.PutText(Stdio.stdout, txt)
  END P;

VAR q: PROCEDURE(txt: TEXT := "Q") := P;
```

Now P = q is TRUE, yet P() prints "P" and q() prints "Q". The interpretation of defaulted parameters is determined by a procedure's type, not its value; the assignment q := P changes q's value, not its type.

In a procedure type, RAISES binds to the closest preceding PROCEDURE. That is, the parentheses are required in:

```
TYPE T = PROCEDURE (): (PROCEDURE ()) RAISES {}
```

B.2.9 Objects

An *object* is either NIL or a reference to a data record paired with a method suite, which is a record of procedures that will accept the object as a first argument.

An object type determines the types of a prefix of the fields of the data record, as if "OBJECT" were "REF RECORD" ($\rightarrow$B.2.7, p. 474). But in the case of an object type, the data record can contain additional fields introduced by subtypes of the object type. Similarly, the object type determines a prefix of the method suite, but the suite can contain additional methods introduced by subtypes.

If o is an object, then o.f designates the data field named f in o's data record. If m is one of o's methods, an invocation of the form o.m(...) denotes an execution of o's m method (→*B.3.2, p. 484*). An object's methods can be invoked, but not read or written.

If T is an object type and m is the name of one of T's methods, then T.m denotes T's m method. This notation makes it convenient for a subtype method to invoke the corresponding method of one of its supertypes.

A field or method in a subtype masks any field or method with the same name in the supertype. To access such a masked field, use NARROW to view the subtype variable as a member of the supertype, as illustrated on page 480.

Object assignment is reference assignment. Objects cannot be derefer-enced, since the static type of an object variable does not determine the type of its data record. To copy the data record of one object into another, the fields must be assigned individually.

There are two predeclared object types:

ROOT   The traced object type with no fields or methods
UNTRACED ROOT   The untraced object type with no fields or methods

The declaration of an object type has the form:

TYPE T =
    ST OBJECT Fields METHODS Methods OVERRIDES Overrides END

where ST is an optional supertype, Fields is a list of field declarations, ex-actly as in a record type (→*B.2.4, p. 473*), Methods is a list of *method dec-larations* and Overrides is a list of *method overrides*. The fields of T consist of the fields of ST followed by the fields declared in Fields. The methods of T consist of the methods of ST modified by Overrides and followed by the methods declared in Methods. T has the same reference class as ST.

The names introduced in Fields and Methods must be distinct from one another and from the names overridden in Overrides. If ST is omitted, it defaults to ROOT. If ST is untraced, then the fields must not include traced types.[3] If ST is declared as an opaque type (→*B.4.6, p. 496*), the declaration of T is legal only in scopes where ST's concrete type is known to be an object type.

The keyword OBJECT can optionally be preceded by "BRANDED" or by "BRANDED b", where b is a text literal. The meaning is the same as in non-object reference types (→*B.2.7, p. 474*).

A method declaration has the form:

m sig := proc

---

[3]This restriction is lifted in unsafe modules (→*B.5.6, p. 503*).

where m is an identifier, sig is a procedure signature, and proc is a top-level procedure constant. It specifies that T's m method has signature sig and value proc. If ":= proc" is omitted, ":= NIL" is assumed. If proc is non-nil, its first parameter must have mode VALUE and type some supertype of T, and dropping its first parameter must result in a signature that is covered (→*B.2.8, p. 477*) by sig.

A method override has the form:

    m := proc

where m is the name of a method of the supertype ST and proc is a top-level procedure constant. It specifies that the m method for T is proc, rather than ST.m. If proc is non-nil, its first parameter must have mode VALUE and type some supertype of T, and dropping its first parameter must result in a signature that is covered by the signature of ST's m method.

Examples. Consider the following declarations:

```
TYPE
  A = OBJECT a: INTEGER; METHODS p() END;
  AB = A OBJECT b: INTEGER END;

  PROCEDURE Pa(self: A) = ... ;
  PROCEDURE Pab(self: AB) = ... ;
```

The procedures Pa and Pab are candidate values for the p methods of objects of types A and AB. For example:

```
TYPE T1 = AB OBJECT OVERRIDES p := Pab END
```

declares a type with an AB data record and a p method that expects an AB. T1 is a valid subtype of AB. Similarly,

```
TYPE T2 = A OBJECT OVERRIDES p := Pa END
```

declares a type with an A data record and a method that expects an A. T2 is a valid subtype of A. A more interesting example is:

```
TYPE T3 = AB OBJECT OVERRIDES p := Pa END
```

which declares a type with an AB data record and a p method that expects an A. Since every AB is an A, the method is not too choosy for the objects in which it will be placed. T3 is a valid subtype of AB. In contrast,

```
TYPE T4 = A OBJECT OVERRIDES p := Pab END
```

attempts to declare a type with an A data record and a method that expects an AB; since not every A is an AB, the method is too choosy for the objects in which it would be placed. The declaration of T4 is a static error.

The following example illustrates the difference between declaring a new method and overriding an existing method. After the declarations

```
TYPE
  A = OBJECT METHODS m() := P END;
  B = A OBJECT OVERRIDES m := Q END;
  C = A OBJECT METHODS m() := Q END;

VAR
  a := NEW(A); b := NEW(B); c := NEW(C);
```

we have that

```
a.m() activates P(a)
b.m() activates Q(b)
c.m() activates Q(c)
```

So far there is no difference between overriding and extending. But c's method suite has two methods, while b's has only one, as can be revealed if b and c are viewed as members of type A:

```
NARROW(b, A).m() activates Q(b)
NARROW(c, A).m() activates P(c)
```

Here NARROW is used to view a variable of a subtype as a value of its supertype. It is more often used for the opposite purpose, when it requires a runtime check ($\rightarrow$*B.6.13, p. 514*).

B.2.10 Subtyping rules

We write T <: U to indicate that T is a subtype of U and U is a supertype of T. If T <: U, then every value of type T is also a value of type U. The converse does not hold: for example, a record or array type with packed fields contains the same values as the corresponding type with unpacked fields, but there is no subtype relation between them. This section presents the rules that define the subtyping relation. For ordinal types T and U, we have T <: U if they have the same basetype and every member of T is a member of U. That is, subtyping on ordinal types reflects the subset relation on the value sets.

For array types,

$$(ARRAY\ OF)^m\ ARRAY\ J_1\ OF\ \cdots\ ARRAY\ J_n\ OF$$
$$ARRAY\ K_1\ OF\ \cdots\ ARRAY\ K_p\ OF\ T$$
$$<:\ (ARRAY\ OF)^m\ (ARRAY\ OF)^n$$
$$ARRAY\ I_1\ OF\ \cdots\ ARRAY\ I_p\ OF\ T$$

if NUMBER(Ii) = NUMBER(Ki) for $i = 1, \cdots, p$.

That is, an array type A is a subtype of an array type A′ if they have the same ultimate element type, the same number of dimensions, and, for each dimension, either both are open (as in the first m dimensions above), or A is fixed and A′ is open (as in the next n dimensions above), or they are both fixed and have the same size (as in the last p dimensions above).

NULL <: REF T <: REFANY
NULL <: UNTRACED REF T <: ADDRESS

That is, REFANY and ADDRESS contain all traced and untraced references, respectively, and NIL is a member of every reference type. These rules also apply to branded types.

NULL <: PROCEDURE(A): R RAISES S for any A, R, and S.

That is, NIL is a member of every procedure type.

PROCEDURE(A): Q RAISES E <: PROCEDURE(B): R RAISES F
if signature (B): R RAISES F covers signature (A): Q RAISES E.

That is, for procedure types, T <: T′ if they are the same except for parameter names, defaults, and the raises set, and the raises set for T is contained in the raises set for T′.

ROOT <: REFANY
UNTRACED ROOT <: ADDRESS
NULL <: T OBJECT ... END <: T

That is, every object is a reference, NIL is a member of every object type, and every subtype is included in its supertype. The third rule also applies to branded types.

BITS n FOR T <: T and T <: BITS n FOR T

That is, BITS FOR T has the same values as T.

T <: T for all T
T <: U and U <: V implies T <: V for all T, U, V.

That is, <: is reflexive and transitive.

Note that T <: U and U <: T does not imply that T and U are the same, since the subtype relation is unaffected by parameter names, default values, and packing.

For example, consider:

```
TYPE
    T = [0..255];
    U = BITS 8 FOR [0..255];
    AT = ARRAY OF T;
    AU = ARRAY OF U;
```

The types T and U are subtypes of one another but are not the same. The types AT and AU are unrelated by the subtype relation.

B.2.11 Predeclared opaque types

The language predeclares the two types:

```
TEXT <: REFANY
MUTEX <: ROOT
```

which represent text strings and mutual exclusion semaphores, respectively. These are opaque types as defined in Section B.4.6, page 496. Their properties are specified in the required interfaces Text (→*C.1.1, p. 525*) and Thread (→*C.1.2, p. 527*).

B.3 Statements

Executing a statement produces a computation that can halt (normal outcome), raise an exception, cause a checked runtime error, or loop forever. If the outcome is an exception, it can optionally be paired with an argument.

We define the semantics of EXIT and RETURN with exceptions called the *exit-exception* and the *return-exception*. The exit-exception takes no argument; the return-exception takes an argument of arbitrary type. Programs cannot name these exceptions explicitly.

Implementations should speed up normal outcomes at the expense of exceptions (except for the return-exception and exit-exception). Expending a thousand instructions per exception raised to save one instruction per procedure call would be reasonable.

If an expression is evaluated as part of the execution of a statement, and the evaluation raises an exception, then the exception becomes the outcome of the statement.

The empty statement is a no-op. In this report, empty statements are written (*skip*).

B.3.1 Assignment

To specify the typechecking of assignment statements we need to define "assignable", which is a relation between types and types, between expressions and variables, and between expressions and types.

A type T is *assignable* to a type U if:

- T <: U, or

- U <: T and T is an array or a reference type other than ADDRESS[4], or

- T and U are ordinal types with at least one member in common.

An expression e is *assignable* to a variable v if:

- the type of e is assignable to the type of v, and

- the value of e is a member of the type of v, is not a local procedure, and if it is an array, then it has the same shape as v.

The first point can be checked statically; the others generally require runtime checks. Since there is no way to determine statically whether the value of a procedure parameter is local or global, assigning a local procedure is a runtime rather than a static error.

An expression e is *assignable* to a type T if e is assignable to some variable of type T. (If T is not an open array type, this is the same as saying that e is assignable to any variable of type T.)

An assignment statement has the form:

```
v := e
```

where v is a writable designator and e is an expression assignable to the variable designated by v. The statement sets v to the value of e. The order of evaluation of v and e is undefined, but e will be evaluated before v is updated. In particular, if v and e are overlapping subarrays (→*B.6.3, p. 507*), the assignment is performed in such a way that no element is used as a target before it is used as a source.

Examples of assignments:

```
VAR
    x: REFANY;
    a: REF INTEGER;
    b: REF BOOLEAN;

    a := b; (* static error *)
    x := a; (* no possible error *)
    a := x  (* possible checked runtime error *)
```

---

[4]This restriction is lifted in unsafe modules (→*B.5.6, p. 503*).

The same comments would apply if x had an ordinal type with non-overlapping subranges a and b, or if x had an object type and a and b had incompatible subtypes. The type ADDRESS is treated differently from other reference types, since a runtime check cannot be performed on the assignment of raw addresses. For example:

```
VAR
  x: ADDRESS;
  a: UNTRACED REF INTEGER;
  b: UNTRACED REF BOOLEAN;

  a := b; (* static error *)
  x := a; (* no possible error *)
  a := x  (* static error in safe modules *)
```

B.3.2   Procedure call

A procedure call has the form:

P(Bindings)

where P is a procedure-valued expression and Bindings is a list of *keyword* or *positional* bindings. A keyword binding has the form name := actual, where actual is an expression and name is an identifier. A positional binding has the form actual, where actual is an expression. When keyword and positional bindings are mixed in a call, the positional bindings must precede the keyword bindings. If the list of bindings is empty, the parentheses are still required.

The list of bindings is rewritten to fit the signature of P's type as follows: First, each positional binding actual is converted and added to the list of keyword bindings by supplying the name of the i'th formal parameter, where actual is the i'th binding in Bindings. Second, for each parameter that has a default and is not bound after the first step, the binding name := default is added to the list of bindings, where name is the name of the parameter and default is its default value. The rewritten list of bindings must bind only formal parameters and must bind each formal parameter exactly once. For example, suppose that the type of P ($\rightarrow$*B.2.8, p. 475*) is

PROCEDURE(ch: CHAR; n: INTEGER := 0)

Then the following calls are all equivalent:

```
P('a', 0)
P('a')
P(ch := 'a')
P(n := 0, ch := 'a')
P('a', n := 0)
```

The call P() is illegal, since it doesn't bind ch. The call P(n := 0, 'a') is illegal, since it has a keyword parameter before a positional parameter.

For a READONLY or VALUE parameter, the actual can be any expression assignable to the type of the formal (except that the prohibition against assigning local procedures is relaxed). For a VAR parameter, the actual must be a writable designator whose type is the same (→*B.2, p. 470*) as that of the formal, or, in case of a VAR array parameter, assignable to that of the formal. Designators are defined in Section (→*B.6.3, p. 506*).

A VAR formal is bound to the variable designated by the corresponding actual; that is, it is aliased. A VALUE formal is bound to a variable with an unused location and initialized to the value of the corresponding actual. A READONLY formal is treated as a VAR formal if the actual is a designator and the type of the actual is the same as the type of the formal (or an array type that is assignable to the type of the formal); otherwise it is treated as a VALUE formal.

Implementations are allowed to forbid VAR or READONLY parameters of packed types.

To execute the call, the procedure P and its arguments are evaluated, the formal parameters are bound, and the body of the procedure is executed. The order of evaluation of P and its actual arguments is undefined. It is a checked runtime error to call an undefined or NIL procedure.

It is a checked runtime error for a procedure to raise an exception not included in its raises set[5] or for a function procedure to fail to return a result.

A procedure call is a statement only if the procedure is proper (→*B.2.8, p. 475*). To call a function procedure and discard its result, use EVAL.

A procedure call can also have the form:

    o.m(Bindings)

where o is an object and m names one of o's methods. This is equivalent to:

    (o's m method) (o, Bindings)

B.3.3 Eval

An EVAL statement has the form:

    EVAL e

where e is an expression. The effect is to evaluate e and ignore the result. For example:

    EVAL Thread.Fork(p)

---

[5]If an implementation maps this runtime error into an exception, the exception is implicitly included in all RAISES clauses.

B.3.4 Block statement

A block statement has the form:

    Decls BEGIN S END

where Decls is a sequence of declarations and S is a statement. The block introduces the constants, types, variables, and procedures declared in Decls and then executes S. The scope of the declared names is the block. (See Section B.4, page 494.)

B.3.5 Sequential composition

A statement of the form:

$$S_1; S_2$$

executes S_1, and then if the outcome is normal, executes S_2. If the outcome of S_1 is an exception, S_2 is ignored.[6]

B.3.6 Raise

A RAISE statement without an argument has the form:

    RAISE e

where e is an exception that takes no argument. The outcome of the statement is the exception e. A RAISE statement with an argument has the form:

    RAISE e(x)

where e is an exception that takes an argument and x is an expression assignable to e's argument type. The outcome is the exception e paired with the argument x.

---

[6]Some programmers use the semicolon as a statement terminator, some as a statement separator. Similarly, some use the vertical bar in case statements as a case initiator, some as a separator. Modula-3 allows both styles. This report uses both operators as separators.

B.3.7 Try Except

A TRY-EXCEPT statement has the form:

```
TRY
  Body
EXCEPT
  id₁ (v₁) => Handler 1
| ···
| idₙ (vₙ) => Handler n
ELSE Handler 0
END
```

where Body and each Handler are statements, each *id* names an exception, and each v_i is an identifier. The "ELSE $Handler_0$" and each "(v_i)" are optional. It is a static error for an exception to be named more than once in the list of *id*'s.

The statement executes Body. If the outcome is normal, the except clause is ignored. If Body raises any listed exception id_i, then $Handler_i$ is executed. If Body raises any other exception and "ELSE $Handler_0$" is present, then it is executed. In either case, the outcome of the TRY statement is the outcome of the selected handler. If Body raises an unlisted exception and "ELSE $Handler_0$" is absent, then the outcome of the TRY statement is the exception raised by Body.

Each (v_i) declares a variable whose type is the argument type of the exception id_i and whose scope is $Handler_i$. When an exception id_i paired with an argument x is handled, v_i is initialized to x before $Handler_i$ is executed. It is a static error to include (v_i) if exception id_i does not take an argument.

If (v_i) is absent, then id_i can be a list of exceptions separated by commas, as shorthand for a list in which the rest of the handler is repeated for each exception. That is:

$$id_1, \cdots, id_n \text{ => Handler}$$

is shorthand for:

$$id_1 \text{ => Handler; } \cdots \text{ ; } id_n \text{ => Handler}$$

It is a checked runtime error to raise an exception outside the dynamic scope of a handler for that exception. A "TRY EXCEPT ELSE" counts as a handler for all exceptions.

B.3.8   Try Finally

A statement of the form:

TRY S_1 FINALLY S_2 END

executes statemenS_1 and then statement S_2. If the outcome of S_1 is normal, the TRY statement is equivalent to S_1; S_2. If the outcome of S_1 is an exception and the outcome of S_2 is normal, the exception from S_1 is reraised after S_2 is executed. If both outcomes are exceptions, the outcome of the TRY is the exception from S_2.

B.3.9   Loop

A statement of the form:

LOOP S END

repeatedly executes S until it raises the exit-exception. Informally it is like:

TRY S; S; S; $\cdots$ EXCEPT *exit-exception* => (*skip*) END

B.3.10   Exit

The statement

EXIT

raises the exit-exception. An EXIT statement must be textually enclosed by a LOOP, WHILE, REPEAT, or FOR statement.

We define EXIT and RETURN in terms of exceptions in order to specify their interaction with the exception handling statements. As a pathological example, consider the following code, which is an elaborate infinite loop:

```
LOOP
  TRY
    TRY EXIT FINALLY RAISE E END
  EXCEPT
    E => (*skip*)
  END
END
```

B.3.11 Return

A RETURN statement for a proper procedure ($\to$*B.2.8, p. 475*) has the form:

    RETURN

The statement raises the return-exception without an argument. It is allowed only in the body of a proper procedure.

    A RETURN statement for a function procedure ($\to$*B.2.8, p. 475*) has the form:

    RETURN Expr

where Expr is an expression assignable ($\to$*B.3.1, p. 483*) to the result type of the procedure. The statement raises the return-exception with the argument Expr. It is allowed only in the body of a function procedure.

    Failure to return a value from a function procedure is a checked runtime error.

    The effect of raising the return exception is to terminate the current procedure activation. To be precise, a call on a proper procedure with body B is equivalent (after binding the arguments) to:

    TRY B EXCEPT *return-exception* => (*skip*) END

A call on a function procedure with body B is equivalent to:

    TRY
        B; *(error: no returned value)*
    EXCEPT
        return-exception (v) => *(the result becomes* v*)*
    END

B.3.12 If

An IF statement has the form:

    IF B_1 THEN S_1
    ELSIF B_2 THEN S_2
        ...
    ELSIF B_n THEN S_n
    ELSE S_0
    END

where the B's are boolean expressions and the S's are statements. The "ELSE S_0" and each "ELSIF B_i THEN S_i" are optional.

    The statement evaluates the B's in order until some B_i evaluates to TRUE, and then executes S_i. If none of the expressions evaluates to TRUE and "ELSE S_0" is present, S_0 is executed. If none of the expressions evaluates to TRUE and "ELSE S_0" is absent, the statement is a no-op (except for any side-effects of the B's).

B.3.13 While

If B is an expression of type BOOLEAN and S is a statement:

WHILE B DO S END

is shorthand for:

LOOP IF B THEN S ELSE EXIT END END

B.3.14 Repeat

If B is an expression of type BOOLEAN and S is a statement:

REPEAT S UNTIL B

is shorthand for:

LOOP S; IF B THEN EXIT END END

B.3.15 With

A WITH statement has the form:

WITH id = e DO S END

where id is an identifier, e an expression, and S a statement. The statement declares id with scope S as an alias for the variable e or as a readonly name for the value e. The expression e is evaluated once, at entry to the WITH statement.

The statement is like the procedure call P(e), where P is declared as:

PROCEDURE P(mode id: type of e) = BEGIN S END P;

If e is a writable designator, mode is VAR; otherwise, mode is READONLY. ($\rightarrow$B.6.3, p. 506) explains designators.) The only difference between the WITH statement and the call P(e) is that free variables, RETURNs, and EXITs that occur in the WITH statement are interpreted in the context of the WITH statement, not in the context of P.

A single WITH can contain multiple bindings, which are evaluated sequentially. That is:

WITH $id_1 = e_1, id_2 = e_2, \cdots$

is equivalent to:

WITH $id_1 = e_1$ DO WITH $id_2 = e_2$ DO $\cdots$

B.3.16   For

A FOR statement has the form:

    FOR id := first TO last BY step DO S END

where id is an identifier, first and last are ordinal expressions ($\rightarrow$*B.2.1, p. 470*) with the same base type, step is an integer-valued expression, and S is a statement. "BY step" is optional; if omitted, step defaults to 1.

The identifier id denotes a readonly ($\rightarrow$*B.6.3, p. 506*) variable whose scope is S and whose type is the common basetype of first and last.

If id is an integer, the statement steps id through the values first, first + step, first+2*step, ..., stopping when the value of id passes last. S executes once for each value; if the sequence of values is empty, S never executes. The expressions first, last, and step are evaluated once, before the loop is entered. If step is negative, the loop iterates downward.

The case in which id is an element of an enumeration is similar. In either case, the semantics are defined precisely by the following rewriting, in which T is the type of id and in which i, done, and delta stand for variables that do not occur in the FOR statement:

```
VAR
  i := ORD(first); done := ORD(last); delta := step;
BEGIN
  IF delta >= 0 THEN
    WHILE i <= done DO
      WITH id = VAL(i, T) DO S END; INC(i, delta)
    END
  ELSE
    WHILE i >= done DO
      WITH id = VAL(i, T) DO S END; INC(i, delta)
    END
  END
END
```

If the upper bound of the loop is LAST(INTEGER), it should be rewritten as a WHILE loop to avoid overflow.

B.3.17 Case

A CASE statement has the form:

```
CASE Expr OF
    L₁ => S₁
| ...
| Lₙ => Sₙ
ELSE S₀
END
```

where Expr is an expression whose type is an ordinal type and each L is a list of constant expressions or ranges of constant expressions denoted by "$e_1..e_2$", which represent the values from e_1 to e_2 inclusive. If e_1 exceeds e_2, the range is empty. It is a static error if the sets represented by any two L's overlap or if the value of any of the constant expressions is not a member of the type of Expr. The "ELSE S_0" is optional.

The statement evaluates Expr. If the resulting value is in any L_i, then S_i is executed. If the value is in no L_i and "ELSE S_0" is present, then it is executed. If the value is in no L_i and "ELSE S_0" is absent, a checked runtime error occurs.

B.3.18 Typecase

A TYPECASE statement has the form:

```
TYPECASE Expr OF
    T₁ (v₁) => S₁
| ...
| Tₙ (vₙ) => Sₙ
ELSE S₀
END
```

where Expr is an expression whose type is a reference type, the S's are statements, the T's are reference types, and the v's are identifiers. It is a static error if Expr has type ADDRESS or if any T is not a subtype of the type of Expr. The "ELSE S_0" and each "(v)" are optional.

The statement evaluates Expr. If the resulting reference value is a member of any listed type T_i, then S_i is executed, for the minimum such i. (Thus a NULL case is useful only if it comes first.) If the value is a member of no listed type and "ELSE S_0" is present, then it is executed. If the value is a member of no listed type and "ELSE S_0" is absent, a checked runtime error occurs.

Each (v_i) declares a variable whose type is T_i and whose scope is S_i. If v_i is present, it is initialized to the value of Expr before S_i is executed.

If (v_i) is absent, then T_i can be a list of type expressions separated by commas, as shorthand for a list in which the rest of the branch is repeated for each type expression. That is:

$$T_1, \cdots, T_n => \text{S}$$

is shorthand for:

$$T_1 => \text{S} \mid \cdots \mid T_n => \text{S}$$

For example:

```
PROCEDURE ToText(r: REFANY): TEXT =
    (* Assume r = NIL or r^ is a BOOLEAN or INTEGER. *)
  BEGIN
    TYPECASE r OF
      NULL => RETURN "NIL"
    | REF BOOLEAN (rb) => RETURN Fmt.Bool(rb^)
    | REF INTEGER (ri) => RETURN Fmt.Int(ri^)
    END
  END ToText;
```

B.3.19 Lock

A LOCK statement has the form:

```
LOCK mu DO S END
```

where S is a statement and mu is an expression. It is equivalent to:

```
WITH m = mu DO
    Thread.Acquire(m);
    TRY S FINALLY Thread.Release(m) END
END
```

where m stands for a variable that does not occur in S. (The Thread interface is presented in Section C.1.2, page 527.)

B.3.20 Inc and Dec

INC and DEC statements have the form:

```
INC(v, n)
DEC(v, n)
```

where v designates a variable of an ordinal type[7] ($\rightarrow$*B.2.1, p. 470*) and n is an optional integer-valued argument. If omitted, n defaults to 1. The statements increment and decrement v by n, respectively. The statements are equivalent to:

```
WITH x = v DO x := VAL(ORD(x) + n, T) END
WITH x = v DO x := VAL(ORD(x) - n, T) END
```

where T is the type of v and x stands for a variable that does not appear in n. As a consequence, the statements check for range errors.

B.4   Declarations

A declaration introduces a name for a constant, type, variable, exception, or procedure. The *scope* of the name is the block containing the declaration. A block has the form:

```
Decls BEGIN S END
```

where Decls is a sequence of declarations and S is a statement, the executable part of the block. A block can appear as a statement or as the body of a module or procedure. The declarations of a block can introduce a name at most once, though a name can be redeclared in nested blocks, and a procedure declared in an interface can be redeclared in a module exporting the interface ($\rightarrow$*B.5, p. 498*). The order of declarations in a block does not matter, except to determine the order of initialization of variables.

B.4.1   Types

If T is an identifier and U a type (or type expression, since a type expression is allowed wherever a type is required), then:

```
TYPE T = U
```

declares T to be the type U ($\rightarrow$*B.2, p. 470*).

B.4.2   Constants

If id is an identifier, T a type, and C a constant expression, then:

```
CONST id: T = C
```

declares id as a constant with the type T and the value of C. The ": T" can be omitted, in which case the type of id is the type of C. If T is present it must contain C.

---

[7]In unsafe modules ($\rightarrow$*B.5.6, p. 503*), INC and DEC are extended to ADDRESS.

B.4.3 Variables

If id is an identifier, T a non-empty type ($\rightarrow$*B.2, p. 470*) other than an open array type ($\rightarrow$*B.2.3, p. 472*), and E an expression ($\rightarrow$*B.6, p. 504*), then:

VAR id: T := E

declares id as a variable of type T whose initial value is the value of E. Either ":= E" or ": T" can be omitted, but not both. If T is omitted, it is taken to be the type of E. If E is omitted, the initial value is an arbitrary value of type T. If both are present, E must be assignable to T.

The initial value is a shorthand that is equivalent to inserting the assignment id := E at the beginning of the executable part of the block. If several variables have initial values, their assignments are inserted in the order they are declared. For example:

VAR x: [0..5] := y; y: [0..5] := x; BEGIN S END

initializes x and y to the same arbitrary value in [0..5]; it is equivalent to:

VAR x: [0..5]; y: [0..5]; BEGIN x := y; y := x; S END

If a sequence of identifiers share the same type and initial value, id can be a list of identifiers separated by commas. Such a list is shorthand for a list in which the type and initial value are repeated for each identifier. That is:

VAR $v_1, \cdots, v_n$: T := E

is shorthand for:

VAR v_1: T := E; $\cdots$; VAR v_n: T := E

This means that E is evaluated n times.

B.4.4 Procedures

There are two forms of procedure declaration:

PROCEDURE id sig = B id
PROCEDURE id sig

where id is an identifier, sig is a procedure signature ($\rightarrow$*B.2.8, p. 475*), and B is a block ($\rightarrow$*B.3.4, p. 486*). In both cases, the type of id is the procedure type determined by sig. The first form is allowed only in modules; the second form is allowed only in interfaces.

The first form declares id as a procedure constant whose signature is sig, whose body is B, and whose environment is the scope containing the declaration. The parameter names are treated as if they were declared at the outer level of B; the parameter types and default values are evaluated in the scope containing the procedure declaration. The procedure name id must be repeated after the END that terminates the body.

The second form declares id to be a procedure constant whose signature is sig. The procedure body is specified in a module exporting the interface (→*B.5, p. 498*), by a declaration of the first form.

B.4.5   Exceptions

If id is an identifier and T a type other than an open array type, then:

>   EXCEPTION id(T)

declares id as an exception with argument type T. If "(T)" is omitted, the exception takes no argument. An exception declaration is allowed only in an interface or in the outermost scope of a module. All declared exceptions are distinct.

B.4.6   Opaque types

An *opaque type* is a name that denotes an unknown subtype of some given reference type (→*B.2.7, p. 474*). For example, an opaque subtype of RE-FANY is an unknown traced reference type; an opaque subtype of UN-TRACED ROOT is an unknown untraced object type. The actual type denoted by an opaque type name is called its *concrete type*.

Different scopes can reveal different information about an opaque type. For example, what is known in one scope only to be a subtype of REFANY could be known in another scope to be a subtype of ROOT.

An opaque type declaration has the form:

>   TYPE T <: U

where T is an identifier and U an expression denoting a reference type. It introduces the name T as an opaque type and reveals that U is a supertype of T. The concrete type of T must be revealed elsewhere in the program.

B.4.7   Revelations

A *revelation* introduces information about an opaque type into a scope. Unlike other declarations, revelations introduce no new names.

There are two kinds of revelations, *partial* and *complete*. A program can contain any number of partial revelations for an opaque type; it must contain exactly one complete revelation.

A partial revelation has the form:

REVEAL T <: V

where V is a type expression (possibly just a name) and T is an identifier (possibly qualified, as on page 499) declared as an opaque type. It reveals that V is a supertype of T.

In any scope, the revealed supertypes of an opaque type must be linearly ordered by the subtype relation. That is, if it is revealed that T <: U1 and T <: U2, it must also be revealed either that U1 <: U2 or that U2 <: U1.

A complete revelation has the form:

REVEAL T = V

where V is a type expression (not just a name) whose outermost type constructor is a branded reference or object type (→*B.2.7 and B.2.9, p. 474 and 477*) and T is an identifier (possibly qualified) that has been declared as an opaque type. The revelation specifies that V is the concrete type for T. It is a static error if any type revealed in any scope as a supertype of T is not a supertype of V. Generally this error is detected at link time.

Distinct opaque types have distinct concrete types, since V includes a brand and all brands in a program are distinct.

A revelation is allowed only in an interface or in the outermost scope of a module. A revelation in an interface can be imported into any scope where it is required.

For example, consider:

INTERFACE M; TYPE T <: ROOT; PROCEDURE P(x:T): T; END M.

INTERFACE MClass; IMPORT M; REVEAL M.T <: MUTEX; END MClass.

INTERFACE MRep; IMPORT M;
  REVEAL M.T = MUTEX BRANDED OBJECT count: INTEGER END;
END MRep.

An importer of M sees M.T as an opaque subtype of ROOT, and is limited to allocating objects of type M.T, passing them to M.P, or declaring subtypes of M.T. An importer of MClass sees that every M.T is a MUTEX, and can therefore lock objects of type M.T (→*B.2.11 and B.3.19, p. 482 and 493*). Finally, an importer of MRep sees the concrete type, and can access the count field.

B.4.8 Recursive declarations

A constant, type, or procedure declaration N = E, a variable declaration N : E, an exception declaration N(E), or a revelation N = E is *recursive* if N occurs in any partial expansion of E. A variable declaration N := I where the type is omitted is recursive if N occurs in any partial expansion of the type E of I. Such declarations are allowed if every occurrence of N in any partial expansion of E is (1) within some occurrence of the type constructor REF or PROCEDURE, (2) within a field or method type of the type constructor OBJECT, or (3) within a procedure body.

Examples of legal recursive declarations:

```
TYPE
  List = REF RECORD x: REAL; link: List END;
  T = PROCEDURE(n: INTEGER; p: T);
  XList = X OBJECT link: XList END;
CONST
  N = BYTESIZE(REF ARRAY [0..N] OF REAL);
PROCEDURE P(b: BOOLEAN)
BEGIN
  IF b THEN P(NOT b) END
END P;
EXCEPTION E(PROCEDURE () RAISES {E});
VAR v: REF ARRAY [0..BYTESIZE(v)] OF INTEGER;
```

Examples of illegal recursive declarations:

```
TYPE
  T = RECORD x: T END;
  U = OBJECT METHODS m() := U.m END;
CONST
  N = N+1;
REVEAL I.T = I.T BRANDED OBJECT END;
VAR v := P(); PROCEDURE P(): ARRAY [0..LAST(v)] OF T;
```

Examples of legal non-recursive declarations:

```
VAR n := BITSIZE(n);
REVEAL T <: T;
```

B.5 Modules and interfaces

A *module* is like a block, except for the visibility of names (→*B.4, p. 494*). An entity is visible in a block if it is declared in the block or in some enclosing block; an entity is visible in a module if it is declared in the module or in an interface that is imported or exported by the module.

An *interface* is a group of declarations. Declarations in interfaces are the same as in blocks, except that any variable initializations must be constant, and procedure declarations (→*B.4.4, p. 495*) must specify only the signature, not the body.

A module X *exports* an interface Int to supply bodies for one or more of the procedures declared in the interface. A module or interface X *imports* an interface Int to make the entities declared in Int visible in X.

A *program* is a collection of modules and interfaces that contains every interface imported or exported by any of its modules or interfaces, and in which no procedure, module, or interface is multiply defined. The effect of executing a program is to execute the bodies of each of its modules. The order of execution of the modules is constrained by the initialization rule on page 503.

The module whose body is executed last is called the *main module*. Implementations are expected to provide a way to specify the main module, in case the initialization rule does not determine it uniquely. The recommended rule is that the main module be the one that exports the interface Main, whose contents are implementation-dependent.

Program execution terminates when the body of the main module terminates, even if concurrent threads of control are still executing.

The names of the modules and interfaces of a program are called *global* names. The method for looking up global names – for example, by file system search paths – is implementation-dependent.

B.5.1 Import statements

There are two forms of import statements. All imports of both forms are interpreted simultaneously: their order doesn't matter.

The first form is

IMPORT X AS Y

which imports the interface whose global name is X and gives it the local name Y. The entities and revelations declared in X become accessible in the importing module or interface, but the entities and revelations imported into X do not. To refer to the entity declared with name N in the interface X, the importer must use the *qualified identifier* Y.N.

The statement IMPORT X is short for IMPORT X AS X.

The second form is

FROM X IMPORT N

which introduces N as the local name for the entity declared as N in the interface X. A local binding for X takes precedence over a global binding. For example,

IMPORT X AS Y, Y AS X; FROM X IMPORT N

simultaneously introduces local names Y, X, and N for the entities whose global names are X, Y, and Y.N, respectively.

It is illegal to use the same local name twice:

IMPORT Y AS X, Z AS X;

is a static error, even if Y and Z are the same.

B.5.2 Interfaces

An interface has the form:

INTERFACE id; Imports; Decls END id.

where id is an identifier that names the interface, Imports is a sequence of import statements, and Decls is a sequence of declarations ($\rightarrow$*B.4, p. 494*) that contains no procedure bodies or non-constant variable initializations. The names declared in Decls and the visible imported names must be distinct. It is a static error for two or more interfaces to form an import cycle.

B.5.3 Modules

A module has the form:

MODULE id EXPORTS Interfaces; Imports; Block id.

where id is an identifier that names the module, Interfaces is a list of distinct names of interfaces exported by the module, Imports is a list of import statements, and Block is a block, the *body* of the module. The name id must be repeated after the END that terminates the body. "EXPORTS Interfaces" can be omitted, in which case Interfaces defaults to id.

If module M exports interface Int, then all declared names in Int are visible without qualification in M. Any procedure declared in Int can be redeclared in M, with a body. The signature in M must be covered by the signature in Int ($\rightarrow$*B.2.8, p. 477*). To determine the interpretation of keyword bindings in calls to the procedure, the signature in M is used within M; the signature in Int is used everywhere else.

Except for the redeclaration of exported procedures, the names declared at the top level of Block, the visible imported names, and the names declared in the exported interfaces must be distinct.

For example, the following is illegal, since two names in exported interfaces coincide:

INTERFACE X;   INTERFACE Y;   MODULE M EXPORTS X, Y;
  PROCEDURE P(); PROCEDURE P(); PROCEDURE P() = ... ;

The following is also illegal, since the visible imported name X coincides with the top-level name X:

INTERFACE X;   MODULE M EXPORTS X; FROM X IMPORT P;
  PROCEDURE P();   PROCEDURE P() = ... ;

But the following is legal, although peculiar:

INTERFACE X;   MODULE M EXPORTS X; IMPORT X;
  PROCEDURE P(...);   PROCEDURE P(...) = ... ;

since the only visible imported name is X, and the coincidence between P as a top-level name and P as a name in an exported interface is allowed, assuming the interface signature covers the module signature. Within M, the interface declaration determines the signature of X.P and the module declaration determines the signature of P.

B.5.4 Generics

In a generic interface or module, some of the imported interface names are treated as formal parameters, to be bound to actual interfaces when the generic is instantiated.

A generic interface has the form

GENERIC INTERFACE $G(F_1, \cdots, F_n)$; Body END G.

where G is an identifier that names the generic interface, $F_1, \cdots, F_n$ is a list of identifiers, called the formal imports of G, and Body is a sequence of imports followed by a sequence of declarations, exactly as in a non-generic interface.

An instance of G has the form

INTERFACE $X = G(A_1, \cdots, A_n)$ END X.

where X is the name of the instance and $A_1, \cdots, A_n$ is a list of actual interfaces to which the formal imports of G are bound. The instance X is equivalent to an ordinary interface defined as follows:

INTERFACE X; IMPORT A_1 AS $F_1, \cdots, A_n$ AS F_n; Body END X.

A generic module has the form

GENERIC MODULE $G(F_1, \cdots, F_n)$; Body END G.

where G is an identifier that names the generic module, $F_1, \cdots, F_n$ is a list of identifiers, called the formal imports of G, and Body is a sequence of imports followed by a block, exactly as in a non-generic module.

An instance of G has the form

    MODULE X EXPORTS E = G($A_1, \cdots, A_n$) END X.

where X is the name of the instance, E is a list of interfaces exported by X, and $A_1, \cdots, A_n$ is a list of actual interfaces to which the formal imports of G are bound. "EXPORTS E" can be omitted, in which case it defaults to "EXPORTS X". The instance X is equivalent to an ordinary module defined as follows:

    MODULE X EXPORTS E; IMPORT A_1 AS $F_1, \cdots, A_n$ AS F_n; Body
    END X.

Notice that the generic module itself has no exports; they are supplied only when it is instantiated.

    For example, here is a generic stack package:

```
GENERIC INTERFACE Stack(Elem);
  (* where Elem.T is not an open array type. *)
  TYPE T <: REFANY;
  PROCEDURE Create(): T;
  PROCEDURE Push(VAR s: T; x: Elem.T);
  PROCEDURE Pop(VAR s: T): Elem.T;
END Stack.


GENERIC MODULE Stack(Elem);
  REVEAL
    T = BRANDED OBJECT n: INTEGER; a: REF ARRAY OF Elem.T END;

  PROCEDURE Create(): T =
    BEGIN RETURN NEW(T, n := 0, a := NIL) END Create;

  PROCEDURE Push(VAR s: T; x: Elem.T) =
    BEGIN
      IF s.a = NIL THEN
        s.a := NEW(REF ARRAY OF Elem.T, 5)
      ELSIF s.n > LAST(s.a^) THEN
        WITH temp = NEW(REF ARRAY OF Elem.T, 2 * NUMBER(s.a^)) DO
          FOR i := 0 TO LAST(s.a^) DO temp[i] := s.a[i] END;
          s.a := temp
        END
      END;
      s.a[s.n] := x;
      INC(s.n)
    END Push;

  PROCEDURE Pop(VAR s: T): Elem.T =
    BEGIN DEC(s.n); RETURN s.a[s.n] END Pop;

BEGIN END Stack.
```

To instantiate these generics to produce stacks of integers:

> INTERFACE Integer; TYPE T = INTEGER; END Integer.
> INTERFACE IntStack = Stack(Integer) END IntStack.
> MODULE IntStack = Stack(Integer) END IntStack.

Implementations are not expected to share code between different instances of a generic module, since this will not be possible in general.

Implementations are not required to typecheck uninstantiated generics, but they must typecheck their instances. For example, if one made the following mistake:

> INTERFACE String; TYPE T = ARRAY OF CHAR; END String.
> INTERFACE StringStack = Stack(String) END StringStack.
> MODULE StringStack = Stack(String) END StringStack.

everything would go well until the last line, when the compiler would attempt to compile a version of Stack in which the element type was an open array. It would then complain that the NEW call in Push does not have enough parameters.

B.5.5 Initialization

The order of execution of the modules in a program is constrained by the following rule:

If module M depends on module N and N does not depend on M, then N's body will be executed before M's body, where:

- A module M *depends on* a module N if M uses an interface that N exports or if M depends on a module that depends on N.

- A module M *uses* an interface X if M imports or exports X or if M uses an interface that imports X.

Except for this constraint, the order of execution is implementationdependent.

B.5.6 Safety

The keyword UNSAFE can precede the declaration of any interface or module to indicate that it is *unsafe*; that is, uses the unsafe features of the language (→B.7, p. 516). An interface or module not explicitly labeled UNSAFE is called *safe*.

An interface is *intrinsically safe* if there is no way to produce an unchecked runtime error by using the interface in a safe module. If all modules that export a safe interface are safe, the compiler guarantees the intrinsic safety of the interface. If any of the modules that export a safe interface are unsafe, it is the programmer, rather than the compiler, who makes the guarantee.

It is a static error for a safe interface to import an unsafe one or for a safe module to import or export an unsafe interface.

B.6   Expressions

An expression prescribes a computation that produces a value or variable. Syntactically, an expression is either an operand, or an operation applied to arguments, which are themselves expressions. Operands are identifiers ($\rightarrow$B.6.3, p. 506), literals ($\rightarrow$B.6.4 and B.6.5, p. 507 and 508), or types ($\rightarrow$B.2, p. 470). An expression is evaluated by recursively evaluating its arguments and performing the operation. The order of argument evaluation is undefined for all operations except AND and OR.

B.6.1   Conventions for describing operations

To describe the argument and result types of operations, we use a notation like procedure signatures. But since most operations are too general to be described by a true procedure signature, we extend the notation in several ways.

The argument to an operation can be required to have a type in a particular class, such as an ordinal type ($\rightarrow$B.2.1, p. 470), set type ($\rightarrow$B.2.6, p. 474), etc. In this case the formal specifies a type class instead of a type. For example:

ORD (x: Ordinal): INTEGER

The formal type Any specifies an argument of any type.

A single operation name can be overloaded, which means that it denotes more than one operation. In this case, we write a separate signature for each of the operations. For example:

ABS   (x: INTEGER) : INTEGER
         (x: Float)   : Float

The particular operation will be selected so that each actual argument type is a subtype of the corresponding formal type or a member of the corresponding formal type class.

The argument to an operation can be an expression denoting a type. In this case, we write Type as the argument type. For example:

BYTESIZE (T: Type): CARDINAL

The result type of an operation can depend on its argument values (although the result type can always be determined statically). In this case, the expression for the result type contains the appropriate arguments. For example:

FIRST (T: FixedArrayType): IndexType(T)

IndexType(T) denotes the index type of the array type T and IndexType(a) denotes the index type of the array a. The definitions of ElemType(T) and ElemType(a) are similar.

B.6.2 Operation syntax

The operators that have special syntax are classified and listed in order of decreasing binding power in the following table:

x.a	infix dot
f(x) a[i] T{x}	applicative (, [, {
p^	postfix ^
+ -	prefix arithmetics
* / DIV MOD	infix arithmetics
+ - &	infix arithmetics
= # <<=>=> IN	infix relations
NOT	prefix NOT
AND	infix AND
OR	infix OR

All infix operators are left associative. Parentheses can be used to override the precedence rules. Here are some examples of expressions together with their fully parenthesized forms:

M.F(x)	(M.F)(x)	dot before application
Q(x)^	(Q(x))^	application before ^
- p^	- (p^)	^ before prefix -
- a * b	(- a) * b	prefix - before *
a * b - c	(a * b) - c	* before infix -
x IN s - t	x IN (s - t)	infix - before IN
NOT x IN s	NOT (x IN s)	IN before NOT
NOT p AND q	(NOT p) AND q	NOT before AND
A OR B AND C	A OR (B AND C)	AND before OR

Operators without special syntax are *procedural*. An application of a procedural operator has the form op(args), where op is the operation and args is the list of argument expressions. For example, MAX and MIN are procedural operators.

B.6.3 Designators

An identifier is a *writable designator* if it is declared as a variable, is a VAR or VALUE parameter, is a local of a TYPECASE or TRY EXCEPT statement, or is a WITH local that is bound to a writable designator. An identifier is a *readonly designator* if it is a READONLY parameter, a local of a FOR statement, or a WITH local bound to a non-designator or readonly designator.

The only operations that produce designators are dereferencing, subscripting, selection, and SUBARRAY.[8] This section defines these operations and specifies the conditions under which they produce designators.

r^   denotes the the referent of r; this operation is called *dereferencing*. The expression r^ is always a writable designator. It is a static error if the type of r is REFANY, ADDRESS, NULL, an object type, or an opaque type, and a checked runtime error if r is NIL. The type of r^ is the referent type of r (→*B.2.7, p. 474*).

a[i]   denotes the $(i + 1 - \text{FIRST}(a))^{\text{th}}$ element of the array a (→*B.2.3, p. 472*). The expression a[i] is a designator if a is, and is writable if a is. The expression i must be assignable to the index type of a. The type of a[i] is the element type of a. An expression of the form $a[i_1, \cdots, i_n]$ is shorthand for $a[i_1] \cdots [i_n]$. If a is a reference to an array, then a[i] is shorthand for a^[i].

r.f, o.f, I.x, T.m, E.id

If r denotes a record, r.f denotes its f field (→*B.2.4, p. 473*). In this case r.f is a designator if r is, and is writable if r is. The type of r.f is the declared type of the field. If r is a reference to a record, then r.f is shorthand for r^.f.

If o denotes an object and f names a data field specified in the type of o, then o.f denotes that data field of o. In this case o.f is a writable designator whose type is the declared type of the field. If M denotes an imported interface, then M.x denotes the entity named x in the interface M. In this case M.x is a designator if x is declared as a variable; such a designator is always writable.

If T is an object type (→*B.2.9, p. 477*) and m is the name of one of T's methods, then T.m denotes the m method of type T. In this case T.m is not a designator. Its type is the procedure type whose first argument has mode VALUE and type T, and whose remaining arguments are determined by the method declaration for m in T. The name of the first argument is unspecified; thus in calls to T.m, this argument must be given positionally, not by keyword. T.m is a procedure constant. If

---

[8] In unsafe modules, LOOPHOLE can also produce a designator.

E is an enumerated type, then E.id denotes its value named id. In this case E.id is not a designator. The type of E.id is E.

SUBARRAY(a: Array; from, for: CARDINAL): ARRAY OF ElemType(a)
SUBARRAY produces a subarray of a. It does not copy the array (→*B.2.3, p. 472*); it is a designator if a is, and is writable if a is. If a is a multi-dimensional array, SUBARRAY applies only to the top-level array. The operation returns the subarray that skips the first from elements of a and contains the next for elements. Note that if from is zero, the subarray is a prefix of a, whether the type of a is zero-based or not. It is a checked runtime error if from+for exceeds NUMBER(a). Implementations may restrict or prohibit the SUBARRAY operation for arrays with packed element types.

B.6.4 Numeric literals

Numeric literals denote constant non-negative integers or reals. The types of these literals are INTEGER, REAL, LONGREAL, and EXTENDED.

A literal INTEGER has the form base_digits, where base is one of "2", "3", $\cdots$, "16", and digits is a non-empty sequence of the decimal digits 0 through 9 plus the hexadecimal digits A through F. The "base_" can be omitted, in which case base defaults to 10. The digits are interpreted in the given base. Each digit must be less than base. For example, 16_FF and 255 are equivalent integer literals.

If no explicit base is present, the value of the literal must be at most LAST(INTEGER). If an explicit base is present, the value of the literal must be less than $2^{\text{Word.Size}}$, and its interpretation uses the convention of the Word interface (→*C.1.3, p. 528*). For example, on a sixteen-bit two's complement machine, 16_FFFF and −1 represent the same value.

A literal REAL has the form decimal E exponent, where decimal is a non-empty sequence of decimal digits followed by a decimal point followed by a non-empty sequence of decimal digits, and exponent is a non-empty sequence of decimal digits optionally beginning with a + or −. The literal denotes decimal times 10^{exponent}. If "E exponent" is omitted, exponent defaults to 0.

LONGREAL and EXTENDED literals are like REAL literals, but instead of E they use D and X respectively.

Case is not significant in digits, prefixes or scale factors. Embedded spaces are not allowed.

For example, 1.0 and 0.5 are valid, 1. and .5 are not; 6.624E−27 is a REAL, and 3.1415926535d0 a LONGREAL.

B.6.5   Text and character literals

A character literal is a pair of single quotes enclosing either a single ISO-Latin-1 printing character (excluding single quote) or an escape sequence. The type of a character literal is CHAR.

A text literal is a pair of double quotes enclosing a sequence of ISO-Latin-1 printing characters (excluding double quote) and escape sequences. The type of a text literal is TEXT.

Here are the legal escape sequences and the characters they denote:

\n	newline (linefeed)	\f	form feed
\t	tab	\\	backslash
\r	carriage return	\"	double quote
\'	single quote	\nnn	char with code 8_nnn

A \ followed by exactly three octal digits specifies the character whose code is that octal value. A \ that is not a part of one of these escape sequences is a static error.

For example, 'a' and '\'' are valid character literals, ''' is not; """ and 'Don't \ n' are valid text literals, """ is not.

B.6.6   Nil

The literal "NIL" denotes the value NIL. Its type is NULL.

B.6.7   Function application

A procedure call is an expression if the procedure returns a result. The type of the expression is the result type of the procedure.

B.6.8   Set, array, and record constructors

A set constructor has the form:

$$S\{e_1, \cdots, e_n\}$$

where S is a set type ($\rightarrow$B.2.6, p. 474) and the e's are expressions or ranges of the form lo..hi. The constructor denotes a value of type S containing the listed values and the values in the listed ranges. The e's, lo's, and hi's must be assignable to the element type of S.

An array constructor has the form:

$$A\{e_1, \cdots, e_n\}$$

where A is an array type (→*B.2.3, p. 472*) and the *e*'s are expressions. The constructor denotes a value of type A containing the listed elements in the listed order. The *e*'s must be assignable to the element type of A. This means that if A is a multi-dimensional array, the *e*'s must themselves be array-valued expressions.

If A is a fixed array type and n is at least 1, then e_n can be followed by ", .." to indicate that the value of e_n will be replicated as many times as necessary to fill out the array. It is a static error to provide too many or too few elements for a fixed array type.

A record constructor has the form:

R{Bindings}

where R is a record type (→*B.2.4, p. 473*) and Bindings is a list of keyword or positional bindings, exactly as in a procedure call (→*B.3.2, p. 484*). The list of bindings is rewritten to fit the list of fields and defaults of R, exactly as for a procedure call; the record field names play the role of the procedure formal parameters. The expression denotes a value of type R whose field values are specified by the rewritten binding.

The rewritten binding must bind only field names and must bind each field name exactly once. Each expression in the binding must be assignable to the type of the corresponding record field.

B.6.9 New

An allocation operation has the form:

NEW(T, ⋯)

where T is a reference type (→*B.2.7, p. 474*) other than REFANY, AD-DRESS, or NULL. The operation returns the address of a newly-allocated variable of T's referent type; or if T is an object type (→*B.2.9, p. 477*), a newly-allocated data record paired with a method suite. The reference returned by NEW is distinct from all existing references. The allocated type of the new reference is T.

It is a static error if T's referent type is empty. If T is declared as an opaque type (→*B.4.6, p. 496*), NEW(T) is legal only in scopes where T's concrete type is known completely, or is known to be an object type.

The initial state of the referent generally represents an arbitrary value of its type. If T is an object type or a reference to a record or open array then NEW takes additional arguments to control the initial state of the new variable.

If T is a reference to an array with k open dimensions, the NEW operation has the form:

NEW(T, $n_1, \cdots, n_k$)

where the n's are integer-valued expressions that specify the lengths of the new array in its first k dimensions. The values in the array will be arbitrary values of their type.

If T is an object type or a reference to a record, the NEW operation has the form:

NEW(T, Bindings)

where Bindings is a list of keyword bindings used to initialize the new fields. Positional bindings are not allowed.

Each binding f := v initializes the field f to the value v. Fields for which no binding is supplied will be initialized to their defaults if they have defaults; otherwise they will be initialized to arbitrary values of their types.

If T is an object type then Bindings can also include method overrides of the form m := P, where m is a method of T and P is a top-level procedure constant. This is syntactic sugar for the allocation of a subtype of T that includes the given overrides, in the given order. For example,
NEW(T, m := P) is sugar for NEW(T OBJECT OVERRIDES m := P END).

The order of the bindings makes no difference.

B.6.10 Arithmetic operations

The basic arithmetic operations are built into the language; additional operations are provided by the required interfaces ($\rightarrow$C.1.5, p. 530). To test or set the implementation's behavior for overflow, underflow, rounding, and division by zero, see the required interface FloatMode ($\rightarrow$C.1.6, p. 533). Modula-3 arithmetic was designed to support the IEEE floating-point standard, but not to require it. To perform arithmetic operations modulo the word size, programs should use the routines in the required interface Word ($\rightarrow$C.1.3, p. 528).

Implementations must not rearrange the computation of expressions in a way that could affect the result. For example, (x+y)+z generally cannot be computed as x+(y+z), since addition is not associative either for bounded integers or for floating-point values.

```
prefix + (x: INTEGER)   : INTEGER
         (x: Float)      : Float

infix   + (x,y: INTEGER): INTEGER
         (x,y: Float)    : Float
         (x,y: Set)      : Set
```

As a prefix operator, +x returns x. As an infix operator on numeric arguments, + denotes addition. On sets, + denotes set union.

That is, e IN (x + y) if and only if (e IN x) OR (e IN y). The types of x and y must be the same, and the result is the same type as both. In unsafe modules, + is extended to ADDRESS.

```
prefix – (x: INTEGER)    : INTEGER
         (x: Float)       : Float

infix  – (x,y: INTEGER) : INTEGER
         (x,y: Float)     : Float
         (x,y: Set)       : Set
```

As a prefix operator, –x is the negative of x. As an infix operator on numeric arguments, – denotes subtraction. On sets, – denotes set difference. That is, e IN (x – y) if and only if (e IN x) AND NOT (e IN y). The types of x and y must be the same, and the result is the same type as both. In unsafe modules, – is extended to ADDRESS.

```
infix * (x,y: INTEGER) : INTEGER
        (x,y: Float)     : Float
        (x,y: Set)       : Set
```

On numeric arguments, * denotes multiplication. On sets, * denotes intersection. That is, e IN (x * y) if and only if (e IN x) AND (e IN y). The types of x and y must be the same, and the result is the same type as both.

```
infix / (x,y: Float) : Float
        (x,y: Set)    : Set
```

On reals, / denotes division. On sets, / denotes symmetric difference. That is, e IN (x / y) if and only if (e IN x) # (e IN y). The types of x and y must be the same, and the result is the same type as both.

```
infix DIV   (x,y: INTEGER) : INTEGER
infix MOD (x,y: INTEGER) : INTEGER
        MOD (x, y: Float)      : Float
```

The value x DIV y is the floor of the quotient of x and y; that is, the maximum integer not exceeding the real number z such that z * y = x. For integers x and y, the value of x MOD y is defined to be x – y * (x DIV y).

This means that for positive y, the value of x MOD y lies in the interval [0 .. y–1], regardless of the sign of x. For negative y, the value of x MOD y lies in the interval [y+1 .. 0], regardless of the sign of x.

If x and y are floats, the value of x MOD y is x − y * FLOOR(x / y). This may be computed as a Modula-3 expression, or by a method that avoids overflow if x is much greater than y. The types of x and y must be the same, and the result is the same type as both.

```
ABS (x: INTEGER) : INTEGER
    (x: Float)       : Float
```

ABS(x) is the absolute value of x. If x is a float, the type of ABS(x) is the same as the type of x.

```
FLOAT (x: INTEGER; T: Type := REAL) : T
     (x: Float; T: Type := REAL)      : T
```

FLOAT(x, T) is a floating-point value of type T that is equal to or very near x. The type T must be a floating-point type; it defaults to REAL. The exact semantics depend on the thread's current rounding mode, as defined in the required interface FloatMode (→*C.1.5, p. 530*).

```
FLOOR   (x: Float) : INTEGER
CEILING (x: Float) : INTEGER
```

FLOOR(x) is the greatest integer not exceeding x. CEILING(x) is the least integer not less than x.

```
ROUND (r: Float) : INTEGER
TRUNC (r: Float) : INTEGER
```

ROUND(r) is the nearest integer to r; ties are broken according to the constant RoundDefault in the required interface FloatMode (→*C.1.6, p. 533*). TRUNC(r) rounds r toward zero; it equals FLOOR(r) for positive r and CEILING(r) for negative r.

```
MAX, MIN  (x,y: Ordinal) : Ordinal
          (x,y: Float)    : Float
```

MAX returns the greater of the two values x and y; MIN returns the lesser. If x and y are ordinals (→*B.2.1, p. 470*), they must have the same base type, which is the type of the result. If x and y are floats, they must have the same type, and the result is the same type as both.

B.6.11 Relations

infix =, # (x, y: Any): BOOLEAN

The operator = returns TRUE if x and y are equal. The operator # returns TRUE if x and y are not equal. It is a static error if the type of x is not assignable to the type of y or vice versa.

Ordinals are equal if they have the same value. Floats are equal if the underlying implementation defines them to be; for example, on an IEEE implementation, +0 equals −0 and NaN does not equal itself. References are equal if they address the same location. Procedures are equal if they agree as closures; that is, if they refer to the same procedure body and environment. Sets are equal if they have the same elements. Arrays are equal if they have the same length and corresponding elements are equal. Records are equal if they have the same fields and corresponding fields are equal.

```
infix <=, >=   (x,y: Ordinal)    : BOOLEAN
               (x,y: Float)      : BOOLEAN
               (x,y: ADDRESS): BOOLEAN
               (x,y: Set)        : BOOLEAN
```

In the first three cases, <= returns TRUE if x is at most as large as y. In the last case, <= returns TRUE if every element of x is an element of y. In all cases, it is a static error if the type of x is not assignable to the type of y, or vice versa. The expression x >= y is equivalent to y <= x.

```
infix >, <   (x,y: Ordinal)    : BOOLEAN
             (x,y: Float)      : BOOLEAN
             (x,y: ADDRESS): BOOLEAN
             (x,y: Set)        : BOOLEAN
```

In all cases, x < y means (x <= y) AND (x # y), and x > y means y < x. It is a static error if the type of x is not assignable to the type of y, or vice versa.

Warning: with IEEE floating-point, x <= y is not the same as NOT x > y.

infix IN (e: Ordinal; s: Set): BOOLEAN

Returns TRUE if e is an element of the set s. It is a static error if the type of e is not assignable to the element type of s. If the value of e is not a member of the element type, no error occurs, but IN returns FALSE.

B.6.12   Boolean operations

```
prefix  NOT  (p: BOOLEAN)    : BOOLEAN
infix   AND  (p,q: BOOLEAN)  : BOOLEAN
infix   OR   (p,q: BOOLEAN)  : BOOLEAN
```

NOT p is the complement of p.

p AND q is TRUE if both p and q are TRUE. If p is FALSE, q is not evaluated.

p OR q is TRUE if at least one of p and q is TRUE. If p is TRUE, q is not evaluated.

B.6.13   Type operations

```
ISTYPE (x: Reference; T: RefType) : BOOLEAN
```

ISTYPE(x, T) is TRUE if and only if x is a member of T. T must be an object type or traced reference type (→*B.2.7 and B.2.9, p. 474 and 477*), and x must be assignable to T (→*B.3.1, p. 483*).

```
NARROW (x: Reference; T: RefType): T
```

NARROW(x, T) returns x after checking that x is a member of T. If the check fails, a runtime error occurs. T must be an object type or traced reference type, and x must be assignable to T.

```
TYPECODE  (T: RefType)          : CARDINAL
          (r: REFANY)           : CARDINAL
          (r: UNTRACED ROOT)    : CARDINAL
```

Every object type or traced reference type (including NULL) has an associated integer code. Different types have different codes. The code for a type is constant for any single execution of a program, but may differ for different executions. TYPECODE(T) returns the code for the type T and TYPECODE(r) returns the code for the allocated type of r. It is a static error if T is REFANY or is not an object type or traced reference type.

```
ORD  (element: Ordinal)          : INTEGER
VAL  (i: INTEGER; T: OrdinalType) : T
```

ORD converts an element of an enumeration (→*B.2.1, p. 470*) to the integer that represents its position in the enumeration order. The first value in any enumeration is represented by zero. If the type of element is a subrange of an enumeration T, the result is the position of the element within T, not within the subrange.

VAL is the inverse of ORD; it converts from a numeric position i into the element that occupies that position in an enumeration. If T is a subrange, VAL returns the element with the position i in the original enumeration type, not the subrange. It is a checked runtime error for the value of i to be out of range for T.

If n is an integer, ORD(n) = VAL(n, INTEGER) = n.

```
NUMBER (T: OrdinalType)     : CARDINAL
       (A: FixedArrayType) : CARDINAL
       (a: Array)          : CARDINAL
```

For an ordinal type T, NUMBER(T) returns the number of elements in T. For a fixed array type A, NUMBER(A) is defined by NUMBER(IndexType(A)). Similarly, for an array a, NUMBER(a) is defined by NUMBER(IndexType(a)). In this case, the expression a will be evaluated only if it denotes an open array.

```
FIRST  (T: OrdinalType)     : BaseType(T)
       (T: FloatType)       : T
       (A: FixedArrayType) : BaseType(IndexType(A))
       (a: Array)           : BaseType(IndexType(a))

LAST   (T: OrdinalType)     : BaseType(T)
       (T: FloatType)       : T
       (A: FixedArrayType) : BaseType(IndexType(A))
       (a: Array)           : BaseType(IndexType(a))
```

For a non-empty ordinal type T, FIRST returns the smallest value of T and LAST returns the largest value. If T is the empty enumeration, FIRST(T) and LAST(T) are static errors. If T is any other empty ordinal type, the values returned are implementation-dependent, but they satisfy FIRST(T) > LAST(T).

For a floating-point type T, FIRST(T) and LAST(T) are the smallest and largest values of the type, respectively. On IEEE implementations, these are minus and plus infinity.

For a fixed array type A, FIRST(A) is defined by FIRST(IndexType(A)) and LAST(A) by LAST(IndexType(A)). Similarly, for an array a, FIRST(a) and LAST(a) are defined by FIRST(IndexType(a)) and LAST(IndexType(a)). The expression a will be evaluated only if it is an open array. Note that if a is an open array, FIRST(a) and LAST(a) have type INTEGER.

```
BITSIZE   (x: Any) : CARDINAL
          (T: Type): CARDINAL
```

```
BYTESIZE (x: Any)  : CARDINAL
         (T: Type) : CARDINAL

ADRSIZE  (x: Any)  : CARDINAL
         (T: Type) : CARDINAL
```

These operations return the size of the variable x or of variables of type T. BITSIZE returns the number of bits, BYTESIZE the number of 8-bit bytes, and ADRSIZE the number of addressable locations. In all cases, x must be a designator and T must not be an open array type. A designator x will be evaluated only if its type is an open array type.

B.6.14   Text operations

```
infix & (a,b: TEXT): TEXT
```

The concatenation of a and b, as defined by Text.Cat ($\rightarrow$C.1.1, p. 525).

B.6.15   Constant Expressions

Constant expressions are a subset of the general class of expressions, restricted by the requirement that it must be possible to evaluate the expression statically. All operations are legal in constant expressions except for ADR, LOOPHOLE, TYPECODE, NARROW, ISTYPE, SUBARRAY, NEW, dereferencing (explicit or implicit), and the only procedures that can be applied are the functions in the Word interface ($\rightarrow$C.1.3, p. 528).

A variable can appear in a constant expression only as an argument to FIRST, LAST, NUMBER, BITSIZE, BYTESIZE, or ADRSIZE, and such a variable must not have an open array type. Literals and top-level procedure constants are legal in constant expressions.

B.7   Unsafe operations

The features defined in this section can potentially cause unchecked runtime errors and are thus forbidden in safe modules ($\rightarrow$B.5.6, p. 503).

An unchecked type transfer operation has the form:

```
LOOPHOLE(e, T)
```

where e is an expression whose type is not an open array type and T is a type. It denotes e's bit pattern interpreted as a variable or value of type T. It is a designator if e is, and is writable if e is. An unchecked runtime error can occur if e's bit pattern is not a legal T, or if e is a designator and some legal bit pattern for T is not legal for e.

If T is not an open array type, BITSIZE(e) must equal BITSIZE(T). If T is an open array type, its element type must not be an open array type, and e's bit pattern is interpreted as an array whose length is BITSIZE(e) divided by BITSIZE(the element type of T). The division must come out even.

The following operations are primarily used for address arithmetic:

ADR (VAR x: Any)   : ADDRESS

+   (x: ADDRESS, y:INTEGER): ADDRESS
−   (x: ADDRESS, y:INTEGER): ADDRESS
−   (x,y: ADDRESS)   : INTEGER

ADR(x) is the address of the variable x. The actual argument must be a designator but need not be writable. The operations + and − treat addresses as integers. The validity of the addresses produced by these operations is implementation-dependent. For example, the address of a variable in a local procedure frame is probably valid only for the duration of the call. The address of the referent of a traced reference is probably valid only as long as traced references prevent it from being collected (and not even that long if the implementation uses a compacting collector).

In unsafe modules the INC and DEC statements apply to addresses as well as ordinals:

INC (VAR x: ADDRESS; n: INTEGER := 1)
DEC (VAR x: ADDRESS; n: INTEGER := 1)

These are short for x := x + n and x := x − n, except that x is evaluated only once.

A DISPOSE statement has the form:

DISPOSE (v)

where v is a writable designator whose type is not REFANY, ADDRESS, or NULL. If v is untraced, the statement frees the storage for v's referent and sets v to NIL. Freeing storage to which active references remain is an unchecked runtime error. If v is traced, the statement is equivalent to v := NIL. If v is NIL, the statement is a no-op.

In unsafe modules the definition of "assignable" for types is extended: two reference types T and U are assignable if T <: U or U <: T. The only effect of this change is to allow a value of type ADDRESS to be assigned to a variable of type UNTRACED REF T. It is an unchecked runtime error if the value does not address a variable of type T.

In unsafe modules the type constructor UNTRACED REF T is allowed for traced as well as untraced T, and the fields of untraced objects can be traced. If u is an untraced reference to a traced variable t, then the validity of the traced references in t is implementation-dependent, since the garbage collector probably will not trace them through u.

B.8 Syntax

B.8.1 Keywords

AND	DO	FINALLY	METHODS	RAISES	THEN	VAR
ARRAY	ELSE	FOR	MOD	READONLY	TO	WHILE
BEGIN	ELSIF	FROM	MODULE	RECORD	TRY	WITH
BITS	END	IF	NOT	REF	TYPE	
BRANDED	EVAL	IMPORT	OBJECT	REPEAT	TYPECASE	
BY	EXCEPT	IN	OF	RETURN	UNSAFE	
CASE	EXCEPTION	INTERFACE	OR	REVEAL	UNTIL	
CONST	EXIT	LOCK	PROCEDURE	ROOT	UNTRACED	
DIV	EXPORTS	LOOP	RAISE	SET	VALUE	

B.8.2 Reserved identifiers

Here are the *reserved* identifiers, which cannot be redeclared:

ABS	BYTESIZE	FALSE	ISTYPE	MIN	NUMBER	TEXT
ADDRESS	CARDINAL	FIRST	LAST	MUTEX	ORD	TRUE
ADR	CEILING	FLOAT	LONGFLOAT	NARROW	REAL	TRUNC
ADRSIZE	CHAR	FLOOR	LONGREAL	NEW	REFANY	TYPECODE
BITSIZE	DEC	INC	LOOPHOLE	NIL	ROUND	VAL
BOOLEAN	DISPOSE	INTEGER	MAX	NULL	SUBARRAY	

B.8.3 Operators

The following characters and character pairs are classified as operators:

```
+        <        #        =        ;        . .        :
-        >        {        }        |        : =        <:
*        <=       (        )        ^        ,          =>
/        >=       [        ]        .        &
```

B.8.4 Comments

A comment is an arbitrary character sequence opened by (* and closed by
*). Comments can be nested and can extend over more than one line.

B.8.5 Pragmas

A pragma is an arbitrary character sequence opened by <* and closed by
*>. Pragmas can be nested and can extend over more than one line. Prag-
mas are hints to the implementation; they do not affect the language semantics.

We recommend supporting the two pragmas <*INLINE*> and
<*EXTERNAL*>. The pragma <*INLINE*> precedes a procedure declara-
tion to indicate that the procedure should be expanded at the point of call.

The pragma <* EXTERNAL N:L *> precedes an interface or a declaration in an interface to indicate that the entity it precedes is implemented by the language L, where it has the name N. If ":L" is omitted, then the implementation's default external language is assumed. If "N" is omitted, then the external name is determined from the Modula-3 name in some implementation-dependent way.

B.8.6 Conventions for syntax

We use the following notation for defining syntax:

X Y	X followed by Y
X | Y	X or Y.
[X]	X or empty
{X}	A possibly empty sequence of X's

"Followed by" has greater binding power than |; parentheses are used to override this precedence rule. Non-terminals begin with an upper-case letter. Terminals are either keywords or quoted operators. The symbols $Ident_{89}$ $Number_{94}$ $TextLiteral_{92}$ and $CharLiteral_{91}$ are defined in the token grammar on page 522. Each production is terminated by a period. The syntax does not reflect the restrictions that revelations and exceptions can be declared only at the top level; nor does it include explicit productions for NEW, INC, and DEC, which parse like procedure calls.

B.8.7 Compilation unit productions

1   $Compilation_1$ $= Interface_2 \mid Module_3 \mid GInterface_4$
               $\mid GModule_5 \mid IInterface_6 \mid IModule_7.$

2   $Interface_2$ $= [$ "UNSAFE" $]$ "INTERFACE" $Ident_{89}$ ";" $\{ Import_{10} \}$
               $\{ Declaration_{13} \}$ "END" $Ident_{89}$ ".".

3   $Module_3$ $= [$ "UNSAFE" $]$ "MODULE" $Ident_{89}$ $[$ "EXPORTS" $IDList_{87}$ $]$
               ";" $\{ Import_{10} \}$ $Block_{12}$ $Ident_{89}$ ".".

4   $GInterface_4$ $=$ "GENERIC" "INTERFACE" $Ident_{89}$ $GFmls_8$ ";"
               $\{ Import_{10} \}$ $\{ Declaration_{13} \}$ "END" $Ident_{89}$ ".".

5   $GModule_5$ $=$ "GENERIC" "MODULE" $Ident_{89}$ $GFmls_8$ ";"
               $\{ Import_{10} \}$ $Block_{12}$ $Ident_{89}$ ".".

6   $IInterface_6$ $= [$ "UNSAFE" $]$ "INTERFACE" $Ident_{89}$ "=' ' $Ident_{89}$ $GActls_9$
               "END" $Ident_{89}$ ".".

7   $IModule_7$ $= [$ "UNSAFE" $]$ "MODULE" $Ident_{89}$
               $[$ "EXPORTS" $IDList_{87}$ $]$ "=" $Ident_{89}$ $GActls_9$ "END"
               $Ident_{89}$ ".".

8   $GFmls_8$ $=$ "(" $[IDList_{87}]$ ")".

9   $GActls_9$ $=$ "(" $[IDList_{87}]$ ")".

10 $Import_{10}$ = "IMPORT" $ImportItem_{11}$ { "," $ImportItem_{11}$ } "; "
                            | "FROM" $Ident_{89}$ "IMPORT" $IDList_{87}$ ";".
11 $ImportItem_{11}$ = $Ident_{89}$ [AS $Ident_{89}$].
12 $Block_{12}$ = { $Declaration_{13}$ }"BEGIN" $Stmts_{23}$ "END".
13 $Declaration_{13}$ = "CONST" { $ConstDecl_{14}$ ";" } | "TYP E" { $TypeDecl_{15}$ ";" }
                            | "EXCEPTION" { $ExceptionDecl_{16}$ ";" }
                            | "VAR" { $VariableDecl_{17}$ ";" }
                            | $ProcedureHead_{18}$ ["=" $Block_{12}$ $Ident_{89}$] ";".
                            | "REVEAL" $Ident_{89}$ ("=" | "<:") $Type_{48}$.
14 $ConstDecl_{14}$ = $Ident_{89}$ [":" $Type_{48}$] "=" $ConstExpr_{65}$.
15 $TypeDecl_{15}$ = $Ident_{89}$ ("=" | "<:") $Type_{48}$.
16 $ExceptionDecl_{16}$ = $Ident_{89}$ ["(" $Type_{48}$ ")"].
17 $VariableDecl_{17}$ = $IDList_{87}$ (":" $Type_{48}$ ":=" $Expr_{66}$ | ":" $Type_{48}$ | ":=" $Expr_{66}$).
18 $ProcedureHead_{18}$= "PROCEDURE" $Ident_{89}$ $Signature_{19}$.
19 $Signature_{19}$ = "(" $Formals_{20}$ ")" [":" $Type_{48}$] [' 'RAISES" $Raises_{22}$].
20 $Formals_{20}$ = [$Formal_{21}$ { ";" $Formal_{21}$ } [";"]].
21 $Formal_{21}$ = ["VALUE" | "VAR" | "READONLY"] $IDList_{87}$
                            (":" $Type_{48}$ | ":=" $ConstExpr_{65}$
                            | ":" $Type_{48}$ ":=" $ConstExpr_{65}$).
22 $Raises_{22}$ = "{" [$QualID_{86}$ { "," $QualID_{86}$ }] "}" " | "ANY" .

B.8.8   Statement productions

23 $Stmts_{23}$ = [$Stmt_{24}$ { ";" $Stmt_{24}$ } [";"]].
24 $Stmt_{24}$ = $AssignStmt_{25}$ | $Block_{12}$ | $CallStmt_{26}$ | $CaseStmt_{27}$
                            | $ExitStmt_{28}$ | $EvalStmt_{29}$ | $ForStmt_{30}$ | $IfStmt_{31}$
                            | $LockStmt_{32}$ | $LoopStmt_{33}$ | $RaiseStmt_{34}$ | $RepeatStmt_{35}$
                            | $ReturnStmt_{36}$ | $TryFinStmt_{39}$ | $TryXptStmt_{38}$
                            | $TCaseStmt_{37}$ | $WhileStmt_{40}$ | $WithStmt_{41}$.
25 $AssignStmt_{25}$ = $Expr_{66}$ ":=" $Expr_{66}$.
26 $CallStmt_{26}$ = $Expr_{66}$ "(" [$Actual_{47}$ { "," $Actual_{47}$ }] ")".
27 $CaseStmt_{27}$ = "CASE" $Expr_{66}$ "OF" [$Case_{42}$] { "|" $Case_{42}$ }
                            ["ELSE" $Stmts_{23}$] "END".
28 $ExitStmt_{28}$ = "EXIT".
29 $EvalStmt_{29}$ = "EVAL" $Expr_{66}$.
30 $ForStmt_{30}$ = "FOR" $Ident_{89}$ ":=" $Expr_{66}$ "TO" $Expr_{66}$
                            ["BY" $Expr_{66}$] "DO" $Stmts_{23}$ "END".
31 $IfStmt_{31}$ = "IF" $Expr_{66}$ "THEN" $Stmts_{23}$
                            { "ELSIF" $Expr_{66}$ "THEN" $Stmts_{23}$ }
                            ["ELSE" $Stmts_{23}$] "END".
32 $LockStmt_{32}$ = "LOCK" $Expr_{66}$ "DO" $Stmts_{23}$ "END".
33 $LoopStmt_{33}$ = "LOOP" $Stmts_{23}$ "END".
34 $RaiseStmt_{34}$ = "RAISE" $QualID_{86}$ ["(" $Expr_{66}$ ")"].
35 $RepeatStmt_{35}$ = "REPEAT" $Stmts_{23}$ "UNTIL" $Expr_{66}$.
36 $ReturnStmt_{36}$ = "RETURN" [$Expr_{66}$].

37 TCaseStmt$_{37}$ = "TYPECASE" Expr$_{66}$ "OF" [Tcase$_{45}$]
                             { "|" Tcase$_{45}$ } ["ELSE" Stmts$_{23}$] "END".

38 TryXptStmt$_{38}$ = "TRY" Stmts$_{23}$ "EXCEPT" [Handler$_{44}$] { "|" Handler$_{44}$ }
                             ["ELSE" Stmts$_{23}$] "END".

39 TryFinStmt$_{39}$ = "TRY" Stmts$_{23}$ "FINALLY" Stmts$_{23}$ "END".

40 WhileStmt$_{40}$ = "WHILE" Expr$_{66}$ "DO" Stmts$_{23}$ "END".

41 WithStmt$_{41}$ = "WITH" Binding$_{46}$ { "," Binding$_{46}$ } "DO" Stmts$_{23}$ "END".

42 Case$_{42}$ = Labels$_{43}$ { "," Labels$_{43}$ } "=¿" Stmts$_{23}$.

43 Labels$_{43}$ = ConstExpr$_{65}$ [".." ConstExpr$_{65}$].

44 Handler$_{44}$ = QualID$_{86}$ { "," QualID$_{86}$ } ["(" Ident$_{89}$ ")"] "=¿" Stmts$_{23}$.

45 Tcase$_{45}$ = Type$_{48}$ { "," Type$_{48}$ } ["(" Ident$_{89}$ ")"] "=¿" Stmts$_{23}$.

46 Binding$_{46}$ = Ident$_{89}$ "=" Expr$_{66}$.

47 Actual$_{47}$ = [Ident$_{89}$ ":="] Expr$_{66}$ | Type$_{48}$.

B.8.9   Type productions

48 Type$_{48}$ = TypeName$_{85}$ | ArrayType$_{49}$ | PackedType$_{50}$| EnumType$_{51}$
             | ObjectType$_{52}$ | ProcedureType$_{53}$ | RecordType$_{54}$
             | RefType$_{55}$ | SetType$_{56}$ | SubrangeType$_{57}$ | "(" Type$_{48}$")".

49 ArrayType$_{49}$ = "ARRAY" [Type$_{48}$ { "," Type$_{48}$ }] "OF" Type$_{48}$.

50 PackedType$_{50}$ = "BITS" ConstExpr$_{65}$ "FOR" Type$_{48}$.

51 EnumType$_{51}$ = "{" [IDList$_{87}$] "}".

52 ObjectType$_{52}$ = [TypeName$_{85}$ | ObjectType$_{52}$] [Brand$_{58}$]
             "OBJECT" Fields$_{59}$
             ["METHODS" Methods$_{61}$]
             ["OVERRIDES" Overrides$_{63}$] "END".

53 ProcedureType$_{53}$ = "PROCEDURE" Signature$_{19}$.

54 RecordType$_{54}$ = "RECORD" Fields$_{59}$ "END".

55 RefType$_{55}$ = ["UNTRACED"] [Brand$_{58}$] "REF" Type$_{48}$.

56 SetType$_{56}$ = "SET" "OF" Type$_{48}$.

57 SubrangeType$_{57}$ = "[" ConstExpr$_{65}$ ".." ConstExpr$_{65}$ "]" ".

58 Brand$_{58}$ = "BRANDED" [TextLiteral$_{92}$].

59 Fields$_{59}$ = [Field$_{60}$ { ";" Field$_{60}$ } [";"]].

60 Field$_{60}$ = IDList$_{87}$ (":" Type$_{48}$ | ":=" ConstExpr$_{65}$ |
             ":" Type$_{48}$ ":=" ConstExpr$_{65}$).

61 Methods$_{61}$ = [Method$_{62}$ { ";" Method$_{62}$ } [";"]].

62 Method$_{62}$ = Ident$_{89}$ Signature$_{19}$ [":=" ConstExpr$_{65}$].

63 Overrides$_{63}$ = [Override$_{64}$ { ";" Override$_{64}$ } [";"]].

64 Override$_{64}$ = Ident$_{89}$ ":=" ConstExpr$_{65}$.

B.8.10   Expression productions

65 ConstExpr$_{65}$ = Expr$_{66}$.

66 Expr$_{66}$ = E1$_{67}$ { "OR" E1$_{67}$ }.

67 $E1_{67}$ = $E2_{68}$ { "AND" $E2_{68}$ }.
68 $E2_{68}$ = { "NOT" } $E3_{69}$.
69 $E3_{69}$ = $E4_{70}$ { $Relop_{75}$ $E4_{70}$ }.
70 $E4_{70}$ = $E5_{71}$ { $Addop_{76}$ $E5_{71}$ }.
71 $E5_{71}$ = $E6_{72}$ { $Mulop_{77}$ $E6_{72}$ }.
72 $E6_{72}$ = {"+" | "–"} $E7_{73}$.
73 $E7_{73}$ = $E8_{74}$ { $Selector_{78}$ }.
74 $E8_{74}$ = $Ident_{89}$ | $Number_{94}$ | $CharLiteral_{91}$ | $TextLiteral_{92}$
                   | $Constructor_{79}$ | "(" $Expr_{66}$ ")".
75 $Relop_{75}$ = "=" | "#" | "<" | "<=" | ">" | ">=" | "IN".
76 $Addop_{76}$ = "+" | "–" | "&".
77 $Mulop_{77}$ = "*" | "/" | "DIV" | "MOD".
78 $Selector_{78}$ = "^" | "." $Ident_{89}$ | "[" $Expr_{66}$ { "," $Expr_{66}$ } "]"
                   | "(" [$Actual_{47}$ { "," $Actual_{47}$ }] ")".
79 $Constructor_{79}$ = $Type_{48}$ "{" [$SetCons_{80}$ | $RecordCons_{82}$ | $ArrayCons_{84}$] "}".
80 $SetCons_{80}$ = $SetElt_{81}$ { "," $SetElt_{81}$ }.
81 $SetElt_{81}$ = $Expr_{66}$ [".." $Expr_{66}$].
82 $RecordCons_{82}$ = $RecordElt_{83}$ { "," $RecordElt_{83}$ }.
83 $RecordElt_{83}$ = [$Ident_{89}$ ":="] $Expr_{66}$.
84 $ArrayCons_{84}$ = $Expr_{66}$ {"," $Expr_{66}$ } ["," ".."].

B.8.11 Miscellaneous productions

85 $TypeName_{85}$ = $QualID_{86}$ | "ROOT" | "UNTRACED ROOT"
86 $QualID_{86}$ = $Ident_{89}$ ["." $Ident_{89}$].
87 $IDList_{87}$ = $Ident_{89}$ { "," $Ident_{89}$ }.

B.8.12 Token productions

To read a token, first skip all blanks, tabs, newlines, carriage returns, vertical tabs, form feeds, comments, and pragmas. Then read the longest sequence of characters that forms an operator (as defined in Section B.8.3, page 518) or an Id or Literal, as defined here. An Id is a case-significant sequence of letters, digits, and underscores that begins with a letter. An Id is a keyword if it appears in Section B.8.1, a reserved identifier if it appears in Section B.8.2, and an ordinary identifier otherwise.

In the following grammar, terminals are characters surrounded by doublequotes and the special terminal DQUOTE represents doublequote itself.

88 $Literal_{88}$ = $Number_{94}$ | $CharLiteral_{91}$ | $TextLiteral_{92}$.
89 $Ident_{89}$ = $Letter_{100}$ { $Letter_{100}$ | $Digit_{98}$ | "_" }.
90 $Operator_{90}$ = "+" | "–" | "*" | "/" | "." | "^" | ":" "=" | "="
                   | "#" | "<" | "<" "=" | ">" "=" | ">" | "&"
                   | "<" "." | "=" ">" | ";" | "," | "|" | "." "." | "." "." "."
                   | "(" | ")" | "{" | "}" | "[" | "]".

91 CharLiteral_{91} = """" (PrintingChar_{96} | Escape_{93} | DQUOTE) """".

92 TextLiteral_{92} = DQUOTE { PrintingChar_{96} | Escape_{93} | " " } DQUOTE.

93 Escape_{93} $\overset{\underline{\ }}{=}$ ' "n" | "\" "t" | "\" "r" | "\" "f" | "\" "\" | "\" """"
     | "\" DQUOTE | "\" OctalDigit_{99} OctalDigit OctalDigit_{99}.

94 Number_{94} = Digit_{98} { Digit_{98} }
     | Digit_{98} { Digit_{98} } "_" HexDigit_{97} { HexDigit_{97} }
     | Digit_{98} { Digit_{98} } "." Digit_{98} { Digit_{98} } [Exponent_{95}].

95 Exponent_{95} = ("E"|"e"|"D"|"d"|"X"|"x") ["+" | "−"] Digit_{98} { Digit_{98} }.

96 PrintingChar_{96} = Letter_{100} | Digit_{98} | OtherChar_{101}.

97 HexDigit_{97} = Digit_{98} | "A" | "B" | "C" | "D" | "E" | "F"
     | "a" | "b" | "c" | "d" | "e" | "f".

98 Digit_{98} = "0" | "1" | ⋯ | "9".

99 OctalDigit_{99} = "0" | "1" | ⋯ | "7".

100 Letter_{100} = "A" | "B" | ⋯ | "Z" | "a" | "b" | ⋯ | "z".

101 OtherChar_{101} = " " | "!" | "#" | "\" | " %" | "&" | "(" | ")" | "*" | "+"
     | "," | "−" | "." | "/" | ":" | ";" | "<" | "=" | ">" | "?"
     | "@" | "[" | "]" | "^" | "_" | """" | "{" | "|" | "}" | "~"
     | $\text{ExtendedChar}_{102}$.

102 $\text{ExtendedChar}_{102}$ = *any char with* ISO-*Latin-1 code in* $[8\_240..8\_377]$.

Appendix C

Library interfaces

C.1 Standard interfaces

The interfaces Thread, Word and Text as well as the floating-point interfaces Real, LongReal, Extended, Float and FloatMode must be provided by every language environment. The interfaces listed here represent the minimum that a Modula-3 language environment must provide; a given environment can extend them.

The floating-point interfaces allow invocation of the floating-point arithmetic of the respective language environment. The terminology employed stems from ANSI/IEEE Standard 754-1985 for floating-point arithmetic. All other interfaces are explained in detail in [Nel91], the source of the interfaces printed here.

C.1.1 Text

A variable of type TEXT references a numbered sequence of characters, where the first character is at position 0. The value NIL does not represent a sequence of characters and is never returned by the following procedures; passing NIL to these procedures as parameter leads to a run-time error.

```
INTERFACE Text;                 (*Copyright (C) 1994, Digital Equipment Corporation. *)

IMPORT Word;

TYPE T = TEXT;

CONST Brand = "Text–1.0";

PROCEDURE Cat(t, u: T): T;
(*Return the concatenation of t and u. *)

PROCEDURE Equal(t, u: T): BOOLEAN;
(*Return TRUE if t and u have the same length and (case-sensitive) contents. *)

PROCEDURE GetChar(t: T; i: CARDINAL): CHAR;
(*Return character i of t. It is a checked runtime error if i >= Length(t). *)

PROCEDURE Length(t: T): CARDINAL;
(*Return the number of characters in t. *)

PROCEDURE Empty(t: T): BOOLEAN;
(*Equivalent to Length(t) = 0. *)

PROCEDURE Sub(t: T; start: CARDINAL; length: CARDINAL := LAST(CARDINAL)): T;
(*Return a sub-sequence of t: empty if start >= Length(t) or
  length = 0; otherwise the subsequence ranging from start to the
  minimum of start+length-1 and Length(t)–1. *)

PROCEDURE SetChars(VAR a: ARRAY OF CHAR; t: T);
(*For each i from 0 to MIN(LAST(a), Length(t)-1), set a[i] to GetChar(t, i). *)

PROCEDURE FromChar(ch: CHAR): T;
(*Return a text containing the single character ch. *)

PROCEDURE FromChars(READONLY a: ARRAY OF CHAR): T;
(*Return a text containing the characters of a. *)

PROCEDURE Hash(t: T): Word.T;
(*Return a hash function of the contents of t. *)

PROCEDURE Compare(t1, t2: T): [-1..1];
(*Return -1 if t1 occurs before t2, 0 if Equal(t1, t2), +1 if t1
  occurs after t2 in lexicographic order. *)

PROCEDURE FindChar(t: T; c: CHAR; start := 0): INTEGER;
(*If c = t[i] for some i in [start .. Length(t)–1], return the
  smallest such i; otherwise, return -1. *)

PROCEDURE FindCharR(t: T; c: CHAR; start := LAST(INTEGER)): INTEGER;
(*If c = t[i] for some i in [0 .. MIN(start, Length(t)–1)],
  return the largest such i; otherwise, return -1. *)
END Text.
```

C.1.2 Thread

A variable of type Thread.T identifies a thread. A MUTEX variable is either not locked or is locked by a thread. A condition variable (i.e., a variable of type Thread.Condition) is a set of waiting threads. A newly created MUTEX variable is not locked; a newly created condition variable is empty. NIL is not a practical value for variables of these three types; it is a checked runtime error to pass the NIL MUTEX, condition, or Thread.T to any procedures in this interface.

For a detailed explanation of these terms, see Chapter 16.

```
INTERFACE Thread;        (*Copyright (C) 1989, 1993 Digital Equipment Corporation *)

TYPE
  T <: ROOT;
  Mutex = MUTEX;
  Condition <: ROOT;

TYPE Closure = OBJECT METHODS apply(): REFANY END;

PROCEDURE Fork(cl: Closure): T;
(*Return a handle on a newly-created thread executing cl.apply(). *)

PROCEDURE Join(t: T): REFANY;
(*Wait until t has terminated and return its result. It is a
  checked runtime error to call this more than once for any t. *)

PROCEDURE Wait(m: Mutex; c: Condition);
(*The calling thread must have m locked. Atomically unlocks m and
  waits on c. Then relocks m and returns. *)

PROCEDURE Acquire(m: Mutex);
(*Wait until m is unlocked and then lock it. *)

PROCEDURE Release(m: Mutex);
(*The calling thread must have m locked. Unlocks m. *)

PROCEDURE Broadcast(c: Condition);
(*All threads waiting on c become eligible to run. *)

PROCEDURE Signal(c: Condition);
(*One or more threads waiting on c become eligible to run. *)

PROCEDURE Pause(n: LONGREAL);
(*Wait for n seconds to elapse.
  To wait until a specified point in time in the future, say t,
  you can use the call Pause(t – Time.Now()) *)

PROCEDURE Self(): T;
(*Return the handle of the calling thread. *)
```

```
EXCEPTION Alerted;
(*Used to approximate asynchronous interrupts. *)

PROCEDURE Alert(t: T);
(*Mark t as an alerted thread. *)

PROCEDURE TestAlert(): BOOLEAN;
(*If the calling thread has been marked alerted, return TRUE and
  unmark it. *)

PROCEDURE AlertWait(m: Mutex; c: Condition) RAISES {Alerted};
(*Like Wait, but if the thread is marked alerted at the time of
  call or sometime during the wait, lock m and raise Alerted. *)

PROCEDURE AlertJoin(t: T): REFANY RAISES {Alerted};
(*Like Join, but if the thread is marked alerted at the time of
  call or sometime during the wait, raise Alerted. *)

PROCEDURE AlertPause(n: LONGREAL) RAISES {Alerted};
(*Like Pause, but if the thread is marked alerted at the time of
  the call or sometime during the wait, raise Alerted. *)

(*Specifying thread stack size.
  Normally Fork uses a default value for the size of the stack of
  the new thread. It is possible to change the default value, and also
  to specify the value used for a particular call to Fork by supplying
  a SizedClosure rather than a Closure. Stack sizes are given as a
  number of Word.Ts. *)

PROCEDURE GetDefaultStackSize(): CARDINAL;
(*Return the current default stack size for new threads. *)

PROCEDURE MinDefaultStackSize(min: CARDINAL);
(*Change the default stack size for newly forked threads to the
  greater of min and the current default stack size. *)

PROCEDURE IncDefaultStackSize(inc: CARDINAL);
(*Increment the default stack size for newly forked threads by inc. *)

TYPE
  SizedClosure = Closure OBJECT stackSize: CARDINAL := 0 END;

END Thread.
```

C.1.3 Word

The type Word.T represents a sequence of Word.Size bits numbered from 0 to Word.Size-1. A value of this type is also a natural number resulting when the bits are interpreted as dual digits (with bit number 0 having the least place value).

```
INTERFACE Word;                    (*Copyright (C) 1989, Digital Equipment Corporation *)

TYPE
  T = INTEGER;      (*encoding is implementation-dependent; e.g., 2's complement. *)

CONST
  Size : INTEGER = BITSIZE (T);                          (*implementation-dependent *)

PROCEDURE Plus    (x, y: T): T;                    (*(x + y) MOD 2^Word.Size *)
PROCEDURE Times   (x, y: T): T;                    (*(x * y) MOD 2^Word.Size *)
PROCEDURE Minus   (x, y: T): T;                    (*(x - y) MOD 2^Word.Size *)
PROCEDURE Divide  (x, y: T): T;                         (*x divided by y *)
PROCEDURE Mod     (x, y: T): T;                              (*x MOD y *)
PROCEDURE LT      (x, y: T): BOOLEAN;                          (*x < y *)
PROCEDURE LE      (x, y: T): BOOLEAN;                         (*x <= y *)
PROCEDURE GT      (x, y: T): BOOLEAN;                          (*x > y *)
PROCEDURE GE      (x, y: T): BOOLEAN;                         (*x >= y *)
PROCEDURE And     (x, y: T): T;                  (*Bitwise AND of x and y *)
PROCEDURE Or      (x, y: T): T;                   (*Bitwise OR of x and y *)
PROCEDURE Xor     (x, y: T): T;                  (*Bitwise XOR of x and y *)
PROCEDURE Not     (x: T): T;                    (*Bitwise complement of x *)

PROCEDURE Shift (x: T; n: INTEGER): T;
(*For all i such that both i and i – n are in the range [0 .. Word.Size –1],
  bit i of the result equals bit i – n of x. The other bits of the result are 0.
  Thus, shifting by n > 0 is like multiplying by 2^n *)

PROCEDURE LeftShift (x: T; n: [0..Size–1]): T;
(*= Shift (x, n) *)

PROCEDURE RightShift (x: T; n: [0..Size–1]): T;
(*= Shift (x, –n) *)

PROCEDURE Rotate (x: T; n: INTEGER): T;
(*Bit i of the result equals bit (i – n) MOD Word.Size of x. *)

PROCEDURE LeftRotate (x: T; n: [0..Size–1]): T;
(*= Rotate (x, n) *)

PROCEDURE RightRotate (x: T; n: [0..Size–1]): T;
(*= Rotate (x, –n) *)

PROCEDURE Extract (x: T; i, n: CARDINAL): T;
(*Take n bits from x, with bit i as the least significant bit, and return them
  as the least significant n bits of a word whose other bits are 0.
  A checked runtime error if n + i > Word.Size. *)

PROCEDURE Insert (x, y: T; i, n: CARDINAL): T;
(*Return x with n bits replaced, with bit i as the least significant bit, by
  the least significant n bits of y. The other bits of x are unchanged.
  A checked runtime error if n + i > Word.Size. *)

END Word.
```

C.1.4 Real

The interface Real defines the representation and range of floating-point numbers in the language environment. There are analogous interfaces for LongReal and Extended. The values of constants are examples and depend on the language environment.

```
INTERFACE Real;                    (*Copyright (C) 1991, Digital Equipment Corporation *)

(*Properties of REAL (for ANSI/IEEE Standard 754-1985).

  This package defines some basic properties of the built-in float type REAL. *)

TYPE T = REAL;

CONST
  Base: INTEGER = 2;               (*The radix of the floating-point representation for T *)

  Precision: INTEGER = 24; (*The number of digits of precision in the given Base for T *)

  MaxFinite: T = 3.40282347E+38;
(*The maximum finite value in T. For non-IEEE implementations, this is
  the same as LAST(T). *)

  MinPos: T = 1.40239846E−45;                       (*The minimum positive value in T. *)

  MinPosNormal: T = 1.17549435E−38;
(*The minimum positive normal value in T; differs from MinPos only for
  implementations with denormalized numbers. *)

CONST
  MaxExpDigits = 2;
  MaxSignifDigits = 9;

(*MaxExpDigits is the smallest integer with the property that every
  finite number of type T can be written in base-10 scientific
  notation using an exponent with at most MaxExpDigits.
  MaxSignifDigits is the smallest integer with the property that
  floating-decimal numbers with MaxSignifDigits are more closely
  spaced, all along the number line, than are numbers of type T.
  Typically,
  MaxExpDigits = ceiling(log₁₀(log₁₀(MaxFinite)))
  MaxSignifDigits = ceiling(log₁₀(Base^Precision)) + 1. *)

END Real.
```

C.1.5 Float

The generic interface Float provides operations required or recommended by ANSI/IEEE Standard 754-1985. They are instantiated as follows:

INTERFACE RealFloat = Float(Real) END RealFloat.
INTERFACE LongFloat = Float(LongReal) END LongFloat.
INTERFACE ExtendedFloat = Float(Extended) END ExtendedFloat.

The comments in the interface only describe how the operations function when their arguments are normal numbers and do not raise exceptions. The IEEE standard explains in more detail how these operations should react to non-numeric values (or *NaNs: not a number*) and to infinite values (*infinity*). Language environments whose floating-point arithmetic does not correspond to the standard should describe these special cases separately.

```
GENERIC INTERFACE Float(R);                (*Copyright (C) 1991, Digital Equipment Corporation *)

IMPORT FloatMode;

TYPE T = R.T;

PROCEDURE Scalb(x: T; n: INTEGER): T RAISES {FloatMode.Trap};
(*Return x2^n. *)

PROCEDURE Logb(x: T): T RAISES {FloatMode.Trap};
(*Return the exponent of x. More precisely, return the unique integer n such that the
   ratio ABS(x) / Base^n is in the half-open interval [1..Base], unless x is
   denormalized, in which case return the minimum exponent value for T. *)

PROCEDURE ILogb(x: T): INTEGER;
(*Like Logb, but returns an integer, never raises an exception, and always returns the
   n such that ABS(x) / Base^n is in the half-open interval [1..Base), even for
   denormalized numbers. Special cases: it returns FIRST(INTEGER) when x = 0.0,
   LAST(INTEGER) when x is plus or minus infinity, and zero when x is NaN. *)

PROCEDURE NextAfter(x, y: T): T RAISES {FloatMode.Trap};
(*Return the next representable neighbor of x in the direction towards y.
   If x = y, return x. *)

PROCEDURE CopySign(x, y: T): T;
(*Return x with the sign of y. *)

PROCEDURE Finite(x: T): BOOLEAN;
(*Return TRUE if x is strictly between minus infinity and plus infinity.
   This always returns TRUE on non-IEEE implementations. *)

PROCEDURE IsNaN(x: T): BOOLEAN;
(*Return FALSE if x represents a numerical (possibly infinite) value, and
   TRUE if x does not represent a numerical value. For example, on IEEE
   implementations, returns TRUE if x is a NaN, FALSE otherwise. *)

PROCEDURE Sign(x: T): [0..1];
(*Return the sign bit x. For non-IEEE implementations, this is
   the same as ORD(x >= 0); for IEEE implementations,
   Sign(−0) = 1 and Sign(+0) = 0. *)
```

PROCEDURE Differs(x, y: T): BOOLEAN;
(*Return (x < y OR y < x). Thus, for IEEE implementations,
  Differs(NaN,x) is always FALSE; for non-IEEE implementations,
  Differs(x,y) is the same as x # y. *)

PROCEDURE Unordered(x, y: T): BOOLEAN;
(*Return NOT (x <= y OR y <= x). Thus, for IEEE implementations,
  Unordered(NaN, x) is always TRUE; for non-IEEE implementations,
  Unordered(x, y) is always FALSE. *)

PROCEDURE Sqrt(x: T): T RAISES {FloatMode.Trap};
(*Return the square root of T. This must be correctly rounded if
  FloatMode.IEEE is TRUE. *)

TYPE IEEEClass = {SignalingNaN, QuietNaN, Infinity, Normal, Denormal, Zero};

PROCEDURE Class(x: T): IEEEClass;
(*Return the IEEE number class containing x. On non-IEEE systems,
  the result will be Normal or Zero. *)

PROCEDURE FromDecimal(
      sign: [0..1];
      READONLY digits: ARRAY OF [0..9];
      exp: INTEGER): T RAISES {FloatMode.Trap};
(*Convert from floating-decimal to type T. *)

(*Let F denote the nonnegative, floating-decimal number
  digits[0] . digits[1] ... digits[LAST(digits)] * 10^{exp}
  = sum(i, digits[i] * $10^{(exp - i)}$)
  The result of FromDecimal is the number $(-1)^{sign}$ * F, rounded
  to a value of type T.
  The procedure FromDecimal is a floating-point operation, just
  like + and *, in the sense that it rounds its ideal result
  correctly, observing the current rounding mode, and it sets flags
  and raises traps by the usual rules. On IEEE implementations, it
  returns minus zero when F is sufficiently small and sign=1. *)

TYPE
  DecimalApprox = RECORD
    class: IEEEClass;
    sign: [0..1];
    len: [1..R.MaxSignifDigits];
    digits: ARRAY[0..R.MaxSignifDigits−1] OF [0..9];
    exp: INTEGER;
    errorSign: [−1..1]
  END;

PROCEDURE ToDecimal(x: T): DecimalApprox;
(*Convert from type T to floating-decimal. *)

END Float.

C.1.6 FloatMode

This interface allows testing the behavior of rounding and numeric exceptions. Some language environments allow changing this behavior for individual threads.

```
INTERFACE FloatMode;          (*Copyright (C) 1991, Digital Equipment Corporation *)

CONST IEEE = TRUE;
(*TRUE for fully-compliant IEEE implementations. *)

EXCEPTION Failure;
(*Raised by attempts to set modes that are not supported by the implementation. *)

TYPE
    RoundingMode = {NearestElseEven, TowardMinusInfinity, TowardPlusInfinity,
                    TowardZero, NearestElseAwayFromZero, IBM370, Other};
(*Rounding modes. The first four are the IEEE modes. *)

CONST RoundDefault = RoundingMode.NearestElseEven;
(*Implementation-dependent: the default mode for rounding arithmetic
    operations, used by a newly forked thread. This also specifies the
    behavior of the ROUND operation in half-way cases. *)

PROCEDURE SetRounding(md: RoundingMode) RAISES {Failure};
(*Change the rounding mode for the calling thread to md, or raise the exception
    if this cannot be done. This affects the implicit rounding in floating-point operations;
    it does not affect the ROUND operation. Generally this can be done only on IEEE
    implementations and only if md is an IEEE mode. *)

PROCEDURE GetRounding(): RoundingMode;
(*Return the rounding mode for the calling thread. *)

TYPE
    Flag = {Invalid, Inexact, Overflow, Underflow,
            DivByZero, IntOverflow, IntDivByZero};

(*Associated with each thread is a set of boolean status flags recording whether the
    condition represented by the flag has occurred in the thread since the flag was last
    reset. The meaning of the first five flags is defined precisely in the IEEE floating
    point standard; roughly they mean:

    Invalid = invalid argument to an operation.
    Inexact = an operation produced an inexact result.
    Overflow = a floating-point operation produced a result whose
    absolute value is too large to be represented.
    Underflow = a floating-point operation produced a result whose
    absolute value is too small to be represented.
    DivByZero = floating-point division by zero.
    IntOverflow = an integer operation produced a result whose
    absolute value is too large to be represented.
    IntDivByZero = integer DIV or MOD by zero. *)

CONST NoFlags = SET OF Flag {};
```

PROCEDURE GetFlags(): SET OF Flag;
(*Return the set of flags for the current thread. *)

PROCEDURE SetFlags(s: SET OF Flag): SET OF Flag RAISES {Failure};
(*Set the flags for the current thread to s, and return their previous values. *)

PROCEDURE ClearFlag(f: Flag);
(*Turn off the flag f for the current thread. *)

EXCEPTION Trap(Flag);

TYPE Behavior = {Trap, SetFlag, Ignore};

(*The behavior of an operation that causes one of the flag conditions is either:
   Ignore = return some result and do nothing.
   SetFlag = return some result and set the condition flag. For
   IEEE implementations, the result of the operation is defined by the
   standard.
   Trap = possibly set the condition flag; in any case raise the
   Trap exception with the appropriate flag as the argument. *)

PROCEDURE SetBehavior(f: Flag; b: Behavior) RAISES {Failure};
(*Set the behavior of the current thread for the flag f to be b,
   or raise Failure if this cannot be done. *)

PROCEDURE GetBehavior(f: Flag): Behavior;
(*Return the behavior of the current thread for the flag f. *)

(***misc.** *)

TYPE
   ThreadState = RECORD
     behavior: ARRAY Flag OF Behavior;
     sticky: ARRAY Flag OF BOOLEAN;
   END;
(*One copy per thread, saved by the thread implementation. *)

PROCEDURE InitThread(VAR s: ThreadState);
(*Initialize the current thread to the default floating-point state. *)

END FloatMode.

C.2   Formatting

C.2.1   Fmt

The procedures of interface Fmt permit converting numbers and other data
to text.

```
INTERFACE Fmt;                    (*Copyright (C) 1994, Digital Equipment Corporation *)

IMPORT Word, Real AS R, LongReal AS LR, Extended AS ER;

PROCEDURE Bool(b: BOOLEAN): TEXT;
(*Format b as "TRUE" or "FALSE". *)

PROCEDURE Char(c: CHAR): TEXT;
(*Return a text containing the character c. *)

TYPE Base = [2..16];

PROCEDURE Int(n: INTEGER; base: Base := 10): TEXT;
PROCEDURE Unsigned(n: Word.T; base: Base := 16): TEXT;
(*Format the signed or unsigned number n in the specified base. *)

(*The value returned by Int or Unsigned never contains upper-case letters, and it never
    starts with an explicit base and underscore. For example, to render an unsigned
    number N in hexadecimal as a legal Modula-3 literal, you must write something like:
    "16_" & Fmt.Unsigned(N, 16) *)

TYPE Style = {Sci, Fix, Auto};

PROCEDURE Real(
    x: REAL;
    style := Style.Auto;
    prec: CARDINAL := R.MaxSignifDigits − 1;
    literal := FALSE)
  : TEXT;
PROCEDURE LongReal(
    x: LONGREAL;
    style := Style.Auto;
    prec: CARDINAL := LR.MaxSignifDigits − 1;
    literal := FALSE)
  : TEXT;
PROCEDURE Extended(
    x: EXTENDED;
    style := Style.Auto;
    prec: CARDINAL := ER.MaxSignifDigits − 1;
    literal := FALSE)
  : TEXT;
(*Format the floating-point number x. *)

(*Overview.

    Style.Sci gives scientific notation with fields padded to fixed widths, suitable
    for making a table. The parameter prec specifies the number of digits after the
    decimal point—that is, the relative precision.

    Style.Fix gives fixed point, with prec once again specifying the number
    of digits after the decimal point—in this case, the absolute precision. The results
    of Style.Fix have varying widths, but they will form a table if they are
    right-aligned (using Fmt.Pad) in a sufficiently wide field.
```

Style.Auto *is not intended for tables. It gives scientific notation with at most* prec *digits after the decimal point for numbers that are very big or very small. There may be fewer than* prec *digits after the decimal point because trailing zeros are suppressed. For numbers that are neither too big nor too small, it formats the same significant digits—at most* prec+1 *of them—in fixed point, for greater legibility.*

All styles omit the decimal point unless it is followed by at least one digit.

Setting literal *to* TRUE *alters all styles as necessary to make the result a legal Modula-3 literal of the appropriate type.* *)

TYPE Align = {Left, Right};

PROCEDURE Pad(
    text: TEXT;
    length: CARDINAL;
    padChar: CHAR := ' ';
    align: Align := Align.Right): TEXT;
(*If Text.Length(text) >= length, *then* text *is returned unchanged. Otherwise,* text *is padded with* padChar *until it has the given* length. *The text goes to the right or left, according to* align. *)

PROCEDURE F(fmt: TEXT; t1, t2, t3, t4, t5: TEXT := NIL): TEXT;
(*Uses fmt *as a format string. The result is a copy of* fmt *in which all format specifiers have been replaced, in order, by the text arguments* t1, t2, *etc.* *)

(**A format specifier contains a field width, alignment and one of two padding characters. The procedure* F *evaluates the specifier and replaces it by the corresponding text argument padded as it would be by a call to* Pad *with the specified field width, padding character and alignment.*

The syntax of a format specifier is:

%[-]{0-9}s

that is, a percent character followed by an optional minus sign, an optional number and a compulsory terminating s. *If the minus sign is present the alignment is* Align.Left, *otherwise it is* Align.Right. *The alignment corresponds to the* align *argument to* Pad. *The number specifies the field width (this corresponds to the* length *argument to* Pad). *If the number is omitted it defaults to zero. If the number is present and starts with the digit "0" the padding character is* '0'; *otherwise it is the space character. The padding character corresponds to the* padChar *argument to* Pad. *It is a checked runtime error if* fmt *is* NIL *or the number of format specifiers in* fmt *is not equal to the number of non-nil arguments to* F. *Non-nil arguments to* F *must precede any* NIL *arguments; it is a checked runtime error if they do not. If* t1 *to* t5 *are all* NIL *and* fmt *contains no format specifiers, the result is* fmt.*)

(***Examples:**

F("%s %s \n", "Hello", "World") 'returns' "Hello World \n".
F("%s", Int(3)) 'returns' "3"
F("%2s", Int(3)) 'returns' " 3"
F("%-2s", Int(3)) 'returns' "3 "
F("%02s", Int(3)) 'returns' "03"
F("%-02s", Int(3)) 'returns' "30"
F("%s", "%s") 'returns' "%s"
F("%s% tax", Int(3)) 'returns' "3% tax"

The following examples are legal but pointless:

F("%-s", Int(3)) 'returns' "3"
F("%0s", Int(3)) 'returns' "3"
F("%-0s", Int(3)) 'returns' "3"
*)

PROCEDURE FN(fmt: TEXT; READONLY texts: ARRAY OF TEXT): TEXT;
(*_Similar to F but accepts an array of text arguments. It is a checked runtime
error if the number of format specifiers in_ fmt _is not equal to_ NUMBER(texts)
or if any element of texts _is_ NIL. _If_ NUMBER(texts) = 0 _and_ fmt
contains no format specifiers the result is fmt. *)

(*_Example:_

FN("%s %s %s %s %s %s",
        ARRAY OF TEXT{"Too", "many", "arguments", "for", "F", "to", "handle"})
returns "Too many arguments for F to handle". *)

END Fmt.

C.2.2   Scan

The procedures of interface Scan support reading numbers and other data from TEXT variables. The procedures read the txt parameter and convert its contents to values of the respective target type. Leading blanks and, for numbers, leading zeros are skipped.

```
INTERFACE Scan;              (*Copyright (C) 1994, Digital Equipment Corporation. *)

IMPORT Word, Lex, FloatMode;

(*Each of these procedures parses a string of characters and converts
  it to a binary value. Leading and trailing blanks (ie. characters
  in "Lex.Blanks") are ignored. "Lex.Error" is raised if the first
  non-blank substring is not generated by the corresponding "Lex"
  grammar or if there are zero or more than one non-blank substrings.
  "FloatMode.Trap" is raised as per "Lex". *)

PROCEDURE Bool(txt: TEXT): BOOLEAN RAISES {Lex.Error};

PROCEDURE Int(txt: TEXT; defaultBase: [2..16] := 10): INTEGER
    RAISES {Lex.Error, FloatMode.Trap};
PROCEDURE Unsigned(txt: TEXT; defaultBase: [2..16] := 16): Word.T
    RAISES {Lex.Error, FloatMode.Trap};

PROCEDURE Real(txt: TEXT): REAL              RAISES {Lex.Error, FloatMode.Trap};
PROCEDURE LongReal(txt: TEXT): LONGREAL RAISES {Lex.Error, FloatMode.Trap};
PROCEDURE Extended(txt: TEXT): EXTENDED RAISES {Lex.Error, FloatMode.Trap};

END Scan.
```

C.3   Input and output streams

Input and output streams (*readers* and *writers*) are explained in detail in [Nel91]. Here we only print the interfaces Rd and Wr.

C.3.1   Rd

A variable of type Rd.T identifies an input stream. After initialization (outside this interface) the stream is *open* and has a current position (initially 0). It can be *closed* later. Reading is not possible from closed streams. The operation GetChar reads a character from the stream and increments the position by one. The stream can be *seekable* or *intermittent*. An explanation of these terms can be found in Chapter 14.

INTERFACE Rd;   (*Copyright (C) 1989, Digital Equipment Corporation *)

IMPORT AtomList;
FROM Thread IMPORT Alerted;

TYPE T <: ROOT;

EXCEPTION EndOfFile; Failure(AtomList.T);

(*Since there are many classes of readers, there are many ways that a
reader can break—for example, the connection to a terminal can be
broken, the disk can signal a read error, etc. All problems of
this sort are reported by raising the exception Failure. The
documentation of a reader class should specify what failures the
class can raise and how they are encoded in the argument to Failure.
Illegal operations cause a checked runtime error. *)

PROCEDURE GetChar(rd: T): CHAR RAISES {EndOfFile, Failure, Alerted};
(*Return the next character from rd. *)

(*Many operations on a reader can wait indefinitely. For example,
GetChar can wait if the user is not typing. In general these waits
are alertable, so each procedure that might wait includes
Thread.Alerted in its RAISES clause. *)

PROCEDURE EOF(rd: T): BOOLEAN RAISES {Failure, Alerted};
(*Return TRUE if rd is at end-of-file. *)

(*Notice that on an intermittent reader, EOF can block. For example, if there are no
characters buffered in a terminal reader, EOF must wait until the user types one before
it can determine whether he typed the special key signalling end-of-file. If you are
using EOF in an interactive input loop, the right sequence of operations is:
- prompt the user;
- call EOF, which probably waits on user input;
- presuming that EOF returned FALSE, read the user's input. *)

PROCEDURE UnGetChar(rd: T) RAISES {};
(*"Push back" the last character read from rd, so that the next
call to GetChar will read it again.
Except there is a special rule: UnGetChar(rd) is guaranteed to
work only if GetChar(rd) was the last operation on rd. Thus
UnGetChar cannot be called twice in a row, or after Seek or
EOF. If this rule is violated, the implementation is allowed (but
not required) to cause a checked runtime error. *)

PROCEDURE CharsReady(rd: T): CARDINAL RAISES {Failure};
(*Return some number of characters that can be read without
indefinite waiting. The "end of file marker" counts as one
character for this purpose, so CharsReady will return 1, not 0,
if EOF(rd) is true. *)

PROCEDURE GetSub(rd: T; VAR str: ARRAY OF CHAR)
  : CARDINAL RAISES {Failure, Alerted};
(*Read from rd into str until rd is exhausted or str is filled. *)

```
PROCEDURE GetSubLine(rd: T; VAR str: ARRAY OF CHAR)
  : CARDINAL RAISES {Failure, Alerted};
```
(*Read from rd *into* str *until a newline is read,* rd *is
exhausted, or* str *is filled.* *)

(*Note that GetLine *strips the terminating line break, while*
GetSubLine *does not.* *)

`PROCEDURE GetText(rd: T; len: CARDINAL): TEXT RAISES {Failure, Alerted};`
(*Read from rd *until it is exhausted or* len *characters have been
read, and return the result as a* TEXT. *)

`PROCEDURE GetLine(rd: T): TEXT RAISES {EndOfFile, Failure, Alerted};`
(*If EOF(rd) *then raise* EndOfFile. *Otherwise, read characters
until a line break is read or* rd *is exhausted, and return the
result as a* TEXT—*but discard the line break if it is present.* *)

`PROCEDURE Seek(rd: T; n: CARDINAL) RAISES {Failure, Alerted};`
(*If rd *is seekable set the current position of* rd *to* n.
Otherwise cause a checked runtime error. *)

`PROCEDURE Close(rd: T) RAISES {Failure, Alerted};`
(**Release any resources associated with* rd *and set* closed(rd) := TRUE.
*The documentation of a procedure that creates a reader should specify
what resources are released when the reader is closed.
This leaves* rd *closed even if it raises an exception, and is a no-op if*
rd *is closed.* *)

`PROCEDURE Index(rd: T): CARDINAL RAISES {};`
(**Return the current position of* rd *)

`PROCEDURE Length(rd: T): INTEGER RAISES {Failure, Alerted};`
(**Return the number of characters in* rd

*If the length is unknown to the implementation of an intermittent
reader,* Length(rd) *returns* −1 *)

```
PROCEDURE Intermittent(rd: T):   BOOLEAN RAISES {};
PROCEDURE Seekable(rd: T):       BOOLEAN RAISES {};
PROCEDURE Closed(rd: T):         BOOLEAN RAISES {};
```
(*Return intermittent(rd), seekable(rd), *and* closed(rd),
respectively. These can be applied to closed readers. *)

`END Rd.`

C.3.2   Wr

A variable of type Wr.T identifies an output stream. After initialization (outside this interface) the stream is *open* and has a current position (initially 0). It can be *closed* later. A closed stream cannot be written to. The operation PutChar writes a character to the stream and increments the current position by one. If the current position equals the length of the stream, the stream size is increased by one. New characters overwrite characters that might have been in the stream before. The stream can be *seekable* or *buffered*. An explanation of these terms can be found in Chapter 14.

```
INTERFACE Wr;                    (*Copyright (C) 1989, Digital Equipment Corporation *)

IMPORT AtomList;
FROM Thread IMPORT Alerted;

TYPE T <: ROOT;

EXCEPTION Failure(AtomList.T);

(*Since there are many classes of writers, there are many ways that a writer can
    break—for example, the network can go down, the disk can fill up, etc. All
    problems of this sort are reported by raising the exception Failure. The
    documentation of each writer class should specify what failures the class can
    raise and how they are encoded in the argument to Failure.

    Illegal operations (for example, writing to a closed writer) cause
    checked runtime errors. *)

VAR
    EOL: TEXT;                                                     (*End of line. *)
(*On POSIX, EOL is "\n"; on Win32, EOL is "\r\n". *)

(*Many operations on a writer can wait indefinitely. For example, PutChar
    can wait if the user has suspended output to his terminal. These waits can be
    alertable, so each procedure that might wait includes Thread.Alerted in
    its raises clause. *)

PROCEDURE PutChar(wr: T; ch: CHAR) RAISES {Failure, Alerted};
(*Output ch to wr. *)

PROCEDURE PutText(wr: T; t: TEXT) RAISES {Failure, Alerted};
(*Output t to wr. *)

PROCEDURE PutString(wr: T; READONLY a: ARRAY OF CHAR)
    RAISES {Failure, Alerted};
(*Output a to wr. *)

PROCEDURE Seek(wr: T; n: CARDINAL) RAISES {Failure, Alerted};
(*Set the current position of wr to n. This is an error if wr is closed. *)

PROCEDURE Flush(wr: T) RAISES {Failure, Alerted};
(*Perform all buffered operations. It is a checked runtime error if wr is closed. *)

PROCEDURE Close(wr: T) RAISES {Failure, Alerted};
(*Flush wr, release any resources associated with wr, and set
    closed(wr) := TRUE. The documentation for a procedure that creates a
    writer should specify what resources are released when the writer is closed.
    This leaves closed(wr) equal to TRUE even if it raises an exception,
    and is a no-op if wr is closed. *)
```

```
PROCEDURE Length(wr: T):    CARDINAL RAISES {Failure, Alerted};
PROCEDURE Index(wr: T):     CARDINAL RAISES {};
PROCEDURE Seekable(wr: T): BOOLEAN RAISES {};
PROCEDURE Closed(wr: T):    BOOLEAN RAISES {};
PROCEDURE Buffered(wr: T): BOOLEAN RAISES {};
```
(*These procedures return len(wr), cur(wr), seekable(wr), closed(wr), and buffered(wr),
   respectively. Length and Index cause a checked runtime error if wr is closed; the other
   three procedures do not. *)

END Wr.

C.3.3 Simple input/output (SIO)

The interface SIO provides a number of auxiliary procedures for frequently
used combinations of procedures from the interfaces Rd, Wr, Fmt and Lex;
they are intended to simplify the use of input/output streams. The procedures have default values for the input/output stream. If NIL is passed as
the stream, then Stdio.stdout is used as output stream and Stdio.stdin as input stream (these streams do not need to be opened and normally write to
the screen and read from the keyboard resp.). The read procedures (except
GetChar) skip all leading blanks and read only to the next blank or to the
next character that cannot be interpreted as the target type. This character is skipped first, but it can be returned with the procedure TermChar
(see comment in interface). The procedure GetChar simply reads the next
character and returns it, without any skipping or interpretation.

INTERFACE SIO;   (*Simple Input / Output 13.04.94. LB*)

(*SIO provides a Reader and a Writer type. Data can be read from a reader by
   Get-procedures, and can be written by Put-procedures onto a writer. For all elementary
   data types Get- and Put-procedures are provided. They advance a (hidden) position
   over reader resp. writer stream. The procedure LookAhead returns the next character,
   without advancing the reader position.

   All Put-procedures flush automtically on stdout. GetText and GetBool terminate with
   any white space character. GetInt, GetReal and GetLongReal terminate with any
   character that cannot be interpreted as a number. Leading whitespaces are ignored.
   (White spaces are: new line, tab, space, form feed and carriage return.) The
   terminating character is removed from the reader, and can be retrieved by the
   TermChar function. At the end of the file TermChar returns the null character.

   The exception Error is raised normally only for readers not connected to Stdio.stdin.
   For Stdio.stdin, which is usually connected to the keyboard, the user is prompted to
   type in a new value. He may repeat the input MaxError-times, afterwards Error
   is raised. He may also interrupt the input by the end-of-file escape (Cntrl-Z or
   Cntrl-D), which causes also an Error exception.

SIO provides some additional functions, such as positioning (seeking) in readers, length and end of readers, flushing of writers etc. Writers are strictly sequential, positioning is not supported. The default value of the reader or writer parameter is always NIL, with the effect, selecting the appropriate standard device.
Standard reader is Stdio.stdin, *which is normally the keyboard.*
Standard writer is Stdio.stdout, *which is normally the screen.**)

IMPORT Rd, Wr;

EXCEPTION Error;

TYPE
  Reader = Rd.T;   (**A Reader is an Rd.T**)
  Writer = Wr.T;   (**A Writer is a Wr.T**)

(***Basic procedures***)

PROCEDURE GetChar(rd: Reader := NIL): CHAR RAISES {Error};
(**Returns the next char.**)

PROCEDURE PutChar(ch: CHAR; wr: Writer := NIL);
(**Outputs a single character.**)

PROCEDURE GetText(rd: Reader := NIL): TEXT RAISES {Error};
(**Reads a text. The terminating character is not appended.**)

PROCEDURE PutText(t: TEXT; wr: Writer := NIL);
(**Outputs all characters in t.**)

PROCEDURE GetLine(rd: Reader := NIL): TEXT RAISES {Error};
(**Reads a line and returns it as a text. The terminating nl is not appended.**)

PROCEDURE PutLine(t: TEXT; wr: Writer := NIL);
(**Outputs all characters in t and appends a new line.**)

PROCEDURE GetInt(rd: Reader := NIL): INTEGER RAISES {Error};
(**Reads a decimal integer.**)

PROCEDURE PutInt(i: INTEGER; length := 3; wr: Writer := NIL);
(**Outputs an integer number. The number is right-aligned in a field of length* length, *i.e.*
  leading blanks are output if the number of digits < length.*)

PROCEDURE GetReal(rd: Reader := NIL): REAL RAISES {Error};
(**Reads a real number.**)

PROCEDURE PutReal(r: REAL; wr: Writer := NIL);
(**Outputs a real number.* *)

PROCEDURE GetLongReal(rd: Reader := NIL): LONGREAL RAISES {Error};
(**Reads a longreal number.**)

PROCEDURE PutLongReal(r: LONGREAL; wr: Writer := NIL);
(**Outputs a longreal number.* *)

PROCEDURE GetBool(rd: Reader := NIL): BOOLEAN RAISES {Error};
(**Reads a Boolean constant.*
  Legal values are: "TRUE" and "FALSE" and any shorthands of them.
  The case of letters is not significant.*)

PROCEDURE PutBool(b: BOOLEAN; wr: Writer := NIL);
(*Outputs a Boolean value.*)

(***Additional procedures***)

PROCEDURE LookAhead(rd: Reader := NIL): CHAR RAISES {Error};
(*Returns the next character, without removing it from the reader.*)

PROCEDURE TermChar(rd: Reader := NIL): CHAR RAISES {Error};
(*Returns the last terminating character or null. At the end of the
  file TermChar returns the null character. There is a restriction on
  the usage of TermChar: it must be applied to the same reader as the
  last read operation, otherwise it returns the null character.
  Therefore, TermChar should not be used in a multi-threaded program.*)

PROCEDURE Nl(wr: Writer := NIL);
(*Outputs a new line.*)

PROCEDURE PutUnsigned(i: INTEGER; length := 6; base: [2..16] := 16;
                       wr: Writer := NIL);
(*Outputs an unsigned number with given base right-aligned
  in a field of length length.*)

PROCEDURE End(rd: Reader := NIL): BOOLEAN;
(*Returns TRUE iff end of reader reached.
  On the keyboard, CTRL-Z on the PC, and CTRL-D in Unix.*)

PROCEDURE Flush(wr: Writer := NIL);
(*Flushes the writer on the file. Not necessary for the standard writer.*)

PROCEDURE Available(rd: Reader := NIL): BOOLEAN;
(*Returns TRUE iff some characters are available.
  Returns FALSE if the condition cannot be checked properly.*)

PROCEDURE Length(rd: Reader := NIL): CARDINAL;
(*Returns the length of the reader or 0 if the length cannot be computed.*)

PROCEDURE Seek(rd: Reader := NIL; position: CARDINAL := 0) RAISES {Error};
(*Sets the reader on position if it is seekable, is otherwise a no-operation.
  Default corresponds to reset a reader.*)

(***Some useful constants***)

CONST
  null = '\000';
  Blanks = SET OF CHAR {' ', '\t', '\n', '\r', '\013', '\f'};
  NonBlanks = SET OF CHAR {'!' .. ' '};
VAR
  MaxError: CARDINAL := 3;   (*Max. number of retrial after erronous input*)
END SIO.

C.3.4 Simple Files (SF)

To simplify the most frequently used file operations, the interface SF provides a number of procedures.

```
INTERFACE SF;                                    (*SimpleFiles 14.04.94. LB *)

(*SimpleFiles provides simple procedures to connect readers and writers with files
  (Open procedures) and to decouple them (Close procedures). OpenRead
  connects a reader to an existing file, OpenWrite connects a writer to a new file.
  If the file with the given name already exists, the user may type in a new name
  or confirm an overwrite. OpenAppend positions the writer at the end of a file.
  The text in parameter prompt is displayed on stdout (screen). The file connected
  to a writer is made permanent by a CloseWrite. SimpleFiles provides a flexible
  mechanism for file naming. If the name parameter is omitted or (NIL) on opening,
  then the opening procedures ask the user for a file name. If the user enters an empty
  line or Standard (actually = "#"), the file defaults to standard I/O, i.e. normally to
  keyboard (standard input device) and screen (standard output device). GetFileName
  provides more explicit control over file naming. *)

IMPORT Rd, Wr;

CONST
   Overwrite   = "!";
   Standard    = "#";
   PromptStart = "Type file name ";
   PromptEnd   = " or NL for standard = ";
   InPrompt    = PromptStart & "for input" & PromptEnd;
   OutPrompt   = PromptStart & "for output" & PromptEnd;
   AppPrompt   = PromptStart & "for append" & PromptEnd;

TYPE
   Reader = Rd.T;
   Writer = Wr.T;

PROCEDURE OpenRead(name: TEXT := NIL; prompt:= InPrompt): Reader;
(*Connects file name to a reader: if name is NIL or file does not exist, prompts
  user for file name until file can be opened; if user enters return or Standard ("#"),
  returns Stdio.stdin *)

PROCEDURE OpenWrite( name: TEXT := NIL; prompt:= OutPrompt;
                     overwrite:= FALSE): Writer;
(*Connects a writer to file name: if name is NIL, prompts user for a file name;
  if user enters return or Standard ("#"), returns Stdio.stdout; if file (specified in
  name or entered by user) already exists and overwrite is false, prompts user for
  another file name or to enter "!" for the constant Overwrite for overwriting; if
  parameter overwrite is true, an existing file with same name is overwritten
  without user confirmation *)

PROCEDURE OpenAppend(name: TEXT := NIL; prompt:= AppPrompt): Writer;
(*Connects a writer to file name: if name is NIL, asks user for file name;
  if user enters return or Standard ("#"), returns Stdio.stdout; if specifed file does not
  exist, creates a new file; if file already exists, positions writer at end *)
```

```
PROCEDURE FileExists(name: TEXT): BOOLEAN;
(*returns TRUE if file name exists *)

PROCEDURE CloseRead(VAR rd: Reader);
(*closes file, assigning NIL to rd unless rd is stdin *)

PROCEDURE CloseWrite(VAR wr: Writer);
(*flushes writer and closes file, assigning NIL to wr unless wr is stdout
  (Close MUST be called if the content of the writer should be made permanent!) *)

PROCEDURE GetFileName(prompt:= PromptStart & PromptEnd): TEXT;
(*asks the user for a file name – actually a simple text (this procedure is used by
  OpenRead and OpenWrite) *)

END SF.
```

Appendix D

Modula-3 language environments

This appendix provides an overview of the available Modula-3 language environments. First of all, we must mention the environment developed by the researchers who developed Modula-3 at the Digital Equipment Corporation Systems Research Center (DEC/SRC). In order to provide all readers with a Modula-3 language environment, we at the University of Klagenfurt (Austria) developed a DOS-PC executable version, which we describe below. Along with the language environment, readers can retrieve the source code to all examples in this book.

D.1 The DEC/SRC language environment

The original Modula-3 language environment consists of a compiler and a very extensive library. This library encompasses modules for system programming, distributed programming, the production of rich graphical user interfaces (complete with animations, video, and speech synthesis), and much more. Together with source code, it is available free for practically all Unix platforms (including Linux), and there is a version for Windows/NT and Windows95.

The environment can be retrieved via anonymous FTP from

```
gatekeeper.dec.com
```

in the directory /pub/DEC/Modula-3. For a detailed description of this environment, refer to the following World-Wide Web site:

```
http://www.research.digital.com/SRC/modula-3/html/home.html
```

This Web site also provides detailed installation instructions.

D.2   A language environment for PCs

For students at the University of Klagenfurt, we developed a lean version
of the DEC/SRC language environment that runs on a simple DOS-PC. This
version is also available for free. It contains most modules of the standard
library and a simple graphical user interface as well as a special editor for
developing Modula-3 programs. This section provides an overview of the
installation and operation of this environment.

D.2.1   Installation

The PC language environment requires a PC with an 80386 (or successor)
processor with a mathematics coprocessor. The PC should have at least 6
Mbytes of RAM; otherwise compile times become intolerably long.

The environment can be retrieved per Internet via anonymous FTP or
from the World-Wide Web. The FTP server is:

```
ftp.ifi.uni-klu.ac.at
```

The necessary files reside in the directory /pub/Modula-3. The examples
in this book can be found in directory /pub/Modula-3/book. This directory also includes a README file that gives the corresponding file name for
each example number.

There are also Web sites describing the PC language environment and
a home page for this book. The PC language environment can be down-
loaded from there. In addition, all the manuals for the environment and
all example programs of this book are accessible. The address of the M3/PC
Klagenfurt home page is

```
http://www.ifi.uni-klu.ac.at/Modula-3/m3pc/m3pc.html
```

The book home page is

```
http://www.ifi.uni-klu.ac.at/Modula-3/m3book/m3book.html
```

The example programs are accessible via

```
http://www.ifi.uni-klu.ac.at/Modula-3/m3book/examples.html
```

Readers without Internet access can procure the language environment
on a set of disks (for the price of reimbursed expenses) from the following
address:

> Institut für Informatik
> Universität Klagenfurt
> Universitätsstraße 65-67
> A-9020 Klagenfurt/Austria
>
> e-mail: m3book@ifi.uni-klu.ac.at

The FTP directory and the first diskette contain the file INSTALL, which gives precise directions for installation. The diskettes also contain the examples in this book. After completed installation, you will have a directory that contains the documentation of the language environment with instructions for the use of all programs and functions described in this appendix.

D.2.2 The programming editor

If everything is installed correctly, the command m3edit from DOS starts the Modula-3 editor.

The majority of the screen is covered by three windows in which you can write source code. At the top is a menu bar, from which you can invoke editor functions via *pulldown menus*. At the bottom is a status bar and space for error messages.

Edit the source code of a program by first clicking with the mouse in a window and then loading a text file into it. Select the menu item *File→Open*[1]. You will be prompted for a file name. If the file does not exist, an empty file is created. Now you can type in the window. With the *cursor* keys you can move in the text and correct typing errors. You must save the source code before you can compile it. Select the menu item *File→Save*.

Instead of waiting for the editor to prompt you for a file name or another parameter, you can write the parameter in another window: if you double-click a word in one of the windows (thereby highlighting it), then this word serves as input for all editor functions that require a parameter. This proves particularly practical if you need to search elsewhere in your program for a character string (e.g., a variable name) that already appears on the screen: double-click it and then select the function *Edit→SearchForward*. The editor will display the next occurrence of the character string in the program.

The documentation directory provides an in-depth description of each function of the editor. They are also accessable on-line via the above Web site. You will find a concise description of the editor functions directly in the *Help* menu.

Compiling programs

The editor is capable of collecting all the files necessary for the compilation of a program (i.e., all interfaces and implementation modules). This requires specifying the name of the main module. All modules imported by the main module (and, in turn, naturally, those imported by the imported modules) are passed on to the compiler. Enter the main module with the

---

[1]Click on item *File* in the menu bar; this opens a submenu. With the mouse button pressed, move the mouse down to highlight item *Open* and then release the mouse button.

menu item *Build→MainModule*. Use the menu item *Build→BuildProgram*
afterwards to compile the program. Even on powerful PCs, this can take
some time.

> A PC with a 50 MHz 80486 processor requires one to two minutes to
> compile a smaller program (as we go to press). The reason for this
> sluggishness is above all the fact that the program is first translated
> into a C program, which is then processed by a C compiler. Future
> versions should correct this drawback.

In the event of compilation errors, error messages appear in the lower
window. The function *Edit→NextError* moves the cursor in the source
code window to the next error location flagged by the compiler. Progress
in this way until you have corrected all errors; then restart by selecting
Build→BuildProgram. If compilation was successful, you can launch the
program with the function *Build→RunProgram*.

D.2.3   The browser

To make the extensive library more accessible, especially for novices, invoke the *browser* from the editor. The browser helps to find interfaces in
the library. You can search interfaces by name, by category (e.g., file management, mathematics, etc.), or by keywords. If you know the name of a
procedure, but have forgotten which interface exports it, the browser helps
to find it. You can display the found interfaces immediately in an editor
window. Press another switch to see the implementation of the module.

You can also publish your own interfaces for the browser. This does
require some typing: in a special window, enter the name, category and
keywords of any additional interfaces that you want to make retrievable
with the browser. The documentation directory also contains a detailed
description of the browser.

D.2.4   A graphical user interface

The library on which the editor is based is available for developing any kind
of program with a similar user interface. The library is quite simple, essentially functioning by linking buttons on the screen with procedures. When
a button is clicked with the mouse, this invokes the corresponding procedure. You can build dialog boxes on the screen for user input. This requires
no new procedures; after they are invoked via a button, library procedures
prompt for values. This allows easy installation of multiple simultaneous
functions on the screen. Primary control remains with a screen manager;
the procedures only execute in small slices (e.g., installing additional dialog
boxes on screen) and must terminate immediately (as quickly as possible).

The documentation directory also contains an introduction to this library, as well as some examples.

D.2.5 Restrictions

The PC language environment necessarily always lags a bit behind the DEC/SRC language environment. Thus the libraries might not be completely up to date with the originals. Network objects, the trestle packet and most modules that offer Unix operating system services are currently unavailable in the DOS-PC version. The scheduler for threads on the PC is not *preemptive* (i.e., it cannot interrupt running threads). However, all the programs in Chapter 16 also run on a DOS-PC.

Bibliography

[And91]   Gregory Andrews. *Concurrent Programming*. Benjamin/-Cummings Publishing Compnay, Inc., 1991.

[ASU85]   A. V. Aho, R. Sethi, and J. D. Ullman. *Compilers : Principles, Techniques, and Tools*. Addison-Wesley, 1985.

[AU92]   A. V. Aho and J. D. Ullman. *Foundations of Computer Science*. Computer Science Press, 1992.

[Bal90]   Henri Bal. *Programming Distributed Systems*. Prentice Hall, 1990.

[BEW94]   L. Böszörmenyi, J. Eder, and C. Weich. PPOST, a parallel database in main memory. In *Proceedings of the Fifth International Conference on Database and Expert Systems Applications*, 1994.

[BNOW94] A. Birell, G. Nelson, S. Owicki, and E. Wobber. Network objects. Research report 115, Digital Systems Research Center, Palo Alto, 1994.

[Bös89]   L. Böszörmenyi. Menschlicher Automat und automatischer Mensch. *Informatik Spektrum*, 1989.

[CDG+89] Luca Cardelli, James Donahue, Lucille Glassman, Mick Jordan, Bill Kalsow, and Greg Nelson. Modula-3 report (revised). Technical report 52, Digital Systems Research Center, Palo Alto, 1989.

[CM81]   F. W. Clocksin and C. S. Messish. *Programming in Prolog*. Springer Verlag, 1981.

[Col69]   Egmont Colerus. *Von Pythagoras bis Hilbert*. Rowohlt, 1969.

[CW87]   L. Cardelli and P. Wegner. On understanding types, data abstraction and polymorphism. *Computing Surveys*, 1987.

[Dat90]   C. J. Date. *An Introduction to Datebase Systems*. Addison-
            Wesley, fifth edition, 1990.

[DDH72]   O. Dahl, E. W. Dijkstra, and C. Hoare. *Structured Program-
            ming*. Academic Press, 1972.

[DFS88]   E. W. Dijkstra, W. H. J. Feijen, and J. Sterringa. *A Method of
            Programming*. Addison-Wesley, 1988.

[Dij68a]   E. W. Dijkstra. Go to statement considered harmful. *Commu-
            nications of the ACM*, 11(3), 1968.

[Dij68b]   E. W. Dijkstra. The structure of the "the" multiprogramming
            system. *Comm. ACM*, 11(5):341–346, 1968.

[Dij75]   E. W. Dijkstra. Guarded commands, nondeterminacy, and for-
            mal derivation of programs. *Communications of the ACM*,
            18(8):453–457, 1975.

[FI85]   Caxton C. Foster and Thea Iberall. *Computer Architecture*. Van
            Nostrand Reinhold Company, third edition, 1985.

[Fra94]   M. Franz. Technological steps toward a software component
            industry. *Programming Languages and System Architectures*,
            1994.

[GH93]   John Guttag and James Horning. *LARCH: Languages and
            Tools for Formal Specification*. Springer Verlag, 1993.

[GR83]   A. Goldberg and D. Robson. *Smalltalk-80, the Language and
            its Implementation*. Addison-Wesley, 1983.

[Har92]   Samuel Harbison. *Modula-3*. Prentice Hall, 1992.

[HKMN94]   Jim Horning, Bill Kalsow, Paul McJones, and Greg Nelson.
            Some useful Modula-3 interfaces. Research report 113, Digi-
            tal Systems Research Center, Palo Alto, 1994.

[Hoa74]   C. A. R. Hoare. Monitors: an operating system structuring
            concept. *Comm. ACM*, 17(10):549–577, 1974.

[Hoa85]   C. A. R. Hoare. *Communicating Sequential Processes*. Prentice
            Hall, 1985.

[Hop79]   John Hopcroft. *Introduction to Automata Theory, Languages
            and Computation*. Addison-Wesley, 1979.

[IK66]   E. Isaacson and H. B. Keller. *Analysis of Numerical Methods.* John Wiley & Sons, 1966.

[KM94]   A. Kemper and G. Moerkotte. *Object-Oriented Database Management.* Prentice Hall, 1994.

[KMP+83]   J. Koch, M. Mall, P. Putfarken, M. Reimer, J. W. Schmidt, and C. A. Zehnder. Modula-R report. Technical report, ETH Zürich, 1983.

[Knu81]   Donald E. Knuth. *The Art of Computer Programming.* Addison-Wesley, 1981.

[Küh84]   Georg Kühlewind. *The Stages of Consciousness.* Linidsfarne Press, 1984.

[Küh90]   Georg Kühlewind. *Der sprechende Mensch.* Vittorio Klostermann, 1990.

[M+62]   J. McCarthy et al. *The Lisp 1.5 Programmer's Manual.* MIT press, 1962.

[Mey89]   Bertrand Meyer. From structured programming to object-oriented design: The road to Eiffel. *Structured Programming,* 10(1):19–39, 1989.

[MMS79]   J. G. Mitchel, W. Maybury, and R. Sweet. Mesa language manual. Csl-79-3, Xerox Palo Alto Research Center, 1979.

[Mös93]   Hanspeter Mössenböck. *Object-Oriented Programming in Oberon-2.* Springer Verlag, 1993.

[Nel81]   B. Nelson. Remote procedure call. Csl-81-9, Xerox Palo Alto Research Center, 1981.

[Nel91]   Greg Nelson. *Systems Programming with Modula-3.* Prentice Hall, 1991.

[PST91]   Ben Potter, Jane Sinclaire, and David Till. *An Introduction to Formal Specification and Z.* Prentice Hall, 1991.

[RBP+91]   J. Rumbaugh, M. Blaha, W. Premerlani, F. Eddy, and W. Lorensen. *Object-Oriented Modeling and Design.* Prentice Hall, 1991.

[RW92]   Martin Reiser and Niklaus Wirth. *Programming in Oberon.* Addison-Wesley, 1992.

[S⁺86]   J. Schwartz et al. *Programming with Sets, An Introduction to SETL*. Springer Verlag, 1986.

[Sch78]   Ernst Friedrich Schumacher. *A Guide for the Perplexed*. Harpercollins, 1978.

[Sch89]   Ernst Friedrich Schumacher. *Small Is Beautiful: Economics As If People Mattered*. Harpercollins, 1989.

[Sed93]   R. Sedgewick. *Algorithms in Modula-3*. Addison-Wesley, 1993.

[SM92]   J. W. Schmidt and F. Matthes. The database programming language DBPL. Technical report fide/92/46, ESPRIT BRA Project 3070, 1992.

[Som92]   I. Sommerville. *Software Engineering*. Addison-Wesley, 1992.

[Tan90]   Andrew Tanenbaum. *Structured Computer Organization*. Prentice Hall, 1990.

[Tan92]   Andrew Tanenbaum. *Modern Operating Systems*. Prentice Hall, 1992.

[Tru88]   J. K. Truss. *Discrete Mathematics for Computer Scientists*. Carl Hanser Verlag, 1988.

[Tur36]   Alain Turing. On computable numbers with an application to the entscheidunsproblem. In *London Math. Soc.*, pages 230–265, 1936.

[Ull82]   J. Ullman. *Principles of Database Systems*. Computer Science Press, second edition, 1982.

[WG92]   Niklaus Wirth and Jörg Gutknecht. *Project Oberon*. Addison-Wesley, 1992.

[WH83]   P. Winston and B. Horn. *Lisp*. Addison-Wesley, third edition, 1983.

[Wir71]   Niklaus Wirth. The programming language pascal. *Acta Informatica*, 1(1):35–63, 1971.

[Wir73]   Niklaus Wirth. *Systematic programming: an introduction*. Prentice Hall, 1973.

[Wir76]   Niklaus Wirth. *Algorithms + Data Structures = Programs*. Prentice Hall, 1976.

[Wir82]   Niklaus Wirth. *Programming in Modula-2*. Springer Verlag, 1982.

[YG66]   D. M. Young and R. T. Gregory. *A Survey of Numerical Mathematics*, volume 2. Addison-Wesley, 1966. Chapter 4.

[Zus92]   Konrad Zuse. A past and present view of computer architecture. Berichte des Departements Informatik, ETH Zürich, 1992.

Index

\# operator, 513
<: declaration, 253, 496
& operator, 68, 516
(* *) (comment), 518
* operator, 511
\+ operator, 510
− operator, 511
. operator, 506
.. in set and array constructors, 508
/ operator, 511
<* *> (pragma), 104, 518
<: relation, 134, 480
= operator, 513
ˆ operator, 244, 506

ABS, 55, 78, 512
abstract data types, 40, 251
abstract modules, 355
abstract superclass, 310
actual parameters, 179, 193
actual type, 250
acyclic graph, 288
Ada, 419
addition, 510
ADDRESS, 249, 475
    assignment of, 484
    operations on, 517
address space, 389
ADR, 517
ADRSIZE, 515
aggregate, see records or arrays
AI, 278
Algol-60, 23, 28, 174
algorithm, 2, 41
aliasing, of VAR parameters, 485
alignment, see packed types
allocated type, 470
allocation, 509

ALU, 4
analysis phase, 15
AND, 60, 514
apostrophe, in literals, 64, 508
Archimedes, 241
arithmetic operations, 56, 510
arithmetic/logic unit, 4
arrays, 140, 472
    assigning, 145, 483
    bidimensional, 142
    constructors, 144, 508
    element, 140
    first and last elements, 146, 515
    indexing, 141, 472, 506
    multi-dimensional, 142, 472
    number of elements in, 146, 515
    operations, 145
    passing as parameters, 485
    relational operations, 146
    sorting, 152
    subarrays, 146, 507
    subscript, 506
    subtyping rules, 481
    unidimensional, 141
    values, 144
artificial intelligence, 4, 278
ASCII, see ISO-Latin-1
assembler, 20
assembly language, 20
assertions with ASSERT, 104
assignable, 483
    READONLY/VALUE formals, 485
    array subscript, 506
    arrays, 472
    in = and #, 513
    in set operations, 510, 511
    in unsafe modules, 517

return value, 489
set/array/record constructors, 508
variable initializations, 495
assignment, 83
assignment compatibility, 135
assignment operation, 41
assignment statements, 483
asynchronous communication, 419
atomic action, 396
attribute, 313
automata, 6

background storage, 228, 349
backslash, 64
backslash, in literals, 64, 508
Backus-Naur form, 28
barrier, 397
base type, 470
    array, 144
    sets, 164
    subrange, 120
BEGIN, 49
binary files, 352
binary number system, 10
binary search, 291
binary search tree, 292
binary semaphore, 414
binary tree, 290, 341
binding power, of operators, 505
bindings, in procedure call, 484
bit, 9, 63
BITS FOR, 170, 474
    in VAR parameters, 485
    subtyping rules, 481
    with subarrays, 507
BITSIZE, 515
blank, 361
block, 48, 494
    module, 500
    procedure, 495
    statement, 486
block structure, 173
BNF, 28
body, of procedure, 179, 475
Boole, George, 40
BOOLEAN, 60, 471

operations on, 514
bottom-up, 17
BRANDED, 475
branded reference, 255
broadcast, 406
buffer, 356
buffered stream, 356
bug, 280
BY, 108
byte, 10, 63
BYTESIZE, 515

call statement, 181
call, procedure, 181, 484
cancellation, 76
CARDINAL, 53, 471
carriage return, in literals, 64, 508
CASE statement, 92, 492
case
    in keywords, 518
    in literals, 507
CEILING, 77, 512
central processing unit, 4
channel, 418, 420
CHAR, 63, 471
character literals, 64, 508
character set, 471
checked runtime error, 469
    INC value out of range, 493
    NARROW, 514
    SUBARRAY, 507
    VAL range check, 514
    assignability, 483
    dereferencing NIL, 506
    failure to return a value, 489
    nested procedure as method, 510
    no branch of CASE, 492
    no branch of TYPECASE, 492
    uncaught exception, 487
    undefined procedure, 485
    unlisted exception, 485
children, in a tree, 288
Chomsky, N., 18
Church, Alonso, 7
circular buffer, 407
circularities

in imports lists, 500
in type declarations, 497
class, 306
class hierarchy, 339
client
of a module, 202
of a RPC call, 419
of an object class, 309
client/server model, 418
Cobol, 22
code sharing, 312
code value, 66
coercions
checked, 514
unchecked, 516
comments, 46, 518
tokenizing, 522
communication, 388, 396
comparison operation, 513
compatibility, 125
assignment, 135
expression, 136
compilation, 36
compilation unit, 37, 42, 210
compiler, 36, 37
compiler-compiler, 37
complete revelation, 496
complexity, 307
composite type, 139
computability, 7
concatenating texts, 68, 516
concrete subclass, 310
concrete types, 496
concurrent processes, 388
condition, 84, 405, 527
condition type, 527
condition variable, 405, 527
conditional GoTo statement, 86
conditional synchronization, 404
CONST, 129
constant expression, 129, 469, 516
constants, 41, 469
declarations, 129, 494
numeric, 507
procedure, 476
constructors

array, 144, 508
record, 157, 509
set, 165, 508
contain (value in type), 469
context, 174
control variable, 108
conventions, 45
conversion
characters and integers, 66
enumerations and integers, 66, 514
to floating-point types, 77, 512
counter, 108
covers, method signatures, 315
covers, procedure signatures, 477
CPU, 4
critical region, 400, 402
CSP, 419
current state, 5
cursor, 44
cyclic imports, 209, 500

Dürrematt, 8
Dahl, O., 24
dangling pointer, 245
data aggregates, 139
Data capsules, 212
data collections, 139
data record, of object, 477
data region, 5
data security, 349
data space, 212
data type, 39
data-parallel algorithms, 397
database system, 140, 349
deadlock, 402, 411
deallocation, 517
debugger, 280
DEC, 54, 66, 118, 493
on addresses (unsafe), 517
DEC/SRC, 21
declaration, 48, 129, 469
recursive, 497
scope of, 494
Declarations, 48
decomposition, 192
decrement, for predecessor, 54

default values
  in record fields, 155, 473
  procedure parameters, 193, 476, 484
deferred methods, 319
delimiters, complete list, 518
denumerably infinite, 72
dereferencing, 244, 506
design phase, 16
designators, 469
  operators allowed in, 506
  readonly, 506
  writable, 506
device drivers, 350
difference, set, 167, 511
Digital Equipment Corporation Systems Research Center, 21
Dijkstra, E.W., 24, 25, 28, 86, 411, 413
dimension, 473
direct file access, 350
directed graph, 288
directory, 350
DISPOSE, 245, 517
DIV, 56, 511
divide-and-conquer, 281, 283
division by zero, 510
division, real, 75, 511
double quote, in literals, 64, 508
doubly linked list, 264
dynamic binding, 310, 311, 325
dynamic data, 241
dynamic data structures, 227, 261
dynamic type, 250, 310

EBNF, 28
eclipse, 174
edge, in a tree/graph, 287
effective, 3
Eiffel, 252
element type, of array, 472
ELSE, 87
ELSIF, 87
empty shape, 144
empty type, 470
encapsulated data types, 251

encapsulation, 257, 308
end of file, 351
entry condition, 97
enumerations, 115, 470
  first and last elements, 118, 515
  number of elements, 118, 515
  operations, 118
  predefined, 117
  range, 117
  selection, 506
  subtyping rules, 480
environment, of procedure, 475
EOF, 351
equality operator, 513
equivalence of types, 133
errors, static and runtime, 469
escape sequence, 64
escape sequences, in literals, 64, 508
Euclidean algorithm, 100
Euler-Venn diagram, 166
EVAL, 194, 485
exception handling, 371
  delayed, 379
  strategy, 382
exceptions, 371, 482
  RAISES set, 378, 485
  RAISE, 376, 486
  TRY EXCEPT, 376
  TRY FINALLY, 379, 488
  declarations, 376, 496
  delegation, 377
  handlers, 376, 487
  return and exit, 482
executable program, 37
EXIT statement, 110, 488
exit-exception, 110, 482, 488
expanded definition (of type), 470
exponent, 73
exporting an interface, 500
EXPORTS, 500
expression, 125, 469, 504
  constant, 516
  function procedures in, 508
  order of evaluation, 504
expression compatibility, 136
EXTENDED, 73, 471

literals, 507
Extended interface, 530
extended Backus-Naur form, 28
EXTERNAL, 518
external state space, 363

factorial, 273
FALSE, 60, 471
Feijen, W.H.J., 28
Fibonacci, 276
field
    object, 313
    record, 155, 473
    selection, records/objects, 506
FIFO, 231
file, 349
    binary, 352
    close, 351
    create, 351
    end, 351
    open, 351
    positioning, 351
    read, 351
    seekable, 356
    type, 352
    write, 351
file access
    direct, 350
    recordwise, 353
    sequential, 350
file format, 359
FileRd module, 355
FileWr module, 355
FIRST, 54, 66, 78, 118, 146, 515
first-in, first-out, 231
fixed arrays, 472
    subtyping rules, 481
FLOAT, 77, 512
Float generic interface, 530
floating-point, 471
    input/output, 78
    literals, 74
    operations, 75
    values, 73
FloatMode interface, 533
FLOOR, 77, 512

flush, 356
Fmt interface, 534
Fmt module, 357
FOR statement, 108, 491
form feed, in literals, 64, 508
formal language, 18, 27
formal parameter, 178
Fortran, 22
FROM ... IMPORT ..., 211, 499
function, 41, 177, 178
    mathematical, 177
function call, 49
function procedures, 42, 178, 475
    in expressions, 508
    returning values from, 489
functional programming language, 21

Gödel, Kurt, 7
garbage collector, 245, 474
generalization, 328
generic interface, 501
generic module, 249, 501
genericity, 249, 257, 340
generics, 501
global block, 174
global variable, 187
GoTo statement, 86
graph, 261
guarded statement, 88

handlers, for exceptions, 376, 487
hash function, 438
hash table, 438
heap, 243
heavyweight process, 389
Hello, world, 44
hexadecimal literal, 507
hidden procedure body, 260
hierarchy, 310
Hoare, C.A.R, 281, 405, 419
human language, 18

identifiers, 48, 126, 469
    lexical structure, 522
    qualified, 499
    reserved, 518
    scope of, 174, 494

syntax, 522
IF statement, 87, 489
imperative programming language, 21
implementation, 43
implementation module, 208
implementation phase, 16
import cycle, 500
imports, 210, 499
IN, 167, 513
INC, 54, 66, 118, 493, 517
increment, for successor, 54
index type, of array, 140, 472
indirect recursion, 279
infinity, 531
infix, 68, 127
information hiding, 43, 203, 205
inheritence, 307, 309
initialization, 48, 132
    during allocation, 510
    in VAR declaration, 132, 495
    modules, 503
    of variables in interfaces, 498
INLINE, 518
Inorder, 294
input parameter, 184
input stream, 353
input/output parameter, 184
installation and maintaince phase, 16
instance, 252, 308
instance variable, 308, 313
instantiation, 40
INTEGER, 53, 471
integer, 39, 53
    division, 56
integration and testing phase, 16
interface
    Extended, 530
    Float, 530
    FloatMode, 533
    Fmt, 534
    LongReal, 530
    Rd, 538
    Real, 530
    Scan, 538
    SF, 545
    SIO, 542

Text, 525
Thread, 527
Word, 528
Wr, 540
interfaces, 43, 202, 207, 498, 500
    exporting, 500
    safe, 503
    unsafe, 503
    variable initializers in, 500
intermittent input stream, 356
intersection, set, 167, 511
intrinsically safe, 503
invariant, 102
invocation stack, 183
Is-a relationship, 134, 307
ISO-Latin-1, 64, 471
ISTYPE, 326, 514

jump, 86

keyword, 45
keyword binding, 157, 484
keywords, complete list, 518

language environment, 36, 37, 547
Larch, 252
LAST, 54, 66, 78, 118, 146, 515
last-in, first-out, 228
lazy evaluation, 128, 151
left-hand side, 135
Lex module, 362
LHS, 135
libraries, 203, 525
life cycle, 307
lifetime, 175
lightweight process, 389
line feed, in literals, 64, 508
linear search, 150
linker, 37
Lisp, 278
list, 238, 240, 262
    doubly linked, 264
literals, 41
    character, 63, 508
    numeric, 73, 507
    syntax, 522
    text, 67, 508

loadable program, 37
loading, of program, 37
local procedures, 475
    as parameters, 485
    assignment of, 198, 483
local variable, 175
location, 469
LOCK statement, 402, 493
logical programming language, 22
logical type, 40, 60
LONGREAL, 73, 471
    literals, 507
LongReal interface, 530
LOOP statement, 110, 488
loop, 97
    body, 97
    condition, 97
    For, 108
    Loop, 110
    Repeat, 105
    While, 97
loop invariants, 102
LOOPHOLE, 516
low-level programming, 20

machine code, 20
Main interface, 44
main module, 43, 44, 499
main thread, 390
maintenance phase, 16
mantissa, 73
masked field, 478
Math module, 79
matrices, 142
MAX, 512
member (value in type), 469
memory, 4
memory cell, 9
memory management, 243
message, 306, 388
message passing, 317, 396, 418
metalanguage, 23, 27, 28
metasymbol, 28
method suite, 477
methods, 306, 308, 506
    declaration deferred, 319

declarations, 313, 478
implementation, 315
invocations, 317, 485
override, 318, 479
specifying in NEW, 510
MIN, 512
MOD, 56, 511
mode, *see* parameter mode
Modula-2, 23
modularization, 223
module, 201
module concept, 202
modules, 42, 208, 498, 500
    for type design, 260
    generic, 249
    initialization, 503
    safe, 503
    unsafe, 503
modulus operation, 56
monitor, 405
multi-dimensional arrays, 472
multiplication, 511
MUTEX variable, 402, 527
MUTEX, 402, 482
mutual exclusion, 400, 402

name conflict, 116
name equivalence, 133
name server, 418
NaN, 531
NARROW, 325, 514
negation, 60
nesting, 85
network objects, 419
NEW, 242, 509
newline, in literals, 64, 508
NIL, 239, 508
node, of a tree/graph, 287
normal outcome, 482
NOT, 60, 514
not a number, 531
NULL, 318, 475
NUMBER, 118, 146, 515
number literals, 126, 507
numerics, 73

Oberon, 23

Oberon-2, 23
OBJECT, 313
object identifier, 430
object-oriented
    applications, 311
    databases, 140
    modeling, 305
    programming, 308
objects, 305, 477
    accessing fields/methods, 317, 477
    allocating, 317, 510
    branded, 478
    declarations, 313
    fields, 306, 308, 317, 506
    invoking methods, 317, 485
    method declarations, 313, 478
    methods, 306, 308, 506
    subtyping rules, 318, 481
    type, 312
Occam, 419
octal literal, 507
oid, 430
on-line, 389
OOA, 307
OOD, 307
opaque types, 252, 260, 496
    rules for design, 260
open arrays, 246, 472
    allocating, 510
    as formal parameters, 485
    loopholing to, 516
    subtyping rules, 481
operand, 125
operating system, 386
operators, 125
    complete list, 518
    precedence, 505
    tokenizing, 522
OR, 60, 514
ORD, 66, 118, 514
order (<, >, ...), 513
order of evaluation, expressions, 127,
        504
ordered binary tree, 292
ordinal number, 66, 118
ordinal types, 53, 470

first and last elements, 54, 515
    subtyping rules, 480
ordinal value, 66, 470
output parameter, 184
output stream, 353
overflow, 57, 75, 510
overloading, of operation, 504
OVERRIDES, 314
overriding methods, 310, 314, 479

package, *see* module
packed types, 170, 474
    VAR parameters, 485
parallel program, 388
parallel programming, 385
parameter
    actual, 179
    default, 193
    formal, 178
    input, 184
    input/output, 184
    named, 194
    output, 184
    passing, 183
    positional, 194
    read-only, 186
parameter mode, 183, 476
parameter passing, 177, 484
parent, in a tree, 287
partial correctness, 103
partial expansion (of type), 470
partial revelation, 256, 260, 344, 496,
        497
partially opaque type, 256, 496
Pascal, 23
path length
    in a graph, 289
    in a tree, 296
path, of a graph, 289
persistent, 150
persistent data structures, 349
persistent variable, 362
Pickle, 367
pipelining, 386
Pkl, 367
pointer, 236, *see* reference

polygon, 219
polymorphism, 310, 325
port, 39
positional binding, 157, 484
postcondition, 86
Postorder, 295
pragmas, 104, 518
pre-emption, 390
precedence, 27
precedence, of operators, 31, 127, 505
precondition, 86
predefined subranges, 122
Preorder, 294
procedural operator, 505
procedural programming language, 22
procedure call, 484
procedure parameter, 198
procedures, 2, 41, 177, 475
    RETURN, 180, 489
    assignment, 195
    assignment of local, 483
    body, 179
    call, 181, 484
    constant, 180, 476
    declarations, 179, 495
    discarding results, 194, 485
    exporting to interface, 500
    head, 179
    inline, 518
    invocations, 181
    operations, 195
    parameter passing, 183, 476, 484
    proper, 178
    pure, 178
    raises set, 378, 475
    signatures, 179, 475, 476
    subtyping rules, 481
    type, 195
    variable, 195
process, 388, *see* thread
program, 1, 10, 18
program region, 5
program system, 14
program text, 37
program translator, 20
program, definition of, 499

programming in the small, 17
programming language, 14, 18, 36
proper procedure, 178, 475
pseudocode, 266
pure procedures, 178

qualified identifiers, 116, 156, 499
quasi-parallel processes, 388
queue, 228, 263
    first-in, first-out, 231
    last-in, first-out, 228
    LIFO, 228
Quicksort, 281
quotataion mark, in literals, 64

RAISE, 376, 486
RAISES, 377, 476
    dangling, 477
    raising unlisted exception, 485
raises set, of procedure, 378, 475
range check, 141
Rd interface, 538
read-only
    designator, 469, 506
    parameter, 186
    variable, 109, 162
read/write buffer, 356
read/write position, 351
reader, 353
READONLY parameters, 186, 485
REAL, 72, 471
    conversions to, 77, 512
    converting to integers, 77, 512
    literal, 74, 507
Real interface, 530
real division, 511
record length, 353
records, 154, 473
    constructors, 157, 509
    defaulting fields, 473
    fields, 156, 506
    operations, 160
    values, 157
recursion, 21, 271
recursive algorithms, 273
recursive data structure, 287

recursive declarations, 497
redeclaration, 174
redefinition
    field, 334
    method, 334
REF, 239
REFANY, 249, 475
reference class, 474
reference semantics, 318
referenced type, 239, 240
references, 69, 228, 241, 474
    TYPECASE, 492
    assigning, 243
    assigning ADDRESSes, 517
    automatic dereferencing, 506
    deallocation, 244
    dereferencing, 244, 506
    generating with NEW, 241, 509
    reference class, 474
    subtyping rules, 481
    traced, 244
    typecase, 327
    typecode of, 514
    untraced, 245
referent, 474
referent type, 475
reflexivity of subtype, 135, 481
register, 10
relational operators, 513
remainder, 56, *see* MOD
remote procedure call, 419
rendezvous, 419
REPEAT statement, 105, 490
resources
    common, 396
    release, 380
    reservation, 380
result type, of procedure, 137, 180, 476
RETURN statement, 180, 489
return type, *see* result type
return-exception, 482, 489
reuse, 16
REVEAL, 254, 496
revelations, 253, 254, 496
    imported, 499
reverse Polish notation, 295

RHS, 135
right-hand-side, 135
ROOT, 318, 478
root class, 339
root, of a tree, 287
ROUND, 77, 512
rounding error, 73
rounding of arithmetic operations, 510
RPC, 419
RPN, 295
run-time error, 121, 375, 469
    checked, 469
    unchecked, 469
run-time support, 37

safety, 503
scalar, 139
scale factors, in numeric literals, 507
Scan interface, 538
Scan module, 357
scanning, 357
scheduler, 388, 390
schema, 308, 428
Schumacher, E.F., 13, 18
scope, 108, 162, 494
    block statement, 486
    exceptions, 496
    locals in FOR, 491
    locals in TRY EXCEPT, 487
    locals in TYPECASE, 492
    locals in WITH, 490
    of formal parameters, 495
    of identifier, 469
    of imported symbols, 500
    of variable initializations, 495
    revelations, 497
search, 150
Searle, J., 371
selection, 428
selection of fields, 506
self, 316
semantics, 18
semaphore, 413
semidynamic data, 241
semifinished system, 308
sentinel, 150

sequence, 84, 87
sequential composition, 486
sequential file access, 350
server
    of a RPC call, 419
server modules, 205
sets, 163, 474
    constructors for, 165, 508
    difference, 167, 511
    equality, 167, 513
    IN operator, 167, 513
    intersection, 167, 511
    operations, 165
    subset, 167, 513
    symmetric set difference, 167, 511
    union, 167, 510
    values, 165
SF interface, 545
shape, of array, 144, 472
shared variable, 388, 396
side effect, 3, 97, 187
sign inversion, 511
signature, 179, 475, 476
    covers, 315, 477
Simple-IO, 360
Simula-67, 311
simulated genericity, 249
simulation, 311
single quote, in literals, 64, 508
SIO, 360
    implementation, 361
    interface, 542
size, of type, 515
Smalltalk, 311
software, 14
software life cycle, 16
sorting
    array, 152
    Quicksort, 281
source code, 37, 46
specialization, 309
specification, 252
    languages, 15
    phase, 15
specification language, 37, 252
square root, 78

SRC, 21
stack, 183, 228, 275
standard interfaces, 525
starvation, 406, 412
state space, 5, 41, 204
state variables, 5
statement part, 209
statements, 48, 49, 482
static data, 241
static data structure, 227
static error, 469
static type, 139, 310, 469
storage allocation, 241, 509
    DISPOSE, 517
strings, 508
structural type equivalence, 133, 160, 470
structure of programs, 35
structured programming, 24, 35, 86, 187
structured statement, 84
style, of programming, 18
SUBARRAY, 147, 507
subclass, 307
subranges, 120, 471
    operations, 122
    predefined, 122
    subtyping rules, 480
subscript operator, 506
subset operation, 513
subtraction, 511
subtypes, 134, 248, 480
    operations on, 135
    reflexivity, 135
    relation, 134
    transitivity, 135
supercall, 323
superclass, 307
supertype, 134, 480
    assignment, 249
symbol-manipulating machine, 6
symbolic constant, 41
symmetric set difference, 167, 511
synchronization, 388, 396
    with barriers, 397
synchronous communication, 419

syntax, 18, 519
Systems Research Center, DEC, 21

tab, in literals, 64, 508
tail recursion, 278
task, *see* thread
termination condition, 97
termination of program, 499
TEXT, 67, 482
Text interface, 525
text files, 352
Text.Compare, 153
Text.FindChar, 358
Text.Sub, 358
texts, 67
    concatenating, 68, 516
    escape sequences, 64, 67, 508
    literals, 67, 508
THEN, 87
Thread interface, 527
thread, 389
    wait state, 403
throughput, 385
time slice scheduling, 390
TO, 108
tokenizing, 522
toolbox, 219
top-down, 17
top-level procedure, 475
total correctness, 103
Towers of Hanoi, 282
traced
    object types, 318, 478
    references, 244, 474
    types, 474
transitivity of subtype, 135, 481
tree, 287, 339
    class hierarchy, 339
    height, 290
tree traversal, 294
triangular swap, 84
trigonometric functions, 78
TRUE, 60, 471
truly parallel processes, 388
TRUNC, 77, 512
truth table, 60

TRY EXCEPT, 376, 487
TRY FINALLY, 379, 488
Turing machine, 6
Turing, Alan, 6
type, 115, 139, 470
    assignable, 483
    composite, 139
    concrete, 496
    declaration of, 131, 494
    empty, 470
    of expression, 469
    of variable, 469
    opaque, 252, 496
    traced, 244, 474
type coercions
    checked, 514
    unchecked, 516
type constructor, 115, 139
type equivalence, 133, 470
type expression, 470
type identification, *see* revelation
type inclusion, 137
type system, 21, 23
TYPECASE, 327, 492
TYPECODE, 514

unchecked runtime errors, 469, 516
undefined procedure, 485
underflow, 75, 510
union, of sets, 167, 510
Unix, 389
UNSAFE, 208, 503
unsafe features, 516
unsafe interface, 208
unsafe module, 208, 245
UNTIL, 105
UNTRACED
    in reference declarations, 475
    in unsafe modules, 517
    objects, 319
    references, 245
UNTRACED ROOT, 319, 478
upcall, 267
uses relationship, 309

VAL, 66, 118, 514

VALUE, 185, 485
value, 40, 469
value parameters, 485
    type checking, 485
VAR, 48
VAR declarations, 132, 495
VAR parameters, 185, 485
variables, 40, 469, 495
    declaration, 48, 132
    global, 187
    initialization, 48, 132, 495
    initialized in interfaces, 500
    local, 175
    procedure, 476
vector, 141
verification, 86, 102
viewport, 221
virtual memory, 228
visibility, 175, *see* scope
von Neumann bottleneck, 387
von Neumann computer, 9
von Neumann, John, 9

wait state, of thread, 403
Weizenbaum, J., vii, 14
WHILE statement, 97, 490
white space, 46, 361
whole number, 39, 53
Wirth, N., 18, 145, 425
WITH statement, 160, 490
Wittgenstein, Ludwig, 18
Word interface, 528
word, 9
word size, of type, 515
Wr interface, 540
writable designator, 469, 506
writer, 353

Xerox PARC, 311

Z, 252
zero, division by, 510
Zuse, Konrad, 10

Springer-Verlag
and the Environment

We at Springer-Verlag firmly believe that an international science publisher has a special obligation to the environment, and our corporate policies consistently reflect this conviction.

We also expect our business partners – paper mills, printers, packaging manufacturers, etc. – to commit themselves to using environmentally friendly materials and production processes.

The paper in this book is made from low- or no-chlorine pulp and is acid free, in conformance with international standards for paper permanency.

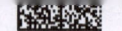